NUVENDALTIN QUHT'ANA:
THE PEOPLE OF NONDALTON

Linda J. Ellanna
Andrew Balluta

Cartographic illustrations by
George K. Sherrod

Smithsonian Institution Press
Washington, D.C.
London

Nuvendaltin Quht'ana: The People of Nondalton

By Linda J. Ellanna and Andrew Balluta
© 1992 Smithsonian Institution

Printed in the United States of America

Library of Congress Cataloging-in-Publication Data

Ellanna, Linda J., 1940 -
    Nuvendaltin Quht'ana : the people of Nondalton / Linda J. Ellanna.
Andrew Balluta, 1930 -
        p. cm
    Includes bibliographical references and index.
    ISBN 1-56098-118-0(pbk)
    1. Dena'ina Indians--History--Sources. 2. Dena'ina Indians-
-Cultural assimilation. 3. Dena'ina Indians--Social conditions.
4. Social change. 5. Nondalton (Alaska)--History--Sources.
6. Nondalton (Alaska)--Social conditions. I. Balluta, Andrew.
II. United States, National Park Service. III. Title. IV. Title:
People of Nondalton. E99.T185E55 1992
979.8'6--dc20   91-16098
                                                      CIP

Cover photo/poster: Anton Balluta of Old Nondalton gets into his canvas-covered *baidarki* *(vaqilin)* in the spring, circa 1928, to hunt moose, caribou, or beaver on the Chulitna River in Alaska.

Funding for publication was provided by the Smithsonian Institution Press and the National Park Service. The National Park Service also funded part of the manuscript preparation.

The authors will realize no profit from this publication.

To Ruth Bobby Koktelash and Albert Wassillie,
without whose knowledge and willingness to teach,
this book would not have been possible.

CONTENTS

LIST OF MAPS

LIST OF TABLES

LIST OF FIGURES

AUTHORS' NOTE

INTRODUCTION

This note is intended to provide guidance to the reader in regard to language or terminology used in this ethnography. Much of the information in this book is in Dena'ina, although English definitions are included in the text when the Dena'ina word is initially introduced. Many of the quotations of Nondalton or Lime Village residents are either in English as it is spoken in Dena'ina communities, or, in the case of biographical chapters, standard middle-American English, with some local expressions. Since this is an ethnography, concepts and other types of information are presented in the terminology of the discipline, social and cultural anthropology. Most technical terms also are defined within the context of the text. However, a glossary, which appears as Appendix C, is available to assist the reader. It includes definitions of some of the Dena'ina terminology frequently used in the manuscript and technical anthropological terms or concepts. It is assumed that terminology not defined in the glossary can be found in most standard college dictionaries.

It was the decision of the authors to present verbatim all direct quotations by Dena'ina speakers in English. To do otherwise would imply, in our opinion, that "village English," as spoken by the Dena'ina, is a substandard form of English. Although it is a distinct form of English, it is considered by us to be completely functional as a means of communication. By our inclusion of such English in direct Dena'ina quotations, we clearly hope to transmit to the reader our view that any form of village English should not be viewed as a substandard version of that language but rather a functional, viable, local linguistic variant.

Biographical chapters, termed "Dena'ina Perspective," were not written verbatim from taped interviews. They were composites of multiple interviews derived from a variety of contexts. They also were focused on elder Dena'ina, who speak Dena'ina as their first language. Therefore, since it was not possible to write these chapters as direct transcriptions of interviews, and for the purpose of making them easily readable, all "Dena'ina Perspective" chapters are written in relatively standard middle-American English. However, many expressions, verb forms, contractions, and other language common to English as spoken by many Dena'ina, were retained in these chapters. These chapters were to be distinct, hopefully in a more humanistic fashion, from the anthropological presentation of the remainder of the ethnography.

In regard to place names, several strategies were used to stress the cultural relevance of inland Dena'ina place names to the relationship of speakers of this language to the land they occupy and use, while assisting the reader unfamiliar with Dena'ina in their location of specific sites on maps included within the text or on other standard Alaska maps. For the serious reader, use of U.S. Geological Survey maps applicable to the areas presented on Maps 1 and 2 within the text may provide more detailed information. Maps 1 and 2 within the ethnography present the location of English and Dena'ina place names used in the text, respectively. These maps would be most useful to the reader if referred to throughout the reading of the ethnography. Additionally, with the first introduction of a place name, it is presented in English with its Dena'ina equivalent in parentheses. This process could have been reversed, but it is expected that more readers will be familiar with English as a language than with Dena'ina. This mode of presentation in no way is intended to imply that the Dena'ina place name is secondary. Subsequent references in the text to particular places are in English if such names exist. Many Dena'ina place names do not have English equivalents. Additionally, Appendix B presents a list of most Dena'ina place names used in the text and their English equivalents, if such exist. It is useful to add that many English place names found on U.S. Geological Survey (USGS) maps are not consistent with predominant local uses in English. For example, although "Iliamna Lake" is the USGS designation for this body of water (Orth 1971), "Lake Iliamna" is the most common name given to this significant body of water when it is designated in English by inland Dena'ina. Therefore, the authors consistently employed "Lake Iliamna" when discussing this location. By way of contrast, local inland Dena'ina refer to "Miller Creek" as "Miller's Creek." Before this site was granted as an allotment to a non-Dena'ina, it was extremely important to the inland Dena'ina as the camp for women and children during fall and early winter trapping periods. Many people living in Nondalton or their ancestors were born there. The use of "Miller Creek" in the text accommodated the view of Lake Clark National Park and Preserve that "Miller's Creek" was incorrect. This discussion of place names highlights the view that "official" place names, as reported and displayed by USGS (a federal agency), normally disregard the names given those places by the indigenous occupants of the area hundreds of years before Euroamerican contact. Each of these Dena'ina place names expresses a wealth of detail about Dena'ina culture, oral tradition, history, ethnogeography, and ideology. It is the hope of the authors that, through time, more and more Dena'ina place names will be incorporated into revised versions of USGS maps.

DENA'INA ORTHOGRAPHY

The inland Dena'ina orthography employed in this ethnography is derived from that of Dr. James Kari (1977), Alaska Native Language Center, University of Alaska Fairbanks, internationally the foremost Dena'ina linguist. He published the first Dena'ina noun dictionary and numerous place names (e.g., J. Kari 1977; Kari and Kari 1982), in addition to theoretical works related to the relationship of Dena'ina to other Athabaskan languages and data regarding the Athabaskan language family in general.

According to J. Kari (1977), there are multiple Dena'ina dialects:

> *Dena'ina is clearly one language. Speakers from all areas can understand one another. However, each Dena'ina dialect area and village has its particular local flavor. There are four distinctive Dena'ina dialect areas (Kari 1975). The Outer Inlet dialect . . . includes Kenai and formerly Kustatan, Polly Creek and Seldovia. The Upper Inlet dialect . . . includes Tyonek (some Outer Inlet speakers also live in Tyonek), Eklutna, Knik, Montana Creek, and formerly Point Possession, Susitna Station, Alexander Creek, Kroto Creek, Talkeetna, and Old Matanuska village. The Iliamna dialect . . . is spoken on the north shore of Lake Iliamna at Pedro Bay and formerly at Old Iliamna village. The Inland dialect . . . is spoken at Nondalton, Lime Village, and by a few people at Stony River, and formerly at Kijik on Lake Clark. . . (J. Kari 1977:10).*

According to J. Kari (1977:12), Dena'ina may be the most dialectically diverse of all Athabaskan languages. Whereas in some cases, the same word is used in all Dena'ina dialects, in other cases each dialect may use a distinct term. Additionally, there is a relatively large number of Russian loan words in Dena'ina, resulting from the intensive period of contact between these two groups from the middle 1700s throughout the majority of the 1800s. Some sounds occur only in Russian loan words (J. Kari 1977:18).

As a language, the Dena'ina alphabet has 36 consonants and 4 vowels, not considering sounds derived from loan words (J. Kari 1977:18). Not all consonants may occur consistently in all dialects. The dialect of interest in this case is that referred to by J. Kari (1977) as "Inland." Based on the orthography of J. Kari (1977), the pronunciation of some Dena'ina words used in the text can be approximated by using the following guidelines.

Dena'ina vowels include those represented by the orthography a, i, u, and e and are described as approximating, not duplicating, the following English words:

a   is pronounced like the vowel in English "f*a*ther"

e   is pronounced like the vowel in English "tick*e*t"

i   is pronounced like the vowel in English "v*i*sa"

u   is pronounced like the vowel in English "t*u*ba"

Dena'ina consonants include those represented by the orthography b, d, dl, dz, j, g, gg, ', t, tl, ts, ch, k, q, t', tl', ts', ch', k', q', l, s, sh, x, h, hh, v, l, z, zh, y, gh, m, and n. We could find no uses of the consonants b and w in inland Dena'ina terminology used in this ethnography. J. Kari (1977) maintains that the consonant w is found principally in the Seldovia dialect and in a few Kenai words, while b is found mainly in the Upper and Outer Inlet dialects. The "glottalized" stops — which are pronounced by the "glottis," or in the upper part of the larynx between the vocal chords — are t', tl', ts', ch', k', and q'. In order presented here, their articulation is from the front to the back of the mouth — from the tip of the tongue touching or approaching the alveolar ridge (t', tl', ts'); the blade of the tongue touching or approaching the alveolar ridge (ch'); and the tongue touching or approaching the roof of the mouth (k' and q'). English equivalents for these sounds are not available. Additionally, the "stops" pronounced with the tongue touching or near the very back of the roof of the mouth or made with the voice box (gg, q, and q') and the fricatives h (which is "voiceless") and y do not have English equivalents.

For the following consonants, similarities to English sounds are attempted:

d is similar to the English consonant in "*d*ollar"

dl impressionistically similar to, but not the same as, the "*cl*ean" for English speakers

dz is similar to the English consonants in "a*dz*e"

j is similar to the English consonant in "*j*ump"

' is similar to the English consonants sounds in the negative response, "*uh-uh*"

g is similar to the English consonant in "*g*un"

t is similar to the English consonant in "*t*en"

tl is impressionistically similar to, but not the same as, the "*gl*ue" for English speakers

ts is similar to the English combined consonants "ha*ts*"

ch is similar to the English consonants "*ch*ild"

k is similar to the English consonant "*k*ill"

ls has no English equivalent, but is impressionistically similar to the consonants "*sl*ow" for English speakers

s is similar to the English consonant in "*s*and"

sh is similar to the English consonants "*sh*oe"

x is similar to the German consonants in "Ba*ch*"

hh is similar to the English consonant in "*h*ere"

v is similar to the English consonant in "*v*est"

l is similar to the English consonant in "*l*and"

z is similar to the English consonant in "*z*ebra"

zh is similar to the English consonant in "a*z*ure" or to the French "rou*ge*"

gh is similar to the German consonant "*Rh*ine" or "he*r*aus" ("to get out")

m is similar to the English consonant "*m*an"

n is similar to the English consonant "*n*asal"

y is similar to the English consonant "*y*es"

The authors hope that this pronunciation guide provides some assistance to those readers wanting to approximate the Dena'ina words used in this ethnography. However, we expect that not all readers will want to undertake this endeavor. We are deeply indebted to Dr. Jim Kari of the Alaska Native Language Center for providing the Dena'ina alphabet (1977) and sound system. In Dr. Kari's absence at the completion of this part of the ethnography, Dr. James Leer, also of the Alaska Native Language Center, was extremely helpful in deriving the similar English vowel and consonant sounds presented above.

ACKNOWLEDGEMENTS

In a project of this duration and scope, it is difficult to identify the many people who provided invaluable assistance in the research, analyses, writing, and rewriting phases of the ethnography. It is our sincere hope that no one has been forgotten in the acknowledgements we offer here.

There is no question that our foremost appreciation should go to the residents of the inland Dena'ina community of Nondalton, Alaska. They were much more than providers of information. They became dedicated to this project as a means of documenting their culture and history, acts which they perceived to be essential to the cultural continuity of the inland Dena'ina. In addition, they provided me, the non-Dena'ina co-author, with enduring warmth, generosity, persistent patience, and friendship. They tolerated my child-like ignorance about inland Dena'ina culture and enculturated me as thoroughly as possible, especially given my status as an anthropologist and, ultimately, an "outsider." Without question, the involvement of a Dena'ina co-author in all phases of the project was important to the members of the community. In particular, some elders should be mentioned by name. Sophie Balluta Austin, both authors' "mom," provided an immeasurable amount of information as well as a home in the community. Agnes Trefon Cusma, "sis" to both authors, gave hours of time, her exquisite smoked sockeye strips and other delicacies, and continued emotional support. Albert Wassillie, Dena'ina historian and intellectual, used his abilities at Dena'ina literacy to work on all phases of the project, including interpreting the Russian Orthodox confessional data and historic photographs. Ruth Koktelash and Pete Koktelash, despite Ruth's serious illness during the research, never wavered in their willingness to provide a wealth of oral historic information. Members of the Nondalton Traditional Council and Kijik Corporation Board of Directors were always cooperative. It is hoped that this ethnography gives the people of Nondalton something which is worthy of their sincere dedication.

During 1985, when the project was not firmly focused, the elders of Lime Village provided significant information and support. Our particular thanks go to Vonga and Matrona Bobby, who dispensed most of what we know about the cultural histories that link the two communities and inland Dena'ina as a people. In addition, we would like to acknowledge Sandy Williams, President, Lime Village Corporation, and Jim Williams for their comments on the manuscript.

There are several individuals who deserve particular note. Ted Birkedal, Regional Archaeologist, U.S. National Park Service (NPS), Alaska Region, became manager of the Lake Clark ethnographic project during the second year of research. Birkedal is an anthropologist with great breadth, depth, and insight, supplemented with an astute sense of history, context, and humor. He supported this project with all of his professional and personal abilities from the second year of research through the days of printing and publication in 1992. The appreciation which he deserves, professionally and personally, is beyond what we can put into words.

Paul Haertel, first Superintendent of Lake Clark National Park and Preserve (LCNPP) and now Associate Regional Director, Resource Services, U.S. National Park Service, Alaska Region, demonstrated unusual insight into and sensitivity toward the inland Dena'ina of the Lake Clark area by seeking funding and supporting, throughout the last six years, an ethnographic research project under the auspices of NPS. To Haertel, knowledge about the indigenous people of the area was as integral to the successful commencement and direction of Lake Clark National Park and Preserve as were its resources, land, and aesthetic beauty. Andrew E. Hutchison, the current Superintendent of Lake Clark National Park and Preserve, deserves mention for his patience and support during the last years of the project.

George Sherrod, Research Associate in the Department of Anthropology, University of Alaska Fairbanks, assisted in each and every phase of the project. He computerized the otherwise unmanageable genealogical data. Sherrod, known as the "man with the boots" by the residents of Nondalton, conducted research in the community, particularly mapping lifetime land use areas for most elders. As extraordinary cartographer and illustrator, he drew by hand the base map and an unpublished genealogy for seven generations of inland Dena'ina. He helped in every phase of the rewriting, by assisting in compiling the comments of multiple and insightful reviewers. Sherrod provided enduring loyalty and support throughout the project.

Although a relative newcomer to the project, Thetus Herndon Smith undertook the monumental task of taking the final draft through all stages, from authors to typesetting to printing. She acted as a patient intermediary between the authors, NPS as the original funding organization, and the Smithsonian Institution as publisher. She read each word and provided the authors with invaluable non-anthropological feedback as well as precise and detailed editorial expertise. Without Smith's tireless efforts and patience with exhausted authors, the publication of the manuscript in 1992 would not have come to pass.

The linguistic expertise of James Kari, Alaska Native Language Center, University of Alaska Fairbanks, was indispensable and fundamental to the successful completion of this project. His *Dena'ina Noun Dictionary* (1977) was used at all stages of the project. Kari provided the original Dena'ina place names list, to which data were added from this project (J. Kari and P. Kari 1982). He assisted in the translation and transliteration, with the assistance of Albert Wassillie and Andrew Balluta, of many relevant Dena'ina texts archived at the Alaska Native Language Center. As a scholar, he is considered the foremost linguist of Dena'ina and some other northern Athabaskan languages.

Catharine McClellan, Professor Emeritus, Department of Anthropology, University of Wisconsin, Madison, and her former student, James Fall, Division of Subsistence, Alaska Department of Fish and Game, provided the most in depth and insightful reviews of the draft ethnography. Although they cannot be blamed for any of its errors, they certainly are responsible for the scholarly quality of many of its contributions.

Other reviewers deserving our appreciation include, alphabetically, Garrick Bailey, Department of Anthropology, University of Tulsa; Ted Birkedal; Muriel Crespi, Senior Anthropologist, NPS; Michael Levin, U.S. Census Bureau; and Alice J. (A.J.) Lynch and Dale Taylor, NPS, Alaska Region.

Other U.S. National Park Service personnel who contributed cultural, organizational, drafting and mapping, and funding expertise and support to the study include, alphabetically, John Christopher (while a student at UAF; now an employee of NPS); Craig Davis; Wendy Davis; Boyd Evison; Paul Gleeson; Leslie Hart; Alice J. Lynch; Diane Reed; Theresa Thibault; Hollis and Pam Twitchell; Larry van Slyke; and Anne Worthington. We also thank Nancy McLoughlin, John Quinley, Claire Willis, and Jim Wood for paving the path to publication.

Many people contributed to the research and/or analyses of data. Most, but not all, of these were administrators/academics, staff, or students from the Department of Anthropology or IMPACT (Instructional Media Production and Communication Technology), University of Alaska Fairbanks. These include, alphabetically, Kathy Arndt; Edmund Cridge; Michael Engelhard; Michael Faugno; Susan Faulkner; Ted Goebel; Joseph Gross; Sara Hornberger; Priscilla Russell Kari; Gary Kontul; Jeff Leer; Sarah J. McGowan; Holly Nickerson; Jim and Mary Pierce; Hugh Richards; Anne Shinkwin; Barbara Smith; Rose Speranza; Julie Sprott; John Stinson; Anne Sudkamp; Polly Wheeler; Richard Veazey; the Walsh Agency; and Tom Wolf. Arndt and Smith were critical in providing Ellanna information about the use of the the Russian Orthodox Church and Russian-American Company archival records, as were Sudkamp and Stinson in translating them. As Ellanna was mailing text from Australia to Alaska during the final stages of writing, Pam Odum provided both editorial and secretarial support. In the last throes of writing, Tracie Cogdill took on the unenviable task of compiling the final bibliography. Both Odum and Cogdill were or are secretaries in the Department of Anthropology, University of Alaska Fairbanks.

Others require acknowledgement for their contributions to making the publication of the manuscript a reality: Lorraine Basnar Elder for her excellent cover design; Daniel Goodwin, editorial director, Smithsonian Institution Press, for his belief in the book's merit for publication; and Diane Dodd and Barbara Holzworth, General Services Administration, for ensuring quality printing.

Lastly, through all stages of research, analyses, writing of the draft, and rewrite of the final ethnography, Ellanna's family and closest friend patiently endured her day and night preoccupation with this project. Therefore, she would like to thank her sons, Dayne and Mischa Ellanna; her daughters, Ookuk, Aleta, and Tara Ellanna; her husband, George Sherrod; and her friend, Polly Wheeler. Without their supportive attitude and assistance, the final product may have been completed much later and with considerably more stress. To them, my love!

PREFACE

Lake Clark National Park and Preserve was established on December 2, 1980, by section 201(7)(a) of the Alaska National Interest Lands Conservation Act (ANILCA) (Public Law 96-487). The park, containing 2,439,000 acres, and the preserve, containing another approximately 1,600,000 acres of what had been designated legislatively as "public lands," included much of the country inhabited and used by the inland Dena'ina Athabaskans of Alaska. Archaeological, ethnohistoric, and sociocultural information, which existed prior to the formation of this federal land unit, was limited in temporal and topical scope and, in some respects, was poorly integrated. However, it demonstrated that the inland Dena'ina had been located in the vicinity of Lakes Clark and Iliamna, the two largest bodies of water within the area, and along the drainages of the upper Stony (a tributary of the Kuskokwim) and Mulchatna (a tributary of the Nushagak) rivers prior to Euroamerican contact in the late 1700s and throughout the historic period (see Map 1 in the "Introduction").

The northern boundary of the area lies approximately 100 miles southwest of Anchorage, accessible only by air or on foot, through formidable, glaciated passes. The park includes almost all of the rugged Chigmit Mountains, which are located at the convergence of the lofty, precipitous Alaska and Aleutian mountain ranges. This terrain effectively had isolated this area from the more intensive nature of the early Euroamerican contact with indigenous peoples that had occurred on the coast. The preserve adjoins the park to the south and west and comprises an area of foothills, a multitude of rivers and lakes, and tundra plains (US, NPS 1984).

As in the case of most United States national parks, the primary intent for the formation of Lake Clark National Park and Preserve was to protect and maintain the resources and wilderness qualities of the area. According to Section 201.4 (a) of ANILCA, Lake Clark National Park and Preserve was to be managed:

to protect the watershed necessary for the perpetuation of the red salmon fishery in Bristol Bay; to maintain unimpaired the scenic beauty and quality of portions of the Alaska Range and the Aleutian Range, including volcanoes,

glaciers, wild rivers, lakes, waterfalls, and alpine meadows in their natural state; and to protect habitats for and populations of fish and wildlife, including, but not limited to caribou, Dall sheep, brown/grizzly bear, bald eagles, and peregrine falcons (US, NPS, LCNPP 1986:10).

Though not specifically mentioned in this mandate, approximately one-third of major planning issues identified for the park and preserve included concerns related to or involving the indigenous Dena'ina. It is this population who resided in or adjacent to the park and preserve and relied economically, nutritionally, socially, and culturally on resources from within this newly formed federal land unit. The most important of the resource management issues related to the research associated with this ethnography were the ". . . management and protection of cultural and archaeological resources and the opportunity for subsistence lifestyles by local rural resident" (US, NPS 1984:4).

Although, by western standards and laws related to land tenure, the area encompassed by the newly formed Lake Clark National Park and Preserve appeared relatively "uninhabited," it, nonetheless, was considered "home" to the inland Dena'ina. As traditional hunters, fishers, trappers, and gatherers, the inland Dena'ina did not erect cities, clear land for cultivation, or otherwise modify the environment in the manner associated with members of agroindustrial societies. Rather, the inland Dena'ina extracted their livelihood, built their camps and villages, sustained a relatively complex social and cultural system, and embraced a world view focused on the land and resources now associated with the park and preserve.

Based on the issue statement quoted above and others listed in the general management plan and environmental assessment (US NPS 1984), it is apparent that US National Park Service (hereafter referred to as NPS) personnel were not unaware of these facts. Paul Haertel, the first superintendent of Lake Clark National Park and Preserve and an administrator of considerable foresight, Leslie Hart, and Craig Davis (Division of Cultural Resources, Alaska Region, NPS) jointly began to seek funding in 1982 for the "Lake Clark Sociocultural Study." This project was conceived as being an important step in complying with relevant provisions of ANILCA (Titles VIII, IX, XIII, and X IV), the American Indian Religious Freedom Act (P.L. 95-341, soon to be updated or replaced by the Native American Graves Protection and Repatriation Act, Public law 101-610, November 16, 1990), the "National Park Service's Cultural Resource Management Guidelines" (U.S. National Park Service 1985a), and, subsequent to the commencement of the study, the Native American Relationships Policy (US NPS 1987b). Research which lead to this ethnography also was conceived to be a means of establishing and maintaining a mutually supportive relationship between NPS and the Dena'ina of the area.

The intent of this study was to provide both ethnographic and ethnohistoric data on the indigenous populations which, from the prehistoric period up to the present, have occupied and relied on land within and adjacent to the newly formed park and preserve. This focus was a deviation from conventional anthropological studies conducted by NPS in Alaska, which had been largely, though not exclusively, archaeological in nature. Notable exceptions to this research trend included relatively more recent subsistence focused studies, which had preceded the implementation of ANILCA (e.g., Behnke 1978; Nelson, Mautner, and Bane 1982). This sociocultural project was an indicator of the growing recognition by NPS personnel in the Alaskan context of the value of human and cultural, as well as "natural," resources. Further, it was an acknowledgment of the relationships, developed over centuries, between indigenous inhabitants and the land and resources upon which they depended.

Although the funding for the research was sought in 1982, it was not until 1985 that the monies were appropriated. In spring of that year, Sara Hornberger, public school teacher and resident of Lake Clark, was hired to conduct research on the non-Native history of the study area. Later that spring, author Ellanna, an anthropologist on the faculty of the University of Alaska Fairbanks, was selected to be the principal investigator. In 1985, the coauthor, Andrew Balluta, a Dena'ina from the community of Nondalton near Lake Clark and the first full-time local park ranger in Alaska hired under the provisions of ANILCA, was assigned to this study. Balluta and Priscilla Kari (an anthropologist who had undertaken previous research with the Dena'ina of Lime Village) commenced the tasks of collecting oral histories,

place names, and other ethnographic data, principally in the community of Lime Village.

This ethnography, *Nuvendaltin Quht'ana: The People of Nondalton*, is but one of several fruits of this research. The first two years' research culminated in a preliminary and unpublished report, which presented initial findings. These included annotated descriptions of Dena'ina place names (an expansion of data gathered by University of Alaska Fairbanks linguist, James Kari), an analysis of the kinship system and demographic history of the study area, and preliminary genealogies of the residents of the communities of Nondalton and Lime Village. Also incorporated into the interim report were case studies of individual lifetime land use and residence biographies, data on the language and dialects of the area, a summary of Euroamerican contact history, an analysis of historic photographs collected from informants, and a comprehensive Dena'ina bibliography.

In addition to the interim report and the ethnography, P. Kari's research on the use of flora by the inland Dena'ina was published in *Tanaina Plantlore: An Ethnobotany of the Dena'ina Indians of Southcentral Alaska* (1987). A videotape, *Chiqilin Q'a: Dena'ina Fish Cache*, depicting a traditional technique for caching fish no longer practiced by the residents of the study area, was produced by Instructional Media and Production Technology (IMPACT), Elmer Rasmuson Library, of the University of Alaska Fairbanks. An extensive computerized data base was developed by anthropologist, George Sherrod, which incorporates family histories gathered from Nondalton and Lime Village residents.

Additional family history and demographic data were retrieved from Russian Orthodox Church archival records at the University of Alaska Fairbanks. These archival data span the period 1847 to 1910 for the village of Kijik on Lake Clark; 1847 to 1887 for one or more villages on the Mulchatna River; 1906 to 1915 for Qeghnilen on the upper Stony River; and 1902 to 1940 for Old Nondalton.

Other components of the research were integrated into the ethnography. For example, information from an expanded and revised Dena'ina place names map appears in the text, as does an illustrative selection of historic photographs. Multiple, taped, historic interviews, collected or archived by the Alaska Native Language Center, University of Alaska Fairbanks, were translated into English and, in some cases, transcribed in Dena'ina. The texts of these translations and transcriptions provide considerable substance to this ethnography. Lastly, lifetime map biographies of land and resource use, collected from most Nondalton male and female elders and including trails and camp sites, were compiled for description and interpretation in this ethnography.

This research has provided a portrait of life in a modern Dena'ina village — a portrait that, hopefully, will provide a record for the children of today's inland Dena'ina and, in turn, those of future generations. For the lay reader and anthropologist or other social scientist alike, the findings of this research are expressed in both a more standard ethnographic and, alternatively, humanistically oriented written account of a modern hunting and gathering society. More specifically for the academic community, this study contributes to an understanding of subarctic Athabaskans in Alaska and, indirectly, in Canada; historic and contemporary indigenous peoples of North America; and contemporary hunters and gatherers in a global perspective.

For NPS and other state and federal agencies that are mandated legislatively to develop and implement policies which balance the multifaceted interests in and demands on the rapidly dwindling "undeveloped" or "wilderness" areas of Alaska and North America, this research provides significant guidance. The holistic perspective of the study has attempted to integrate the frequently dichotomized concepts of "human" and "cultural" versus "natural" resources. In this regard, the research findings have provided insights into an understanding of the relationships between indigenous populations and their environments. Additionally, the ethnography addresses the question of how exigencies of the modern industrial world have influenced subarctic Athabaskan social and cultural patterns developed over millennia. Lastly, research data illustrate why federal bureaucracies should maintain knowledge of indigenous populations and be cognizant of the lessons which all humanity potentially can learn from them.

Figure 1. Kijik residents posed for a photograph in front of the St. Nicholas Russian Orthodox Church at Kijik, circa 1901. (left to right) Yvdakia Karshekoff, Mary Ann Trefon, Trefon Balluta, Wassillie Trefon (front), Gabriel Trefon (front), unidentified female, Evan Koktelash, four unidentified individuals (two front, two back), Zackar Evanoff, and eight unidentified males and females. This photograph was taken shortly before most Kijik residents commenced their move to the site of Old Nondaltin on Nuvendaltin (Six-Mile Lake). *Photograph Courtesy of Cook Inlet Region, Inc.*

CHAPTER 1

INTRODUCTION

I was going trapping every year until my first son went to school . . . . We [Martha and her huband] stayed right about — you know where that trail comes down from Mulchatna [River]? Right there we stayed. We trapped up there winter time . . . . The last year we trapped in Kijik. We was coming back down and you know how Igiugig, on this side, how it gets no more ice way out and you get into that icky mud? Well, we crossed up here by the islands and was coming down on the ice when we hit Igiugig when we went over that portage. We hit that mud . . . , and Billy was mad because he had to push the sleigh, and I took Billy Jr. out the sleigh and I was packing him on my back. And I was walking way off on that tundra. And then Billy said, "never again will I take you trapping," and I said, "fine, Jr.'s going to school next year." He was hollering at me so I was hollering at him, "fine, Jr.'s going to school next year." Then he [Billy] says, "look at my feet," and his feet were just huge with that mud and just stuck to him. Then when the dogs hit that ice, boy they wanted to go. They started pulling and he was hollering, "hurry up" . . . . I ran over there and threw Jr. in the sleigh, and before I could jump on there, he started off, so I was half hanging on out and dragging. That was the last time I went trapping. I never went trapping no more after that.

Martha Hobson Trefon, 1986

AN AWARENESS OF CONTEXT AND MEANING

As we sat in a tent on a warm, sunny evening during the summer of 1986 at her fish camp on Lake Clark, Martha Hobson Trefon, an inland Dena'ina woman from Nondalton in her mid-40s, in an animated and humorous style, recalled this and many other stories about the changes which had occurred during the course of her life. In many respects, such recollections provided us only glimpses into the complex myriad of changes which, as a relatively young woman, she has experienced over the last four decades.

Over the years, Martha has participated in multiple and diverse ways of life. As a young girl and, later, woman, up until the early 1960s when she was newly married, Martha spent much of the year engaged in a relatively nomadic annual cycle

of residence at hunting, trapping, and fishing camps, with periodic returns to the community of Nondalton a — pattern common to many other Nondalton families into the 1960s. Later, she and her husband, Billy, spent a period of time in Alaska's urban center, Anchorage, where both were employed and Martha learned to be a village health aide (i.e., a trained, local health practioner). Life in Anchorage was not the choice that Martha and Billy ultimately perceived to be in the best interests of their family. Rather, they returned to Nondalton, where they have maintained a home in the village into the 1990s.

However, in large part, living from the land and at camps has not ceased for Martha and Billy, who commonly can be seen travelling by four-wheeler (i.e., all-terrain vehicles), boat, or snowmachine, frequently in the company of adult children and grandchildren, on trips out of "town" to hunt, fish, and gather — activities which they perceive to be both economically, socially, and recreationally important to the overall well being and standard of living of their extended family.

During spring, summer, and fall months, they live at various camp sites, most commonly at their accessible and more permanent "home" on Lake Clark at Chayi Point ("the point where we boil tea") (see Maps 1 and 2). Here amenities include a small steam bath and new tarp covering an extended main tent. This structure has a plywood floor and houses the kitchen, general living, and sleeping areas. It is Martha's, Billy's and their adult children's desire that one day, soon, they can convert this seasonal camp into a year-round residence, with Nondalton being a short boat or snowmachine trip away. In this way, they believe, they, and their children after them, can select the best from both ways of life. That is, they can more regularly and intimately interact with the land they love. At the same time, they have more expeditious access to local resources. Hunting, fishing, trapping, and gathering provide a quality to life, as they perceive it, as well as products on which members of the Trefon family still depend. Yet, they remain near enough to a Dena'ina community where medical, educational, commercial, and sporadic wage earning opportunities are available.

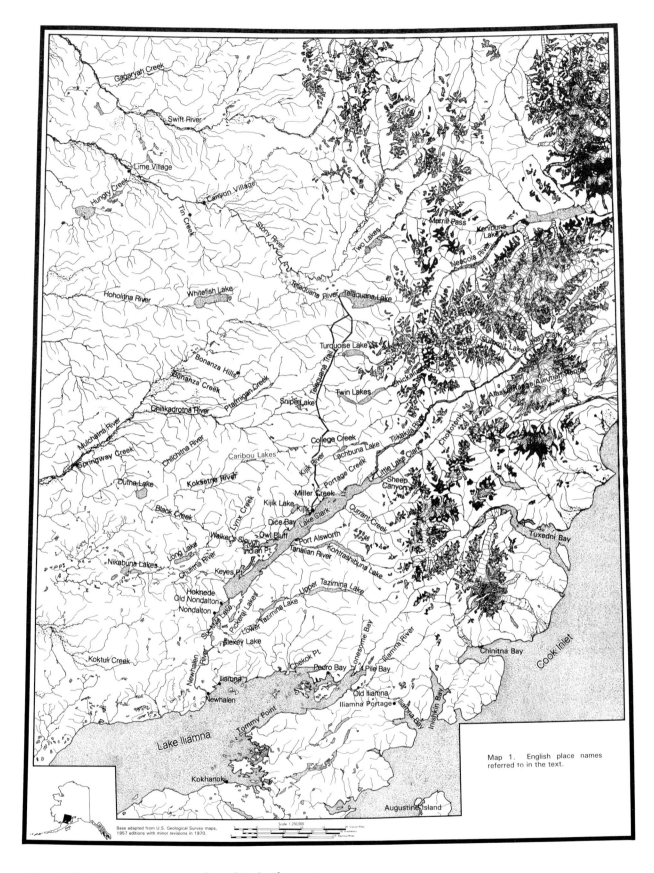

Map 1. English place names referred to in the text.

Map 1. English place names referred to in the text.

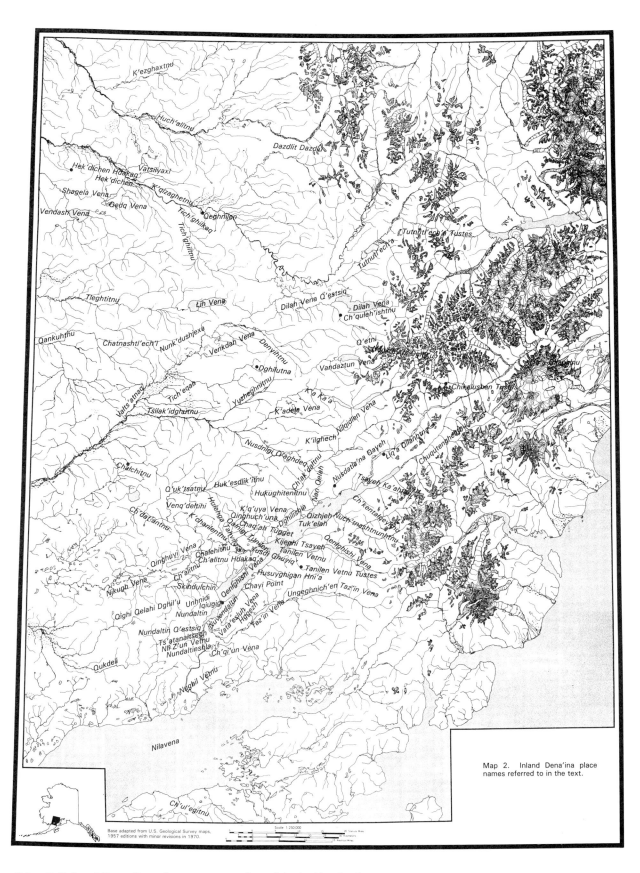

Map 2. Inland Dena'ina place names referred to in the text.

Map 2. Inland Dena'ina place names referred to in the text.

How easy it was for us, the ethnographers, to envision this tale of life spanning a few decades, while located in this setting at Martha's camp — there, at Chayi Point, away from the village and the disruptive sounds of radio, television, all-terrain vehicles, airplanes landing on the bush strip, and, yes, even trucks and cars in this community with less than ten miles of road. Here at the camp, the life that Martha and Billy and many other Nondalton people experienced was somewhat vicariously lived by one of us — a non-Dena'ina anthropologist — and relived by the other, a Nondalton Dena'ina.

For the ethnographer from outside Dena'ina society, the stories Martha told and the aura of life in her camp put flesh on and breathed life into the sterile bones of ethnographic fact and detail. The Dena'ina researcher was learning to record his own culture and history in a written, rather than the traditional oral, form, hopefully to be transmitted to the young people of Nondalton. For him, these stories recalled the poignant remembrances of the years in which Martha's recollections summoned memories of his own youth and early adult life.

It was in the early to middle 1960s that the Nondalton Dena'ina, who were still moving across the land in accordance with the rhythms and cycles of the seasons and the availability of resources, became, in many cases reluctantly, more committed to year-round village life. In doing so, they knew that it had become somewhat necessary to abandon the seasonal round as they had known it since childhood — a cycle which, as we shall see, appears to have been grounded far into the past. It was not that they ceased hunting, trapping, fishing, and gathering, but rather they adapted new technologies and strategies that enabled them to go further in shorter periods of time, thereby accommodating the mandated schedules and demands of more permanent and sedentary village life.

In many cases, no longer did entire families customarily go from camp to camp. Women often remained in the village with young children and elders, except during the late spring and summer, Russian Orthodox Christmas and Easter, or other school or church holidays. While residing in Nondalton, women, younger children, and elders still put up fish at nearby camps on Six-Mile Lake or the Newhalen River, gathered berries and greens in the surrounding countryside, or fished through the ice on the lake or at the mouths of rivers in the vicinity of the community. Young and middle-aged men ran the trap lines and hunted

caribou and moose, returning with greater frequency and for longer durations to the village. In this way, the demands of the western world for the Dena'ina to send their children to school, to attend church regularly and with devotion, and to obtain employment, if and when available, were integrated, to a greater or lesser extent, into the more nomadic way of life remembered wistfully, but with vivid acuity, by elders of the community.

Martha's was only one of a multitude of insights gathered from the contemporary residents of Nondalton during the course of this study. From other residents, we collected life, land use, and residence histories; discourses on the importance of kin, being generous, working hard, and knowing, in detail, the natural world of which all Dena'ina are a part; the characteristics of Dena'ina leadership; and detailed commentaries on the changes which have resulted from contact with the western world and being a part of a large, agroindustrial nation-state.

Dilemmas faced by the inland Dena'ina throughout the contact period have been multiple and diverse. For example, they have tried to accommodate mandatory school and Russian Orthodox church attendance and associated values. They have had to find the means to accommodate expanding requisites for cash and the acquisition of skills and access to occupations for which wages are paid. They have had to develop the abilities to deal with representatives of the non-Dena'ina world successfully and without the loss of cultural pride, identity, and a sense of self sufficiency. Lastly, they have had to bear the costs and sense of loss involved in being tied to a settlement, when their overriding preference and overall economic well-being have been integrally connected to being out on the land.

These social, cultural, and ideological shifts and resulting conflicts are problems needing resolution. They are common among most foraging peoples in the world today. "There can be no doubt that, one way or another, all [hunter-gatherer studies] describe societies coping with the impact of incursions by foreign forces into their territories" (Schrire 1984:18). An important question to social scientists is, then, what can modern hunters and gatherers tell us about the commonalities found among humans worldwide? As Schrire (1984:18) states the question:

> *. . . are the common features of hunter gatherer groups, be they structural elements such as bilateral kinship systems or behavioral ones such as a tendency to share food, a product of interaction with us? Are the features we single out and study held in common, not so much*

because humanity shared the hunter gatherer lifestyle for 99% of its time on earth, but because the hunters and gatherers of today, in searching for the compromises that would allow them to go on doing mainly that, have reached some subliminal consensus in finding similar solutions to similar problems?

In the evolutionary perspective of hunter and gatherer studies, which has a lengthy history within the discipline of anthropology, foraging populations, who are "contemporary at any given point in time," often have been viewed as being significant, primarily or solely, because they forge a tangible link with the heritage of humankind. For example, they provide a useful context for assisting the processes of archaeological interpretation — specifically, through the method of ethnographic analogy.

It is widely acknowledged among contemporary scholars of human evolution that the face of modern day humanity has been molded by the processes of adaptation through time of ancestral hunters and gatherers. Therefore, despite the acknowledged usefulness of ethnographic analogy and ethnohistory in interpreting prehistory and early contact history, it is unquestionably an ill conceived notion that modern foragers somehow have been encapsulated and timelessly, ahistorically, transported from the past to the present in order to shed light on the questions raised by the scholars in their attempts to reconstruct our species' history. Further, it is erroneous to assume that the demographic, social, economic, political, and other sociocultural patterns of present day hunters and gatherers have continued to mirror those of the past, since the dynamic nature of all cultures through time and space has been adequately demonstrated.

Nonetheless, despite the fact that modern day hunters and gatherers "can not their ancestors be," they do provide knowledge of the past and of different human adaptations to those of us enmeshed in the web of the "civilized," industrial world. For example, the study of modern foragers can provide both insights into our evolutionary past as a species and significant lessons about the responses of human societies to sociocultural change.

Modern day hunters and gatherers illuminate many questions about the capacity of humans to extract a living from the land and its natural (non-cultivated) resources. They demonstrate the diversity of ways in which humans can adapt sociocultural systems and related ideologies to a dependency on wild resources for the energy and intellect necessary to sustain human life as we know it today. The demographic histories of hunter and gatherer groups temporally and geographically provide a measure of the success of this economic focus by indicating how long people live, how many children they have, how large and sedentary their communities are, and other relevant information. Modern foragers also shed light on the nature of human sociocultural change, including the actual or illusory phenomenon of worldwide westernization and its related correlate — the loss of cultural diversity.

The significance of documenting the cultural history of the inland Dena'ina in this context cannot be understated and was the specific focus of the research. Additionally, this ethnography was intended to provide a case study of a single group of subarctic Alaskan Athabaskans. Importantly, however, it also was conceived to be a contribution to understanding other modern foragers in northern North America and throughout the world and, if analogies are cautiously employed, the history of humanity in a more general sense. In this respect, then, contemporary hunting and gathering populations like the inland Dena'ina effectively provide insights into the past, present, and future of our species.

Within this ethnography, the inland Dena'ina provide the opportunity for the reader to explore a way of life that is somewhat unique and, importantly, to do so to some extent through the eyes of those who have lived it in the past and present. The temporal dimensions of this study span, through the oral history of Nondalton people, the period from approximately 1890 to the early 1990s — a century of relatively rapid change. Additionally, information about inland Dena'ina cultural history was gathered from early published and unpublished (archival) sources, which expanded the temporal framework for limited topics back to approximately the mid-1800s. Additional but limited data were derived from archaeological sources.

The ethnography itself, a method and tool of anthropological inquiry and communication from the earliest days of the discipline, is a format which has become more complexly conceived, innovatively used, and substantively critiqued in the anthropology of the 1980s (e.g., Marcus and Fischer 1986; Wolf 1982). The ethnographic process and product, then, deserve further comment in regard to how they were employed in this context.

THE ETHNOGRAPHY AS
A CULTURAL PORTRAIT

Formal fieldwork related to *Nuvendaltin Quht'ana: The People of Nondalton* spanned a five year period, 1985 through 1990, and included a cumulative total of approximately 18 months in Nondalton and surrounding areas. Data were gathered through the traditional methodologies of cultural anthropology, including extensive and highly active participant observation, the collection of oral histories, structured interviews, biographical mapping and residence history interviews, incalculable hours of informal discussions and observations, and the collection of individual life and family histories.

As Nelson (1973:8) perceptively noted in his study of the Gwich'in (also referred to as the "Kutchin" in the literature) of the Chalkyitsik area of Alaska, participant observation among Athabaskans requires that ". . . . the ethnographer attempts to replicate the behavior involved in the activities he [or she] is documenting and to learn to perform each technique at least at a minimal level of proficiency." The Gwich'in, the Dena'ina, and most other documented hunting and gathering peoples also educate their young, both male and female, by this technique of "active participation." That is, verbal instruction is limited or absent. A novice, including, of course, any newcomer into the society, is expected to watch, attempt the tasks involved, be corrected for any mistakes, and good naturedly accept the humorous but pointed jokes about his or her efforts – an example of nonwestern "on-the-job-training" of sorts.

However, as Nelson (1973) and many others have pointed out, there are difficulties inherent in the "active participation" method of conducting anthropological research. The most obvious, but least complicated to resolve, involves excessive and, often conflicting, temporal commitments. That is, while undertaking productive activities with and for members of the study population and oneself, little time remains for note taking. Keeping notes and journals – the "data" of sociocultural anthropologists – often occurs during stolen moments late at night or early in the morning, frequently with negligible privacy. Even when important activities are not in progress, observations of interpersonal interactions or discussions further add to the problem of finding adequate time for taking notes or for reflecting upon what one has learned in any given day.

More potentially complicated is what Nelson (1973) suggests is the "loss of objectivity" resulting from the level of intense involvement with members of a study population. On the face of it, this, indeed, could be perceived to be a perplexing obstacle, particularly if one naively assumes that the anthropologist in the field is capable of maintaining the total objectivity implicit in the ideals of cultural relativism. In reality, as has been well documented by the earliest generations of field workers in the discipline (e.g., de Laguna 1957; Malinowski 1922), it is never possible, nor necessarily desirable, to fully discard the cultural "glasses" through which the anthropologist sees the world of others. In fact, innovative ethnographers in the 1980s have argued that one's cultural perspective can be critically applied to the ethnographic process and product (Marcus and Fischer 1986). Such contemporary approaches to ethnography have incorporated less traditional perspectives in the process of ethnographic data gathering and description, variously integrating views which were once seen to be dichotomous (such as the "native" versus the "anthropologist," the "insider" versus the "outsider," the "emic" versus the "etic").

The traditional role of the anthropologist as being solely responsible for analyzing data and drawing conclusions is open to question. In the view of some contemporary ethnographers, the reader inevitably is involved in this analytical process – that is, in arriving at cross cultural conclusions based on the data which are presented by the social scientist (Marcus and Fischer 1986). The problems confronting the anthropologist in relating to members of a study population and their way of life are, in and of themselves, legitimate subjects of inquiry. In discussing the organization of this ethnography below, some of these points are highlighted as they applied to this context.

Although the majority of field data were gathered by the authors, several non-local and local research assistants were involved in both data collection and analyses. However, most meaningful for these purposes is to note that many members of the community became an integral part of the study process. They expressed a vested concern in the outcome of all phases and facets of the study and were not hesitant to express their opinions about the content and conclusions when reviewing draft manuscripts. They spontaneously offered their own analyses of externally derived events and changes over which they perceived that they lacked influence. They gave of their time willingly for the purpose of documenting what it meant to them to be inland Dena'ina, both in a collective and individual sense. They saw the products of the research to be a means of recording their cultural heritage and expressing their concerns about the future of their children and grandchildren, their community, and their culture.

The level and breadth of community involvement in this study is not common in anthropological research. For this reason, it is possible that the nature of some of these data may be more indepth, albeit potentially different, from those resulting from research conducted solely by an ethnographer, who, in a more traditional style, has retained full control of the research, analytical, and reporting processes in conducting cultural inquiry (Marcus and Fischer 1986).

Since one of the authors was a local, bilingual Dena'ina, as a team we had a decided advantage in interviewing elders who spoke only their Native language. Although an attempt was made to translate, verbatim, interviews which were conducted solely in Dena'ina, unquestionably secondary interpretation from the perspective of the Native author occurred. Similar interpretation obviously occurs when the language of the ethnographer is employed in interviews with bilingual speakers of another language. In this respect, then, both authors were active within a primary level of the analytical process based principally upon language and related conceptual differences.

Early on in the course of conducting this study, it was decided that the ethnography would be researched and written in a manner more appealing to a diverse audience than would be a standard academic monograph. One means of accomplishing this goal was to adapt the model established by Brody in *Maps and Dreams* (1982) — that is, by interspersing the academically oriented chapters with those written in a more humanistic genre.

Specifically, it was decided that those chapters entitled "Dena'ina Perspective" would be researched and conveyed in a manner which approached the communication of the "insider's" point of view to as great a degree as was feasible. It was intended that these chapters parallel the substance of the more academically analyzed and composed chapter or chapters that preceded them. Most of the "Dena'ina Perspective" sections of the ethnography were more or less biographical in orientation. Interviews from which they emerged were purposefully structured with this end in mind.

Marcus and Fischer (1986) have discussed ethnography as both a process and product within the discipline. The different ways in which ethnographies can be used to portray varying social realities have been highlighted in this discourse. Marcus and Fischer (1986) portray anthropology as a discipline and its practitioners as having become more sophisticated and aware of ways in which they inflict their academic models on the processes of data gathering, analysis, and portrayal. They have suggested that endeavors to portray the "native" or "insider" perspective, however well intended, remain colored by the approaches and analytical categories of the discipline — that there are many social realities and these may all be anthropological in nature, albeit approached from a variety of new and innovative techniques.

With these cautions in mind, the "Dena'ina Perspective" chapters of this ethnography were intended to portray the Dena'ina world view as it applied to a variety of topics — such as, characteristics of Dena'ina leaders, marriage and the family, patterns of land and resource use, and participation in introduced western market activities. Additionally, the use of biographical histories in this context addressed another concern of Marcus and Fischer (1986) — namely that ethnography not portray its subjects in an ahistorical vacuum. Since both the researchers and the Dena'ina shared a common interest in cultural change through time and space, a consistent attempt was made to set Dena'ina culture and society today in their historical, social, political, and economic contexts.

OTHER METHODOLOGICAL NOTES

In many respects, it was fortuitous that the interests of the U.S. National Park Service, as described in the preface, and those of the Dena'ina of Nondalton merged in this study. Both had vested interests in the land and resources of the Lake Clark area and mutual, albeit somewhat different, concerns about potentially conflicting uses resulting from the formation of this national park and preserve. In addition to Nondalton, Lime Village and the Athabaskan people of the Iliamna area also had historical and contemporary vested interests in the lands encompassed within the newly formed park and preserve. The Nondalton sociocultural study provided a vehicle by which information about the historical and contemporary culture of the inland Dena'ina could be documented. Simultaneously, this information provided the U.S. National Park Service with data critical for their management decisions and interpretive programs related to the indigenous populations or human resources of the area.

The success of the project was unquestionably facilitated by local Dena'ina coauthorship. His participation was central in gaining access to local communities, generating resident interest in the study, successful data gathering and analysis, and the local reviews of interim and final manuscripts.

The choice of Nondalton as the community of focus can be explained most clearly in an historical context. In the initial year of research (1985), primarily residential histories, information on land and resource use, and family histories were gathered in Nondalton, Lime Village, Chekok Point, and Pedro Bay. It soon became clear that temporal and fiscal restrictions of the project mandated focusing the research on a single community. Since previous anthropological studies had been undertaken by Townsend (1965) in Pedro Bay and P. Kari (1983) in Lime Village, and because Nondalton is the most proximal community to Lake Clark National Park and Preserve, the choice of this community as the focus of research was relatively straightforward.

Based on previous research and preliminary data analysis, it was clear that contemporary Nondalton residents and their ancestors were representative of a much larger Dena'ina population distributed over a more expansive geographic area. The largest segment of Nondalton's ancestral and contemporary populations originated on the Stony River, including those from the contemporary community of Lime Village. Additionally, new Nondalton is the most recent site of the centralization of other Dena'ina populations or their descendants originating from communities and camps on the Mulchatna River, Telaquana Lake and River, and at Kijik on Lake Clark (see Maps 1 and 2).

Lastly, several resource management issues had focused on the use of fish and game by Nondalton residents. Most importantly, however, it was assumed that the greatest potential for mutual impact of the newly formed park and preserve on the inland Dena'ina and the Dena'ina on the park and preserve, especially in regard to access to land and resources, would involve Nondalton residents.

The Nondalton sociocultural study was multidimensional. Its central end product was conceived to be an ethnography, including a substantial ethnohistoric component. The application of multiple and diverse data sets to a specific question or group of related questions provides a useful example of how information gathered during this study was integrated. One principal objective was to explain inland Dena'ina land and resource use in a diachronic perspective. In order to undertake this task, the researchers needed information about inland Dena'ina concepts of land tenure and related sociocultural institutions. It was fundamental for the researchers to comprehend intercommunity and intracommunity and local and regional band distribution, exchange networks, and the composition of production units. This information necessitated the collection of family histories and genealogies by means of informant recall and the translation and transliteration of Russian Orthodox Church archival confessionals, priest travel reports, and vital statistics for the study areas. In addition, since the contemporary Nondalton population was highly mobile between the study community, Lime Village, and Anchorage, it was necessary to gather comparable data on the transient portion of this larger "community." The intent was to depict, through time and space, a society or community of inland Dena'ina now focused around the settlement of Nondalton. Hence, this research could be neither synchronic nor limited to members of the village during the study period, as both would have created artificial boundaries in delineating the study population.

The demographic and genealogical data were critical to interpreting changing population structure and residence patterns and the relationship of these variables to the inland Dena'ina kinship system. Residents of Nondalton were fascinated with the draft genealogy and its extension backward through time based on the Russian Orthodox records — a database which had to be computerized for analysis because of its size and problems with the identification of Russian and English orthographic depictions of Dena'ina and early Russian names. Genealogical, demographic, and kinship data were analyzed by a modified set of programs designed for the analysis of small, geographically or culturally isolated societies. The draft genealogy was corrected by elders and used in the school in conjunction with matriclan (matrisib) terminology to explain genealogical links and clan affiliation to younger members of the community. Demographic analysis involved the use of the Statistical Package for the Social Sciences (the version referred to by the acronym SPSSX). The analyses of these data yielded information concerning the role of kinship in Dena'ina marriage of the recent past and present. Kinship terminological systems and related obligatory behaviors were analyzed in conjunction with demographic and land use information to provide a greater comprehension of the overall inland Dena'ina sociocultural systems of past and contemporary periods.

The patterning of inland Dena'ina land and resource use through time and in response to introduced economic and political factors (such as the development of the Bristol Bay commercial fishery, the fur trapping and trading post eras, and territorial and state resource management) were of major theoretical interest in this context. Consequently, lifetime map biographies were completed for most male and some female residents of Nondalton over the age of 50 and selected other younger individuals for comparative purposes. These data were gathered by means of the mapping methodology described in Ellanna, Sherrod, and Langdon (1992). Individual map biographies were gathered according to segments of the seasonal round, as perceived by the inland Dena'ina, rather than by the more commonly used method of mapping by species. This seasonal cycle was analytically derived from land and resource use data collected prior to the majority of mapping interviews. In a few cases, personal rather than composite maps were analyzed for different time periods representing changes in individual life status (such as marriage, ill health, or advanced age). However, most mapped data, which appear in this ethnography, are presented in the form of composites.

Prior to this study, the land use patterns of the inland Dena'ina were much less well documented than that of their coastal cultural "relatives" on Cook Inlet. Insights derived from reconstructing and recording these patterns diachronically were, in part, used to explain the phenomena of mobility and band fusion and fission for a northern Athabaskan population reliant on both relatively abundant and recurrent runs of sockeye salmon and, in more recent years, expanding populations of large game such as moose and Mulchatna caribou.

In hunting and gathering societies, among whose members knowledge of the natural environment is detailed and pragmatically, spiritually, and socially significant, indigenous place names yield a proliferation of ideological data. Place names not only surrender extensive oral historic information about natural and social environments, human populations, and their histories, but they are also essential to a cognitive analysis of world view. Although it was critical to gather Dena'ina place names in order to properly analyze the more mundane aspects of geographic and land and resource use data, throughout the ethnography

place names have played a key role in providing insights into the inland Dena'ina world view and their perceptions of the empirical and nonempirical features of the environments which they inhabit.

A preliminary place names data set was provided by linguist, James Kari, of the Alaska Native Language Center, University of Alaska Fairbanks. The Nondalton study provided additional names, annotations for new and existing names, and raised some semantic and orthographic questions which may require additional linguistic analysis. Only a portion of the total place names data base which included in excess of 600 names at the culmination of this study appears in the context of the ethnography (see Map 2).

During the first (1985) field season, research assistant, P. Kari, gathered data on the ethnobotany of the inland Dena'ina of the study area to supplement previously compiled and published information for both coastal and inland areas of contemporary Dena'ina distribution (Kari 1977). The previously published work was updated and republished, as a product of this study, under the title, *Tanaina Plantlore* (P. Kari 1987). Data from this component of the research is not reiterated, for the most part, in the ethnography but could be consulted by readers with a particular interest in the plants gathered by the Dena'ina and their uses.

Until the introduction of salting as a prevalent supplementary means of fish preservation approximately in the early 1900s, the inland Dena'ina cached some salmon and their heads and eggs in spruce and birch bark lined pits in the ground as one means of preservation. This method, in addition to smoking and drying, offered dietary variety and insurance against ecological fluctuations which could, and did, result in periods of "hard times" or starvation. As part of the Nondalton study, construction of this caching technique was both video and audio taped by the Instructional Media Production and Communication Technology (IMPACT) division of the Elmer Rasmuson Library, the University of Alaska Fairbanks. The Dena'ina portions of the narrative were translated and relevant tapes transcribed into English. The videotape, entitled "*Chiqilin Q'a,* Dena'ina Fish Cache" was made available to the community, the local school system, external secondary and post-secondary educational institutions, and Lake Clark National Park and Preserve.

Historic and contemporary photographs of the study area were employed as a source of data, as a means of portraying culturally relevant phenomena in a more humanistic format and as a research tool for eliciting oral histories and other information from Nondalton residents. The historic photographs principally were gathered from current and previous residents of Nondalton and, for the most part, previously had not been placed in archival collections. Both video and still photographs were filmed during the multiple years of field work. Many of the still photographs are included in the context of the ethnography to illustrate particular people, places, and events.

During the initial two years of the project (1985 and 1986), a local historian was employed to conduct interviews focused on the non-Dena'ina history of the Lake Clark area. Although these data were not published separately, they were applied to the analysis of Euroamerican contact and related inland Dena'ina cultural change within the context of the ethnography.

During the course of gathering the family history data, a relatively high per capita incidence of morbidity and mortality from cancer was documented. Since it was the intention of the researchers to use information which would benefit the inland Dena'ina, the U.S. Public Health Service, Center for Disease Control (CDC), was contacted regarding the cancer data. This contact, and the expressed interest and concern on the part of the Nondalton Traditional Council, stimulated CDC's involvement in a survey and analysis of potential carcinogenic substance exposure in Nondalton. Supplemental data were gathered and the findings presented by medical anthropologist, Sprott (1986).

Finally, whereas the interim report (Ellanna 1986) contained a keyworded, pan-Dena'ina bibliography, citations included in this context were intended to provide a comprehensive review of anthropological and historical references related specifically to the inland Dena'ina of the Lake Clark, upper Stony, Mulchatna, and Telaquana

rivers, and, to a lesser degree, the Lake Iliamna area. As such, the bibliography is not limited to references cited. Although a few specific archaeological references, of particular relevance to historical interpretations, are included, this bibliography is not intended to be inclusive for the prehistoric period.

As a final note, it is hoped that this ethnography will achieve many goals for different audiences. For the inland Dena'ina of Nondalton and elsewhere in the study area, it is a documented interpretation of their sociocultural history and contemporary society and culture. As such, hopefully it will be used as an educational tool for transmitting Dena'ina culture to younger generations faced with a rapidly changing world. For Dena'ina leaders, it may serve to provide guidance in decision making which may involve implicit or explicit contradictions and mandates. For the U.S. National Park Service, this document serves to educate the public who visit the park and preserve and the staff who plan, make, and/or implement policies. Hopefully, this ethnography will increase the awareness within that governmental agency of the importance of indigenous people as cultural and human resources. For the lay reader interested in gaining broader cultural insights in a rapidly shrinking world, the Dena'ina Athabaskans of the Lake Clark area provide an opportunity to view, through multiple perspectives, a different way of life, which has changed in many ways but not become homogenized, westernized, or extinct in the sense predicted by explorers, adventurers, and early social scientists. Lastly, this ethnography provides the academic community with a portrayal of a modern foraging population — in this case of subarctic northern North America. In this ethnography, the authors have strived to achieve the mandates of holism — in spatial, temporal, and topical dimensions — which have inspired the peculiar nature of the discipline of anthropology.

Figure 2 (above). A summer aerial view of Qizjeh Vena, or Lake Clark, 1986. **Figure 3** (below). The upper or northeastern end of Qizhjeh Vena, or Lake Clark, during mid-winter. *Photographs Courtesy of Lake Clark National Park and Preserve.*

CHAPTER 2

THE INLAND DENA'INA: ENVIRONMENT, LANGUAGE, AND CULTURAL IDENTITY

Another time, long ago, they went to a place called Liq'a Qilanhtnu, which is called now ... Big River [or Tlikakila River]. They went all the way up to the glacier and found a crevasse when it was getting dark. A sled went into the crevasse, and the sled had a little baby in it, and the baby fell into the crevasse. Then they put a rope down in there and lowered one guy down. He said, "Don't go too fast, drop me really slow, all the way down in case I get stuck in the side there. Lower me down really slow." They lowered him and lowered him until he could hear the baby crying. He had a caribou tallow candle on the string and they kept him down there, in the cold down in there. And then they lowered him down and he heard that baby crying, and then he had that little stick. He landed right where it was, and he grabbed that kid. He got that baby back, and there was nothing wrong. He lived .... He was still in a basket wrapped up real good. If it would have lasted another ten more minutes, that kid would have frozen to death.

Steve Hobson, Sr., in an interview
with Priscilla Kari, 1981

BEYOND THE COASTAL RANGE

The quotation by Steve Hobson, Sr., above, taken from the wealth of oral history which has been collected from the inland Dena'ina, recounts one of the many attempts of the people from the Lake Clark area to traverse the glacially chiseled Lake Clark Pass on foot, using dogs for pack and human power for hauling their hand-hewn, double-ended sleds. This pass, today a major flight path for small aircraft travelling between Anchorage and Lake Clark, historically provided critical transportation and communication corridors between the inland Dena'ina and their relatives, who resided on the coast of Cook Inlet. However, it was, in part, the isolating influences of the formidable mountain barriers separating the inland and coastal Dena'ina that gave birth to their traditional linguistic, social, and cultural divergence and to a meaningfully different course of contact history with Euroamericans.

In order to arrive at an understanding of the history, culture, and society of the inland Dena'ina, a narrative and visual portrayal of the current configuration of the habitat occupied, for centuries if not millennia, by the inland Dena'ina is of extreme relevance in this context. Unquestionably, biologists, geologists, paleontologists, zoologists, botanists, climatologists, and many other formally trained specialists could describe more precisely this habitat in the terminology of western science. For these purposes, however, a portrait of the always scenic and yet, successively, placid and tumultuous Lake Clark, its drainages and those of the Stony and Mulchatna rivers, is painted primarily by the images, features, and impressions of this natural setting reiterated by the inland Dena'ina in their ongoing, daily conversations. It is this land and its features, its animal and plant life, and the weather and water conditions, so central to the everyday lives and cultural traditions of these indigenous inhabitants, that were the focus of these discussions in Nondalton in the last half of the 1980s.

The most prominent characteristics of the Lake Clark area, contributing to its dynamic nature, are its formidable mountainous boundaries and, relatedly, its volcanic and glacial origins. Lake Clark proper is located west of the jutting mountains that emerge from the northeast as the Alaska Range and, running southwest, become the Aleutian Range. Specifically, the Chigmit Mountains east of Lake Clark include three active volcanoes — 11,100 foot Mount Spurr, 10,197 foot Mount Redoubt, and 10,016 foot Mount Iliamna. This area forms the base of the Alaska Peninsula, which eventually subsides into the sea, becoming the myriad of islands of the Aleutian archipelago. The volcanic origins of this area, commencing as early as 180 million years ago (Hirschmann 1986:25), and glacial weathering continue to change the face of the terrain, even within the collective memory of the Dena'ina. For example, the glacier in the story above told by Steve Hobson, Sr., no longer obstructs Lake Clark Pass. Elder residents remember its retreat and the demise of the lake which contained its melting waters.

In the 1980s, as in the past, the mountains played a major role in funneling strong winds from Cook Inlet to Bristol Bay in the winter and in the opposite direction during spring and summer months, another theme of daily observation and speculation on the part of Dena'ina residents of Nondalton. The mountains also serve to partially negate the moderating influences of the coast on weather patterns of the area. These mountains frequently act as a conduit for storms, roaring through the sinuous passages between Bristol Bay and Cook Inlet that incorporate the Kvichak and Newhalen rivers, Lake Iliamna and Lake Clark, Lake Clark Pass (Qizhjeh Vena Tustes), and the Chokotonk (Chuqutenghetnu) and Tlikakila or "Big" rivers.

Geologists speculate that Lake Clark itself, with a known minimum depth of nearly 1,000 feet and a length of approximately 63 miles, was once connected to the sea, as Iliamna Lake was part of Bristol Bay during the beginning of the Pleistocene (Hirschmann 1986:41). Many of its contemporary features have resulted from what is termed the "Brooks Lake glaciation," occurring between 25,000 and 12,000 years ago — a period preceding the collective oral historic tradition of the inland Dena'ina. In the 1980s, with a few exceptions, all glaciers within the Lake Clark and Lake Iliamna areas were maintaining their size or retreating. Lastly, the lake has fluctuated in depth through time, thereby influencing the location of sites of human habitations along its banks.

As any local adult Dena'ina resident is aware, with the clarity borne of years of intimate familiarity, Lake Clark itself is somewhat disparate in appearance. This was noted, as well, by one of the earliest non-Dena'ina to document information about the lake (Osgood 1904a, 1904b) during his reconnaissance of the area at the beginning of the 1900s. The lower or southwesterly portion is relatively shallow, with less dramatic relief along its shores. At this end it is more similar to the connecting Nuvendaltin or Six-Mile Lake on which the contemporary community of Nondalton is located (see maps 1, 2, and 3). The northeastern (or upper) portion of the lake is characterized by its blue gray color — the result of heavily flowing glacial silt which enters Lake Clark from its mountainous origins. The mountains bordering the lake at its lower end are dwarfed by the increasingly lofty peaks to the north and east. The configuration of Lake Clark reveals the tug and pull of tectonic uplift and volcanic building countered by the erosive activities of wind, precipitation, glaciers, and associated streams.

To the inland Dena'ina, these are the natural features with which they have become familiar throughout their past, as poignantly represented in oral histories. In fact, Qizhjeh Vena, as the inland Dena'ina know Lake Clark , with its islands and multiple tributaries, has been a primary source of food and raw materials, a route of travel

in both summer and winter, and the location of communities and camp sites for the entirety of the inland Dena'ina's collective history. Additionally, the lake and its environs significantly have molded the overall world view of these indigenous occupants (see Figures 4 and 5).

There are several major, and multiple smaller, river systems, of significance to the Dena'ina in the northern part of what is now referred to as Lake Clark National Park and Preserve (as depicted below in Map 3). For example, from the Cook Inlet side, there is the eastward flowing North Fork of the Big River, which carries glacial debris over a 46 mile course into the head of Lake Clark. This river is replaced by the southwest flowing Tlikakila River, west of Summit Lake, paralleled along part of its course by the Chokotonk River. Both of these rivers have glacial valleys, follow branches of a fault line that runs along Lake Clark to the northeast end of the lake, and enter the lake at its northeastern end. The Tlikakila River has deposited sand and silt in such large quantities at the upper end of the lake that it has resulted in the formation of a wide delta separating an upper portion of the lake, referred to in English as "Little Lake Clark," from the main body of water. Little Lake Clark and the main lake are connected only by a narrow channel, navigable when the rivers and lake have adequate water levels and by those travellers with adequate boating skills and knowledge of this narrow waterway.

The southern part of the inland Dena'ina country borders Lake Iliamna (Nilavena). This area and the portage from Iliamna Bay on Cook Inlet to the village of Old Iliamna and from Lake Iliamna to Lake Clark were described in some detail by Osgood (1904a) during his 1902 biological reconnaissance of the lower Alaska Peninsula.

The portage trail leads up the narrow valley of a small stream flowing into the head of the bay, and after 3 or 4 miles crosses a low mountain pass possibly less than 1,000 feet high. On the other side it runs down through several mountain meadows. . . , around a small lake, and along a stream draining toward Lake Iliamna. Passing for 3 or 4 miles through a good growth of spruce timber, it terminates at Iliamna River, opposite the native village of [Old] Iliamna. From the head of Iliamna Bay to Iliamna is about 12 miles. Outfits and supplies are easily taken across by pack horses, or natives from Iliamna village may be secured to "pack" them. The Iliamna River is a stream of fair size flowing from the mountains east of Iliamna Pass, and at the village is about 50 yards wide. Six miles farther on it enters Lake Iliamna. . . .

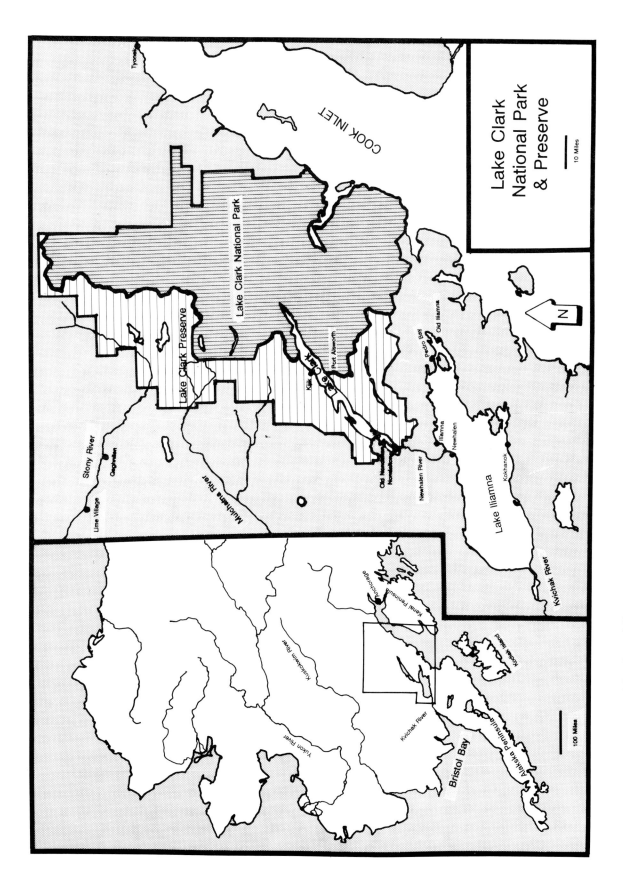

Map 3. Lake Clark National Park and Preserve.

Figure 4 (above). Sophie Austin's long-term home and present summer camp located at Chaq'ah Tugget, a bay across Lake Clark from the present community of Port Alsworth, summer 1986. **Figure 5** (below). The mouth of the Tanalian River (Tanilen Vetnu), near the present day community of Port Alsworth, summer 1986.

Lake Iliamna is about 60 miles [sic] long and from 15 to 25 miles wide. It can not be more than a few feet above the level of the sea, as the Kvichak River, its outlet to Bristol Bay, is navigable for small sloops. At its upper end it is rather shallow and contains many small islands, while the lower end is an uninterrupted expanse of comparatively deep water. The southeast shore is rather mountainous. . . .

In going from Lake Iliamna to Lake Clark a portage of about 6 miles is necessary in order to avoid the Petroff Falls in the lower part of the Nogheling [Newhalen] River. The carry begins a few miles east of the mouth of the Nogheling and crosses the triangular peninsula to the river above the falls. The first half of the trail is rather swampy open country and the last through open forest on comparatively hard ground. Above the portage there is one stretch of a third of a mile of swift water, easily descended by canoes but difficult of ascent except at low water when "tracking" is practicable; otherwise the river is ascended without great difficulty although the current is strong. The entire length of the Nogheling is from 25 to 30 miles (11-12).

Lake Clark is joined to Six-Mile Lake by another narrow channel, which is complex to navigate with modern water craft during periods of the year in which the lake is at lower depth levels. Six-Mile Lake is the site of both the "old" and "new" communities of Nondalton — the latter located near the mouth of the lake where it empties into the Newhalen River (Nughil Vetnu) and the former approximately five miles northeast along the same shore. The Newhalen River, the upper segment of which is the long term site of inland Dena'ina summer fish camps (also described by Osgood in 1904 for the year 1902), is only partly navigable to Iliamna Lake because of the rapids. Lake Iliamna, in turn, drains into the Kvichak River, which flows into Bristol Bay on the southwestern coast of Alaska. The Tazimina River (Nughilqutnu), Lower and Upper Tazimina lakes (Taz'in Vena and Unqeghnich'en Taz'in Vena, respectively), and South, Middle, and North Pickeral lakes (Vata'esluh Vena, Q'aghdeq Vata'esluh Vena, and Unqeghnich'en Vata'esluh Vena, respectively) are also important tributaries of Six-Mile Lake and sites of inland Dena'ina historic and contemporary resource harvesting activities (see Maps 1 and 2).

Only a few of the multitude of other rivers and lakes, which are places of importance in the context of inland Dena'ina residence and land use, are referenced in this general discussion, although some are considered in greater detail in specific narratives below. Those which drain into Lake Clark include: Tanalian River, which enters the lake at the site of the contemporary, principally non-Dena'ina community of Port Alsworth (Figure 5); Miller Creek (Nan Qelah Vetnu) (locally referred to in English as Miller's Creek), a location of fall and winter hunting and trapping camps and the beginning of the well known and used Telaquana trail; Kijik River (Ch'ak'daltnu), the delta of which was the location of the historic community of Kijik; Kijik Lake (a misnomer for K'q'uya Vena or "red salmon lake," as Kijik or Qizhjeh is actually the Dena'ina name for Lake Clark), this smaller lake being located near the site of a more ancient village and fish camp near Kijik Mountain; Chulitna River (Ch'alitnu), which approximately bisects the northern and southern halves of Lake Clark, provides an important transportation corridor to the Mulchatna River, and drains Nikabuna Lake (Nikugh Vena), an important trapping area; Currant Creek (Nuch'tnashtnunhtnu), which has its headwaters in mountain glaciers east of Lake Clark; and the Koksetna River (Q'uk'tsatnu), locally referred to as "Caribou Creek" and a tributary of the Chulitna.

There are other major drainages which remained important areas for inland Dena'ina resource harvesting and associated camping activities throughout the 1980s. North of Lake Clark, these drainages include the Stony River, of which Telaquana River (Dilah Vetnu) (which originates at Telaquana Lake or Dilah Vena) is a tributary, and the Swift River (Huch'alitnu), both of which eventually flow into the Kuskokwim River — one of Alaska's largest riverine systems. The Telaquana area has served as an important site of caribou calving in recent years, was the location of a community throughout the first three decades of the 1900s, and remained a productive fishing site in the 1980s. The upper reaches of the Stony River are the sites of Qeghnilen, an earlier inland Dena'ina community and contemporary fishing location, and Lime Village (Hek'dichen Hdakaq). The Swift River endures as an important location for hunting, trapping, and fishing for Dena'ina residing on the Stony River (P. Kari 1985). As in the cases of the Lake Iliamna and Newhalen River areas, these drainages were points of both peaceful and hostile interface between Yup'ik (Eskimo) and Dena'ina populations.

The third major drainage inhabited and used by the inland Dena'ina was that of the Mulchatna

(Valts'atnaq') and Chilikadrotna (Tsilak'idghutnu or "Middle Fork") rivers, tributaries of the Nushagak River, which flow into Bristol Bay near the modern community of Dillingham. Mulchatna River was the site of several inland Dena'ina communities, all of which were abandoned by the end of the 1800s. Three important lakes — Turquoise (Vandaztun Vena) (Figure 6) and Twin (Nilqidlen Vena) lakes, located approximately 28 miles and 18 miles north of Lake Clark, respectively — drain into the Mulchatna River. Turquoise Lake is an important site of caribou calving, as indicated by the Dena'ina term for the lake and its outlet (Vandaztuntnu or "caribou hair stream"). As is demonstrated in this example, as in many others, inland Dena'ina place names demonstrate the cognizance of these indigenous peoples of critical ecological facts associated with particular areas and sites.

The mountain passes, which historically made the coast accessible to the inland Dena'ina, are of particular interest in this context. Of primary importance to Dena'ina living south of the Stony River was Lake Clark Pass (Figure 7). It is through this pass that many inland Dena'ina portaged to the Cook Inlet side of the mountains during the early Euroamerican contact period, into the area referred to today as West Forelands, and on to the trading facilities at Tyonek.

Oral historic accounts commonly record the treacherous travel through the Lake Clark Pass with its multiple glaciers. To cross a glacier, the Dena'ina recount that they used poles to locate crevasses. They would then camp on the glacier and bridge crevasses with these poles. Then they walked to the coast and remained in Tyonek for a long time, until they were well rested, then returning home (Steve Hobson, Sr., 1981). Lake Clark Pass glacier extended across this pass within the memory of Nondalton elders — the glacier in the story told by Steve Hobson, Sr., and in many other oral accounts.

Other passes north of Lake Clark Pass, between the inland, high plateaus, and the coast, are referenced in oral historic accounts as routes of travel leading specifically from the Lake Clark, Telaquana, and upper Stony River areas to the coast of Cook Inlet. These passes include Telaquana (Dilah Vena Tustes) and Merrill (Tutnutl'ech'a Tustes). The former connects Neacola River (Nikugh Vetnu) on the east with Telaquana River to the west, and the latter is situated between Kenibuna and Two (Tut-nutl'ech'a) lakes. These are narrow, 3,100 foot passes between precipitous mountains that range from 6,000 to 8,000 feet in elevation (Hirschmann 1986:22, 24). For many years, Merrill Pass has functioned as a common route for most small aircraft travelling between Cook Inlet and the interior of Alaska.

Oral historic accounts relate that the Tyonek people used Telaquana Pass in earlier times to gain trading access to the people of the Lake Clark, Telaquana, and upper Stony River areas, especially when Lake Clark Pass was less accessible as a result of glaciation. Current elders of Lime Village and Nondalton, who were born on the upper Stony River, remember stories about Dena'ina going from Qeghnilen over Merrill Pass to Tyonek on Cook Inlet to get gun powder, shells, lead, tobacco, and other trade goods. Some older people remember trapping in these passes as young children.

Another pass, Chickalusion (Chikalushen Tustes), named after Chief Simeon Chickalusion from Kustatan and Tyonek, goes from the Tlikakila River to the head of Twin Lakes. This pass served as a connecting link to Lake Clark Pass. The name of Chickalusion Pass suggests the importance of trading relationships between the inland Dena'ina and those of the coast.

There are numerous oral historic accounts of the inland Dena'ina — who resided in the historic communities of Kijik, Telaquana, and Qegh-nilen — visiting the Iliamna Dena'ina in Old Iliamna village, located at the head of Iliamna Lake. Such visits had both social and economic functions, including the acquisition of trade goods. According to elder informants in Nondalton and Lime Village in the 1980s, the Iliamna Dena'ina lived in an area which bordered that occupied by the historically hostile *Dutna* (translated into English as meaning "Aleut" but used to refer to the Yup'ik speaking people who reside in the vicinity of the Naknek River and the southwestern end of Lake Iliamna). This term is distinct from *Ulchena*, which was used by the inland Dena'ina for the Alutiiq or Sugpiaq Yupik of Prince William Sound, the eastern half of Kenai Peninsula, and Kodiak Island.

The Iliamna Dena'ina were different, according to informants, from the people who lived on the Mulchatna, Lake Clark, Telaquana, and upper Stony River drainages. The residents of Old Iliamna and, in the early decades of the 1900s, new Iliamna, had sustained contact, not only with the

Figure 6. A fall view of Turquoise Lake located on the Mulchatna River drainage. *Photograph Courtesy of Lake Clark National Park and Preserve.*

Figure 7. An aerial view of Lake Clark Pass and the Tlikakila River, summer 1986.

Dutna but also with Russian fur hunters and traders. The latter conducted trade activities fromt he coast via the primary southern portage between Lake Iliamna and Cook Inlet-Iliamna Bay Pass, the 12-mile portage between the community of Old Iliamna and Iliamna Bay.

During the last half of the 1800s and early decades of the 1900s, freight was commonly hauled by dog sleds or horse drawn wagons between Iliamna Bay on the coast and Old Iliamna. Access to Old Iliamna was through a pass called Tanilen Vetnu Tustes, a pass from Tazimina Lake to Lake Clark at the mouth of the Tanalian River. There are oral historic accounts of avalanches occurring in this pass, killing many people and leaving survivors to tell the tale. The other route to Lake Iliamna was along the Newhalen River and over the portage which bypasses the rapids.

This discussion has included only some of the major terrestrial travel routes of the inland Dena'ina in order to give insight into the extent of their mobility. There are many other passes and trails, which once were traversed by men, women and children on foot, pulling sleds and using dogs as pack animals and, later, by families travelling by sled and dog team. Additionally, rivers, streams, and lakes functioned as travel corridors for skin and bark covered boats during periods of open water and on foot and by dog team during times of the year when ice covered waterways. Although in the 1980s, small aircraft served as an important means of transportation, it was well into the late 1930s before the inland Dena'ina regularly saw airplanes and the 1940s and 1950s before this mode of transportation was occasionally used.

The weather in the Lake Clark area is transitional between the maritime climate of Alaska's southwestern coast and the aridity and seasonal temperature extremes of the interior. The location of Lake Clark across the Alaska and Aleutian ranges contributes to weather patterns which are colder with less precipitation than those of the coastal areas. For example, average annual precipitation in the mountainous region along the coast ranges between 40 and 80 inches, whereas only 17 inches fall at Port Alsworth on Lake Clark and 26 inches at Iliamna (Hirschmann 1986:47). In large part, this results from the fact that the mountains, with peaks nearing 11,000 feet, provide an effective barrier to precipitation.

Throughout the period from January to June, the cold, dry air of the interior dominates the climate of the Lake Clark area, because of high pressure systems which emanate from the north. For example, winter temperatures at Port Alsworth range between a recorded low of –55 degrees F., occurring on February 23, 1971, and a record high, associated with moist coastal air, of 54 degrees F. on January 21, 1963. The average winter high and low at Port Alsworth are 22 and 1 degree F., respectively (Hirschmann 1986:54).

Contrastingly, between July and December, moist and warmer Aleutian Island storms dominate the climate, with August and September generally being the rainiest months of the year. Where as it is not uncommon for interior Alaskan temperatures occasionally to reach highs of 100 degrees F., July, the warmest month at Port Alsworth and Iliamna, has an average high of 68 and 62 degrees F., respectively (Hirschmann 1986:54). As can be seen by these data, the proximity of the Lake Clark area to the southwestern coast moderates both high and low temperature extremes.

Prevailing north and northeasterly winds in winter are cold and often reach high velocities. Wind directions and speeds are a continual topic of conversation among the inland Dena'ina. The practice of weather forecasting on the part of inland Dena'ina male and female adults is common, although couched in terms of considerable respect for nature. Cloud formations over Lake Iliamna, Lake Clark, and particular mountains provide critical information to individuals speculating about future weather conditions.

Because of the seemingly changeable nature of the climate between different years, there is considerable variation of months and weeks during which ice forms on Lake Clark and the conditions under which it is thick enough to permit safe crossing. In some years, there are only segments of the lake which are frozen to a depth permitting crossing by snow machine, dog team, all-terrain vehicles, or truck. Ice forms first in shallow bays and later over segments of the lake with greater water depth. However, areas of the lake most directly influenced by northern winds, in some years, may have too much surface disruption for the ice cover to form until late January, if at all. Breakup of the ice on Lake Clark generally occurs in April or May. Oral histories indicate that the depth and extent of ice coverage in the last couple of decades have been considerably less than was the case in the early 1900s.

Since transportation by boat, snowmachine, all-terrain vehicle, truck, or on foot is essential to hunting, fishing, trapping, and gathering activities, the conditions of Lake Clark, Six-Mile Lake, Lake Iliamna, the many rivers and streams of the area, and trails and passes are common and important topics of conversation throughout the year. Extreme wind storms during summer months make boat travel on the larger lakes potentially treacherous and mandate sophisticated knowledge of the location of sheltered beaches or harbors at which travelers can land and wait out storms. Since the inland Dena'ina have become more reliant on small commercial aircraft travel to Anchorage, Bristol Bay, or other villages over the past two decades, weather conditions in regard to flying are also important to contemporary residents of Nondalton. The ability to travel by small aircraft frequently is variable within any given day throughout the year, particularly since flights through the narrow mountain passes to the coast normally depend on visual navigation. Additionally, high wind velocities and "icing" conditions disrupt the use of small aircraft year round.

The varying nature of the climate between years greatly affects the growing seasons and insulative effect of snow on locally available wild flora. These, in turn, influence the distribution of fauna, which are key to the economy of the inland Dena'ina. Though domestically grown vegetables were not an important food source in the 1980s, potatoes and several other garden crops were planted by a few Nondalton families. However, as in the case of wild flora, domestic produce is also affected by variable weather conditions, and the growing season can range between 60 and 90 days.

As in the case of the weather patterns of the Lake Clark area, the flora are also transitional between the boreal forests of the interior of Alaska and the microvegetation of the tundra which dominate coastal habitat north of the Alaska Peninsula (see P. Kari 1987 for more detail on the Dena'ina use of local flora). To some degree, elevation is analogous to latitude in regard to the distribution of wild flora. By boreal forest standards, there are relatively abundant stands of timber, including both deciduous and coniferous varieties, surrounding the entire area encompassed by and adjacent to what is now Lake Clark National Park and Preserve (Figures 8 and 9). As Osgood (1904a) noted at the turn of the century:

> A good growth of timber surrounds the entire lake and runs up the mountain sides from 500 to 1,500 feet. . . . The black spruce . . . , which was not found about Lake Iliamna, however, is

> quite abundant on Lake Clark. This is particularly the case about the lower end of the lake, from the head of the Nogheling [Newhalen] River to Keejik [Kijik], where there is more or less low, moist ground suited to the tree. The aspen . . . is also found in a few places near the Nogheling and about Lake Clark. On the steep mountain sides of the lake, the white spruce is the principal tree, and in many places composes the entire forest. On the north side it is also abundant, but the deciduous poplars and birches are largely mixed with it. . . . Many of the small, low peninsulas projecting into the lake on the north side are almost entirely occupied by groves of poplars. . . . A beautiful open forest of birch and spruce is found in some localities, and much of the ground in such places produces tall grass. . . in great abundance. Devil's club. . .occurs in a few dark, sheltered places near the head of the lake, and perhaps reaches the northwestern limit of its range there. Willows and alders abound in their respective relative positions, while smaller shrubs and boreal plants are in characteristic profusion (13-14).

More specifically, Osgood (1904a) noted at the turn of the century that the banks of the Chulitna River, an important site of spring harvesting by the inland Dena'ina, hosted relatively small hills, brush, and grass, with a wide, grassy swamp providing excellent waterfowl habitat near its lower reaches. He noted that the vegetation changed from the scrubby black spruce and brush along the lower reaches of the river, where banks were poorly defined, to drier areas upriver with more diverse vegetation.

As is the case in inland Dena'ina beliefs about animals, geological and geographical features, climate, and many other characteristics of the natural environment, the relationship between people and plants is a very integral and personal part of inland Dena'ina cosmology. The Dena'ina emphasize the importance of treating all plant life with respect and the avoidance of wasting or abusing any types or portions of plant life. This relationship between humans and flora is accentuated by a set of rules associated with the proper treatment of certain plants and the potential consequences resulting from inappropriate behaviors in this context (Kari 1987:20; see Nelson 1983 for similar views among Koyukon Athabaskans). Among these rules is the principle that the decreased use or non-use of meaningful flora may result in the ultimate disappearance of that species in areas inadequately or not utilized. This principle has important ramifications for potential conflict between inland Dena'ina and western biological management of floral resources in this area.

The inland Dena'ina, like their coastal relatives, are keen botanists and, in addition to having rules for the proper treatment of floral species, apply their own taxonomic scheme in organizing wild flora in a systematic fashion:

> *In the Dena'ina language the concept of the plant kingdom is conveyed by the noun hdenłyahi, which translates as "that which grows." The Dena'ina distinguish plant life from other forms of life in very much the same way modern western man does. . . . Divisions within the plant category, however, are not necessarily the same in the Dena'ina plant system as in the western scientific system or western folk systems* (P. Kari 1987:22).

In the Dena'ina scheme, minimally nine major categories or classes of plants are identified.

Although the harvest of flora as a source of food is of less relative quantitative importance than large terrestrial mammals and salmon (Behnke 1982), the significance of plant life as a source of dietary diversity and essential nutrients, fuel, raw materials for the construction of dwellings and tools, traditional medicine, decoration, dyes, and an essential component of Dena'ina cosmology cannot be over emphasized. The distribution of northern Athabaskans is normally associated with boreal forest habitat. In fact, the presence or absence of necessary stands of spruce (white and black), Kenai and paper birch, mountain hemlock, tamarack, common mountain juniper, balsam poplar, quaking aspen, mountain and thin leaf alder, willow, and dwarf birch played a primary role in group decisions regarding the location of villages and camps throughout the history of the inland Dena'ina (P. Kari 1987).

Spruce was an essential and highly valued type of flora and the subject of considerable local knowledge. Osgood (1970 [1940]) documented the same phenomenon among the Ingalik Athabaskans of the Yukon River in the 1930s. Prior to the use of western plank housing, semi-subterranean winter and more temporary summer dwellings incorporated the use of locally available spruce frames and, in many cases, bark covering for floors, roofs, and siding. Fuel for heat and light was derived from spruce, birch, willow, and other varieties of trees, depending upon purpose and availability. After Euroamerican contact, the use of hand and machine hewn spruce logs for western style housing continued the traditional reliance on this resource. Additionally, spruce continues to be used for fuel, constructing caches, steam baths, fish racks, fish wheels, and many other items of customary and more contemporary technology (J. Kari 1977; P. Kari 1987). In the past, both spruce and birch bark were used for constructing underground fish storage caches (*chiqilin q'a*), a preservation technique widely used in the early 1900s and remembered by only a few elders in the 1980s.

Other traditional inland Dena'ina technology (much of which is still used) fabricated from locally available plants included, but certainly was not limited to, the following. For example, dip nets were made of spruce root and set nets from willow bark. Spruce frames were used for birch bark and skin covered tents and water craft, including both single or double hatched kayak-like boats. Spruce also was used in the construction of the frames of seasonally covered moose hide boats, employed in hauling meat downriver in the spring or in moving freight. This type of wood was also the essential material for the construction of highly valued double-ended sleds. Spruce roots were used for any purpose served by rope, twine, or string in the 1980s, including ice scoops, baskets, and fish snares (P. Kari 1987). Grass was used for making baskets, insulation for clothing and footwear, mats, and floors and was burned as a mosquito repellent. Birch bark was made into basins for hot water, baby carriers, storage barrels, and food platters. Wooden pegs, rather than nails, were employed for a variety of purposes in construction.

Lastly, dietary, medicinal, and artistic uses of flora were abundant in the past and remained so in the 1980s. Wild fruit (locally referred to generically as "berries") was harvested from minimally 20 different species of plants (P. Kari 1987:60), many of which were the primary ingredient of *nivagi* (Indian "ice cream") — a favorite and traditional dish of the inland Dena'ina. Blueberries, lingon berries, cloudberries, and lowbush cranberries were among the most prized varieties in the 1980s, although most of the other species described by P. Kari (1987) were gathered where and when available and eaten, stored, or used for medicinal or aesthetic purposes. For example, crushed cranberries were commonly applied to sore throats. Many other plant foods — such as wild celery, wild onion, sour dock, wild rhubarb, and wild potatoes — had retained a meaningful role in the life of the inland Dena'ina in the 1980s (see P. Kari 1987 for more detail).

Figure 8 (above). A view of the Chulitna River area and vegetation during spring from the hills northwest of the channel which connects Six-Mile Lake and Lake Clark, 1986. **Figure 9** (below). A cow moose and her calf enjoying a winter meal of willows along the Chulitna River. *Photograph Courtesy of Lake Clark National Park and Preserve.*

The importance of salmon as a dependable and abundant resource in relationship to the demography, settlement patterns, and economies of Pacific drainage northern Athabaskan societies has been discussed widely in relevant literature (Hosley 1977; McKennan 1969; Osgood 1936; VanStone 1974). During the 1970s and 1980s, Nondalton residents harvested more pounds in edible weight of salmon than any other locally available resource (Behnke 1982; Morris 1986). Earlier diachronic but nonquantified data have demonstrated the pivotal importance, particularly of sockeye salmon in the Lake Clark drainage. This species provided a food source which was easily stored in summer for human and canine consumption throughout the entire year and between years and, less significantly, was a source of raw materials.

Despite these data, residents of Nondalton viewed themselves primarily as hunters and consumers of large game in the 1980s. This view is compatible with the interior orientation of the inland Dena'ina, as contrasted with that of their coastal relatives on Cook Inlet. This conceptual dichotomy is further reflected in the language and other social and cultural traditions of the coastal and inland groups. Nonetheless, in the 1980s, the inland Dena'in were cognizant of the central role of salmon in their economic and social systems. The dependability, predictability, and quantity of this resource played a major role in enabling the inland Dena'ina to conduct other aspects of their seasonal round of hunting, trapping, fishing, and gathering activities and events of social significance, such as potlatching (Figures 10 and 11).

The Bristol Bay coast of southwestern Alaska is the site of the world's largest sockeye salmon runs. Lake Clark and its tributaries are linked to Bristol Bay by way of the Kvichak and Newhalen rivers. The Kvichak River and its drainage are by far the largest producers of sockeye salmon vis-a-vis the Bristol Bay run. In the peak year of 1965, 74 percent of the Bristol Bay catch were heading for the Kvichak River, based on Alaska Department of Fish and Game estimates (Hirschmann 1986:100). However, these runs are cyclical and are dramatically lower in some years. Tagging experiments in 1983 revealed that 31 percent of that year's Kvichak run crossed Lake Iliamna and ascended the Newhalen River, spawning on the bed of that river, the shallow areas of Lake Clark and Alexey (Ch'qi'un Vena) and Kijik lakes, up the Tazimina, Kijik, and Tlikakila rivers, or into other smaller tributaries (Hirschmann 1986:101). These waterways have been a single species (sockeye) salmon system throughout the historic period. When the commercial fishery commenced in Bristol Bay in the early 1880s, the practice of blocking the mouth of the Kvichak River with fish traps resulted in years of little or no escapement into the rivers and lakes used by the inland Dena'ina, bringing about famine or the need to rely on salmon from the Kuskokwim and Nushagak associated drainages.

Throughout the history of the inland Dena'ina, reliance on sockeye salmon was accentuated by the movement of local people to fish camps on the upper reaches of the Newhalen River and on Lake Clark in summer and to the area near the outlet of the Kijik River and the abandoned community of Kijik for taking spawned-out sockeye in the fall (Figure 11). Oral histories are abundantly endowed with references to the importance of sockeye salmon to the well being of Dena'ina and their dogs. Additionally, involvement in the commercial salmon fishery at Bristol Bay provided a primary source of cash to the community of Nondalton in the 1980s.

The two other salmon systems used by the Dena'ina — that of the Nushagak/Mulchatna and the Kuskokwim/Stony/Swift rivers — were not only supplemental to the Kvichak/Newhalen river runs and the source of specifically desired species, but they were the most proximal and available to the Dena'ina living on the former two drainages. The Nushagak/Mulchatna river system supports multiple salmon species. Oral historic accounts reveal that inland Dena'ina from the Lake Clark area went to the Mulchatna specifically to obtain king and silver salmon. King salmon were valued for their flesh, skins (which were made into waterproof boots), and oil, which was rendered from boiled heads. Telaquana Lake and River are a part of the third drainage — that of the Stony River — which flows into the central Kuskokwim River near the contemporary village of Stony River, approximately 40 river miles upriver from the Yup'ik community of Sleetmute. Steep river gradients and other conditions on the upper Stony River required the use of dip rather than set nets to harvest salmon at fish camps located in the canyon near the historic community of Qeghnilen. Both the Stony and Swift river drainages provided commonly used *nusdlaghi* or silver salmon.

Figure 10 (above). Caribou from the Mulchatna herd grazing on a grassy slope typical of their summer habitat within Lake Clark National Park and Preserve, 1985. **Figure 11** (below). Spawned-out sockeye salmon in late August or early September 1985. *Photographs Courtesy of Lake Clark National Park and Preserve.*

In the case of all drainages, multiple items of technology were used for harvesting salmon. Although presently mandated as illegal by the state's fish and game management system, fish traps were most commonly used for taking salmon in the Kvichak and Mulchatna drainages prior to the introduction of commercially made nets or netmaking materials. Historically, both set and dip nets were made of spruce roots and sinew. King salmon were taken with a harpoon-like spear constructed with a head attached to a line and shaft — a tool referred to in Dena'ina as *dineh*. The head penetrated the king salmon, turned sideways, and the line allowed retrieval of the king salmon in much the same way that marine mammal harpoons functioned in Yupik, Inupiat, and Dena'ina occupied coastal areas. Salmon and other fish species were also taken with snares made out of eagle feather stems, used both in summer and under the ice in winter. Since commercially made nets became available through trading facilities (largely in association with the Bristol Bay commercial fishery), they have become the most common item of technology used for taking salmon in the Lake Clark area. Fish wheels, introduced by miners at the turn of the century, have continued to be used on the Stony River for taking salmon throughout the 1900s.

Many other species of fish have remained important resources to the inland Dena'ina throughout their history, particularly in seasons and localities in which they were a primary source of fresh food (such as at spring camp on the Chulitna River.) These other fish resources, used historically and throughout the 1980s, have included five species of whitefish, arctic grayling, northern pike, rainbow and lake trout, Dolly Varden, two species of char, burbot, least cisco, stickleback, and, occasionally, long nose sucker (see Appendix A). Stories about the importance of these species when multiple salmon runs or terrestrial game species were minimal or absent, for dietary diversity, and as a source of fresh food abound in the oral historic record. Obtaining these fish during all seasons was also a source of considerable pleasure, according to accounts of informants. As in the case of salmon, traps, with mouths of the appropriate diameter for the size of the fish, were the most commonly used item of technology, although multiple other means of taking fish were known and employed. For example, spruce roots were woven into a basket, which was placed under water or ice with a long pole. When it could be

ascertained that the basket-like device contained fish, it was pulled up from the water or ice. Fish were also taken with spears or willow and sinew fish nets. In the 1980s, women, men and children from Nondalton actively jigged for fish under the ice on Six-Mile Lake or Lake Clark, during spring months in the light and warmth of the lengthening days. They used hand-held lines, weighted and baited with fish eggs. Fish eggs were both thrown into the hole prior to fishing and attached to the hook or other types of lures. Some people occasionally fished with sport gear (i.e., rod and reel) in the 1980s.

Both male and female inland Dena'ina in the 1980s perceived Mulchatna caribou and moose (Figures 10 and 9, respectively) — the latter having expanded their presence in the area in more recent years — to be highly valued sources of food and raw material. They perceived the hunting of large game in general, including brown and black bear and Dall sheep, to be the most prestigious foodgetting activities, despite the quantitative importance and reliability of salmon.

The long term use of these species — particularly Mulchatna caribou — and the overall relative scarcity of large game at the end of the 1800s and early 1900s have been documented in both early and oral historic accounts. Osgood (1904 a:27, 28) reported the harvest of several caribou in July 1902, 20 miles northwest of "Keejik" on Lake Clark and their presence at the upper end of the lake and along the Chulitna River. However, in his opinion, they were not available in great abundance. Murie's (1935) study of Alaskan caribou herds in the 1920s was undertaken to assess the status of the resource and make recommendations regarding the management of these herds and the relationship between introduced reindeer and caribou, which utilized the same ecozone and interbred when the opportunity arose.

Since the purchase of Alaska from Russia in 1867 the caribou herds have vastly decreased over a large part of the Territory, but with a few exceptions they are now doing well. Although they are gone from the Kenai Peninsula, are dwindling on the Alaska Peninsula, and are disappearing from what is now the range of the reindeer, the principal herds of the interior are thriving. . . . There has indeed been much speculation as to the number of caribou in the Alaskan herds and much disagreement over various estimates. Enthusiastic observers speak of "millions" or of "countless thousands." These estimates are usually based on general impressions, but it is difficult to find any other basis. When one considers the large territory occupied by caribou, the scattered distribution, and the almost constant and erratic movements of the animals, the difficulty of making a caribou census becomes evident (Murie 1935:5).

Although his research was focused more on the well-being of prospectors and miners than Native people, Murie (1935) noted the importance of the caribou for human survival in Alaska and emphasized that non-Natives would have been unable to survive if it had not been for caribou. He drew an analogy between caribou and the bison of the western states in regard to the dependency of human populations. Of course, the use of caribou by prospectors and miners at the turn of the century involved market hunting (i.e., taking caribou for sale as a food source) and incurred waste (Murie 1935:2), thereby possibly contributing to the decline of the herds, which was already underway as part of the process of natural demographic cycling of this species. Murie (1935) commented upon the hardship to Native people that resulted when the herds were seasonally unavailable. He reported animals at the heads of the Stony and Mulchatna rivers and noted that the numbers were few. He described the common Athabaskan method of taking caribou by the use of a pole fence (surround) and sinew snares placed at intervals or gaps between poles — a hunting method known but never practiced by older inland Dena'ina of the 1980s.

A comprehensive assessment of the Mulchatna and other caribou herds was undertaken in the 1960s by Skoog (1963), at which time he estimated that the Mulchatna herd numbered 5,000 animals. In the late 1960s and early 1970s, virtually all caribou herds in Alaska had reached the nadir of their decline. In more recent years, joint monitoring of the Mulchatna herd by the U.S. National Park Service and Alaska Department of Fish and Game has indicated a continued increase in the size of the herd. In 1986, it was estimated that the Mulchatna herd included minimally 45,000 animals based on data derived from photo censuses. By 1990, similar data indicated a herd size of 80,000 animals.

The calving ground for the core of the Mulchatna caribou herd extends from the Alaska Range to the east and through the hills around Turquoise and Twin lakes, westward toward Snipe Lake (K'adala Vena) and in the vicinity of Little Bonanza Creek (Tich'eqantnu Gguya) and the Bonanza Hills. Calving occasionally occurs in the Koksetna Hills near Fishtrap Lake (Nunch'qelchixi Vena) (Hirschmann 1986:79).

The overall range of the herd also is expanding. In spring 1986, caribou were available in large numbers and hunted within visual proximity of or a short snow machine trip from Nondalton. The expanding access and increased numbers of caribou provided abundant food for community residents as well as for relatives in other villages and Anchorage.

Traditionally and contemporarily, caribou have been hunted as a primary source of meat and raw materials. In the 1980s, caribou and moose were eaten fresh and were frozen and dried for later consumption to such an extent that imported beef was insignificant in the local diet. In previous years, caribou hides were used in multiple ways, including as coverings for spruce-framed dwellings or kayak-like boats (referred to as *baidarki* by Russian fur traders and hunters) and as material for bedding, footwear, rawhide lines, clothing, and many other purposes. Caribou leg and shank bones and antlers were used to make spears, which, in turn, were deployed for taking fish, beaver, and other land fauna. Bone was preferred for making points, as it was less subject to fracture and more flexible and durable than lithic materials. Caribou sinew was an essential source of sewing material prior to the availability of commercially produced thread, floss, string, and twine. Caribou stomachs, as well as those of bear, were used as drag floats by hunters taking large game animals in the water.

Oral historic accounts abound with examples of caribou hunting techniques involving the use of caribou fences or surrounds and snares. After being taken in the rawhide snares, caribou were dispatched with sinew-backed bows and arrows or spears. Caribou were also stalked by individual or paired hunters and dispatched with bows and arrows or spears in the past and firearms throughout most of this century.

Imported reindeer were transplanted to the Lake Iliamna area in the early 1900s as part of Sheldon Jackson's economic and social transformation scheme for "civilizing" Alaska Natives by teaching them to domesticate animals. The introduction of reindeer influenced the Iliamna Dena'ina, but reindeer distribution did not extend into the majority of the area occupied by the inland group. Although there were occasional references to the use of reindeer meat, hides, and horns by Nondalton residents, they generally were elicited from individuals who had spent part of their lives in the Lake Iliamna area.

Osgood (1904a:30, 45) documented that there were comparatively "... small numbers [of moose] in the region of Lakes Iliamna and Clark" and noted that the Dena'ina reported that moose were not abundant in these areas in the past. Prior to the end of the 1920s, according to local informants, moose rarely were seen in the Lake Iliamna or Lake Clark regions. Since they were present on the upper Mulchatna and Stony river drainages, the inland Dena'ina travelled to these areas to harvest these infrequently available but highly valued animals. By the 1980s, however, moose range had expanded, encompassing the Lake Clark and adjacent areas. By that decade, moose also had become relatively abundant in localities in which the inland Dena'ina hunted. Moose population levels and breeding patterns also have been monitored by a joint effort of the U.S. National Park Service and Alaska Department of Fish and Game. Brown bears were the major predators of both adult moose and calves in the 1980s, especially in years in which there was extensive snowfall. However, moose population levels and calf ratios suggested considerable productivity of the species in this region.

Throughout inland Dena'ina collective oral history into the 1980s, moose, like caribou, were a choice source of red meat. Moose meat was eaten fresh or frozen and dried into strips for subsequent consumption. Most parts of the moose were consumed, including the majority of its internal organs and other portions (such as the nose and tongue). As in the case of caribou, unmodified or dehaired moose hides were used for many purposes, such as footwear, rawhide line, and the covering of large, open spruce frame boats. In the case of Lake Clark area Dena'ina, the large moose or caribou hide covered boats were made at spring camps for hauling meat, other animal products, and freight downriver to Indian Point at the mouth of the Chulitna River, where people travelling home from spring camps awaited the breakup of ice on Lake Clark. Moose horns were cut into the shape of platters and the ends decorated.

Additionally, Osgood (1904a) reported that people of the study area took Dall sheep in the mountains between Lake Clark and Cook Inlet. Dall sheep were harvested during the fall and deemed to be a significant resource by the inland Dena'ina in the 1980s. Prior to the availability of commercially manufactured coats, sleeping bags, and woolen stockings, Dall sheep provided not only a highly valued source of meat but also the raw materials for the clothing and bedding essential to living in this environment. In the 1980s, during caribou and moose hunting, fishing, and trapping excursions, the inland Dena'ina commonly attempted to sight the location of Dall sheep. Several parties of young to middle-aged men hunted Dall sheep during the fall months of 1985, 1986, and 1987. Successful Dall sheep hunters were knowledgeable of the appropriate altitude and areas at which sheep are likely to be located, access trails, and successful strategies for pursuing these animals adept at traversing steep, mountainous terrain. The stamina and skills necessary to travel into the mountain habitat — including safe maneuvering at high elevations and on crags, pinnacles, and ridges — were requisites for Dall sheep hunting in this region.

The other major large game animal taken by the inland Dena'ina historically and contemporarily was the brown bear, although the harvest of this resource legally has been severely restricted by state management regulations in recent years. Black bears were taken as well but were not considered as essential a resource by the inland Dena'ina as they were by related coastal populations (Osgood 1976 [1937]). Oral historic accounts emphasize the fact that brown bears were a critical source of meat when caribou or moose were scarce or unavailable. More importantly, however, brown bear fat was rendered into an oil — a condiment accompanying the consumption of most dried meat and fish and mixed with greens or berries in many Dena'ina dishes. Functionally, for the inland Dena'ina, the oil rendered from the fat of the brown bear had the significance of seal oil in coastal Dena'ina, Yupik and Inupiat diets or butter and margarine in the meals of the average American or European (Behnke 1981). In the 1980s, many inland Dena'ina consistently complained about not having adequate access to bear fat and bemoaned the inadequacies of margarine or butter as a substitute.

During fall hunting trips, swimming brown and black bears were taken at waterways in the mountains by means of harpoon-like spears or *dineh*. In late fall or early spring, they were taken at their dens with spears, bows and arrows, and, rifles or trapped in snares or steel traps (Osgood 1976 [1937]). Besides providing fat and meat, these animals were notable sources of other raw materials. For example, brown and black bear intestines were cleaned, inflated, cut open, dried, and made into waterproof raincoats. These were analogous to the use of seal intestines as rain gear by coastal Dena'ina and Yupik. Additionally, bear intestines also were valued as the most useful raw material for making windows in both traditional and post-contact Dena'ina houses prior to the importation of glass. The intestines were oiled so that they retained their pliability and remained air tight during heavy winds. Bear stomachs were inflated and used as floats for hunting game in the water or fishing.

Furbearing animals were trapped for local use and for barter or sale by the inland Dena'ina, both prior and subsequent to Euroamerican contact. It is nearly impossible to reconstruct the amount and range of time in each annual subsistence round dedicated by the Dena'ina to trapping furbearers prior to the commencement of the Russian fur trade era. However, it is likely to have been less than that committed to trapping during the historic period until the fur market declined subsequent to World War II. Nonetheless, in the 1980s, many young men trapped to provide their families with a supplementary source of cash or to obtain pelts for contemporary Dena'ina clothing or for the production of arts and crafts.

Some of the species trapped for their pelts also provided a sumptuous source of meat (particularly beaver), especially at spring camps when winter meat supplies were depleted. Species trapped historically and into the 1980s included beaver, muskrat, arctic ground squirrel, "rabbit" (snowshoe hare), arctic hare, porcupine, marmot, red and cross fox, marten, short-tailed and least weasel, mink, wolverine, river otter, and lynx. Although wolves were occasionally taken if caught accidentally in a trap set for another animal, they were not purposely pursued. In the 1980s, Nondalton residents believed that wolves are actually a human-like group which look after the well-being of the Dena'ina and share food with them. Therefore, if they were trapped inadvertently, they required special treatment. Some species, such as beaver and muskrat, were both trapped and hunted, depending upon the time of year and conditions of harvesting.

More detailed information about particular species are plentiful in the oral historic record, and only a few examples are provided here. In the case of Lake Clark area Dena'ina, beaver were particularly significant as a source of both food and pelts, harvested during the spring primarily on the Chulitna River. In the 1980s, beaver was eaten in most households and the pelts were used for the construction of distinctive headgear in both Non-

dalton and Lime Village as well as for other items of clothing. "Rabbits" are mentioned throughout the oral historic record as an emergency food source relied upon when the Dena'ina were unsuccessful in obtaining large game — starvation fare, as it were. During fall hunting periods in which men went into the mountains in search of caribou, moose, and Dall sheep, women trapped ground squirrels with snares or, more recently, small steel traps. Women recalled using up to 100 snares for trapping ground squirrels, carried about for logistical placement on a special woman's cane. The meat from ground squirrels was eaten on the spot and preserved traditionally in moose stomachs. Ground squirrel pelts were made into underwear and, with beaver and muskrat, into outer coats and pants. When adequate supplies of Dall sheep hides were not available, the hides of ground squirrels, muskrats, and hares were sewn together to be used as blankets. Although Athabaskans generally did not make pottery, elders reported making food containers from beaver hair mixed with sand and clay. Beaver teeth were used for making arrowheads, some spear points, and special carving knives. Beaver and porcupine scapulae were often made into implements because of their sharpness. Porcupine provided both a highly desired meat and quills, lavishly used in various forms of decoration. In the 1980s, the importance of trapping and the associated by-products remained significant in the perception and practice of the inland Dena'ina.

A total of 135 species of birds have been estimated to appear seasonally throughout the Lake Clark and Lake Iliamna areas (Hirschmann 1986:94). Of these, in excess of 30 species or subspecies were named and used by the inland Dena'ina and commonly familiar to both young and old in the 1980s, as in the past. The importance of ducks and geese and a few sea bird species and subspecies and their eggs in the spring, when other meat resources were depleted and as the first source of fresh meat in the annual cycle, was paramount to the inland Dena'ina in the past and remained so in the 1970s and 1980s (Behnke 1978, 1982). Ducks, geese, spruce hens, and "rabbits" were the only meat available during times when no moose or caribou were harvested for any one of multiple reasons. Additionally, most elders keenly remembered stories and actual occurrences of famines — times when they had to range far in search of large game and depended heavily on small game and fish. The use of migratory waterfowl, seabirds, and the eggs of both in the spring by the inland Dena'ina have been at odds in recent years with nationally and internationally mandated restrictions on the spring harvesting of these species.

In all the data gathered on land and resource use for purposes of this ethnography, it was evident that most inland Dena'ina did not travel to the coast to harvest marine resources. The few who hunted, fished, gathered, or used marine resources along the coast of Cook Inlet were the offspring of at least one Iliamna Dena'ina parent or individuals who spent part of their lives at Lake Iliamna as a result of adoption, marriage, or other social arrangements. Coastal resources harvested or used by inland Dena'ina included saltwater seals, belukha, black bears, and ducks and seabirds and their eggs. Freshwater seals have been available in Lake Iliamna for minimally the entirety of the historic period and were occasionally harvested in small quantities by the inland Dena'ina, normally in conjunction with visits to or social connections with Lake Iliamna residents. For the most part, the inland Dena'ina relied upon traditional trade and kinship networks to acquire marine sources from coastal groups.

Lastly, there were other resources used by the inland Dena'ina, only some of which are mentioned in this context. The shell of the dentalium deserves special note, as, at least in the post-contact period, its use on items of clothing, such as belts and shirts, was a symbol of wealth and high status among the inland Dena'ina. Although dentalia were often obtained via trade between the coast and inland areas, they also were available in a lake at the head of Swift River. Minerals, particularly those which fracture in a way amenable to making items of lithic technology, were commonly used by the ancestors of the inland Dena'ina during the precontact period. However, lithics, horn, stone, bone, antler, and tooth were readily replaced as the raw material from which implements such as points, axes, blades, scrapers, and adzes were made after the introduction of iron and, later, steel. Black, white, and red ochres — used for the decoration of many items of technology, clothing, and the human body — were derived from local minerals. Coal was known and occasionally employed as a source of fuel where it occurred, such as by a mountain on the Stony River referred to in Dena'ina as Nizdlu Dghil'u.

Resources discussed in this chapter are listed by their common, western scientific, and inland Dena'ina names in Appendix A. Dena'ina and English place names are inventoried in Appendix B.

THE INTERFACE OF LANGUAGE, CULTURE, AND SOCIETY

The delineation of human populations into families, communities, societies, bands, tribes, or multiple other types and sizes of groups meaningful to social science research is often arbitrary and problematic, particularly if the classificatory criteria are not defined in some detail. It has been recognized by contemporary sociocultural anthropologists that the composition and structure of human groups made by practitioners of the discipline are commonly not identical or similar to those conceptualized by the members of this or that group. In fact, from the perspective of the participant, the group with which he or she identifies may differ radically depending upon the timing and reason for stating a particular association. For example, the group affiliation of the person to whom the identity is being revealed, social status of either parties, or the purposes of identification are but some of many factors influencing emic conceptions of association.

With these ground rules in mind, the criteria by which the group of people, referred to in this context as "the inland Dena'ina," are overtly stated. Although other chapters of this ethnography explore in depth, diachronically and synchronically, the role of kinship, economics, the allocation of power, and world view in the overall social organization of this group, it is necessary here to build the foundations for more detailed discussions below.

The diachronic criteria, which have been employed herein to distinguish the inland Dena'ina from other Dena'ina, Athabaskans, Alaska Natives, Alaskans, North American Indians, and so on, have principally been language and dialect, genealogical connections, spatial distribution and related land use patterns (including a set of commonly used place names), self identity, political affiliation, economic unity (distribution and exchange networks), and additional aspects of cultural or subcultural similarity. The relative significance of these criteria and their interconnectedness deserve additional, albeit succinct, comment.

Of the criteria mentioned above, language and dialect may be the most significant, as they provide insights into many of the other measures of group affiliation. For example, the distribution of a dialect over a specific geographic area suggests that its speakers have had more linguistic contact with one another than they have had with neighboring populations. In other words, a community, band, or some other organizational unit may be the social correlate of a dialect (Krauss and Golla 1981). Of course, as Krauss (1978) has pointed out, linguistic divergence does not necessarily imply either linguistic isolation or historic taxonomic relationships. Therefore, the use of lines separating languages on maps is an artifact of convenience, which obscures transitional intelligibility, multilingualism, and the degree of dialectical or language relatedness.

The ability to make use of the indigenous language or languages of a group for purposes other than linguistic classification has been recognized as a key component of anthropological research since its inception as a discipline. For example, since linguistic distribution relates to the spatial distribution of people, it is not surprising that research into place names discloses information regarding territoriality of specific groups, as place names tend to be a relatively conservative part of the lexicon of specific languages or dialects (Kari and Kari 1982). Secondly, it is through eliciting the names used by one group of people for those of other areas that it is possible to derive information about perceptions of social identity. Additionally, the collection of kinship terms is essential to revealing the nature of socially perceived and biological family relationships, as well to reconstructing, for example, the composition of economic production units or exchange and distribution networks.

Non-linguistic means of ascertaining sociopolitical affiliations and boundaries can be used to determine group identity. For example, lifetime map biographies are an indispensable tool for developing composite, visual representations of group distribution and associated identity (Ellanna, Sherrod, and Langdon 1992). Data on political unity in the face of a common adversary reveals much about levels of group affiliation. Many other kinds of cultural data, such as similarities in marriage patterns, adoption, the use of personal names (Shinkwin and Pete 1984), technological production, recognized access to sites of resource harvest, and the sharing of goods and services, are essential sources of data on group identity and distribution.

Based on the criteria discussed above, the identity of the inland Dena'ina, as distinct from other populations, is asserted in this context. As a starting point, the term "Athabaskan" (also variously spelled "Athapaskan," "Athapascan," and "Athabascan" in the literature) is used to refer to a group of North American Indian

languages and the people who spoke them historically and contemporarily. Athabaskans are distributed throughout the interior of Alaska, the western interior of Canada, at a few locations on the northwestern coast, and in the southwest of the contiguous United States.

It is currently hypothesized by some scientists, based on linguistic, genetic, dental, and archaeological evidence, that the ancestors of the Athabaskans were part of the second most recent migration of people from Asia to the Americas by route of the Bering land connection or Beringia (Greenburg, Turner, and Zegura 1986). The identification of linguistic ancestors of contemporary Athabaskans, speakers of Proto-Athabaskan-Eyak-Tlingit or NaDene (a reconstructed, ancestral language family originally proposed by Sapir in the 1920s [Krauss 1973; Krauss and Golla 1981]), with archaeological remains has been problematic. In the case of eastern central Alaska, the Athabaskan archaeological tradition has been defined as principally consisting of the sequential Tuktu and Denali complexes, with Tuktu being the oldest in this case (Clark 1981:113). In a very simplistic overview, both the Denali and Tuktu archaeological complexes, the former dated minimally as early as 10,500 years ago in its earliest stages (Clark 1981:109), included a distinctive wedge shaped and tabular microblade core and blade technology.

There are significant problems in correlating linguistic and archaeological prehistoric data. Linguists, using their own dating methods, have postulated the migration of both the ancestral NaDene language and people into Alaska by 6,000 to 7,000 years ago (Krauss and Golla 1981). It is not uncommon for linguistic methods to render more conservative dates than those derived from archaeology. Additionally, archaeological evidence cannot be linked, at least with any degree of certainty, to ethnicity (Powers pers. comm. 1990).

A succinct review of one principal contemporary theory regarding the prehistory of the Proto-Athabaskan-Eyak-Tlingit or NaDene language family places Athabaskans in a linguistic context. Because of the distinctiveness of Tlingit from Athabaskan and Eyak, and its problematic relationships to both, it is postulated that Tlingit was the first to diverge from this ancestral linguistic group. The separation of Proto-Athabaskan from Proto-Eyak, according to this theory, occurred approximately 3,500 years ago (Krauss and Golla 1981:68). By 2,500 years ago, Proto-Athabaskan was still undifferentiated and exhibited no significant Eskimo language influence, suggesting the separation of proto-Athabaskans from ancestral Eskimo and Aleut peoples. Based on the premise that the area of greatest linguistic complexity is also the region of longest term linguistic time depth, Krauss (1980) argued that eastern interior Alaska and adjacent western central Canada were probably the Athabaskan linguistic "homeland." By minimally 1,500 years ago, this language family had diversified into three significantly different subfamilies – Apachean, now located in the southwestern United States; Pacific, virtually extinct but pockets of which occurred on the coasts of Washington, Oregon, and California; and northern, of which the contemporary Athabaskan languages of Alaska and Canada are a part. Krauss stressed that one should not view existing northern Athabaskan languages as substocks – analogous to branches stemming from a common tree trunk (Krauss 1978; Krauss and Golla 1981). Rather, northern Athabaskan languages should be viewed as a linguistic complex, with boundaries representing greater or lesser degrees of mutual unintelligibility, with both merging and diverging processes at work and no total isolation between bounded units (Krauss and Golla 1981:68).

The northern Athabaskan languages of Alaska and Canada in the 1980s were heterogeneous. One of these languages, Dena'ina – most commonly misrepresented by the convention "Tanaina" in the literature – means "the people" to speakers of that language and was their name for themselves in the 1980s (J. Kari 1975a). Osgood (1976 [1937]), who conducted important ethnographic research in the Cook Inlet area in the 1930s, gathered comparative vocabularies from six Dena'ina subgroups. However, in large part because he was not trained as a linguist, Osgood (1976 [1937]) failed to recognize the distribution of this language and its speakers on the Stony River and the distinction between the dialects of Lake Iliamna and Lake Clark residents and to accurately record all of the languages' phonemes using an appropriate orthography (Hoijer 1963; Krauss 1973). However, the existence of the Dena'ina as a distinctive linguistic group was recognized a century earlier by Russian explorers, traders, and missionaries (VanStone 1962).

The distinctiveness and diversity of the Dena'ina language and its dialects, as compared with other Athabaskan languages and dialects, are suggested by systematic contemporary linguistic research (Kari 1977). The Dena'ina language is generally not intelligible to neighboring groups, either Athabaskan or Yupik. In fact, historically it was common for Dena'ina to learn to speak the language of their neighbors, but there is evidence that rarely did the reverse situation occur (Kari 1977). The impact of the Russians on the Dena'ina, particularly along the coast of Cook Inlet, is marked by the approximately 300 Russian loan words which could be identified in the language in the 1980s (Krauss pers. comm. 1990).

A modern orthography for Dena'ina was developed by Krauss and J. Kari in 1972 and extensive research commenced. Based on these scholarly inquiries during the 1970s and 1980s, it can be concluded that, notwithstanding a linguistic miracle, the language is moribund (Krauss and Golla 1981). In fact, there were only 250 speakers remaining in 1974 and 150 in 1982 (Krauss 1978; Krauss pers. comm. 1990), most of whom were located in Nondalton and Lime Village. Since the youngest speakers were in their late teens (at Lime Village) and late 20s or early 30s (at Nondalton) by the end of the 1980s, one can easily calculate the approximate time at which the Dena'ina language will no longer be spoken. Those areas on Cook Inlet inhabited by the Dena'ina and most intensely subjected to Euroamerican contact were the first to experience language extinction and related community and territorial disruption.

Dena'ina, as one of the most internally diverse of the Alaskan-Athabaskan languages, has been subdivided dialectically by linguists. The distribution of dialectical subdivisions has been used conjecturally to reconstruct the prehistory and early contact history of the Dena'ina. There is linguistic and oral historic evidence that the Dena'ina were expanding their territory prior to and at the time of Euroamerican contact, including movement into the coastal areas of Cook Inlet. Linguistic interpretations strongly support the contention that the Dena'ina were originally an interior oriented people who inhabited the high, inland plateau west of the Alaska Range (Kari and Kari 1982; J. Kari 1985), rather than a coastal population who moved across the mountains to escape the oppression of Russian contact (VanStone and Townsend 1970). Unfortunately, there has not been enough archaeological research undertaken in the area to allow interpretive consensus between linguistic, oral historic, and archaeological data.

Dena'ina dialects have been subdivided into two major groups – the upper and lower inlet. In the 1980s, the upper inlet dialect was thought minimally to include the modern and historic communities of old and new Tyonek, Alexander

Creek, Susitna Station, Old Susitna, Yentna River villages, Kroto Creek, Talkeetna, Montana Creek, Knik, Cottonwood Creek, Eklutna, and Point Possession, as well as several other historically or archaeologically defined seasonal or annual village sites (Fall 1987; Kari and Kari 1982; Townsend 1981). Linguistic research, primarily undertaken by J. Kari, indicates that upper inlet Dena'ina is the most diverse of the dialects and has been heavily influenced by the neighboring Ahtna language (J. Kari 1977), also a subdivision of Athabaskan.

There are actually three subdivisions of lower inlet Dena'ina, referred to as outer, Iliamna, and inland. The most divergent and annihilated of these is outer inlet, which historically included multiple communities on the Kenai Peninsula — such as old and new Seldovia, Kenai, Kasilof, and Kalifornsky — and those of the western coast of Cook Inlet, such as old and new Kustatan and Polly Creek (Kari and Kari 1982). The Iliamna dialect was spoken in the vicinity of Lake Iliamna, including the communities of Old Iliamna, Pedro Bay, Chekok Point, Lonesome Bay, and Pile Bay at various times in the 1900s (Kari and Kari 1982; Townsend 1981). Inland Dena'ina, the dialect of greatest concern in this context, was spoken in the historic and contemporary communities of the Mulchatna River, old and new Nondalton, Kijik, Telaquana, Qeghnilen, and Lime Village (J. Kari 1975; Kari and Kari 1982). In the 1970s and 1980s, there were also some inland speakers in the linguistically mixed communities of Stony River Village, located at the confluence of the Stony and Kuskokwim rivers (P. Kari 1985), and the primarily Yup'ik community of Newhalen, located on the Newhalen River. The latter was originally the site of a Dena'ina community, according to oral historic accounts, and population movements in the area of the former have been very complex and are not yet fully understood. The Iliamna dialect is closer to that of the outer inlet than to inland Dena'ina, suggesting that contact between members of groups residing on or near Lake Iliamna and those located on the shores of western Cook Inlet were more frequent and intense than were the relationships of either to the inland Dena'ina. The case for geographic isolation of the inland Dena'ina is also reflected in their dialect, which has the fewest number of Russian loan words within this language.

The distribution of these dialects can be used to delineate major Dena'ina subgroups or societies and has been applied to the use of the term "inland" for describing the historic and contemporary populations which are the focus of this ethnography. Townsend (1981:625) included both upper inlet and western coastal outer inlet dialects in what she termed the "Susitna society." This area is tangential to the ethnography so is not commented upon further (see Fall 1987 for a detailed historical discussion of the upper inlet Dena'ina). Townsend's (1981:625) "Kenai society" included only outer dialect speakers who resided on the Kenai Peninsula. Exception is taken to her inclusion of the speakers of both Iliamna and inland dialects in an "interior society" (Townsend 1981:625). Oral historic, historic, and contemporary sociocultural data derived from this research strongly support the view, held by residents of Nondalton and Lime Village in the 1980s, that they identified with one another and were, without question, a distinct group of Dena'ina.

Lastly, all three major drainages occupied by the inland Dena'ina historically and in the 1980s had boundaries shared with Yup'ik peoples, a population which VanStone (1962, 1967, 1974) argued was expanding at the time of Euroamerican contact, into the interior, country previously occupied by Athabaskans. Therefore, at the time of contact, it is likely that the inland Dena'ina occupied the entirety of the Stony River (according to VanStone 1962) but definitely from Hlsit to the river's headwaters in the Alaska Range. They also occupied the upper reaches of the Hoholitna River (Tleghtitnu) and the Swift River, from its confluence with the Gargaryah River (K'ezghaxtnu) to its headwaters (Kari and Kari 1982). Oral historic accounts of contact with Yup'ik and Kuskokwim Athabaskans during certain seasonal hunting and trapping activities were common. The Kuskokwim River, into which these three rivers drained, provided a boundary between the inland Dena'ina and the Yup'ik people of the Kuskokwim, whom they referred to as *Kusquqvagmit* or *Dutna*; the Kuskokwim Ingalik, *Deg Hit'an* or *Kenaniq' Hit'an*; and the Upper Kuskokwim Athabaskans, *Yun'eht'an* (J. Kari 1977). It is clear that despite some intermarriage with Yup'ik and other Kuskokwim Athabaskans (Figure 13), the inland Dena'ina remained dominant and maintained their identity on the Stony River. Some Lime Village Dena'ina were multilingual, speaking and/or comprehending Dena'ina, Ingalik, Yup'ik, and/or English.

On the Mulchatna River, the Dena'ina occupied the upper part of the river, generally above Mosquito Creek (Nuch'nastninhtnu) (Kari and Kari 1982). It was in this area that they shared a boundary with Yup'ik people, whose descendants now reside in or near the modern community of New Stuyahok on the Nushagak River. Mulchatna Lake was considered to be a part of Dena'ina country. Neighboring Yup'ik also were referred to as *Dutna* by the inland Dena'ina.

To the south and southwest, the Iliamna Dena'ina, referred to as *Ilavnaht'an, Nilamnaht'ana,* or *Nilanvenaht'ana* (Kari 1977), occupied an area adjacent to the Lake Clark group (Figure 12). However, the lower end of Iliamna Lake, at or near Tommy Point (Liq'a T'el'iht) according to oral accounts, was the boundary between the central Yup'ik or *Dutna* and the Iliamna Dena'ina. The Kvichak River was always occupied by *Dutna*, according to local informants. In the 1980s, the communities of Igiugig, Kokhanok, and New-halen, located on or near the southwestern, eastern, and northeastern shores of Lake Iliamna, respectively, were also considered to be *Dutna*, despite the fact that these communities were established in areas recognized by the Dena'ina as once having been within their territory. The inland Dena'ina also had frequent contact with residents of the Naknek area, also referred to as *Dutna*. The people of Igiugig, Kokhanok, and Naknek referred to themselves as "Aleuts" when speaking English in the 1980s, but some Newhalen residents had reinstituted the ethnonym "Yup'ik."

The inland Dena'ina distinguished between the *Dutna* and the Alutiiq (Yupik) peoples of Prince William Sound and the eastern half of the Kenai Peninsula, whom they called *Ulchena* (Kari 1977). Aleuts from the Aleutian Islands were referred to as *Hl'ana* or "downriver ridge people" by the inland Dena'ina. However, there appeared to be some differentiation, on the part of the inland Dena'ina, between *Dutna* and "Eskimos" or "Yup'ik," who were known to be "the ones with round faces." The *Dutna* do not have round faces

like the Eskimos, according to elder inland Dena'ina. It is possible that the inland Dena'ina were recognizing regional Yup'ik variation in making this distinction or reflecting the contemporary confusion which exists regarding uses of the names "Aleut" and "Yup'ik" or "Eskimo" in reference to group identity.

The discrepancies involved in the use of these terms of self identification are comprehendible in historical context. The residents of Prince William Sound, Kodiak Island, the eastern half of Kenai Peninsula, and some of the inhabitants of the Bristol Bay area were referred to as "Aleut" rather than "Yupik" by early Russian fur hunters and traders. Therefore, there were multiple populations and cultural and linguistic groups, including the indigenous residents of the Aleutian Islands and the southwestern tip of the Alaska Peninsula, which were grouped together into a single ethnic category by outsiders — that of "Aleut." These circumstances have carried over to contemporary issues of self-identification. Therefore, whereas all of these once culturally and linguistically distinctive groups referred to themselves as "Aleuts" in English in the 1980s, linguists have accommodated this preference for named identity with the term "Alutiiq" for the people of Kodiak Island and Prince William Sound and "Aleut" for residents of the Aleutian and Pribilof islands proper and the lower Alaska Peninsula.

Lastly, the inland Dena'ina clearly distinguished between themselves and other Native people, "white people," and "black people." The terms for the latter two were *Gasht'ana* and *Dashtl'ech'na*, respectively, in the 1980s (Kari 1977). The inland Dena'ina saw themselves as being the "real people," in contrast to others, who were considered to be not quite as authentic variations of humankind — an ethnocentric bias common among most known human groups.

Figure 12 (above). This photograph depicts the chief of Old Iliamna Village and his family, probably in the early 1920s. Inland Dena'ina in the 1980s did not remember their names. *Photograph Courtesy of the Alaska Historical Library, James Carter Collection.* **Figure 13** (below). Parascovia Pitka, also known as Chuk'al, in 1943. Elders recount that Parascovia came to the Stony River from the Kuskokwim or Yukon rivers after marrying an inland Dena'ina man. Parascovia is the maternal grandmother of Vonga Bobby of Lime Village. She was in her late 80s when she died in 1949. *Photograph Courtesy of Vonga and Matrona Bobby.*

Figure 14 (left to right). Ben Trefon, Gustingen Constantine, Katherine Constantine, and Agnes Trefon, at a camp near Lime Village in 1930. Agnes and Ben Trefon are Gustingen's and Katherine's great grandchildren. In Dena'ina, Ben was referred to as *kuya* and Agnes *tsiya* by both great grandparents. *Photograph Courtesy of Agnes Cusma.*

CHAPTER 3

DENA'INA PERSPECTIVE: *NANUTSET NAKENAGHECH' SUTDU'A*
(STORIES AND HISTORY BEFORE OUR TIME)

Those children, your children, sometimes you should advise them. When you give them advice on what kind of person they should be, they will think in that manner. They will then become that kind of person. If you don't advise them, they will become people in their own self image. As people then we give advice to each other and the people can try to improve. There is no new generation that has not been trained to be people since the beginning of the earth . . . . Now we people no longer do this. We should give a little advice to one another and that will be good enough. Then this village will be good.

Gabriel Trefon, interviewed by Clark Davis, 1961

THE IMPORTANCE OF ORAL HISTORY

Dena'ina was not a written language until recent years, when linguists developed an orthography and analyzed the grammar of the language, making literacy possible. Traditionally and into the 1980s, the majority of Dena'ina history was passed down orally from generation to generation, primarily by storytellers. In the quotation at the beginning of this chapter, chief Gabriel Trefon was bestowing upon those of his generation, and younger, the wisdom of chiefs of the past. He was telling other Dena'ina the importance of conveying to members of younger generations the rules for living, because only through such knowledge can life be good. He was, in fact, using a *sutdu* as a mode of instruction.

From these stories, young people learned many things about how the world came to be what it is today; the substance of Dena'ina relationships with other animals, aspects of nature, and their neighbors; how to behave properly toward one another and toward other beings of the empirical and non-empirical environments which they occupy; the origin of clans; and what were the consequences of being stingy, boastful, foolish, untruthful, or lazy. In Dena'ina tradition, there was no time in which the world did not have both humans and animals. These stories describe how people and animals have certain qualities which they may share and what forces influence and direct all living things and the world of spirits. They also relate how certain places and features of

the country — such as mountains, rocks, islands, lakes, rivers, and other things — have special meaning to the history of the inland Dena'ina as a people. They communicate both historic and more modern events, such as wars with neighboring *Dutna*, where such conflicts took place, who the war leaders were, and what was the nature of their exploits. These stories describe the *Gasht'ana*, who came into Dena'ina country in recent times. This is but an example of the breadth and extent of knowledge embodied within inland Dena'ina oral history.

Included in these stories, then, are tales of long, long ago, when animals became people and people became animals. There also are accounts of more recent times, when humans and animals had mutual respect and provided mutual assistance but were usually distinct from one another. Lastly, they describe historic times, when inland Dena'ina travelled to visit, trade, and war with other people and when the *Tahtna* (Russians) came from the bottom of the sea. This is the nature of the education which the elder Dena'ina hope to pass on to the younger generations outside of the western schools and classrooms in which they spend so much of their year. This is their heritage as inland Dena'ina.

Many *sutdu'a* and more recent histories of the Nondalton Dena'ina have been collected in both the Dena'ina and English languages by anthropologists, linguists, folklorists, historians, and others. Some of the Dena'ina versions have been translated into written English and, even fewer, transliterated into written Dena'ina. A few of these histories have been published (for example, see Osgood 1976 [1937]; Tenenbaum 1984; Vaudrin 1969). In this context, the selected stories present inland Dena'ina perspectives of the natural and cultural histories of their world and the people who inhabit it.

LONG, LONG AGO, WHEN ANIMALS WERE PEOPLE AND PEOPLE WERE ANIMALS

Among the inland Dena'ina, the raven was a very important figure in the stories from the distant time. He usually was described as a very clever male, with the ability to transform himself from being a raven to whatever other form of life he wished to be. When he changed form, he attempted to mimic the behavior of the human or animal he had temporarily become, but, in the end, he was usually unsuccessful in reaching his desired goals. He used lies and tricks, usually for selfish reasons, to outwit people or other animals. However, he generally got caught and, when found out, immediately turned back into a raven and flew away.

Among the inland Dena'ina, raven stories commonly were intended to teach children about what was considered to be "good" or "not so good" behavior. These stories were often told to children at night when family members were sitting around together, usually by elders such as grandmothers (*chida*) or grandfathers (*chada*). Raven's exploits were considered to be examples of improper Dena'ina behavior — lessons to be learned about how not to behave. In the 1980s, Nondalton Dena'ina considered raven to be somewhat of a loser and self-centered although extremely clever. However, it was not appropriate to kill or harass ravens in their animal form. The Dena'ina recognized that the raven described in the stories and the raven as a living animal are one and the same.

The following story was told by Anton Evan and recorded by him in February 1981. It was translated by James Kari and Andrew Balluta in 1985 at the Alaska Native Language Center, University of Alaska Fairbanks. In this case, as in all other stories presented in this chapter, the narratives have been presented in inland Dena'ina English rather than modified in accordance with the rules of standard American English. This choice has been made to reiterate the point that, although there are alternative forms of English which may deviate from standard American English, they are considered equally viable and valid as forms of communication by the authors of the ethnography and by the Dena'ina.

CHULYIN VEJEX SUTDU'A: THE STORY OF RAVEN AND CARIBOU

This is another story, we call *chulyin* (raven) story in our language. That's supposed to be a raven story. The *chulyin*, he started flying around. He was flying around every day, all over, just looking around for something to eat. And he started flying around on the mountainside and he see the person. He [the person] killed some things, so the raven started flying low and he flew over that man. He [the man] got a caribou and was cutting the

caribou. So the raven, he flew away and he landed on the other side of the hill. After he land there, he make himself [into] a person. He make himself [into] a young, young person.

So he started walking to that person cutting the caribou meat. So he went over there and that man told him, "Gee, I've never seen a human around here, so where'd you came from?" The raven said, "I was walking around here too, so I was hunting too."

The man said, "Yeah." That man was cutting that caribou, big caribou, a nice and fat caribou. That raven, he was sitting there watching him cutting that meat. And the raven told him — that man — "I got grandma not too far on the other side of this mountain. My grandma's over there. We got nothing to eat."

So that man, he cut it up, all the good stuff. They got some ribs, some brisket, and the kidneys. And tongue and marrow. He told him, "You take it back to your grandma, this one." The raven said, "Okay." And raven, he was sitting there, and he was thinking, he was thinking which way to tell him, that man there. So he told that man, "The one I'm talking about, my grandma, she's not too old. If you want to see her, you can come to our place and you can see my grandma." He told him, "I wish you were married to my grandma." And that man never said nothing to him.

That raven, what he was thinking, he wish he [the man] came to their camp, so he could see his grandma. He wish he'd get married to his grandma. So that man, after a long time, he said, "Married tomorrow? At what time, I'll go over there. I'll see you guys." The raven told him, "Okay, you sure do that."

See that raven, when he [the man] gave him [the raven] the meat, he went back to his grandma. And his grandma, she was in the house — in the brush house. She see that meat. "You bring that meat?" She asked him where he got it, though. The raven told her, "The man, he killed something so he gave me this meat. He's going to see us tomorrow. I told him to come to our camp, so he's going to come tomorrow." So he told his grandma, he said, "Grandma, you got to make a cap for yourself [out of] the one you were catching, the squirrel. Tonight you got to clean it and make it soft and make a cap for yourself, so you look good." After they've eaten, his grandma cleaned all the skins, enough for the cap. She made the cap herself.

So the next day, the raven, she stayed home, his grandma. She went back to her snare to look at the squirrel snare. And that man, he came to their camp. The raven told him, "My grandma, she's out to look at her snares. She'll come back pretty soon." That man told him [raven], "Okay." They were sitting there, not too long his grandma came back. The raven, he wished he'd [the man] would marry his grandma. And that man, he married his [raven's] grandma and he stayed with them. All summer that man, he was out hunting. He killed moose, caribou, black bear — boy, they got lots of meat and fat. But late in the fall, the *chulyin*, the raven, he got tired of packing meat. He told his grandma, "I'm getting tired of packing meat, grandma. My back's really hurting."

That man, one day he went out hunting again. After he left for a long time, the raven, he took off. He looked for that man there. He looked, he flying around, he flying around, then he seen him. Way steep mountains, high mountains, pretty steep, right down below, he's [the man] got caribou, he's cutting caribou there. So the raven, he land, way above him on the mountain, on top the mountain. So he walked around and looked and seen that man. He walked around, he looked for big rocks. He found really big rocks. He keep on pushing, pushing, pushing. Then they dropped, them rocks, rolled down on the mountain, right down on the mountain, right straight to that man, the one's cutting caribou. That man, he didn't expect that rocks. He didn't even hear it. They hit that man. That man, he got killed. And that raven, he know he killed that man.

Then he took off and came back to his grandma's. His grandma told him, "Where you was?" "Oh, I just walking around." And it's getting dark. His grandma told him, "I don't know why he stay a long time, that man there. He supposed to come back before dark." The raven said, "I don't know." And that night, that man, he didn't come back. Next day, next day, that man didn't come back.

That's what they call, my grandma use to tell me this raven, raven story. That's what they call *chulyin* stories.

Another story from long, long ago focuses on the brown bear, another animal of great importance in inland Dena'ina *sutdu'a*. The brown bear was respected as being more spiritually and physically powerful than humans. Therefore, great care always was taken in the way the inland Dena'ina spoke about them, hunted them, and cared for them after they were trapped and/or dispatched. When a hunter approached a brown bear, he

thought to himself, *"Cheyatda* [grandfather], I know that you are greater than I am, but I am here to hunt you with respect. My people are hungry and we need what you can provide." The bear was able to understand what the hunter was thinking or saying to himself, so he studied the hunter to see if his thoughts or remarks were a product of fear or meant to be sincere. If the bear thought the hunter was sincere, he would take his coat (hide) off and throw it toward the hunter, thereby giving himself up. The hunter took only his hide and flesh, but the bear's spirit remained alive and, in time, moved into another body. The spirit observed how the hunter handled his hide and flesh. If proper care were taken, the next time the hunter went after bear, he would be able to obtain another. Conversely, if he behaved inappropriately and disrespectfully toward the bear, on his next hunt he would be minimally unsuccessful or risk being killed or badly injured by the bear — a truly unworthy hunter.

The story below explains how coastal or saltwater brown bear came to be separate from the inland brown (grizzly) bear. This story also illustrates the great respect the Dena'ina had in the past and still had in the 1980s for brown bear. Lastly, it teaches young people not to lie or deceive others.

This story was told by Andrew Balluta. It is similar to another version of the story told by Anton Evan in the early 1980s to Joan Tenenbaum (1984:23-33).

NUTIHNA DEGHK'ISNA SUTDU'A: THE STORY OF TWO WOMEN

Two women were living at the edge of the ocean. One man was their husband. Every morning their husband went hunting out at sea. He always killed all kinds of things. Whatever he got, seal, belukha, he always killed every kind of thing.

Then it happened that their husband began to get sick. He was sick. And then their husband told them, "I'm never going to get well again. When I am gone, up there, there on the sand bank at the top of the hill, right on the edge, you will bury me," he told them. My covered skin boat and all my hunting gear, bow and arrows, spear and all, the throwing spear and everything, you'll put it in, under the cover. And a pole, put a long one inside it this way, and on top of me. You'll turn it [the skin boat] upside down [over him]," he told them. And the next morning he was dead; so they buried him as he had asked.

Up on top of the hill, in a sandslide on the very top of the hill, right there they buried him in that way. And his skin boat too, they prepared just as he had said. They put everything he had used in under the cover with him. Then they turned it all upside down over him. Those two women walked backed down, and they cried and cried. Every morning, the two of them always cried.

And then a chickadee alit outside on a branch near them. "What's the matter with you?" he said to them. "Our husband is gone. That is why we're doing this." "Why," he said to them, "your husband is fine. He's quite well; you shouldn't be doing that," he said to them.

"Tell us about it. We'll make a cap for you," they said to him. "All right," he said. He flew away, that chickadee. That day the two women made a cap for the chickadee. That evening he came flying back to them. "Here's the cap we made for you," they told him. The chickadee put it on [this is why the chickadee has a black head — it is his cap]. "Go on, tell us about it. Are you telling the truth, that our husband is well?" they said to him. "Yes," he said. "Your husband is at the seashore over where there is a reef along the water and a village, there he lives, and he has a wife. It's him for sure, the one you're mourning," he told them. "Is that so!" they said. "All right," they said to him. The chickadee flew away again.

In the morning they woke up early. The sun hadn't risen yet but they woke up. They got dressed, both of them. Brown bear skins, they wrapped brown bear skins around themselves, both of them. And then they started walking to the place he [chickadee] had told them about. They walked over the mountains to the shore. They walked and walked and they walked over a mountain. They came out on top of it, and down there on the beach was that village.

They were up above the brush line where there was no brush. Down to where they could be seen they went and they were eating berries, being brown bears. Down below in the village, "There are brown bears walking around up there," they said. Then their husband said, "Let me go after them!" "All right," they told him.

He took his bow and arrows and his spear. Up, he started running up. He went on and on; he reached the top and then there at the brush line were two brown bears eating berries. Then he stalked them slowly, and he kept going until he got very close to them, right behind them, stalking, stalking. He put an arrow in his bow. One of them

walked by him exposing her flank and he raised his bow and he pulled back the bowstring. When he pulled back the bow string, the brown bear turned to face him and pushed back her hood. She pushed back her hood and it was his wife both of them. They each pushed back their hoods, and there were his two wives.

Right there he dropped his bow and arrow and started running toward them, trying to get hold of them. As he ran up close to them, they pulled their hoods back down. They turned back into brown bears. They charged him and killed him.

Then down the mountainside, toward the village they started running. They came down into the village. They killed some of the people and some ran away. All the houses in the village they destroyed. They demolished every last one of the houses. They started back up. They got back up to the top, where they had eaten berries. "Now I will be an inland brown bear," said one woman. "Very well," the other said to her. "And what about you?," said the first. "As for me, I'll be a coastal [saltwater] bear," she said to her. And that is what happened to both of them. That is the story.

TIES THAT BIND: DENA'INA AND ANIMAL MUTUAL RESPECT AND COOPERATION

Many inland Dena'ina *sutdu'a* are important because they tell of hard times when humans or animals are in need of assistance. In situations such as these, the Dena'ina often turned to an *el'egen* (shaman or "medicine man") to make right what had gone wrong in their world. Since *el'egen* could be helpful or harmful, it was important to go to one who was adept and trustworthy — referred to as "good" shaman in English by the inland Dena'ina. Such a powerful person usually called upon spirit helpers to accomplish his or her feats.

In times of fish or game shortage, the inland Dena'ina realized that starvation was always a possibility. They also knew that times of food scarcity usually resulted from "evil spirits." To determine the source of the problem, people had to go to someone with great powers — spiritual powers greater than those of the "evil spirits" causing the shortage of fish and game.

The following story is a composite of a version told by Ruth Koktelash to Priscilla Kari in June 1981 and another told by Pete Koktelash, with comments interjected by Ruth, to the authors in August 1986. Another version of this story was told by Alexie Evan and published in Tenenbaum (1984).

CH'IDUCHUQ'A *SUTDU'A*: "MEDICINE MAN" STORIES

One time long ago in the fall, all the people went up in the mountains to hunt, and when they got to the mountains they didn't see nothing. They walked all over, but they didn't even see a ground squirrel. So they told Ch'iduchuq'a, a medicine man, to see what's going on. When he looked, he saw mountain people. The mountain people had put all the game in a mountain called Nduk'eyux Dghil'u or Telaquana Mountain. This place is at the head of Vandaztun Vena, or Turquoise Lake. Nduk'eyux Dghil'u means "animals go in the mountain." The medicine man took along *q'ich'idya* or "rock rabbit" [pika] with him. They walked and walked until they got to Nduk'eyux Dghil'u. There was no doorway of any kind it was all rocks. Ch'iduchuq'a took his cane and struck it on top and then a door opened a little. As soon as the door opened a little, he put his cane in between the crack.

Q'ich'idya, rock rabbit, went in first and then he [the Ch'iduchuq'a] went in behind him. Inside of the mountain, there were all the animals on earth, all walking around inside. They were hungry. Ch'iduchuq'a was dancing and *q'ich'idya* was singing. The mountain people were excited, and all of them were looking at Ch'iduchuq'a. Ch'iduchuq'a told *q'ich'idya* to go sing and make lots of fun. In your song, name each species of animal. *Q'ich'idya* sang and he called the *gunsha* [ground squirrel], the *vejex* [caribou], the *yeghedishla* [black bear], everything, he name it. Soon as he named the animal, it went out through the door.

The mountain people started to realize what was happening. And then they started to close the door. Ch'iduchuq'a went back out and put his cane in between the door. While *q'ich'idya* was going out, the door closed. When the door closed, it closed when the *q'ich'idya* was halfway out, so part of it went outside and the other half went inside of the mountain. The front part of him fell in amongst the rocks, fell in all over amongst the rocks in the Alaska Range.

All the animals went out and were eating above the timber line in the mountain. All the animals were eating and eating and Ch'iduchuq'a went home. If Ch'iduchuq'a hadn't done that, there wouldn't be any animals, if he hadn't let them out of the mountain. That's why we've got wild game. All the wild animals out in the country, Ch'iduchuq'a had let out. That's all.

Another story relating to human and animal mutual respect and cooperation involves the wolf. The inland Dena'ina considered wolves to be their brothers. Wolves were thought to have once been people and, as such, they all belonged to one of the inland Dena'ina clans — *ggahyi* (raven clan), according to some elders. In the past, when people were short of food and hungry and they heard a wolf howling, they went to where the wolves had been consuming game and took the portion of the meat which had been left behind. The Dena'ina believed that the wolves had notified them by howling that there was food there and had deliberately left part of their harvest for their brothers, the inland Dena'ina.

Because of the nature of this relationship, wolves were greatly respected and neither deliberately hunted or trapped. If a wolf were taken in a trap accidentally and not injured mortally, some trappers released it. If it were seriously hurt and had to be killed, the trapper talked to the wolf first. He apologized for trapping the wolf, stating that it had been accidental. The trapper then explained that he had to take the wolf's life.

After killing the wolf in the most humane fashion, the trapper carefully skinned the animal, quartered it, and hung every piece of the wolf in young trees — birch, willow, spruce, alder, cottonwood, or whatever was growing in the area in which the wolf had been killed. In this way the trapper was giving every part of the wolf, including the spirit, to nature. The spirit of the wolf was then satisfied and did not bring bad luck to the trapper or hunter. If a man did not treat the remains of a wolf properly or failed to explain and apologize for its unavoidable killing, bad luck resulted, and the hunter or trapper was unable to support himself or herself.

This story was told by Andrew Balluta based on versions related to him by elders as he was becoming an adult. Another version of this story was published by Vaudrin (1981:66-75). Although Vaudrin (1981) did not credit story tellers for specific oral histories, he stated in the preface that Michael and Jean Richteroff were responsible for the plots of most of the stories as they appear in his publication.

TIGIN SUTDU'A: WOLF STORY

Early one spring, a young man and his wife walked up a mountainside far from their village packing a small baby. They made camp near the top. They spent some time making snares out of eagle feathers for snaring ground squirrels. After the snaring started, they were usually gone from their camp most of the day.

One evening they came back late after spending a long day on the mountain. The young man was leading the way with his wife following behind packing the baby. When they reached their brush shelter at camp, the young man held open the skin door for his wife to go inside. When she stood up inside the brush shelter, the young woman was completely taken by surprise. Lying there just in front of her was a large, gray wolf. Her husband was still outside. She didn't know what to do, but she didn't scream or holler. She knew that wolves and people were closely related. She stooped down and laid the baby right beside the wolf. "Here's your little brother," she said to the wolf. "We just found him."

The wolf started licking the baby's face. When the young man stepped inside, he saw what had happened and spoke to the wolf. As he talked, the wolf laid his ears back, so the young couple knew he understood what they were saying. From that time on, the wolf stayed with the family and hunted with them high on the mountain. The couple treated him like a son, and the wolf accepted their child as his baby brother. Sometime he would take the baby from the cradle and carry it out into the woods or off around the mountain for hours at a time. Whenever the father went hunting for caribou, he took the wolf with him. When they'd spot a herd of caribou, the wolf took however much meat they needed, so the family never went without.

As the boy grew older, the wolf taught him how to hunt. The boy learned fast, but the wolf pushed him harder and harder to hunt better. The wolf made the boy run and work until he was faster and stronger than any boy his age had ever been. The boy was so quick, he could catch birds as they were flying in the air.

After a while, the boy's father began to grow jealous of the wolf. The boy was always going after the wolf, and the man's wife was always saying what a good hunter the wolf was. So one day, when the boy's father was feeling mean, he took the wolf out with him to hunt some caribou. It wasn't long before they came upon a herd, and the man sent the wolf off after them. In a few minutes, the wolf had killed four caribou, and the man followed along behind cleaning them. It had always been the man's habit as he cleaned the caribou to wash off the liver and give it to the wolf. However, this time he left the liver bloody and threw it at the wolf, hitting him in the face. "You're no wolf," said the man. "You're half dog. We don't have to wash everything for you all the time." The wolf just sat there looking at him. He didn't eat the liver. When the man had finished loading up his pack, he put it on his shoulders and started off for the camp. The wolf still sat there with blood on his face, getting madder and madder. He watched until the man was far off in the distance. Then he leaped up and went off after the man. The wolf caught up with the man and killed him there with the pack still on his back.

When the man didn't come home for supper that night, his wife suspected that something had happened to him. Later that evening, she went to the door and found the wolf lying there with blood all over his face. "I guess the wolf has killed my husband," she thought to herself. Kneeling beside the wolf, she began washing off his face while she talked to him. "What happened to my husband?," she asked. "Did you kill him?" Both of the wolf's ears twitched forward, so she knew that that was what had happened.

After she fed the wolf, he lay down near the doorway and fell asleep. Later on while the woman was nursing the boy, she started feeling angry about what the wolf had done. "I'll get even with him for killing my husband," she thought. So while he slept, the woman took her own milk and rubbed it all over the wolf's paws. She knew that after a while, the milk would make his feet so soft, he wouldn't be able to walk. She didn't want to kill the wolf, but she wanted to make him sorry for what he'd done. When she had finished, the woman began gathering up her belongings in the brush shelter. Soon the wolf woke up and the woman said, "There's no use in my staying around here any more. I'm going back home to my village. You won't be able to go along, of course."

The wolf sensed her bitterness now, and so he turned into a man and explained to her exactly what had happened. As he told his story, the wolfman stood beside the boy holding on to him. The woman began to feel sorry for what she had done to his feet, but she was afraid to tell him about it. The wolf said he realized that because he was a wolf, he couldn't come into the village to live with them. He promised that he would still do what he could to care for the boy. "Whenever you fellows are having a hard time in the village," he said, "and you don't have enough food, just listen for a wolf howling. Go to where the sound is, and you will find meat." Then he left them.

A year passed and the young boy and his mother didn't see the wolf again, even once. The following winter, a famine struck the village. The women set snares out all over the forest, but there weren't any rabbits. The men hunted clear back into the mountains, but the country was empty of game. Then one night, as the men returned empty handed from a hunting trip, they heard a wolf howling not far from the village. They thought nothing of it, but the young woman heard them talk about it and knew what it was.

Early the next morning, she rushed out to where the wolf had been heard and found him waiting. "I've brought meat for you," he said. Then the wolf turned into a man and cleaned the game for her. He hung it up until she could return for it with others from the village. She took part of the meat with her. When she finished loading up her pack, the young woman said to the wolf, "The men from the village will be coming here after this meat. You'd better not be around or they'll kill you." "I only came to make sure you have enough meat," the wolf said. "I'll be gone before they come." As he turned away, the woman saw that he was limping and she knew that his feet were getting softer. But she didn't know how to tell him what she had done.

That afternoon when she got back to the village, the woman told everyone where the meat was. The men went out to pack it in. There was plenty to last until the hunting got good again, and everyone was happy. Life was better in the village after that, and the winter months passed quickly. But by spring, the people in the village started missing food. Some of the people said they had seen a wolf in the village. Others said it had stolen from them. After much talking, the men said they would hunt it down and kill it.

When the young woman heard about it, she ran out to look for the wolf. She knew that she must find him before the hunters did. Finally, after hours of searching, she found him. He walked over to her and sat down. Then he lifted a covering like a hood from his face and turned into a man. "Look at my feet," he said. "They are all raw." He told her that he had been stealing meat from the village. His feet were so sore that he couldn't hunt for himself.

The young woman finally told him what she had done to his feet, but she said she was really sorry and promised to help him. She took some pieces of skin out of her sewing kit and put them under his feet. When she spit on them, they stayed on, and the wolf's feet were all right again.

So he put his hood back on again and changed back into a wolf. He was so happy that he forgave the young woman for what she had done. He even told her that if they ever needed meat in the village again, he would still be glad to get it for them. The woman told him he'd better keep out of sight for awhile, because the men were out hunting for him. She also told him he should not take any more meat from the village. "It might be poisoned," she said. So they split up and the woman went back home to her son. The boy was getting older now, so she told him what had happened. After that, the boy always went along whenever the wolf left food for them. Sometimes he went out alone to meet the wolf, and the two of them went hunting together.

As the years passed, the time came when the boy was no longer a child but had become a man. He married and built a sod and spruce bark house for himself on the shore of the lake, not far from his mother's village. It was then that the wolf decided to have a serious talk with him. "I am your brother," the wolf said. "I have taught you a great deal and you have learned well. But now you must go on your own. You are a great hunter. I'm getting old now, and you could even outdo me. But one day all the animals will make war with you — because I have taught you and you have taken so many of them — and you cannot out fight them all. So you must prepare yourself for that day. The first thing you must do is make a shelter and cache enough food on an island, so you can escape there. Be sure you have a skin boat ready at all times. When the animals attack, you can jump into the boat and row out to the island."

The young man hurried to carry out his brother's instructions. Having lived with the wolf for all those years, he knew that whatever he said was true. Before long, everything was ready. Then one night when he and his wife were asleep, the young man was awakened by strange noises coming from the woods. He woke her, they hurried down to the beach, and they got into the skin boat. They had barely pushed out from shore when the clearing around his shelter was filled with raging animals. Among the animals was a large gray wolf. After the man and his wife were too far to hear, the wolf said, "You see! I told you we couldn't catch him.

He's too fast." The rest of the animals didn't know that the man was the wolf's brother.

Several nights later, a skin boat moved quietly across the water from the island and landed just below the man's shelter. The man stepped onto the beach, moved quietly up the shore to his house, and peered in through the window. All the animals were inside having a feast on some food which the man had left behind. The leader of the animals sat at the head of the table. Putting an arrow to his bow, the man drew back and shot the animal leader in his heart. He dropped dead. The shelter was in an uproar. All the other animals jumped up and were moving around. By the time some of them got outside to catch the man, he was already in his skin boat paddling back to the island. Once again the old wolf told them, "You see, I warned you that we could never catch him."

A few nights later, the young man returned in the boat with his wife. Again he sneaked quietly up to his house. But when he reached the doorway, someone was waiting for him there in the shadows. It was the old wolf. He'd been expecting him. The wolf handed the young man a bear bone club and said, "You may kill them all or let some escape — whatever you want."

The man understood. He pulled down the skin over the entrance and rushed inside, swinging the club left and right. He didn't stop until he had killed every animal he could reach and the house was quiet with death. Only a few had escaped. Finally, when his anger and strength were gone, the man walked outside. The wolf was satisfied.

"The few that got away talked to me before they left," the wolf told the man. "They said to tell you they'd forgive you and that they're going to have a party in two years at the dead leader's house. You and your wife are invited." "What are they going to do?," the man asked. "It's a trick. They are going to try to kill you then," said the wolf. But the wolf said he would be back before the time came to talk with the man about it. "Meanwhile, I'll watch out so that nothing happens to you or your family. You should get prepared for that party. You should take a brown bear and some caribou. Soak the bones in oil to make them strong and save them for the party."

The months passed quickly, summer and winter, and before long the two years were up and the wolf returned. "They're getting all ready now," the wolf said, sitting down. "The party will be in about two days, so you must fix up your equipment and be ready. The animals will be ready for you, but I'll

do what I can to help. When you find them, I'll be there."

So the young man hurried to get everything ready. He gathered together the oiled clubs and fixed up his bow with plenty of arrows. His wife was busy sewing waterproof boots and clothing for their trip to the party. When the weapons and clothing were finished, the man and his wife gathered them up and walked to where the party was going to be.

Just before they got there, the young man stopped at the home of an old woman, who lived in a foxhole right under the trail. He told his wife to wait outside the door for him. Inside, the old woman was sitting down. She lived all by herself. "Who are you?" she asked. He told her his name. She told him the animals were going to make war on a man by that name. "I'm the one," the man said. "I killed your leader." The old woman started to scream, but he knocked her down with his oiled club and smashed her throat before she could make any noise. She died. The young man called to his wife as he began skinning the old woman out. Together they waited in the foxhole until night time. Then he put the old woman's skin over himself and picked up her cane and left with his wife for the party. His wife didn't need a disguise, because the animals didn't know her.

Pretty soon they came to the place where the party was being held. It was a little settlement a village of animal people. When the young man and his wife entered the dead leader's house, the wolf, who was there before them with his own wife, recognized his brother. "That's your brother-in-law," he whispered to his wife. "Go invite them over."

So the young man and his wife went over and sat down with the wolf and his wife. Later in the evening the two brothers left the party together and had a talk outside. "They'll all be starting home now pretty soon," said the young man. "They don't think I'm coming, so I'll have to wait right here by the door in the dark and kill them as they leave." The wolf told him not to kill all the animals, so they would not die out completely. Then the wolf went back inside and began talking each of the party guests into leaving, one or two at a time, while the man stood outside, killing some and letting some go. When the house was about half empty, those left inside sensed something was wrong. They began escaping from the house in any way possible.

The man and his wife went inside and walked all around, taking whatever they wanted. "You're too smart for me," said the wolf. "What do you mean?" asked the young man, turning to his brother. "I thought they would get you. But now there won't be any more war again, ever. I must go now," the wolf said, "for I am getting old. But there is one thing you must always remember. Whenever any animal attacks or charges you, just think of me. I'll be right by your side. None of them will be able to catch you or hurt you in any way." This agreement between the wolf and the young Dena'ina has been good for many generations of their descendants.

DEEDS OF OUR ANCESTORS: STORIES FROM HISTORIC TIMES

In the recent past, but before the *Gasht'ana* or "white men" came, the inland Dena'ina and the *Dutna* of the Bristol Bay area warred with one another. The *Dutna* from Bristol Bay came up to the Lake Iliamna and Lake Clark areas in an attempt to take the country and women from the Dena'ina who lived there. The Dena'ina were good warriors, but among them emerged one man, Ts'enhdghulyał. Although he was born of a woman but his father was unknown, Ts'enhdghulyał became a great leader in all Dena'ina wars.

Some stories recount a raid by the *Dutna* on the settlement of Kijik and, later, on Kijik Lake at a time Ts'enhdghulyał was not present. During this raid, in which some women were captured, the *Dutna* were victorious, although most of the Dena'ina escaped. The following story tells about the Kijik raid and the retaliation of the Dena'ina on the *Dutna* of the Naknek River area.

This story was told by Andrew Balluta. It is a composite of several Ts'enhdghulyał stories, which Balluta learned from elders during his lifetime.

THE DENA'INA RAID ON A NAKNEK RIVER VILLAGE

I actually don't know what time of the year — it could have been fall, summer, or spring when this happened. They [the *Dutna*] brought their *baidarki* and open skin boats across the portage into the Newhalen River. They came up Lake Clark and into where it is called Chaq'ah Tugget [the site of Sophie Austin's camp] — that's before the name came to be Chaq'ah Tugget. And Chaq'ah Tugget is where they landed and pulled up all their skin boats. There were some old people that were along with them. They were left

at that place to look after the skin boats and equipment there — that is why the place came to be Chaq'ah Tugget, "the place where equipment is left."

Very early in the morning when they started up toward Dghilishla [a mountain south of Kijik Lake], they went up the mountain northwest of Kijik village. They went on top of the mountain, up to the other end of the mountain, and right there below them is where the Dena'ina fish camp and fish village were. The men were all out hunting except for the few who were left in the village fishing. The fish camp is now called "Kijik Lake," which means "salmon lake." The villagers, the Kijik villagers, didn't realize the Aleuts [*Dutna*] were coming until they were near the fish camp. All their men folks were gone, and they were sort of in trouble. They couldn't figure out how they could get away from the warriors.

When the Aleuts [*Dutna*] approached closer, an older man told them to set fire to a smokehouse that had fish in it. The elder people told them that when you set a fire to that smokehouse and when the wind is just right for the smoke to go across the river, then escape in the smoke. When they set the smokehouse on fire, it was a heavy smoke, and it blew across the river. When the smoke was thick enough, they took their children and some of their belongings and escaped across the river, and went into the timber. This is where they [the *Dutna*] took some women, young women, captive and took them back to Naknek as hostages — or back to Savonoski — some place in there.

There was one young girl whom they took captive. This girl they took captive, they took her back down. Naknek — I really don't know the original traditional name for Naknek — but that's where they took this young girl. The girls and women that they took captive, they kept in sort of a prison that they called a steam bath, a little room off the house. The women they kept in the steam bath, they'd use them, they'd use their bodies, the young men went in and helped themselves to these women. These women were used as — just for young men to come and use them as they wanted.

There was one Aleut [*Dutna*] old lady who made friends with this one young Indian girl. She told this young girl that these, my people, are not very good for capturing other women. This old lady told the young girl to prepare for escape. This Aleut [*Dutna*] old lady started preparing this young girl for her journey back, like moccasin soles, material to sew new soles on her boots. This old lady started preparing things for this young girl, like needles, things that she can eat, that she can preserve, and getting her ready. She prepared her with food and all the material that she can carry. One night, after all the men folks went hunting and it was quiet at night, when things were quiet at night, this old lady helped the young girl escape and sent her off. After she escaped from the village, she just continued on toward Lake Iliamna outlet, Nilan Q'estsiq'. I really don't know how she crossed the river. After she crossed the outlet of Iliamna Lake, she walked all the way back up to Kijik.

When she got back to the village, she told the story of how they were treated by the men and the Aleuts [Dutna]. She told the story of what was happening down in that Aleut village, and that's when Ts'enhdghulyal and all the council and the chiefs gathered and had a meeting and said if this keeps up, it won't be any good. So the tribe decided they were going to declare war. All the tribes from different villages all gathered near Lake Iliamna on the Newhalen River. From there, they crossed Lake Iliamna by baidarki and skin boats, niggiday [open caribou skin-covered boats]. They crossed Iliamna Lake to what they call "medicine man creek," Ch'ul'egitnu [also called Dennis Creek]. From there, they went on foot toward Naknek. They had a sort of convoy, supply people, who packed skins, skin boats, and groceries, and women who could sew. All these people who were along were doing something. Ts'enhdghulyal's warriors were up ahead.

As they were portaging from Lake Iliamna to Naknek, the Naknek people were out hunting. As they were going along, they spotted some hunters, some of Ts'enhdghulyal's men. When Ts'enhdghulyal looked, he recognized the men. He told them that was Jilughun [the Dutna war hero]. He told his men, "I'm going to try to capture Jilughun myself, and you guys capture the others."

So Ts'enhdghulyal started chasing Jilughun. Jilughun was himself a great warrior too. There just wasn't anybody who could get a hold of him. Jilughun was one of the greatest warriors in the Aleut [Dutna] tribe. Ts'enhdghulyal started chasing him. Jilughun headed for a swampy area, and that's where he was running. While he was running in the swamp, he dived into the ground and came up some other place. The place that he was diving into was sort of an underground creek where the grass was grown over, over where you can't see it. He dived under there and he knew exactly where to go and come up some other place. As the game was going on, Ts'enhdghulyal finally

figured him out, what he was doing. So while he was chasing him, he figured him out. So when Jilughun dived under the ground again, Ts'enhdghulyal figured just about where he was going to come up as far as he could hold his breath, where he was going to come up. He figured him just right, where he came up, came up right in front of him. Ts'enhdghulyal grabbed Jilughun. Jilughun didn't fight back — he just looked back and told him, "You got me."

They captured him but they didn't kill him right there. They made a pack for him to torture him. They cut him on the shoulders where the strings would be cutting into his flesh and made him pack skins for skin boats. So they told him to lead them to his village. So they came to Naknek River across from his village. Jilughun told Ts'enhdghulyal that there was nobody in the village here, that everybody was upriver hunting. Then they tied him to a tree.

As the hunters came back down the river, the Indians would kill the men and bring each body to Jilughun and ask him to identify the body. They just about went through all the hunters that came down river, and killed them and showed each one of them to Jilughun. They asked him if this was the man that raised him, and he just shook his head. And then, just about at the end, here comes a baidarki with a child and a young boy in the baidarki with a man. When they started shooting arrows at him, he turned the baidarki over while he was sitting in it and then flipped it back. When he turned himself over in the canoe, when he came right back, right side up, he was so fast with the bow and arrow, he killed two or three Indians before they could shoot an arrow at him. Then they finally hit him with a bow and arrow and killed him. Then they brought the body to Jilughun and asked him who this man was. And he said, "Yes, that's the man who raised me." So he told them, "Now, now you have ruined me and you can kill me." And then they killed him; he had asked them to kill him.

And then they went across to the village to see if everybody was still there. They didn't kill off any children or women, they didn't kill off any others, and they left the village. They went with skin boats and baidarki and went back upriver. They returned to their village. That's the kind of story they use to tell of Ts'enhdghulyal.

Before the days of the Gasht'ana, the inland Dena'ina travelled overland, covering miles of country on foot and dragging sleds behind them during the winter time. During the precontact period, they did not use dog traction, although dogs were used as pack animals. Sometimes they travelled to visit relatives, to attend ceremonies, or to trade. Their travels included trips to the coast. Since the Lake Clark area is surrounded to the north and west by mountains, the inland Dena'ina had to travel through mountain passes and over glaciers to reach coastal destinations. After the *Gasht'ana* came, the Dena'ina began to use dogs for pulling sleds. This story is an account of one of the trips to the settlement of Tyonek during the historic past.

This story was told and recorded by Anton Evan in 1980. Andrew Balluta had him retell it on tape in 1985. It is this latter version which appears in this context.

THE STORY OF A GLACIER IN LAKE CLARK PASS

Long ago before our time, at Kijik village there were no airplanes, no cars, no motors. They [the Dena'ina] used to travel by rowing a boat with oars. In the winter time, they used to travel between Tyonek and Lake Clark Pass. They used to travel through Lake Clark Pass for a visit long ago. People from Kijik were travelling to Tyonek. They went to Tyonek and visited with Tyonek people during the winter.

They started back through Lake Clark Pass. About halfway in that pass, there is a glacier. There were many crevasses in places that were five feet wide and they were snow covered. There was a man who had two sleighs behind him, and he had a child in one sled. The sled that was ahead made it across the crevasse, and the sleigh that was behind fell in. The sleigh went down into the crevasse. The man had three dogs; that stopped the sled from going all the way down. They pulled the sled up, but when they got the sled backup, they found the child wasn't in the sled. It looked like the child had fallen out of the sled.

The Dena'ina took all the sleigh lashings and the extra ropes they had — rawhides — and spliced the ropes. The rawhides are real strong like a rope. The child's dad told them to tie the rope around his waist and lower him down. And then they tied the rope around his waist and started lowering him down. It was pretty near the end of the rope when, just about then, he shook the rope. And they pulled him up out of the crevasse, and he had the child with him.

They went below the glacier down toward Lake Clark and made a camp. When the child was in the crevasse, he put his hand out of the covers. His hand was frozen. In those days, there were no doctors. The child lost his hand. And then they came back to the village and the child grew up. He became a man, but his parents, father and mother, had died. The man was handicapped with only one hand. He grew up and had children. He lived to be an old man and died. They used to tell about these paths that they used to travel through. They used to tell about this.

THE DENA'INA STORYTELLER

The ability to tell Dena'ina *sutdu'a* in the proper ways and at the appropriate times has always been an important part of inland Dena'ina culture. Although not everyone was considered an expert storyteller, all adults used stories during their lifetimes to pass on information to other adults or, more importantly, to children.

For the inland Dena'ina of the 1980s, storytelling was both a personal and group experience. As such, the content and style were conditioned by the timing, setting, audience, kinship and social status of the storyteller, and the events that stimulated the need to recount the specific oral historic incident. Although children and young adults were obliged to listen intently without interrupting the teller, adults having some relationship with the storyteller, at times, felt free to interject details that they perceived to be essential and omitted from the version being presented. These conditions, in part, account for variations between versions of the same story.

To the inland Dena'ina of the 1980s, storytelling served multiple functions. Most apparent to the outsider, storytelling was a source of recreation and entertainment — a means of spending leisure time in a traditional and social manner. As is well known by social scientists, oral histories were the means by which peoples, termed by westerners to be "nonliterate," conveyed both general and specific knowledge and their cultural heritage between generations. In the case of the inland Dena'ina, storytelling was the principal method of instructing children and young adults about acceptable social behavior and associated norms and cultural values. In this function, stories normally focused on events and behaviors from the past that were analogous to the situations at hand. That is, such education was generally indirect, involving the behaviors of third party actors.

Western historians are preoccupied with the accuracy of accounts of the past as documented in written form. Despite the fact that interpretations of written histories are of great significance within the interests of practitioners of this discipline, the underlying paradigm — that there is only one correct version of an historic event — is a key concept within the discipline. Variation is commonly attributed to the subjective perspectives of the historian providing the account or the genre in which he or she is writing.

By way of contrast, oral histories exist in the collective memories of group members. Not only are stories commonly not related identically by the same storyteller or by all adults of his or her generation, such oral histories vary geographically within the same group and through time. Since Dena'ina histories were never put into print until recent years, developing methodologies for measuring change through time and, therefore, the accuracy of historic accounts are speculative, at best. Comparisons of the same story, as told by members of different subgroups during a comparable period of time, may provide more cultural and historical insight.

Different perceptions of the nature of history by the inland Dena'ina and western scholars provide a meaningful example of cultural contrast. The western system of objective logic dictates the existence of one "real" or "genuine" account — a single reality. To the inland Dena'ina, there is no contradiction of logic if multiple variations of the same recounted event exist simultaneously or through time and space. All accounts are equally valid, genuine, and representative of the event, given the contexts in which they are presented. When adults interject the telling of a story, it is not perceived usually to be a correction of the storyteller's account, but rather is seen to enhance or emphasize certain events being recalled. In the case of the inland Dena'ina, stories are not the property of individuals but are rather the collective memory of members of a particular kinship or socioterritorial group at any given point in time. Therefore, there is no one historic account or storyteller who represents a singular truth or reality.

Within the last decade, many inland Dena'ina expressed a solemn concern for the future of their oral histories and what they perceive to be the associated future of their culture. They expressed the opinion that, as they have become increasingly drawn into the realm of influence of the *Gasht'ana* world, the use of oral histories or stories as a means of transmitting knowledge has declined. In their view, the functions of inland Dena'ina storytelling seemingly have been replaced or made secondary to modes of information dissemination and recreation emanating from school teachers and other artifacts of western educational institutions, non-Dena'ina members of councils and boards, politicians, televisions, and radios.

At a community meeting during the summer of 1991, adults of all ages expressed the concern that the young people were spending less time both listening to those who know the Dena'ina past and learning how to be effective storytellers themselves. As one young woman lamented, "If younger people do not learn the importance and skills of Dena'ina oral history, much of the knowledge of our past will be lost as well as our ability to transmit our histories through traditional means. This, indeed, would be a sad thing for our people."

Figure 15. Residents of Old Nondalton, who were travelling from the village to Severson's trading post in Iliamna, circa 1931. Individuals in the photograph are (left to right) Marka Karshekoff, Jenny Drew, Evan Nudlash, Maxim Cusma, Vadlunga (Yenlu) Severson holding Martin Severson, and Annie Severson. The child standing behind Vadlunga is thought to be Mary Severson. *Photograph Courtesy of Agnes Cusma.*

CHAPTER 4

INLAND DENA'INA DEMOGRAPHIC CHANGE: POPULATION SHIFTS, SEDENTISM, AND EUROAMERICAN CONTACT

INTRODUCTION: WHAT CAN BE LEARNED FROM THE INLAND DENA'INA CASE?

It generally has been observed that contact between Euroamericans and the Native peoples of the arctic and subarctic of northern America has been followed by greater centralization of the latter. That is, in the postcontact period, indigenous peoples of the north have taken up residence in fewer, more permanent, and larger settlements. To some degree, this trend has been documented in the case of other hunting and gathering societies worldwide. However, it cannot be assumed that increased sedentism and a decline in nomadic activities are necessarily correlated with greater centralization. The nature of the relationship between centralization and sedentism, and between these variables and demography (population size and structure), are examined in the case of the inland Dena'ina in this chapter.

The ways in which centralization, sedentism, and demographic change are manifested in different hunting and gathering societies depend upon multiple variables. These include the nature of precontact settlement patterns; population sizes and distributions; characteristics of seasonal and annual migratory rounds; intensity, duration, and content of contact experiences; and social, economic, and political alternatives to more traditional settlement and demographic arrangements.

The primary questions in this context are what changes have been identified in inland Dena'ina settlement and associated demographic patterns through time and in what ways do these changes relate to introduced Euroamerican social, economic, and political institutions and events? The detailed and temporal dimensions of inland Dena'ina settlement, demographic, and genealogical data are exceptional by way of comparison with other hunting and gathering populations and of utility in answering these questions.

Several models have been proposed for examining changes in hunter and gatherer settlement patterns and associated demography as a result of

Euroamerican contact. One common model used in explaining demographic transformations of indigenous hunters and gatherers, who have become increasingly urbanized or, in western terms, "modernized," is that termed "demographic transition" (Freeman 1970, 1971). According to this model, immediately following Euroamerican contact, there is a stage of initial population reduction due to the effects of introduced epidemic diseases. This is followed by a stage of rapid population growth.

According to the theory of the demographic transition, both mortality and fertility are affected by the sequelae of economic development . . . . Early in this development stage, death rate begins to decline dramatically as a result of improvements in health, material and communication levels, but birthrate appears more refractory. The reasons for this differential response appear to be social: societies traditionally accept the ideal of minimizing suffering and death, but no such consensus exists regarding the desirability of producing fewer children. The net effect of this dramatic decline in deaths with an unchanging birth rate is to produce a "population explosion" (Freeman 1971:217).

Subsequently, there is a stage of population reduction.

Changes associated with modernization in time begin to erode certain traditional beliefs and practices. Those members of the society who place increasing value on maximizing the new occupational, material and political goals presented will in varying degrees adopt the lifestyle of apparently successful members of the modern society. Thus, generally, new norms of behaviour, including reproductive behaviour, diffuse through the modernizing society from the more progressive, and often elitist, elements, to the emerging urban proletariat, so that eventually the birthrates and death rates of the modernizing society will approach those of the dominant modern nation-state (Freeman 1971:217).

A question to be asked in this context is to what degree is demographic transition, as described above, applicable to population and settlement shifts among the inland Dena'ina since the time of Euroamerican contact. Secondly, have the inland Dena'ina attempted to mimic Euroamerican modes of behavior in general, as suggested by demographic transition theory?

There are other questions or assumptions which have emerged from the study of contemporary hunting and gathering societies. One of these is the implication in demographic transition theory and others that the "westernization," "industrialization," or "modernization" of hunting and gathering societies following Euroamerican contact is assumed to be natural and an inevitable outcome, normally associated with centralization and decreased mobility (e.g., Chance 1990; Murphy and Steward 1968 [1956])).

In addition, data derived from contemporary hunter-gatherer research have revealed that culturally defined goals, rather than merely physical survival, play a vital role in demographic structures and processes through time. Many contemporary hunting and gathering populations live well below the biological carrying capacity of the environments they occupy (Sahlins 1981 [1972]). They practice a variety of social arrangements that result in lowered fertility, not solely for reasons related to the food supply (Zubrow 1973). Rather, Freeman (1970) and others have emphasized the role of optimum population in light of the desire on the part of hunters and gatherers to facilitate mobility. Models which unduly stress starvation and anxiety about food as the driving forces in hunter-gatherer demographic and settlement patterns tend to ignore, or consider secondary, social, ideological, and historic factors.

It is suggested here that processes of centralization, related changes in the size and composition of social units, and value sets that support either decreased or increased levels of mobility are all significant variables in understanding the demographic and settlement history of any hunting and gathering society. In other words, whereas the end products of Euroamerican contact on hunters and gatherers are commonly assumed to include centralization, sedentism, ultimately decreased fertility, and nuclear family dominance, the alternative view to be examined here is that these are actually complexly related variables in their own right. Lastly, since the relationships between these variables are not inextricably linked nor unidirectional in nature — predictable stages in some scheme of social evolution — the occurrence of any one does not imply or mandate the existence of any other.

SETTLEMENT AND POPULATION HISTORY OF THE INLAND DENA'INA

PRECONTACT SETTLEMENT AND DEMOGRAPHY: SOME CONSIDERATIONS

The origins of the Dena'ina, as distinct from neighboring Athabaskan and Yupik populations, and the relationships between contemporary Dena'ina subgroups or societies and those of the precontact period are unclear. In part, this problem results from the limitations of archaeological method and theory in associating socially, culturally, and, unless skeletal evidence is available, genetically distinct populations with material, structural, and contextual remains. Townsend (1974a) and VanStone and Townsend (1970) discussed this problem specifically in relationship to making Dena'ina and Yup'ik distinctions based on excavations at the Kijik site and at Yup'ik occupied areas of the same period on the Nushagak and Kuskokwim rivers. Workman (1978) had similar questions regarding the identification and interpretation of cultural and paleontological remains in relationship to prehistoric and historic occupations of Kachemak Bay on the lower Kenai Peninsula. In the case of the inland Dena'ina, there are additional problems related to the paucity of available archaeological data for the areas that they occupied (VanStone pers. comm. 1985). Additionally, preservation of Athabaskan remains in general is considered problematic by many northern archaeologists (Dumond 1978).

A concise summary of archaeological research in the area occupied by the inland Dena'ina highlights the relatively limited nature of the existing prehistoric and early historic data base. In 1966, archaeologists VanStone and Townsend (1970) excavated the foundations of all but two of the structures at historic Kijik village. At the end of the season, VanStone undertook limited archaeological tests in the north and south meadows of the outlet river from Kijik Lake, comprising the historic component of the Kijik fish camp. In 1975, historic Kijik village and cemetery, Kijik Mountain, and Kijik fish camp were recorded by the Cook Inlet Historic and Cemetery Sites project in conjunction with the Alaska Native Claims Settlement Act (ANCSA) (Brelsford 1975). An archaeological survey of prehistoric and historic sites was undertaken for the Lake Clark area by Smith and Shields in 1976 (1977). This survey added 54 additional sites and trails to the

Figure 16. The community of Old Nondalton, circa 1929. The population of Old Nondalton relocated to the present site of Nondalton in the early 1940s. *Photograph Courtesy of Ida Carlson Crater.*

Figure 17. The first Old Nondalton school photograph, 1931, taken by teacher Mr. Liese. Individuals in the photograph are (back row, left to right) Ruth Bobby, Martha Richteroff, Jean Karshekoff, Edward Severson, Macy Hobson, Sophie Balluta, and Anton Balluta; (second row, left to right) Agnes Trefon, Harry Balluta, Paul Cusma, Bertha Koktelash, Sophie Cusma, Bob Balluta, Nicholai Wassillie, Ben Trefon, George Wassillie, and Mrs. Liese; and (front row, left to right) Alice Balluta, Mary Balluta, Serfean Balluta, Vera Balluta, Anisha Evanoff, Frank Evanoff (holding pennant), Clarence or Harold Balluta, unknown girl, Tatiana (Frances) Hobson, unknown boy, Clarence or Harold Balluta, and Albert Wassillie. *Photograph Courtesy of Ida Carlson Crater.*

existing and, still relatively sparse, cultural inventory of the area. In 1978, cultural geographer, Steven Behnke, while on a pedestrian reconnaissance of the Kijik area, discovered the foundations of several old, semisubterranean houses in a heavily wooded area about one kilometer north of historic Kijik village (Behnke pers. comm. 1979). This site appeared to be the prehistoric settlement reported by Osgood (1904a:329) during his 1902 explorations, in which he mentioned "very ancient traces of a large village of former times." In 1979 and 1980, U.S. National Park Service (NPS) anthropologists from the Cooperative Park Studies Unit, University of Alaska, Fairbanks, assisted by the Bureau of Indian Affairs, surveyed the Kijik area in more detail. At that time, much of the low lying area near the base of Kijik Mountain had been inundated by beaver dams. During this same research period, historic Kijik and cemetery, North Kijik, and Kijik fish camp sites were mapped and described by Lynch (1982). In 1983, NPS personnel Alice Lynch and John Branson made a surface reconnaissance near the base of Kijik Mountain. There they located and mapped the sites of three old Dena'ina settlements. A fourth site, the remains of a large and extensive settlement, was also recorded. Investigation of these archaeological features was delayed until 1990, when an NPS archaeological and surveying party mapped and described the surface attributes of three of these reported sites (Birkedal pers. comm. 1991).

While this archaeological research has provided important cultural information, to date it has not led to the definitive formulation of general theories relating prehistoric intergroup migrations and relationships involving the inland Dena'ina and neighboring populations. As a result, there are multiple competing theories about Dena'ina prehistory and many variations on these interpretive schemes.

Based on their excavations at Kijik, VanStone and Townsend (1970) concluded that the inland Dena'ina were once coastal residents of Cook Inlet, who had moved inland no earlier than the 1600s or 1700s and, possibly, subsequent and in response to Russian contact. Based on archaeological research on Cook Inlet, Workman (1978) and Dumond (1978) suggested a relatively recent (500 to 900 year) occupation of the coast by these Athabaskans, in large part because of the absence of earlier evidence which can be identified unequivocally with the Dena'ina. Since this is an area and topic of active archaeological research, theories and dates change with considerable

rapidity, as new data become available and undergo analysis. Recent unpublished information suggests even greater longevity of the Dena'ina in the Cook Inlet area (K. Workman pers. comm. 1991).

Based on ethnogeographic, structural linguistic, and oral historic data, J. Kari (1975a, 1977, 1985; Kari and Kari 1982) has argued for an inland, mountainous origin of the Dena'ina in the piedmont plateau west of the Alaska Range, an area of the upper Stony and Mulchatna rivers referred to as Hlsaynenq' or "first land" by the Dena'ina. Interestingly, von Wrangell (1970 [1839]), manager of the Russian-American Company from 1830 to 1835, postulated a mountainous origin for the Dena'ina as well. Based on principally linguistic evidence, Kari (1985) proposes a long term occupancy of the plateau area (perhaps 3,000 or more years), with later dispersal into the Lake Clark, Lake Iliamna, and Cook Inlet areas — into regions potentially occupied during earlier times by Alutiiq and Central Yup'ik populations.

Dialectical divergence between Dena'ina populations in the latter part of the 1900s, analyzed by J. Kari (1975a), suggests closer ties between the Lake Iliamna, Lake Clark, Telaquana, and Stony River populations than between them and the populations of Dena'ina who resided on Cook Inlet. However, the Dena'ina spoken on the Kenai Peninsula more closely resembles that spoken by the Lake Iliamna and inland populations than does the dialect spoken on upper Cook Inlet (Fall pers. comm. 1990).

Specifically, many prehistoric inland Dena'ina settlements may not have survived the changing nature of the environments in which they were located. For example, as Smith and Shields (1977) pointed out, factors, such as the fluctuation of Lake Clark's shoreline by as much as several hundred feet, undoubtedly affected human occupation along the shoreline of the lake and elsewhere. This point is emphasized by the fact that only a few of the sites Smith and Shields (1977:5) located on the lake could possibly be considered "prehistoric," and even those were not likely to be earlier than the mid-1700s.

Ultimately, additional archaeological, linguistic, oral historic, ethnographic, and related paleoscientific research can be expected to shed light on these larger questions of Dena'ina prehistory. Therefore, with the majority of the prehistoric period remaining somewhat of a mystery in regard to societal boundaries, settlement patterns, and populations, we turn to ethnohistoric data to reconstruct the postcontact settlement and demographic history of the inland Dena'ina.

Based, then, on ethnohistoric reconstruction, it appears that approximately 100 years ago, inland Dena'ina society consisted of minimally four closely related bands, all having one or more relatively permanent settlements and multiple associated seasonal camps. These bands were distributed geographically on the middle to upper reaches of the Stony River (including the settlements described today as Hlsit and Qeghnilen), at or near Telaquana Lake, along the Mulchatna River, and in the vicinity of the historic village of Kijik on Lake Clark (see Maps 1 and 2).

During the late 1880s and early 1900s, there were major changes in these settlement patterns (similar to those noted by Fall [1987] on upper Cook Inlet). The four bands consolidated into two, one at Lake Clark and the other on the Stony River. Kijik on Lake Clark was the site of relocation of the majority of the inland Dena'ina. The history of these changes in settlement size and number and corresponding demographic shifts, described in detail below, provide insight into contemporary residence patterns and demography of the inland Dena'ina.

THE EARLY YEARS: FUR TRAPPING, TRADING, AND MISSIONIZATION

Prior to direct Euroamerican contact, it is unlikely that the inland Dena'ina were ever isolated, socially and culturally, from neighboring populations. In fact, oral and early historic, linguistic, and archaeological evidence suggest the existence of precontact trade networks, through which distribution of aboriginal and early European material goods and, assumably, ideas occurred. Trade and other social networks extended minimally to coastal Dena'ina, the Ahtna Athabaskans of the Copper River, and the Yupik (Alutiiq) of southwestern Alaska, Kodiak Island, and Prince William Sound. In fact, it was the effective role of indigenous trade networks, in which the inland Dena'ina played the role of "middlemen," that pressed the Russians into interior exploration and the resultant establishment of inland redoubts and *odinochka* (small trading posts) (Sarafian and VanStone 1972).

Oral histories depict the longstanding existence of disputes and warfare, as well economic exchange and intermarriage, in early contact inland Dena'ina culture. Such warfare occurred mini-

mally between the inland Dena'ina and neighboring Yupik populations of Bristol Bay and Prince William Sound, with slaves being taken by both sides. Intermarriage sometimes occurred between raiders and female captives (Townsend 1979). While societal endogamy was the norm, intermarriage during times of peace periodically occurred between the Dena'ina and other Athabaskan and neighboring Yupik populations (Townsend 1981:623).

Oral historic, historic, and archaeological information indicate that, at time of contact, all Dena'ina societies maintained relatively permanent villages with large, semisubterranean, multiple family dwelling. However, the inland Dena'ina spent most of each annual cycle hunting, fishing, gathering, and trapping from seasonal camps. The timing and location of these seasonal activities were patterned to accommodate the availability of animal and plant resources, which varied from season to season and from year to year. The villages themselves were really semipermanent. For example, changes in local ecological conditions, such as diverted river channels, fluctuating beach levels on a lake, or the availability of a particularly important animal species, encouraged resettlement. Additionally, an unusually large number of human deaths at any point in time, warfare, the depletion of proximal resources such as firewood, the overall quality of a settlement site after years of occupation, or modification in the seasonal cycle as the result of cultural factors stimulated the relocation of communities. The existence of settlements, however, provided "... a continuity of social and political interaction among village members, which contributed to the evolution of ranking and other complex forms of village life" (Townsend 1981:624).

Lastly, based on what was noted during the Russian contact period (e.g., von Wrangell 1980 [1839]), it can be conjectured that kinship was a driving organizational feature of early postcontact inland Dena'ina societies. The large semisubterranean houses were occupied by multiple, related families. The persistence of the matrilineal clan and moiety systems into the 1990s and their existence in historic accounts suggest their importance to the social organization of early contact inland Dena'ina groups.

What was the course of contact history specifically in the case of the inland Dena'ina? Captain James Cook was the first documented European to sail in 1778 into the inlet now bearing his name. He traded with the coastal Dena'ina and observed

Figure 18. Alexie Evan's house at Lime Village, 1939. Individuals in the photograph are (from left to right) Nick Alexie, William Evanoff, Sergei Evan, Okzenia Alexie, Annie Alexie, Valanja Alexie, and Parascovia Alexie. The house is made of round logs, with moss chinking and a sod roof. Everyone is wearing caribou skin boots. A wooden model of an early "bush" plane on skis is in the foreground. The Alexie and Evanoff families relocated to Nondalton in the 1940s. *Photograph Courtesy of Vonga and Matrona Bobby.*

Figure 19. The Bobby family with Russian Orthodox priest Father Zackar Guest at Lime Village, circa 1963. Individuals in the photograph are (back row, left to right) Evan Bobby, Katherine Bobby, Father Zackar Guest, Vonga Bobby, Matrona Bobby, and Alice Bobby; (second row, left to right) Bedusha Bobby, Dolly Bobby, Helen Bobby, Mary Bobby, and David Bobby; (in front) Pauline Bobby. The Russian Orthodox church at Lime Village did not have a resident priest but periodically was visited by priests from the Kuskokwim River. This is an occasion of such a visit. *Photograph Courtesy of Vonga and Matrona Bobby.*

that they were already in possession of iron and trade beads. However, it was Russian fur hunters or trappers and traders, *promyshlinniki*, who were the first Europeans to have "contact," directly or indirectly, with the inland Dena'ina, primarily through the introduction of trade goods. At least during the earliest years of Russian occupation of the area, such goods passed through indigenous trade networks. Although relations between the coastal Dena'ina and the Russians were often uneasy or outright hostile (Andreyev 1952; Fall 1987:15), the earliest part of the trade period may have had negligible impact on the settlement patterns and related demography of the inland Dena'ina. It is likely that they became increasingly involved as middlemen in trade to the interior and developed an intensified reliance on western goods. These factors may have influenced specific details of seasonal movements to access or redistribute items obtained from Russian sources or encouraged a greater commitment to trapping vis-a-vis other resource harvesting activities.

After the arrival of Shelikhov at Kodiak Island in 1784 and the establishment of a post (the Shelikhov Company) at Three Saints Bay near the southwestern end of the island, this facility served as a base from which the Russians had greater direct contact with the coastal Dena'ina. In fact, Shelikhov attempted to subject the Kenai Peninsula Dena'ina to a system of control and suppression similar to that already established among the Aleuts and Koniags. The response to such efforts was not friendly on the part of the coastal Dena'ina and resulted in an attack on the Russian settlement on Kodiak in 1786 (Tikhmenev 1978 [1861-63]:16-17).

In part as a result of this incident and his concern about trading relations with the Dena'ina, Shelikov founded a settlement, Aleksandrovskiy Fort, at the present site of English Bay on the Kenai Peninsula in 1786. The following year, a representative of the rival Lebedev-Lastochkin Company founded a trading station, Georgiyevskiy Redoubt, near the mouth of the Kasilof River (Black 1981). In 1791, another group from the same company established Nikolayevskiy Redoubt on the Kenai River near the present day community of Kenai. During the 1790s, two additional outposts at Lake Iliamna and Bristol Bay were constructed (Black 1981), providing more or less permanent sources of trade goods and more sustained contact with people living within the coastal and Lake Iliamna segments of Dena'ina territory. By 1797, there were approximately 650 Russians engaged in fur

trapping, hunting, and trading in Alaska (Fedorova 1973), with the Cook Inlet area being a major focus of attention.

Townsend (1965, 1979) concluded that prior to the construction of the Iliamna *odinochka*, Dena'ina from that area travelled to trading posts established on the Kenai Peninsula. It is not known if the people of the Lake Clark or Stony River areas made similar journeys during these early years of Russian contact. However, it is unlikely that major relocations of inland Dena'ina in response to the establishment of permanent trading facilities within coastal Dena'ina country occurred prior to the 1800s.

In the 1790s, employees of the Lebedev-Lastochkin Company had direct contact with the inland Dena'ina, when they travelled through their country from Lake Iliamna to the Kuskokwim River. During this journey, they recorded information about Kijik (Klichikh) and drainages to the north such as the Khukhlitna (the context suggests this to be the Hoholitna River) and Khagylin (possibly the Stony or Kuskokwim rivers), the latter which ". . . flows into the sea" (Davydov 1977 [1810-1812]:200; Zagoskin 1967 [1847]:79). They recorded four villages north of Kijik, with between 40 to 60 men and a densely populated village in the vicinity of the "Khukhlitna" (Davydov 1977 [1810-1812]:200).

In the late 1790s, two Russian outposts were destroyed by the Dena'ina, one at Iliamna and the other at "Tuiunuk," the latter which Fall (1987:17) believes may have been located at North Foreland on the Cook Inlet coast. There were 20 Russians and almost 100 Native subjects killed (Tikhmenev 1978 [1861-1863]:46). It is apparent that by the late 1790s the Lebedev-Lastochkin Company had established themselves in the Iliamna area and had direct contact with the inland Dena'ina, although Russian and Dena'ina relationships involved hostilities. However, it was into the second decade of the 1800s before the Iliamna Dena'ina permitted the establishment of another Russian trading post in their country (VanStone and Townsend 1970).

Changes in the nature of Russian contact primarily resulted from the commencement of Russian Orthodox church activity in Alaska and the organization of an administrative and trade monopoly in the form of the Russian-American Company. The priests encouraged more humane treatment of Alaska Natives, including the Dena'ina. The clergy also documented important ethnographic and linguistic data, introduced systems of writing some Native languages in Cyrillic orthography, and travelled into remote areas in order to bring Russian Orthodoxy, its liturgy and sacraments, into Native communities. Since at that time the Dena'ina were within the Kodiak administrative clerical district of the church, the contact experience emanated from there in those early years.

In regard to the conduct of fur trading, trapping, and hunting, Baranov was appointed manager of the Shelikov Company in 1792. As such, he was successful in bringing about the organization of the Russian-American Company and a decree in 1799 that gave this firm the power to act as a trade and administrative monopoly on behalf of the tsar. With that charter came a greater degree of control over the conduct of Russian fur related activities in Alaska until its sale to the United States in 1867.

The headquarters of the Russian-American Company moved south from Kodiak to Sitka in 1804. Nonetheless, the expansion of fur exploration and the establishment of trading facilities north of the Alaska Peninsula in the second decade of the 1800s increased reliance on and access to trade goods on the part of the inland Dena'ina. More specifically, in 1818 Korsakovskiy and a party of Russians and Aleuts under his command ascended the Kvichak River to Lake Iliamna, Lake Clark, and the upper Mulchatna River. They noted that the Dena'ina were already very familiar with Russian goods (recorded by Khromchenko in VanStone [1973]). This exploration resulted in the establishment of Aleksandrovskiy Redoubt in 1819, located at the mouth of the Nushagak River in territory occupied by Aglegmiut and Kiatagmiut Yup'ik groups. The establishment of this post was significant to the inland Dena'ina, since the Mulchatna River, along which one band resided, was also a part of this same drainage.

This redoubt also provided a base for further interior exploration. By the 1830s, the Russian-American Company directed Kolmakov, administrator of Aleksandrovskiy Redoubt, to explore the Kuskokwim River. He was to barter for beaver hides and select a site for an *odinochka* (Sarafian and VanStone 1972). By these acts, the Russian-American Company increased its ability to trade directly with people in the interior, thereby cutting out Native middlemen. In 1832, an *odinochka* site was located establishing another direct point of contact with the inland Dena'ina via the Stony River. By 1834, the post, Kolmakovskiy Redoubt, was functioning as an active center of trade from its location approximately 60 miles

south and downriver on the Kuskokwim from its confluence of the Holitna River. During this period of Russian-American Company history, "creoles" — the offspring of Russian men and Native women — like Kolmakov effectively were employed by the firm in trading, as they provided a link between Russian and Native societies. It was assumed by the Russians that at some point in the future, creoles would replace the Native population (Fedorova 1973).

Contact between Russians and inland Dena'ina were indicated in numerous historic documents of this period. For example, the Russian-American Company in 1838 recorded the need for a Dena'ina translator at Aleksandrovskiy Redoubt to facilitate inland trade. Von Wrangell (1970 [1839] 1980 [1839]:5) the chief manager of the Russian-American Company from 1830 to 1835, documented ethnographic and demographic data regarding the Dena'ina.

The *odinochka* at Iliamna was reported as functioning from minimally 1821 to the end of the Russian occupation of Alaska (Townsend 1970:57, 1979). After a smallpox epidemic, which lasted from 1836 to 1840, missionary activity in the areas occupied by the Dena'ina intensified (Townsend 1965:57-58). A Russian Orthodox mission was established at Aleksandrovskiy Redoubt in 1842 (Sarafian and VanStone 1972) and at Kenai in 1845. The monk in charge of the Kenai mission, Nicholas, visited all Dena'ina villages (Tikhmenev 1979 [1861-1863]:303-304). By 1847, confessionals from the Russian Orthodox Church included baptismal and individual and family records gathered by clergy at Kijik and, after 1853, at Mulchatna as well. In 1853, the Lake Iliamna, Lake Clark, and Mulchatna regions were transferred administratively from the Kenai to the Nushagak mission. The clergy attempted to visit villages in their parishes at least once every two years. In many years, however, this schedule was not met due to logistical and travel rigors.

During the latter years of the Russian period pertinent in this context, the inland Dena'ina persisted as middlemen in trade, despite the expansion of the Russian-American Company's activities. For example, in the 1830s, the Dena'ina of the Stony River actively remained engaged in the fur trade between Cook Inlet and the Kuskokwim River. Because of the location of the *odinochka* at Lake Iliamna and redoubts on the Kuskokwim and Nushagak rivers, the inland Dena'ina were spending a greater portion of each year trapping, making trips to trading facilities located in areas to which they traditionally may not have travelled, and bartering some subsistence resources for commercial goods.

After the sale of Alaska to the United States in 1867, and until the turn of the century, Euroamerican contact was minimal. For the territory overall, this first 20 years of American ownership of Alaska is often referred to as "the period of neglect" (Bancroft 1970 [1886]). The Russian Orthodox church retained some presence in Alaska. For example, the Holy Cross chapel was constructed at Kijik in 1884. Confessional data, vital statistics, and other general information documented in the priests' trip reports provided continuing documentation of the inland Dena'ina and marked an ongoing source of contact between them and representatives of the western world.

American explorations were primarily military. They focused on locating and assessing mineral resources and gathering other geological and geographic data (e.g., Glenn 1900). A need for census and related economic information stimulated the 1891 expedition into Lake Clark by J.W. Clark of the Alaska Commercial Company and A.B. Schanz, enumerator for the U.S. Eleventh Census (Osgood 1904b). This expedition provided the first more comprehensive, but still relatively limited, description of the area. The U.S. government did not establish schools for Dena'ina not located on the coast until 1905, when one was founded in Old Iliamna.

After 1867, the principal Russian-American Company post at Kenai came under the control of the Alaska Commercial Company, which maintained subordinate operations at several locations on Cook Inlet (Townsend 1965:62). The company's Iliamna facility was located on Cook Inlet at Iliamna Bay (a site referred to as A.C. Point), approximately 12 miles over the portage from the community of Old Iliamna. Western Fur and Trading Company, a competing firm with posts at most locations in which the Alaska Commercial Company operated, sold out in 1883, negatively influencing fur prices according to Townsend (1965:161). In 1900, Hans Severson founded a trading post at the site of present day Iliamna, returning the Lake Iliamna area to its former position of prominence in regard to Euroamerican trade.

The development of the Cook Inlet and Bristol Bay commercial salmon fisheries in the 1880s had multiple impacts on the inland Dena'ina. Since in some years the canneries blocked the entire drainages of major river systems, such as the Kvichak and Nushagak, there was no escapement to the Lake Clark and Mulchatna areas. Consequently, there were years in which the inland Dena'ina had limited or no access to salmon, except along the Telaquana drainage to which salmon migrated via the Stony River from the Kuskokwim. A depletion or decline in salmon available to the inland Dena'ina was exacerbated by the already existing dissipation of game and furbearers, a by-product of ongoing fur trade. Additionally resource availability to the inland Dena'ina was affected by their trading of locally harvested resources for Euroamerican trade goods and habitat alteration as a result of intensive beaver trapping. Canneries also purchased quantities of salmon caught by the Dena'ina. These salmon normally would have been used for local consumption. Dena'ina elders recall accounts of their parents seeking wage employment in the canneries before 1900.

HISTORIC INLAND DENA'INA SETTLEMENT PATTERNS AND DEMOGRAPHY

What were the implications of this early contact period for inland Dena'ina settlement patterns and population? By the end of the 1800s, increasing reliance on Euroamerican trade goods and participation as middlemen in trade and in the Bristol Bay fishery encouraged some inland Dena'ina to centralize in localities more accessible to trading posts and canneries. During this time, Dena'ina travelled principally on foot during winter months and by birch bark canoes and skinboats in late spring and summer, all of which required considerable time effort and a degree of physical fitness or necessary assistance to those who were unfit, very young, or very old. Dog traction was not a common mode of travel until well into the 1900s. Renowned anthropologist Osgood (1976 [1937]:72) observed that the coastal Dena'ina did not use dogs to pull sleds in the early 1930s. Though the inland Dena'ina continued to value mobility, there was a decrease in the number of winter settlements, and these villages were located in different areas.

At historic Kijik, a site of relocation, traditional semisubterranean, multiple family dwellings with attached bath houses (*nichil*) mostly were replaced with smaller, above ground, Euroamerican style log cabins. In approximately 1900, historic Kijik village consisted of 12 of these hand hewn log dwellings, 5 bath houses, and 47 cache pits. While the Kijik cabins were smaller than traditional inland Dena'ina houses, they maintained some of their basic configurations. For example, Kijik dwellings were described by Clark and Schanz in 1891 as having windows made of the intestines of mountain sheep (Smith and Shields 1977). Bath houses, used by multiple families, provided continuity to the social and physical configurations of the past. A small Russian Orthodox church, also constructed of hand hewn logs, separated the village from the cemetery. Most artifacts found in and around the houses by archaeologists were of European manufacture, such as knives, a stone pipe, cartridge cases, glass bottles, pottery cups and saucers, bullets, and buttons. However, some traditional items, including whetstones, hammerstones, bone awls, net sinkers, and skin scrapers also were associated with this community (VanStone and Townsend 1970). Kijik was located near an idyllic fall salmon fishing site and at the head of the major trail to Telaquana. It was also within ready access to the mountains in which fall hunting occurred.

Kijik was an inland Dena'ina settlement from at least the late 1700s until the measles and associated influenza epidemic of 1901 to 1902. Shortly after that time, most Kijik residents commenced relocation to Six-Mile Lake at the site of what is now called "Old Nondalton." One large, extended family settled across the lake at Tanalian Point, near the contemporary community of Port Alsworth. As families moved, they dismantled the logs from most of the dwellings and floated them to the new village. The resettlement was complete by approximately 1909, with chief Zackar Evanoff being one of the last to leave. Old Nondalton was more proximal to important fishing sites on the upper Newhalen River, Iliamna's trading facilities, and the Bristol Bay commercial fishery.

In the 1980s, Nondalton elders offered many explanations for this resettlement. Some said that people had become accustomed to using coffee, tea, and other goods and wanted to be where they could access them more readily, especially since game was very scarce during that time. Others explained that the "ground around the village was really old and worn out and it was time to find a new place to live" — a point most commonly associated with declining timber proximal to the community. Most recounted that it was too hard to get to Bristol Bay from Kijik, because they lacked outboard motors in those days. Some elders said that there had been so many deaths in Kijik from the epidemic that the cemetery was full. Influencing the Dena'ina was the fact that most of the Russian Orthodox clergy had encouraged

them to leave. Lastly, most everyone who recalled stories from that time reported that there were bad spirits at Kijik, as evident by the death of so many people. Despite the many explanations for this relocation, the site of the historic settlement of Kijik remained of utmost importance to the Nondalton people in the 1980s. Old Nondalton eventually attracted some previous residents of the upper Stony River and Telaquana as well.

Less is known about the group of inland Dena'ina who resided on the Mulchatna River. In large part, this relates to the fact that this area was more isolated from Euroamerican contact and therefore basically undocumented. Although Russian Orthodox clergy, under the auspices of the Nushagak parish, recorded Mulchatna populations for the years 1854 to 1888, trip reports suggest that priests did not visit the Mulchatna River during most of these years. Additionally, Russian Orthodox clerical records did not specify the number of settlements represented by their population data. It is likely that the clergy acquired populations for this area secondhand, possibly from residents who were recorded as visiting Kijik for purposes of confession.

Because of the nature of documentation, it is not known how many Mulchatna Dena'ina villages there were, exactly where they were located in most cases, whether or not they were occupied simultaneously, and whether census statistics were composites of all communities or, rather, representative of one or the other of several settlements. The census of 1880 reported more than one Mulchatna village, although Petroff (1884) failed to gather these data first hand and did not explain what he was referring to as the "Mulchatna villages." Kari (1985) proposed that there were three village sites on the Mulchatna River — one at the mouth of Springway Creek (Shehtnu) (referred to in Dena'ina as Shek Kaq'), one at the mouth of the Chilchitna River (Chalchitnu) (known as Chalchi Kaq'), and the last at the mouth of the Chilakadrotna (Tsilak'idghutnu) (known as Niłaghedlen or Tsilak'idghut-nu Hdakaq). Kari (1985) proposed that all of these settlements were separated by approximately 8 to 10 nautical miles.

The Russian Orthodox priest, Fr. Vasilii Shishkin, noted in 1887 that he encouraged Mulchatna residents to abandon the area due to a lack of food resources (ARCA 1847-1900), which they did the following year according to church accounts. Since elders depict the Mulchatna River to have once been a resource rich area, Shishkin's (ARCA 1888) report suggests the possibility of postcontact game depletions.

In 1986, two Nondalton elders (Agnes Cusma and Sophie Austin) who knew the country and thought they could locate one of the villages, accompanied the authors by helicopter to Moose Creek (Hqak'elaxtnu). Just above the Moose Creek and near Springway Creek, they located one of the village sites. The settlement was difficult to detect, because it was situated on a slough and surrounded by trees rather than in an open area on the creek proper as they remembered it. Upon landing, they noted that the helicopter was resting in the center of the remains of a single large semisubterranean house. The elders had been told that all residents of this settlement resided in this single, large structure. They recalled that an old man, Pete Delkittie, who died in the 1940s, had come from there but said that everyone had left the village for Kijik because of sickness — "a kind of influenza."

Lastly, information from Alaska Commercial Company records indicated shipments of trade goods to "Mulchatna" in 1889 and 1891. However, by 1896, Mulchatna no longer was listed in these shipping ledgers. These data conform with oral historic accounts suggesting the depopulation of the Mulchatna village or villages in the 1890s, with former residents moving primarily into Kijik.

Oral historic and archaeological data are much more complete for the Telaquana area, which was the location of a village occupied by some contemporary Nondalton residents in their youth. This site, referred to as Trail Creek (Ch'qul-ch'ishtnu) by the Dena'ina , is located approximately 74 miles northeast of modern Nondalton and near Telaquana Lake (Dila Vena or Vek'dilah Vena). When surveyed by U.S. Bureau of Indian Affairs archaeologists in 1985 (US DOI, BIA 1987a, 1987b), the remains of eight structures and numerous pit caches (*chiqilin q'a*) were mapped and described. However, some Nondalton elders remembered this settlement as having had four to five large plank houses, with many adjacent log caches and smokehouses. Others recalled the community as having six "mud and birch bark" houses, suggesting the earlier semisubterranean, multifamily dwellings described for the prehistoric Kijik settlement and Mulchatna River.

In the memory of Nondalton people, Ch'qulch'ishtnu was the home of the Trefon family, considered by many to be its founders; the Balluta family, who originally had come from the Mulchatna River area; and the Kankanton family, who previously had lived in Qeghnilen on the upper Stony River. This community ceased functioning as a quasi-permanent settlement in approximately 1910. Some elders attributed the relocation of some of its members to the desire of Trefon Balluta, a Dena'ina leader, to have his sons educated in American schools and to be located closer to Bristol Bay and a Russian Orthodox church. By the early 1900s, others recalled, resources were more available and abundant at Lake Clark. This site continued to be used by some Nondalton residents for salmon fishing, trapping, or other harvesting activities into the 1990s.

Near the village is Telaquana fish camp, located at the mouth of Telaquana Lake, along the north bank of the Telaquana River (Dilah Vetnu). A path leads from the settlement to the fish camp. Nondalton residents recalled summer salmon fishing at this camp when the settlement was occupied. In 1937, a log house and fish wheel remained at the camp. Several Nondalton elders described the location of graves on a ridge behind the fish camp as well, but archaeologists were unable to locate this cemetery in 1985 (US DOI, BIA 1987b). Both the fish camp and village sites were connected to Kijik by the Telaquana trail.

The location of the last of the four bands was centered on the Stony River. The Stony River also provided an important trade route for the inland Dena'ina to Kolmakovskiy Redoubt. Many Nondalton elders were born on the Stony River, specifically at the settlement of Qeghnilen or Canyon Village. This site is about 23 miles upriver from modern Lime Village. Qeghnilen is a central focus of much of the oral history and land use of the inland Dena'ina. Other Nondalton elders from the Stony River were born downriver from Lime Village at a site referred to in Dena'ina as Hlsit. This community, located on a stream flowing from Tishimna Lake (Hlsit Vena) to the Stink River (Vendashtnu), was occupied by an Ingalik speaking family. When the settlement dissolved in the 1930s, some people moved to Lime Village. Based on oral histories, Qeghnilen was occupied as a settlement minimally during the latter half of the 1800s until the 1930s. By this time, most families had relocated to Lime Village or to the Lake Clark area after a series of migrations (P. Kari 1983). Qeghnilen continued to be an important fish camp for Lime Village residents into the 1990s. Since there has been virtually no archaeological research focused on the prehistory of this area, reconstructions about Dena'ina settlements are based almost solely on linguistic data (e.g., J. Kari 1985), including oral historic accounts.

Although population totals for all Dena'ina have been estimated by various sources (see Fall [1987:16] for a compilation of these data), the size of the inland Dena'ina population specifically has not been established. Population totals prior to 1900 were derived from early documentation, U.S. census data for 1880 and 1890, archaeological and oral historic estimates (VanStone and Townsend 1970), and, most importantly confessionals, vital statistics, and travel reports of Russian Orthodox clergy from the Kenai parish between 1847 and 1853 and the Nushagak parish from 1854 to 1900. The use of Russian Orthodox and other historic records required complex, multifaceted methodologies. A more detailed discussion of these methodologies is published in Ellanna (1990).

Table 1 presents population estimates for the inland Dena'ina for the period 1854 to 1900. During these years, there were no published censuses for Qeghnilen or Telaquana. It was not uncommon for the Telaquana Dena'ina to come to Kijik for receiving sacraments, so in some years they may have been included in the Kijik confessional records.

Kijik was better known by Euroamericans who travelled through the area. Although there were more censuses for Kijik, the reliability of the population data for the 1800s is questionable. Townsend's (1965) "impression" that Kijik had a minimal population of between 150 and 175 during the period 1875 to 1895 was conjectural, since it was not based on enumeration. Additionally it conflicted with lower population estimates reported by Russian Orthodox clergy. Townsend (1965) also suggested that the U.S. eleventh census count of 45 in 1890, reported for a community by the name of "Nikhkah," was not for the settlement of Kijik — an opinion also supported by VanStone (VanStone and Townsend 1970). Other plausible explanations for this seemingly low population include the possibility that there may have been another community on Lake Clark with the name "Nikhkak," heretofore unidentified, that people may have been absent from Kijik because of seasonal camping, that the census information may have been gathered at one such camp, or that the data were misrecorded.

Mulchatna's population was recorded irregularly by the clergy of the Russian Orthodox church between 1854 to 1888. The Russian Orthodox confessionals reflect that Mulchatna was visited only in the years 1847 and 1851 by clergy from the Kenai parish and in 1881, 1882, 1886, and 1887 by Fr. Shishkin of the Nushagak parish. Fr. Shishkin designated a population of 177 in 1881, 75 in 1882, 67 in 1886 and 72 in 1887. In 1876, Mulchatna's population was reported to be 56 and in 1877, 230. It is impossible for these data to reflect natural population growth for a one year period. Plausible explanations which could account for this phenomenon include visitors from another community, under-enumeration in previous years, relocation of another Dena'ina group to the Mulchatna River area, or the inclusion of one or more other Mulchatna settlements, members of which previously were not included in census accounts.

Because of incomplete demographic data for the inland Dena'ina in the 1800s, only a few speculations related to overall population size can be made. Based on the early 1800 decline of coastal Dena'ina populations due to introduced epidemic diseases (Fall 1987), it could be postulated that a similar decline occurred among inland populations. Although the latter were more isolated, their trade relations with coastal people and contact with Russian exploration and trading parties would have made the dissemination of infectious diseases a possibility. For example, while it is known that a smallpox epidemic documented for the period 1836 to 1840, reduced the coastal Dena'ina population by half (Fall 1987; Townsend 1965), it is not known to what degree the inland Dena'ina specifically were affected. Population estimates from multiple sources suggest that 1845 was the year that the coastal Dena'ina decline reached its nadir (Fall 1987). It is documented in Russian Orthodox vital statistics and other sources (such as Glenn 1900; Petroff 1884) that tuberculosis (consumption), influenza, syphilis, and other contagious diseases also were impacting Dena'ina prior to 1845. It is well established that the 1900 measles and related influenza epidemic directly affected the inland Dena'ina (Wolfe 1982).

Sex and age profiles were calculated for Kijik in 1897 and for all inland Dena'ina in 1875 and 1900 for purposes of comparison with similar information from the 1900s and the contemporary period (1985 to 1990). These data for the late 1800s and 1900 are depicted in Figures 20, 21, and 22, respectively. They indicate that there was a slightly greater percentage of females to males (55 to 45 percent, respectively) in the 1875 overall population and the 1897 Kijik profile (52 percent

TABLE 1. POPULATION OF THE INLAND DENA'INA DURING THE 1800S

Year	Kijik	Mulchatna	Telaquana	Qeghnilen	Inland Dena'ina
1800	ND	400[a]	100-150[b]	ND	ND
1856	16[c]	48[c]	ND	ND	ND
1857	16[c]	47[c]	ND	ND	ND
1858	16[c]	41[c]	ND	ND	ND
1859	16[c]	47[c]	ND	ND	ND
1860	46[c]	32[c]	ND	ND	ND
1861	22[c]	38[c]	ND	ND	ND
1862-1867	ND	49[c]	ND	ND	ND
1868	ND	50[c]	ND	ND	ND
1875	ND	ND	ND	ND	546[d]
1875-1895	150-175[e]	—	—	—	ND
1876	ND	56[c]	ND	ND	ND
1877	33[c]	230[c]	ND	ND	ND
1878	78[ac]	188-208[c]	ND	ND	ND
1879	78[c]	144[c]	ND	ND	ND
1880	91[f]	180[f]	ND	ND	ND
1880	81[c]	145[c]	ND	ND	ND
1881	40-102[c]	142-177[c]	ND	ND	ND
1882	102[c]	75[c]	ND	ND	ND
1883	98[c]	75[c]	ND	ND	ND
1883	140[g]	ND	ND	ND	ND
1884	96[c]	78[c]	ND	ND	ND
1886	82[c]	67[c]	ND	ND	ND
1887	100[c]	72[c]	ND	ND	ND
1888	102[c]	70[c]	ND	ND	ND
1889	138[c]	ND	ND	ND	ND
1890	137[c]	ND	ND	ND	ND
1890	42[h]	ND	ND	ND	ND
1891	134[c]	ND[i]	ND	ND	ND
1894	134[c]	ND	ND	ND	ND
1895	101[c]	ND	ND	ND	ND
1896	117[c]	ND	ND	ND	ND
1897	106[c]	ND	ND	ND	ND
1897	103[d]	ND	ND	ND	ND
1898	106[j]	ND	ND	ND	ND
1899	98[c]	ND	ND	ND	ND

[a] Gabriel Trefon, oral history, based on information passed on from his mother's mother who was from there.

[b] Data derived from an oral historic account, Pete Koktelash, personal communication, 1985.

[c] These data are derived from Russian Orthodox Church confessional records, Kenai and Nushagak parishes (ARCA 1847-1900). Different data for the same year reflect multiple clerical visits during different seasons.

[d] Calculated for selected years only from a computerized data base, which was generated by Russian Orthodox records and family histories.

[e] Townsend (1965).

[f] Petroff (1884).

[g] The 1883 data are derived from a priest's report, who said that this was the number of people who took communion. Oral histories affirm that Mulchatna and Telaquana people came to Kijik for communion, so this may not represent merely Kijik's population.

[h] Townsend (1965) and VanStone and Townsend (1970).

[i] During this decade, other data suggest that the Mulchatna River area was abandoned as an area of permanent settlements. The exact year or years in the 1890s are unknown, but there were still people there in 1891 according to Alaska Commercial Company records.

[j] Glenn (1900:740) quoting Unalaska Russian Orthodox church records, which referred to this as the population of Clark's Lake or "Kuchik."

ND No data.

female to 48 percent male). These ratios are reversed in the overall inland Dena'ina profile of 1900, when there were 56 percent males and 44 percent females. These changing ratios may be merely a by-product of small numbers, although hunting and gathering societies generally have a slightly higher percentage of males to females (Lee and DeVore 1968). However, the sex ratios were not greatly imbalanced relative to the small size of the overall populations for these years.

Some information regarding household size and composition are reflected in the demographic data. Russian Orthodox church confessionals for the years 1877, 1881, and 1882 indicate household sizes of 19.5, 9.4, and 18.5, respectively. During that period, most inland Dena'ina still resided in large, multifamily, semisubterranean dwellings. These were associated with substantially larger household sizes than those reported either in oral historic data or generated from Russian Orthodox confessionals for Kijik in 1897. In the Kijik case during this year, there were 19 dwellings occupied simultaneously, 10 of which were composed of extended and 9 of nuclear families. Average household size in Kijik during this year was 5.4, with a range of 2 to 10 members. There are multiple feasible explanations for shifts in household size and composition. Archaeologically and oral historically, it has been well documented that the older, semisubterranean, multiple family dwellings mostly had been replaced by smaller, Euroamerican style, hand hewn log houses at historic Kijik. This change in house style may have corresponded with an overall decrease in household size. Such a change might have been associated with a more Euroamerican mode of domestic unit size and nuclear family composition considered to be the norm by traders, priests, and other representatives of western society. Additionally, it is possible that the organization of individuals into households in the confessionals may have been a product of the recording process rather than a reality of social order.

The 1875 data (Figure 21) for the total inland Dena'ina and the 1897 information (Figure 20) for Kijik indicated that some people were living to be well into their late 60s or older. However, the population profiles for these two years were not as broad based for the cohorts under the age of nine as would be expected for a healthy population, possibly reflecting the high rate of postcontact infant mortality reported in Nondalton and Lime Village family histories and early documented

sources. Figure 22, depicting the total inland Dena'ina population in 1900, reflects deaths in all cohorts related to the measles and accompanying influenza epidemic. The loss of all cohorts over the age of 59 and the relative depletion of the cohort of children aged 5 to 9 are noteworthy. Some normally productive and reproductively active, middle-aged adult cohorts of both sexes also were absent from the population profile. These included women aged 35 to 39 and men 40 to 44. Other cohorts with potentially reproductively active members were imbalanced sexually or were representative of few individuals during this year (see the glossary for more detailed information about population pyramids).

Dependency ratios are the ratio between the dependent segment of a population, assumed to be children aged 14 and adults aged 60 and over, and productive adults aged 15 through 59 multiplied by 100. Such ratios are considered by demographers to be most balanced as they approach a value of 100 (i.e., one dependent for each producer). The ratios for the inland Dena'ina in 1875 and 1900, respectively, were .58 and .59, and, for Kijik in 1897, .49. From what is known about hunting and gathering societies worldwide, these ratios indicate that there were adequate producers to support a nonproductive component of the population for these years. However, the populations pyramids suggest that there may have been inadequate cohorts of young people to take over productive and reproductive functions in the future.

Figures 23 and 24 are scattergrams (see glossary) of age at death by year of birth and age at death by year of death, respectively. These figures, which present the data in an alternative form, shed light on longevity, as viewed longitudinally, of the inland Dena'ina. Age at death by year of birth information (Figure 23) indicates that longevity among this population was not a phenomenon restricted to more recent years or a direct outcome of improved Euroamerican medical care and way of life. In fact, longevity beyond the age of 60 was demonstrated for all periods of time represented in this figure. Using longevity as one measure of a population's well-being, it is suggested that historically the inland Dena'ina were a relatively successful population adaptively (Laughlin 1972). The clustering of deaths below and above late middle age during the period 1840 to 1889 indicates that individuals generally died in childhood or in early years of adulthood. If they

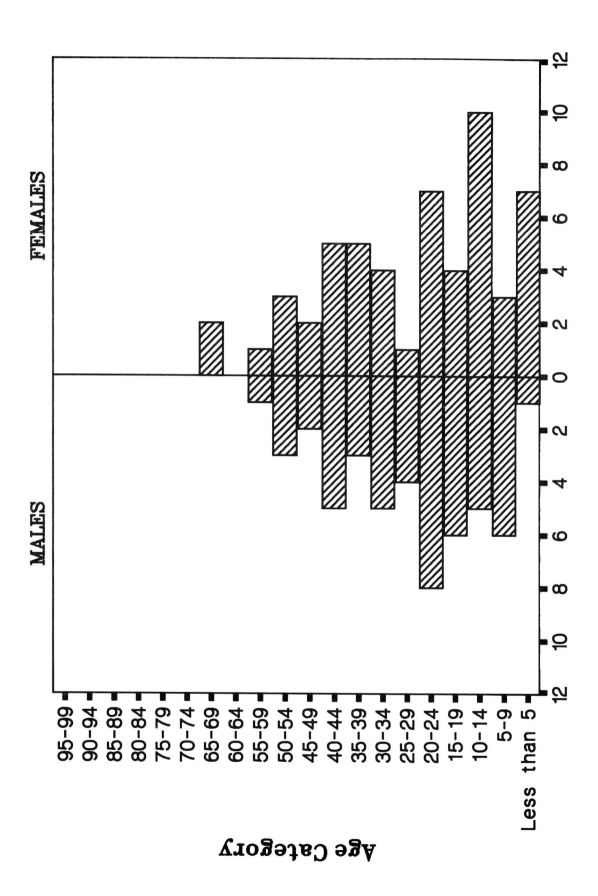

Figure 20. Kijik Dena'ina population by age and sex, 1897.

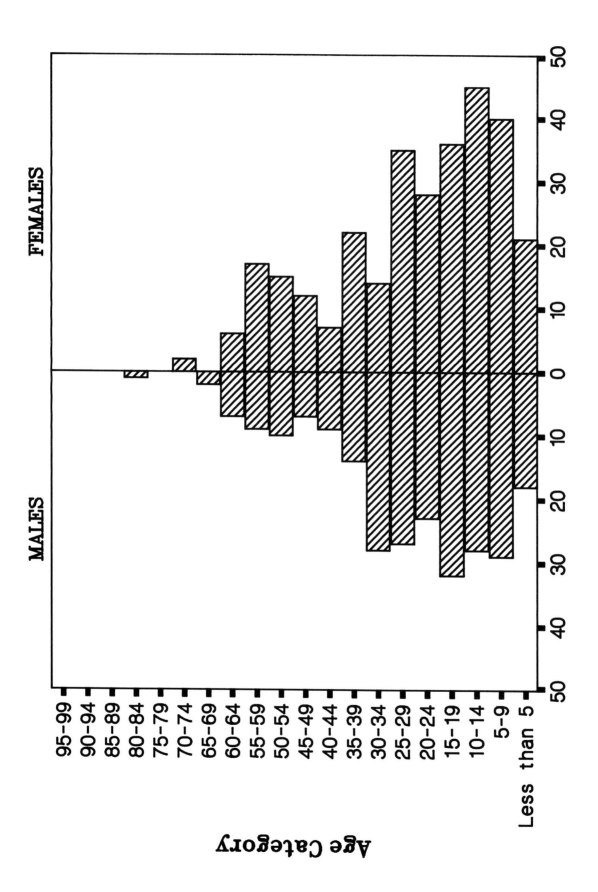

Figure 21. Total inland Dena'ina population by age and sex, 1875.

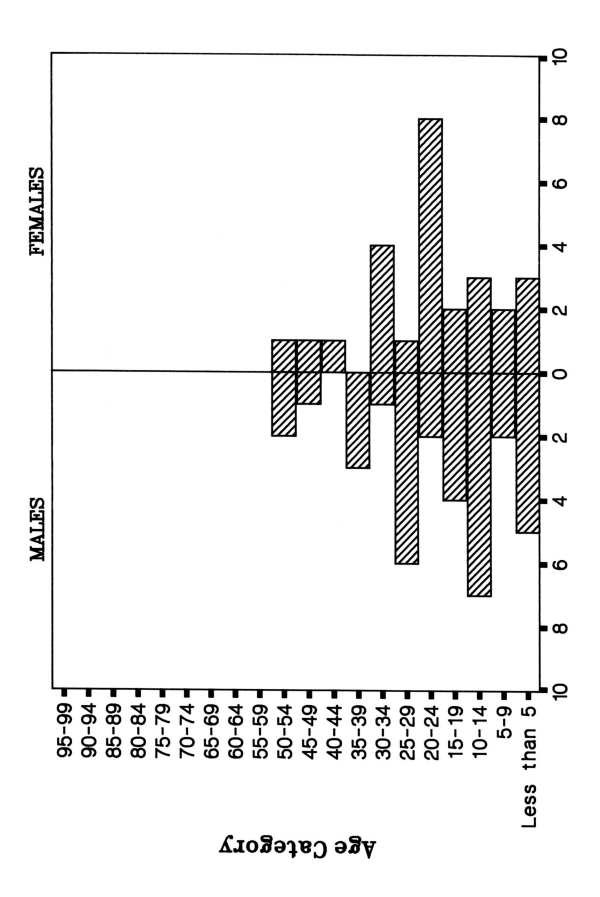

Figure 22. Total inland Dena'ina population by age and sex, 1900.

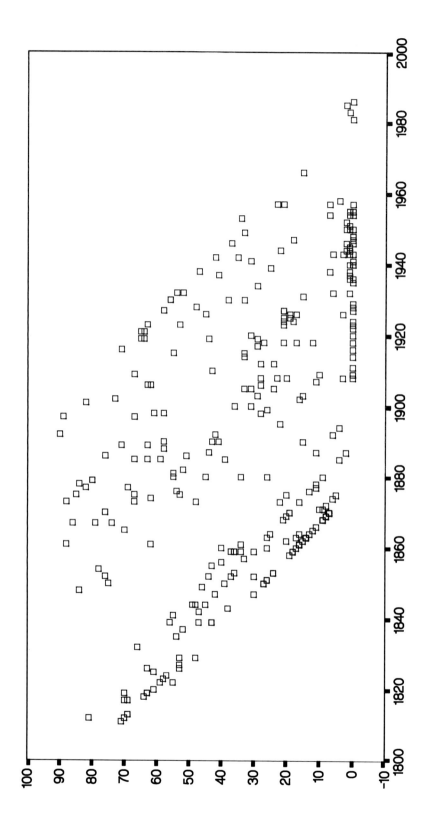

Figure 23. Age at death by year of birth for the inland Dena'ina, 1800 to 1987.

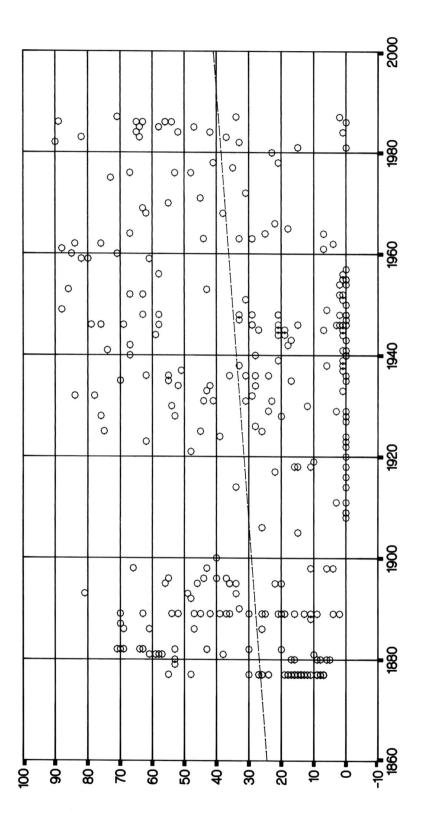

Figure 24. Age at death by year of death for the inland Dena'ina, 1860 to 1987.

survived, then they generally had a relatively long life span. Additionally, infant mortality markedly increased after 1900, suggesting that the ravages of infectious diseases outweighed the benefits of potentially available western medical care.

Figure 23, depicting age at death by year of birth, reveals years in which epidemics may have impacted the inland Dena'ina. For example, 34 members of the population died in 1877, 12 in 1882, and 23 in 1889. These statistics indicate substantially high mortality for any single year given small populations. The clustering of deaths in 1877 and 1882 may have been related to the outbreak of "consumption" (most likely, tuberculosis or pneumonia) described by the Russian Orthodox clergy in the former case, and to the 1880 smallpox epidemic in the latter. Again, the impact of measles and associated influenza after 1899 is apparent.

In regard to fertility, a review of life histories indicates that inland Dena'ina younger women had fewer children than did their mothers. However, because of a decrease in infant mortality, they raised approximately the same number of offspring. It was not uncommon for women to have had from 6 to 10 children in the early part of the 1900s, with half or less of them surviving to adulthood. Generally speaking, inland Dena'ina women, who were over the age of 60 in 1987, at any given time normally had no more than 2 children dependent on them or another adult family member for feeding, dressing, and other assistance. In fact, some older women overtly commented on the difficulties inherent in a woman having more than one dependent infant simultaneously. Such infants required carrying, since so much of inland Dena'ina transport was by foot until very recent years. Therefore, it was common in the early 1900s for female children 12 years of age or older to play a major role in the care and nurturing of younger siblings.

Natality is a statistic useful for comparative purposes and is based on the ratio of children to women of reproductive age. To calculate such ratios, the number of children aged 0 to 4 is divided by the number of women between the ages of 15 and 50, with the product then multiplied by 1,000. Theoretically, if each woman in that age category were to have a single child, the natality statistic would equal 1,000. It is important to note that some demographers employ the adult female age range 15 to 44 in calculating this ratio. However,

inland Dena'ina female childbearing histories indicated the inappropriateness of this range for this case.

Inland Dena'ina historic natality or child-woman ratios were as follows: Kijik in 1897, 286; all inland Dena'ina in 1875, 253; and all inland Dena'ina in 1900, 471. The Kijik 1897 ratio of 286 indicated that theoretically there were approximately 3 infants for every 10 women of reproductive age. Since this ratio is very similar to that of all inland Dena'ina in 1875, the 1900 ratio of 471 may be an anomaly rather than a reflection of actual increased fertility. Additionally, the 1900 ratio for all inland Dena'ina is unquestionably a product of a decreased number of reproductively active women in 1900 due to the measles and influenza epidemic (see Figures 22, 23, and 24.) That is, the number of women declined in relationship to the number of babies who were born during this year.

Figure 25 depicts inland Dena'ina mothers' ages at birth for mothers born prior to 1900, those born between 1900 and 1929, and those born after 1930. The number of births for all mothers born prior to 1900 and up to 1987 is also plotted. In the case of mothers who were born prior to 1900, childbearing years began very early, commencing at age 11, peaking in the late teens and early 20s, then gradually falling off in the late 40s. These data suggest early marriage and childbearing and a lengthy period of fertility for inland Dena'ina women.

Lastly, for the interval beginning with the earliest contact and ending in 1900, other factors influencing settlement and demographic patterns included Russian Orthodox condemnation of the practice of polygyny, the preferential marriage of kin (usually cross-cousins), and marriage between individuals of different generations. Though polygyny was suppressed overtly, reciprocal, clan-based patterns of marriage involving cousins persisted in some cases into the 1900s.

CENTRALIZATION AND CHANGES IN MOBILITY IN THE 20TH CENTURY

By the first decade of the 1900s, some centralization of the inland Dena'ina had occurred. The Mulchatna band had dispersed, with its populations settling primarily in Kijik but also at Telaquana and on the Stony River at Qeghnilen. In the first decade of the 1900s, the residents of

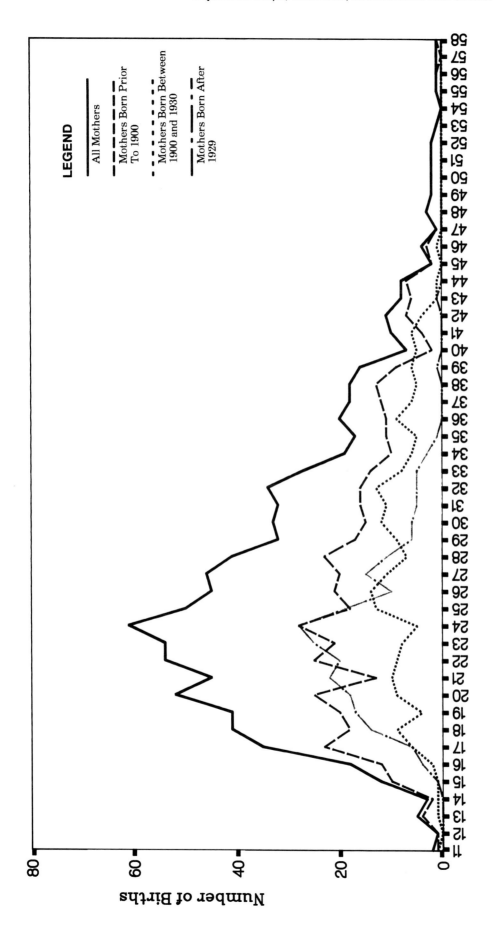

Figure 25. Mothers' ages at birth for inland Dena'ina women.

Kijik began and completed their relocation to the site of Old Nondalton. Subsequently, the Telaquana band resettled at Old Nondalton, with the exception of the large family of Trefon Balluta, who established their home at Tanalian Point. During these early years of the 1900s, many people moved to the Lake Clark area from Qeghnilen, primarily, Nondalton elders said, to be closer to trading posts and the Bristol Bay fishery. A school was established in Old Iliamna in 1908, although few inland Dena'ina attended.

Up to this time, centralization of inland Dena'ina into fewer settlements had occurred in response to Euroamerican contact, including access to trading facilities and reciprocal involvement in commercial trapping participation in the Bristol Bay commercial fishery; the establishment of Russian Orthodox churches and related mandatory attendance; population declines brought about by introduced epidemics; and, in the case of a couple of families, brief attendance at the Old Iliamna school. However, declining mobility had not accompanied centralization. In fact, it can be postulated that because of the increased reliance of the inland Dena'ina on trade goods, and the limited means by which they could be obtained, a commitment to trapping may have been a factor in increased mobility during the first three decades of the 1900s. The inland Dena'ina were now using as extensive a land area from two villages as they once covered from four or more settlements. The use of dog traction provided an opportunity to run longer traplines, sometimes in excess of 100 miles, from a base camp and still access the village periodically during the winter months for commercial supplies, attending Russian Orthodox church holidays and other, more traditional, Dena'ina events of significance such as potlatches. Furthermore, more Dena'ina were going to Bristol Bay during the summer. There is no evidence, then, that the inland Dena'ina had become more sedentary as their populations became more concentrated. In fact, the evidence argues for increased nomadism during the first three decades of the 1900s (c.f., Fall [1987] for a discussion of similar patterns on upper Cook Inlet).

What were the most instrumental factors affecting inland Dena'ina settlement and demographic patterns in the 1900s? The Bristol Bay commercial fishery mineral exploration and the institution of western schools were among the most significant influences in this context.

The inland Dena'ina participated in commercial fishing since the first Alaska Packing Company cannery was established at the mouth of the Kenai River in 1882. Other canneries, such as the Northern Packing Company and Pacific Steam Whaling Company, moved into the Cook Inlet area in 1888 and 1897, respectively. In later years, inland Dena'ina participation in commercial fishing was limited to Bristol Bay.

Initially, only men worked in Bristol Bay canneries, although they were not employed as fishermen in the early years. Cannery laborers included Chinese, Mexicans, Filipinos, Yupik, Aleuts, and many other ethnic groups in addition to the Dena'ina. Gaining and retaining employment was difficult for the Dena'ina, in part because many knew very little English. Young men accompanied their fathers, brothers, and uncles to Bristol Bay when they were 13 or 14 years of age, while women were left behind with younger children and elders to put up salmon for domestic consumption. Men returned to the Lake Clark area in August after the commercial fishery was over to complete the task of putting up fish for dogs, since transport by dog sled now was essential for inland Dena'ina mobility.

Ironically, this early source of cash or trade goods was the same activity which caused shortages of salmon in the drainages which fed into Bristol Bay. For example, the Nushagak River was the focus of activity of the Alaska Packers Association, Pacific Steam Whalers, the Alaska Fishermen's Association, and Whitney's salting station (Elliott 1900). The Alaska Packers Association had an immense trap inside the mouth of the Nushagak River. It was reported to Elliott (1900:788) in 1899 that there were 700,000 fish which had been killed and "wantonly destroyed," because cannery owners were unable to ship them off before they spoiled. Since the Mulchatna River was part of the Nushagak drainage, it is highly likely that these commercial fishing practices played a role in forcing the relocation of the inland Dena'ina residing there to the Lake Clark area.

By the 1930s, inland Dena'ina men were hired by the canneries to fish from company owned boats and with company owned gear. Some of the Nondalton elders fondly remembered the days of fishing on cannery sailing craft prior to the use of diesel powered boats. Non-fishing employment involved the processing of fish. Fish processing was not the preferred activity of men, since it was perceived to be women's work. Once inland Dena'ina men were able to fish for the canneries, there was even more impetus for them to go to Bristol Bay during the summer.

To access Bristol Bay, Dena'ina men had to travel in the spring with boats and dogs to help transport the boats across portages. Therefore, proximity to the Newhalen River, a commonly used travel corridor, was valued highly. The journey to Bristol Bay involved descending the Newhalen River, traversing the portages adjacent to the rapids crossing, Lake Iliamna, and floating down the Kvichak River to Bristol Bay.

The involvement of the inland Dena'ina in commercial fishing intensified during World War II. In approximately 1942, and as a result of the war, aliens were restricted from working at Bristol Bay canneries. This provided an opportunity for inland Dena'ina women to enter the commercial fishery as processors.

In regard to Nondalton, from the mid-1900s to the 1990s, frequently entire families went to Bristol Bay to earn money. Men fished from boats with drift nets, and women were employed as fish processors or fished from set net sites located on the beaches. The latter activity generally was considered to be appropriate for women, children, and older people. Some younger people of both sexes continued to pursue employment as fish processors, especially if they lacked drift net or set net fishing opportunities. With increased participation of the inland Dena'ina in the commercial fishery, those who remained behind in the village were normally women with extremely young, dependent, and unemployable children; and older or disabled individuals, who were unable to work at commercial fishing because of its strenuous nature. Most residents remaining in the Lake Clark area moved to summer fish camps, where they conducted subsistence fishing and processing. As snowmachines were introduced to the area in the 1960s, the need for fish as a source of dog food declined.

The participation of inland Dena'ina in the commercial fishery seriously and irreversibly was curbed or eliminated by the implementation by the state of a limited entry system for the commercial fishing of salmon in 1973. The limited entry system was implemented to set an upward, fixed limit on the number of individuals participating in commercial salmon fishing. Permit applicants were judged by a point system based on a set of criteria designed by the state. Not only did the application process require fluent control of English literacy, but the criteria were complex and designed on a western market economic model. The outcome of this process was the immediate disenfranchisement of many Alaska Natives from commercial salmon fishing. Others were given interim permits until the applicants could provide "acceptable" evidence as to why they met minimal qualifications. In 1990, many interim claims remained unsettled. Since 1973, permits acquired a substantial market value, with Bristol Bay drift permits being worth in excess of $130,000 by the end of the 1980s. Many Native fishermen, who were successful recipients of permits in 1973, subsequently lost them. Such losses were related to the fisherman's inability to understand and plan for federal tax obligations, indebtedness related to high capital investment in fishing boats and associated gear, family emergencies making the cash sale of the permit an attractive option, and controversies as to the disposition of a single permit from a father to one of multiple, potential heirs. All of the conditions leading to lost Native permits potentially arose from cross-cultural differences or misunderstandings.

In the case of the inland Dena'ina, many men, who had been long-term commercial fishermen, were disenfranchised by this system. Although commercial fishing remained the primary source of income for a few Nondalton residents, in 1987, after the implementation of the limited entry system, fewer individuals and family groups participated in the fishery. Some males, faced with the loss of their permits, returned to Bristol Bay as crew on boats of non-Native, non-Alaskan permit holders, or, less prestigiously, to undertake fish processing for wages as cannery employees.

Mining exploration and extraction also affected the inland Dena'ina. As noted by Fall (1987:21), the earliest prospectors in the Cook Inlet region left few records of their activities. However, as early as 1876, miners were moving inland into Dena'ina country along river drainages. The Russian Orthodox clergy noted that some independent traders and gold, coal, and copper prospectors began to penetrate the Kenai Peninsula and Lake Iliamna areas by approximately 1896. According to clerical records, some Dena'ina were hunting moose for sale to traders and miners. Prospectors in search of valuable minerals frequently started forest fires, thereby destroying habitat used by the Dena'ina (Townsend 1974a). As early as 1890, several prospectors were reported to have ascended the Mulchatna River for a distance of approximately 200 miles (Ellanna 1986). In 1901, minimally three prospectors established a copper claim six miles southwest of Old Iliamna.

At the turn of the century, U.S. Geological Survey (USGS) sponsored expeditions into the Cook Inlet region (e.g., Glenn 1900) in search of mineral deposits and geological and geographic knowledge. However, most of these expeditions did not survey Lake Clark, Lake Iliamna, and the Mulchatna and Stony river drainages (Capps 1930).

There was a short burst of intense mining activity on the Mulchatna River and at Bonanza Creek beginning in 1908. After that year, knowledge of gold in the Mulchatna and Lake Clark areas stimulated an interest in a trading facility on the Mulchatna River to be serviced by a river-steamer — a venture which never came to fruition. In 1909, 16 men went up the Mulchatna, and in 1910, 15 to 20 did the same (Capps 1930). The first recorded gold claim in the Lake Clark area was that issued to Brown Carlson in 1911 for a placer site on Portage Creek. For the next five years, numerous claims were filed including at least one in the names of two inland Dena'ina. Some of the claimants combined commercial fishing in Bristol Bay with mining activities. Subsequent to 1916, however, mining activities in this area dwindled significantly. By 1928, only a few prospectors visited the more accessible parts of the Lake Clark area. Therefore, the region remained relatively undeveloped as it was at the turn of the century.

It was the lure of gold, the nearby commercial fisheries, and an interest in trade, however, that stimulated the settlement of the first *Gasht'ana* among the inland Dena'ina. This settlement was a significant form of contact, as it involved the first documented intermarriages between non-Native men and inland Dena'ina women. Prospectors Jack Hobson and Brown Carlson were in Kijik during the measles epidemic and credited by some Nondalton elders with saving the lives of many of the children (Ellanna 1986) (Figure 26). By 1911, two other prospectors, O.M. (Doc) Dutton and Joe Kackley, were living on Lake Clark, where they remained until their deaths in the mid-1940s. Dutton and Kackley instructed some of Trefon Balluta's children to read and write and encouraged the Dena'ina to garden. Another prospector, Brooks, married Matrona Nudlash from Old Nondalton. When he knew his death was imminent, he sent for his friend Hans Severson to care for his family. It was this event which stimulated Severson's trading career on Lake Iliamna.

Communication with non-Natives was more frequent and intense as a result of the establishment of a settlement and trading facility on Lake Iliamna. It was said that in Old Iliamna village,

during the early decades of the 1900s, there were three streets, each dedicated to either Dena'ina, *Dutna,* or *Gasht'ana* residents (Hornberger, field notes 1985). By 1914, a trading post was established at even the most remote site of Qeghnilen (Smith 1917).

Lastly, the introduction of formal western education was, for some families, the most significant impetus for restructuring their annual nomadic seasonal round. The Old Iliamna school directly encouraged the relocation of at least one Telaquana family to Tanalian. The parents desired to be closer to their son who lived with relatives and attended school in Old Iliamna for one year.

However, in general, the impact of schools on Nondalton and Stony River Dena'ina was later in time and less intense than was the case in the Iliamna area. The second teacher in Iliamna, Hannah Breece, noted in 1910, that based on communication with Chief Zackar Evanoff and others, the "Noondalton children were scattered at least part of the year in small settlements outside of the villages of Old Nondalton, Telaquana, and Qeghnilen. During other parts of the year, they were in fall, winter, spring, and summer camps. She also noted that "Noondalton" [sic] children are too few in a place and too many miles apart to establish any central school and to employ teachers and erect buildings for two or four children . . ." (US Bureau of Education 1908-12). Later that same year, she documented in official correspondence that there were 12 children between the ages of 5 and 20 living, at least some part of the year, in Old Nondalton and 2 additional children from there attending school at Old Iliamna (U.S. Bureau of Education 1910). Breece campaigned vigorously to get funds from the U.S. Bureau of Education to carry on summer teaching activities at Old Nondalton after ostensibly getting the support of Chief Zackar Evanoff (US Bureau of Education 1908-12).

In the summer of 1910, Breece set up school in tents at the fish camps on the Newhalen River near the outlet of Six-Mile Lake commenting, in correspondence to the Bureau of Education (1910), that ". . . the children and adults were eager to learn." She not only instructed the children in reading, writing, and arithmetic but also taught the adults gardening as an alternative means of food production. According to Breece's letters, Zackar Evanoff and other men "beseeched her" to

Figure 26. Jack Hobson and Brown Carlson sitting beside the former's log house in Old Nondalton, circa 1939. Jack Hobson married Tatiana Constantine from Qeghnilen, where they lived until 1915. At this time, they moved to Old Nondalton. Brown Carlson settled in Kijik, where he married Christine Balluta in 1906, later moving and opening a store in Old Nondalton. *Photograph Courtesy of Ida Carlson Crater.*

provide additional education the following summer, so she returned to Old Nondalton's fish village during the summer of 1911. As in the case of most teachers of the time, she was a proponent of Christian proselytization and assimilation of Native peoples, acted as a provider of medical care, and served the functions of a cultural broker throughout her contact with the inland Dena'ina (US Bureau of Education 1908-1912).

According to Nondalton elders, the option of their children attending the Old Iliamna school was not viewed as being a preferential or permanent arrangement. Generally, the few who attended did so for only a period of one to two years. It was not until 1930 that formal western education commenced in a school at Old Nondalton. Despite the presence of this school in the village, most families were reluctant to give up the mobility and way of life associated with necessary hunting, fishing, trapping, and gathering. Some families adopted alternative strategies, such as leaving school-aged children with elders in the village. Other children never attended school at all or did so only when their families were temporarily in the village. Elders recalled that education beyond the fourth or sixth grade, or when a child reached an economically productive age, was considered unnecessary and in conflict with the traditional Dena'ina learning process.

During the late 1930s, the Old Nondalton school closed until a facility was constructed at the new site of Nondalton. Despite the presence of the school in the village, however, some families clung tenaciously to cycles of intermittent camp and community residence until the early 1960s. A few children attended boarding schools at Eklutna on Cook Inlet or Wrangell Institute in southeastern Alaska at the insistence of village teachers and other territorial officials. The inland Dena'ina on the upper Stony River did not have a school at Lime Village until the early 1970s.

In the late 1960s and early 1970s, the state government more aggressively pursued alternatives for rural education. Inland Dena'ina children from Nondalton were sent to boarding schools within and without Alaska. Beginning in the late 1960s, under the auspices of what was referred to as the "Boarding Home Program," teenagers were sent to live with families in Anchorage or other urban areas to attend public schools. Since there was no elementary school in Lime Village, in 1969 the state began sending children as young as six and older to McGrath on the upper Kuskokwim River to get an education while living primarily with non-Native boarding families. In later years, children also lived with Native and non-Native families in Anchorage and in the Yup'ik community of Sleetmute for purposes of attending school. When Lime Village finally got an elementary school in the 1970s, teenagers still were forced to leave home to receive secondary educations. In both communities, many chose not to attend school after the mandatory age of 16. Some children opted to leave school to accompany parents and other relatives in their pursuit of seasonal hunting, fishing, trapping, and gathering activities.

During the late 1930s and early 1940s, when schools initially were established as more or less permanent western institutions in the area occupied by the inland Dena'ina, accompanying and significant residence shifts also occurred. Qeghnilen, as a settlement, was "abandoned" in the 1930s. While two large families moved to Old Nondalton, others settled at Lime Village, located approximately 63 miles upriver from the confluence of the Stony and Kuskokwim rivers. Nondalton elders recalled family trips by dog sled to visit relatives on the Stony River from the 1930s to the early 1960s, maintaining mutually supportive kinship ties during church holidays, funerals, memorial potlatches, and other less formal occasions. From the 1960s to 1990, small aircraft travel between the two communities was the norm.

The relocation of Old Nondalton to the new site in the late 1930s under the direction of the first and second chiefs was stimulated by multiple factors. These included the formation of a sand bar in front of the old village site, making it difficult to land watercraft in close proximity to the community. Moreover, timber — essential for building tool construction and fuel — had become depleted in the vicinity of the settlement. As in the case of historic Kijik, many people recalled that the village site had become "old" and the graveyard too full.

Population movements in the Iliamna area are noteworthy, because it is there that most trading activities took place and commercial transport to Bristol Bay was organized. Old Iliamna village remained the primary source of contact with Cook Inlet and traders until approximately 1910. By that time, Severson's trading facility at the current site of Iliamna was established, and the decline of Old Iliamna commenced. Although this settlement was not abandoned totally until the 1930s, residents began moving into new Iliamna,

Pile Bay, and, after 1935, Pedro Bay (Townsend 1965).

The new site of Iliamna was much more central-ized as a trade and transportation hub for Dena'ina, "Aleuts," Yup'ik, and the few locally residing non-Natives from a vast area. Iliamna also proved to be located strategically vis-a-vis Bristol Bay. The trading connections between Cook Inlet and the inland and Iliamna Dena'ina were superseded by those which linked the inte-rior to Bristol Bay. By the late 1920s, float planes began servicing the Iliamna and Lake Clark areas. By the middle of the 1960s, Iliamna was a major center for air traffic originating in Anchorage and other locations statewide. In the 1980s, the major-ity of the Iliamna Dena'ina resided in the small, extended family community at Chekok Point, the heavily Anglicized community of Pedro Bay (Townsend 1965), and the largely non-Native com-munity of Iliamna, with Newhálen being composed of both Yup'ik and Dena'ina residents. Accompanying the use of snowmachines, all-ter-rain vehicles, outboard motors, "bush" aircraft, and the construction of a dirt road between Iliamna and the outlet of Six-Mile Lake of the Newhalen River, by the 1980s, contact between the Iliamna area and the Dena'ina increased in frequency and intensity.

Lastly, the non-Dena'ina settlement of Port Alsworth was established on Lake Clark in 1944, when Babe and Mary Alsworth homesteaded on Hardenburg Bay near Tanalian Point where the Trefon family had lived. By the early 1980s, Port Alsworth also became the headquarters of Lake Clark National Park and Preserve and multiple commercial sport fishing vendors. The U.S. Cen-sus Bureau first recorded Port Alsworth in 1960, with a population of 34 (Townsend 1965). In 1970 it had a documented population of 22. Although at that time, some residents were of Alaska Native ancestry, none self-identified as "Dena'ina." An effort in the 1980s to establish Port Alsworth as a non-Dena'ina "Native" community under the aus-pices of the Alaska Native Claims Settlement Act met with some resistance from both Nondalton residents and the U.S. National Park Service. In 1990, the majority of the population of Port Alsworth was associated with the park, and its concessions remained seasonal.

Table 2 presents the population of inland Dena'ina communities from 1903 to 1982. Dis-crepancies in census data for any given year or between years may relate to the methodologies of the agency undertaking the enumeration. For ex-ample, methods of the clergy, U.S. Census Bureau enumerators, and anthropologists differ greatly.

By 1900, the role of the Russian Orthodox clergy as census takers, in large part, had been replaced by the U.S. Census Bureau. Throughout the years and up until 1990, U.S. census data have been recognized to be inaccurate for small rural popula-tions, resulting generally in under enumeration.

In Table 2, Kijik data reflect the population de-cline associated with the 1900 to 1902 measles and influenza epidemics, the relocation of most of Kijik's population during the first decade of the 1900s to the site of Old Nondalton, and inaccurate counts associated with seasonal mobility of the inland Dena'ina. Population data for Old Nondal-ton were recorded first in 1907. From 1903 to 1920, the Russian Orthodox clergy reported the Dena'ina of Lake Clark to be residents of Kijik, while the Bureau of Education documented them as occupants of Old Nondalton.

Data gathered at the new site of Nondalton indi-cate that the population doubled between 1950 and 1960 and peaked in 1974, followed by a subse-quent decline. Dwindling of Nondalton's population after 1974 reflected, in part, outmigra-tion and transience to Anchorage for secondary education and some wage employment.

Lime Village maintained a relatively small popula-tion throughout the historic period. However, in 1969, state officials predicted that the community would be abandoned totally within the next decade. Such was not the case. The village remained viable into the early 1990s.

Figures 27, 28, and 29 reflect the composition of the total inland Dena'ina population by age and sex for the years 1925, 1950, and 1975 respectively. Twenty-five year intervals were used for purposes of comparison. Members of this "total inland Dena'ina" population depicted in these figures, were residing in Qeghnilen and Old Nondalton until the mid-1930s, Lime Village and Old Nondal-ton until 1940, and Lime Village and Nondalton up until 1975.

The 1925 data portrayed in Figure 27 depict a relatively balanced population by sex (52 percent male and 48 percent female) with a total popula-tion of 130. By 1925, there was a considerable overall percentage of children under the age of five, as depicted in the broad base of the popula-tion pyramid. Longevity had increased relative to 1900, with a small number of both males and fe-males surviving into their 70s. The small number

TABLE 2. INLAND DENA'INA POPULATION, 1903-1982

Year	Nondalton	Lime Village[a]	Old Nondalton	Kijik
1903-1905	N/A	N/A	ND	44 [b]
1907	N/A	N/A	44[c]	39 [b]
1909	N/A	N/A	44[d]	N/A
1910	N/A	N/A	ND	43 [b]
1920	N/A	N/A	69[e]	N/A
1929	N/A	N/A	24[ef]	N/A
1939	N/A	38[f]	82[e]	N/A
1950	103[e]	29[e]	N/A	N/A
1960	205[e]	15[g]	N/A	N/A
1970	184[e]	25[e]	N/A	N/A
1974	253[h]	26[h]	N/A	N/A
1975	215[i]	ND	N/A	N/A
1976	200[j]	40[j]	N/A	N/A
1979	ND	42[k]	N/A	N/A
1980	173[e]	48[e]	N/A	N/A
1981	171[l]	ND	N/A	N/A
1982	176[m]	ND	N/A	N/A

[a] There are no documented data for Qeghnilen except for the years 1908 (47 total with 22 males and 25 females); 1914 (48 total with 25 males and 23 females); and 1915 (52 total with 26 males and 26 females). This information was taken from the Qeghnilen Russian Orthodox confessional lists.

[b] Russian Orthodox church confessional data (ARCA 1847-1900).

[c] U.S. Bureau of Education (1908-1912).

[d] Townsend (1965).

[e] U.S. Bureau of the Census (1972).

[f] Capps (1935); Old Nondalton data included two "Whites."

[g] P. Kari (1983).

[h] Personal communication, Kijik Corporation, 1986. These data were the numbers enrolled in the village corporation in 1974.

[i] Taken from van Horne (1975).

[j] Behnke (1978).

[k] U.S. Public Health Service unpublished data (1980).

[l] State of Alaska, Department of Community and Regional Affairs (1982). These data reported that 93.1 percent of this population was "Native," most of whom were Dena'ina.

[m] State of Alaska, Department of Labor (1983).

N/A Not applicable.

ND No data.

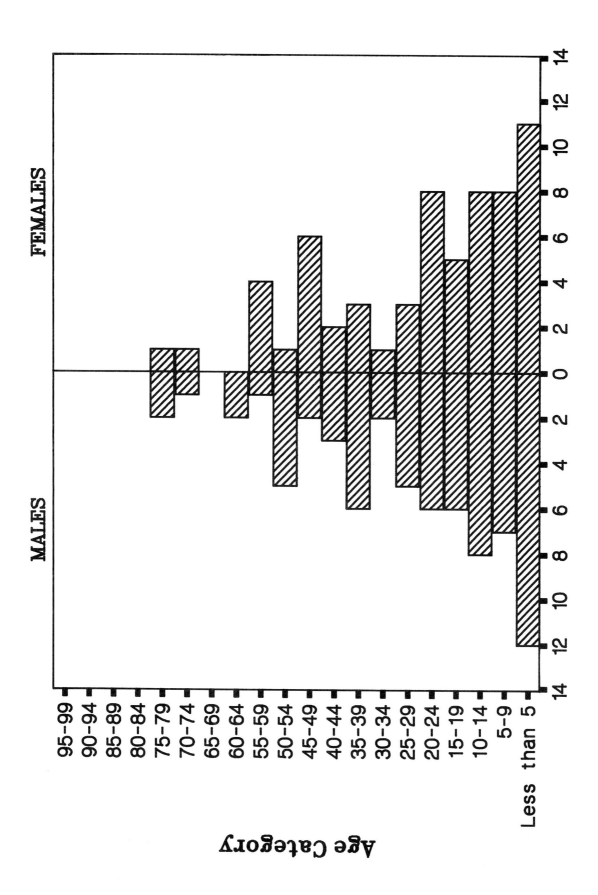

Figure 27. Total inland Dena'ina population by age and sex, 1925.

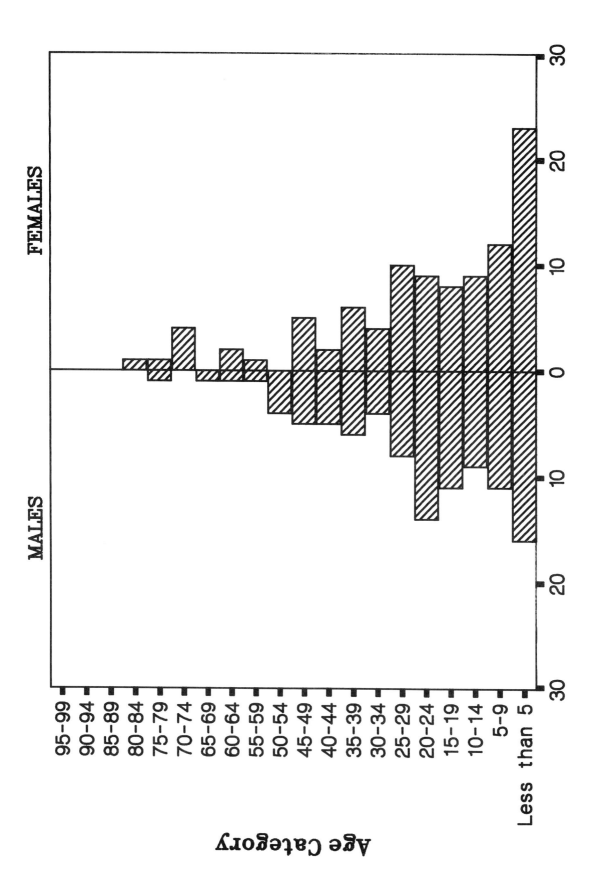

Figure 28. Total inland Dena'ina population by age and sex, 1950.

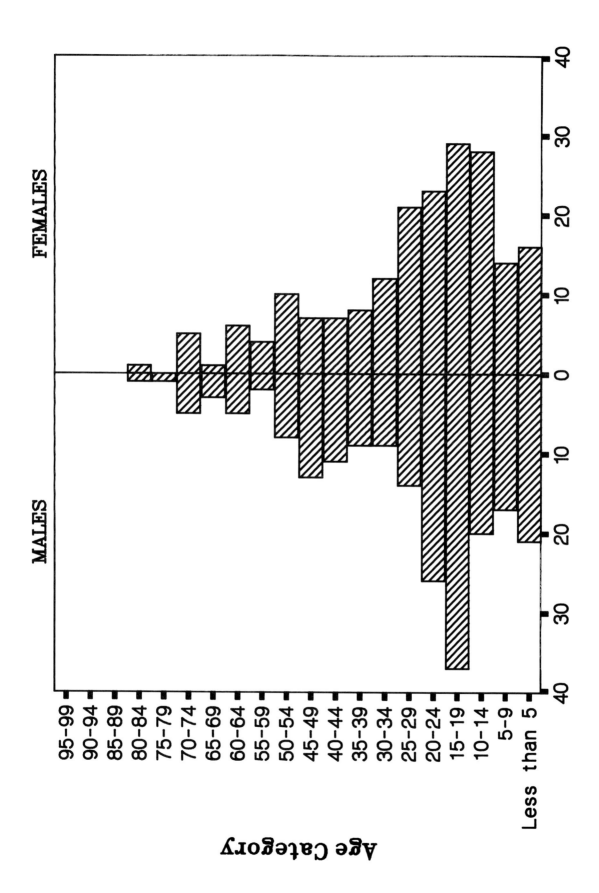

Figure 29. Total inland Dena'ina population by age and sex, 1975.

of both males and females in the cohort 30 to 34 may reflect some outmigration associated with employment or marriage, but such practices were uncommon at that time. It is more likely that under-representation of this cohort reflected mortality associated with epidemics at the turn of the century.

The 1950 data depicted in Figure 28 also present a balanced sex ratio (50 percent each for males and females) and a total population of 194 — an increase of approximately 49 percent from 1925. This figure approaches a standard population pyramid, with some people living to be 80 years or older. By 1950, many people were suffering from tuberculosis. Treatment within and outside Alaska had commenced at that time under the auspices of the U.S. Public Health Service. It was common during these years for adults to be sent away from their families and the community for lengthy periods of time to undergo surgery and convalescence.

Figure 29 presents the 1975 population for all inland Dena'ina. As in the case of 1950, the demographic balance between males and females was equitable (51 percent and 49 percent, respectively). The total population had grown to 394, an increase of 103 percent over 1950. In this case, the rate of population growth had doubled, indicating reduced mortality associated with more accessible western health care. The increased rate of population growth between 1900 and 1975 and decreased fertility after 1960, when western birth control techniques first were promoted, fit the demographic transition model, as described at the beginning of this chapter.

The populations of Old Nondalton and Nondalton remained ethnically Dena'ina throughout the 1900s. The first *Gasht'ana* to marry into the inland Dena'ina population, Jack Hobson and Brown Carlson, were two of very few cases of marriages between Dena'ina and non-Natives, other Athabaskans or Yup'ik (*Dutna*) over the years. Interestingly, women living in Nondalton, who referred to themselves as "part Dena'ina," married only Dena'ina males through 1987 (the final year of our family history data base). Cases that violated this pattern involved inland Dena'ina who relocated to Anchorage or other non-Dena'ina communities.

Systematic data regarding household size and composition for the period 1903 to 1982 are not available. However, information for some exemplary years exists. Nondalton data are available

for 1970 and 1976 (Alaska, Department of Community and Regional Affairs 1974, 1979, 1982; Behnke 1978). In these years, the average household size in Nondalton was 6.3 and 6.7 for 1970 and 1976, respectively. These household sizes were larger than those of Kijik in 1897, smaller than the early contact estimates for the inland Dena'ina, and considerably greater than that of many Alaska Native and non-Native communities in the late 1970s and 1980s (c.f. Wolfe and Ellanna 1983).

Dependency ratios were calculated for the inland Dena'ina for the years 1925, 1950, and 1975. These ratios were 88, 88, and 58, respectively, for these years. The first two ratios more closely approached one producer per dependent than did the ratio for any other period of time documented for this population. An increase in this ratio can result from either a greater proportion of older, post-productive individuals, younger or pre-productive individuals, or both. In the case of the inland Dena'ina, for the period 1925 to 1950, the increased dependency ratios were a product of the combined effects of a relatively fixed fertility rate, reduced infant mortality, and a resultant rapid population growth. The .58 figure for 1975 suggests the introduction of western contraceptive devices and/or techniques. Not only has this case followed the theory of demographic transition (Freeman 1971), but the 1975 ratio approached that calculated for the early contact period. As such, it more closely approximated that of other hunting and gathering societies.

Natality rates were computed for 1925, 1950, and 1975 in order to compare, longitudinally, a facet of inland Dena'ina demography. These rates indicate a marked increase in fertility between 1875 and 1950. Specifically, whereas in 1900 the natality rate was 471 for all inland Dena'ina, nearly a twofold increase over the 253 statistic for 1875, the 1925 rate was 821. This rise in fertility peaked between 1950 and 1975, since the 1950 rate was 886. By 1975, the rate declined to 348, in association with the encouragement of birth control and smaller family size as promoted by non-Dena'ina medical practitioners, educators, and social service workers.

Figures 23 and 24 provide some additional insights into mortality during the first 80 years of this century. Infant mortality showed a marked decline just prior to 1960, correlating with institutionalized non-Native prenatal health care and western concepts of "family planning." The apparent absence of infant mortality during the period 1880 to 1900 may be a result of poor data, such as the reluctance of mothers to discuss deceased infants and their underenumeration in Russian Orthodox confessionals. In the 1980s, it was not uncommon to encounter female elders — either mothers or close relatives of mothers — who could not remember or declined to account for the exact years of birth or specific causes of death of infants miscarried, born dead, or "lost" at a very early age.

CONTEMPORARY INLAND DENA'INA DEMOGRAPHY

Nondalton in the late 1980s and 1990 is depicted in photographs (Figures 30 and 31) and diagrams (Figures 32 and 33). In the case of Nondalton, there were 219 persons in 1987, with a sex distribution of 56 percent males and 44 percent females (Figure 34). The mean ages by sex were 27.1 and 26.0 for males and females, respectively. The overall mean age of the residents of the community was 26.6. In comparison with the 1975 pyramid (Figure 29), the 1987 population profile suggested that birthrates markedly increased over the past decade. The relatively large size of the youngest two cohorts (newborns to age nine) indicated a trend of return migration to Nondalton of single adult parents with their offspring. Additionally, the expanding number of young children seemingly paralleled an overtly stated interest on the part of many young adults in remaining in the village, marrying Dena'ina, and having large families.

Given the relatively high incidence of death in earlier years associated with introduced diseases and accidents, unavoidable among hunters and gatherers, a surprisingly large number of people born 60 or more years ago were still alive in 1987. Those elders, who survived the ravages of nonindigenous diseases and continued the active ways of life implicit in more traditional Dena'ina culture, exhibited extraordinary longevity from the earliest documented accounts to the 1980s — particularly as compared with other hunting and gathering societies worldwide. Unfortunately, some residents of Nondalton succumbed in recent years in relatively large numbers to "modern" illnesses, such as cancer, associated with western ways of life (Sprott 1987).

Figure 35 depicts the Lime Village population in 1985. In that year, the Lime Village population profile represented primarily the members of one large extended family, who occupied multiple dwellings in the community. The population totaled 48 and was 58 percent male and 42 percent female. The sex ratio was weighted more heavily toward males than that of Nondalton, possibly reflecting greater female outmigration. The mean age of 25.6 was somewhat lower than that of Nondalton for males but higher at 28.9 for females. There was an overall mean age of 26.7. The population profile did not form a normal pyramid, as there were no boys in the cohort 5 to 9, no girls in the cohort 15 to 19, and no individuals in the cohort 45 to 49.

In 1987, the transient Anchorage inland Dena'ina population, with membership from both Nondalton and Lime Village, totaled 150, 47 percent of whom was male and 53 percent female (Figure 36). This sex ratio was not surprising, given the greater tendency of females to outmigrate, particularly as a result of marriage to non-Dena'ina. The mean age of males was 26.3, females 25.8, and the overall population 26.1. The profile did not reflect a normal pyramid, with the cohorts 25 to 34 being extraordinarily large relative to the rest of the population. This was not unexpected, given the interest of members of this age group in seeking employment and training opportunities not available in either Nondalton or Lime Village.

The overall inland Dena'ina population (i.e., Nondalton, Lime Village, and the transient inland Dena'ina in Anchorage combined), as depicted in Figure 37, was 417 for the period 1985 to 1987. The sex ratio was 53 percent and 47 percent for males and females, respectively. The mean age was 26.4 for males, 25.9 for females, and 26.1 overall. The sex ratio was similar to that of other rural Alaska Native populations. The population profile was not a symmetrical pyramid, because of constriction of the cohorts 10 to 24. Cohorts newborn to age nine reflected the existence of a normal, healthy population.

Table 3 depicts self-identified ethnicity of Nondalton and the transient inland Dena'ina population in 1987. This table indicates that the vast majority of Nondalton and transient inland Dena'ina populations considered themselves to be "Dena'ina." In the 1980s, an overt preference for marrying other Dena'ina was expressed intensely by most younger people in Nondalton. In Table 3, if all Nondalton residents who referred to themselves as "Dena'ina" in 1987 were combined, they totaled 198 or 90 percent of the total population. Of the transient Anchorage population, 127 or 85 percent referred to themselves as "Dena'ina." Those who referred to themselves as other than "Dena'ina" were inmarried spouses or, in some cases, adopted individuals. School teachers and other transient non-Natives were not included in

Figure 30 (above). The community of Nondalton during summer 1986. **Figure 31 (below).** Competitive dog races on Nondalton's main street during spring carnival, 1986. This event, usually held in March or early April, attracts Dena'ina from throughout the Lake Clark, Stony River, and Lake Iliamna areas as well as *Dutna* and Yup'ik neighbors.

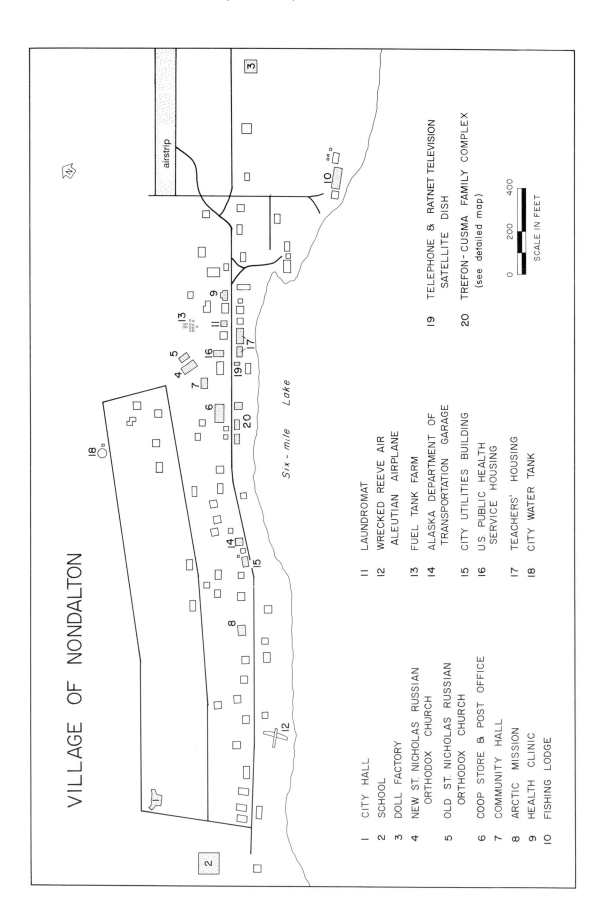

Figure 32. A field diagram of the village of Nondalton during early summer 1991.

VILLAGE OF NONDALTON

airstrip

Six-mile Lake

1 CITY HALL
2 SCHOOL
3 DOLL FACTORY
4 NEW ST. NICHOLAS RUSSIAN
   ORTHODOX CHURCH
5 OLD ST. NICHOLAS RUSSIAN
   ORTHODOX CHURCH
6 COOP STORE & POST OFFICE
7 COMMUNITY HALL
8 ARCTIC MISSION
9 HEALTH CLINIC
10 FISHING LODGE

11 LAUNDROMAT
12 WRECKED REEVE AIR
   ALEUTIAN AIRPLANE
13 FUEL TANK FARM
14 ALASKA DEPARTMENT OF
   TRANSPORTATION GARAGE
15 CITY UTILITIES BUILDING
16 U.S. PUBLIC HEALTH
   SERVICE HOUSING
17 TEACHERS' HOUSING
18 CITY WATER TANK

19 TELEPHONE & RATNET TELEVISION
   SATELLITE DISH
20 TREFON-CUSMA FAMILY COMPLEX
   (see detailed map)

0   200   400

SCALE IN FEET

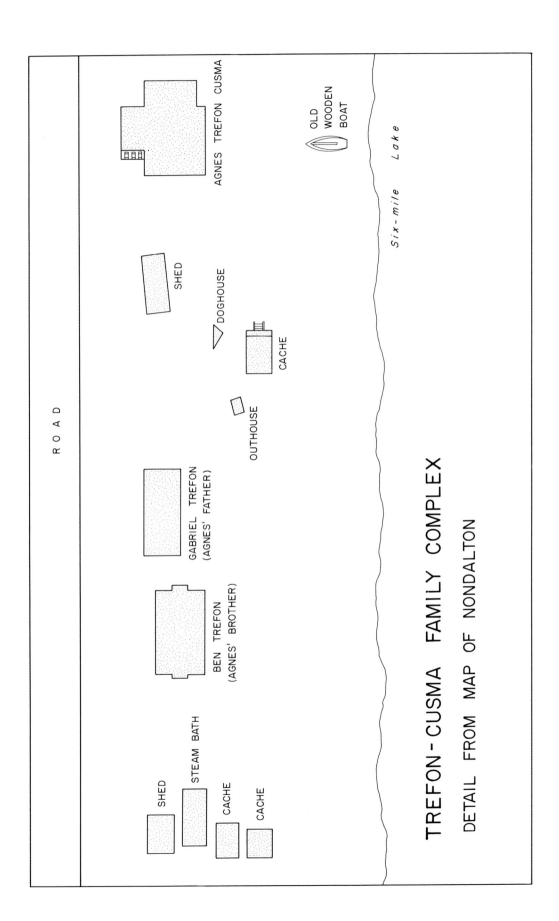

Figure 33. The Trefon-Cusma family complex with associated structures – a typical example from Nondalton, summer 1991.

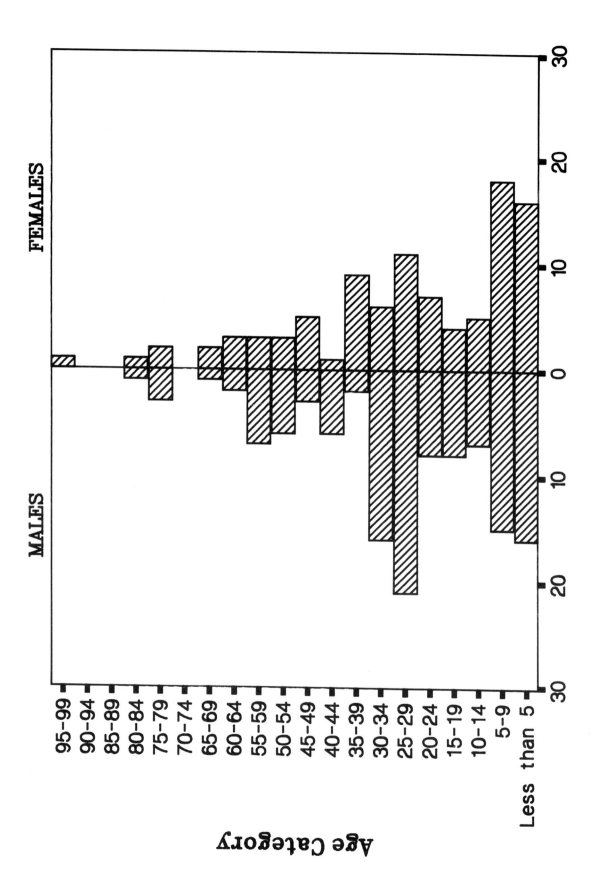

Figure 34. Nondalton population by age and sex, 1987.

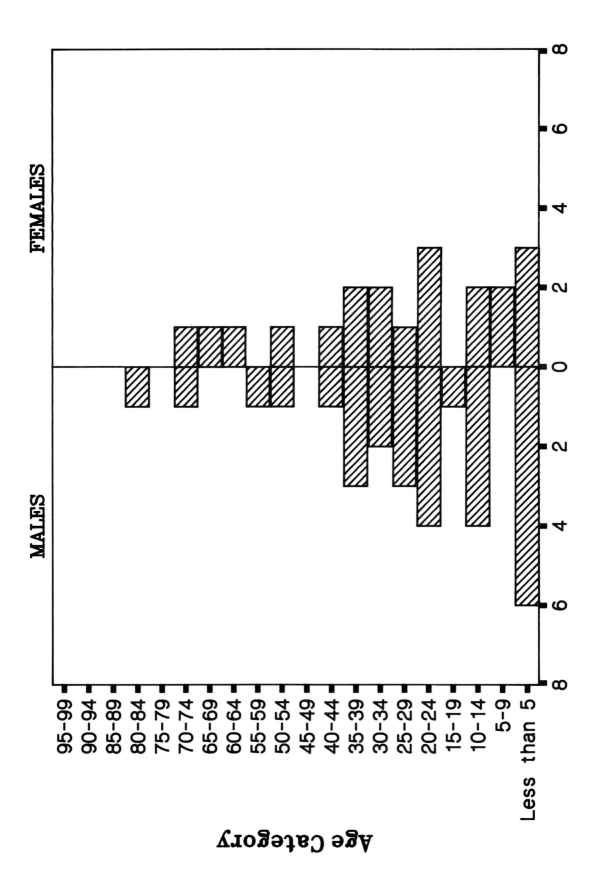

Figure 35. Lime Village population by age and sex, 1985.

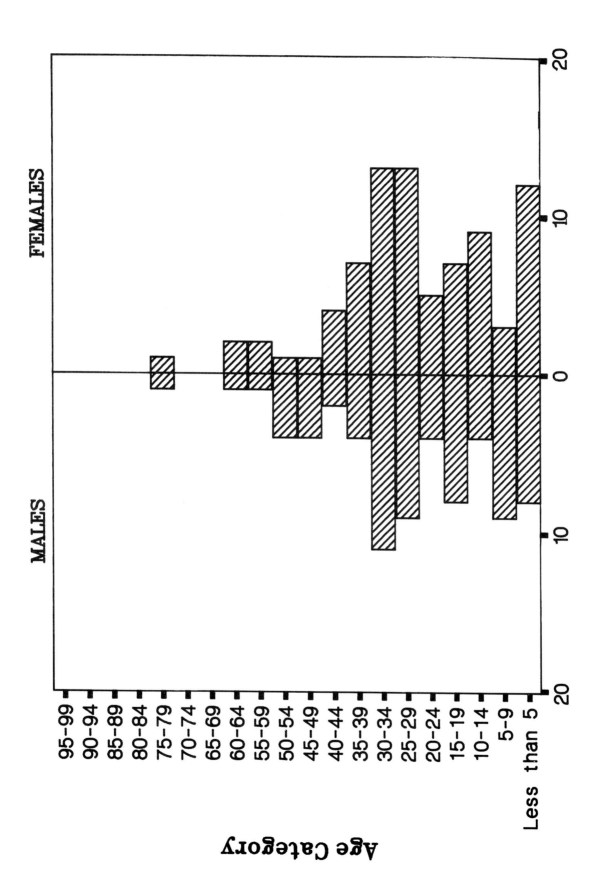

Figure 36. Transient Anchorage inland Dena'ina population by age and sex, 1987.

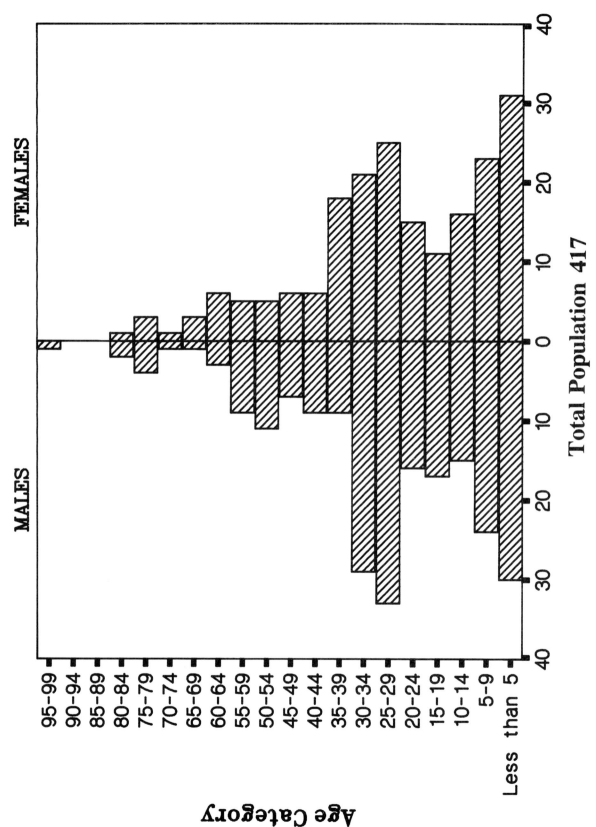

Figure 37. Total inland Dena'ina population by age and sex, 1985-1987. This figure represents the compilation of Lime Village data for 1985 and Nondalton and the transient Anchorage populations for 1987.

TABLE 3. INLAND DENA'INA ETHNICITY, 1987[a]

Ethnicity	Nondalton 1987	Anchorage 1987
Dena'ina	44	34
Caucasian	5	12
Yup'ik	3	0
Athabaskan (non-Dena'ina)	0	1
Other	13	10
Dena'ina/Caucasian	52	54
Dena'ina/Yup'ik	12	3
Dena'ina/Athabaskan	14	3
Dena'ina/other	46	19
Caucasian/Dena'ina	7	1
Yup'ik/Dena'ina	1	0
other/Dena'ina	22	13

[a] Definitions applied to the data in these categories are necessary to understanding this table. Those listed as Dena'ina, Caucasian, Yup'ik, Athabaskan (other than Dena'ina), and other are those individuals who say that their ethnicity is fully that named. That is, they reported that they were "full-blooded" within the category in which they are portrayed. Cases depicted as mixed ethnicity, such as Dena'ina/Caucasian, refer to individuals who say they are 50 percent or more Dena'ina. The same applies to all other categories based on the ethnicity placed before the slash. The category "other" can include any ethnicity with the exception of Dena'ina that is not represented by at least 50 percent of ethnic ancestry in that individual. For example, a person listed in the category "other" may have one-eighth each of many ethnic affiliations, such as Yup'ik, Caucasian, etc. No one part of their affiliation, however, is greater than 50 percent as they reported. The individuals in all categories including the designation "Dena'ina" usually referred to themselves as such, despite the degree to which this ethnicity was reflected in their ancestry as self-reported (or reported by parents for their children).

these data, as they did not function as part of Dena'ina society.

In regard to household composition, the residents of the study communities overtly stated their preference for extended family domestic units. By way of contrast, pressure on residents by state and federal housing program administrations, the encouragement of the nuclear family model by transfer payment funding program policies and their representatives, and the promotion of that grouping as the "normal" social unit in formal western education resulted in drastically changed household sizes. In 1985, Nondalton had 53 households, having an average size of 4.3 members. In 1987, there were 56 households with an average size of 4.1. Among Anchorage inland Dena'ina, there were 50 households, with an average size of 3.0 in 1987. In Lime Village in 1985, there were 12 households, having an average size of 4.0.

These statistics may be misleading in that they reflect the occupation of domiciles rather than functional households. In all cases, household sizes were larger than that of the non-Native populations of rural and urban Alaska. In fact, the use of the western "household" rather than the functional household as a unit of analysis is problematic. For example, in cases in which families had "old" and "new" houses, younger unmarried or newly married adults slept in the "old" house but ate and conducted most social activities in the household of his or her parents or other relatives. The smaller household size in Anchorage was not surprising, since commonly young men and, less frequently, women, acquired temporary apartments in Anchorage while attending school, receiving medical care, or undertaking short term employment. Some elders had assumed residency in the State of Alaska's Pioneer Home (a public facility for the elderly) or, in a few cases, nursing homes, thereby lowering the overall average household size.

Normally, adult children who were newly married, formally or informally, participated in activities with the family members of either the male or female or both. In many cases, young couples remained within the household of parents until they had more than one child. Most frequently, residence was with the family of the woman. Such couples later moved to a separate residence. In the historic past and even in the 1980s, the Dena'ina considered the practice of males residing with their wives' families to be bride service in most cases. Living away from one's family definitely was considered deviant in contemporary Nondalton. Young children continued to spend a lot of time or were adopted into the households of their mother's brothers and, less frequently, mother's sisters.

Dependency ratios were calculated for Nondalton and transient Anchorage inland Dena'ina in 1987 and Lime Village in 1985. These ratios were 74, 50, and 85, respectively. Based on these data, dependency ratios were expanding as a result of increased fertility.

Natality rates for the three populations also were calculated. Nondalton, with a rate of 744, exhibited a 114 percent increase over the rate in 1975. The Lime Village rate in 1985 was 1,000. The transient Anchorage inland Dena'ina population had a natality rate of 400, not unexpected due to the age and sex composition of that group and their reasons for being temporarily outside of home villages. The overall inland Dena'ina natality rate of 744 for the period 1985 to 1987 was the same as that of Nondalton.

As depicted in Figure 25, mothers born after 1930 exhibited similar birth patterns as those born prior to 1900, with fertility peaking at 23.5 years of age. In the case of mothers born after 1930, fertility dropped off dramatically during their late 20s. In general terms, mothers born after 1930 had their initial child at an older age than those born in 1900 and ceased having children at a much earlier age than mothers born at any period.

URBAN TRANSIENCE AND THE DEMOGRAPHIC FUTURE OF THE INLAND DENA'INA

The introduction of trading posts and the potential for conducting activities by which trade goods could be obtained (trapping, cannery work, etc.) influenced the number of inland Dena'ina villages, reducing them from minimally 4 in the 1870s to 2 by 1901. Centralization, then, preceded the actual location of trading posts, churches, or schools in communities inhabited by the inland Dena'ina.

Centralization did not involve increased sedentism, minimally until schools began to operate within inland Dena'ina communities. In fact, the need for trade goods and/or cash may have encouraged increased mobility associated with spending a greater percentage of the year running trap lines than would have been the case prior to western indirect and direct contact.

Demographic data suggest population growth between the 1850s and 1870s. However, this may be a function of a scanty data base for the earlier period resulting from the use of Russian Orthodox confessionals. The large number of deaths in 1877 and the population decline after 1882 suggest that the inland Dena'ina were experiencing morbidity and mortality related to western contact. However, the expected rapid population growth associated with demographic transition (Binford and Chasko 1976; Freeman 1971) did not occur in association with centralization among the inland Dena'ina. This suggests that centralization without associated sedentism may lead to very different demographic conclusions.

Low reproductivity among women born between 1900 and 1930 may be related to the advantages of having a small number of dependent children under conditions of seasonal nomadism, even when the population had centralized in fewer settlements. However, what has been interpreted here as low productivity, in fact may be a representation of the poor survivability of newborns.

Rapid population growth corresponded with the restructuring of nomadic strategies associated with mandatory school and church attendance and more accessible western health care. This growth rate declined between 1950 and 1970, conforming to demographic transition models, but was on the increase again in the 1980s. These more recent data challenge the unidirectional and assimilationist assumptions that are key to demographic transition paradigms.

Westernization and centralization, even in the absence of sedentism, superficially resulted in a decline of household size and increasing similarity to the nuclear family household model common in industrialized societies. However, such analysis may be misleading because of a lack of attention to the more culturally relevant concept of "functional domestic group."

Fertility data suggest that reproductive patterns among the inland Dena'ina, in part, have responded to sedentism and westernization. There appears to be an inverse relationship between the length of the total reproductive period of inland Dena'ina women and recency of their year of birth. In addition, reproductive peaks occurred at an earlier age among mothers born since 1930 than among those born before 1900 but not after 1930. The lengthy reproductive period for mothers born prior to 1930, as compared with those born after that year, may be related to centralization in the absence of sedentism and the need to maintain low dependency ratios for purposes of facilitating mobility while still assuring population replacement.

Longevity data indicate that the inland Dena'ina were able to support individuals of advanced age from the early contact period through the 1980s. There is no evidence that the study population practiced either infanticide or senilicide — both common among some northern North American populations with comparable or even lesser degrees of nomadism. This factor, in part, may relate to the relative abundance of the inland Dena'ina resource base, especially in regard to plentiful and reliable supplies of sockeye salmon.

Infant mortality was a factor of inland Dena'ina demography throughout the historic period until the onset of rural, modern health delivery. When the inland Dena'ina were more nomadic, such mortality may have benefited the population through providing natural population limitations. However, the onset of a more sedentary way of life negated this connection. It is of interest to note that higher rates of infant mortality reappeared after 1980 — a phenomenon recorded for the United States overall.

Figure 38. (left to right) Ben Trefon, his father's brother or *dada* (in Dena'ina), Alex Trefon, and his sister, Agnes Trefon (Cusma), circa 1934. This photograph was taken next to the cabin of Doc Dutton and Joe Kackley, neighbors of Gabriel Trefon and his family at Tanalian Point. *Photograph Courtesy of Agnes Cusma.*

CHAPTER 5

FAMILY, CLAN, AND BAND: THEMES OF INLAND DENA'INA SOCIAL ORGANIZATION

On a beach in a river, there was a village. One man, he had a sister. This sister lived across the river by herself opposite the village. Her brother lived in the village. This woman had one dog. When she ran out of food, he had a dog pack for her dog. She took the dogpack and tied it on the dog. Then she spoke to the dog, "go swim across to the village to my brother and he will put some food in your pack." So the dog swam across and came to this man. Without a question, he filled the dog pack with food. . . . Another day when she ran out of food, she did the same thing. . . . So the dog swam across. Just when he swam to the beach, there were some village people watching the dog. They filled the dog pack with rocks and told the dog to swim back. The dog started back, but halfway in the river, its pack filled up with water and the current took the dog underwater. The woman was watching the dog and went back in the house. She lived there with very little food.

Afterwards, she noticed that she was pregnant. She did not have a husband. She had triplet pups — there were two males and one female. She started raising them. . . . Everyday she would go out in the woods and pack a bundle of wood for the fire. After she came back, she'd see kids' tracks on the ashes in the fire pit and knew that the pups made the tracks. As the pups slept, she started sewing some caribou, rabbit, and squirrel skins making kids clothes, enough for three kids. After she made these clothes, she hid them.

In the morning, she went after wood again. She kept packing wood and started piling it by the door. She piled it high in such a way so she could watch the pups as they played. As she was packing the last bundle, she saw three kids run out of the house — two boys and one girl. . . . Then she ran out from her hiding place and grabbed the kids. As she was going back into the house, the little girl squirmed out of her grasp and ran back in the house. The two boys started to cry. While she was holding them, she ran in the house and saw the little girl turn back into a little pup. . . . She looked by the fire pit and saw two puppy skins laying there. She grabbed them and threw them into the fire. Then the two boys spoke to her and said, "Mother, why did you throw our clothes into the fire?" "What will we wear?" The woman said, "I made you some clothes," and she brought them out. . . .

One day as they were playing outdoors, there was no more sound from them. . . . Then she heard a grunting noise as if they were working hard. There was a flap on the door and they pushed it aside and said, "Mother, what is this?" She rushed to the door and they had a live caribou and were hanging onto it by the antlers. She grabbed a spear and speared the caribou. After this she made them a bow and arrows and spear. Then she trained them how to use the bow and arrows and spear. She told them, "these are weapons that your grandfather used to get animals for food. So next time, don't try to grab a live animal. . . .

As they grew up, they started to hunt. The female pup never stayed behind. Wherever they hunted, she was always along. One day they went hunting again. They stayed all day and it was getting dark. She started to go outdoors and listen for them, but they never returned. Towards morning, she went out again and heard the pup barking. . . . While she was listening, the sound was coming from the sky. She looked up in the sky and saw these two boys running on both sides of a bear and the little pup running behind barking. . . . She cried and cried until it became daylight. Then she said, "Well, what can I do now? Let me turn into a morning star in the memory of my kids." She became a morning star. And where the boys went across the sky became the Milky Way.

Anton Evan, 1976, translated by
Albert Wassillie

KINSHIP AND KINSWOMEN: THE ORDERING OF SOCIETY

This story, as told by elder Anton Evan, illustrates several essential themes of inland Dena'ina social organization existing in the historic past and persisting as an underlying motif of society in the 1980s. This account portrays the most basic principle of inland Dena'ina social organization — that of the importance of ties of kinship in binding together and organizing members of society. That is, the kinship system defines a number of individual statuses and their connectedness according to a variety of rules. These statuses and their behavioral correlates or roles distinguish kinsmen, or those who are perceived to be related, from non-kin, or those who are not. Kinship, as perceived by the inland Dena'ina, may or may not be based on assumptions or models of biological or "blood" relatedness, common in the American kinship system.

This narrative also suggests that the inland Dena'ina determine descent (i.e., how groups of people are related through parental and child or sibling bonds) matrilineally rather than bilaterally, common in modern industrialized American and European societies, or patrilineally, common among some other hunting and gathering groups. Based on matrilineality, each individual traces relatedness to a particular subgroup of the larger society, each of which have many corporate functions. Kinship linkages between individuals are established through women or, more specifically, mothers by both males and females. In cases of matrilineal descent, brothers and sisters always belong to the same descent group or clan (sib). Since such societies are not matriarchies (i.e., groups in which women wield the majority of power), males generally assert overt authority in the functioning of the social system. Therefore, a woman's brothers and her mother's brothers are the most significant men in her life. Conversely, a woman's offspring are the most significant children to her brothers and her mother's brothers. This kinship system is novel as contrasted to that of mainstream America and nations with related European cultural origins.

Additionally, this story can be interpreted as providing several less obvious insights into inland Dena'ina kinship. For example, it covertly illustrates potential conflicting loyalties, in matrilineally structured societies, between a man and his relatives and those of his wife. A man's relatives always belong to a different kinship group from that of his wife, most commonly because of prohibitions on marrying members of one's own clan. Therefore, ties of marriage (affinal links) tend to be weaker than bonds of descent in matrilineally organized societies (Schneider and Gough 1974). An adult male's obligations and productivity are directed more toward the welfare of his sister and her children than that of his wife and their children. In the account by Anton Evan, the villagers may have put rocks in the dog's pack in response to such divided loyalties.

Given the fact that a man, as husband and father, has such divided loyalties, it is not surprising that the closest ties within the domestic family are between a woman and her children. The strength of the bonds between women and their children in inland Dena'ina society are symbolically illus-

trated in the narrative of Anton Evan by the fact that this woman, in the absence of a husband or brother, taught her sons to make food procuring technology (e.g., a bow, arrows, and spear) and skills of hunting, most commonly but not exclusively associated with males. Her intense grief at the loss of the children, culminating in her transformation into the morning star to be near them, is yet another indication of the strength of maternal bonds.

Lastly, this oral historic account reveals that the scope of kinship extends beyond the realm of humanity to include other creatures and features of the universe. This perception typically is found among contemporary hunting and gathering peoples worldwide (e.g., McClellan 1987; Nelson 1983; Williams and Hunn, 1982). The offspring in the story were interchangeably puppies and human beings. In the end, the entire family became stellar bodies – a representation of inland Dena'ina perceptual relatedness to other aspects of the universe.

ELUSIVE QUESTIONS AND RIVAL RESPONSES

There are multiple, fundamental questions about matrilineality in hunting and gathering societies. These have included inquiries into the temporal and spatial distribution of matrilineal descent systems, the observation that this kinship pattern occurred and persisted in some cases and, alternatively, was absent or seemingly disintegrated in others. Hypothetical answers to these questions are based, in part, on the assumption that it is possible to reconstruct indigenous social systems and to identify their causes. Matrilineality is relatively uncommon worldwide and, specifically, among hunters and gatherers.

The assumption that prehistoric indigenous social systems can be reconstructed, by means of comparisons with similar cases in the historic period (i.e., ethnographic analogy) and with evidence derived from archaeology and biological anthropology, is subject to considerable debate. Similarly, the assumption that the "causes" of particular indigenous social systems can be ascertained is equally questionable (e.g., Asch 1980; Schneider and Gough 1974). Additionally, an understanding of the sociocultural change of indigenous cultures and societies resulting from Euroamerican contact must rely on these questionable reconstructions. Lastly, and importantly, scholarly classifications of kinship systems as being "matrilineal," "patrilineal," "bilateral" or any other analytical reality may elude the complexity, flexibility, and dynamic nature of social processes in favor of neatly defined taxonomic classification (Keesing 1975).

With these qualifications and cautionary remarks in mind, some major theoretical responses to these very elusive questions deserve comment. June Helm (1965), an authority on northern Athabaskans, evaluated the earlier contributions of Julian Steward (1955) and, subsequently, Elman Service on the topic of the social organization of hunting and gathering societies:

A decade ago, Julian Steward reiterated his identification of socioterritorial organization of the Arctic Drainage Dene [Athabaskans]. . . of Canada's Northwest Territories as of the "composite hunting band" type. For the Northern Athapaskans, he identified as "bands" only certain reported "social aggregates of several hundred persons.". . . In his dichotomous classification of "primitive bands" there is the implication that the "composite hunting band" wherever found is essentially a departure, brought about by special ecologic or sociodemographic circumstances, from the principle of virilocal residence [postmarital residence with a male spouse's family] that creates the "patrilineal band." The structural principles of Steward's "composite society" are nebulous; such a society is composed of "many unrelated nuclear or biological families," integrated "on the basis of constant association and cooperation rather than of actual or alleged kinship" (Steward 1955:143). Service . . . has recently reevaluated Steward's formulation from an evolutionary perspective. Accepting for the historic period the validity of Steward's concept of the composite band as composed of unrelated families, Service makes it explicitly into a residual category — the consequence of the destruction of the virilocal principal [sic] by catastrophes resulting from European contact, notably, in the Northern Dene case, population loss through disease (Helm 1965:361).

Helm (1965), while ostensibly arguing that it is not possible to reconstruct the precise nature of precontact socioterritorial arrangements, countered Steward's and Service's assumption that post-contact Athabaskan bands were composed of unrelated members. Based on data from four Canadian arctic drainage Athabaskan groups representing three linguistic divisions (i.e., Hare, Slavey, and Dogrib), Helm (1965) demonstrated that, to the contrary, families which made up these bands exhibited a high degree of relatedness, primarily through the existence of parent-child and sibling bonds, between one or more spouses in

each conjugal unit. She also argued for the ecological adaptability of this type of organization. In this model, bilaterality (e.g., determining one's kin through both mother and father) and flexibility of postmarital residence were considered more adaptive than principles of unilineal descent, particularly in light of post-contact human population decimations and long-term fluctuations in critical resource availability.

What I am stressing is not merely that aboriginal Dene populations were small in size and low in density, but that population was unstable, with decimation through famine occurring at what may have been rather cyclical intervals. When such disaster struck, "multiple kinship avenues" to new affiliations as old ones collapsed may well have been crucial in permitting quick and socially coherent regrouping of survivors. I suggest that population instability militates more stringently against societal integration through one track rules of affiliation than does a population size and density which is merely continuously checked at a low level. This argument does not contravene Service's position that virilocal residence, in combination with reciprocal band exogamy through cross-cousin marriage, is an inherently optimal mode of societal organization for the hunting band society. But it may be necessary to maintain the proviso: **environmental conditions permitting** *[emphasis is Helm's]. We must, at least, be wary of assuming that all human kind at the hunting and foraging level have been allowed by the nature of their environmental resources to achieve a unilocal, band-exogamic system of societal integration* (Helm 1965:382).

Helm's concepts, reiterated by other anthropologists providing comparative hunter-gatherer perspectives (Lee and DeVore 1968), resulted in the preeminent view among western anthropologists that the social organization of hunters and gatherers was principally bilateral in regard to descent, bilocal (e.g., postmarital residence with either the kin of the wife or husband) in regard to locality, and generally flexible in nature (Bishop and Krech 1980). For the most part, such arguments assumed the strong role of ecological factors in conditioning the form of hunter and gatherer social organization.

Evidence from other Athabaskan research offered competing theories of hunter and gatherer social organization, both in the past and present times. McKennan (1969), based on his research in the 1930s, like Helm, disagreed with Steward's (1955) contention that northern Athabaskan social organization was composite and bilateral. More specifically, McKennan (1969) did not agree with

Steward's (1955) suggestion that matrilineality and matrilocality, or uxorilocality, among northern Athabaskans were the result of diffusion from the northwest coast of North America (Krech 1979). By way of contrast, McKennan (1969) argued that matrilineality, including exogamous matriclans and a tripartite division of such clans into three larger units, were very ancient, existing in proto-Athabaskan societies. Since famines and wars existed prior to contact, McKennan (1969), unlike Helm (1965), saw no reason to postulate major post-contact demographic catastrophes as the major or sole explanations for apparent changing principles of social organization.

McKennan's (1969) position in regard to the antiquity of principles of matrilineality in northern Athabaskan social organization basically were accepted by noted anthropologist, Catharine McClellan (1964). McClellan (1964) further argued in favor of the ecological adaptability of matrilineality and initial matrilocal postmarital residence, mandated by the practice of bride service (common among northern Athabaskans). McClellan's (1964) argument concluded that in times of ecological stress, males, as primary producers, had knowledge of land and resource availability and use in two rather than a single area — that of their own parents and that of their in-laws.

Both McClellan (1964) and McKennan (1969) noted an increase in individual as opposed to cooperative hunting after the introduction of the rifle and an escalating emphasis on furbearer trapping. However, McClellan (1964) did not suggest that these economic changes stimulated any decline in the social significance of matrilineality in most northern Athabaskan societies (see also de Laguna 1971). Contrastingly, McClellan commented upon the perseverance of matrilineality as a social principle among northern Athabaskans into the 1960s (McClellan 1987).

More contemporary arguments, such as those of Asch (1980), Krech (1979), Bishop and Krech (1980) are based both on field data and a review of the evidence and conclusions derived from earlier research. Krech (1979) and Bishop and Krech (1980) reconstructed indigenous patterns of northern Athabaskan social organization, to identify causal factors and to explain shifts from matrilineality and matrilocality to bilaterality and bilocality. Krech (1979) and Bishop and Krech (1980:36) accepted the antiquity of matrilineality and/or matrilocality among proto-Athabaskans. They postulated that there were numerous, identifiable, historical reasons for the relatively rapid development of what they perceived to be more flexible bilocal-bilateral social organization among subarctic peoples in the 1800s and 1900s.

In interpreting assumed shifts from matrilineality and matrilocality to bilaterality and bilocality among northern Athabaskans, Krech (1979) and Bishop and Krech (1980) employed an adaptive, causal model. This model used a broad definition of "environment," to include ecological, sociocultural, and other variables. Krech (1979) and Bishop and Krech (1980:36-39) proposed that shifts from matrilineality and matrilocality were a product of the "sheer depletion of traditional resources," including caribou and "musk oxen"; a change of subsistence focus from big game to "unreliable" fur-bearing and fish resources; relocation to residence around trading posts and associated expanded reliance on trade goods; and relatively massive human population declines related to introduced epidemic diseases. Meaningfully, it is apparent from a review of competing theories that some of the same evidence is used to substantiate conflicting interpretations.

Bishop and Krech (1980) dismissed as too simplistic McClellan's (1964) conclusion that matrilocality was adaptive, primarily because the major producers (males) were familiar with dual territories and harvesting and distribution procedures. Bishop and Krech (1980) fundamentally agreed with McClellan (1964) that matrilineality was much more adaptive to precontact seasonal, annual, and multiannual faunal cycles, in which nadirs of resource availability for multiple species coincided in time and space. Additionally, they argued, the distribution of related males within multiple small bands or microbands, that collectively composed a larger socioterritorial unit (macroband) via the mechanism of matrilocality, aboriginally facilitated the use of multiple territories and access to supportive relatives and distribution networks over a broad area. Such an organization thereby eliminated many of the risks of localized resource and related harvest and distributive failures.

Finally, and in stark contrast to the position of Bishop and Krech (1980), is that of Asch (1980). Asch (1980) arrived at some general observations of Athabaskan social organization by the application of data he gathered from research in a single Slavey community in northwestern Canada. He argued that principles of social organization were embedded in the ideology of and rights to the means and modes of production in Athabaskan societies and not merely the end product of normative behavior. In fact, Asch (1980) reiterated extreme caution in attempting ecological or any other causal explanations of lineality and locality, and their correlation to other facets of culture, particularly in the absence of information on the ideology of group formation. Unless extensive data can be gathered regarding this ideology and its relationship to principles of social organization for contemporary and historic Athabaskan groups, Asch (1980) argued that it was fruitless to attempt grandiose schemes of reconstructing precontact patterns of socioterritorial organization. Based on his data for the Slavey, he rejected the concept of "nodal kindred" (i.e., a bilateral social unit based on affinal and genealogical ties between siblings and sibling groups) postulated by Helm (1965) as the basis of northern Athabaskan residential groups. In fact, according to Asch's data (1980), residents of the Slavey community chose certain kin linkages over others to establish the relatedness of males married to a group of related females.

Given this limited but relevant discussion of some prominent attempts to explain Athabaskan social organization, we turn to the nature of kinship among the historic and more contemporary inland Dena'ina. As Asch (1980) argued, and we agree, specific behavioral and ideological data are essential for coming a step closer to fleshing out broader theoretical skeletons of the social order of northern Athabaskan and other hunting and gathering societies.

TIES THAT BIND: THE NATURE OF KINSHIP

KINSHIP AND DESCENT: A REVIEW OF SOME FUNDAMENTAL PRINCIPLES

There has been considerable debate among various scholars about the nature of "kinship" in human societies. One of several conceptual frameworks for viewing this universal human phenomenon is presented in this context. For these purposes, then, kinship is defined as a network of relationships between members of human groups. This network is created by genealogical and affinal relatedness and a wide array of other social and ideological ties (such as adoption, naming, marriage). Many kinship bonds, both in non-western and western societies, are neither genealogical or affinal, although scholars of kinship disagree as to whether or not they are biologically modelled upon what western science views as the "natural" relations of

genealogical parenthood (procreation) and associated marriage (cf, Keesing 1975; Needham 1971; Schneider 1980).

Kinship terminology is normally defined in anthropology with reference to one particular individual, usually termed "ego." Kinship relations occur in all known human societies and, differing from descent, are normally bilateral (i.e., they include relatives on both mother's and father's side from the perspective of ego). From an individual's (ego's) perspective, the group of people she or he deems as "kin" are referred to as that individual's "kindred."

By way of contrast, membership in descent groups (e.g., matrilineal clans) is defined in reference to a common human or nonhuman ancestor or ancestress; is culturally recognized in only some human societies; connects, through bonds of relatedness, only a limited segment of ego's relatives (as opposed to the breadth of "kin" recognized as "kindred"); generally results in functioning corporate entities; and is absolute in the sense that one is or is not a member (Keesing 1975:21). If descent is determined through the parent of one sex only, that system is referred to as being "unilineal" (literally, "one line"). If the line of descent is traced through ego's mother (and her mother, in turn), the pattern is referred to as "matrilineal." Siblings in matrilineally organized societies are members of the same "lineage" (a segment of the larger matrilineal group or "clan") and clan (also referred to as "sib").

There are qualifications which are central to understanding the nature and functioning of matrilineal descent groups, within and outside of inland Dena'ina society. The first of these has to do with the fact that there are no known human societies in which women principally hold overt key political power — a phenomenon termed a "matriarchy." In all known matrilineally organized societies, significant political power governing the form and function of the descent groups (clan or lineage) is in the hands of male members of that group related to one another through females. However, examples of both covert and overt power of females in societies with matrilineal descent have been underestimated in earlier literature, based on more recent analyses of the functioning of such societies. Nonetheless, although descent, in terms of group membership, is transmitted to both males and females through women (mothers specifically), the inheritance of power and property most commonly is transmitted from mother's brother to sister's children.

Other principles of matrilineal organization include, most commonly, rules of clan "exogamy." This means that marriage norms require people to marry outside of their own descent group to avoid perceived incestuous relationships. Therefore, husband and wife are, by definition, members of different descent groups. The corollary to this condition is that mothers, as opposed to fathers, have primary responsibility for their children, since they are born into her descent group rather than into his. This is not to imply that children do not recognize natural or social fathers as being "relatives" or part of their kindred. Because of the nature of descent in matrilineally organized societies, consequentially, the ties between a woman and her husband are usually somewhat at odds with her bonds to her brother, who represents her descent group. In part, the same could be said for the ties between children and their mother's husband as opposed to their mother's brother, since they belong to the descent group of the former, not to that of the latter (Schneider and Gough 1974 [1961]). In fact, it is not unusual for the biological contribution of the husband or the male role in conception to be ignored in societies with matrilineal descent systems. Nonetheless, the emotional and affectionate interest of a father in his own children, as opposed to those of his sisters, at times may constitute a source of strain. Most usually, however, relationships between children and their fathers take the form of bonds of affection rather than those of authority.

The degree to which the authority of male members of a matrilineal descent group is localized or dispersed is, in large part, a function of rules of postmarital residence. In matrilineally organized societies, post-marital residence is variable. It normally includes a period of bride service, during which time a potential male spouse resides in the household of his bride to be. During this time, he provides a source of economic assistance to the female's family, and both he and the potential wife are mutually evaluated as having achieved the skills and maturity necessary for marriage. Bride service may terminate with the birth of one or two children or may persist, in which case the residence is termed "avunculocality." Other forms of postmarital residence include a young married couple living in the household of the husband's father (referred to as "patrilocality") or with his family in general ("virilocality"). If the young married couple continue to reside with the wife's mother, this is technically referred to as "matrilocality" (or with the wife's family, "uxorilocality"). Lastly, and rarely in nonwestern societies, a newly married couple might establish residence apart from both families. This latter form of postmarital residence, considered the norm in middle American society, is referred to as "neolocality."

AS AN INLAND DENA'INA, WHO ARE MY KIN?

It was noted by Osgood in the 1930s (Osgood 1976 [1937]) that the people whom he referred to as "Tanaina," living on the coast of Cook Inlet, reckoned kinship bonds matrilineally. However, he concluded that early Russian and, later, American contact notably had eroded this system by the time of his research. Since Osgood had not conducted inquiries directly with those people referred to in this context as the "inland Dena'ina," he made negligible specific reference to the historic communities of Kijik, Telaquana, Qeghnilen, and Mulchatna.

In the 1960s, Townsend (1965) commenced initially archaeological and, later, ethnographic research focused on cultural change among the Iliamna Dena'ina of Pedro Bay and surrounding areas. Therefore, three decades after Osgood, she became the first to systematically document and assess principles of social organization and cultural and social change among a Dena'ina population more proximal to those of Lake Clark and the Stony and Mulchatna river drainages.

Based on research in the 1960s, Townsend (1970b:85) made the following assessment of pan-Dena'ina social organization of the precontact period:

> *In aboriginal times it is probable that the Tanaina society was composed of at least eleven matrilineal sibs [clans] divided into two moieties [a dual division of society into two segments composed of multiple, related clans]. One function of a moiety was at the time of a death. The members of one moiety prepared the body and did other necessary jobs for the opposing moiety. Richardson (1851:406), who described the sibs and moieties in the first half of the nineteenth century, also remarked that a child belonged to the "race" (sib) of the mother. It is very doubtful that a sib organization of the magnitude described could have developed only during the first fifty years of Russian contact. Portlock (1789:113), at the time of very early contact, noted that the Indians wore red and black face paint. Osgood (1937:53) identified red and black face paint as sib markings. Further, matrilineal sibs are known from other Na-dene peoples of southern Alaska . . . including the Tlingit.*

Residence patterns are particularly unclear from aboriginal times. Folk tales from my informants suggest that residence was matrilocal or possibly bilocal. Matrilocality appears to have been more of a tendency than a hard-and-fast rule. Davydov (1812:148), who observed the Tanaina before much change from Russian influence could have occurred, stated that a boy went to a girl's home and presented her parents with a gift. He then slept with the girl. If the girl wanted to stay with her parents, she and her husband would build an addition to the girl's parents' house and assist them.

It can be concluded from the above quotation that Townsend (1970b) found early and oral historic data and ethnographic analogy to be evidence for tentatively reconstructing a precontact, pan-Dena'ina kinship system. She paid negligible attention to regional variation among the Dena'ina, comparative Athabaskan data, or to problems in ethnohistoric methodology in arriving at conclusions.

Townsend (1970b:86-87) went on to assess the impact of fur trade and more contemporary cultural contacts on patterns of Dena'ina social organization:

Matrilineal sibs continued to function through the nineteenth century. Osgood (1937) provides considerable information on them, and my informants recalled some aspects of them. Until 1850, inheritance still tended to be matrilineal (Richardson 1851:406), but in the final half of the nineteenth century, apparently a shift began. Osgood (1937:141, 143) had conflicting evidence. Some informants maintained that inheritance was from parent to child. However, subtle evidence suggested that property was owned by the matrilineal sibs. Evidences from other sources (Learnard 1900:667) suggest that by the end of the nineteenth century some property began to be passed from father to son.

Another indication of social organization in a state of change was the uncle-nephew relationship. The uncle still assisted in the training of the boy, but it no longer had to be the mother's brother; an uncle from either the father's or mother's side of the family could be in charge. . . .

In the last half of the nineteenth century, the residence patterns and the way of obtaining a wife were also shifting. About 1850, bride service was performed for a year. Then it was said that a boy could return "home" with his bride (Richardson 1851:406-407). It is not certain whether "home" referred to patrilocal or neolo-

cal residence [residence apart from the family of both husband and wife]. . . . A boy had to accumulate property and experience before he could acquire a wife, and he might be as old as thirty before this was possible. . . .

This perceived trend toward the erosion of matrilineal kinship and other associated features of the social and ideological systems of the Iliamna group was extended by Townsend (1970b) to the entirety of the population speaking the language identified as "Tanaina" and was postulated to have continued full force into the 1960s. She concluded that after 1900:

Sibs have become progressively less important. They may still function occasionally at a death and marriage tends to respect sib exogamy. . . . A wife is obtained in ways similar to those of Western civilization. . . . Residence has become neolocal, although the couple may live in the village of one or both sets of parents. House structures began to be single family dwellings after 1900 and remain such today (Townsend 1970b:89-90).

Data on kinship and descent, collected from Lake Clark and Stony River Dena'ina during the 1980s, were at variance with many of Townsend's interpretations and inferences about a pan-Dena'ina indigenous kinship system and its changes through time. The overgeneralizations of her data on Dena'ina social organization, in part, resulted from inadequate recognition of Dena'ina regional variation. Townsend (1965) not only included coastal data (Osgood 1976 [1937]) in arriving at conclusions, but, in much later years (1981), she continued to refer to the Dena'ina of Lake Iliamna, Lake Clark, and the Mulchatna and Stony river drainages as members of the same "society."

Lastly, however, is the nagging concern that Townsend (1965) may have been postulating a too rapid rate or simplistic a model of cultural change, acculturation, or assimilation, particularly regarding fundamental principles of social organization. Her conclusions seemingly predicted or assumed the total demise of matrilineal descent and associated features of Dena'ina society and culture by a time in the not too distant future from the perspective of the 1960s. Townsend (1965) failed to consider the basically conservative nature of those aspects of social structure, ideology, and language, that form the core of society, in the formulation of her conclusions (Keesing 1975).

Figure 39 (above).   (left to right) Katie Trefon, Ida Carlson, Agnes Trefon, Ben Trefon, Charlie Trefon, Pete Trefon, and the Trefon family's sled dog, Suzy. This photograph was taken at Mary Ann Trefon's log cabin at Tanalian Point in 1928. *Photograph Courtesy of Agnes Cusma.*   **Figure 40** (below). (left to right) George Evan Wassillie, Albert Cusma Wassillie, (slightly behind) Nicholai Kolyaha, and Agrafina Kolyaha. This photograph was taken beside Nicholai's cabin at Old Nondalton in 1939. *Photograph Courtesy of Albert Wassillie.*

What insights do the inland Dena'ina of the 1980s and the historic period shed on questions of matrilineal organization among northern Athabaskans and, more broadly, post-contact hunters and gatherers? From the perspectives of both normative behavior and ideology, principles of matrilineal descent and related social institutions were alive and well and firmly grounded in inland Dena'ina cultural traditions of the 1980s.

In the 1980s, the inland Dena'ina residing in Nondalton and Lime Village recognized affiliation with one of eight named matrilineal clans. These clans included *nuhzhi* (translated into English as meaning the "clean" or "neat" clan), *qqahyi* ("raven" clan), *k'kali* ("fishtail" clan), *yusdi gulchina* ("end of the point" clan), *q'atl'anht'an* ("head of the lake" clan), *tulchina* ("water" clan), *kukuht'an* ("downriver" clan), and *chishlaht'an* ("independent" or "paint" clan) (J. Kari 1977). In all cases, clan membership was derived from one's natural or social mother. All adults with whom clan affiliation was discussed knew not only the clan to which they and their parents and siblings belonged but also those of most other members of the community. Adults frequently critiqued the level of knowledge of clan affiliation and appropriate behavior mastered by individuals in their late teens or younger. However, considerable insights into the functional features of this matrilineal descent system were revealed by more youthful members of society. Such knowledge was expressed particularly in the context of ceremonies, courtship and marriage, behavior associated with structured reciprocal relationships between individuals, deference to particular people, patterns of economic exchange, the use of appropriate kin terminology, and many other facets of everyday life.

Elders in the 1980s reported that the *nuhzhi, qqahyi, k'kali,* and *yusdi gulchina* clans were more closely related to one another than they were to the *q'atl'anht'an, tulchina, kukuht'an,* and *chishlaht'an* clans, the latter four of which formed a similarly connected group. Inland Dena'ina oral history refers to a connection between *nuhzhi, qqahyi, k'kali,* and *yusdi gulchina,* derived from the names of female children born sequentially to the same mother. The descendants of these children eventually formed a single group of clans perceived to be the "opposite" of the second four clans presented above. Although elder informants could not remember whether or not these two clan groupings were specifically named, patterns of reciprocal relationships, and widespread reference in English on the part of the inland Dena'ina to some clans being the "opposite" of others, suggest the existence of moieties in the recent past (cf, Guédon 1974). Additionally, residents of the area verbalized ideal principles of both clan and moiety exogamy.

While all eight clans were easily identified by most inland Dena'ina in the 1980s, one, *k'kali,* was defunct in Nondalton and another, *yusdi gulchina,* had only a single surviving male representative. Additionally, *chishlaht'an* had one male and three female members in the 1980s. As Guédon (1974) observed among the Upper Tanana, clans were not immutable. The matrilineal kinship system was flexible enough to accommodate, through time, demographic imbalance between the membership of different clans and moieties. Therefore, it is expected that some of the eight reciprocal clans recorded in the 1980s may have been replacements for others which had previously become defunct. However, information on clan succession was not provided by Nondalton residents in the 1980s.

In the 1980s, other mechanisms were employed by the inland Dena'ina to assure the continued viability of waning clans. For example, several non-Dena'ina inmarried females were adopted, with appropriate ceremonial behaviors, into clans considered opposite those of their husbands. Such adoptions were explained as being essential in order to assure that the offspring of such unions would have affiliation with a descent group, therefore being fully functional in inland Dena'ina society. Concern was expressed on the part of elders that arrangements be made for the clan adoption of all inmarried females residing in the community and for some males, although the urgency of incorporating husbands from outside inland Dena'ina society was obviously not as great a priority.

Figure 41 and Table 4 present, diagrammatically and descriptively, respectively, the kinship terminological system of the inland Dena'ina in the 1980s. Based on cousin terminology, this system is described by anthropologists as a relatively rare variant of what is referred to as the "Crow system." For those people most familiar with the kinship terminology typical of western European and nonindigenous American societies, this system for naming one's relatives may seem difficult to comprehend and somewhat exotic.

Anthropologists have attempted to establish direct connections between types of kinship terminology and the social organization of society, but, for the most part, the relationships have proven to be elusive. Debates regarding this topic are of limited utility in this context. However, it is important to present information about the terminology by which kin refer to each other, since there are normally reciprocal behavioral expectations between individuals who stand in a particular relationship to one another.

Anthropologists distinguish between "descriptive" and "classificatory" kinship terminological systems. As defined, "descriptive" systems distinguish between lineal relatives (such as, grandmother, father, mother, and son) and those considered collaterals (such as, father's brother, mother's sister, or the offspring of either). By way of contrast, "classificatory" systems include some lineal and collateral kin within the same kinship categories. For example, the inland Dena'ina refer to father and father's brother by the same term, *dada*. In American kinship terms, there is a distinction made between the term for "father" and that for his brother ("uncle"). However, Americans normally lump together father's brothers, mother's brothers, and the husbands of father's and mother's sisters as "uncles" as well. The inland Dena'ina do not. There is no indication that any one of the many terminological systems documented in the world is any better or more "advanced" than any other.

Members of many non-western societies employ "classificatory kinship terminologies." The distinction between descriptive and classificatory kinship terminologies is often confused with the inability of members of particular groups to distinguish between the biological ties of individuals who share the same kinship term. Such is not the case. For example, in the American kinship system, mother's sisters', mother's brothers', father's sisters' and father's brothers' children are all termed "cousins," without any distinction being made between the sex and relationship of the parents of such "cousins" to ego or to his or her parents. In this case, genealogically distinct relatives are lumped together under a single term and perceived to be somewhat equal in their relationship to ego. The clumping of all cousins into a single category does not imply that Americans lack the ability to distinguish between the sex of these relatives or that of their parents' siblings. By the same token, the Dena'ina use of the term *dada* for their father, their father's brother, and several other male relatives, both

consanguineal (relatives by "blood" or biology) and affinal (relatives by marriage), and of different generations, does not suggest their naivete or ignorance of the western "facts" of procreation. Importantly, then, in all of these examples, the kinship terminological system reflects the nature of reciprocal social relationships within a group and the expected, related behavioral norms (Keesing 1975). Reference to Figure 41 and Table 4, at various points in this discussion, will clarify the issues discussed in relationship to the inland Dena'ina.

What makes the Crow system so difficult to comprehend and strange looking from a western perspective is the fact that, if you look at mother's brother and father's sister and their descendants in Figure 41 (and Table 4), you see that relatives who are in different genealogical generations are classed together. That is, there is "cross-generational equivalence" or "generational skewing." Examples from the inland Dena'ina system include the terminological equating of a woman's brother and her son or a father's sister and her daughter in kinship reckoning.

Crow kinship terminological systems are commonly, although not solely, found in societies which determine descent matrilineally. One explanation for this seemingly peculiar cross-generational skewing is that the terminology differentiates between relatives who are members of ego's clan and those who are not — the latter category being the only socially acceptable group into which ego can marry because of principles of descent group exogamy. Examples from the inland Dena'ina system include the fact that ego, his mother, his mother's sister and brother, and the children of his mother's sister are all members of the same clan. Conversely, ego's father and his sister and brother are of a different clan than that of ego. Therefore, because descent is determined through females, ego's father's sister's children, for example, are never of the same clan as ego and were preferred marriage partners in the past, and, to some degree, more contemporarily. Again, conversely, father's brother's children take the clan of their mother rather than their father so may be of the same clan as ego. The fact that father's brother's children are called "brother" and "sister" by ego suggests that they may be of the same clan — a distinct possibility based on what is known about clan reciprocity in inland Dena'ina society. The important point from the perspective of the inland Dena'ina is that principles of descent (i.e., clan affiliation)

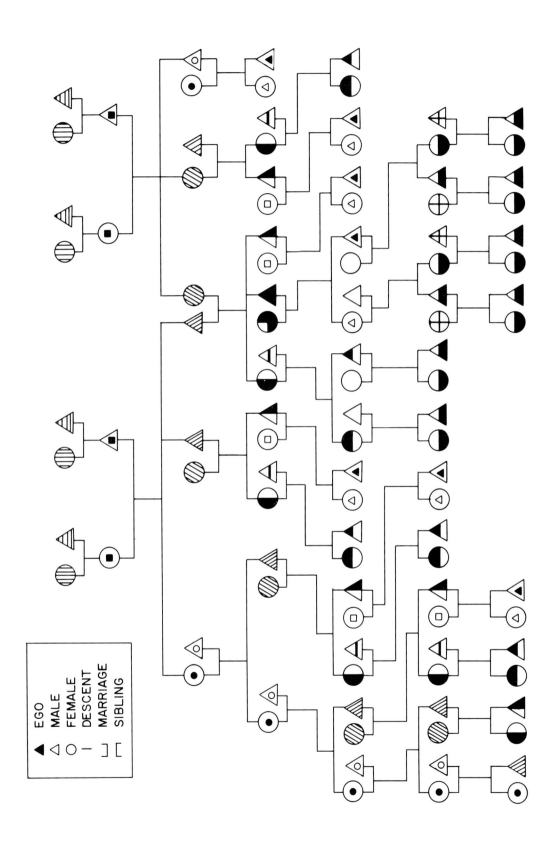

Figure 41. Inland Dena'ina kinship relationships in 1987. The terminology associated with each category of kin is described with the appropriate kinship term and narrative in Table 4.

TABLE 4. NONDALTON KINSHIP TERMINOLOGY, 1987[a]

Dena'ina Kin Term	English Equivalent[b]
N/A	ego
udla	older Z; MZ's, FB's, FZS's, FZDS's, FZDDS's daughters (if older)
daja	younger Z; same relatives specified for *udla* (if younger)
ala	older B; MZ's, FB's, FZS's, FZDS's, and FZDDS's sons (if older)
kela	younger B; same relatives specified for *ala* (if younger)
shełkugheduna	my "really" or "blood" B or Z
'u	wife
ena	M; MZ; FB's, FZS's, FZDS's, and FZDDS's wife (wives)
shunda	my M (term of reference, applies to all *ena* specified above)
dada	F; FB; MZH; FZ's, FZD's, FZDD's, and FZDDD's sons
shtuda	my F (term of reference, applies to appropriate males of the same generation as F)
tutda	F (as distinguished from *shtuda* or "my father"), FZ's sons (applied to classificatory fathers of the same or younger generation than ego)
zhala	MB; FZ's, FZD's, FZDD's, FZDDD's, and FZDD's husband(s)
shezh'a	my MB (term of reference, applies to all *zhala* specified above)
vach'ala	FZ, FZ's, FZD's, FZDD's, and FZDDD's daughters; MB's wife (wives)
ey'a	S; B's, MB's, MZS's, FBS's, FZSS's, and FZDSS's sons
shey'a	my S (term of reference, applies to all *ey'a* specified above)
tsa'a	D; B's, MB's, MZS's, FBS's, FZSS's, and FZDSS's daughters
shtsa'a	my D (term of reference, applies to all *tsa'a* specified above)
uzha	ZS and ZD; FBD's and MZD's sons and daughters; FZSD's and FZDSD's sons and daughters
shuzha	my sister's sons and daughters (this term applies to all *uzha* specified above)
chida	MM; FM (can apply to other females of the same generation)
chada	MF; FF (can apply to other males of the same generation)

TABLE 4. CONTINUED

Dena'ina Kin Term	English Equivalent[b]
neɬeghyeh chida	MM's, MF's, FM's, and FF's mother (often termed "great great" in English; can apply to other females of the same generation)
neɬeghyeh chada	MM's, MF's, FM's and FF's father (often termed "great great"; can apply to other males of the same generation)
kuya	S's, D's, BS's, BD's, ZS's, ZD's, sons and daughters (all members of the next descending generation)
shkuya	my "grandchildren" and "great grandchildren" (applies to all *kuya* specified above)
shgguya	my "baby" (an alternate term for females related to ego as Z's daughter; a pseudo-kin term
gha or shgha	man's or woman's sisters-in-law the second version is "my sisters-in-law"), a term used if there is no other more appropriate term (such a woman actually may be a man's *vach'ala* or preferred marriage partner)
ɬen or shɬen	man's or woman's brothers-in-law (the second version is "my brothers-in-law"), a term used if there is no other more appropriate term (such a man actually may be a woman's brother's son)

a   These data were gathered by the authors throughout the course of the research and, more systematically, from Sophie Austin and Albert Wassillie in January 1987. They were recorded using the Dena'ina orthography of the Alaska Native Language Center (J. Kari 1977) by Albert Wassillie. They were used to diagram the kinship terminological system presented in Figure 41. For some categories of relatives, terms of reference are distinguished from terms of address. All terms were elicited from the point of view of a male ego.

b   The symbols used in the table are as follows: F = father, M = mother, B = brother, Z = sister, S = son, and D = daughter.

seemingly take precedence over principles of generational equivalence, thereby resulting in the skewing of generations in kinship terminology.

There is a greater emphasis on generational equivalence among the inland Dena'ina in the case of terms applied to the second and third ascending and descending generations — grandparents and great-grandparents and grandchildren and great-grandchildren, respectively. As is illustrated in Figure 41 and described in Table 4, grandparents and great-grandparents are distinguished only by sex but not by descent affiliation. Terms for both grandmother and grandfather (*chida* and *chada*, respectively), with common use of the English equivalent "great great" for great-grandparents of either sex, illustrate this point. At the level of grandchildren and great-grandchildren, there is no distinction made by either sex or generation from the perspective of ego — that is, all are called

by the same term, *kuya*. The simplification of this terminological system at more distant generational levels may be explained in several ways. For example, elders normally are held in esteem despite their clan affiliation. Secondly, in cases in which more traditional, prescribed Dena'ina marriage practices were followed, ties between ego and his or her grandparents might be simplified by the use of terms distinguished only by sex. Lastly, fewer people survive across this number of generations, therefore diminishing their involvement in the more mundane day-to-day issues of clan affairs and accentuating their responsibilities to the community at large.

Systems of kinship terminology are difficult to understand in isolation. Therefore, for these purposes, the inland Dena'ina system is considered in the context of marriage, the rearing of children, and clan reciprocity. Since the ideological basis of the terminological system is expressed in perceptions and behaviors, a discussion of these topics demonstrates the social and cultural significance of particular categories of kin.

MARRIAGE AND RESIDENCE: WHAT OUR ELDERS SAY

Marriage in inland Dena'ina society historically, and, to a lesser degree, in the 1980s, was perceived principally to be a union between opposite clans and extended families rather than a bond solely between individuals. In the collective memory of elders in Nondalton and Lime Village, marriages were arranged by appropriate adult members of each kinship group and ideally were not perceived to be a matter of individual preference. Although there was certainly more overt individual choice in the selection of mates in the 1980s, the parameters within which a young adult could make a socially acceptable selection remained clearly delineated in a more covert fashion. Additionally, those who offended important principles were ridiculed publicly via the medium of gossip and, in more serious cases, were subjected to overt and covert ostracism. Failures of marital unions and misfortunes affecting both a married couple and their children most frequently were attributed to the inappropriate choice of partners.

According to oral historic accounts, traditional marriages were marked by a period of bride service and coresidence, rather than by ceremonial recognition. Although bride service endured into the 1980s, Russian Orthodox clergy encouraged church sanctioning of marital unions among the inland Dena'ina since the early 1800s. In the 1980s, many young people recognized the significance of and their ultimate desire for a ceremonial wedding within the Russian Orthodox church and were keenly aware of clerical disapproval of premarital coresidence. Nonetheless, the practice of coresidence as an expression of bride service and as a means of ensuring success of the union persisted.

There were several significant rules which governed inland Dena'ina mate selection and marriage. The most noteworthy of these was the principle of clan exogamy. That is, marriage between members of the same clan was opposed and failed to receive full family and community sanction.

Of 202 inland Dena'ina marriages recorded for nearly the past two centuries, clan affiliation of both spouses was identified in 102 cases. Of these, eight were clan endogamous. Half of the marriages which violated the principle of clan exogamy were contemporary (i.e., occurring within the past four decades). Of these, two were explained as resulting from inadequate knowledge of the system on the part of younger people, who had received a formal western education outside of the community. In the third case, cultural norms were violated but not without critique and regret. In the fourth case, those involved voiced a conscious intent to violate rules of clan exogamy in an effort to cast off traditions in favor of the rules of "modern," non-Dena'ina society. All cases were viewed as tempting potential family misfortune or contributing to probable marital disfunction or failure.

While marriages to non-Dena'ina occurred in the minority in the 1980s and, in part, were sanctioned, such unions were not perceived to be ideal. The formal adoption of spouses from outside the community was intended to operationalize the marriage within Dena'ina society. Multiple cases of marital dissolution were attributed publicly to the fact that one of the spouses in each couple was not Dena'ina. Such unions, which had sustained through time, were neither overtly opposed nor enthusiastically endorsed.

According to elders, not only was a proper, early post-contact, Dena'ina marriage outside of one's clan but also specifically between a man and his father's sister or, more commonly, with this woman's female descendants, related to ego as *vach'ala* (Figure 41 and Table 4). In this way, principles of clan exogamy were assured, as father's sister and her female descendants were ideally never of the same clan as ego. Additionally, if a man were to arrange a marriage between his son and his sister or, more practically, his sister's daughter, then he was able to consolidate affinal ties with his genealogical son. That is, since children belonged to their mother's clan, this may have been the only avenue by which a man could bring about the effective unification of influence and wealth involving his own conjugal family and that of his own clan.

The Russian Orthodox church adamantly opposed marriage between individuals viewed as either "first" or "second" cousins from the perspective of western kinship terminology. Unquestionably, the heavy pressure put upon the inland Dena'ina by clergy of the church may have altered this practice substantially during the nearly 200 years of both sporadic and more sustained interface. However, despite the influence of the church, it is significant to note that 29 percent of males born in the 1950s married women related to them as *vach'ala.* The persistence of this marital practice into recent decades suggests the tenacity of inland Dena'ina cultural norms in the face of long-term, continuous, and intense opposition on the part of Euroamerican individuals and institutions.

The likely early post-contact organization of inland Dena'ina clans into two, reciprocal halves or moieties (Osgood 1976 [1937]; von Wrangell 1980 [1839]), influenced marriage patterns as well. Although names of these social units were not identified by von Wrangell (1980 [1839]), Osgood (1976 [1937]), or the authors, as they were for other Athabaskans such as the Upper Tanana (Guédon 1974), in the 1980s it was commonly stated that proper marriages occurred only between members of "opposite" clans.

An analysis of marriages suggests that if moietal exogamy existed in inland Dena'ina society, this rule was possibly eroding within the historic period. By 1900, some people were marrying members of what is now described as the "same" as opposed to the "opposite" side, while still maintaining principles of clan exogamy. Of the 102 marriages described above, in which clan affiliation was determined for both spouses, approximately 21 percent were moiety endogamous. That is, in these cases marriages occurred within, rather than outside of, the group of clans considered to be most closely related to one another. Conversely, the fact that 79 percent of these marriages were between clans of "opposite" sides provides evidence that principles of moiety-like social organization were still functioning. If such were not the case, one would expect marriage between clans of the "same" side and between those of "opposite" sides to be approximately equal. Additionally, since both Guédon (1974) and Fall (1987) noted historic clan shifts among the Upper Tanana and upper Cook Inlet Dena'ina, respectively, it is possible that the violation of what appears to be moiety exogamy at the beginning of the 1900s may reflect incomplete clan data for the inland Dena'ina for that period of time. In analyzing adherence to ideal rules of either clan or moiety exogamy, nonconformance may have been practical and necessary responses to epidemic diseases and associated population reductions rather than the disintegration of traditional cultural principles.

Other features of marriage were described by elders but no longer overtly exercised. Changes in these traditional marriage practices occurred principally because of the influences of the Russian Orthodox church, teachers, and overall western Christian morality and ideology, thrust upon the inland Dena'ina by a host of outsiders. For example, traditional inland Dena'ina marriage conventions included the practices of polygyny (i.e., the marriage of one man to two or more women simultaneously); more rarely, polyandry (i.e., the marriage of one woman to two or more men simultaneously); the sororate and levirate (i.e., the marriage of a widow or widower to a classificatory sister or brother of the deceased spouse, respectively); and the relatively young ages of brides at first marriage. It was widely known by inland Dena'ina in the 1980s that, in the past, men who were good hunters and relatively wealthy frequently had more than one wife. Often multiple wives were sisters, a practice referred to as sororal polygyny. Sisters were considered to be more compatible and productive as cowives, since they were of the same lineage or clan and had worked cooperatively throughout their younger years. Overt or formalized polygyny was not only discouraged by western agents of cultural change but also made illegal by territorial and, later, state and federal laws. Mutually approved conjugal-like relationships between unmarried and/or married individuals, who were not formally spouses, existed for temporary periods of time at seasonal camps or during movements from one site to another.

Both formalized and non-formalized cases of the sororate and levirate occurred well into this century and generally were not considered in the 1980s to violate principles of introduced Christian morality. In fact, the effectiveness of this marriage practice in maintaining the reciprocal relationships between different clans was both recognized and highly valued in recent years, as in the past. Such arrangements were seen to be in the best interests of children, since a mother's sister and father's brother, in the Dena'ina kinship system, already were perceived to be social parents. Therefore, it was expected that they would care for the offspring of their siblings with the same devotion, concern, and responsibility as did "natural" parents. This ideology was also reflected in adoption patterns.

Lastly, within the collective memory of elders, it was not uncommon for women to marry and have children shortly after puberty. One woman poignantly recalled being sent from her home village at the age of 11 to live with a sister, who had married into another inland Dena'ina community, in preparation for an arranged marriage. Figure 25 demonstrates that the age of women at the birth of their first child had markedly increased in recent decades. Since the birth of children was associated with Dena'ina conceptions of "marriage," this information suggests younger ages of matrimony in earlier years as compared with those of more recent decades. In part this trend was related to greater participation of the inland Dena'ina in institutional, non-local, western education, particularly at the secondary level. However, it is similar to a social and demographic trend which has occurred synchronically throughout rural Alaska in the last two decades.

Intermarriage between the inland Dena'ina and those of Cook Inlet and the Lake Iliamna area, though not exceedingly common, had considerable temporal depth. Throughout oral historic accounts, the theme of three Tyonek sisters, who married into the Stony River and Lake Clark areas, persisted. In the 1980s, these women were described as the ancestresses of many members of the contemporary population.

Early inland Dena'ina marriages with Tyonek and Lake Iliamna Dena'ina are attributed by elders to contact resulting principally from trade at Russian American Company and, later, Alaska Commercial Company facilities in these areas. It was common among the Canadian Athabaskan Tagish, Tahltan, and Tutchone, inland Tlingit, and Ahtna Athabaskans to arrange marriages for their daughters inland in order to facilitate trade relationships (McClellan 1987; McClellan pers. comm. 1990). It is likely that similar strategies existed between the inland and coastal Dena'ina.

More recently, spouses who have come from the Iliamna area frequently were regarded as more distantly related to others in the community than inland Dena'ina were to one another. In times of social conflict, commonly they were perceived to be the sources of problems and the focus of gossip. However, these caveats should not obscure the fact that many inland Dena'ina saw Iliamna and Cook Inlet cultural and linguistic relatives to be both friends and kin, particularly when compared to non-Dena'ina. Such perceptions can be understood as increasingly more distant rings of concentric circles representing kinship and other social and economic bonds.

Marriage to non-Natives or non-Athabaskans, although also not common, had considerable temporal depth. For example, during the early 1900s, a few prospectors settled in the area and married inland Dena'ina women. Generally, these men were respected for their abilities to learn aspects of inland Dena'ina culture and language,

and, in part, they influenced the interface of Native and non-Native history. In most cases, they were not perceived to be disruptive to the local way of life. More recent examples of marriage to non-Natives, with some exceptions, also involved inmarrying males rather than females. These individuals were participant, to a greater or lesser degree, in the social and economic life of the community. For example, in the 1980s, some had assumed positions of permanent, full-time wage employment generally not highly desired by local residents or considered incompatible with other kin-based obligations (e.g., the village police officer or mayor). Others began entrepreneurial careers, such as air taxi services or retail outlets for imported goods. Since the children of such unions were perceived to be members of their mothers' clans, the apparent ease in which such non-Native males were integrated into inland Dena'ina society only underscores the relatively low priority placed on genealogical paternity as opposed to kinship group affiliation.

Remarriage after the death of a spouse and divorce were not unknown among the inland Dena'ina throughout this century. The practice of the sororate and levirate remained preferential into the 1980s, although such unions were not always possible because of western prohibitions on polygyny or polyandry and out-marriage. Divorce in this context refers to the separation of a conjugal pair. The concept of "divorce" in Dena'ina society necessarily did not entail a formal, western, legal action in recent decades, although traditionally it was socially recognized by the cessation of coresidence. All cases of inland Dena'ina divorce could not be analyzed statistically for the historic period. However, the majority of those incidents occurring in approximately the past 50 years involved remarriages to individuals who were members of the same clan or "side" as that of the previous spouses. Meaningfully, in many cases remarriages involved males and females who stood in the same or similar kinship relationship to one another as did the former pairs prior to divorce. The corollary of this is that, in many cases, sequential spouses also had similar kinship statuses.

Some scholars of matrilineal descent systems have argued that clan bonds take precedence over affinal ties in societies with such organization (Keesing 1975; Schneider and Gough 1974 [1961]). Others, however, have noted that divorce is uncommon among northern Athabaskans (McClellan pers. comm. 1990; Osgood 1976:165

[1937]). It is possible that the incidence of divorce noted among the inland Dena'ina of the 1900s reflected shifting cultural norms and related behavioral correlates associated with western contact. In any event, if divorce does not break the linkages between clans, as inland Dena'ina data suggest, its practice was not incompatible with principles of clan solidarity through time. Additionally, until 1990, it was more common and socially acceptable to divorce spouses who were not inland Dena'ina than those who were.

In the case of divorces in which a conjugal pair had borne children, these offspring normally remained with their mother or mother's family. Cases in which children remained with their father or father's family generally were identified with incidents of divorce in which the mother remarried outside of inland Dena'ina society. There remained a high priority on the retention of Dena'ina children within their own society in the 1980s, both in cases of divorce or adoption.

The question of postmarital residence is complex in the case of the inland Dena'ina. As Gough (1974:545) stated, determination of residence is dependent upon the focus of discussion. That is, one may look at the residence of children in relationship to older kin, of married couples at different stages in their life cycle or at different seasons of the year, or at the minimal economically productive or independent group. Determining what unit to examine in the case of the inland Dena'ina is somewhat problematic. That is, the social composition of groups changed during the course of the annual seasonal round, through the life cycle of the conjugal and extended unit, and in conjunction with shifting patterns of mobility through time. For example, the centralization of multiple inland Dena'ina communities into a fewer number of larger villages may have obscured some patterns of residence which existed in the historic past. Participation in commercial trapping, in which males were the primary producers and used the same or longer traplines for multiple and sequential years, influenced residence patterns as well (Krech 1981). Shifts in the economic roles of males and females were influenced by many factors affecting residence, including the participation of first the former and then both in commercial fishing at Bristol Bay. A greater cultural stress on non-mobile wealth — such as log trapping cabins, permanent fish camp dwellings and associated structures, Native allotments, or other forms of individually owned property may have influenced people to be less willing to abandon such capital assets, thereby also

affecting settlement patterns. Lastly, sporadically available sources of wage labor came to play an important role in the selection of residence after marriage during particular seasons of each year and between years.

The tenacious adherence to norms of bride service resulted in initial matrilocal or uxorilocal residence in the majority of cases. In the 1980s, young couples commonly lived with the wife's parents or in a proximal separate dwelling. If they resided separately, their house often was an older structure belonging to the female's family. In either case, the potential husband and wife worked for the female's family. This period of residency normally ceased at the birth of the first or second child, depending on multiple circumstances.

Approximately 90.5 percent of the population of Nondalton and Lime Village (eliminating teachers, preachers, and shopkeepers, most of whom were temporary residents) were inland Dena'ina in the 1980s. The converse of this is that only 9.5 percent of the population were inmarried. These data suggest that the inland Dena'ina were highly endogamous as a social unit and population. Therefore, residence in one or the other of the two communities representing this society in the 1980s served the mandates of being both uxorilocal (or matrilocal) and virilocal (or patrilocal), since, for the most part, married couples were residing with both wives' and husbands' kin groups.

More meaningfully, an examination of the composition of social groups at various times of the year in relationship to productive activities reflects a residence pattern characterized by flexibility. Commercial trapping areas were generally inherited, based on principles of usufruct rights, from a man to his classificatory sons. However, trapping groups commonly were composed of brothers, their wives, and offspring; brothers-in-law, their wives, and children; fathers-in-law and sons-in-law and their families; a man's and his mother's brother and their respective immediate kin; and other combinations of relatives. An unmarried male usually was attached to a conjugal pair, one member of which was either a brother or sister. Unmarried males also formed distinct hunting parties during winter and spring trapping periods. If a man were married into inland Dena'ina society, he usually trapped with his wife's kin. Those men with more accumulated capital assets for trapping tended to pull in a greater number of kinsmen from both their own and their wives' clans.

Generally, males hunted with either classificatory brothers, their mother's brothers, or "partners." The inland Dena'ina commonly reported that some men, who were neither related nor close kin, had hunting luck together and therefore formed productive partnerships while still young. These partnerships reportedly lasted throughout a man's lifetime. Although fathers played a role in teaching young sons to hunt, productive units formed solely of an adult man, his male siblings, and father were uncommon in the accounts of elders in the 1980s. Although men often hunted in territories which had been used by their father or father's father, they seemed equally familiar with areas used by their mother's male kin and their wife's father and his male kin as well. Some hunting areas, such as those in which all sheep were taken, were used in common by virtually all male members of inland Dena'ina society based in a particular community. During fall hunting, separate camps were established for the wives and children of all males involved in a hunting group.

Salmon fishing provided a large proportion of food for both humans and their dogs. At least in the 1900s, most of the domestic fishing effort was conducted by females, older children, and older males, since young and middle-aged men generally went to Bristol Bay to commercially fish. At summer fish camps, generally a common seine net was used by multiple, smaller, related family groups. Female members of such groups also jointly processed the abundant quantities of salmon taken during summer months. The women who cooperated in summer fishing and processing were generally members of the same or related descent group. Clearly, principles of matrilocal or uxorilocal residence were primary during this period of the annual cycle. This was an important time for female kin and their children to interact in the 1980s. Interestingly, women's set net commercial fishing sites at Bristol Bay and their composition followed similar principles of social and spatial organization. Additionally, women usually conveyed set net permits to daughters, while male commercial fishermen generally transferred permits to sons or sisters' sons.

There has been considerable controversy in the anthropological literature regarding potential correlations between matrilocality and matrilineal descent and between post-marital residence and the primary mode of production (e.g., Gough 1974). Matriorganization is most commonly found in societies with an economic base of cultivation, and it is within the context of these societies that most theoretical explanations have occurred. Theories correlating mode of production and residence patterns, stressing the importance of kinship ties between those who are primary producers, shed little insight into understanding matrilocality in relationship to the composition of hunting and gathering groups.

Thus, several key themes of post-marital residence among the inland Dena'ina emerge. Flexibility of residence was more important, at least during the historic and contemporary periods, than any other single factor. Factors of Euroamerican contact may have influenced aboriginal patterns of residence. Such has been the case among some cultivators (Gough 1974). Lastly, in the inland Dena'ina case, neither patrilocality nor neolocality (common among many hunting and gathering societies worldwide) were predominant or marked residential principles. Thus, the inland Dena'ina example may enhance an understanding of relationships between variations in matrilineal organization, the composition of productive groups, and post-marital residence.

PRECIOUS COMMODITIES

Long ago, children, especially boys, when they'd start growing up, when they'd reach up to ten years old, that's when they'd start doing their exercises and training. They'd do regular physical exercise, leg strength and arm strength, also their back. They use to make themselves strong. They'd jump over poles, and also run. They use to have a pole across two trees and they use to pull themselves up with it, like a chinning bar. That's the way they'd strengthen their arms. To strengthen their backs, they use to lift one another or carry one another. That's the way they exercised their backs. For a game, to strengthen their legs, they use to do, what we nowadays call "Indian leg wrestle." When a child was small, they use to take him by one hand and pick him up and lift him right up. That's the way they'd strengthen the baby's arms. That was a normal exercise. . .

When the young children, or young boys, are doing their exercises, they didn't let them eat hot stuff, like hot soup; they didn't let them eat hot soup. Even the soup had to cool off before they could eat it. If they drank hot stuff or ate hot soup, they claimed that it would shorten their wind. Their lungs are not developed so they had to eat nothing but cold, warm food. That way, when they ran, they'd have long wind. Their breathing was stronger and better. During childhood, the boys, when they'd get old enough, before they'd grow up to be men, they'd start teaching them how to hunt, and how to go for game.

They use to teach them to use a bow and arrow and use a spear. They didn't use a regular spear for training, but they had a pole, a regular stick, a long pole with a sharp point on it. They bundled grass, straw, not too big, about as big as a ball, and they'd make a bundle out of that, and throw it at the ones that they're training. They'd throw it at them and they had to spear it as if something were coming to it. They'd spear it with this spear they had in their hands. Some of the trainees were pretty clumsy, some didn't hit the bundle of straw that they'd throw at them. For some it was natural, they'd spear that thing fast. That's how they use to train the young people to use a spear (Anton Evan, interviewed by Priscilla Kari in 1981 and translated by Andrew Balluta in 1985).

Anton Evan's account of the traditional inland Dena'ina training of young boys illustrated several important points about the value of children in this society. For this group, the most significant product of human labor was its children, in whom the emotional, social, cultural, economic, and biological future of the group rested. Oral history was one of the many means used by inland Dena'ina adults to ensure that subsequent generations were well prepared to provide for the continuity of society and tradition. Other methods included providing good models for behavior appropriate to particular sex and age cohorts, informal instruction through allowing children to assist in adult tasks, and formal guidance in particular skills, such as processing fish or hunting skills in the cases of girls and boys, respectively.

Until very recent times, education of the young was provided in the context of the domestic unit, the extended family or kin group, and the community. One older woman described how children were taught in the evenings after they had stopped playing. It was "just like school," she recalled. The children's evening tasks, such as chopping wood and feeding dogs, were supervised by adults. Afterward, many hours were devoted to recalling events of the past, providing children with a template for acting out their lives of the future.

As soon as young boys were able to dress and feed themselves and, therefore, not a burden, they were taken in boats or on sleds to accompany their fathers, elder brothers, and mother's brothers on hunting or trapping forays. At a very young age, boys were expected to learn to handle their own dogs and sled, beginning with only three or four dogs and gradually controlling a full-fledged team. Young girls learned to care for less mature children in the family, fish with nets, operate small watercraft used in tending a fishing site, deftly handle the semilunar woman's knife or *vashla* in processing meat and fish, tan the hides of moose and caribou, sew clothing, and set snares for ground squirrels. Both girls and boys gathered wood and fed dogs. So that females were not totally dependent on male provision of food and raw materials, many young girls also were taught how to use shotguns, traps, and rifles for hunting birds, large and small game, and furbearers; and for self-defense against the formidable brown bear. Most young women also knew how to handle a dog team by the time they reached adulthood. After marriage, travelling with a family required that both a husband and wife take separate sleds and teams for hauling children, supplies, and other camping necessities.

Children learned much more than the practical tasks of daily life in inland Dena'ina society. Equally as important was the acquisition of knowledge of the appropriate behaviors toward one's kin and non-kin alike. As in all human societies, the inland Dena'ina had a code of behavioral etiquette that governed relations between individuals holding particular social statuses. For example, a man and woman, who were related as brother-in-law and sister-in-law, were typically expected to maintain a warm but often raucous joking relationship, characterized by teasing with considerable sexual innuendo. Children learned that relationships with their fathers, who were not members of their descent groups, were characterized by warmth and affection and negligible or gentle discipline. In fact, older Dena'ina women say that many hesitated to remarry after the death of a husband if children were young, as it was generally believed that stepfathers normally did not treat children well unless they were the classificatory brothers of the deceased parent. It was believed that mother's brothers' role was to provide exacting instruction of their sisters' children, as the affectionate bond between father and child interfered with the strict discipline necessary for transmitting successfully skills and abilities essential to survival.

At a very early age, children learned the meaning of being a member of their mother's clan. They knew that their overall position in the community was dependent, not only on their own unique individual skills and abilities, but also on the social status of their matrilineage and clan. Children learned covertly and overtly at a very young age that individual well-being was related to the wealth, social status, and qualities of leadership represented in the membership of their descent groups. The more material goods clan members possessed, both to consume and, more importantly, give away, the higher their overall rank in relationship to members of clans of their own "side," those of the "opposite," and to society at large. Additionally, wealth and leadership were intrinsically linked. The survival and flourishing of descent groups were as dependent on the transmission of tradition regarding their origin, relationships to particular features of the human and natural world, and appropriate ethos as on more pragmatic knowledge.

Prior to the adoption of western naming practices, young children were usually referred to by kinship terms and nicknames, until such time that their actions or some event, occurring before or after their birth, provided the source of their personal name. Throughout the life cycle of the individual, they were able to acquire other "nicknames" based on events which distinguished them. For example, one highly respected man, who could walk from Miller's Creek to Telaquana along the Telaquana Trail in a single day, was given a Dena'ina name which translated into English as "one who walks fast." Conversely, features of the physical environment were often named after individuals who undertook some notable task at that particular site.

To be without children in inland Dena'ina society was to be decidedly unfortunate and possibly poor, particularly in latter years of life. Even in the 1980s, most inland Dena'ina of all ages perceived that it was difficult to imagine a condition of greater misfortune than to be left childless by an inability to reproduce, because of the untimely death of all or most of one's offspring, or by most children growing up and leaving the community. Children were considered to be the source of most happiness. To be childless was, without question, a condition of both perceived and real abnormality. Their loss was mourned more poignantly than that of any other relative.

In association with mobility, it was important that groups, responsible for domestic production, were not burdened by having too many small, helpless infants at any one point in time but adequate older children to assist in essential maintenance of the extended family. In this regard, introduced diseases exacted a heavy toll on society by bringing about high levels of infant mortality, thereby disrupting the demographic balance of the inland Dena'ina population. However, an increase in reproductive rates and a decline in infant

mortality were consequences of western medical care and centralization. During certain periods of time, there were larger conjugal families than probably was the case in the early contact past.

One way of assuring that all families had children and children had families, particularly in the case of children who were orphaned, was the mechanism of adoption. Adoption was perceived to be the generous sharing of a most important social commodity – a child. Adoption also was a mechanism for maintaining ideal demographic balance within family units. Adopted children were not isolated from their natal family, but, in fact, benefited by their close relationship to two conjugal and larger kinship groups. As in most other forms of social interaction, patterns of adoption were influenced by principles of descent and kinship. Ideally, a child's adoptive parents were of the same clans as were his or her natural parents. However, it was most important that the adoptive mother be of the same clan as the child's natural mother, ideally her classificatory sister, since such an arrangement allowed the adoptee to remain within the context of the same descent group.

In inland Dena'ina genealogical data, there were 43 recorded adoptions. Unquestionably, many more cases were not documented, as adoptive children were generally not distinguished from natural children in historical data. In the 1980s, many children spent long periods of time in households of kin other than that of their natural parents, most commonly with mother's siblings or grandparents. Of the 43 documented cases, the genealogical relationships between the child in question and the adoptive parent were identified in 20 cases. Of these 20 examples, 35 percent of the adoptive mothers stood in the relationship of mother's sister to the child. An additional 30 percent were related to the child as mother's mother, reflecting the high priority of assuring that older kin of the appropriate descent group were not left childless. In 25 percent of the documented cases, the adoptive father was a classificatory mother's brother. The remaining 10 percent included cases of the adoptive parent standing in the relationship of mother's mother's brother and mother's father's sister, both of whom were classificatory grandparents. Therefore 90 percent of documented adoptions occurred between kin of the proper descent relationship, and the other 10 percent involved grandparents, who may or may not have been members of the same clan as the child.

Adopted children were expected to learn appropriate modes of behavior within their new familial context. According to elders, children were guided in the development of appropriate personality traits, such as patience, cooperation, generosity, industriousness, and humility. Older orphans were most closely monitored in this respect, since many of their personality traits already had been formed. Adopted children suffered no diminished potential for achieving positions of high status and leadership within their adoptive families and the community at large.

Inland Dena'ina always have preferred that adoptions occur within their own society. However, they were often intimidated by well-meaning but misguided teachers, preachers, and, more recently, social workers into adopting their children into "white homes in which they would receive a better upbringing." Such perspectives formed the foundation of the assimilationist policies which dominated relationships between principally non-Natives and Natives throughout this century and earlier. Interestingly, many of the children, who were adopted outside of the community, returned as adults. Many others, however, were socially "lost." Through the 1980s, most Dena'ina believed that adoption was a family and community matter rather than the concern of state and federal agencies. Consequently, many people were reluctant to undergo formal, "legal," western adoptions. Since 1978, federal legislation restricted legal adoptions outside of American Indian "tribes." This legislation — the Indian Child Welfare Act — has been very effective in diminishing the number of children taken away from their kin and culture, since adoptees not claimed by relatives are placed in other homes within the community by "tribal" councils. There was no evidence in the 1980s that principles of inland Dena'ina adoption or the high value placed upon children eroded or were significantly modified by western contact.

AFFILIATION AND RECIPROCITY: THE SIGNIFICANCE OF THE "OPPOSITE" CLAN

Throughout this chapter, reference has been made to the reciprocal nature of relationships which existed between sets of matrilineal clans in inland Dena'ina society. Matrilineal clans crosscut socioterritorial units or bands and, as such, had corporate interests and investments. Under certain circumstances, the viability and goals of any particular clan or its lineage components potentially could have stimulated divisiveness within the larger, non-kinship based group. Alternatively, the existence of unilineal descent groups also has been viewed as bringing about social cohesion, primarily because of principles of mandatory reciprocity between kinship groups at all social levels. Examples of bonds of reciprocity are offered in defense of the thesis that, in the inland Dena'ina case, matrilineal clan organization functioned more as a source of unity than as one of divisiveness.

Because of the rule of descent group exogamy, all domestic units represented the coalition of minimally two descent groups. In inland Dena'ina society, bonds between affines were commonly characterized by mutual cooperation and emotional and economic aid related to the nature of the division of labor and the role of the conjugal family in enculturating the young. For the most part, affinal relations prevalently were characterized by mutual affection.

In times of life crises, particularly when someone died, members of the opposite clan were called upon to wash and dress the body of the deceased, make food for and clean the house of his or her family, carve the Russian Orthodox cross, and dig the grave. Violations of such obligations were considered to be a major social transgression. Examples of other important life cycle events, in which opposite clan reciprocity remained functional in the 1980s, included the birth of a child, baptism, the time and disposition of a boy's first game harvest, and adoption of an in-married spouse or child. Similarly, the inheritance of a deceased adult male did not go to his own lineage or clan relatives but rather to members of the opposite clan. Distribution of the belongings of the deceased not only included items of clothing, hunting gear, and household goods but also more valuable material possessions, such as cabins or houses. Property such as houses, cabins, boats, outboard motors, sleds, snowmachines, set nets, and trucks typically were distributed to clan members within the domestic unit. Since the recipients of the more labor or capital intensive goods were usually sons, such items were distributed to members of the opposite clan. Trapping territories were inherited in this same fashion in more recent years. The distribution of potlatch goods to members of the opposite clan was considered to be repayment for services provided to the immediate relatives of the deceased. In describing the funeral potlatch, one elder stated, "In this way, things just keep going round and round, so you can stay involved with one another — it's just a circle."

Reciprocity established bonds beyond the level of the conjugal or extended family, localized descent group, and settlement. Large scale technology used for production — such as fish traps, caribou fences, or corrals, camp dwellings and caches, and, in more recent years, seine nets — were "owned" by particular individuals and thereby accessible to members of that person's descent group. They also were shared with members of opposite clans by means of alternating periods of use. Additionally, since the yield of an extended family was shared with kin of all clans represented in the unit of production, distribution systems were also reciprocal in much the same sense. Potlatch invitations were offered to people from throughout the community of the deceased as well as residents of other settlements. Age and kinship affiliation were important determinants of the relative value of gifts given at the potlatch and the order in which food and material wealth were distributed. However, all who attended were recipients of both favored foods and other presents. In cases of community carnivals, dog races, or fund-raising events in the 1980s, both clan unity and reciprocal obligations were evident in the distribution of labor within and between years.

Within the inland Dena'ina "society," the clan system was shared and reciprocal relationships respected. Therefore, marriage, the distribution of goods, trade, ceremonial events, adoption, and many other benefits of same clan affiliation crosscut settlement boundaries. In the 1980s, this phenomenon was notably apparent between residents of Lime Village and Nondalton and between members of both of these communities and transient inland Dena'ina periodically located in the Anchorage area. To a more limited degree, the contemporary Dena'ina of the Lake Iliamna area and Tyonek, Eklutna, and the Kenai Peninsula on the coast of Cook Inlet participated in this system (Fall 1987; Townsend 1965).

KINSMEN AND COUNTRY

Helm (1965; 1985), based on her research among the Dene (Athabaskans) of northwestern Canada, made a memorable contribution to the study of northern and worldwide hunter and gatherer social organization by her introduction of the concepts of the "local band" and "regional band." Employing measures of size, duration, and the percentage of primary ties, and settlement pattern, "the local band" was described as follows:

> *The local or linked-family band tends to form from or around a nuclear family set — a set of adult siblings, with the father and his wife, if living, included in the constellation. One male of the sibling set or the father of the set may be clearly the dominant figure. . . . The ethnographic evidence available suggests that it is often the sentiment of primary consanguine solidarity, especially when focused about one dominant figure, that precipitates the formation of the linked-family band as a territorially and socially distinct entity, holds the band together through time, and serves as a point of recruitment for male affines (as wives' brothers and as husbands of the females of the sibling set). Herein in the basis for the higher percentages of primary consanguinities between all conjugal pairs in recently formed local bands. . . . As the primary consanguines of the founding generation are lost through death, more cousin and other distant relationships emerge as the closely consanguine ties between living dyads. . . . The present evidence suggests that today about one dozen is the maximum number of linked families that are likely to maintain residential cohesion without the additional and, in terms of intra-Indian society, extraneous inducement of a Euro-Canadian installation such as a trading fort or school (Helm 1965:375-376).*

In the case of the local band, kinship, composed of consanguineal ties, principally through siblings, provided the connecting link for this socioterritorial unit. A local band, as defined by Helm (1965), had flexible membership and a life span limited by the longevity of connections between its members.

Within the historic period and prior to centralization, inland Dena'ina society was somewhat similarly organized but only at particular times of the year. The inland Dena'ina case differed from that of Helm (1965), in that her data were derived from a group which determined descent bilaterally. Therefore, unilineal affiliations (e.g., lineages and clans) were not structurally available to expand networks of relationships at the local level.

In contrast to the local band, Helm (1965) distinguished the "regional band" as being:

> *. . . best viewed from a different perspective than that of the local band. The local band is predicated on a set of sibling relationships which result in a physical grouping together. At the regional band level, some of the constituent members may be spatially and socially oriented as sibling clusters and with links to a*

preeminent sibling cluster. But the shared orientation of the regional band **in toto** *is to an extensive exploitative zone or territory, its biotal resources, their sites, and the routes of access (mainly waterways) to those sites . . . , which determine the stations and movements of various groupings. Traditionally, from the patterns of human ecology that the region imposed on the Indians exploiting it, the region and the people were socially defined. . . . Even in the days before extensive fort-dwelling brought about deterioration of band identity, local and regional, it does not seem that the immediate constituents of a regional band were necessarily a series of local (linked family) bands. The weight of the scanty evidence indicates that a significant portion of the Dene population lacked the minimum degree of group stabilization here attributed to the local band (376-377).*

Inland Dena'ina data conformed to Helm's (1965, 1985) view that social units larger than the local band in Athabaskan society were associated with geographically focused, largely undefended land and resource use areas. The inland Dena'ina had intensive kinship and descent relationships across local bands, which apparently did not exist in the arctic drainage Canadian case (Helm 1965). Kinship and descent played a significant role in the organization of this larger socioterritorial unit in the inland Dena'ina example and, therefore, must be included in the criteria used for identifying such groups.

Hence, in this context, the use of the term "society" for describing this larger socioterritorial unit, based on models developed for conceptualizing similarly structured Inupiaq and Yup'ik groups (Burch 1975), had more applicability than that of the "regional band" as defined by Helm (1965). That is, the "regional band" was composed of unrelated local bands, whereas the group we have referred to as the "inland Dena'ina" was not. As McKennan (1969) and Fall (1987) recognized in their treatment of data derived from the Alaskan Gwich'in and Upper Tanana, in one case, and the upper inlet Dena'ina in the other, respectively:

. . . because of the practice of unilineal descent, the structure of the Alaskan band differed somewhat from Helm's model for the Arctic drainage. . .

The regional band, then, although far from a closed unit, tended to be an intermarrying and kin-connected group, and this in turn reinforced the feeling of unity and preserved minor cultural distinctions that might develop (McKennan 1969:100, 105).

Another question related to the association of descent group and territoriality is whether or not families, lineages, or clans were perceived to be the "owners" of particular tracts of land or associated resources. The inland Dena'ina case suggested that, although there was an association between particular related local groups and residence in specific areas, there was no conception of clan "ownership" of particular resources or the locations in which they were found. According to elders, food storage areas and structures were associated with particular individuals and localized clans. However, even commercial trapping areas, which had value in western, market terms, were maintained within family groups only on the basis of usufruct rights as opposed to outright ownership. Cabins, lines, caches, and traps, as well as summer fish camps and associated paraphernalia (e.g., fish racks, fish bins, cutting tables, smokehouses, tent frames, stoves, and even, on some occasions, nets and boats) were considered available if abandoned for minimally two or three years by the related family groups who had used them in the past. Exceptions to this rule applied only under conditions in which hardships had temporarily prevented occupancy and use of the areas and/or associated technologies.

The inland Dena'ina extended the concept of kinship beyond human society to incorporate features of the natural environment in which they lived and on which they depended for sustenance. For the most part, inland Dena'ina viewed themselves as having originated from features or characteristics of the natural environment. Multiple examples from their cosmology abounded in both oral historic and contemporary accounts. Wolves were believed to have been a group of people who looked after the inland Dena'ina, sharing portions of their harvests with them. They were referred to as "brothers" and treated with great deference and respect. Brown bears were considered to be "grandfathers" of the inland Dena'ina, possessing considerable nonempirical power. A hunter wanting to take a brown bear for its hide, meat, and fat addressed the bear, saying "grandfather, my family needs your coat." The nature of relationships between Dena'ina and other phenomena was based on a kinship model. Natural phenomena included animals, plants, rocks, geographical features, and spirits. Many of the reciprocal obligations and behavioral norms expected in the case of human interactions were applied to relationships with non-human entities who shared their environment.

PERSISTENT PRINCIPLES IN A CHANGING WORLD

Despite nearly 200 years of Euroamerican contact and attempts on the part of outsiders to modify any and all aspects of kinship and descent not acceptable from a western perspective, the inland Dena'ina tenaciously have retained the core of both the ideological constructs and behavioral norms associated with these systems. Why has this been the case given the depictions and prophecies of disintegration and extinction of similar kin-based societies?

One component of an answer to this question involves the nature and methodologies of particular studies. Because the inland Dena'ina were very participant and vested in the content of this research and because they viewed kinship and descent to be at the basic core of their lives, the topical and temporal depth of these data may be more substantial than in some other ethnographic accounts. As Asch (1980) suggested, more data are necessary before sweeping generalizations regarding the demise of "traditional" social organizations can be formulated. As the history of the discipline of anthropology has proven, the balance between adequate data and theory formation is delicate and often difficult to ascertain and maintain.

The intensity and duration of contact were postulated as significant factors in the disintegration of principles and practices related to kinship and descent in other contexts (e.g., Townsend 1965). Based on this premise, the inland Dena'ina case suggested that the quality and quantity of contact experiences between this society and non-Dena'ina were minimal enough to defend early historic social organization from forces of change. If isolation, in part, were to be a useful explanation in this regard, one could point to the inland Dena'ina's maintenance of early historic seasonal settlement patterns, land and resource use, and mobility throughout the first six decades of this century. Given this premise, survival of these aspects of inland Dena'ina culture may reflect their social organizational underpinnings.

Closely related to explanations based on cultural change theory are those which postulate the diffusion of principles of social organization as a by-product of contact between two differently organized societies. As Aberle (1974 [1961]) described this kind of change in kinship and descent systems:

Matriliny, however, may spread from one society to another. If a cluster of societies of similar organization exists under virtually identical technico-environmental conditions, and if matrilineal descent groups originate in one society and spread across such a unitary area, the situation conforms fundamentally to the model of origin **ab initio** *[from the beginning] and requires no further discussion. We cannot, however, refuse to recognize the possibility that kinship forms diffuse. It is one thing to assert that peoples do not say, "Go to, now, let us borrow that pretty kinship system," and quite another to eliminate any theoretical possibility of inter-societal transmission. Kinship organization, like many other forms of social organization, represents an adaptation to the cultural as well as to the natural environment of a society. Two kinship-based societies have as one major method of articulation the development of connections between their kinship systems. Where one of these societies is dominant, or where the kinship forms of one society are highly suitable to its natural ecology, and the other society exists in a setting which permits several possible forms of kinship organization, then there may be at least a partial adoption of the forms of the first society by the second. At a minimum, those forms which tie together groups, rather than those which organize the local community, may spread. . . (660-661).*

The fact that matriliny and the importance of kinship in the organization of inland Dena'ina society remained prominent suggests that these were more functional principles of social organization than bilateral descent and the nonkinship basis of the modern and industrialized western world. In other words, in this scenario, mechanisms of diffusion were summoned to explain the otherwise inexplicable.

The view that economic and attendant cultural and social change, particularly involvement in market economies, commonly has been postulated as adequate explanation for the demise of matriorganization worldwide (Schneider and Gough 1974 [1961]). In essence, these are functional explanations for mutations and transformations of kinship and descent principles and practices. However, to discuss meaningfully the adaptability of particular social conditions, one must have substantial data regarding both the context in which they arose and functioned and, conversely, the conditions under which they have undergone change. Furthermore, such an explanation must take into account the fact that sociolinguistic data suggest that aspects of kinship and descent are relatively stable features of societal organization. Therefore, it is not adequate to assert that lack of functionality suffices as an explanation for change. Rather it must be demonstrated that conditions of dysfunctionality exist in order to apply such an interpretive model.

In summary, matrilineal descent and corporate descent groups, methods of determining one's kin and potential mates, the central role of kinship in all aspects of inland Dena'ina culture and ideology, and the functioning of reciprocal obligations were unequivocally alive and operative in inland Dena'ina society in the 1980s. These sociocultural principles also were significant in the maintenance of societal unity between residents of Nondalton and Lime Village and their transient kin in the urban setting of Anchorage. Whatever the reason for this example of cultural conservatism under conditions encouraging transition, the inland Dena'ina perceived that the maintenance of matrilineality and the kin-based nature of their society was essential to their identity and well-being as a distinct, unique, and valuable human group.

Figure 42. Agnes Cusma recalling the past from the steps of her cache during a video interview with the authors, summer 1986. *Photograph Courtesy of IMPACT, Rasmuson Library, University of Alaska Fairbanks.*

CHAPTER 6

DENA'INA PERSPECTIVE:
A WOMAN'S VIEW OF FAMILY LIFE AND MARRIAGE

BEFORE MARRIAGE

When I was born in Old Nondalton in 1921, I was given the name Agnes Trefon. By this time, the Dena'ina of this area often followed the *Gasht'ana's* practice of taking our father's last name, although some people still took their father's first name as their surname. In the old days, I would have been given a Dena'ina name, either when I was born or in the future when I became known for something which happened to me or some characteristic I had which was unusual. I also was given another English name, Mary, as a church name when baptized in the Russian Orthodox church.

I was the oldest child and, as it later turned out, the only daughter of Gabriel Trefon and Katherine Hobson Trefon. I have lived 67 years in the Lake Clark area, except for brief stays in Anchorage and, when I was younger, Iliamna. Old and new Nondalton always have been my home. In my lifetime, I have seen many changes facing Dena'ina women. I hope that if I tell you something about my family, before I was married, and my husband and children as I got older, it will help you get a better idea of what my life, and that of other Dena'ina women, have been like over the years.

My father, Gabriel Trefon, was born in 1897 in the village of Telaquana. He was the eldest of the seven surviving children of Trefon and Mary Ann Balluta. My grandparents had two other children who died as infants, but I don't think that they were older than my dad. My dad took his surname Trefon from his father's first name, a common practice when both my father and I were young. My *chada* (grandfather) Trefon was born at Telaquana, a village north of Lake Clark, in the mid 1860s. My grandmother (*chida*) Mary Ann was from the Mulchatna area. When my dad was born, he was given to his father's sister to raise, since she was childless. However, she died when my dad was only three years old, so he was raised, first in Telaquana and then at Tanalian Point, by his parents and with his sisters and brothers. As the oldest boy, he had a lot of responsibility for helping his mom and dad. After my grandpa

Trefon died, my grandma Mary Ann raised the children and provided food and other things that the family needed. My dad was a big help to her in taking care of his sisters and brothers, both before and after he was married.

In about 1901 or 1902, my grandfather and other families at Telaquana, such as the Balluta family, decided to move to the larger village of Kijik. However, the Kijik people were also moving to a new village located on Nuvendaltin Lake, because so many people were sick and had died. People in those days were afraid of what was causing the sicknesses and deaths. The priest had encouraged them to move as well. Also, everyone wanted to live closer to the trading post at Iliamna, so that they did not have to travel so far for commercial fishing at Bristol Bay. They were able to get jobs at the canneries there. However, my grandparents only stayed a short time at Kijik. Then they moved their family to Tanalian Point across Lake Clark, near where Port Alsworth and the park (NPS) headquarters are today. My grandfather knew that Tanalian was close to Kijik, where everyone went for fall fishing, and close to Telaquana, where he and his father had always hunted and trapped throughout their lives.

My grandfather also was concerned about his children having both a Dena'ina and white man's education. If he lived at Tanalian, he would be closer to Old Iliamna Village, where a school had been started in the early 1900s. My grandfather wanted my dad to go to school at Old Iliamna and live with his grandmother on his mother's side. As it turned out, my father went to school but only for one year — really only 11 months. Neither he nor my grandpa thought that life at Old Iliamna was very good. Old Iliamna was quite a big town for someone who had been born and raised in the sticks, and at that time there was quite a bit of drinking there.

Instead, my grandfather asked two white prospectors living at Tanalian, Joe Kackley and Doc Dutton, to teach his children to read and write, which they agreed to do. Although my father only went to a white man's school for one

Figure 43. (left to right) Agnes Cusma, Andrew Balluta, and Ruth Koktelash placing birch bark over an underground fish cache (*chiqilin q'a*), 1986. *Photograph Courtesy of IMPACT, Rasmuson Library, University of Alaska Fairbanks.*

year, he was very smart, even compared to educated people today. He was always willing to listen to new ideas and try new things. When he was older, he managed the Alaska Packer's store in Nondalton for 10 years. He was so good at math that when he tallied the store's money every month, he was never short. He could figure in his head. My brother Benny was like that, too. Today you can ask many people, and they still remember what a smart man my dad was. Although he was smart and always provided for us throughout his life, he was always very generous to others who were in need of help. Later on, when I was older, that is why he became chief when the other chief became disabled.

Even after my grandfather's death in about 1925, my grandmother stayed at Tanalian and raised her children there. She was a very strong woman, who not only cared for her children but helped with her grandchildren as well after her own children were grown. She was able to chop wood, haul water, plant gardens, fish, trap, and even hunt small game. I remember a lot of things about her.

My mom, Katherine, was born in approximately 1904, on the upper Stony River at Qeghnilen. Her father was Jack Hobson, a *Gasht'ana* who had come to Bristol Bay as a teenager on a sailing ship and later went up to Lake Clark. I think he was looking for gold. While he was up on the upper Stony River, he met and married my grandmother, Tatiana Constantine. She was the daughter of Gustingen and Katherine Constantine, who were the founders of Lime Village. When my grandfather met my grandma, she was a widow with two children. My grandfather Jack found it very hard to make a living on the upper Stony River, as there were no jobs or other ways to make money except for trapping. He started going to Bristol Bay each spring to commercial fish, make some money, and buy groceries and other goods at the canneries or at the trading post in Iliamna. He made the trip all the way from the upper Stony River to the bay by dog team — a very long distance. In 1914, when my mother was only about 10 years old, my grandfather finally decided that it would be easier for the family if they moved to Old Nondalton, the new village where Kijik people had settled. It was at Old Nondalton that my dad met my mother and married her in 1920.

My dad was about 24 years old and my mother 16 when they got married. They lived together at Old Nondalton for 40 years, and I really don't remember them fighting. I heard them argue and

stuff like that, but I never really saw them fighting. All married life is like that. You have got to have an argument once in a while.

I was the oldest of the two children that my mom and dad had together. My brother Ben was born in 1923. He was always very close to me until he died in 1985. After Benny was born, I don't think my mom and dad could have any more children. But they decided to adopt one other boy and they raised two more, so I had more brothers. I still was the only girl, though. The boys that they adopted or raised were all related to my mom or dad or to both. Evan Charles Trefon, whom we called Charlie, was the son of my dad's sister Agafia. Agafia died when Charlie was about four years old. In the Dena'ina way, a woman's brother has a lot of responsibility for his sisters' children. It was not surprising that dad and mom adopted Charlie. Luther Hobson was another boy they raised. His father was my mother's brother. Luther's mother died when he was an infant, so my mom and dad decided to raise him. Then there was Phillip Balluta. Phillip was Sophie's son. Sophie was my mother's sister, whom I called "mom" in the Dena'ina way. Sophie was widowed when her five children were small. We took Phillip to help her out and also, I guess, because my parents wanted more children.

Although we had a house at Old Nondalton, when the kids were young, our family hardly every stayed home in the village. We really had nothing to stay home in the village for at that time. We went from the Chulitna River or Nikabuna Lakes in the spring, where we trapped beaver and hunted muskrats, ducks, and geese, to summer fish camp on the Newhalen River. There we put up our year's supply of salmon. Then we went to Kijik on Lake Clark in the fall, where we camped in our cabin at Miller's Creek. That's where Alaska's ex-governor, Jay Hammond, lives today. The men folks got meat, especially moose and caribou, and the women picked berries and trapped squirrels. The men went after all sheep and brown bear, before fish and game people told us we couldn't hunt brown bear very often any more. Brown bear were very important for us, since we used their fat with almost everything we ate — just like *Gasht'ana*s use margarine or butter. Everyone helped get fall fish at Kijik. Then we went out on winter traplines or the men left the women and children at Miller's Creek, while they trapped along the Telaquana Trail. We all stayed out there trapping until spring camp, when it would all start again. That was our life. That is what we all did.

I remember one year — I think 1926 — when I was young and we were trapping out of Telaquana in February and March. My brother Benny and I were trapping rabbits and squirrels, while my father was running his trapline. I use to put my dad's sheepskin mittens on my feet, so that I could check my traps. That was the year Alexie Evan and Vonga Bobby came all the way from the upper Stony River in deep snow to tell us that the game warden was travelling through the country. The game warden was taking away pelts from anyone whom they suspected was trapping illegally, and everyone was afraid of them. Alexie and Vonga had come to help my dad pick up his traps so that his furs wouldn't be taken away. When Benny and I tried to get our traps out so that the game warden wouldn't get us, one of them got stuck. We couldn't get it out. Dad came up to where we were to help us. Boy, we were glad to know that the game warden was not going to get us.

In 1930, they started a school in Old Nondalton. One thing the teachers couldn't do was to keep people from getting their meat and fish. My dad, like some other people at Old Nondalton, never completely stopped travelling around the country with us kids. Whenever people wanted to take their kids out of school, they did. It was the only way we really could make a living. There wasn't the meat and fish we needed in the village. So, I guess, we didn't really stay until the end of school most of the time. In my case, I started school when I was 10 years old and went through fifth grade. Then we all thought that I had had enough white man's education.

I was the oldest of all my cousins. Actually, many of us called each other "brother" and "sister" in the Dena'ina way. Because I was the oldest, I spent much of my life baby-sitting my own brothers and the children of relatives like "mom," Aunt Sophie, who really needed help since she had no husband. Phillip always called me "mom," which use to make me mad, since I was a single girl. When I was young, we kids were sometimes left behind in the village to go to school, while my mom and dad went out in the country to get us food and other things we needed. "Mom," Aunt Sophie, sometimes watched us. Once I turned 13, I was old enough to watch the younger kids, including my aunt's kids, while she ran the mail and freight by dog team to make some money for her family. She didn't want to remarry when her children were young, because she believed that a stepfather never treated children, who were not his own, as well as did their own father.

Even though my mother and those of us who were school-age remained most of the winters in Old Nondalton, we still went with my dad to spring, summer, and fall camps. I remember going by dog team with my family to Lime Village in 1930 for the whole winter, the following spring, and summer. I was only about nine years old. That was about the first time I had worn a pair of store bought shoe packs. I walked around and around, looking at my feet and at the tracks of the shoe packs behind me. Before that, we had worn only moose and caribou skin boots, which really didn't leave tracks. I remember those shoes, because they had little buttons rather than laces and very high tops. Also, they seemed very heavy.

Anyway, that year we had gone to Lime Village to help look after my mother's parents, who were getting very old. There were no animals, like moose and caribou, that year — nothing. In the spring, we got a lot of trout. Then we went down to where they put up fish near Qeghnilen. I remember eating fish only once. The fish had come in, but the water was too high for people to put in nets or a fish wheel. There was too much wood drifting in the river. My dad went all the way down the Stony to the Kuskokwim River without an outboard motor. On the Kuskokwim River, there was a trading post, where he bought 10 dried fish. That's all we had for seven dogs and we didn't lose even one. Everyone, including our family, had to feed their dogs berries mixed with a small amount of fish stored in underground caches lined with spruce and birch bark. I don't remember how long those fish had been in the ground. They were just red, and everyone in the village got a bucket of fish to mix with berries to feed their dogs.

That fall when we went up into the mountains, my mom and the others had their hooks to fish for brook trout for our dogs. My mom also had squirrel traps. Benny and I stayed home at the camp fishing for brook trout for our dogs. We'd cut the tails off, which we sold to the fish and game guys for money. Those fish and game guys paid a bounty on trout tails until the 1940s. Then Benny and I decided to cook up the trout for our dogs. We built a fire. My mom was way up on the mountain and saw smoke coming from camp. Well, she started running down, since she couldn't holler from too far away. She fell down with her 22 rifle and cut her hand. When she got back to our camp, Benny and I had a fire going, boiling the pot of fish. We had added flour to make gravy, but we had put too much in. The bottom almost was burning by the time my mom got there. She didn't get mad at us or anything, because she knew that we were trying to get some kind of food for our dogs. My mom said, "What you guys doing." "We're cooking for our dogs," I replied. She took the pot off the fire, put some more water in, and mixed it all up. That probably was about the first time in my life I tried cooking for dogs without help. I was only nine years old that year.

My father and his father and others, such as the Balluta family, continued spending much of each winter in Telaquana well into the 1930s. Although the village had been abandoned, they built another cabin southeast of the old settlement. They used this cabin for trapping. My father also went to Telaquana for fish, especially when there weren't any in Lake Clark or the Newhalen River. Telaquana Lake drains into the Stony River, so fish come there from the Kuskokwim River rather than from Bristol Bay. There are different species of salmon at Telaquana, not just reds like we got at Kijik on Lake Clark. They fished at the head of the lake or in a bay at its outlet, where there was an old fish village. They were also able to get pike there.

I remember making my last trip to Telaquana with my father in 1934. He was going after beaver, and he and his brother Alex took two sleds for the trip. We stayed at Telaquana the entire spring, beginning in March month, and lived in tents. My dad and his brother trapped beaver from canoes in open water after the ice melted. They weren't the only ones trapping, though, because my mom and I were also trapping. We went to the beach and found a place where the beavers went for food. We set a steel trap near the place where we thought that the beavers were eating. Then we connected the trap to a burlap sack filled with rocks. We called this sack a "drowning sack." It was connected to the trap by twine or anything that was strong enough. When the beaver got trapped, he went back into the water and drowned. My mom and I knew how to use this kind of beaver trap.

That was the year we ran into some Lime Village people trapping along the Stony River as far up as they could go. There were three families, that of old Alexie Evan, the Evanoffs, and Sergei Evan. That was the last year those families went there to trap, as some moved down to Nondalton shortly after this time.

During that trip to Telaquana, my mom and I did other kinds of things as well. My mom was picking *k'tl'ila*. I don't know what they call this plant in English. *K'tl'ila* is a vine that grows in river beds

and tastes sweet. We used to boil it in water or fry it in oil. It tastes something like sweet potatoes.

My dad was always a good provider. Part of the time, he continued hunting, trapping, and fishing with his brother or with my mother after I was old enough to watch the younger children. He never stopped going up to Telaquana for trapping, as this was the area he knew best. He also worked at the store and fished at Bristol Bay. Our family never went without anything. As he got older, he stayed in the village more, especially after he became chief and had more responsibilities for other people living there. He was a good father, and I always had a lot of respect for him. However, when I got older and it was time to marry, he and I had some disagreements.

COURTSHIP AND MARRIAGE

My father was very old fashioned and believed that members of the family should choose husbands and wives for their children. This is not the way it is done today. Actually, my father was very stingy when it came to me or my brothers. He was not anxious for us to get married. Benny was 30 years old when he married Irene. I began going with Paul when I was about 16 years old, but my dad didn't want me to marry him. I finally had a chance to go out to the states with the teachers, Mr. and Mrs. Leise. They had been teaching in Nondalton since the school first opened and wanted to take me out of Alaska.

At that time, I had been going with Paul for seven years. My dad didn't seem to care for him or something. Paul had lost his mother when he was five years old. His dad, Maxim Cusma, and his dad's sister Yvdakia Karshekoff had raised him. Paul knew how to fish and build things with wood. He built sleighs, boats, or anything. Well, my dad was like other Dena'ina fathers and took Paul out hunting and trapping to see if he could support me. But my dad still didn't want me to marry Paul. Maybe it was because Paul and his dad had come from down south. People from the south were called by a Dena'ina word which translates as something like "southern people" (*Duntsiht'an* or *Dunch'ench'dna*). Maybe it was because Paul's stepmother, Daria Koktelash Balluta, didn't care for me either and had someone else picked out for him to marry. She had married Paul's father after her husband and Paul's mother had both died. Anyway, no one seemed to want us to get married.

Figure 44. Agnes Cusma, making her first visit to Telaquana since 1934, accompanied by her mother's sister, Sophie Balluta, and the authors. Since Nondalton residents usually have not travelled the Telaquana Trail in recent years, this helicopter visit to the village and fish camp sites stimulated poignant memories of the past for Agnes and Sophie. In the photograph, Agnes is holding old traps.

Finally, I told my dad, "I was 19 years old long time ago. If I don't marry that guy or something, then I'm going to go out to the states. I'm going to find somebody down there and I'll live down the states," I told him. I really wanted to go, but my dad didn't want me to leave. Here I was, staying at home without having a child, 23 years old. I guess my dad thought I wasn't supposed to have any babies. Then I went down to Iliamna for two years. I was keeping house for the people who were running the Iliamna Trading Post. They didn't have any kids. The man was running the store, and she was postmistress. Finally they had a meeting in Nondalton about Paul and I getting married. Many of the older people were there discussing the marriage. I told them that if they didn't let us get married, I would leave Nondalton and go to the states. They finally agreed that I could marry him. It's a good thing he married me. The other girl his stepmother had picked out for him died a long time ago. I used to tell Paul, "Gee, if you had married her, you would be a widower already."

In 1944, Paul and I were married at Pedro Bay, where a territorial commissioner lived. Sergei Evan also got married that same day with us. My dad and younger "brother," Aunt Sophie's son Andrew, attended the wedding. It was performed in a proper way by the commissioner. At that time, a Russian Orthodox church wedding was not considered legal. We had to get married by a commissioner and later could be married within the church. However, it was the church wedding that was important to us.

RAISING A FAMILY

It was spring when we got married, so we decided to go to lower Tazimina Lake for our honeymoon. There we trapped beaver for two weeks. That's where I had my honeymoon. This was where *chada* Maxim, Paul's father, had his camp. Beaver prices were $85 to $90 a pelt at that time. It was possible for us to make as much as a $1,000 in those days. That was big money. The limit was 10 beaver per trapper, but each family could have several trappers. The women were trappers as well as the men. We stayed up there two weeks on our honeymoon, trapping away.

After that, we spent the spring at Nikabuna Lakes, the same camp to which I had gone before I was married. Then we went to my dad and his family's fish camp. We stayed at this camp until I had my first daughter, Hilda, in 1946. Before I had had my second daughter, we had made our own fish camp at Ch'ghitalishla, where it is located today. It is on that creek which is only about one mile south of Nondalton. That is where we made the video tape of putting the fish into the bark lined pits. Then we went to Dutna Lake and a mountain north of Long Lake (Qinghuy Dghil'u) for fall hunting. I still have that camp today. Then we went with everyone else to Tuk'elah, which is the south creek of Kijik River, for catching fall fish. I still have that camp today, too. Harry Balluta and his family stayed at the same camp all fall where the little steam bath was. Harry and Paul and I built fish racks there. We filled the racks with fish. Boy, we must have been good workers. During these years, the men were hunting by boat. They had gotten lazy about packing things on their backs. They didn't go up the mountain after Dall sheep any longer. Then we went back to the village for awhile.

After I was married, I got my house where my brother's house is now (Figures 32 and 33). I never was away from my mom and dad. It was the same with my brother — we always lived close together. I don't think that my brother and I were ever separated from each other, except when we went to Bristol Bay for a month or two. Our family always stayed close together.

I had four children — three girls and one boy. My girls were Hilda, Linda, and Betty. Then I had Paul junior in 1953. He was my only boy until I adopted Willy from my father's brother Pete Trefon and his wife. I raised Willy from the time he was a small child.

When our first daughter, Hilda, was born, it was during World War II. Paul had to make her a handmade crib. She never wore shoes until she was about two years old. I had to make boots for her. My second daughter, Linda, was the first to have a crib purchased from a store. We got it from the people I had worked for in Iliamna, Art and Helen Lee.

When my adopted son, Willy, was only about three weeks old, his mother, Mary Trefon, became ill with tuberculosis and was hospitalized in Anchorage for nine months. We took care of him, because his father, Pete, was my father's brother or like a father to me in the Dena'ina way. I called him *dada*. Mary was Paul's sister. Since Pete was my *dada*, Willy was considered to be my brother. When his father came down to pick him up for lunch or in the evening after work at five, Willy just cried because he was used to us taking care of

Figure 45. Paul and Agnes Cusma's trapping cabin at the mouth of the Chilchitna River, 1949. *Photograph Courtesy of Agnes Cusma.*

Figure 46. (left to right) Paul Cusma, Jr., Betty Cusma, Linda Cusma, and Hilda Cusma, 1957. The children, standing beside their log home in Nondalton. *Photograph Courtesy of Agnes Cusma.*

him. Mary would stand outdoors rocking him, trying to get him to stop crying for me. My girls were the same. Every evening when Willy left, they'd all go upstairs and cry for the baby. Everybody was crying for the baby. The girls decided they wouldn't go to Bristol Bay in the summer if we couldn't take Willy. Finally, my *dada*, Pete, told them, "What are you going to do, stand outdoors all hours of the night just to keep him [Willy] quiet. He needs to lay down and rest."

Well, I guess Mary tried it for one whole week. But Willy wouldn't get use to his sisters or brothers or to anything. So finally *dada* came back from the store. He told his wife, "You dress that kid and you take him back where you picked him up from." That's what he told her. Mary dressed Willy. Pete said, "The baby was only 24 days old when you went to the hospital. Nine months away from him — it won't work. Even though you take him back, he'll never forget the one who's been his mother these past months." So, Pete and Mary brought him back into our house. She put him down, right at the doorway. He was crawling. Boy, he was hollering and he crawled right over to me, because he thought I was his mama. Mary felt bad, but Pete said, "We're living here right in the same village. You might as well just say you're not going to try to take him back no more." The next day I left for Egegik on Bristol Bay with everyone including the baby. We went to where I had a set net fishing site.

After we had children, Paul used to leave me in the village after November and go out into the country by himself. Sometimes I went with him during those short days to help him trap. These were the only ways we had to make a living, as times were hard. We had a little camp at the mouth of Moose Creek. Everyone of our camps had a steam bath if we spent a month or more of each year there. Every year in the late fall, my husband also went up to our cabin on the Mulchatna River to trap fox, otter, mink, and other animals for their pelts. He remained there until January, making only a couple of trips back to Nondalton during this time. In February, he brought all of us up to the cabin above the Chilchitna River for beaver trapping. We had a steam bath there and a cache. We stayed there until nearly the end of March. Then we moved to the Chulitna again for spring camp. We all looked forward to the time just before the ice would go out on the lake. It was then that the *Dutna* and all the Dena'ina of the area got together at Indian Point at the mouth of the Chulitna River, where we played games, shared our food, and gossiped. This was the time when we saw people we knew from the past and caught up on what had happened over the last year. Spring at Indian Point was a very important time for everyone — men, women, and children.

My mother's father, Jack Hobson, died in 1948. Linda, my second child, was only three days old. My grandpa baby-sat my oldest daughter. He must have died on January 19th, because I remember that we were in Mulchatna. He was pretty sick, and I was in labor with the baby. The family didn't want to worry him because of his illness, so no one told him that I was in labor. My grandpa knew that something was wrong and asked my grandma if I were sick. My grandma said that I had been feeling poorly for two days, but they hadn't wanted to tell him. After *chada* Hobson died, my grandma lived a long time. She didn't die until 1962.

In 1949, we were all up on the Mulchatna River trapping beaver in the spring. We had two dog teams to carry our family out to hunt and trap. I drove seven dogs and Paul drove nine. He carried two of the children and I carried the other. There was so much snow that year that I couldn't walk with the three kids when Paul went out to check traps. So I just stayed home in our cabin, and Paul went snowshoeing down the river.

After he had left one day, I saw a whole bunch of spruce hens by the cabin. So I went out to see if I could get them. I told the kids to watch me through the window. I had my automatic 22 rifle and just started shooting. I really didn't know when to stop. I just kept going after them. Paul heard the shooting and thought that something had happened to me or the kids. He started running back in the deep snow with his snowshoes on. Meanwhile, I looked around, and there were spruce hens laying all over the place. I didn't know what to do with all of them. So I put a dishpan in the middle of the floor and told my girls, "Come on, you guys; clean the spruce hens." They all dived into that little dishpan, while I went back out and started shooting some more. My youngest daughter, Betty, was just a baby that year. She just was sitting up and not even crawling. The other two, Hilda and Linda, were pretty much the same size. Well, my husband got to the camp and asked me what had happened. I told him that there were lots of spruce hens. I think he could have knocked my head off, because he hadn't even had time to check his traps or anything. We came in the house, where the kids were trying to pluck the spruce hens. The floor was nothing but feathers. What a sight!

My husband and I went to Bristol Bay every summer. He fished for the cannery in the days of sailing boats. Later, he became an independent fisherman and fished for 30 years. I had a set net site at South Naknek. When summer time came and the fish began to run, the entire family went to Bristol Bay. I fished the set net site every year except 1974, when there was a union fisherman's strike. That summer they closed down the fishery and, at the last minute, opened it after the fourth of July. When the limited entry system for salmon was begun in 1973, Paul received a permit. However, before he died of cancer, he was worried about me and the family being able to get along. So he sold his permit to pay off any bills and gave me enough money to live. I kept the set net site at South Naknek, although my daughter Betty has been fishing it in recent years. Two of the years we were married, I fished with my husband in a boat as well.

My dad had been a fisherman for most of his life. He didn't quit until his brother Was Trefon fell off his boat in Bristol Bay and drowned before anyone could help him. All of Was' children, who were my cousins, quit fishing as well. Because Was was my dad's brother, he was also like *dada* to me. I was really like a sister to his children. I told them that I wouldn't quit fishing. I would fish until I couldn't fish any more. I didn't care what happened. I told them that I would walk those mud flats and I did. I walked the mud flats for 20 years. However, after his brother fell overboard, my dad didn't want me to fish in the big boat any more and I didn't.

My husband became one of Nondalton's chiefs during the later years of our marriage. There had been several changes in chiefs over a short period. In 1930, our chief, Zackar Evanoff, was too old. He had to be held by the hand and led around. Then Alexie Balluta, whom we called *dada ka'a*, became chief, and my dad was second chief. Later, after my dad became chief, Nick Karshekoff was named second chief. After Nick died, my father made my husband, Paul, second chief. My husband learned about being a chief from my dad. Of course, everyone in the community had to make a decision in a meeting about who was qualified for the job of chief. The one they picked had to know what he was doing and be willing to stay with the job for a long term. Harry Balluta was the last traditional chief. After Harry became chief, it was turned over to the white man's way. A council took the place of the chief in about 1964.

I will never forget 1964. It was the year that I almost had a nervous breakdown, because that was when my father died. I remember exactly when he died. I'll never forget the hour or the minute. I only have forgotten the seconds. My brother Benny was close to my mom, but I always was devoted to my dad. For one whole year, I didn't remember anything. Nothing! I didn't even remember the holidays. My husband knew something was wrong. It was just like I was sleeping. When I woke up, I had been to Bristol Bay. I didn't even know that I was there fishing. Then it was just like I woke up. When I tried thinking back, I couldn't remember anything. If it weren't for my mom, I might have been in the "nuthouse." I had had all my kids already. It was a terrible feeling. I was close to my dad — real close. That was also the last year I travelled by dog team. That was the last time I drove the sleigh away from Mulchatna and pulled it up outside my house. I unhooked the dogs and that was it. Since then I haven't hooked up a dog again.

When my mother died, I told my husband that he had better go away with me for awhile. So we moved to Anchorage for three years. Paul worked at Elemendorf Air Force Base, where he made shipping crates. I left Nondalton because I wanted to stay away from that nervous breakdown.

My daughter Betty married a *Gasht'ana* and moved to Anchorage, where she lived with her husband and children until recently. My daughter Linda married into the Roehl family from Iliamna. Her husband is part Dena'ina, Yup'ik, and *Gasht'ana*. They lived on the Kenai Peninsula for over five years. My daughter Hilda was married with two children, but she died a few years ago. My son Junior married a Yup'ik woman from the coast. They live here in Nondalton with their six children. My husband died in 1983. I spend my time these days helping care for my grandchildren here in Nondalton or in Anchorage or Kenai when their parents are travelling. Sometimes I just go for a visit. I also spend a lot of time with "mom," Aunt Sophie, fishing with her on the ice in front of town and sometimes staying with her at her house on Lake Clark during the summer. I still put up dried fish in the summer at my fish camp near Nondalton.

In recent years, I have come to realize that there have been many changes in the Dena'ina way of life. There are lots of things that kind of make me mad too, conveniences such as running water and electricity. All I have to do is touch a switch, and it lights up the whole house. All I have to do is turn on a faucet, and I have enough water to last a day. And then there are oil stoves. Some Dena'ina really don't need to get wood any more, although many people are going back to wood because fuel oil costs so much. But when my grandma and my parents were living, we didn't do that. I had to run up to my grandma's and grandpa's house when I was a child. I filled their Coleman lantern with gas, lit it for them, then ran down to my mom's and did the same thing to get their lamp going. Then I ran back over to my house and did the same thing. My aunt forgot she had electricity when we first got it. In the evening, she waited for somebody to come in so that they would fill her Coleman lamp. She had a flashlight and found her way around the house until her husband got off work. He would come home from work, and there would be no light. He'd walk in and turn the switch on and my aunt would say, "Hey, I forgot I had electricity in here." There she was, with a flashlight in her hand, cooking. It is the same thing with water. A lot of people here forgot that they had water in their houses. They wanted to go and carry in their water. When I raised my family, it wasn't like when my parents raised us. We are taking it easy. Our parents took a beating, I think. But us, we're just sitting down and getting everything. If you want to go some place, well you jump into an airplane and take off.

The young people today, including my own children, don't like to live the way I did when I was their age. They think that work was too hard during those days. You had to run out and feed your dogs, cook for your dogs, and feed them. Young people today park their snowmachine, cover it up, and the next morning they pull the cover off and jump on it and go. But we didn't. We had to feed our dogs. In the morning we had to hook every one of them up. If you had nine dogs, then you would take all nine. That's too much for these young people. Just like the older people say today, if we had no more groceries, no more stores or airplanes, the younger peoples are the ones that would perish first. Not us, because we older people know how to live off the country for months and months if we needed and wanted to. We wouldn't starve. But not these younger people. They'd rather run to the store, into the freezer, or refrigerator. Also, we always helped older people. Not the younger people today. They usually won't help older people unless they get a dollar. You have to have dollars in your pocket for young people to do you a favor. I did that this summer. I had one kid carry wood in for me. For two armloads, he wanted a dollar. I gave him the dollar. That's the way it is now. That is why it is so important for me to tell about the history and way

of life of the past, so that the young people can learn what it was like.

A POSTSCRIPT

On August 23, 1986, NPS and the authors arranged to take Agnes Cusma and Sophie Austin by helicopter to visit the old village sites of Telaquana and Mulchatna. When we asked Agnes if she wanted to accompany us, initially she seemed hesitant. She stated, somewhat wistfully and emotionally, "When you guys ask me these questions, I start remembering the past." In thinking it through, she decided to go, because she had not been to Telaquana since the last trip with her father in 1934. Also, she had not seen the camp she shared with her husband and family on the Mulchatna River area for over two decades. In planning the trip, Agnes and Sophie began talking about where we would go and what we would take to eat. Eventually everyone had reached a peak of enthusiasm.

When we finally spotted the overgrown clearing that once was Telaquana village, Agnes and Sophie were filled with anticipation. For Agnes, seeing the village and walking among its collapsed and decaying houses evoked powerful memories of her father and the life her family had lived before they settled down in Old Nondalton. Agnes, with Sophie's help, was able to reconstruct the remains of the village in her mind, visualizing the now collapsed houses as they once stood. Empty rifle cartridges, pots, pieces of barrels, steel traps, and other debris at the old village site all stimulated an intellectual journey into the past. Agnes and Sophie spent the entire stay remembering life as they knew it then, both the good times and the bad. Agnes said that it was her belief that she would never see Telaquana again. The association of Telaquana with her father and her childhood was obviously intense.

On the other hand, from Agnes' perspective, the visit to the very obscure and difficult to locate Mulchatna village site was most meaningful, because it was located in the vicinity of her cabin on the Chilchitna River. This was a place with many memories of Paul and their children. It represented the life that they had once lived before becoming more settled at Nondalton.

It took us some time to find the village, as it once was located on the main river and now had been cut off from the primary channel by an oxbow lake. Beaver houses abounded everywhere, attesting to the wealth of this area for beaver trapping. At the

Mulchatna village site, only a depression of the lengthy, semisubterranean house and some cultural debris remained. We began to head back toward Port Alsworth. In the course of flying out, however, we accidentally but fortuitously flew over Agnes' beaver trapping camp. The cache was still standing and the site remained relatively free of vegetation. When Agnes saw the camp, she asked the pilot to return, so that she could look at the site a second time. He turned around and flew the helicopter directly over the camp. Tears came to Agnes' eyes. She was very quiet for a long time on our trip back to Port Alsworth that late afternoon in August.

Since the beginning of this research, Agnes has shared every possible memory with us, both about her own family and about the inland Dena'ina in general. Through our asking about the past, we hit upon emotions and events that had not been spoken of for many years. Yet, she willingly shared the past — the pain and the happiness, the mourning for those lost, and the humor. At the very beginning of the research for this ethnography in 1985, Agnes lost her beloved brother Benny. Near the end in 1988, when these chapters were being constructed around the stories that Agnes and many others had told us, her adopted son, Willy, and her daughter's son suffered untimely and tragic deaths in a snowmachine accident on Six-Mile Lake. To Agnes, this was not only the death of a son and grandson but the loss of the baby whom she had nurtured since he was only three weeks old, the last child to reside in her home, the young man who always had a smile for anyone, and a person who had brought years of happiness to her house.

Though to us this seemed to be more loss and pain than anyone could bear, it is not an uncommon experience for inland Dena'ina women. They frequently are faced with the unexpected and untimely loss of husbands, children, siblings, and significant others. Agnes faced this most recent misfortune with the extraordinary strength and courage characteristic of older Dena'ina women. Such strength, stoic courage, adaptability, and willingness to do whatever is necessary to provide both the necessities and qualities of life are hallmarks of older Dena'ina women. Though some of the older people are pessimistic about the abilities of younger generations to go forward in their lives with this same strength, caring, and courage, hopefully the necessary values and emotional skills have been transmitted across the generations. Younger women today are confronted, in part, by a much different set of problems. While it is true that the Dena'ina woman of the 1980s only needed to manipulate a switch for light, turn up a furnace for heat, and get on an all-terrain vehicle, snowmachine, or airplane to travel, they basically remained Dena'ina in their cultural perspectives and values.

Figure 47. Anton Balluta getting into his canvas-covered *baidarki* (*vaqilin*) in the spring, circa 1928, to hunt moose, caribou, or beaver on the Chulitna River. *Photograph Courtesy of Sophie Austin.*

CHAPTER 7

LIVING WITH THE LAND: THE INLAND DENA'INA YEAR

In fact, the wildland and the village are inseparable, at least in human terms. From the forest and waterways, Athabaskan people have drawn their physical and cultural and spiritual sustenance for millennia. Their traditional lifeway has emerged and exists in concert with the force and stimulus of the surrounding environment, in an ancient process of adaptation that continues today.

Richard Nelson, ***Raven's People***, 1986

RHYTHMS AND PATTERNS THROUGH TIME AND SPACE

Historically and contemporarily, western ideology regarding land and resources embraced the view that humans were apart from the natural world and the domesticators and conquerors of nature's bounty. The romantic image of pioneers, advancing into the frontier, harvesting nature's bounty, pushing back and taming the wilderness, and making the land productive, suggests the omnipresent influence of this world view and associated values within the context of modern nation-states (Brody 1982). This ideology has resulted in the modification of the vast majority of the surface of the earth considered habitable or otherwise valuable, including those areas rich in renewable and non-renewable resources alike. Such a philosophy guided the introduction of Euroamericans into the country inhabited by the inland Dena'ina and resulted in the exploitation of the fauna, and in some cases, flora on which they relied, such as sockeye salmon, furbearers, large game, and timber.

Within the last half of this century, a growing awareness on the part of Euroamericans of rapid environmental modification of the world has led to alternative ideologies, embracing the values of the wilderness as an aesthetic, non-consumptive, and recreational commodity. Highly trained specialists and lay followers embracing this conservationist ideology have emerged, with a mission dedicated to keeping nature natural and curbing the seemingly insatiable human appetite for consuming, dominating, and developing the earth (Livingstone 1981). This conservationist ethic appears to be contradictory to a developmental view of nature. However, the fundamental premise that humans control nature, whether it be for consumption or benign appreciation, remains central to both philosophies.

Conservationist movements have stimulated a complex debate as to whether or not American Indians possessed and followed an environmental ethic prior to Euroamerican contact (cf, Callicott 1982; Krech 1981; Martin 1978; Nelson 1982; Tanner 1979). Problems inherent in reconstructing precontact ideologies of non-literate peoples contribute to the speculative nature of this debate. Although this is not an appropriate context for a detailed exploration of this controversy, only some major positions are mentioned. Both early Euroamericans who first encountered American Indians and scholars throughout history and from multiple disciplines have maintained that American Indians traditionally were unregulated predators of natural resources and have remained so into modern times, facilitated in this goal by what westerners perceive to be more efficient industrial technology. In this view, only relatively small populations and "primitive" technologies in the precontact period provided limitations on the abilities of indigenous people to exterminate entire species (e.g., Malthus 1803[1798]). Others have distinguished between non-western land use ideologies and practices and argued against a universal American Indian ethos in this regard. In the perception of some, American Indian environmental ethics and practices were based more on fear of retribution than true respect for nature or an ambiguous combination of both (Regan 1982). Proponents of these views have attributed the unchecked harvest of furbearers, for example, to a corruption of traditional ideologies and/or practices resulting from Euroamerican contact (Martin 1978) — to some, the downfall of the "noble savage." Lastly, others advocate a traditional American Indian environmental ethic which has persisted into the contemporary period and, for the most part, regulates the harvest of natural resources (e.g., Callicott 1982; Nelson 1983).

*The retributive factor does not suggest, to me at any rate, that American Indian **world views** did not, therefore, include a land ethic (Martin's claim), or even that there is, therefore, an "ineradicable layer of ambiguity" in the average, manifestly restrained, behavior of traditional Indians toward nature (Regan's* *claim), an ambiguity which makes it impossible for us to decide if their restrained relations with nature were genuinely moral or merely selfish. Such restraints were doubtlessly of both the moral and selfish sorts and the balance between these behavioral poles varied from person to person and, with respect to a given person, probably from time to time. The point is, American Indian **cultures** provided their members with an environmental ethical **ideal,** however much it may have been from time to time or from person to person avoided, ignored, violated, or for that matter, grudgingly honored because of fear of punishment (Callicott 1982:317-318).*

It is only in more recent years that anthropologists have focused on the complex relationships between world views of contemporary hunters and gatherers and the ways in which they interact with and obtain an existence from the natural environments of which they are a part (e.g., Brody 1982; Nelson 1983; Tanner 1979). For the most part, contemporary anthropologists have tended toward the conclusion that the central focus of the world views of most modern hunters and gatherers is that humans are a part of nature. Therefore, it is perceived as requisite that they live in harmony with animate and inanimate, empirical and non-empirical, human and non-human aspects of the natural world. The very use of these dichotomous terms in modern English for describing the universe of contemporary hunters and gatherers could be viewed as a portrayal of the biases and inadequacies of western science in describing the nature of American Indian relationships with their natural environments.

Regardless of the context of these theoretical debates, the inland Dena'ina continued to rely on local natural resources for making a living into the 1980s. Such economic endeavors influenced the social organization of their society, again into the present decade. These behaviors were representative of an associated ideology. The next three chapters describe the ways in which the inland Dena'ina lived on and with the land and the fauna and flora for approximately the past century.

The inland Dena'ina year represented here was depicted by residents of Nondalton in the 1980s. It represented the tempo of their relationships to land and resources from their earliest memories and oral histories, passed on from their parents and grandparents to children and grandchildren through time. Translated into years, the pattern of seasonal resource use described here was applicable to a composite period of time from approximately 1890 to 1990.

Without question, the nature of the inland Dena'ina seasonal cycle was dynamic and underwent changes associated with the introduction of formal education, trading posts, the Russian Orthodox church, and changing technologies. However, the inland Dena'ina year, as represented here, persisted with modifications well into the late 1960s and, in many respects, throughout the 1980s. This was achieved in more recent years through the use of modern technology to maintain mobility under the constraints of village life.

The seasonal round is depicted in Figure 48. A composite map of camps and trails, reported by residents of Nondalton for the period 1890 to 1990, is presented in Map 4. A comprehensive list of animals used by the inland Dena'ina, including Dena'ina, English, and scientific names, is in Appendix A. English and Dena'ina place names referred to in this description of seasonal activities are depicted on Maps 1 and 2, respectively. The areas used by the inland Dena'ina in relationship to Lake Clark National Park and Preserve are illustrated in Map 3.

ŁITLEN NUCH'ETDEH: SPRING CAMP

The inland Dena'ina year began with the onset of spring. The days became long, human hardship dissolved with the ever rising temperatures and melting snow and ice, and the cycle of life began anew. Since the onset of regular Russian Orthodox contact in the 1840s, by mid-April winter camps already had been abandoned and small groups of related families returned to their home villages. People left winter camps with the products of their trapping efforts. Depending upon the timing of Russian Orthodox Easter, some family groups moved directly from winter camps to spring camps, or *litl'en nuch'etdeh,* while some members returned to their village for Russian Orthodox services. The number of family members who returned to the community depended upon snow and ice conditions, the related ease of transportation, the degree to which families were in need of harvesting fresh resources, and the number of people desiring transport. Easter services were combined with potlatching and socializing, events wanting during fall and winter months when small groups were more isolated from each other.

For the Dena'ina of the Lake Clark area, the most important spring camp sites were distributed along the Chulitna River from Nikabuna and Long lakes, Caribou Creek or the Koksetna River, Chun

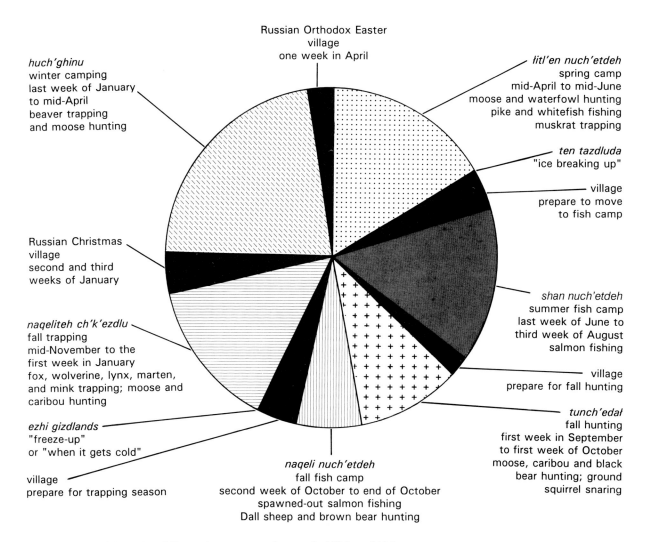

Russian Orthodox Easter
village
one week in April

litl'en nuch'etdeh
spring camp
mid-April to mid-June
moose and waterfowl hunting
pike and whitefish fishing
muskrat trapping

ten tazdluda
"ice breaking up"

village
prepare to move
to fish camp

huch'ghinu
winter camping
last week of January
to mid-April
beaver trapping
and moose hunting

shan nuch'etdeh
summer fish camp
last week of June to
third week of August
salmon fishing

village
prepare for fall hunting

Russian Christmas
village
second and third
weeks of January

tunch'edał
fall hunting
first week in September
to first week of October
moose, caribou and black
bear hunting; ground
squirrel snaring

naqeliteh ch'k'ezdlu
fall trapping
mid-November to the
first week in January
fox, wolverine, lynx, marten,
and mink trapping; moose and
caribou hunting

ezhi gizdlands
"freeze-up"
or "when it gets cold"

village
prepare for trapping season

naqeli nuch'etdeh
fall fish camp
second week of October to end of October
spawned-out salmon fishing
Dall sheep and brown bear hunting

Figure 48. The inland Dena'ina seasonal round, 1890 to 1990.

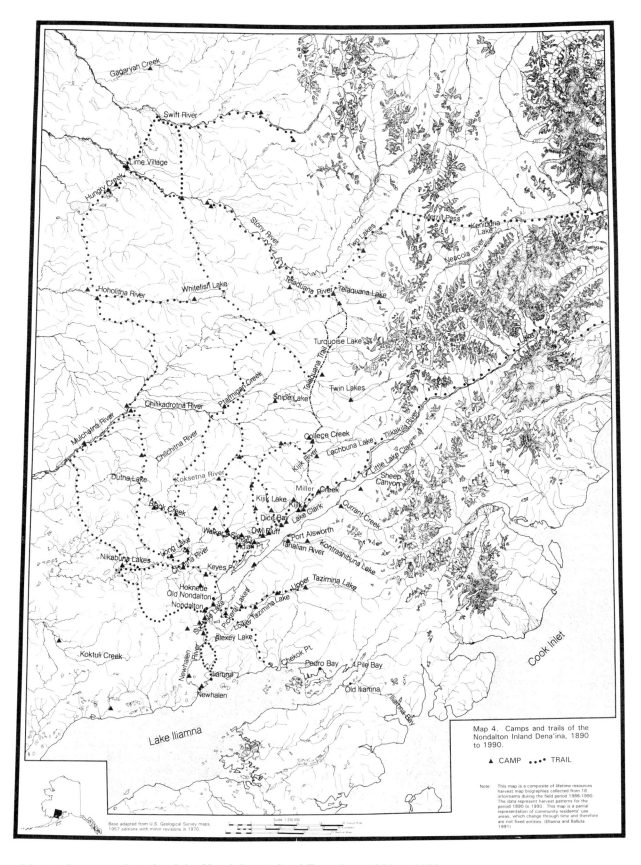

Map 4. Camps and trails of the Nondalton inland Dena'ina, 1890 to 1990.

Figure 49. A freight sled travelling along Six-Mile Lake in early spring 1930. *Photograph Courtesy of Agnes Cusma.*

Figure 50. Mary Ann Trefon and her daughter Katie Trefon at the mouth of Walker's Slough on the Chulitna River in spring, circa 1927. Their catch of whitefish and pike is in the foreground. Katie is holding muskrat pelts destined for sale, and a canvas windbreak is in the background. *Photograph Courtesy of Agnes Cusma.*

Talen (the south fork of the Chulitna delta), Hulehga Tahvilq'a (a slough on the north fork of the Chulitna delta), Qalnigi Tunilen (a creek that runs into Chulitna Bay), to Indian Point. Some people went across Six-Mile Lake to the south shore and to nearby south Pickeral Lake. At these locations, grayling spawned in great number. In a single night, as many as 2,000 could be taken by groups of three or four men and women with seines. Depending upon the abundance of cached foods by spring, grayling were important protein for both humans and dogs as needed in any given year. Grayling were driven down the creek by part of the group and then taken in small mesh, specially prepared seine nets positioned across a creek. The nets were held at either end by one or two adults on each side of the creek bank. In the 1940s, occasionally Nondalton people went to Peck's Creek and Kukaklek Lake in the Iliamna area. These were traditionally *Dutna* trapping areas. However, they were used by the inland Dena'ina when Lake Clark drainages were closed to beaver trappers by territorial regulation in the mid-1940s. At this time of year, beaver was an important source of food and pelts for sale. The cash received for beaver pelts was necessary to restock commercial grocery supplies at the end of winter. For the people of the upper Stony River, spring camps were situated along Hungry Creek, from Shagela Vena to its mouth and including White-fish Lake (Lih Vena).

Trout, whitefish, pike, and grayling fishing; beaver hunting and muskrat and beaver trapping; and migratory waterfowl hunting were the most important factors in the selection of spring camp-sites. The fervor of the Dena'ina for the warmth and freshness of spring was expressed in their use of tents instead of cabins as dwellings, since living outdoors was highly valued after the lengthy dark and cold of the winter months. Steam baths were built soon after camps were set up. Areas used for spring fishing, hunting, and trapping by Nondalton residents from 1890 to 1990 are depicted in Map 5.

The selection of camp sites was based largely on the traditional use of areas by particular families, a tenure system based on usufruct rights. Though kinship links were largely determined by relationships between men and their fathers, they were also associated with women and their fathers. Normally a spring camp was composed of members of one extended family, although it was not uncommon for related families or the families of hunting partners to live together at a particular site. In the memories of many Dena'ina in the

1980s, the selection of camp sites was decided by consensus before people left the village and made public knowledge via communication with and through the chief. Families wishing to join other families, which held more established rights to a particular spring camping area, stated their interests in joint occupancy in terms of mutual benefit. Therefore, conflicts over land use were rare to non-existent. Men who recognized a kind of luck in their unified action chose to camp together. Conversely, men who recognized the absence of luck in common action chose to camp apart.

Before the river ice went out, men and older boys were occupied constructing the frames of canoes from spruce. Women and girls cleaned moose or caribou hides for covering the boat frames constructed by the men and boys. In more recent years, canvas was used to cover canoes instead of moose or caribou hides. Men were responsible for covering the boat frames.

Moose or caribou found in the area were taken in small numbers to provide only for immediate consumption, since storage conditions were not advantageous at this time of year. Females pregnant or accompanied by young calves were avoided. Hides taken from moose also were used to cover the large *niggiday* or semi-permanent open skin boats. These large, open boats were used to transport meat, hides, and belongings downriver from spring camps at the end of the season. Although moose or caribou were not the targeted species in the spring, the appearance of an animal in the vicinity of camp was perceived as advantageous, since fresh meat from large game was scarce during this season. A moose taken in spring was widely shared by members of a single camp and with members of adjacent camps as well.

At the mouth of creeks, the outlets of lakes, or wherever open water was found early in this season, nets or traps (*taz'in*) were used to harvest whitefish, pike, and grayling. In the days before cotton netting was commonly available, an area 15 to 20 feet in length — located along a creek with stretches of shallow, open water — was fenced off — with wooden stakes, thereby forming a weir. Funnel-shaped doors were placed in the fence at the end of the weir from which the fish were approaching. Trapped freshwater fish were removed from shallow water, usually with dip nets (*nch'equyi*). Then they were strung through the gills and hung to dry or taken back to the camp to eat fresh.

From mid-April until mid-May, flocks of Canada geese and a diversity of ducks landed in feeding

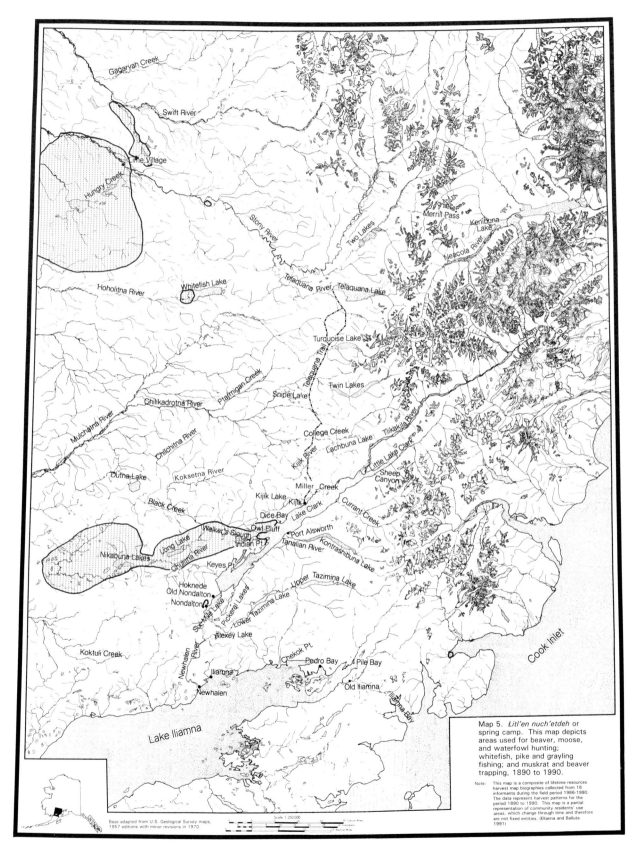

Map 5. *Litl'en nuch'etdeh* or spring camp. This map depicts areas used for beaver, moose, and waterfowl hunting; grayling, whitefish and pike fishing; and muskrat and beaver trapping, 1890 to 1990.

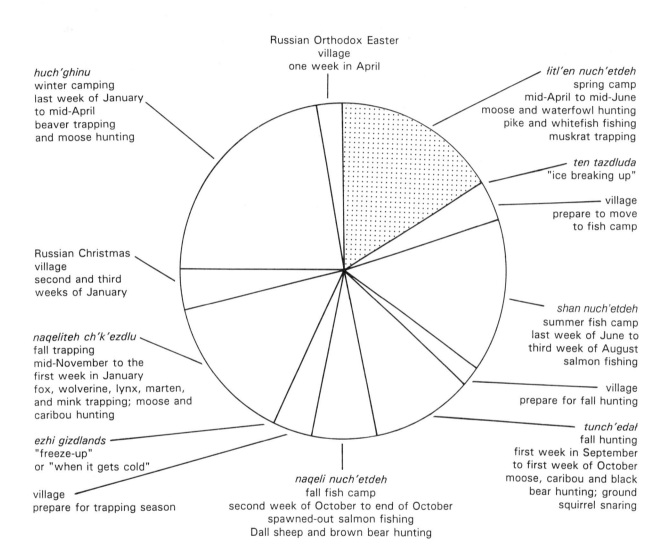

huch'ghinu
winter camping
last week of January
to mid-April
beaver trapping
and moose hunting

Russian Orthodox Easter
village
one week in April

łitl'en nuch'etdeh
spring camp
mid-April to mid-June
moose and waterfowl hunting
pike and whitefish fishing
muskrat trapping

ten tazdluda
"ice breaking up"

village
prepare to move
to fish camp

Russian Christmas
village
second and third
weeks of January

naqeliteh ch'k'ezdlu
fall trapping
mid-November to the
first week in January
fox, wolverine, lynx, marten,
and mink trapping; moose and
caribou hunting

shan nuch'etdeh
summer fish camp
last week of June to
third week of August
salmon fishing

village
prepare for fall hunting

tunch'edał
fall hunting
first week in September
to first week of October
moose, caribou and black
bear hunting; ground
squirrel snaring

ezhi gizdlands
"freeze-up"
or "when it gets cold"

village
prepare for trapping season

naqeli nuch'etdeh
fall fish camp
second week of October to end of October
spawned-out salmon fishing
Dall sheep and brown bear hunting

Map 5. (continued) Key to Map 5.

areas. The inland Dena'ina harvested them using small steel traps or firearms. Geese and ducks provided a welcomed change of diet from winter provisions of smoked and dried salmon, caribou, and moose or the occasional fresh large game taken during midwinter. Often women saved the feathers of ducks and geese for bedding, and meat was consumed shortly after harvest in order to prevent it from excessively drying out or spoiling. Generally, the Dena'ina did not take ducks or geese after they began laying eggs, and seldom were duck eggs harvested. However, seagull eggs were taken from nests on grassy islands on larger lakes, such as Lake Clark and Lake Iliamna.

The ice began to disappear, first from small creeks and then, more suddenly and quietly, from the sluggish and shallow Chulitna River. Men and older boys, travelling in skin-covered canoes alone or in pairs, went out on the rivers to hunt beavers with firearms or trap them on beaches. Spring beaver trapping initially involved locating beaver lodges. Once a lodge was sighted, men identified the path which beavers were taking to go to their food supply on the beach. Throughout this century, steel traps were set at points at which beavers came ashore to access their food supply. A small burlap sack, filled with rocks or a large rock, was attached to the trap by twine or string. The chain on the trap was extended by a rope, so that it was approximately six to eight feet in length from where it was solidly attached to a stake or tree. When a beaver was trapped, it headed for the water with the attached sack and, subsequently, drowned from the weight. Trappers checked their traps daily, recovering the beaver by pulling in the rope or chain line.

Beaver hunting occurred at the same time and in the same places as trapping. Beavers were hunted with small-caliber firearms, such as 22s. Beaver hunting and trapping forays occurred in the long spring evenings or early mornings when the prey were out feeding on birch, willow, cottonwood, or alder. Beaver meat, more resistant than moose or caribou to deterioration in the warmth of the spring, was smoked and dried and taken back to the village.

Beaver was perceived to be one of the most important animals taken by the inland Dena'ina. Not only did they provide an essential source of fatty, rich food, but they also provided pelts important for clothing, including caps, gloves, lining, trim, or, in some cases, entire outfits. Since the onset of Russian American Company trading in the Cook Inlet and Lake Iliamna areas, and until fur prices

began to fall after World War II, beaver trapping provided an important means by which people obtained trade goods or, in more recent years, cash. After the 1950s, beavers were taken primarily for food and pelts for Dena'ina clothing, principally because of their low market value.

As the rivers became navigable, families camping upriver completed the large, open boats. They loaded them with meat, fish, pelts, camping equipment, and people to float downriver to Indian Point. Dogs were turned loose to follow the boats as they made their way downriver, and sleds were usually left behind for use the following winter. Indian Point was the location of a large temporary camp, where everyone awaited breakup of the ice on Lake Clark. Even the *Dutna* of the Newhalen area, who had camped at Koktuli Creek (Qukdeli) and Nikabuna Lakes, came downriver by open skin boat and joined the inland Dena'ina at this gathering place.

Although trips for hunting beavers and ducks were made from Indian Point, the significance of this camp was mostly social. Visiting, catching up on gossip, playing games of chance (such as the stick game or *ch'enlahi*) and physical prowess, common meals with special dishes, courtship, and other events of social significance took place within this camp. Residence at Indian Point could last as long as two weeks, depending upon ice conditions on Lake Clark. Warm temperatures and long days honeycombed the ice on the lake. Stiff winds sometimes piled it upon the beach leaving the lake navigable. Men and older boys went to fall camps up the lake or back to the village to pick up spruce plank boats, in recent years, or skin-covered or birch bark canoes in the past. These were used to transport women, children, meat, hides, and camping gear back to the villages in preparation for summer salmon fishing.

Variations on the themes described above occurred. On the upper Stony River, the Dena'ina returned to either Qeghnilen or Lime Village or moved directly to summer fish camps. They did not have a staging area comparable to Indian Point. Nondalton people originally from the Lake Iliamna area, or having relatives residing there, went to the coast of Cook Inlet during the spring to dig for clams or harvest salt water seals.

SHAN NUCH'ETDEH: SUMMER FISH CAMP

The return from spring camp signaled the anticipation of the arrival of the first sockeye migrating

Figure 51 (above). Pete Delkittie's fish camp in the early 1930s, located approximately five miles down the Newhalen River from the present site of Nondalton. A smokehouse with a bark roof, two white canvas wall tents, two fish caches, a sod-roofed cabin, and fish racks are visible. *Photograph Courtesy of the Alaska Historical Library, James Carter Collection.* **Figure 52 (below).** Salmon backbones drying on a rack (*liq'a k'eyena zggeni*), to be used as dog food in the winter, and a log platform cache. *Photograph Courtesy of Ida Carlson Crater.*

upstream and commencement of summer fishing. The first fish to arrive, even if it were only a single salmon, was cooked and shared in the context of a potlatch. Newhalen people informed the people of Nondalton when they harvested their first fish, which then permitted the Lake Clark area people to gauge the time that they had before the sockeye arrived at their area.

Most families remained in the village for approximately one week, while they prepared for their fish camps. The majority of Nondalton camps were on Six-Mile Lake, near the headwaters of the Newhalen River, or on the river itself as far as six miles downstream, to a place referred to by the Dena'ina as Nundaltinshla. For the residents of the upper Stony River, summer fish camps were located above the Qeghnilen village site in the middle of the actual canyon. The term, *qeghnilen,* means "the river flows through a canyon" (J. Kari 1977). After the people moved to the present location of Lime Village, fish camps were established below the canyon but above the old Qeghnilen village site (see P. Kari 1983 for a more detailed description of summer fishing on the upper Stony River).

Day trips were made from the village to the fish camps to repair tent frames, place wall tents on frames, gather spruce bark to mend the roofs of smokehouses, repair smokehouses and drying racks, and construct storage fish bins and cutting tables. Wood was gathered for smoking sockeye, heating steam baths, and other domestic uses. Traffic between fish camps and the village was by canoe, baidarki, and wooden skiffs or dories (also sometimes referred to by the Russian term, *valgas*).

In normal years, the first sockeye arrived at Six-Mile Lake in the middle of June. By the second week in July, the Newhalen river was churning with schools of sockeye in eddies and sloughs, making their way to Six-Mile Lake and on to Lake Clark. The first sockeye arrived on the upper Stony River normally about the first of July. Kings were not abundant in the upper Stony River drainage. However, if there were a king run, it arrived at the same time as the sockeyes, to be followed later in the summer by chums and, less abundantly, silvers at the end of the season. On the upper Stony River, salmon did not form dense congregations to the extent that they did in the Lake Clark area, largely because of the gradient of the river and the swiftness of its flow.

Since the late 1800s, involvement in the Bristol Bay commercial fishery was an integral part of the inland Dena'ina seasonal round. In the years prior to World War II, only men and boys went to "the bay." After that time, some younger women began to go as well to seek employment in canneries. Prior to leaving Nondalton for Bristol Bay, men moved their families to summer fish camps, *shan nuch'etdeh,* between the middle and third weeks of June. Middle-aged women directed the subsistence fishery at summer camps, assisted by older men and women and children of both sexes.

Inland Dena'ina summer fishing areas and camp locations are depicted in Map 6. Prior to the abandonment of Kijik, most summer fish camps were located at the outlet of what is now called Kijik Lake, four miles upriver from the old village site. Summer salmon fishing at this location was a community endeavor. Sockeyes were taken by weirs and dip nets in much the same manner as that described for grayling spring fishing. Other salmon fishing camps were situated at the outlet of Telaquana Lake. Even after the people resident there relocated, the summer fish camp remained important as an alternative source of salmon species derived from a different drainage from that of Lake Clark. No oral historic or documented information is available regarding summer fish camp locations on the Mulchatna River. In the case of the family which remained at Tanalian Point after leaving Kijik, their summer fish camp was located at the mouth of the Tanalian River.

In the 1960s, families began moving their summer fish camps up the Newhalen River, closer to the present site of Nondalton. This shift resulted from the desire of residents to be closer to the village. Additionally, as more and more adult men, and a greater number of young men and women, went to Bristol Bay, those family members at summer camps were increasingly isolated. Lastly, for the past three decades, Nondalton residents perceived sockeye fishing to be more productive near the origin of the Newhalen River at the outlet of Six-Mile Lake.

Summer fish camps typically included from two to five extended families, with three being the most common. Each family unit had a separate tent, smokehouse, drying racks, and cache, but the steam bath was shared by all members of a camp. Multiple adjacent camps shared a beach seine, but boats, bins, and processing tables were held individually by extended family units. During warm, dry days, many activities, such as midday meals, were shared by camp members. Fishing, though a critical activity, was not continuous. Trips to the village for church, berry picking, and other activities were interspersed with periods of intensive fishing. Fish taken during this time were processed only for human use.

By the first week of August, men returned to the fish camps from Bristol Bay. Sockeyes were still abundant and in good condition. Men and older boys took over fishing responsibilities from the women, children, and elders and began harvesting and smoking salmon to be used primarily for dog food. Most families had dog teams and relied on cached smoked salmon for dog food, from approximately the end of October until late April when fishing began at spring camp. Most families minimally processed 60 bundles, at 40 fish per bundle.

The use of 40 as the number of fish comprising a "bundle" began during the American trading period, when traders bought fish for resale to transient prospectors and trappers. Into the 1940s, some men chose not to go to Bristol Bay but rather to put up fish for sale to traders. This practice was prohibited by territorial fish and game regulations in the early 1940s.

At the end of the summer, women continued to cut fish. The men hung salmon, cut wood, and maintained smokehouse fires. By August, blueberries, salmon berries, and moss berries had ripened and were gathered in buckets, pots, and pans by women and children in the vicinity of fish camps. Berries were stored in wooden barrels with oil rendered from bear fat and mixed with caribou or moose tallow.

Fish heads were strung on spruce roots and left in water for about three days. Then they were placed in birch and spruce lined pits in the ground or, in later years, large pots. Hot stones were put into the pits or pots were placed over fires and the water boiled until oil was rendered and floated to the surface. In earlier days, the oil was stored in brown bear stomachs. In more recent years, it was put into glass jars and cans, to be consumed later with dried fish or used in waterproofing boots and skin boats.

Before the 1880s, men stored fish, which already had dried, in family caches in preparation for fall and winter. After the introduction of salting by commercial fishing canneries as an alternative preservation technique, some fish were salted and placed in wooden barrels. However, salting did not replace the storage of salmon in pits, smoking, or drying as means of preservation, especially on the upper Stony River where underground caches were used into the 1960s. In the 1980s, soaking salmon in brine usually preceded smoking procedures.

Fermented fish and heads from underground pits were considered a delicacy. They were often dug up after a couple of months. Fish prepared in this fashion were slightly fermented but in firm condition. They were eaten after being washed and dipped in boiling water. Some fish stored in this manner frequently were left for a year or two, or even multiple years, to be used as an emergency food supply during lean times.

By the third week of August, summer fishing ended. Tents and other equipment were stored in smokehouses at camp sites. The majority of smoked sockeyes, the mainstay of the Dena'ina winter diet, was left cached. Families took two to three week supplies of the smoked fish with them throughout various periods of the winter and spring, as they moved into other parts of the country during the course of their annual cycle. From summer camps, the inland Dena'ina loaded various kinds of water craft with fish, equipment, and people to return to the village, where they began preparation for fall hunting.

TUNCH'EDAL: FALL HUNTING

The inland Dena'ina prepared for fall hunting (tunch'edal) by repairing or sewing caribou hide packs for dogs, purchasing drygoods (such as flour, sugar, rice, tea, and ammunition), and sewing waterproof boots fabricated from dehaired caribou hides. Most strong and healthy members of extended families left the village and went to fall camps. The ill and elderly, who were left behind, were cared for by young men and women. Young children joined their families on the trek to fall camping areas. People normally departed the village during the first week of September. Map 7 depicts the areas used by Nondalton residents for fall hunting throughout their lifetimes, or during the period 1890 to 1990.

In the case of the Nondalton Dena'ina, families generally travelled by boats to the northeastern shore of Lake Clark. The ultimate objective during this season was accessing the high country to hunt caribou, moose, and black bears and to snare ground squirrels. Boats were left at various sites along the shore of the lake, including Miller Creek, Qalnigi Tunilen, Lynx Creek (K'chanlentnu), Long Lake, and other locations. On the upper Stony River, the Dena'ina went on foot from the village to various places at the head of the Swift

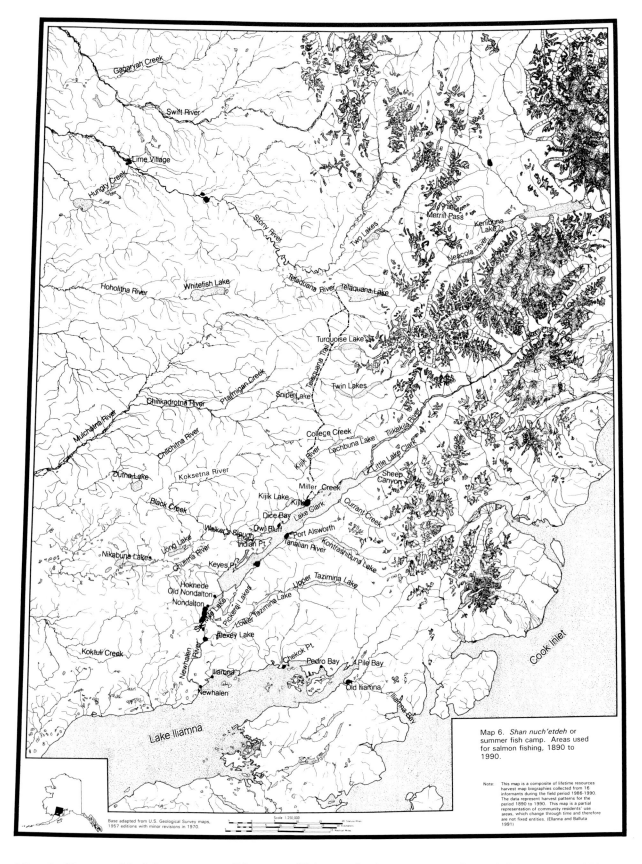

Map 6. *Shan nuch'etdeh* or summer fish camp. Areas used for salmon fishing, 1890 to 1990.

Note: This map is a composite of lifetime resources harvest map biographies collected from 16 informants during the field period 1986-1990. The data represent harvest patterns for the period 1890 to 1990. This map is a partial representation of community residents' use areas, which change through time and therefore are not fixed entities. (Ellanna and Balluta 1991)

Base adapted from U.S. Geological Survey maps, 1957 editions with minor revisions in 1970.

Scale 1:250,000

Map 6. *Shan nuch'etdeh* or summer fish camp. This map depicts summer salmon fishing areas, 1890 to 1990.

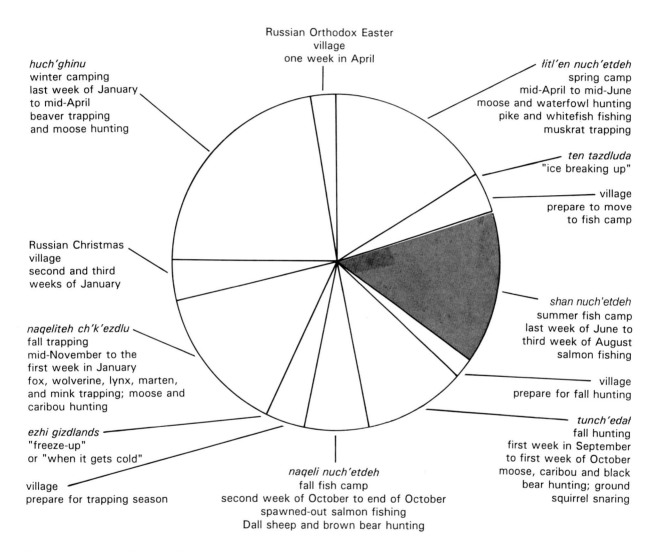

Russian Orthodox Easter
village
one week in April

huch'ghinu
winter camping
last week of January
to mid-April
beaver trapping
and moose hunting

litl'en nuch'etdeh
spring camp
mid-April to mid-June
moose and waterfowl hunting
pike and whitefish fishing
muskrat trapping

ten tazdluda
"ice breaking up"

village
prepare to move
to fish camp

Russian Christmas
village
second and third
weeks of January

shan nuch'etdeh
summer fish camp
last week of June to
third week of August
salmon fishing

naqeliteh ch'k'ezdlu
fall trapping
mid-November to the
first week in January
fox, wolverine, lynx, marten,
and mink trapping; moose and
caribou hunting

village
prepare for fall hunting

tunch'edał
fall hunting
first week in September
to first week of October
moose, caribou and black
bear hunting; ground
squirrel snaring

ezhi gizdlands
"freeze-up"
or "when it gets cold"

village
prepare for trapping season

naqeli nuch'etdeh
fall fish camp
second week of October to end of October
spawned-out salmon fishing
Dall sheep and brown bear hunting

Map 6. (continued) Map 6 key.

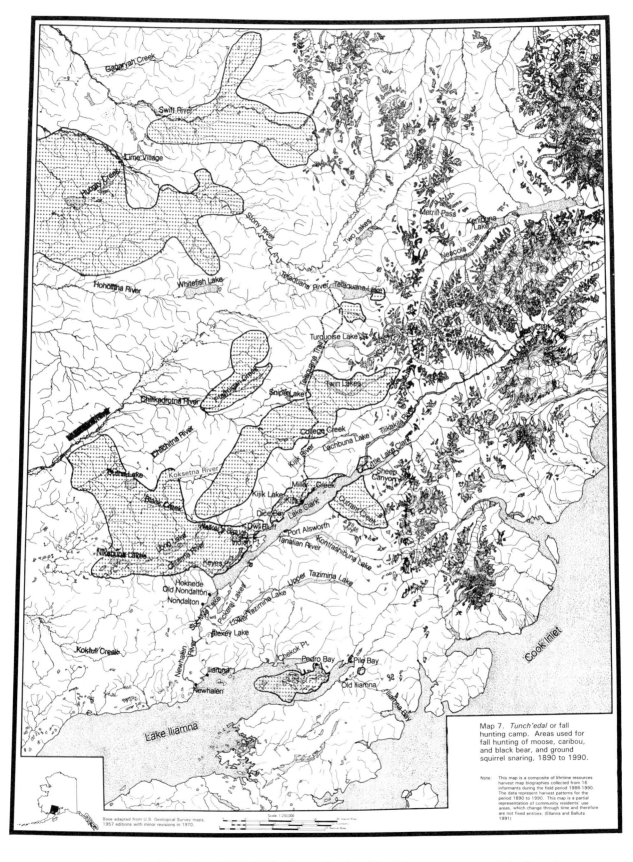

Map 7. *Tunch'edal* or fall
hunting camp. Areas used for
fall hunting of moose, caribou,
and black bear, and ground
squirrel snaring, 1890 to 1990.

Note: This map is a composite of lifetime resources
harvest map biographies collected from 16
informants during the field period 1986-1990.
The data represent harvest patterns for the
period 1890 to 1990. This map is a partial
representation of community residents' use
areas, which change through time and therefore
are not fixed entities. (Ellanna and Balluta
1991)

Base adapted from U.S. Geological Survey maps.
1957 editions with minor revisions in 1970.

Scale 1:250,000

Map 7. *Tunch'edal* or fall hunting, 1890-1990. Areas depicted in this map were used for hunting moose,
caribou, and black bears in the fall. Ground squirrels were also snared, principally by women.

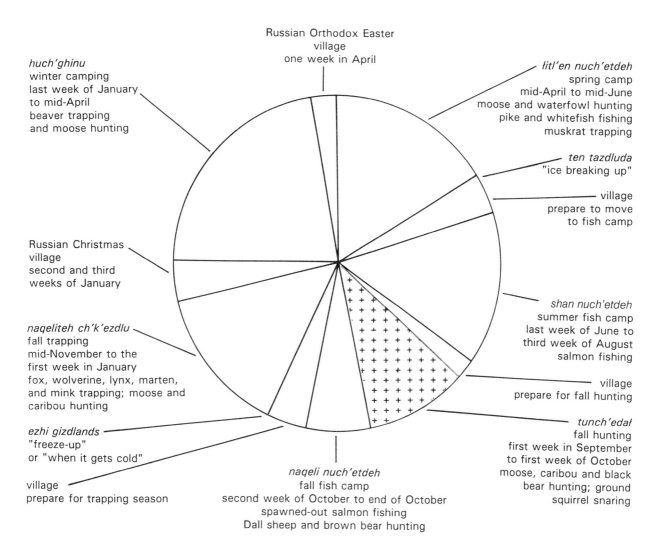

huch'ghinu
winter camping
last week of January
to mid-April
beaver trapping
and moose hunting

Russian Orthodox Easter
village
one week in April

litl'en nuch'etdeh
spring camp
mid-April to mid-June
moose and waterfowl hunting
pike and whitefish fishing
muskrat trapping

ten tazdluda
"ice breaking up"

village
prepare to move
to fish camp

Russian Christmas
village
second and third
weeks of January

shan nuch'etdeh
summer fish camp
last week of June to
third week of August
salmon fishing

naqeliteh ch'k'ezdlu
fall trapping
mid-November to the
first week in January
fox, wolverine, lynx, marten,
and mink trapping; moose and
caribou hunting

village
prepare for fall hunting

tunch'edał
fall hunting
first week in September
to first week of October
moose, caribou and black
bear hunting; ground
squirrel snaring

ezhi gizdlands
"freeze-up"
or "when it gets cold"

village
prepare for trapping season

naqeli nuch'etdeh
fall fish camp
second week of October to end of October
spawned-out salmon fishing
Dall sheep and brown bear hunting

Map 7. (continued) Map 7 key.

Figure 53. The Balluta family travelling to fall hunting camp in 1939. *Photograph Courtesy of Agnes Cusma.*

Figure 54. Alex Trefon hunting moose during late fall at Dice Bay on Lake Clark, 1931. *Photograph Courtesy of Agnes Cusma.*

River (Huch'altnu) and its tributaries, such as Gargaryah Creek.

In the Lake Clark area, people beached their boats and travelled on foot into the mountains, packing babies and young children. They were assisted in transporting their gear by pack dogs. Hunting and camping locations were selected on the basis of several criteria. A man's familiarity with an area, used by him and his father in previous years, provided essential knowledge of caribou and moose feeding preferences and resource abundance in particular locales. Also, the availability of black bears and ground squirrels influenced decisions about the location of fall hunting camps. Many families hunted at Chilikadrotna River or Middle Fork, others went to the Mulchatna River for caribou and moose, and yet others travelled to Venq'deltihi (a mountain range on the north side of the Chulitna River near Lynx Creek).

Elders reported that when they were young, they had to travel long distances from the village to get large game, as caribou were scarce and moose rare in the vicinity of Lake Clark in the early decades of the 1900s. For the people of the upper Stony River, Dazdlit Dazdlu, located at the head of the Swift River, was an important location for hunting caribou, moose, black bears, and Dall sheep.

Fall camp sites normally were established by a stream or small lake, where alders and willows were abundant. The camps were situated along the edge of the wooded area, thereby providing some protection from predominating cold north winds and storm-bearing east winds.

A dome-shaped frame of alder poles, approximately 12 feet in diameter, was constructed. The size was dependent upon the number of individuals occupying the dwelling. Alder roots or, in more recent years rope or twine, connected intersecting poles of the structure. Alder boughs with intact leaves were woven into the framework, resulting in a thatched, dome-shaped dwelling. If spruce were available, boughs were used as flooring. If they were not, such as at higher altitudes, grass served the same purpose for covering floors. The hearth was placed in the middle of the lodge, with the smoke hole in center of the domed roof. There was more than one entrance to this type of structure, assuring the circulation of fresh air. Grass mattresses and caribou hides were placed toward the periphery of the shelter, while cooking and other activities common to the group occurred toward the center.

Meat racks were constructed approximately 75 to 100 yards from the camp to protect residents from raiding predators. In more recent years, such dwellings were replaced by white canvas wall tents, but local materials commonly were used for poles and flooring as they had been in the past.

Camp sites generally were occupied by one or two nuclear or extended families, most commonly a man and his brothers, all with their families. At times, men travelled and camped with their wives' male relatives. Single men often were attached to camps of their fathers, if the latter were still active hunters, or to those of married brothers. Because of the relative scarcity of large game, camp groups were composed generally of 10 people or less. Once the camp was established, it remained a base for all hunting and squirrel snaring activities, although men frequently went for two or three day trips away from the camp. However, if a caribou herd or multiple moose were encountered on a hunt, a decision was made to move the camp to the game rather than pack large quantities of meat to the camp.

In the mountains, caribou generally were pursued by paired hunting partners. Skillful hunters were aware of the locations at which caribou fed in late summer. They left camp on foot and traversed high country, from where they could observe game foraging below in lowlands or stream drainages. Bulls were hunted before they went into rut, usually at the end of September or early October. Cows and calves usually were targeted later in the season. Hunters approached caribou as close as possible, being cautious to remain downwind. They were aware of the fact that caribou are generally curious and not likely to run unless they detect a human scent. The inland Dena'ina also did not like to run down game, as they believed that the levels of excitement and activity incurred in the chase were detrimental to the quality and flavor of the meat. When caribou were accessible, hunters shot multiple animals with bows and arrows in earlier times and firearms in more recent years. Harvest levels were associated with need and, therefore, related to family or hunting camp size. The inland Dena'ina had a strict ethic prohibiting the harvest of more animals than a hunting group could process, store, consume, or distribute to others from the community.

Another method of hunting, requiring the participation of a greater number of individuals from the village at large, involved the construction of spruce or birch pole fences across a ridge, intersecting the migratory paths of caribou. Snares made of rawhide were placed at open spaces between poles of the fence, in order to entrap animals as they tried to escape through these gaps. In some cases, the snares were attached to fixed or stationary poles. Therefore, when caribou became entangled, they were immobilized and dispatched quickly with a spear or bow and arrow. In other cases, snares were attached to loose poles set on top of the fence. This technique, referred to as drag pole snaring, enabled caribou to get away from the fence, thereby minimizing the possibilities that they would disturb other animals or destroy portions of the barricade. The pole slowed the animal down or, on occasion, strangled the caribou. In either case, caribou were dispatched with spears and bows and arrows in a timely manner, primarily to prevent them from fighting the snares for any length of time. Although no one in the 1980s had observed this method of hunting caribou, elders remained knowledgeable about the strategies and technology associated with this highly effective harvest method. The inland Dena'ina systematically did not hunt caribou at crossing places in lakes or streams. However, if a caribou were spotted swimming across a lake, river, or creek, hunters usually awaited their landing before attempting to take them with bows and arrows or spears. If a hunter were unable to land his boat on the beach before his prey emerged from the water, he shot or speared the caribou while it was still swimming. Taking caribou while they were swimming was considered by the inland Dena'ina to be a lazy way to hunt.

By the early 1900s, when moose became available in inland Dena'ina country, almost everyone possessed and used firearms for hunting. During the fall, hunters conducted surveillances for tracks and sought swampy areas with thick bottom grass in which moose commonly fed. From the downwind edge of such areas, hunters, in protective wooded or brushy cover, watched for moose to emerge in the early evenings or mornings. They shot them from as close a range as possible. Moose were known to be more wary than caribou. Therefore, successful hunters took considerable effort to prevent moose from either smelling or seeing them. Generally, hunting partners, as well as individuals, took moose by this method.

Elders recalled a technique of snaring moose, occasionally used to assure success, as moose were highly prized and relatively scarce. This method of snaring, involving the use of a "spring pole," required that a single hunter or hunting partners locate a moose trail. A rawhide or rope snare was set between two trees on opposite sides of the game trail. The hunter climbed the most young and flexible of these two trees and attached one end of the snare to the top. Once snared, the moose attempted to walk away with the snare around its neck or its antlers. The tree to which the snare was attached bent elastically until the tension was too great. At that point, the tree recoiled, pulling the moose back into its trail. Such a snare was checked daily and predominantly used by older or infirm hunters, not capable of travelling great distances. This method also was employed by any hunter needing game but unable to hunt far afield because of travel conditions.

Black bears, an important source of both meat and fat, were hunted during the fall in open, high country as they foraged for berries. Prior to the introduction of firearms, spears, rather than bows and arrows, were more customarily used by hunters stalking bears. Hunters using this technology attempted to approach the animal silently, thereby having the advantage of surprise. Young men were educated about bear behaviors and developed appropriate physical skills necessary to undertake this relatively risky type of hunting activity with success. After the introduction of firearms, spear hunting was uncommon, but the need to approach bears as closely as possible before shooting them remained a requisite part of hunting strategies. Additionally, the need to advance toward bears in the appropriate manner remained important in hunting techniques in modern times, not only to ensure successful hunting, but also to reinforce Dena'ina views regarding the skill and bravery associated with taking this nutritionally and spiritually important species.

The Dena'ina ate some fresh bear meat and hung the remainder to dry partially, retaining it for later consumption. Dried or fresh bear meat always was boiled before it was consumed. The fat was highly prized and considered a delicacy, as the Dena'ina used it for preserving berries, cooking and as a condiment into which dried fish and meat were dipped. The uses of bear fat were functionally similar to the uses of rendered seal or eulachon oil in coastal areas.

One woman customarily cared for small children at hunting camps, while the remaining women and children snared ground squirrels and picked cranberries. Women were responsible for cutting, hanging, and smoking meat brought back to the camp by hunters. They skinned ground squirrels, preserving the meat of these animals as well. The hides of caribou and squirrels were dried after scraping, whereas moose hides initially were dehaired and then scraped and dried. Caribou and moose hides were essential for clothing, bedding, and watercraft covering. In many respects, the harvest of hides was more central to fall hunting than the harvest of meat. This was particularly true prior to the introduction of commercially manufactured clothing, bedding, boats, and housing.

NAQELI NUCH'ETDEH: FALL FISH CAMP

By the first week of October, it began getting cold at higher elevations. The Dena'ina were anxious to travel to fall fish camps to harvest spawned-out sockeyes. If the fall hunting camp site had been used in previous years, a raised log cache already existed. If not, one had to be constructed to store the harvest of this season. Except for a small portion needed for more immediate consumption, the majority of meat and hides were cached at fall camps until rivers, streams, and lakes froze and the first snowfall facilitated transportation. At this time, meat and hides were then ferried by dog team back to the village or to fall and winter trapping camps. Pack dogs were loaded with food and equipment. Mothers packing babies and small children, other women, men, and older boys and girls commenced a two day trek, heading down the mountains to specific sites on lakes or rivers where they had beached their boats.

By approximately the second week in October, the inland Dena'ina established their fall fish camps (*naqeli nuch'etdeh*), from which they put up spawned-out sockeye and hunted brown bear and Dall sheep. Areas used for these activities between 1890 and 1990 are depicted in Map 8. Lake Clark area fall fish camps were located at sites such as Kijik village, Tuk'eleh (the south fork of the Kijik River on the delta), Qalnigi Tunilen, and the lower Tanalian River. Since there were no spawning areas on the upper Stony River in the vicinity of Qeghnilen, some families went to the northeastern end of Telaquana Lake.

Fall fishing sites were always selected in prime spawning areas. According to elders, these were commonly locations used by a man's father before him. Usufruct rights to fall fishing sites, passed from father to son, may have been influenced significantly by associated hunting areas. In other cases, fishing sites were jointly occupied by a man or men and their sisters, with the families of all concerned. Frequently, more than one family re-

sided at a fall fish camp, and these were often the same families which composed fall hunting groups. In general, a greater degree of aggregation occurred during this time of year, since fall fishing camps were somewhat larger than fall hunting camps. During this season, people lived in white-walled canvas tents and constructed steam baths, but there were no caches at these sites.

Men were the primary harvesters of spawned-out salmon. Elders reported that before commercially made fish nets were available, spawned-out sockeye were taken with barbed fish spears, or *tuqesi,* at fish ponds and rivers where spawning occurred. Once imported netting materials or commercially made nets were available, sockeye were taken with gill nets on lakes or at mouths of rivers. It was in these locations that salmon congregated into schools for spawning or preceding their travel upriver to spawn. People reported that the water distinctively was bright red, filled with the humped bodies and beaked-nosed fish. Some fish taken had spawned already, while others still had soft eggs intact. Women cut, split, and filleted these salmon in the same manner as they had at summer fish camps. However, rather than being smoked and dried, spawned-out sockeye or, *nudelvegh,* were dried on a spruce pole fish rack which was A-shaped and had multiple rungs. *Nudelvegh* were considered to be a delicacy, usually consumed with rendered bear fat. Salmon taken at this time of year were valued, not as a primary source of everyday food, but rather as a special treat. They were shared with visitors or consumed on special occasions. A domestic unit typically took only 150 to 200 fish during this time of year.

While women and older girls were processing the salmon, men and older boys from the Lake Clark area initially went by boat to the head of the lake and climbed into the mountains in search of Dall sheep. During these four or five day trips, hunters camped in tents and harvested sheep on the slopes of mountains. More specifically, they frequently went to Sheep Canyon (Tsayeh Ka'ahtnu) at the outlet of Little Lake Clark, Kontrashibuna Lake (Qenlghishi Vena), or Ch'kentalqeyitnu (a creek north of Currant Creek). Approximately four sheep per domestic group generally were taken. Sheep pelts were used for winter clothing, such as mittens and socks; sleeping bags or blankets; and linings for coats. Dall sheep meat was a highly valued food item as well. Because the weather was cold during this time of the year, sheep meat was merely hung for immediate consumption. The upper Stony River Dena'ina generally hunted sheep at the head of Swift River (see P. Kari, 1983, for a more detailed description of upper Stony River sheep hunting).

At the end of the fall fishing and hunting period, brown bears were about to hibernate. Since they were still eating salmon, as they had throughout the summer, they were in prime condition and had considerable fat to sustain life during the winter. Therefore, they were a highly valued prey during this temporal window. Brown bears were stalked, usually by small groups of three or four hunters, on moonlit evenings at fish ponds where they fed. Hunters often constructed blinds of grass or scaffolds of spruce, depending upon the terrain. From these vantage points, bears were shot by waiting hunters.

Prior to the introduction of firearms, hunters with dogs tracked bears to their dens. Bear dens were monitored until the hunters were assured that the animals had commenced hibernation. Subsequently, a group of men approached the den. Younger, stronger, and more skillful hunters were positioned closest to the den. An object covered with human scent was thrown into the den to attract the attention of the bear. Since the bear had just entered its den on a more less seasonally permanent basis, it had not yet fallen into the type of sleep characteristic of full hibernation. Being alarmed by the human scent, the bear emerged to protect its territory. In most cases, the most skillful hunters speared it. If the bear were not killed by the initial attack, other hunters farther away from the den undertook a secondary assault.

Brown bears, being larger than black bears, provided a more abundant source of fat and meat. Brown bear meat was hung outside in the cool autumn days and nights and was distributed to anyone short of food. Generally, bear meat was not used for dog food. The inland Dena'ina stated that dogs avoided eating brown bear, river otter, wolverine, and weasel meat, except in unusual cases. Pieces of fat were placed in large containers with small amounts of water and boiled slowly. As in the case of fish oil, rendered fat from bears was stored in cleaned bear stomachs, glass jars, or metal cans.

By the end of October, the temperatures were very cold and travel by boat was marginal. The severity of climate at this time of year was the major determinant of when the inland Dena'ina decided to leave fall fish camps by boat and return to their home communities. Dried spawned-out salmon and meat and processed hides were loaded in boats along with camping gear. Almost everyone moved back to the village. Dogs ran along the beach following the boats. People remained in the village approximately through the first half of November or until conditions for travelling on ice and snow were suitable and preparation of equipment and clothing for fall and winter trapping and hunting were complete.

Women soaked and cleaned moose hides, taking off remnants of meat and fascia with tibia scrapers in earlier times and long knives more recently. These hides usually had been dehaired previously. Some hides were cut into strips or *babiche* approximately three-eighths of an inch wide. The strips were then stretched and freeze-dried between trees and poles. After four or five days in cold weather, the rawhide was soft and used for multiple purposes, such as lashing together wooden components of sleds, webbing for the portion of snowshoes in which the foot was positioned, and lines for packs. Other hides were soaked in moose brain or, more recently, also detergent. After soaking, they were cleaned and freeze-dried intact. The soles of boots or *k'qa* were cut directly from dried hides. Other hides were smoked and used for sewing mittens, gloves, the upper part of boots, and slippers. Women also processed caribou hides by dehairing, cleaning, and freezing them. Some caribou hides, like moose, were cut into narrow strips for snowshoe webbing and other purposes.

During these first two weeks of November, men left villages to gather birch wood for constructing sleds and snowshoes. The birch was split and hewn with a metal ax prior to the introduction of whip saws. In more recent years, it was sawed into appropriate sizes and shapes for making sled parts, such as runners, stanchions, battens, and railings. Wood to be used for snowshoes was split, hewed with an ax, shaped with a whittling knife, put on a jig, and seasoned by drying. After the wood dried, men removed it from the jig, reshaped it, added the foot piece, and drilled holes for attaching webbing. Women usually joined the caribou strip webbing to the frame, although sometimes both men and women worked cooperatively to accomplish this task. Men also gathered firewood for the elderly, sick, and disabled, who were left behind in the village during fall trapping activities. By the middle of November, the inland Dena'ina were prepared to go to fall trapping camps.

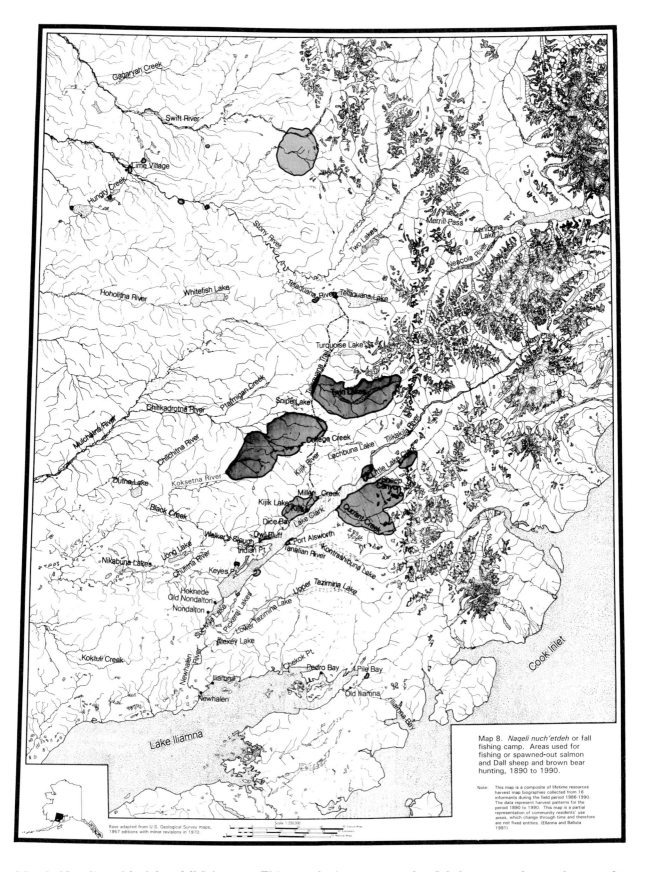

Map 8. *Naqeli nuch'etdeh* or fall
fishing camp. Areas used for
fishing or spawned-out salmon
and Dall sheep and brown bear
hunting, 1890 to 1990.

Note: This map is a composite of lifetime resources
        harvest map biographies collected from 16
        informants during the field period 1986-1990.
        The data represent harvest patterns for the
        period 1890 to 1990. This map is a partial
        representation of community residents' use
        areas, which change through time and therefore
        are not fixed entities. (Ellanna and Balluta
        1991)

Base adapted from U.S. Geological Survey maps,
1957 editions with minor revisions in 1970.

Scale 1:250,000

Map 8. *Naqeli nuch'etdeh* or fall fish camp. This map depicts areas used to fish for spawned-out salmon and
to hunt Dall sheep and brown bear, 1890 to 1990.

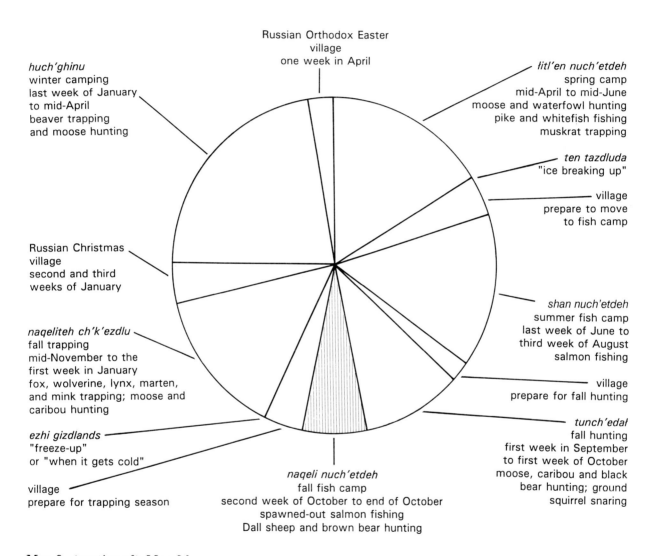

huch'ghinu
winter camping
last week of January
to mid-April
beaver trapping
and moose hunting

Russian Orthodox Easter
village
one week in April

litl'en nuch'etdeh
spring camp
mid-April to mid-June
moose and waterfowl hunting
pike and whitefish fishing
muskrat trapping

ten tazdluda
"ice breaking up"

village
prepare to move
to fish camp

Russian Christmas
village
second and third
weeks of January

shan nuch'etdeh
summer fish camp
last week of June to
third week of August
salmon fishing

village
prepare for fall hunting

naqeliteh ch'k'ezdlu
fall trapping
mid-November to the
first week in January
fox, wolverine, lynx, marten,
and mink trapping; moose and
caribou hunting

ezhi gizdlands
"freeze-up"
or "when it gets cold"

village
prepare for trapping season

tunch'edał
fall hunting
first week in September
to first week of October
moose, caribou and black
bear hunting; ground
squirrel snaring

naqeli nuch'etdeh
fall fish camp
second week of October to end of October
spawned-out salmon fishing
Dall sheep and brown bear hunting

Map 8. (continued) Map 8 key.

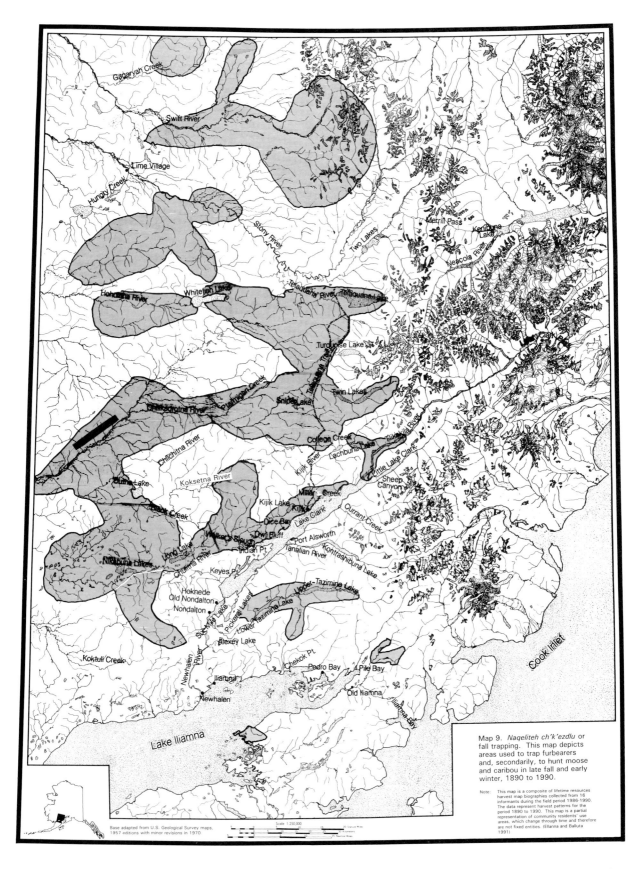

Map 9. *Naqeliteh ch'k'ezdlu* or fall trapping. This map depicts areas used to trap furbearers and, secondarily, to hunt moose and caribou in late fall and early winter, 1890 to 1990.

Note: This map is a composite of lifetime resources harvest map biographies collected from 16 informants during the field period 1986-1990. The data represent harvest patterns for the period 1890 to 1990. This map is a partial representation of community residents' use areas, which change through time and therefore are not fixed entities. (Ellanna and Balluta 1991).

Base adapted from U.S. Geological Survey maps, 1957 editions with minor revisions in 1970.

Scale 1:250,000

Map 9. *Naqeliteh ch'k'ezdlu* or fall trapping. This map depicts areas used to trap furbearers and, secondarily, to hunt moose and caribou in late fall and early winter, 1890 to 1990.

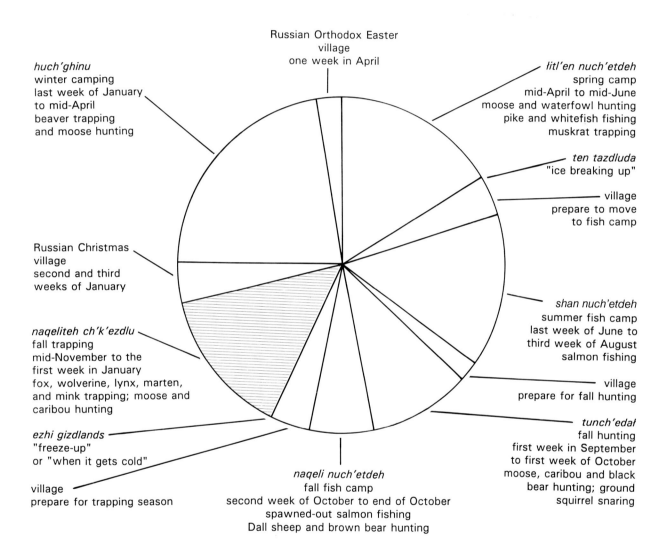

huch'ghinu
winter camping
last week of January
to mid-April
beaver trapping
and moose hunting

Russian Orthodox Easter
village
one week in April

litl'en nuch'etdeh
spring camp
mid-April to mid-June
moose and waterfowl hunting
pike and whitefish fishing
muskrat trapping

ten tazdluda
"ice breaking up"

village
prepare to move
to fish camp

Russian Christmas
village
second and third
weeks of January

shan nuch'etdeh
summer fish camp
last week of June to
third week of August
salmon fishing

naqeliteh ch'k'ezdlu
fall trapping
mid-November to the
first week in January
fox, wolverine, lynx, marten,
and mink trapping; moose and
caribou hunting

village
prepare for fall hunting

ezhi gizdlands
"freeze-up"
or "when it gets cold"

tunch'edał
fall hunting
first week in September
to first week of October
moose, caribou and black
bear hunting; ground
squirrel snaring

village
prepare for trapping season

naqeli nuch'etdeh
fall fish camp
second week of October to end of October
spawned-out salmon fishing
Dall sheep and brown bear hunting

Map 9. (continued) Map 9 key.

NAQELITEH CH'K'EZDLU: FALL TRAPPING

According to the inland Dena'ina, there was a sense of exhilarating anticipation associated with the commencement of fall trapping or *naqeliteh ch'k'ezdlu* and associated hunting. Map 9 illustrates the areas used for furbearer trapping and,

secondary moose and caribou hunting, during late fall and early winter, 1890 to 1990. Multiple related families and associated single men travelled together and resided collectively and cooperatively in cabins located at specific sites. In some cases, a family with small children moved with only one dog team. However, if there were other single adult males living with them, the former most commonly drove their own teams. In some families, wives drove their own teams and competently handled both dogs and sleds. By the middle of November, days were relatively short. Sled dogs had diminished endurance because of inactivity during summer and early fall months. Additionally, young children were part of this seasonal group. For these reasons, the distances which camping groups travelled in any given day usually did not exceed seven miles.

Camp locations were selected on the basis of usufruct rights established by a man's father and his father before him. During this time of year, rarely did men trap and hunt in areas associated solely with wives' kin. Because of reciprocal marriage between clans, however, both husband and wife may have had familial ties to the same area. Exceptions to this rule usually involved men married into the area of the inland Dena'ina from another location, such as Lake Iliamna. In other cases, men may have elected to hunt with their wives' kin when their own male relatives were too old or not exceptionally good providers.

Fall trapping camps most commonly used by Nondalton Dena'ina during the period 1890 to 1990 included Miller Creek, where there were four cabins in the early decades of the 1900s; Owl Bluff (Kijeghi Tsayeh), Qalnigi Tunilen; Chaq'ah Tugget, a bay on Lake Clark across from Tanilen Point; Lynx Creek; and Nikabuna Lakes. With the exception of Miller Creek, all of the other trapping sites had only a single cabin in the historic period. Some trappers left their families at Miller Creek and ran trap lines between Lake Clark and Telaquana Lake along the Telaquana Trail. These trappers normally had trap line cabins at K'a Ka'a, a valley on College Creek; Snipe Lake (K'adeła Vena); Denyihtnu, a canyon on the Mulchatna

River; and Telaquana Lake. The upper Stony River Dena'ina travelled into the headwaters of the Swift River or to the Hoholitna River for trapping and hunting from tents during this time of year (see P. Kari, 1983, for further information about fall trapping and associated hunting by the people of the upper Stony River).

Men, women, and children first established provisions at the main camps where they had cabins. Men and older boys gathered wood and made certain that grocery supplies were adequate to last several weeks. Boys generally were 11 or 12 years of age before they were allowed and able to accompany their classificatory fathers or older brothers on trap lines. However, in some cases a younger male was taken along if he were mature, skillful, and able to get along with little assistance in daily tasks such as dressing appropriately. Such a young man also was expected to ready himself in a timely fashion to go out for a day's trip and to demonstrate qualities of endurance. He also was required to participate in trapping and hunting without complaining in the face of difficult conditions. Women without children typically accompanied their husbands on trap lines.

While in late fall and early winter camps, women and older girls snared "rabbits" (hares); hunted grouse with 22 caliber rifles; jigged through the ice for grayling, whitefish, lake trout, and pike; gathered additional wood; hauled fresh water to the camp; and sewed clothing. Most of the game they harvested was eaten fresh, thereby serving as an important addition to their staple diet of smoked salmon, dried meat, and the remains of game from fall hunting. Cached fall game meat and hides were hauled to trapping camps at intermittent periods by men with teams during the course of trapping.

Trap lines generally ran from the site of fall trapping camps to the areas in which men had hunted earlier in the fall. An average trap line was 25 to 30 miles in length during short winter days. A man running a trap line took from 7 to 9 dogs. He remained away from the main camp for a period lasting from 10 days to a couple of weeks. By the end of the 1800s, steel traps had replaced traditional deadfalls and snares as means of taking furbearers. Furbearers most frequently harvested included fox, lynx, and martens, although weasels, wolverines, and other species were occasionally trapped as well. With the exception of wolves, furbearers were skinned at "spike" (i.e., secondary) camps and the carcasses discarded. In times of privation, lynx were sometimes eaten.

The inland Dena'ina had a high degree of respect for wolves and considered them to have been previously human. Wolves were known to save human lives in times of starvation, when they left part of their prey behind for people in need. Therefore, they were not usually trapped by the inland Dena'ina. If they were accidentally taken in a trap, they were skinned carefully, quartered, and the pieces hung in young stands of birch, spruce, willow, and other trees. It was thought that if a trapper talked to a wolf unwittingly trapped before killing it, assuring it of respectful treatment and the return of its body to the natural world, the wolf would not bring bad luck to the trapper and his family.

During this time of the year, the cold temperatures and short days made large game hunting difficult. Snow conditions were such that hunters pursuing an animal made considerable noise, whether by dog team or on snowshoes. Hunters travelling by dog team left sleds and animals some distance from where they attempted to pursue large game.

Moose prevalently spent their time during these months in valleys where willows and alders were abundant sources of food. An optimal hunting party was composed of four to five individuals. After spotting the tracks of a moose going into a valley, the hunting party split into two groups. Three or four men selected an observation point, from which the activity of the moose was monitored. One or two other hunters circled around the moose and came down the valley making loud noises by hollering. This activity was intended to scare the animal out of the cover of the valley's floor to where the hunter-observers were waiting. This was a fairly effective and efficient means of taking moose. A harvested moose was field dressed, divided among the families represented by the hunters, and taken back to the main trapping camp.

During late fall and winter, caribou predominantly were found in open, flat country, where mosses and lichens were not covered by deep snow because of their exposure to wind. If caribou tracks were spotted, normally four or five hunters, each with a team and sled, made the decision to follow the herd. Because of diminished sunlight, hunters were able to travel for only four or five hours per day, camping in a tent along the way. On average, it took several days to catch up to the herd. Decisions as to whether to go on foot or by dog team were made based on the freshness of the tracks. If the tracks were only hours old or the herd spotted, the dogs and sleds were left behind,

and hunters proceeded on foot. Hunters remained downwind of the caribou. Noise was not a problem, as the animals themselves were not quiet while feeding. Hunters approached as closely as possible before shooting. Prior to the use of firearms, hunters with bows and arrows split into two groups. One group circled the herd and drove it back toward the remaining men, who were armed and ready. As in the case of moose, caribou were field dressed, distributed between families represented in the hunting party, and hauled back to the main camp or to the village for Russian Orthodox Christmas holidays.

The occurrence of Russian Orthodox Christmas during the second week of January encouraged the movement of inland Dena'ina to villages for the second and third weeks of January in order to participate in this Christian holiday. In the past and during some years, only adult males returned to the community, leaving women and children behind at trapping camps. The decision as to whether or not entire families returned to the village was derived from multiple factors, including travel conditions and the health and age of family members. Prior to the celebration of Russian Christmas, the longer days and warmer temperatures of late winter signaled the move to winter beaver camps. Therefore in the historic period, time in the village for Russian Orthodox Christmas became a transitional period between late fall and early winter trapping camps to winter camps or *huch'ghinu*. During late winter, beaver trapping became the primary activity.

HUCH'GHINU: WINTER CAMP

At the end of January and beginning of February, men relocated camps to areas which provided good access to beavers. Equipment and food supplies were moved and tents pitched before families were taken to these camps. Then families and associated supplies were transported by dog team. Group composition at these camps mirrored that of the previous season. Map 10 depicts *huch'ghinu* or areas used for beaver trapping and occasional moose hunting, 1890 to1990.

As in the case of late fall and early trapping and hunting locations, winter camp sites were selected on the basis of usufruct rights between related males, as culturally defined. In the case of the Nondalton Dena'ina, key winter camp sites were located along the Mulchatna River and its tributaries, including the Chilchitna and Chilikadrotna rivers and Ptarmigan Creek (Yuzheghnitnu).

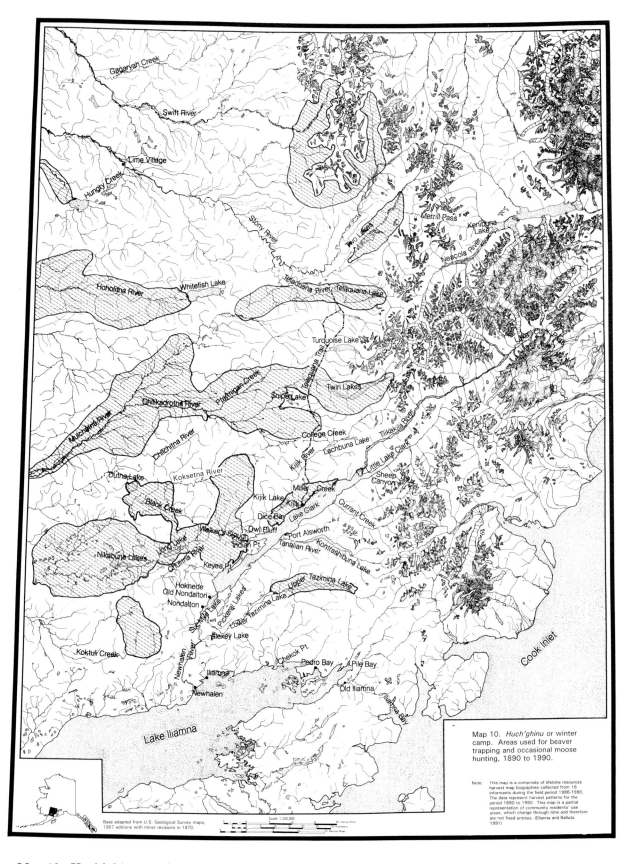

Map 10. *Huch'ghinu* or winter camp. Areas used for beaver trapping and occasional moose hunting, 1890 to 1990.

Note: This map is a composite of lifetime resources harvest map biographies collected from 16 informants during the field period 1986–1990. The data represent harvest patterns for the period 1890 to 1990. This map is a partial representation of community residents' use areas, which change through time and therefore are not fixed entities. (Ellanna and Balluta 1991)

Base adapted from U.S. Geological Survey maps, 1957 editions with minor revisions in 1970.

Map 10. *Huch'ghinu* or winter camping. This map depicts areas used for beaver trapping and occasional moose hunting, 1890 to 1990.

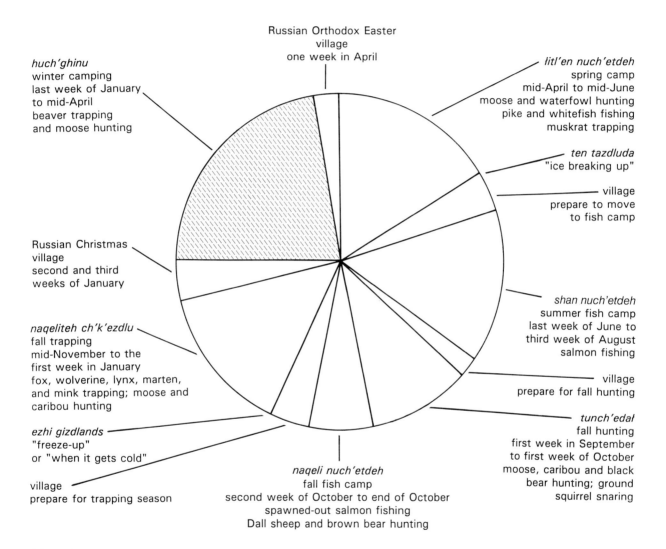

huch'ghinu
winter camping
last week of January
to mid-April
beaver trapping
and moose hunting

Russian Orthodox Easter
village
one week in April

litl'en nuch'etdeh
spring camp
mid-April to mid-June
moose and waterfowl hunting
pike and whitefish fishing
muskrat trapping

ten tazdluda
"ice breaking up"

village
prepare to move
to fish camp

Russian Christmas
village
second and third
weeks of January

shan nuch'etdeh
summer fish camp
last week of June to
third week of August
salmon fishing

naqeliteh ch'k'ezdlu
fall trapping
mid-November to the
first week in January
fox, wolverine, lynx, marten,
and mink trapping; moose and
caribou hunting

village
prepare for fall hunting

ezhi gizdlands
"freeze-up"
or "when it gets cold"

village
prepare for trapping season

tunch'edał
fall hunting
first week in September
to first week of October
moose, caribou and black
bear hunting; ground
squirrel snaring

naqeli nuch'etdeh
fall fish camp
second week of October to end of October
spawned-out salmon fishing
Dall sheep and brown bear hunting

Map 10. (continued) Map 10 key.

Figure 55. Bill Wilson, Sr., and Ben Trefon, Sr., at beaver camp, located on the Mulchatna River, in 1943. They are sitting in front of a white canvas wall tent commonly used during this part of the year. *Photograph Courtesy of Agnes Cusma.*

Other camps were situated along the tributaries of the Chulitna River, including the Koksetna River or Caribou Creek, Black Creek (Ch'dat'antnu), and Huk'esdlik'itnu, a creek that runs into the Koksetna River from the south. All of these sites were habitats for abundant numbers of beaver. For the upper Stony River Dena'ina, winter camps were located on the upper Swift and Hoholitna rivers (see P. Kari, 1983, for a more detailed description of winter trapping in the case of Dena'ina from the upper Stony River).

As a rule, winter camps were made up of two related families, each of which had its own tent. In some cases, single men had separate tents as well. Beaver trapping normally took place from the winter camp, usually within a single day's travel or 20 to 25 miles. Spike camps were established for overnight stays away from the main camp. Men in pairs usually trapped beaver and travelled the extent of their trapping area by dog team.

Trappers travelled along rivers, creeks, and the shores of lakes. As they journeyed, they searched for beaver cuttings. Such cuttings provided an indication that beaver had taken their food supply late in the summer and early fall in that area. Trappers expected beaver lodges to be located very near these cuttings. Holes were cut in the ice near the lodge and traps or snares set with bait. Steel traps were set on a pole. Fresh bait of newly cut willow, alder, birch, or cottonwood was tied in place near the top of the pole. The pole was placed through the hole in the ice and set into the bottom of the creek or river. It was positioned so that the trap was located approximately six inches below the surface of the ice. Beavers were trapped when they became attracted to the fresh bait. The bait was much more tantalizing than the old supply of food stored the previous fall along the shore under the ice.

In the case of steel snares, the ice hole was placed near the runway between the beaver lodge and its food supply. Three snares attached to poles were placed horizontally on the surface of the ice. They were set six inches or so below the ice perpendicular to the poles at angles which formed a triangle. A freshly cut piece of willow, birch, alder, or cottonwood was set in the bottom of the creek or riverbed through the middle of the ice hole and frozen in place. When the beavers attempted to recover the bait, they tried to gnaw it free from the ice. In doing so, they were unable to avoid entanglement in one of the snares, thereby drowning.

Beavers were pulled out through the ice hole and returned to the main winter camps before they were skinned, usually by the trapper. The hides were fleshed by women, and men stretched them on willow or alder hoops or stretching boards made from split or hewn trees. Some pelts were made into clothing. Others were sold in the spring at trading posts or to fur buyers who came to the village. The meat was hung from poles outside, where it froze and was eaten as needed. Beaver provided the primary source of protein at this time of year, unless a moose opportunistically was taken.

Prior to the introduction of steel traps and snares, the inland Dena'ina did not hunt beavers at this time of year. Alternatively, they awaited the arrival of spring by hunting small animals, such as "tundra" (arctic) and snowshoe hares, porcupines, and ptarmigans, and, occasionally, migratory caribou.

Elders remembered that hibernating black bears were taken during this season. Dens were relatively shallow and located in swampy areas. They were apparent to an observant hunter because of their hummocky appearance and frost above breathing holes. Hunters blocked the entrance to the den by thrusting two poles through the top, each perpendicular to the other. Another hole was cut in the top of the den, awakening the bear. When the bear was unable to escape from his entrance because of the poles, he attempted an exit from the newly cut hole in the top of the den. At that point, in more recent years, the bear was shot or, in the past, was speared by awaiting hunters.

Occasionally moose were hunted in deep snow at this time of year. Hunters were unable to pursue them, except when traversing the country on snowshoes. When the wind came up, it rustled the trees, thereby obscuring sounds of the hunter. Moose tracks were followed and intercepted by hunters travelling in small, semispherical paths. Therefore, hunters crossed the moose trail from side to side at regular intervals (Osgood 1976 [1937] and Nelson 1973 described this hunting method among the coastal Dena'ina and Gwich'in, respectively). Once a hunter no longer intercepted the tracks, he doubled back in order, hopefully, to locate the moose bedded down. Once a moose was found, his escape from the hunter was hampered by the depth of the snow. It is reported by the inland Dena'ina that a strong man on snowshoes eventually can run down a moose in deep snow. A moose taken during this season was welcomed as a source of fresh meat. Parts of the animal not consumed immediately were deboned, frozen, and hauled to spring camps or villages at the end of this segment of the annual cycle. The hides covered the frames of open freight boats, used to haul people, food, and all supplies back to the villages in spring.

Although in the 1970s and 1980s, most Nondalton families were not spending entire winters or springs at beaver camps, one elder wished to relive this part of the annual cycle while his health was still good enough to do so alone. In 1971, he flew to the Chilchitna River with his tent, snowshoes, traps and snares, a firearm, a saw, and a few food items, like coffee, sugar, and tea. According to his own account, he "lived like a hermit," not even taking a radio. He remained there trapping during February, March, and April. In April he sent for his sister's son, and they took home a full load of beaver pelts and meat to the village. In the 1980s, this event was recalled and admired by inland Dena'ina of all ages.

The timing of Russian Orthodox Easter, an important church event, varied by as much as a month, normally from the first week of April to the first week of May. As a rule, people remained in winter camps until Easter, at which time they returned to villages by dog teams. Returning families transported meat for consumption during the holidays and pelts of furbearers for trade or sale. The inland Dena'ina year had come full cycle.

VARIATIONS ON A THEME

The inland Dena'ina year — as portrayed in the narrative, maps, and figures in this chapter — is a composite. It was generated primarily from the lifetime seasonal rounds of individuals who were living in Nondalton in the 1980s. The significance of this chapter to an understanding of the inland Dena'ina did not lie solely in specific details, such as names of camps and resource harvest locations, technologies, resources utilized, or strategies. Rather, the portrayal of this seasonal round afforded insights into relationships between the Dena'ina and the natural world of which they were, and remained, a temporal, spatial, and ideological part. Unlike the static nature of this description, the inland Dena'ina seasonal round was dynamic. For example, seasons changed gradually, blending one into the other. Faunal and floral populations and distributions fluctuated within any given year or cyclically across the years. Human populations varied in size, composition, and spatial arrangement, in large part in response to introduced diseases, western social institutions, migration, and other factors over which the Dena'ina had little control. Technologies altered with the seemingly irrevocable involvement of the Dena'ina in world market systems.

Nonetheless, the key themes which emerged from this consideration of the inland Dena'ina year were the adaptive nature of this culture and people and the tenacity of their relationships with the natural world, despite the disruptive events of the last century. Some readers might critique the temporal dimensions (i.e., one century) portrayed in this composite seasonal round in favor of one which highlighted diachronic cultural change. Alternatively, the composite seasonal round portrayed here existed in the mental constructs and collective behaviors of the inland Dena'ina of the 1980s. That is, the continuity of ideology and practice overshadowed discontinuity or change at either level.

Figure 56. Andrew Balluta, lifetime resident of Nondalton, coauthor of *Nuvendaltin Quht'ana: The People of Nondalton*. Andrew was previously a park ranger at Lake Clark National Park and Preserve. *Photograph Courtesy of Lake Clark National Park and Preserve.*

CHAPTER 8

DENA'INA PERSPECTIVE:
A RESIDENCE HISTORY BIOGRAPHY OF ANDREW BALLUTA

I didn't know exactly where my father's and mother's camps was, but that's the area they hunted, they trapped. My interest was going there again, by myself. Nobody was interested in that area anymore. But my interest was going back there and seeing what it looked like. I was too small when they took me up there. I wanted to get back in there and learn that country, asking different people what's the country like, what it looks like, and then have them tell me the names of the places.

Andrew Balluta, 1986

IN THE BEGINNING: 1930 TO 1938

My mother, Sophie, told me that I was born in the dead of winter, January 9, 1930, at a place that we called Nan Qelah, referred to as "Miller's Creek" by non-Dena'ina people. Nan Qelah, in Dena'ina, means "where there is moss." Today that place is the home of the former governor of the Alaska Jay Hammond. But at the time I was born, it was a main fall trapping camp for the Nondalton Dena'ina. Women and children usually remained there from the middle of November until Russian Orthodox Christmas in early January. Sometimes they went there earlier if their husbands, older sons, and brothers were fall hunting from this camp as well as trapping. Nan Qelah was often visited by families who were not camped there, because it was located on the main trail to Telaquana.

The year I was born, my mother didn't go back to Old Nondalton for Russian Christmas. I was about to be born, and travel conditions were poor. My father, Anton Balluta, and his younger brother Ralph were out on their trap line with my mother's sister's husband, Gabriel Trefon, and Gabriel's brother, Wassillie. We also called him Was. My sister Betty, who's two years older than I, was with my mother. I was the eldest son. My father's mother, Daria, my mother's sister Katherine, and Mary Trefon helped my mother at my birth. My brother Jimmy was born in 1932, my sister Anisha was born in 1934, and my brother Phillip was born in 1936.

In 1930, my father's mother, Daria Koktelash Balluta, had just lost her husband. She lived in her own cabin with another son Harry and daughter Vera. The other people in camp that winter of 1929 to 1930 were my mother's sister Katherine, her husband, Gabriel, and their children, Agnes and Ben. This family was like my own, because, in the Dena'ina way, Katherine was like a mother to me, her husband like a father, and their children like my sister and brother. Wassillie and Mary Trefon and their son Henry were also in the camp.

Gabriel and Katherine Trefon and Wassillie and Mary Trefon occupied two log cabins. These cabins were chinked with moss and joined together by a common wall. My family's log house was located uphill from a old beach ridge. It was a single room, with caribou hide mattresses on wooden bed frames and calico covered rabbit skin or caribou hide blankets. By the time I was born, people were using tables and benches, wooden cabinets constructed of gasoline boxes, and a wood-burning stove made out of galvanized iron from the canneries in Bristol Bay. Firearms, ground squirrel parkas, sheepskin or smoke-tanned moose hide mittens and boots, and caribou legging cold weather boots hung within the arctic entry way, ready for use at all times.

That winter there was heavy snowfall. The trail back to Old Nondalton was not good. It was decided that the women and children would remain at camp, despite Russian Christmas, because of these poor travel conditions. The men and older boys returned to the village for Christmas. Normally, snow covered the countryside this time of year. Temperatures ranged from –10 to +30 F° during the month of January. Qizhjeh Vena, known today as Lake Clark, was usually frozen at this time of year. Travel was by dog team or on foot using snowshoes. We had mostly north and northeast winds during this season, making travel even more cold and difficult.

My mother had come from the upper Stony River and was born in the Dena'ina village of Qeghnilen. She was calm, kind, and loving to us. She never raised her voice. She was a hard working woman and never stopped from dawn to dark. She taught us many things that we needed to learn as

Figure 57. (from left to right) Andrew Balluta, Sophie Balluta, and Jimmy Balluta, at Pete Delkittie's fish camp on the Newhalen River. They were enroute to Iliamna, 1939. *Photograph Courtesy of Agnes Cusma.*

Figure 58. (left to right) Ralph Balluta, Paul Cusma, Larry Drew, Pete Trefon, and Anton Evan in front of a warehouse at Pile Bay on Lake Iliamna, 1939. They were employed to haul freight from Pile Bay to Iliamna for trader Hans Severson. *Photograph Courtesy of Agnes Cusma.*

Dena'ina children. Her father, a *Gasht'ana* or "white man," by the name of Jack Hobson had come to Alaska from the midwest as a young man on a sailing ship, seeking his fortune. While he was trapping and prospecting, he ended up on the upper Stony River in the early 1900s, where he met and married my mother's mother, Tatiana Constantine. Tatiana, or my *chida,* was a widow with two children. Together they had five more, two older and two younger than my mother. My mother was born in 1910. My *Gasht'ana* grandfather spent his entire life on the upper Stony River and, in later years, in Old and new Nondalton. He died in 1949 and was buried in Old Nondalton. He had learned to speak Dena'ina and, in many ways, lived like a Dena'ina man. Though he often swore and was loud, he was a kind man and especially very good to children.

My father was born in the village of Telaquana in 1905. He was the eldest son of Andrew Balluta and his wife, Daria. My father was kind to others and liked by most people in the village. He was a good hunter and trapper and tried to teach us what he thought we should know when we were very young. His father, Andrew, had spent most of his life at Telaquana. He was known to be a good hunter and provider as well. His grandfather on his mother's side had been a chief of Mulchatna village. *Chida* Daria was from the old village of Qizhjeh (Kijik) on Lake Clark. However, little is known today about her history.

My mother and her family moved from the upper Stony River to Old Nondalton in 1915. That's where she was living when she met and married my father in 1927. They were married first by a Territorial Commissioner at Goose Bay on Lake Iliamna. Later, they were married in the Russian Orthodox church in Old Nondalton. My grandfather Hobson had followed the Dena'ina custom of having a potential son-in-law live with them. This man was referred to as *k'eniquzdun* or "man performing bride-service." My dad hunted and trapped with my mother's father and brothers, in order to show them that he was capable of supporting my mom. Two previous suitors had not passed this test. After he had proven himself, my dad was given permission to marry my mom. After their marriage, they moved to live with dad's family. From this time on, they followed the seasonal cycle of hunting, trapping, and fishing which my dad had learned from his father. They moved from camp to camp and camp to the village, as needed. My father and mother always were good partners during the years I can remember. I never heard them argue with one another.

My family's seasonal round for the years 1930 to 1938 is shown in Map 11. The camp at Nan Qelah was for fall and winter trapping and a base for fall hunting in the high country. We came there by boat from Old Nondalton in early September and generally remained until the end of March. My first memories when I was about five years old were of the houses at Nan Qelah. I remembered being packed by my dad across the swift, high waters of the Kijik River in September. We were leaving the main camp on our way to a temporary fall hunting camp at K'ilghech', a valley south of College Creek, where we stayed in tents. My father, my uncle whom I also called *dada*, Gabriel Trefon, and Gabriel's brothers Alex and Pete also were hunting moose and caribou.

I remembered my dad skinning out a moose. I asked my mom how my dad had gotten the moose so close to camp. She told me how and why my dad took that moose. My dad had been on the side of a mountain looking for caribou. He saw a moose approaching camp. The moose was very close to my mom and the kids. The moose lowered his antlers at my mom. Because the moose was in rut, he was attracted to the camp by the sound of my mother and her sister chopping wood. He thought that he heard another bull. Even though my dad had told them not to chop wood at this time, my mom and her sister were doing it anyway. They thought that my father was up in the mountains. My father needed to get us meat but was also worried about the moose going into the camp. He rushed from where he was watching to the bottom of the valley to shoot the moose before it entered camp. My mom asked him if he had caribou. He said, "No, I came to shoot this moose." It was foggy, rainy, and cold. It was dark by the time that the moose was butchered, so my dad couldn't go back after caribou that day. This was a time of great excitement for all of us.

We usually stayed in the mountains for the entire month of September and then returned to Nan Qelah. Other years my family and I went to Qinghuch'una. This was a mountain at the head of the first creek from the north, which runs into the Chulitna River. In other years, we went to Venq'deltihi, a mountain with a lake on it, northeast of the Koksetna River.

At the end of September, we hiked back to the boats. We were carrying meat, caribou and moose hides, and the berries and squirrel skins which my mother and the other women had gathered and snared. The adults had to make several trips, but the children went only on the last one. From my earliest memories, my dad had his first outboard motor, a 4-horse Johnson. He used it on our 20 foot, spruce plank boat. Having the outboard motor made it easier for us to travel from Old Nondalton to Nan Qelah and from Nan Qelah to Tuk'eleh, the south creek on the Kijik River delta.

Tuk'eleh was our fall fish camp, an exciting place to go. We often had visitors passing through the country by boat. It was the place we went to put up spawned-out sockeye. During these years, our family often went there with my father's unmarried brothers, Ralph and Harry, and their unmarried stepbrother, Paul Cusma. Paul was a stepbrother to my father and his brothers, because his father had married my father's mother after my grandfather had died. Spawned-out sockeye were taken by gill nets in Lake Clark and in fish ponds near our camp. My mom cleaned them with my dad's and uncles' help and hung them to dry. Dogs were fed these fall fish while we were at this camp, rather than the precious smoked fish which we put up earlier in the year.

Later in the fall, while we were still camped at Tuk'eleh, my father and his brothers travelled by boat to Nuch'tnashtnunhtnu or Currant Creek. There they left their boat and climbed the mountains to get to Dall sheep hunting areas. If hunting was not successful there, they travelled farther up the lake into Little Lake Clark and then into Tsayeh Ka'ahtnu, also known as Sheep Canyon. The year that I was about six years old, I was allowed to go with them on the boat. My dad stayed with me at Little Lake Clark. My uncles, whom I also called *dada* or father, went into the mountains in the morning. By evening, they returned with the meat and the hides of two sheep. It was late, so we camped on the beach, having a delicious dinner of sheep ribs roasted in an open fire. We didn't have tents but slept under a canvas tarp in sleeping bags. The next day we returned to Tuk'eleh, where they hung the meat and dried the hides. Dall sheep hides were used to make sleeping bags, mittens, socks, or lining for coats.

Later in the fall, before my family moved to trapping camp or went back to Old Nondalton, my father and his brothers went brown bear hunting. I was too young to go during these years. They travelled on foot about two miles north across the mountains to K'q'uya Vena. This place is referred to as Kijik Lake today, but that's not really its name. According to the Dena'ina, it should be called "sockeye salmon lake." Kijik Lake is actually Lake Clark.

They found fish ponds where sockeye were spawning and located spots where tracks and trails led to places that brown bears were feeding. They waited until moonlit evenings or nights on the opposite side from where the bears entered the fish pond. The light from the moon enabled them to see the bears. They shot one bear and waited until daylight to skin it. First they took off the hide, which was rarely saved, and then they removed the fat. The fat, later rendered into oil, was the main reason for taking the bear. The meat was quartered, taken back to Tuk'eleh, and used or shared with neighbors who were short of food.

By the end of October, it was getting cold. We were getting ready for another move. The men made a fast trip back to Old Nondalton by boat to get supplies of flour, sugar, rice, and smoked salmon, which had been cached there at the end of summer. The men brought my father's sister Vera with them when they returned. My family and my dad's brothers and sister travelled by boat about four miles southwest of Tuk'eleh to Chaq'ah Tugget. Chaq'ah Tugget is a bay on Lake Clark, where my dad had a trapping cabin at that time and my mom has a home today. The cabin was small, but they pitched a tent alongside it with a stove. That was where my uncles stayed. The bay was where men and women prepared for fall and early winter trapping. My father and his brothers repaired or built sleds, snowshoes, tow lines, and dog harnesses. My mother sewed and mended winter clothing for all members of the camp. The children played and learned what we would be required to do when we were older by watching and helping adults. We also hauled water and brought in wood that had been cut and split by the men. We fed the 16 to 18 dogs in the two teams. The men used the dogs for running trap lines and providing transportation for the family. A few dogs and a sled were left behind at the camp, so that the women and children could haul wood in the absence of the men. Caring for dogs was a real chore but one I really liked to do.

After the lakes, rivers, and creeks froze and there was enough snow on the ground, my dad and his brothers left the main camp for as long as a week to 10 days. They trapped for red and cross fox, lynx, wolverine, marten, river otter, and mink. They also made temporary small camps. These are called "spike camps." The trail they followed went from Chaq'ah Tugget to Hukughitenitnu, a creek

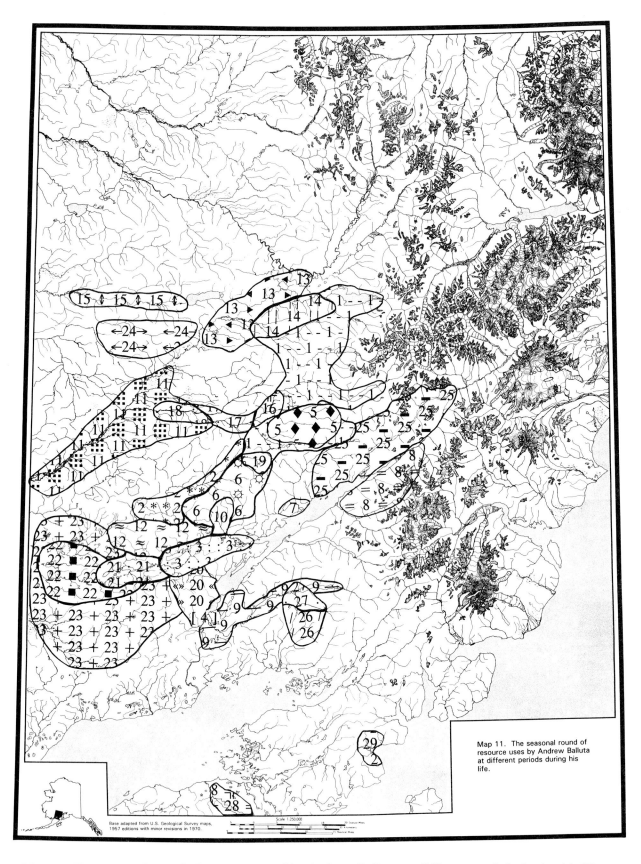

Map 11. The seasonal round of resource uses by Andrew Balluta at different periods during his life.

Map 11. The seasonal round of resources used by Andrew Balluta at different periods during his life.

Seasonal Round	1930 to 1938	1940 to 1953	1962 to 1990
Fall trapping, or *Nageliteh ch'k'ezdlu.* Areas used to trap furbearers and to hunt moose and caribou.	1, 5, 14, 16, 19	2, 9, 10, 11, 12, 18, 22, 23, 27	11, 18, 22, 23
Winter camping, or *Huch'qhinu.* Areas used for beaver trapping and moose hunting.	2	3, 8, 11, 13, 14, 15, 18, 21	3, 16, 17, 18, 21, 22
Spring camp, or *Litl'en nuch'etdeh.* Areas used for beaver, moose, and waterfowl hunting; grayling, whitefish, and pike fishing; and muskrat and beaver trapping.	3	3, 21	3, 21
Summer fish camp, or *Shan nuch'etdeh.* Areas used for summer salmon fishing.	4	4	4, 7
Fall hunting, or *Tunch'edal.* Areas used for hunting moose, caribou, and black bears, and for snaring ground squirrels.	5, 6, 10, 19	6, 10, 19	6, 10, 19
Fall fish camp, or *Naqeli nuch'etdeh.* Areas used to fish for spawned-out salmon and to hunt Dall sheep and brown bears.	7, 8	7	7, 8
Big game hunting. Areas used for big game guiding			24, 25, 26, 27, 28, 29

Map 11. (continued) Map 11 key.

that runs into the head of K'q'uya Vena. Then they went to Nusdnigi Q'aghdeq or Caribou Lakes, which are located in a valley on the Koksetna River. Then they went on to Tsilak'idghutnu, called the Chilikadrotna River on *Gasht'ana* maps. This route also was used for hunting moose and caribou during late fall and early winter.

Uncle Harry often stayed behind with my mom and us kids. Because of the short days, they trapped fox and lynx right around Chaq'ah Tugget and K'q'uya Vena, both within walking distance of our main camp. My Aunt Vera, who was my *vach'ala,* was 10 or 11 years old. She was old enough to care for me and my younger brothers and sister. During these years, I was too young to go with my dad.

We stayed at this camp until the end of January or early February. Sometimes, the entire family went back to Old Nondalton during Russian Christmas, which occurred during the first two weeks of January. We especially liked to go when a priest was visiting the village. When we moved our camp during those years, it was usually to Q'uk'tsatnu, now called the Koksetna River. My dad didn't have a cabin there, so we lived in a white canvas wall tent with a Yukon stove. This kind of stove usually was made out of gasoline cans, which could be taken apart and were light and easy to carry around.

By the mid-1930s, my father's youngest brother and sister remained in the village with their mother in order to go to school. My family and my dad's brother Ralph were the only ones to move to winter camp. The men trapped beaver under the ice on the Q'uk'tsatnu River and Ch'dat'antnu or Black Creek during overnight trips from our main winter camp. My mom kept the main camp going and cared for my younger brothers and sister. My dad and his brother brought beavers back to the main camp, where they skinned them and stretched the hides. My mom hung the meat to freeze. I remember that Uncle Ralph used to haul some of the beaver meat back to the village for his mom and the younger kids. We stayed at this camp until Russian Easter, which usually occurred sometime in April. Before we went to the village, we hauled the camping gear to Qinghuyi Vena or Long Lake, where it was left until we returned to spring camp.

During the Easter holiday, many families from Old Nondalton returned to winter camps. It was fun to get back together with other children my age. Besides the Easter services in the Russian

Orthodox church, the adults had potlatches. At potlatches, members of one clan cooked food for the opposite clan. My clan, which I inherited from my mother's side, was *nuhzhi*. My father belonged to the opposite clan, *kukuht'an.* My father's father also had belonged to the *nuhzhi* clan.

A day or two after Easter Sunday, I remember that our family sometimes left the village with other families to go to spring camp. One year, Pete Delkittie, his son Nicholai, and Nicholai's family wanted to go with us to the same area. Nicholai and my dad agreed to use the same spring camp. We called Nicholai by another name, Gulia. That same year, Alexie Balluta and his family and Gabriel Trefon and his family also left the village with us. About one day out from the village, we stopped to camp. We built a steam bath and everything. We were there maybe a week waiting for breakup, so that we could travel by canoes and *baidarki*s.

When we were ready to go again, Alexie and Gabriel and their families followed a different trail, which led to another spring camp. My dad and Ralph hauled a load of freight to our spring camp at Qinghuyi Vena before taking the family. My dad brought his three-hatched, canvas-covered *baidarki*. We had travelled for three days, in part because we were visiting with the other families. The time it took to get to spring camp depended upon travelling conditions and how often we stopped to visit others on the way. By the time we got to the Chulitna River, the ice already was getting pretty rotten. My dad had to use the *baidarki* to transport both families across the open water, while the dogs swam. We left one sled behind on the opposite shore and the other we floated across for hauling gear. Then we hiked over the portage to Qinghuyi Vena. The dogs hauled our gear on the sled, even though there was no snow left on the ground. My dad packed his *baidarki* on his shoulders.

At the camp, we set up three tents. One was for my dad and mom and their family. Gulia and his family had their own tent. Pete Delkittie, Gulia's father, had a third tent. There was a steam bath at the camp, which had to be repaired by the adults. Having a steam bath at camp was very important to the Dena'ina, as we used them to bathe every other day or so. As soon as the camp was set up, my dad and Pete Delkittie built a moose-hide covered canoe with a spruce frame. Moose hides were put on the frame while still raw. The hides dried on the frame. While they were drying, my dad and Pete kept rubbing them with oil and moose tallow. The oil was rendered from the boiled heads of salmon. Both oil and tallow were rubbed along the seams joining hides. After the hides dried, Pete and his son used the canoe. My dad used his *baidarki* to hunt and trap beaver, fish for whitefish and pike, and trap muskrat and for transportation.

During the spring of 1936, I was six years old. I was not allowed to use a firearm without my mom or dad being with me. I was taught to use a single shot 22-caliber rifle. Gulia's son, also named Nicholai, was a little older than I. He and I used to set small steel traps for ducks or muskrats. Most of the time we got only ducks. Sometimes my dad took me in his *baidarki* when he was hunting beaver and let me try to shoot, but I still was not a good enough shot to get one. I was not allowed to shoot from the *baidarki*. My dad was afraid that I might shoot a hole in the boat. We would go near a beaver lodge and sit on shore, waiting for beaver to come up. One day we went across the lake to a small creek where there was a beaver lodge. We sat and waited for one to come out. My dad shot the first beaver that poked his head up. It was a large animal. I asked my dad if I could shoot the next one. When it came up, he let me shoot. I missed it and felt like I was going to cry. My dad was patient and told me to wait for another. The wait seemed like hours, although I know it wasn't really very long. Finally, another beaver came up. I shot at it, and, to my surprise, I had killed the beaver. It was only a little, small beaver, but I was really proud. When we brought it back to camp, my dad told me to give the beaver to the old man, Pete. I could barely carry it because I was small, but I dragged it over to the old man. My dad told Pete that it was my first beaver. Pete skinned it out and cooked it, but I was not given even one piece. I already had been told that a boy never shares in eating the first game animal he takes. He only gives it to others.

The spring I took my first beaver, Gulia and his wife, Stephanita, had three children, two boys and one girl. The girl, whose name was Olga, was less than two years old. She became ill while we were at spring camp. The adults did everything they could to help her recover, but they did not have any *Gasht'ana* medicine. When her condition got worse, my dad carried his *baidarki* across a portage to the Ch'alitnu. The portage made his trip to another camp at Nikugh Vena shorter, as he did not have to follow every bend of the river. He and I went in his *baidarki* upriver to Nikugh Vena, where Chief Alexie Balluta and Gabriel Trefon were camped. In the case of an accident, sudden death, or serious illness, a neighbor was notified. Dena'ina chiefs always made an effort to go wherever there were problems or trouble involving their people. Alexie Balluta and his son Bob, Gabriel Trefon and his son Ben, and Alex Balluta followed us back to our camp in moose-hide canoes. By the time we arrived, the baby already had died. My dad and the baby's father went across the lake where there was good timber. They split some spruce trees and hewed them out with an ax to make lumber for a coffin and a cross. The other men stayed in camp and dug the grave with wooden shovels and axes. We didn't have metal shovels at that time. A Russian Orthodox prayer was said. Everyone sung a song, and the burial was complete.

During these years, life was expected to go on as normal even though a death had occurred. This was the Dena'ina way. Even the mother of the child who died was expected to continue to prepare food and carry on with her daily work, although she cried and sadness showed in her face. My mom assisted her in preparing food for a meal after the funeral. This meal was to thank the men from the other camp for coming to help with the burial. Alexie and Gabriel and their sons and Alex Balluta remained with us for a couple of days before returning to their camp. Because the little girl who had died was a member of her mom's and my mom's clan, they were expected to provide the meal of thanks to the men of other clans for assisting in the burial and funeral services.

Spring had come to the Lake Clark area. It was warmer, leaves began to bloom, and ice and snow melted. The smell of spring was in the air. By now it was late May and time to move our spring camp downriver. My dad and his brother constructed the frame of a two moose skin *niggiday* or large boat, which was used to transport our meat, beaver pelts, and camping equipment to Ch'alitnu Hdakaq at the mouth of the Chulitna River or to Yusdi Ghuyiq'.

Yusdi Ghuyiq' is known today as Indian Point. This was where the inland Dena'ina from spring camps all over the area got together, often with our *Dutna* neighbors from Newhalen, to await the breakup of ice on Qizhjeh Vena or Lake Clark. At spring camp, each family had a wall tent approximately 10 by 12 feet in size. The tents were heated with wood-burning stoves. Single men had separate sleeping tents but ate with their families. This was a great time for everybody, adults and children. I got to see my friends, and the adults got to see each other and play games, such as stick gambling games or *ch'enlahi*. My friends and I carved pieces of wood shaped like boats, attached them to strings, and played along the shore, pretending that we were going up rivers or travelling up the lake. We also played with toy bows and arrows. We used empty ammunition cartridges to make arrow heads for taking spruce hens. We also speared grass balls to improve our skill, an activity called *k'ighali*. We played many other games as well. We stayed at this camp for about two weeks until the ice went out.

Gabriel Trefon and his son and Kerosim Balluta returned to Old Nondalton on foot to get their boats, while the women and their children remained at the camp. When they came back up to Yusdi Ghuyiq', they were accompanied by my mother's brothers, Macy and Steve Hobson, who also brought their boat. All the plank boats had outboard motors. They towed the *niggiday* and canoes back to Nondalton. My dad was the only one with a *baidarki*, and he and I travelled back to Old Nondalton in his boat. We followed the beach in the *baidarki*, so that the dogs followed us back to the village. Preparation for summer fishing was about to begin.

At the village, my dad put his plank boat in the water. All the men left for Hans Severson's trading post at Iliamna. They used their winter furs and beaver pelts to trade for flour, sugar, lard, coffee, tea, ammunition, gasoline for the outboard motors, bolts of cloth for my mother to sew into pants and shirts for us, and, occasionally, a few items of store-bought clothing. My friends and I weren't interested in going to Iliamna with the men. We had more fun playing together in the village after being separated for most of the year.

As soon as the men returned from Iliamna, we began to move our supplies and gear to our summer fish camp, which was located about one mile upriver from Ts'atanaltsegh, a creek below Fish Village on the Newhalen River. My mom's mother's brother's daughter Ruth Bobby Kok-telash and her husband, Pete, camped with us as did Simeon Kankanton, or Singha, and his second wife, Agafia, whom we called "Mrs. Singha." I called her *chida* or grandmother. Simeon and his wife were elderly and they were alone. Most of their children had died, and their only surviving son lived with his wife's family. The men repaired the smokehouses and fish racks, put up the framed, white wall tents, cut wood, and put the fish bins and cutting tables back on shore where they could be used by the women for processing sockeyes. Then my dad and most of the younger men left for Bristol Bay, where they fished or worked as processors for the canneries.

A week or so before the first salmon came, my mom, Ruth Bobby Koktelash, and some of the children who were older went up on the mountains overnight. We trapped ground squirrels and generally took a "vacation." The younger children were left behind in the care of older girls. We also went from camp to camp by boat visiting people. Finally, word spread from downriver that the first salmon had come to Newhalen. Early in the season, the older people, kids, and women set gill nets when the runs of sockeye were still small. Later in the summer when large numbers of fish began to run, my mom and the other woman began seining using a common net. The fish schooled up at night, so everyone usually seined in the mornings. If we couldn't find enough fish, we used to row along the beach looking for schools of sockeye. If there were lots of salmon, my mom put up as many as 200 fish in a day. I followed my mom everywhere she went by boat, helping her by pulling in the lead lines, holding the rope from shore while the adults set the seine, hanging fish, tying fish backbones, cooking food for the dogs, and cutting wood for the smokehouse. Sometimes I was lazy and would sneak off to play. One time I climbed on top of the smokehouse. My mom got real mad and took a belt to me. She told the other kids that I deserved the spanking for not behaving. The activities at summer fish camp went on throughout the month of July.

The first of August, my dad and the other men returned from Bristol Bay. This was a great time for me. This was probably the only time they purchased candy. Sometimes, the men brought candy back in barrels to last the winter. Sometimes he brought us canned fruit instead of candy. We all had fun being together for a day or so, and then the work started again. The men put up fish for dog food for the winter. They made getting the fish fun by doing the work in a playful manner. There was a lot of joking, pushing one another in the water, and loading up anyone's boat with fish. The men really enjoyed one another's company. The women remained back in the camp, gutting and filleting salmon after salmon, while the men hung them in the smokehouse. After 10 days, we usually had enough fish. We stayed around another week or so until the fish had dried. Then everything was cached, the boats loaded, and we returned to the village. By now it was the end of August.

In Old Nondalton, we lived in a one room log house which we shared with my dad's two unmarried brothers. My dad and his brothers prepared to leave for Iliamna by boat, accompanied by six or so pack dogs. They travelled by boat to a point below the first rapids on the Newhalen River. From there, they travelled on foot for nearly six miles overland to reach Iliamna. Sometimes my mom went with them if she had someone to care for us kids. In Iliamna, my family shopped for their winter supply of dry goods. These included 300 pounds of flour, 300 pounds of sugar, 100 pounds of rice, a case of tea, 20 to 30 gallons of gasoline, and various other foods, such as coffee and lard, and ammunition. While at Iliamna they camped near the Newhalen River, as Iliamna, as it is known today, was nothing but Severson's Trading Post. They needed to make several trips to pack the supplies from the camp on the Newhalen River over the portage, even with the help of the dogs. Each dog packed 50 pounds of flour, 25 pounds on each side. Three to four days later, the boats were loaded and my family travelled back to Old Nondalton. By this time, we were looking forward to going back to the mountains for fall hunting. Fall time was the most enjoyable period of the year for me. The seasonal round, for my family, had come full circle.

THE LOSS OF MY FATHER AND A TIME OF CHANGE

The year 1938 was a time of major change for me and my family. Shortly after summer fishing in 1937, my father began to have stomach pains while we were in Old Nondalton. A float plane coming from Anchorage stopped at the village to refuel on its way to Dillingham. Its arrival was fortunate, as the pilot was able to take my father to the U.S. Public Health Service Hospital at Kanakanak near Dillingham. My dad had his appendix removed, and he returned in late September. We didn't go fall hunting that year, because my dad was in the hospital. But my Uncle Ralph, who was also my *dada,* went hunting and brought meat back to the family. When my dad returned from the hospital and seemed to be well enough to travel, my family moved to Chaq'ah Tugget for fall trapping. He began fixing up the cabin and got prepared for running his trap line. However, he didn't seem to recover and wasn't feeling well. Sometime during the fall, he slipped on the ice and ruptured his surgery. In March, my family returned to Old Nondalton. Airplanes were uncommon at this time. My dad was unable to get to the hospital until late March, when an airplane on skis happened to land in Old Nondalton. When my dad arrived at the hospital, he was too ill to be helped, so they sent him home in early April.

From this time on, he got much sicker. On May 10, as spring had just come to the village, Alex Balluta and I were out on the mud flats trapping ducks and playing around. We heard the church bell ring, which let us know that someone in the village had died. Since I knew my dad was sick, I was afraid that the bell was for him. Alex and I hurried to my house and learned that my father had died. To all of us in the family, including my father's brothers and sister, his death was a great loss. This was especially true for my Uncle Harry and Aunt Vera, whom had been raised by my dad and mom. For years, I thought that Harry and Vera were my brother and sister. It was long after my dad died before I knew they were really my uncle and aunt.

My Uncle Ralph took over as the main provider for our family. He was always a cheerful, kind, and well-liked man. Ralph always provided for our family and was very close to my father. Chief Alexie Balluta came to Ralph and told him that his brother's family needed his help now more than ever. The chief explained that it was Ralph's responsibility to care for us now. Also, before my dad died, he had asked Ralph to care for my mom and the children, and he had promised to do so. That summer, Ralph moved us to fish camp as usual. Then he and Harry both went to Bristol Bay, where Ralph was fishing and his brother was working as a cannery processor.

While my dad was ill and knew he was going to die, he had asked Gabriel and his wife, Katherine (my mom's sister), if they could raise my brother Phillip. My mom was pregnant and dad knew she would have a difficult time with two small children. Of course, Katherine was the same clan as my mother and as Phillip, since children followed their mother's side. In addition, my father called Gabriel *ala* or older brother, because he was the son of my father's father's mother's brother. Family links remained intact, and Phillip was young enough to adjust to the change. Gabriel's daughter, Agnes whom I called "sis," was the one who really cared for Phillip. Since she was just a young girl at the time, Agnes was dismayed that Phillip always called her "mom."

Life went on as usual and Tony, my youngest brother, was born 10 days after my dad died. For the next two years, my mom stayed in the village during the fall, winter, and spring, while Ralph and my Uncle Macy on my mother's side became hunting, fishing, and trapping partners. They went out for two weeks or a month at a time, to the same areas my dad and family had used in the past. They supplied us with abundant food during those years. I was now between 8 and 10 years old, and

Harry was in his mid-teens. We often went along with Ralph and Macy on hunting and trapping trips. Although I had tried to go to school for a couple months after Russian Christmas in 1936, it wasn't meant for me. I wanted to go with my family to winter camp, and they had no desire to leave me behind in the village. By the time we were staying in the village between 1938 and 1940, the school had closed down. People were getting ready to move the community to a new location closer to the mouth of the Newhalen River on Six-Mile Lake. My mom spent most of her time taking care of the children.

However, bad luck came to my family again. During fall hunting in the mountains in 1940, Ralph was accidentally shot by another hunter. Paul Cusma and Harold Kankanton were hunting with Ralph and me. We were travelling in one boat and were hunting in Qinghuch'una for moose and caribou. It was rainy and foggy on the mountain where we were camped. Ralph and I went out hunting in one direction and Paul and Harold went in another. They mistook us for caribou, and Ralph was shot in the confusion. He was not killed instantly. We tried to stop the bleeding and get him back to the village. He died nine hours later, as we were carrying him out on a stretcher. We took him back to the boat and went on to Old Nondalton. It took us two and a half days to get back, travelling night and day without rest. My mother and the family took this second loss very hard. It was to change our life in a way nothing else had in the past. For me, I felt that I suddenly had to become a man at the age of 10 as the eldest son. The chief and the elders encouraged my mom to remarry, since she had so many young children. This was the Dena'ina way. However, my mother feared that a stepfather would not treat her kids as well as he should, and that she must raise them on her own. She became both mother and father to our family.

ANDREW COMES OF AGE: 1940 TO 1953

In the fall of 1942, my mom, the rest of the family, and I moved from Old Nondalton to the new village site. We spent the first two winters in a white wall tent. In the fall of 1944, I began gathering logs that my dad and Ralph had cut before they died. They were to be used for building a new house. Mom and I made a log raft and towed it by boat about two miles to the village. We started the foundation for the house. Gabriel Trefon and Pete Koktelash helped us build it with the occasional assistance of other villagers. During the 1940s, we had a 9-dog team and sled; a 20-foot spruce plank boat, which Gabriel and Ben Trefon helped us build; and my father's 4-horse Johnson outboard. All the kids in the family attended school but me.

My mother tried to support us. To get cash, she hauled mail by dog team from Iliamna to Nondalton, Port Alsworth, and other locations on Lake Clark. The mail route took her about three days. She made the run once a month, retaining this job for two years. She also ran a trap line for red fox, land otter, and mink in the vicinity of Nondalton. Her trap line stretched down the Newhalen River, to Pickerel Lakes, and to Alexey Lake. All of these locations were one-day trips from Nondalton. She cut cordwood for the school and hauled freight from Iliamna to various places around the lake, making additional cash needed by the family. I always accompanied her, and Betty was now considered mature enough to care for the younger children. The village became our main residence year-round, except for summer fish camp. When I was about 13 years old, I took over the family dog team. When I was 14, I began going to Bristol Bay to work in the canneries. I had to fib about my age, since workers had to be 18 years old before they could be employed.

Alex Balluta was about the same age as I and had gotten his first moose when he 12 years old or so. Kids teased me and said that I might not learn how to hunt because I had no father. I felt hurt, because both my dad and uncle had died. I went home feeling sad one day. My mom asked me what was wrong. I told her what the kids had said. The next day the wind was blowing and the weather was mild. It was unusually warm for January month. My mom told me to get ready to go out hunting. We often went porcupine, grouse, and rabbit hunting, and I thought that that was what we were going to do that day. Surprisingly, my mom told me to take my 30-06 rifle, which had belonged to my dad, along. We travelled with our team down the Newhalen River to Nli Z'un Vetnu, the second creek below Fish Village, where we left our dogs. Then we travelled on snowshoes up into the hills, following fresh moose tracks. Before we got to the two moose, they began to move away. They heard us approaching. My mom told me that I should try to shoot before they got out of range, if I thought I could hit one. I shot and saw a cow stumble and go down, much to my mom's surprise. My mom wanted me to go right over, in case the moose might only be stunned or slightly injured. When I got there, the moose was dead. We skinned it out, cleaned it, quartered it, and took a small

Figure. 59. (left to right) Pete Koktelash and Andrew Balluta, on the mountain, Qinghuch'una, where Ralph Balluta accidentally was killed. The photograph was taken in early October 1940. Pete and Andrew had returned to the site of the accident two weeks after it had occurred to retrieve the camping equipment. *Photograph Courtesy of Agnes Cusma.*

piece of meat back to the sled, because it was already dark. Mom told me to take the meat we had brought back to Gabriel Trefon, since boys were expected to give the first large animal they successfully hunted to others. The next day many people from the village went to get the meat, as it was thought to be a major event when a young man got his first moose. My family got a share of the rest of the moose once it was hauled back to the village, a good thing as we were living on dried fish. I was the only one who couldn't have any of the moose. After this time, the kids stopped teasing me, and I became a successful hunter.

Between 1942 and the fall of 1946, I seasonally hunted and trapped in different places. I began fall hunting for moose up the Ch'alitnu by boat with Pete Koktelash, who was adopted and considered to be my mother's brother. His own mother had died when he was very young. We no longer went to the mountains to hunt caribou or moose, and I never hunted sheep again until after I was married. I hunted black and brown bears with Gabriel and Ben Trefon by boat in the Kijik area. These trips away from the village lasted from one to two weeks. However, there were problems in hunting from late October until December from Nondalton. In October and November, boating on Lake Clark was very cold. Also, the lake normally remained ice free until late December or early January, making travel across ice impossible. When conditions were good, my mom and I occasionally hunted and trapped with Gabriel Trefon. Our trapping areas changed from those used by my dad to new places, such as Skihdulchin, a creek which runs from the mountain which we called Unhnidi. This place is referred to as Hoknede on *Gasht'ana* maps today. Unhnidi was a one-day trip from Nondalton. It was convenient for us to go there, since the younger children were in the village going to school. I also travelled with other people to places such as K'chanlentnu, a valley west of Lynx Creek. I went to other locations in the Ch'alitnu area, because it was close to Nondalton. In the spring I went to Ch'alitnu with Pete Koktelash, who became my spring trapping partner. Our summer fish camp remained in the same place.

These years were difficult for my mom. Supporting such a large family was not easy, especially for an unmarried woman. The school closed down again in 1946, since the Bureau of Indian Affairs had no teacher for Nondalton until 1950. The last year the school was open, the teacher told my mom that she should send the younger kids to a boarding school to get an education. My mom didn't want to send her kids away and was really talked into doing it by this teacher. He tried to convince her that boarding school was better for the children. From my mother's point of view, the teacher was suggesting that she was unable to properly care for her own children.

In the late summer of 1946, Jimmy and Tony, my brothers, and Anisha, my youngest sister, were sent to a boarding school in Eklutna by the Bureau of Indian Affairs, where they stayed for a few months. Then they were transferred to the Jesse Lee Home in Seward, something like an orphanage run by the Methodist Church. They stayed there for the remainder of the school year. They were not allowed to come home in the summer. During the summer of 1947, they were then sent to Wrangell Institute, another Bureau of Indian Affairs school. This boarding school was located in southeastern Alaska. We were not allowed to see the children again until the fall of 1948, when I made enough money fishing to take my mom to Wrangell for a visit.

In the spring of 1946, Betty went to work at Kanakanak Hospital near Dillingham. In September, my mom and I joined her there and also worked for the hospital. I remained in Dillingham until fishing season and then returned to Bristol Bay. Mom and Betty set nets in Nushagak Bay during the summer of 1947. In the winter of that year, we all moved to Anchorage. I went to work for the Alaska Railroad, and mom and Betty worked at Providence Hospital doing laundry and housekeeping. I fished every summer during the rest of these years. The younger children were moved from Wrangell to Mt. Edgecumbe in Sitka in 1948. They remained there until I paid their way back to Anchorage in 1949. Jimmy returned to Nondalton, and Anisha and Tony stayed with mom in Anchorage. It was there that she met and married a military man in 1952. She left Anchorage for her first "visit" to the "lower 48," a visit that lasted two years. It was during this period that all of the kids, except for Tony, got married and went their separate ways. Only Tony remained with my mom and her new husband. Our family was now spread across the United States. We had been forced to adjust to a totally new way of life, so different from that of our Dena'ina upbringing.

EPILOGUE

In 1953 I returned to Nondalton and the following year married Dolly Karshekoff. This marriage was arranged by Chief Gabriel Trefon and other elders on both my dad's and mom's sides. I later learned that my mom, who was absent from the village at the time, would not have approved of this marriage if she had been at home. Dolly's father had died, and she was of an acceptable clan, *ggahyi*. However, although her clan was from the "opposite side," it was not the "opposite clan" of my clan, *nuhzhi*. Some people considered Dolly to be a proper Dena'ina woman ready for marriage. We lived in Nondalton until we were separated in 1964. We had three children, two boys and one girl. Andrew, the youngest boy, died in 1964 of meningitis. The other two, Marilyn and Ralph, were raised in both Nondalton and Anchorage.

During the years of my marriage, my family remained village based. The fur market had fallen, with the exception of beaver. Therefore, late fall and early winter trapping was no longer profitable. I continued to trap beaver but no longer went back to areas used by my dad. Instead, I trapped in the Ch'alitnu area with Paul Zackar, my wife's stepfather. I had to raise new dogs, as we had given away our team when we left the village. I hunted moose by boat during the early fall up the Ch'alitnu or at the head of Lake Clark. I began hunting sheep again at Tsayeh Ka'ahtnu and Ch'kentalgeyitnu. I no longer hunted in the mountains but pursued brown and black bears around Lake Clark by boat. I built my own fish camp at Nundaltinshla, where other people had summer fishing sites. My family and I shared our camp with Gabriel Trefon, Agnes Cusma and her family, and Benny and Irene Trefon and their family. Irene was my father's sister's daughter. I continued to commercial fish in Bristol Bay as an independent fisherman after 1954.

From 1962 to 1979, I became a big game guide for moose, caribou, Dall sheep, and brown and black bear hunting. Some of the areas I guided in were the same as those I had used during my lifetime for subsistence hunting. I was unsuccessful in my bid to get a commercial fishing limited entry permit when they were issued by the state for Bristol Bay in 1973. I did not qualify, because I had not been a boat captain for the two years prior to the beginning of the permit system. In 1983, I was employed as a local hire in the position of park ranger for Lake Clark National Park and Preserve. Tony was still living with my mother. After his death in 1985, I took over fishing his drift permit for Bristol Bay.

My knowledge of the land and resources of the area in which I was brought up were applied to my job as a park ranger and to reconstructing the cultural history of my people in this book. I still hunt and fish as well as work for wages. My mother returned to the Lake Clark area in 1966 and remains heavily dependent on the products of hunting, fishing, gathering, and trapping for her well-being and survival. Her primary home is at Chaq'ah Tugget, although she recently had a small house built in Nondalton.

Throughout the course of my life, the extent of the area with which I became familiar included Ungeghnich'en Tazin Vena, or Upper Tazimina Lake to the southeast; Qukdeli to the southwest; Tleghtitnu, or the Hoholitna River, to the northwest; and Two Lakes, or Tutnutl'ech'a, the outlet of Merrill Pass, in the northeast. Despite the fact that my life has undergone many changes which have affected my use of the land in which I was born and raised, its meaning to me personally and to my children and their children after them and to the other Dena'ina of my village was in no way less important in the 1980s than it was in the past. This was and remains the home of the inland Dena'ina.

Figure 60. Ralph Balluta, Andrew Balluta's eldest son, standing on the stairs of the community hall in Nondalton in 1958. *Photograph Courtesy of Agnes Cusma.*

Figure 61. (left to right) Ruth Koktelash, Sophie Austin, and Agnes Cusma, processing sockeye salmon at Agnes' fish camp at Ch'ghitalishla, July 1986. This site is located approximately one-half mile south of Nondalton. The women are processing fish on a typical cutting table. *Photograph Courtesy of IMPACT, Rasmuson Library, University of Alaska Fairbanks.*

CHAPTER 9

THE SOCIAL DIMENSIONS OF INLAND DENA'INA ECONOMICS

*This mixture of cash and subsistence econo-
mies has brought a kind of stability to interior
villages that never existed in the past. The spec-
ter of severe shortages and starvation is now
gone, because people can depend on imported
foods if necessary. But Athabaskans are not
satisfied with a steady diet of "white man
grub," because they strongly prefer traditional
foods and consider them more healthful. . . .
Athabaskan people not only prefer to eat Native
foods, but they have also made them a central
part of their social lives through networks of
sharing that bind families and neighbors to
one another. Subsistence foods are an essential
part of social and ceremonial events, such as
potlatch feasts, which symbolize intense connection between villagers and the wild
resources they depend on. In the conclusion of
his speech at a village feast, a Koyukon elder
summarized this dependence by saying, "Food
is the meaning of our lives."*

Richard Nelson, ***Raven's People,*** 1986

A CONCEPTUAL NOTE

Western analytical models commonly have been
applied in contemporary studies of modern hunter
and gatherer economic systems. Specifically, the
household, usually defined as the residential unit,
has been employed in analyses of production,
distribution, and consumption. However, anthropological data have indicated that the modern
"household," members of whom reside in a single
dwelling, cannot be equated with these respective
economic functions (cf, Altman 1987; Behnke
1982; Morris 1986; Nietschmann 1973). In some
cases, the terms "family" or "domestic unit" have
been used without definition, leading the reader to
the assumption that "household," "family," and
"domestic unit" are synonymous.

In the inland Dena'ina case, the English term
"family" was used by an individual to refer to a
category of people whom he or she considered
"relatives." Members of an individual's "family"
were rarely co-resident at any given point in time.
Additionally, the term "family" was used in
varying contexts to denote all relatives, a group
referred to by anthropologists as the "kindred" of
an individual, or a smaller group with whom one
had close emotional ties and day-to-day interactions. In other words, an understanding of the use

of the concept "family" among the inland Dena'ina
required knowledge of context.

Among the inland Dena'ina of the 1980s, the
membership of a residential unit (i.e., a house) was
fluid, commonly changing during any given day,
week, month, year, or between years. For want of
a better term, in this context "household" was
applied to those people who resided together at
any given point of time in the same structure.
However, the fluidity of this unit, by western"
nuclear family" standards, cannot be understated.
In no case were the members of a single
"household," as defined here, economically self
sufficient in terms of production, distribution, and
consumption.

Anthropologists have struggled with a definition
of the concept "domestic unit," which encom-
passes multiple and diverse functions attributed to
this group in literature from throughout the
world. In the inland Dena'ina case, the concept
of "domestic unit" was applied to a body of
individuals who functioned productively and
reproductively. That is, the members of this unit
were principally responsible for the economic functions of production, distribution, and
consumption and for the procreation and
enculturation of younger members of society. In
an attempt to define the social dimensions of
Dena'ina economics, the "domestic unit" was the
most meaningful and self-sufficient unit.

THE SOCIAL ORGANIZATION OF PRODUCTION

THE DIVISION OF LABOR

The division of labor in the subsistence sector was
termed by Sahlins (1981) "the domestic mode of
production." In the Dena'ina case, this division of
labor was based primarily on criteria of age and
sex. Table 5 presents a breakdown of inland
Dena'ina production for particular age and sex
cohorts for the period 1890 to 1990. The
organization of production in inland Dena'ina
society demonstrated considerable stability
through time. Factors such as seclusion and
related taboos at first menses or pregnancy, in the
case of women, were included in this analysis of
production for particular habitats and activities.

TABLE 5. SUBSISTENCE PRODUCTION AND HABITAT USE KEYED TO AGE AND SEX COHORTS AND FERTILITY STATUS OF FEMALES, INLAND DENA'INA, 1890 - 1990 [a]

Sex and Age Cohort[b]	Riverine or Lacustrine Fishing (Shore-Based, with Gill or Seine Net or Fish Wheel)	Fish Trap Fishing	Ice Fishing	Open Water Set Hook
Old and/or infirm males	+	+	–	+
Old and/or infirm females	–	–	+	+
Pregnant women	–	–	+	+
Male children (under 12)	+	–	+	+
Female children (under 12)	–	–	+	+
Females, first menses	–	–	–	+
Young to middle-aged males	+	+	+	+
Young to middle-aged females	+	+	+	+

[a] Format adapted from Laughlin (1972).

[b] + indicates participation; – indicates nonparticipation; and (+) indicates limited or sporadic participation

Sex and Age Cohort	Dip Netting	Salmon Processing (Human Use)	Salmon Processing (Dog Use)	Bristol Bay		
				Drift Net	Set Net	Cannery
Old and/or infirm males	–	+	+	–	–	–
Old and/or infirm females	–	+	+	–	–	–
Pregnant Women	–	+	+	–	+	+
Male children (under 12)	–	(+)	(+)	–	(+)	–
Female children (under 12)	–	+	+	–	–	–
Females, first menses	–	–	–	–	–	–
Young to middle-aged males	+	+	+	+	+	+
Young to middle-aged females	(+)	+	+	–	+	+

TABLE 5. CONTINUED [a]

Sex and Age Cohort	Large Game (Mountains)	Large Game (Village or Camp)	Game Processing (Village or Camp)	Small Game Snaring	Small Game Hunting
Old and/or infirm males	–	+	–	–	+
Old and/or infirm females	–	–	+	+	+
Pregnant women	–	–	+	+	+
Male children (under 12)	–	–	+	+	+
Female children (under 12)	–	–	+	+	+
Females, first menses	–	–	–	–	–
Young to middle-aged males	+	+	–	+	+
Young to middle-aged females	–	(+)	+	+	+

Sex and Age Cohort	Trapping (Furbearers and Beaver)	Waterfowl Hunting	Wood Cutting	Plant and Berry Gathering	Care of Dogs
Old and/or infirm males	–	(+)	+	(+)	+
Old and/or infirm females	–	–	–	+	–
Pregnant women	–	–	+	+	(+)
Male children (under 12)	–	+	(+)	+	+
Female children (under 12)	–	–	–	+	(+)
Females, first menses	–	–	–	+	–
Young to middle-aged males	+	+	+	(+)	+
Young to middle-aged females	(+)	+	+	+	(+)

[a] In all cases portrayed above, the table depicts normative behavior for this time period. Cases of idiosyncratic variation occurred but are not noted in this table.

Salmon fishing quantitatively provided the primary and most dependable source of food for the inland Dena'ina. The abundance and diversity of salmon harvested differed by areas. Sockeye was the only species in the Lake Clark drainage, while sockeyes, kings, dogs, and silvers were available and used on the upper Stony and Mulchatna river drainages. The successful production of salmon required a balanced division of labor between those who fished and those who processed the fish. Prior to participation in the Bristol Bay fishery, young to middle-aged males were the primary fishers. Traps in association with weirs were set in spawning areas until the early 1900s. Gill nets and seines were employed during most of this century, although nets were made out of local raw materials as well prior to the availability of commercial netting or twine. Even after participation in the Bristol Bay fishery became the norm principally for males residing in Old and new Nondalton, those who went to Bristol Bay returned to summer camps after commercial fishing ended. They put up fish for dogs and cached the smoked salmon which had already been processed.

Table 5 indicates that despite the technology used for obtaining salmon for domestic use — gill nets, seines, traps, or dip nets and fish wheels on the upper Stony River — young to middle-aged males and adult females were the primary producers. This production was supplemented by the efforts of older or infirm, but not incapacitated, males, who assisted in maintaining fish traps in the past or in gill netting or seining in more recent years.

Freshwater fish were important seasonally in the overall economy of the inland Dena'ina. This was particularly true in the spring, when smoked sockeye from the previous summer's cache were depleted. In earlier times, fish traps were used for freshwater fish as well as for salmon. During most of this century, however, gill nets, seines, jigging through the ice, and open water set hooking were the primary means by which freshwater fish were taken. Species valued most highly included whitefish, grayling, pike, lake and rainbow trout, and Dolly Varden. As can be seen in Table 5, adult males, using nets and with the assistance of older males and boys, were the primary producers of freshwater fish. However, all sex and age cohorts set hooks for fish in open water. Old, young, and adult women, except girls in their first menses, jigged for fish under the ice.

During years when Dena'ina families were short of dog food for their teams in the spring, most of the freshwater fish taken during this time of year was consumed at camp by people and their dogs. Commonly, however, a month's supply was dried and stored to tide the group over until salmon started running in the summer. The harvest of freshwater fish in spring was dependent upon the amount of smoked salmon remaining in each family's cache, the success of fall and winter hunting, family and population size, and other key variables. However, it was not uncommon for a domestic unit at spring camp to net approximately 1,000 freshwater fish of all species. One elder reported getting 2,000 grayling for his dogs in one day with a single net at Pickerel Lakes.

Hunting of large and small game quantitatively provided the second most important source of food and raw material for the inland Dena'ina. Qualitatively, however, the inland Dena'ina perceived themselves to be hunters and consumers of large game. They believed that if their supplies of fresh or dried meat were exhausted and they had only fish to eat, people were not getting an adequate diet. In fact, such a situation was perceived to be tantamount to starvation. To be without meat, especially fresh meat, was considered a perilous condition. Additionally, relying solely on smoked salmon depleted the amount of food a domestic unit had cached to last members an entire year. In addition, the hides of caribou and moose were essential to the construction of adequate cold weather clothing, skin-covered watercraft, summer housing materials, *babiche*, and many other items of technology. For the most part, these raw materials were not accessible from fish.

Young to middle-aged males normally were the sole harvesters of large game, especially during the productive fall hunt. They were also the principal sex and age cohort running trap lines. The maintenance of lengthy trap lines provided not only the opportunity to hunt large game in the course of trapping, but also yielded small mammals used for food. Not all households included young to middle-aged males but most domestic units did. Therefore, multiple households depended upon the distribution of game from others within the domestic unit. In rare cases, elderly people or individuals with few relatives required resources produced by members of other domestic units. Elders estimated that during an average year in the 1940s, domestic units with one or more active hunters took approximately 3 caribou, 2 moose, 1 brown and 1 black bear, and 10 beaver, not including other small game. If an example of contemporary

Figure 62 (above).   Martha and Olga Nudlash processing salmon next to a birch log fish bin at Ch'ghitalishla, a creek one mile south of present Nondalton, between 1910 and 1920. *Photograph Courtesy of the Alaska Historical Library, James Carter Collection.* **Figure 63** (below). Agnes Cusma and Andrew Balluta checking a gill net at Ch'ghitalishla from a 16-foot aluminum Lund boat, July 1986. *Photograph Courtesy of IMPACT, Rasmuson Library, University of Alaska Fairbanks.*

Figure 64 (above). Sockeye backbones drying on a fish rack near Ch'ghitalishla, summer 1986. **Figure 65** (below). Sockeye roe drying on a rack near Ch'ghitalishla, summer 1986. *Photograph Courtesy of IMPACT, Rasmuson Library, University of Alaska Fairbanks.*

Figure 66 (above). Agnes Cusma's smokehouse at Ch'ghitalishla, the location of her fish camp near Nondalton, summer 1986. **Figure 67** (below). The inside of Agnes Cusma's smokehouse at Ch'ghitalishla, filled with sockeye which are being smoked, summer 1986.

Figure 68. Agnes Cusma holding a processed sockeye, which she is about to place in the spruce bark-lined pit for storage (*chiqilin q'a* or underground fish cache). Fireweed leaves are placed between the layers of fish or fish heads to improve their flavor and aid in the storage and fermentation process. Birch bark is used to cover the pit, and the sod is replaced. *Photograph Courtesy of IMPACT, Rasmuson Library, University of Alaska Fairbanks.*

conversion figures is used to calculate edible weight of this harvest (Behnke 1982), each domestic unit was taking conservatively 1,810 pounds of meat without hides. Some households and domestic units were much more productive than others.

By way of contrast to the hunting of large game, older men, women of all ages, and young boys and girls, except for the latter in their first menses, were productive in hunting or snaring small game, such as ground squirrels, hares, ptarmigans, grouse, and porcupines. Ground squirrels and hares were essential sources of both meat for food and hides for clothing.

As in the case of salmon, the economic cycle involving the use of large and small game began with the harvesting of the animal and ended with the cutting of the meat into smaller units suitable for transporting, drying, or freezing, depending upon the season. These activities were followed with the processing of hides of particular species and desirable sex and age cohorts of specific animals. Again, the balanced division of labor between males and females was requisite to successful production, since females of all ages were the primary processors of meat and hides.

For the inland Dena'ina of both Lake Clark and upper Stony River, birch and spruce trees were the primary sources of fuel for heat in the past and remained so in the 1980s for in excess of 75 percent of Nondalton and 100 percent of Lime Village households. Even many households using oil heat in the 1980s also relied upon wood. Many of those who were using oil heat in the 1980s were elderly or community residents with full-time wage employment.

Reference to Table 5 indicates that wood cutting was a task for older and younger adult males and females, even when the latter were pregnant. Cutting wood was considered to be good exercise for any adult. Being short of wood for fuel was deemed to be a sign of laziness on the part of household members. Comparisons between the wood piles of different households were common topics of conversation in the 1980s and encouraged people to be productive.

Gathering plants and berries was principally a task undertaken by females of all ages and young boys. However, often men expressed the view that gathering berries was both productive and recreational, although few believed that they had the patience to undertake this activity on a regular or systematic basis. The wide range of plants and berries used by the inland Dena'ina was described in detail by P. Kari (1987) and is not repeated in this context. Plants and berries provided not only sources of food but also of traditional medicines and raw materials, many of which continued to be used in the 1980s. Plant and berry gathering, occurring primarily in the late summer and early fall, was considered to be an important female social activity as well as one of economic significance. In addition to plants and berries, spruce and birch bark were collected. The use of bark for construction or tool manufacture decreased markedly in recent years with the availability and selective adoption of features of Euroamerican technology.

During the years before snowmachines were introduced to the inland Dena'ina, and for years after in the case of some domestic units, dog traction provided the central means of transportation during winter months. Additionally, dogs were important as pack animals during the summer. Their feeding, watering, and overall care was indirectly related to resource productivity for these reasons. Generally, drivers cared for their own dog team in winter months. It was considered to be a way of establishing positive relationships between dogs and their owners during the most intensive canine work period. During summer, women and older children assisted in the care of dogs, particularly when men were away from the village. Generally young girls were not permitted to handle or care for dogs, although several exceptions to this rule were documented orally by residents of Nondalton and Lime Village. Some adult women, particularly from the upper Stony River, learned to drive dog teams and continued to do so into the 1980s. The use of dog teams for racing, recreation, and, in some cases, trapping was on the increase in the 1980s, as compared with the previous decade.

Until the early 1940s, only young and middle-aged adult males went to Bristol Bay. They initially worked in canneries and, in subsequent years, began fishing from sail-powered cannery boats. Sailing fishing craft were converted to gasoline and diesel power, beginning in the early 1950s. During World War II, the demand for local cannery workers increased, and females became an acceptable source of labor. Males were involved in the war effort, the conflict disrupted the transportation of the Asian work force to Bristol Bay, and, in general, the employment of foreigners during this time was discouraged. It was during these years that the first inland Dena'ina women

Figure 69. Sophie Austin peeling the outside layers on a piece of spruce bark. This bark was used for lining a fish caching pit. The bark was taken near Sophie's house at Chaq'ah Tugget on Lake Clark, June 1986. *Photograph Courtesy of IMPACT, Rasmuson Library, University of Alaska Fairbanks.*

Figure 70. Kristy Balluta (foreground) and her sister, Cherie (background), picking fireweed to provide leaves for the storage of sockeye in the bark-lined underground fish cache at Ch'ghitalishla, summer 1986. *Photograph Courtesy of IMPACT, Rasmuson Library, University of Alaska Fairbanks.*

went to Bristol Bay as cannery workers. Their participation in cannery processing and, later, set net fishing varied in the intervening period. With a very few exceptions, Dena'ina women did not play a role in drift fishing from boats in the past or in the 1980s.

In considering hunting and gathering economic systems, the question arises as to whether there is evidence for individual specialization in production. In the case of the inland Dena'ina, a conceptual dichotomy between economic specialization and political status in the early contact period is somewhat arbitrary.

Fall (1981) provided an excellent discussion of the traditional upper Cook Inlet Dena'ina *qeshqa*, usually translated "rich man." Nondalton elders reported that the functions of the *qeshqa*, before the coming of the Russians, related to the leadership of his extended family house group. He played a role in coordinating fishing, hunting, and other resource harvesting activities essential to the survival of the group. His role was of particular importance in productive activities requiring coordination and planning, such as building a fish weir and associated trap or constructing a caribou fence. The *qeshqa* also organized people to drive caribou into the surround.

Fall (1987) and residents of Nondalton reported that the *qeshqa* was instrumental in encouraging people, over whom he had influence, to be productive. He employed positive sanctions by disproportionately rewarding more industrious members and chastising or initiating negative sanctions, through the forum of gossip, of those whom were deemed to be lazy. As an economic leader, he was able to accumulate greater wealth. Wealth, in turn, contributed to aiding his political position and overall social status. The *qeshqa* was expected to be as good or better a hunter, fisher, and coordinator than those over whom he had influence. The *qeshqa* was never a female in Dena'ina society.

The position of the *qeshqa* was seen as meshed historically with that of the post-Russian *duyun* (Russian *toyen*), also described for the upper Cook Inlet Dena'ina by Fall (1987). This person acted as a intermediary between Dena'ina elders, other members of society, and the Russians or other *Gasht'ana* for purposes of trade and the organization of labor. The *duyun* mutually reinforced his positions of political power and wealth with that of economic leadership in the subsistence and trade sectors of the economy. If competent, he achieved a successful but delicate balance between generos-

ity — a virtue integrally connected to leadership and the ability to accumulate wealth. By these means, he set himself apart from others in his household, domestic group, or community and reinforced his status. In addition, the *duyun* also attempted to elevate the status of his kin and followers to the forefront of the community and to establish his community as exemplary among other Dena'ina settlements. As in the case of the *qeshqa*, the *duyun* had to be a good provider, although not necessarily or strictly an illustrious hunter.

The distinction between being a good hunter and good provider remained a theme in discussions of male economic specialization in Nondalton in the 1980s. Example after example was provided by residents of individuals who were not necessarily "good hunters" but who were "good providers" and, contrastingly, individuals who were excellent hunters or trappers but poor providers. The crux of this distinction seemed to relate to the overall abilities of a man to obtain and maintain necessary resources. Throughout the historic period, "necessary" resources included both those available and consumed locally and trade goods or, more recently, cash. Both *qeshqa* and *duyun* also were expected to provide for people in need outside of their domestic units. In conversation, residents of Nondalton in the 1980s demonstrated a high degree of consensus about who was and who was not a good provider. Being a good provider required the ability to cache the products of a man's efforts, or not "run out" of necessary supplies; complete projects in a timely manner; maintain economic autonomy; and avoid laziness.

All adults were expected to perform the tasks associated with their age and sex cohorts, unless ill or incapacitated for some other reason beyond their control. Individuals who could not support themselves or kin were referred to as a *ch'qidet-nik'en* or a "lazy person." They were drifters, who went from one relative to another seeking support. In the case of men who behaved in this fashion, wives and children often abandoned them for new male supporters. Sometimes parents assumed the care of their daughters and grandchildren, but non-productive husbands were ordered out of the household or domestic unit. The same principal applied to women who refused to sew, cook, or care for husbands and children. Such women were abandoned, and often their parents refused to take them back into their natal households. There was a community obligation to prevent any family from starving or suffering other privations as the result of a non-productive parent or parents. However, during times of the year when people were dispersed in camps, there were instances in which the elderly, ill, and their caretakers, remaining in the village, did not have adequate resources to care for lazy people.

The cultural value placed upon economic productivity, the Dena'ina work ethic, persisted into the 1980s. The antithesis included an inability to provide for oneself and family adequately and to care for one's food supply, equipment, and other necessities of life. Elders expressed great concern for the abilities of young men and women to become good providers as adults. It was generally felt that many young adults lacked the values and skills necessary to become productive members of inland Dena'ina society. However, the factors blamed for this perceived condition of many younger people were commonly externally introduced and/or outside the realm of Dena'ina control. Such factors included mandatory formal western education, modern technology, the presence of commercially available food, cash available from "welfare" sources, and the excessive use of alcohol. According to elders, many of these were considered to be *Gasht'ana* models of behavior, resulting in general laziness.

This discussion about the division of labor in inland Dena'ina society suggests a static nature to economic production that, in fact, did not exist. There were numerous examples of women who had lost husbands early in the cycle of their family of procreation and never remarried. Whereas in the past, it would have been likely for such women to remarry as part of the practice of the levirate, historic and contemporary disruptions to traditional marriage practices affected the economic dimensions of social organization as well. In such cases, women often assumed many roles in production normally held by adult males. These included hunting large game, the construction of technology normally associated with males (such as snowshoes and sleds), long distance travel with their families by dog team, remaining at fall camps and trap lines in the absence of a husband or other appropriate male relative, and working at wage paying occupations normally reserved for men. Such women relied heavily on older female children to help care for those who were younger. In addition, the participation of males in the Bristol Bay commercial fishery mandated the assumption of the majority of the domestic production of sockeyes by females. The important point here is that the economic system permitted variation. Women who assumed male roles as a result of economic exigency were respected rather than condemned by others. The role of Athabaskan women was explored for Koyukon Athabaskans of Alaska in Nelson, Mauntner, and Bane (1982), providing many parallels to what has been described here regarding the role of women in Dena'ina economics.

UNITS OF PRODUCTION

Units of domestic production for the inland Dena'ina were patterned. These patterns were somewhat disrupted by a decline in the number of inland Dena'ina villages, increased sedentism in communities, and other socioeconomic and demographic factors. However, they continued to function for shorter and more frequent hunting and fishing forays in the 1980s. Although patterned, the composition of production groups was flexible and shifted in accordance with the exigencies of available relatives of the appropriate age and sex cohorts, health conditions of group members, numbers and ages of children, participation in sporadic wage employment, and other factors.

Nondalton residents reported that units of production were forged primarily from kinship networks. Since the composition and size of production groups changed seasonally, models presented here reflect periods within the annual round of resource harvesting. These representations are abstractions of what was described as the normative patterning, but not all groups conformed to the types depicted herein.

During the period of spring camp (*litl'en nuch'et-deh*), the most common composition of a domestic unit included a man, the eldest male in his family of orientation; his younger brother; and an elder or younger sister. Each of these adults was accompanied by his or her spouse or spouses and children. This unit of production is depicted in Figure 71. This description of the composition of spring camps excluded the social organization at Indian Point, when multiple production units, societies or bands, and ethnic groups joined together to socialize and await the breakup of the ice on Lake Clark. In most cases, the eldest male of those brothers, holding usufruct rights to the area inherited through their father, coordinated the productive activities of the group. He had amicable relations with his sister's husband, rarely arguing. The brother-in-law was recipient of the eldest male's first take of each species for the season. Based on rules of marriage, a man and his

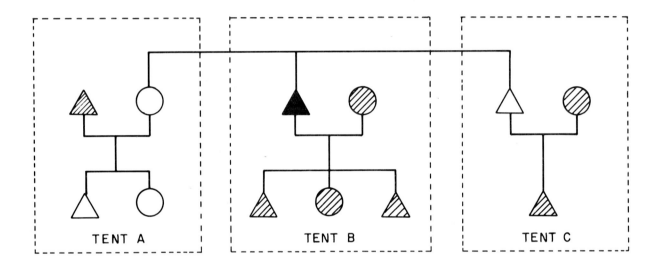

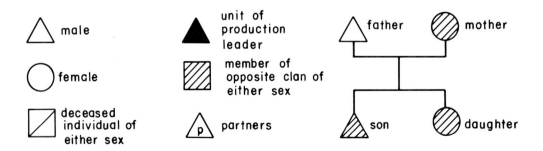

Figure 71. Normative composition of an inland Dena'ina spring camp (*litl'en nuch'etdeh*), 1890 to 1990.

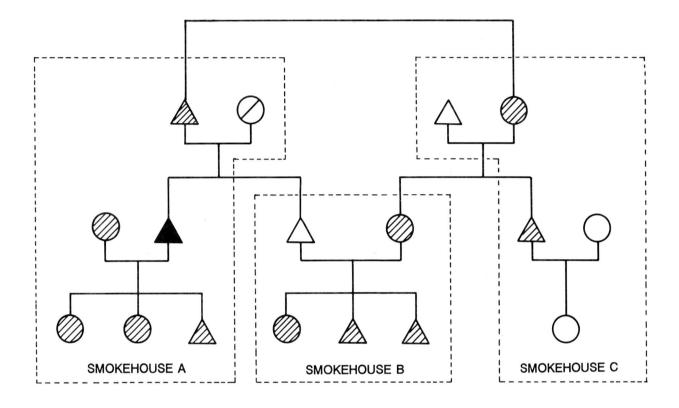

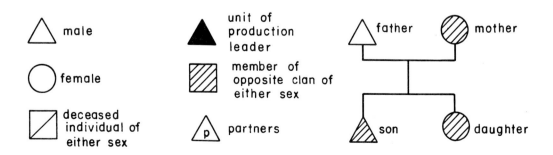

Figure 72. Normative composition of an inland Dena'ina summer fish camp (*shan nuch'etdeh*), 1890 to 1990.

sister's husband were, of course, members of opposite clans and, therefore, had reciprocal obligations. These mutual obligations included the responsibility of teaching one another's children. Figure 71 depicts the fact that the male in one household was of the same clan as that of the children of the other, if the adult members of a camp included a man or men and their sister or sisters. A man and his sister's husband (*len*) generally had a joking relationship. The women in such a group cooperated in female productive roles and, usually, enjoyed being together. Each nuclear family slept in a separate tent, but often the entire camp group consumed meals in common.

Summer fish camps (*shan nuch'etdeh*) were larger than those of spring. The camp leader or coordinator was generally the eldest son of a man who used the camp before him. Often the elderly father and mother, if they were still living, resided in the fish camp but were no longer primary producers. Camps were most commonly composed of the eldest son of the previous camp user; his younger brother or brothers; their spouses and children; one or both of their wives' parents; and one or more of the wives' brothers, spouses, and children. This production unit is depicted in Figure 72. Although each of the nuclear or extended residence groups depicted in Figure 72 had one or more white wall tents, fish processing tables and bins, and, a smokehouse, all camp members shared a common gill or seine net and fished together. As in the previous spring example, some meals were shared by all members of the camp. Also, as in the spring camp example, brothers and their sisters' husbands had amicable relations and mutual obligations regarding the instruction of one another's children. If elderly parents were present in the camp, the eldest son was given advice about the efficient and proper conduct of productive activities. Each nuclear or extended family group cached its own fish separately, unless a couple was newly married and had not yet acquired independent fish processing paraphernalia. Conflicts within the fish camp unit rarely occurred. Since the onset of inland Dena'ina participation in the Bristol Bay commercial fishery, either the wife of the eldest son or an elderly parent, if at the camp, became temporary head of the domestic fishery until the men returned.

The fall hunting (*tunch'edal*) productive unit had the fewest members of any camp group in the annual seasonal round. It commonly was composed of a man, whose father had usufruct rights to the general area in which hunting occurred; his hunting partner; the wives and children of both men; and the lead male's and/or his wife's unmarried older or younger brothers. This unit of production is depicted in Figure 73. The ideal number of hunters, for achieving the greatest productivity in a fall hunting camp, was three or four. Unmarried males contributed to the meat cache of the family group to which they were attached by kinship ties.

Fall fish camps (*naqeli nuch'etdeh*) were flexible in composition. They had larger populations and were composed of four or five tents. The people who resided together at fall hunting camps usually remained a domestic unit at fall fish camps, although they were joined by other groups autonomous during the previous period. The composite group formed by multiple fall domestic units at a fall fish camp was not perceived to be necessarily related. In addition, the selection of fall fishing sites was dictated by proximity to abundant numbers of spawning or spawned-out salmon. Under most circumstances, each domestic unit caught and put up its own fish.

Fall and winter trapping (*naqeliteh ch'k'ezdlu and huch'ghinu, respectively*) camp compositions were normally the same. The size of these domestic units was larger than that of fall hunting groups but smaller than that of summer fish camps. Such groups moved from fall trapping to winter trapping camp sites, after going back to the village for Russian Christmas, if travel conditions permitted. Normative composition for these camps included a man holding usufruct rights to the trapping area, his elderly parents, one or two unmarried brothers, and his wife's brother or brother's spouses and offspring. This group is depicted in Figure 74. Each nuclear family with children resided separately, unmarried males generally shared another shelter, and elderly parents normally had their own dwelling. Typically two of the men in this group ran a trap line together, each with his own team and traps. As in the previous examples, the eldest son of the man with trapping rights acted as productive group coordinator but depended heavily upon consensus in making decisions. Such decisions included the placement of traplines or the timing of movements from one camp to another. Meat was cached in common, but pelts belonged to the individual who trapped the furbearer.

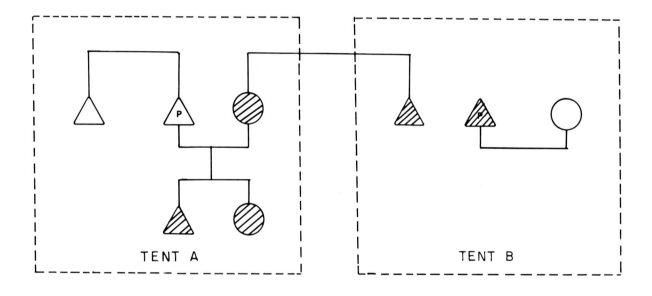

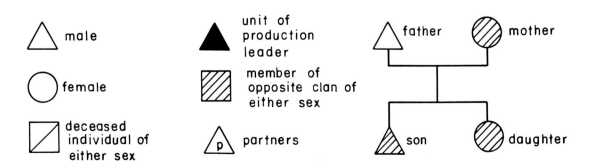

Figure 73. Normative composition of an inland Dena'ina fall hunting (*tunch'edał*) camp, 1890 to 1990.

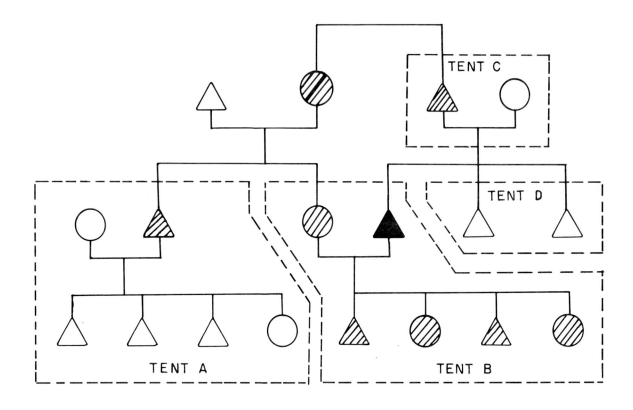

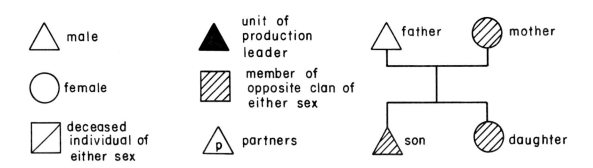

Figure 74. Normative composition of inland Dena'ina fall and winter trapping camps (*naqeliteh ch'k'ezdlu* or *huch'ghinu,* respectively), 1890 to 1990.

A critical principle of the social organization of production was that of partnerships between males (*ida*). The ideal criteria for establishing partnerships included the absence of perceived consanguineal and affinal kinship links; opposite clan affiliation; mutually beneficial "luck" at hunting, trapping, and fishing; amicability; and endurance of the relationship through time. All men had one or more partners, and these relationships normally were established before a male passed through puberty. Although partners theoretically produced cooperatively during any season, fall hunting was the most common collaborative activity for men of this relationship. Because partners were of the opposite clan, their wives were as well. Therefore, all adults involved in this affiliation had expectations of mutual responsibility and obligation to one another and to their respective children.

The institution of male partnerships was mirrored in female productive roles. In the case of women, the partner most commonly was termed "friend," "good friend," or "best friend" in English. However, in Dena'ina, this relationship was also described as one between *ida*s. The criteria described for the determination of male partners had applicability to relationships between women partners as well. Such affiliations generally spanned multiple years, although occasionally disputes focused on interpersonal jealousies resulted in the reorganization of female *ida* dyads. Principles of partnership affiliation remained important in the organization of productive activities of Nondalton Dena'ina in the 1980s and involved associations which were not strictly economic in nature.

THE SOCIAL ORGANIZATION OF DISTRIBUTION

In inland Dena'ina society, distribution occurred within households, within and between family groups and domestic units of the same community, and between communities. Distribution networks were very patterned and integrated within the overall sociocultural system. Distribution among inland Dena'ina did not involve everyone sharing products equally as need and available resources dictated. Similar non-random, formal distribution has been well documented for economic systems of other hunting and gathering societies (e.g., Altman 1987; Morris 1986; Nelson 1978; Wolfe and Ellanna 1983).

Inland Dena'ina society was stratified economically and socially. Concepts of property stewardship and rights existed at multiple levels, although the western idea of "ownership" was generally avoided, except in relationship to very personal items of technology such as a woman's sewing kit. Concepts of property and resources spanned a continuum. Resources and property at one end of this continuum were associated very distinctly with individual rights of access and control. Those at the opposite end were held in common by a society, or even possibly multiple societies, at large. Resources and property between these extremes were controlled and accessed by households, kindred, clan members, domestic units, communities, and spatially defined ethnic groups.

The concept of individually held or controlled property was conceptually very limited within inland Dena'ina society. In the case of married males, a man's bed, clothing, rifles or other hunting implements, and basic tools were, in essence, private property. They were not to be taken by anyone without the permission of the owner. This restriction on the use of a man's personal property was particularly applicable to women, especially wives, sisters, or daughters of the owner. In cases of need, hunting equipment and other items belonging to a man were commonly loaned to other males temporarily, if the borrower were deemed to be trustworthy. A high value was placed on caring for borrowed technology. Those who were careless with property belonging to someone else rapidly developed a negative reputation, resulting in refusals of subsequent requests for use of other person's equipment. If such loans resulted in damage or destruction of property loaned, the borrower was expected to repair or replace the item. An irresponsible borrower sometimes returned a damaged or destroyed piece of equipment at night unobserved and, thereby, avoided any discussion of its condition with the lender.

Adolescent males were provided necessary technology, normally by their mother's eldest brother, when they were considered old enough. They were strictly admonished to care for it by their maternal uncles and rarely found themselves in a situation of needing to borrow from their fathers or other males in the household or larger family. It was not uncommon, however, for a father to "spoil" his son by lending him equipment or assisting him in repairing technology carelessly used. By way of contrast, mothers' brothers were expected to be harsh critics and very straightforward in their teachings about the care and use of property.

A woman's property included her sewing case, which was never left behind or put in an inaccessible location, despite her conditions of residence or travel. Her other most important possession was her snowshoes, normally made by her husband or, if unmarried, by her father or father's brother. The maker was always a male of the opposite clan. She kept her snowshoes with her at all times, and no one was allowed to borrow them. In addition, a woman's property included her clothing and domestic technology, such as baskets, dishes, pots, and pans. These were never taken by another woman without permission, although, as in the case of male technology, they were loaned to women in need considered to be careful with the property of others.

In general terms, fish, meat, vegetable foods, and raw materials to be used for clothing, housing, or other domestic purposes were considered the responsibility of women once brought into households or domestic units. Although women were responsible for distributing resources of households or domestic units, they did so on the basis of strictly defined principles. Distribution varied depending upon the species; relative abundance within the household, domestic unit, camp, or community; the general rule that a woman's husband's elderly relatives rather than her own had priority in the distribution of scarce, highly valued, or essential commodities; and a community-wide or camp responsibility for caring for the sick, elderly, very young, or otherwise incapacitated.

Each domestic unit or household had its own food cache at particular sites and periods of the seasonal round, including above ground caches, meat and fish racks, smokehouses, fish pits, and others. There were no forms of caching food or raw materials, either in seasonal camps or at villages, which guaranteed community-wide access in the absence of permission of the social unit controlling the stored resources. All members of a household or domestic unit theoretically had access to the food or raw materials which were retained in their caches. However, if the elderly parents of a male head of a domestic unit or his wife were present, they normally had ultimate say over the disposition of resources held by the social group of which they were a part. Although children normally were fed upon request, they were not allowed free access to food from caches but rather made requests to adults. If their requests were made within the context of acceptable Dena'ina behavior and availability of resources, their perceived needs were almost always satisfied.

In times of starvation or periods in which essential food and raw materials were scarce, all resources were rationed to last for as long as possible, while meeting the needs of all who relied upon the cache. If shortages were really severe, particularly in the case of food, men, considered the primary producers, and male children were given preference. It was logical to the Dena'ina that existing or potential food producers must be kept in good condition in the hope that they would be capable of performing tasks requisite for group survival. The maintenance of a minimal number of dogs necessary for transporting people and freight, whether by sled or pack, was seen as essential to the well-being of people. Therefore, dog food was distributed accordingly. Elders reported that in the past, before goods from trading posts were available, periods of temporary food shortages were not infrequent. Often the elderly and female children most severely suffered the consequences of this deprivation.

During spring camp, the group leader was given the first game taken by his sister's husband. This man then cooked what he had been given and shared it with everyone in the camp. The next day, camp members from other domestic units were told where to locate remaining moose or caribou meat. Virtually all members of the camp took their pots and buckets and went together to the site of the harvest. There they shared in a common feast, consuming as much meat as they were able to eat at one time. The remaining meat was hauled back to the camp or village site. Even camp members, who were unable or unwilling to go to a harvest site, were given a portion of the take. No one was left without adequate meat at this time of year, when game was scarce and many domestic units had run out of stored sockeye from the previous summer. It was difficult to store meat in the spring because of warm temperatures. Therefore, widespread distribution of all game was the rule. Distribution sometimes involved adjacent camps, if there were more meat than was readily usable by the producers.

Persons responsible for harvesting game always gave it to members of their opposite clan. They said, "I thought you might want some of this fresh meat," upon making a presentation to one or more influential males of an opposite clan resident in the camp. In response, the recipient group's head male said, "This is the one [animal] that my brother-in-law took, my sister's husband." However, before distributing meat to other camp members, the head man selected parts of the animal which he preferred and made it well known to group members that these choice portions were not available to others. Such select cuts normally included the heart, kidneys, backbone, ribs, and brisket. In turn, parts of game animals considered to be delicacies were presented to elders of the domestic unit by the head productive male. Elder consanguineal or classificatory siblings were given adequate and choice pieces of game by the wife of the head male.

If a spring camp had only one net or fish trap, freshwater fish were divided equally among all domestic units. However, frequently each domestic unit had its own net or trap. Therefore, its catch remained the property of that social group. Because of competition between male producers of different clans, it was uncommon for a man's sister's husband to depend upon access to the net or trap of his brother-in-law. The same was true of women of different clans in reference to set hook fishing or jigging at spring camps. It was never thought to be advisable to depend solely or primarily on distribution of resources from in-laws at spring camp without the ability to reciprocate.

The people left in the winter village to care for the sick or elderly or, after the commencement of village-based education, school-aged children also were given provisions. Members of domestic units located at spring camps made regular trips back to the village to share the food which they had procured. A man's parents, if left behind, were the first to be asked if they needed any food or raw materials. It was thought that when a man performed requisite bride service prior to marriage, his and his wife's economic commitments to the latter's parents had been dissolved for all practical purposes. The wife's parents, in turn, were expected to depend on their sons' and respective wives' productive capacities.

A man had special and reciprocal obligations to his wife's mother's brother. If preferential marriage patterns were followed (i.e., marriage of a man to his *vach'ala*), a wife's mother's brother was, consanguineally or terminologically her husband's father (*dada*). In cases in which a man's parents were well off and not in need, they directed their son and his wife to share, in part or in whole, the game or fish which they had brought into the village with the wife's natal family.

At summer fish camp, more than one group shared the use of a beach seine and fished cooperatively. When sockeyes were running in large numbers, members of multiple camps purse seined with the net. Most domestic units had their own skiffs. The skiff arriving at the site of the net first was filled with fish, as were the rest until all skiffs were full. There was no particular order in which skiffs were allocated fish from the common net. The important point was that each household or domestic unit with a smokehouse had a full skiff of fish. Then fishing ceased until all salmon taken were processed. At this point in time, the cycle was repeated, until all domestic units had enough fish for the remainder of the year. In some cases, such as newly married couples, household members had a smokehouse but no skiff. The chief went around and directed those with skiffs to share their fish with members of such a social group to "help give them a start." However, one or more adult members of the household needing fish but lacking a skiff were expected to assist in the actual seining process. Generally, salmon were not shared with domestic units capable of putting up fish but which failed to do so because of laziness involving no assistance in fish or lack of foresight in failing to prepare fish bins, cutting tables, drying racks, and smokehouses in a timely fashion. Once the fish were unloaded in a bin, they entered the realm of the household or domestic unit. At this point, the fish were no longer considered common property.

At fall hunting camps, partnerships were essential in the distribution as well as production phases of the economy. This was a period in the annual cycle in which both men and women assessed the needs of the domestic unit. Assuming that there were at least two good hunters at a camp, each made decisions regarding the focus of their efforts. For example, if a man knew that his wife needed leggings for new boots or his son a new blanket, he specifically sought caribou with hides that could be made into suitable leggings or young animals with hides appropriate for constructing blankets. Women did the same. If a wife thought that her husband needed a new coat, she set a personal quota of 100 ground squirrel skins requisite for making this item of clothing. The Dena'ina pursued such goals with confidence and competence. This is how people became "well off" by inland Dena'ina standards. In earlier times, obtaining raw materials was as important or more important than harvesting meat during the fall hunting period.

As in the case of spring camps, a man's sick or elderly parents had priority access to any raw materials or meat obtained. In the case of elders lacking consanguineal or classificatory sons, they became the responsibility of the community as a whole. The chief and second chief determined the needs of these couples and designated other domestic units as their providers.

Partners were of the opposite clan and had reciprocal obligations. Partners jointly were committed to assuring that both families obtained adequate products from the fall hunt to carry them through the annual cycle.

During the late fall and winter trapping seasons, furbearer pelts were the primary targets of production and belonged to the domestic units of the men who harvested them. Large game, opportunistically taken during the course of trapping, and beaver meat were subject to the same rules of distribution described for sharing game and freshwater fish at spring camps. In both the aboriginal and contact period, furbearer pelts commonly were distributed beyond the community, either for barter for non-local items or, in more recent years, for cash.

The persistence of intracommunity distribution of locally harvested resources into the late 1980s was important and noted, for earlier periods of time, by others (e.g., Behnke 1982; J. Kari 1983; Morris 1986). Behnke's (1982) arguments for a continuity of intracommunity distribution of resources in 1973 and the early 1980s were based, in part, on non-random surveys of fish and wildlife harvest and use. These data suggested that consistently, a larger number of households used locally produced fish and game than did those which harvested these resources. Although Behnke (1982:45) estimated that fewer than 70 percent of Nondalton households procured the full range of resources available in the area, he concluded that overall productivity per capita in the community was relatively high compared to other rural Alaskan communities. He also noted that non-producing households were utilizing the resources taken by other domestic units. Although Behnke (1982) systematically did not gather quantitative distributive data, he cited several examples of moose sharing in 1981. In one case, a moose was taken during early fall and was shared between eight people in two households. These households were headed by a father and his son. In another case, five related households shared a fall moose taken during a fly-in hunt along the northeastern end of Lake Clark.

Morris (1986:140) reported that in the period 1982-1983, 90 percent of the households in Nondalton harvested caribou and 38 percent harvested moose. She also estimated that 89.3 percent of food exchanges in Nondalton during this period occurred within the community rather than between Nondalton and other communities in the Iliamna area (Morris 1986:137).

P. Kari (1983:50) noted that in Lime Village in 1982, people shared large game animals more regularly than small game and fish. In addition, she noted that the distribution of large game was closely correlated with the need for such resources by particular domestic units. For example, two men, related distantly through affinal links, shot four caribou. One of the hunters took two of the caribou, because he had harvested a negligible quantity of meat earlier in the season. The other hunter already had cached a significant amount of game. He took all of the third caribou and butchered the fourth, taking part for his own household and that of his father-in-law. He and the other hunter gave an uncle permission to retrieve the remaining meat available from the fourth caribou. In another instance, three hunters, travelling by dog team and snow machine, took a moose 20 miles out of the village. It was divided among all households in the community, except for one with members who had recently harvested fresh meat and not shared with others (P. Kari 1983:49).

Although quantitative data on distribution of locally produced food and raw materials were not gathered in the course of this research, both informal interviews and lengthy periods of participant observation revealed a continuity of resource sharing until 1990. In every Nondalton household visited during the period 1985 to 1990, members were observed either receiving or disseminating locally acquired resources. Although moose and caribou were most commonly the objects of distribution, freshwater fish, smoked salmon, canned salmon, berries, dried meat, bear fat, beaver, migratory waterfowl, ptarmigan, spruce grouse, clams, and other resources were also objects of intracommunity exchange. The primary principles patterning the distribution of resources during this period were multiple. These included the following rules: opposite clan reciprocity; support of the elderly and sick, particularly the parents of a male head of household; sharing between genealogical and classificatory fathers and sons, maternal uncles and nephews, same sex siblings, and brothers-in-law; and community-wide support for households in need, particularly those headed by females or non-productive males. These, in large part, mirrored the principles of distribution described by elders for earlier periods of time.

Townsend (1965), based on her fieldwork in Pedro Bay in the 1960s and ethnohistoric documentation, argued for the existence of precontact aboriginal intercommunity trade. She concluded that it usually ". . . added commodities which the Tanaina [Dena'ina] could not or did not produce locally, and widened their cultural inventory" (Townsend 1965:155). She stated that trade beads and iron fragments were found ". . . in an otherwise completely aboriginal Tanaina [Dena'ina] cultural inventory at the Pedro Bay site, which dates to the early part of the 1700's [sic] . . . " (Townsend 1965:157), suggesting a precontact trade network from Siberia which reached the inland Dena'ina. Townsend (1965) also noted Dena'ina trade for native copper with the Ahtna Athabaskans of the Copper River. However, the Davydov (1977 [1810-1812]:199) document she used in support of this argument implied that the reference was to Dena'ina living on the coast, particularly in the upper Cook Inlet and Susitna River areas. Nondalton elders in the1980s gave no accounts of trade with the Athabaskans of the Copper River. However, local Dena'ina knew of and had terms for the Ahtna and Tlingit. They also discussed cultural features which they shared, particularly clan affiliation.

The inland Dena'ina traded regularly with the coastal Dena'ina and the *Dutna* residing on Bristol Bay, the southwestern shores of Lake Iliamna, and the Nushagak and Kuskokwim river drainages. The inland Dena'ina traded ground squirrel, moose, caribou, and wolverine hides; birch bark technology; dentalia; and products manufactured from Dall sheep for coastal foods and raw materials. Coastal trade goods included clams; halibut; sea mammal products; and technology, such as the multi-hatched *baidarki*.

Some Nondalton residents reported travelling overland to the Cook Inlet coast for trade by way of Lake Clark and Telaquana passes; or from the head of Little Lake Clark, up a valley to the south, through the Chigmit Mountains, and into Tuxedni Bay (Behnke 1982). Others gave accounts of crossing the portage from Old Iliamna to Iliamna Bay. From the bay, they navigated up Cook Inlet, using Kalgin Island and points along the western shore of the inlet and Kenai Peninsula as landings. The use of landings allowed them to traverse the treacherous tidal fluctuations in the most safe and expedient fashion. In the 1980s, some trade and potlatching with the Dena'ina of Cook Inlet living at Tyonek and on the Kenai Peninsula still occurred, but all travel was by aircraft.

Travel into *Dutna* country occurred down the Hoholitna to the Stony River and on to the Kuskokwim; directly down the Stony to the Kuskokwim River; down the Mulchatna River to the Nushagak; through Six-Mile Lake, down the Newhalen River, across the portage that bypasses the rapids, and to Lake Iliamna; and from the Tanalian River to Tazimina Lakes, going either south to Chekok or up to the head of Tazimina Lakes and downriver to Pile Bay, both located on Lake Iliamna (Behnke 1982). Other routes undoubtedly were known and used as well. Contact and trade with *Dutna* of the Bristol Bay and Lake Iliamna areas were intensified by the participation of inland Dena'ina in the Bristol Bay commercial fishery and the location of trade and communication centers on Lake Iliamna.

Trade with the *Dutna* of the Lake Iliamna and Bristol Bay areas remained economically and socially viable throughout the 1980s and took many diverse forms. In many cases, this trade was referred to as "visiting" by both *Dutna* and Dena'ina, despite the fact that goods and cash were exchanged between the visitors and hosts. The most common occasions for "visiting" and direct economic exchange included Russian Orthodox Christmas ("Slavi"), Easter and the sometimes associated spring carnival, midwinter carnivals, and important socioreligious events such as Russian Orthodox funerals and weddings.

During these occasions, Nondalton residents acted as both hosts and visitors. In either case, visitations had structured expectations of hospitality on the part of visitors and hosts alike. Visitors were provided with substantial food, mostly in the form of meals in individual households or community-wide potlatches. Visitors also were provided places to sleep and other amenities at no cost. Other exchanges included resources available or abundant in one area but not the other, presented as gifts by both visitors and hosts. Individual households receiving visitors with inadequate food or other necessary resources were aided by the community at large, the church, or kin. Cash exchanges normally occurred within the context of competitive gaming, particularly card playing. A marked similarity existed between economic exchanges occurring during church holidays, ritual events, or carnivals in the 1980s and those of the recent historic period at Indian Point. Games changed from primarily Dena'ina or

Dutna events involving skill or chance, such as *ch'enlahi* or *k'ighali*, to card playing. Correspondingly, winner's pots changed from dentalia, furs, or items of technology to cash. However, the principles remained similar. During winter and spring carnivals in 1987 and 1988, elders encouraged participants to play traditional games as well. For example, bow and arrow marksmanship and the "flat game" were popular. In the latter example, circular pieces of birch were thrown onto burlap covered targets by two teams made up of male and female throwing partners.

For the period 1982-1983, Morris (1986) reported that 67 percent of all "visitors" to Nondalton from the Iliamna area were from Newhalen and 33 percent from the community of Iliamna. Nondalton respondents reported visiting Iliamna, Newhalen, and Pedro Bay.

Distribution of locally derived food and raw materials between the residents of Nondalton and Lime Village or between Nondalton and Lime Village inhabitants and their relatives in Anchorage was common in the past and remained so in the 1980s. The designation of this type of distribution as intracommunity or intercommunity is arbitrary and dependent upon what is defined to be the "community" of inland Dena'ina. In this context, the "community" was defined to include residents of both villages and their transient sectors. The degree of perceived relatedness, the dynamic nature of residence patterns, and the frequency of intercommunity communication precluded the static assignment of transient individuals to any one of these inland Dena'ina groups.

The location of individuals involved in intracommunity and intercommunity exchange networks influenced the nature of goods which were traded. For example, Lime Village residents' tenacity in maintaining skills necessary for the production of traditional items of Dena'ina technology, such as birch bark containers and locally produced sleds, provided them with marketable commodities in both Dena'ina and non-Dena'ina exchange networks (P. Kari 1983). By way of contrast, temporary inland Dena'ina residents of Anchorage frequently had access to wage employment. The product of this effort, cash, was used to acquire commercially produced goods, some of which were introduced into traditional distribution networks. Nondalton residents had the most lucrative access to caribou, moose, and sockeye of the three settlements, providing them with both processed and unprocessed items of exchange. In

the case of Nondalton Dena'ina residing temporarily in Anchorage, there was no hesitancy to call upon appropriate kin in the village to supply them with food or raw materials. Alternatively, kin in Nondalton sometimes called upon those in Anchorage to provide commercial goods unavailable or more costly in the local store. The Anchorage-based air taxi operator who services Nondalton attested to the frequency with which such exchanges were transported by informal arrangement between residents of the two locations. Exchange networks also provided the principles by which housing was sought by visitors from one settlement to another. Although long-term residents of Anchorage, originally from Nondalton or Lime Village, were not excluded totally from distribution patterns, they participated less frequently in the 1980s.

The Dena'ina potlatch was not solely an economic activity but also was structured around opposite clan reciprocity, the social recognition of important rites of passage, and the reaffirmation of Dena'ina world view and associated values (cf. Mauss 1967[1925]). The first systematic ethnographic description of Dena'ina potlatching was documented by Osgood in the early 1930s (Osgood 1976 [1937]). However, it is of limited use in this context, since it concentrated on potlatch phenomena from Kachemak Bay, the Kenai Peninsula, and Tyonek. The assumption that all Dena'ina conducted similar potlatching is untenable, given the variation which Osgood found in these three coastal locations. In addition, potlatching observed in recent years and recorded in oral histories or ethnographies (Osgood 1976 [1937]; Townsend 1965) demonstrated the influences of Russian Orthodoxy and the availability of Euroamerican goods.

Potlatching was the most formal, public, and ritualized means of economic distribution in Nondalton in the 1980s. P. Kari (1983) reported the same phenomena for Lime Village in the early 1980s. Osgood's (1976 [1937]) description of a Tyonek potlatch as being moiety related was applicable to the Nondalton potlatch. Since the moiety structure in Nondalton had survived as a recognition of two related groups of opposite clans, perceptions of potlatching in this community in the 1980s focused on reciprocal obligations between members of these two groups. The emphasis on opposite clan reciprocity permeated memorial potlatches or "feasts for the dead." As one informant reported, "Potlatch is a thing that when a man loses his loved one, you know, he's not satisfied until he pays everybody that was

Figure 75. A Nondalton memorial potlatch associated with the death of Benny Trefon, a member of the *nuhzhi* clan. It was intended to honor him and distribute his personal belongings and other goods to members of the opposite clan, *q'atl'anh'an*, September 1986. This potlatch involved considerable feasting, with foods provided primarily by members of his own clan.

concerned — then it cost him lots of money" (Dick Mishakoff, interview, 1961). However, smaller potlatches — locally referred to as "potlucks" in English and held on the occasions of church or secular holidays, marriages, birthdays, a young man's first game harvest, and fund raising events — also involved principles of opposite clan reciprocity, though less clearly delineated.

There were two kinds of funeral potlatches performed in Nondalton in the 1980s. The first usually occurred on the day of the burial and, closely was associated with that event and related procedures. Members of the opposite clan of that of the deceased always were expected to care for the person whose death was imminent. They were also obligated to prepare food for visitors to the household of the dying person, contact the Russian Orthodox priest, prepare the body for burial, dig the grave, carve the Russian Orthodox cross grave marker, and make the coffin. Recently, the Nondalton village corporation, Kijik, began providing commercially made coffins to the family of the deceased, thereby eliminating one of the opposite clan functions. Even after coffins were provided from this outside source, it was the responsibility of members of the opposite clan to contact Kijik and arrange for the delivery of the coffin, flowers, other clothing or necessary goods. Opposite clan members also arranged for the transport of relatives to Nondalton for the funeral.

Occasionally deaths of Nondalton residents occurred in Anchorage or services were held in Anchorage following autopsies. In these cases, opposite clan members made appropriate arrangements with the Anchorage Russian Orthodox priest, funeral parlors, airlines, florists, and other Anchorage based concerns, as well as arranging for burial in the village. Members of what was perceived to be most properly the opposite clan sometimes were assisted by other clans "on the same side," another suggestion of an operative moiety division of inland Dena'ina society.

The funeral potlatch was the culmination of a stage in the continuum of life, death, and the proper dispensation of souls. It involved the repayment of members of the opposite clan from within and without the village for their participation in the processes related to the death. In reality, all members of the community were invited to share in the food, but those of the opposite clan of the deceased were fed first, offered the most choice dishes, and given special deference during the entire potlatch.

The primary or memorial potlatch normally was held 40 days after a death. People came to Nondalton from Lime Village; sometimes from the communities of Stony River or Tyonek, depending upon their relationships to the deceased; Pedro Bay; Iliamna; Newhalen; and occasionally other *Dutna* communities. At these potlatches, members of the opposite clan particularly were honored with food, gifts, and overt displays of deference. It was during these potlatches that the personal belongings of the deceased were distributed to members of the opposite clan. These included clothing, hunting equipment, tools, furniture, boats, snow machines, all-terrain-vehicles (ATVs), occasionally a truck, and household goods. In addition, an enormous quantity of newly purchased blankets, towels, dishes, canned goods, cigarettes, ammunition, locally gathered and processed foods, cash, and many other valuable commodities also were disbursed. These events required the amassing of large amounts of wealth. The most valuable items went directly to members of the opposite clan as strictly defined. Less valuable gifts went to members of other clans of the opposite side. Lastly, members of all clans, except that of the deceased, were accorded some small gift. It was not considered proper for members of the clan of the deceased to participate in the receipt of gifts, although they shared in the feast. Young people occasionally demonstrated their ignorance of principles of clan reciprocity by seeking inappropriately to be gift recipients. In most cases, those breaking norms were admonished by elders. The entire process was very formal, requiring considerable planning and coordination, primarily on the part of clan elders. Since the onset of Christianity, potlatching became intermeshed with appropriate Russian Orthodox Church ritual. At one 40-day potlatch in 1986, a funeral song and previous chief's speech were played at the end of the event. This was perceived as an expression on the part of those present that potlatching in the future should include more traditional songs and dance. The timing of the memorial potlatch at 40 days following death is a syncretism between Russian Orthodoxy and Dena'ina tradition. That is, 40 days is an appropriate day for feasting in the memory of the deceased in the Russian Orthodox church, but the principle of potlatching is distinctively Dena'ina in origin.

In the 1980s, many elders were concerned that young and middle-aged adults were not sharing material resources and labor to the degree expected within traditional inland Dena'ina society. In particular, some elders expressed a concern that the rules of opposite clan reciprocity, respect for those of greater age, and care of those who can no longer adequately produce for themselves were not understood or respected in practice by younger people. One widowed and elderly woman reported that male children of her deceased husband's sister provided her little fresh game. Additionally, she was given a "bloodshot" portion of meat, or that piece near the entry point of the bullet. In earlier times, according to elders, respect for age was indicated by the quality and type of the piece of a large game animal provided by a younger, productive hunter. Such disregard of distribution rules was considered insulting to the widow, particularly since she carefully recalled sharing freshwater fish, which she had harvested, with this family of the opposite clan. From an outsider's perspective, however, the continuity of Dena'ina distribution patterns and associated values remained normative and strongly reinforced by positive and negative sanctioning in Nondalton throughout the 1980s.

THE SOCIAL ORGANIZATION OF CONSUMPTION

Consumption, or the act of consuming that which is produced, generally is downplayed in the analyses of non-western economics in favor of production and distribution or exchange. As in the case of production and distribution, consumption, as a sector of an economy, cannot be understood as distinct from the whole sociocultural matrix of which it is a part. Therefore, some general statements about the non-market sector of the Dena'ina economy, and its relationship to Dena'ina society, are necessary as a prelude to discussing the social organization of consumption.

The non-market sector of the inland Dena'ina economy is essentially what Mauss (1967 [1925]) and Gregory (1982) termed a "gift economy" as opposed to a "commodity economy." A gift economy differs from a commodity economy in several respects. In the latter, there is a fundamental distinction between things and persons. That is, property is held by individuals and is alienable and exchangeable. There is a sharp contrast between a thing and its owner, and concepts of private property predominate in describing the relationships between the two. In the case of the inland Dena'ina, concepts of personal or private property were extremely limited, as was the idea of

"ownership." These phenomena are similar to those occurring in what Gregory terms a "clan-based economy." In a clan-based economy, there is no private property, and people do not have alienable rights over things (Gregory 1982:18). As Mauss (1967 [1925]) astutely observed, in such an economy, objects are never really completely separated from the people who exchange or distribute them.

Distribution or exchange in a commodity economy establishes a relationship between the objects which are exchanged. By way of contrast, in a gift economy, exchange establishes a relationship between the giver and receiver, since the object which is given is not alienable. Since objects are not alienable, what is given away must always be returned in some form. Thus, a gift creates a debt that has to be repaid, and the aim of a gift giver is to acquire as many gift debtors as possible (Gregory 1982:19). In reality, what the gift giver gets as a result of the act of giving is a personal relationship created by economic exchange. It is only in this context that Dena'ina consumption can be clearly understood.

The act of consuming food for the inland Dena'ina was a necessary condition for survival and self-replacement, a prerequisite for the continuance of society through time and space. The results of deprivation in regard to food were common topics of conversation in the 1980s. The emphasis of the inland Dena'ina on particular values, such as hard work, a disdain for laziness, "always having enough," "never being without," caring for what one has, and generosity in hard times, can be explained by the reiterated fear of individual and group deprivation.

The other facet of consumption, which is the relationship between the giver or provider and the recipient or consumer, was of greater significance in the Dena'ina context. As Gregory states, "Consumption in a gift economy, then, is not simply the act of eating food. It is primarily concerned with the regulation of relations between people in the process of social and biological reproduction" (1982:79). For the inland Dena'ina, the focus of interest was reciprocal obligations and responsibilities between "opposite" social groups based on kinship affiliations. The exchange and consumption of food, raw materials, and other goods between opposite clan members carried forth obligations for repayment. Success or failure in fulfilling such commitments was reflected in the social status of individuals, households, domestic units, families, and clans.

Figure 76. Mary Balluta Evanoff, wife of Kijik Chief Zackar Evanoff, and her adopted daughter Yvdakia Balluta Evanoff. Since Yvdakia was Mary's sister's daughter, she already was a classificatory daughter of Mary. The woman's dress in the background is lavishly decorated with dentalia and beads, both of which were evidence of wealth in inland Dena'ina society. Yvdakia appears to be wearing a dentalia and bead necklace. The stylish western women's clothing of the late 1890s provides another indication of the wealth and status of this domestic unit. This photograph was taken in Kijik in the late 1890s. *Photograph Courtesy of the Alaska Historical Library, James Carter Collection.*

In one sense, the inland Dena'ina were egalitarian. That is, there was no evidence that a particular clan or group of clans economically or politically dominated another for any lengthy period of time. People at all social levels, from the individual to the community, were expected to be productive and share the fruits of their labors. In another sense, however, the inland Dena'ina were highly stratified. Some domestic units were considerably more wealthy than others. Some men were termed *qeshqa* ("rich man" or "respected man") and some women *qiy'u* ("rich woman"). Their domestic units and localized clan segments or lineages reflected their relative wealth and status.

Those without were forced to depend on the generosity of those more capable of successful production. Less wealthy individuals or groups acquired debts which were sometimes difficult or impossible to repay. For example, some men requested to hunt with others, who were known to have "luck" in hunting. Less affluent individuals often had to borrow items of technology essential to the successful production of food and raw materials. In some cases, domestic units required direct donations of food or raw materials from others in the camp or community. This assistance usually was coordinated by the chief or second chief. Fall (1987) reported that chiefs tended to be among the most wealthy in Dena'ina society. Becoming rich was a typical Dena'ina goal (Fall 1987).

If a domestic unit or localized clan were impoverished temporarily as the result of ill health, the death of a major producer, or merely a period of "bad luck," the domestic unit or clan was able to recover by repayment of its indebtedness to its benefactors. Repayment and the associated recovery of status and prestige often required the assistance of the debtor's more affluent clan members. Since generosity was a virtue, and prestige and social status resulted from giving, the ability to be more frequently on the giving rather than the receiving end of a transaction was desirable. Therefore, it is clear that a fine line, or balance, was maintained between the accumulation of wealth by members of a domestic unit or kinship group and related conspicuous consumption and the giving away of this same wealth to those in greater need.

A position of wealth or poverty of any social group did not remain static through time, although some individuals and groups were more consistently successful than others in having both material and social wealth in the short term. The balance between reciprocal relationships shifted as the result of multiple factors. These included commonplace, or day-to-day transactions; ostentatious potlatch displays and related distribution; trading transactions; and gambling success. Additionally, other mechanisms included the use of women as a source of obtaining wealth through a non-caste form of hypergamy (i.e., marrying one's daughter to a man of higher social status), extending one's kinship network, effective coordination of localized clan productivity, and success in controlling trading and other interactions with different ethnic and cultural groups.

Stratification based on both material grounds and social status existed in Nondalton in the 1980s. Although access to cash influenced the type of wealth which could be acquired, the mechanisms and associated values related to consumption as opposed to distribution remained relatively intact. In contemporary Nondalton, there were those who were poor and those who were rich by Dena'ina standards. There were also those who were generous and those who were stingy. The real economic problem with tremendous social implications remained how to achieve the appropriate balance — that is, to be wealthy and generous simultaneously.

Figure 77. Wassillie Trefon with his freight sled at Mary Ann Trefon's cabin at Tanalian Point, circa 1939. It is likely that Wassillie was heading for his cabin at Miller Creek when this photograph was taken. This cabin was the base from which he trapped up to Telaquana Lake. His trapping equipment included a small, wooden sled carried on the freight sled, skis, steel traps, a beaver hat, food and other supplies necessary for a lengthy stay, and his dog team (tied in the background). *Photograph Courtesy of Agnes Cusma.*

CHAPTER 10

THE ECONOMICS OF EUROAMERICAN CONTACT

When the people of an unstratified native society barter wild products found in extensive distribution and obtained through individual effort, the structure of the native culture will be destroyed, and the final culmination will be a culture-type characterized by individual families having delimited rights to marketable resources and linked to the larger nation through trading centers.

Robert F. Murphy and Julian H. Steward, *Tappers and Trappers: Parallel Processes in Acculturation*, 1968 [1956]

THEORIES AND PERCEPTIONS OF ECONOMIC CHANGE: IN SEARCH OF THE "RATIONAL MAN"

The hypothesis, represented in the quotation above, emerged from a comparative study of economic change. The authors (Murphy and Steward, 1968 [1956]) described the economic and cultural results of contact between the western market system and the "traditional" economies of the Mundurucu of South America and Montagnais of North America. The Mundurucu were rubber tappers and the Montagnais furbearer trappers in relationship to the Euroamerican market economy. Murphy and Steward (1968 [1956]) clearly recognized the relationships between economic and social systems in small-scale horticultural and hunting and gathering societies. Their model predicted the rapid demise of community and family subsistence production subsequent to the opportunity to participate within a western market economic matrix. Additionally, they suggested the parallel transformation of the social systems forming the foundation of the traditional economies. This classic argument suggested that when commercial goods become available to those who function in subsistence or "gift economies" (cf, Gregory 1982), people turn their attentions away from the traditional economic cycle in their eternal quest and insatiable desire for western commodities. They become devoted to efforts that result in obtaining trade goods. In doing so, producers in such societies develop debtor relationships with traders. Consequently, this dependency prevails over social bonds operative in the traditional economy. In this scenario, production shifts from collective to independent efforts. Concepts of personal ownership over resources or

resource areas become dominant over principles of group ownership and usufruct rights. The implication of Murphy and Steward's (1968 [1956]) conclusion was that, whereas specific details may differ, processes and outcomes of economic change of traditional, subsistence economies and societies are similar in the face of access to market or commodity economies.

Neoclassical economic theory is dominated by general analyses of the universal laws of consumer choice or consumer behavior under conditions of unlimited wants and limited resources. This body of theory might offer similar explanations of the phenomena described by Murphy and Steward (1968 [1956]). That is, once exposed to the benefits of a commodity economy, "rational" non-western people can be expected to attempt to maximize their economic condition by acquiring ownership over resources, restricting the consumptive unit to the nuclear family, and accumulating personal wealth. These changes occur at the expense of the social organization and associated economic behavior characterizing subsistence or domestic production, distribution, and consumption. This behavior was viewed as being merely normal or "rational" in the paradigm of western "economic man."

The role of rationality in economic behavior has been applied by non-economists to the involvement of subarctic American Indian hunters and gatherers in fur trapping and associated trading after Euroamerican contact. Portrayals of subarctic American Indians as being traditionally conservationists, who managed the resources upon which they depended by adjusting demands to avoid environmental degradation, elicited critique. For example, the historian, W. H. Hutchinson, made the following observations:

... the Indian revered nature because he had no other choice; ... he perceived nature as being controlled by supernatural forces that he was obliged to propitiate if he hoped for success in life; failure to perform the proper rituals, adhere to taboos, and conduct ceremonies was tantamount to inviting disaster. We ought to dry our eyes and recognize that the Indian was above all a self-centered pragmatist when it came to land use (Hutchinson, as interpreted by Martin [1981:14]).

Additionally, Hutchinson concluded:

If the Amerind was a truly dedicated ecologist, why did he so succumb to the artifacts offered him by Europeans that he stripped his land of furs and pelts to get them? ... He did so because he was only human. The white man offered him material goods — iron and woolens and gewgaws and alcohol — which he could not resist. These riches, which is what they were, gave his life an expanded dimension it had never known before. No power on earth could keep him from getting these things by raid or trade, once he had been exposed to them. To ask him to have refrained from making his material life fuller and richer is to ask him for far more than we ever asked of ourselves (cited in Martin [1981:14]).

This argument typified the essence of ethnocentric, western bias in evaluating "rational economic behavior" on the part of most postcontact American Indians.

Many anthropologists critiqued the application of western values and neoclassical economic theory to explanations of aboriginal, non-market economies and their apparent or assumed transformation as a result of contact with Euroamericans. Of specific interest is the concept of the universality of "rational economic behavior." In part, applications of this concept to indigenous peoples emerge from confusing the nature of "rational" decisions with the content of "rational" desires:

Rationality requires that individual decision makers choose their "top" or more preferred alternative. These alternatives will be ranked in terms of their value to enable the individual to secure his or her preferences. Rationality says nothing about the content of these preferences (Bates 1983:369).

Further, it is assumed that the intent of rational economic behavior is to maximize returns — that is, to get the most of a desired product by the least expenditure of effort. However, it is mistakenly assumed that desired products take the form of material wealth, usually interpreted as commercial western commodities when such are available. This definition of wealth, by its very nature, excludes traditional values and non-material goods such as social status or group solidarity.

A final point is that defining "irrationality" or "rationality" in economic or any other terms requires that criteria be established for making such evaluations. Needless to say, it is difficult to identify criteria that apply universally to all ideological and related social systems. However,

even if widely applicable criteria could be validated, there is a second problem related to the concept of what is perceived to be rational, individual economic decision–making. Can it be assumed that rational economic choices on the part of individuals result in rational economic outcomes for society at large? As Bates (1983:371) astutely pointed out, "... individual choices, even when rational, do not necessarily lead to socially rational outcomes."

Various interpretations of economic change, specifically in the case of subarctic Athabaskans and usually focused around fur trapping and associated trading, were advanced. For example, based on ethnohistoric data for the eastern Kutchin (Gwich'in) between 1800 and 1860, Krech (1976) argued that Athabaskans and other subarctic Indians were not mere passive recipients of cultural change in regard to the fur trade era. Instead, they were active "problem solvers" and "problem creators," who made contributions to the nature of such trade. Indians played a role in shaping the character of their relationships with traders. Such was the case, in part because the latter were dependent upon Indians for communication skills and provisioning. This dependency was based on the ineptitude of traders in learning local languages and survival skills in the contexts of the social and physical environments in which they were newcomers and in which they conducted business. Krech (1976) argued that the Indians were selective about the trade goods they wanted. They integrated them into existing sociocultural patterns rather than overhauling their societies to fit newly acquired technology.

Helm (1985) asserted that among the arctic drainage Slavey, cultural and social change related to commercial trapping and trading with Euroamericans was minimal for nearly a century. She referred to this as the "contact-traditional" period, lasting well into the 1950s.

To characterize the classic contact–traditional era: the only Whites in the land are the personnel of the trading post and, in the course of time, the mission. Both are usually at the same site. Indians have no permanent dwellings at the trading "fort" or elsewhere. They live out in the land, taking moose and caribou, fish, and the snowshoe hare. By 1905 or so, a few begin to build log cabins at the fort or at a major fishery or other site occupied for several weeks during the year.... But, generally, Indians remain mobile, with ammunition, nets, and a few staples (flour, tea, tobacco) from the trader, often on credit.... Subsistence hunting, fishing, and snaring is combined with taking of furs during the winter. Trading gangs come to the fort at New Year's and debts are paid with furs. With new supplies, they return to bush camps or hamlets. . . . Ingatherings at the fort are occasions for festivities: feasts, dances, gambling games (Helm 1985:12–13).

Such a model proposed greater cultural and social conservatism on the part of subarctic Athabaskans in the face of access to western trade goods than commonly was assumed by scholars of culture change.

A somewhat contradictory view emerged from McKennan's (1969) analysis of the impact of trapping and the establishment of trading posts on the Chandalar Kutchin (Gwich'in) and Upper Tanana Athabaskans of northeastern Alaska. Although he admitted that precontact trade and trade goods had minimal effects on these people, the institutionalization of trade was very disruptive in his opinion:

Before the coming of white fur traders to the region there was some trade with the Russian redoubts on the coast. Although the bulk of this trade was conducted through intermediaries, some was direct. . . . While I doubt that this early trade had any appreciable effect upon the traditional subsistence pattern, it may well have reinforced status distinctions based on wealth and thus strengthened the positions of the traditional band leaders.

Once trading posts were established in the territory, however, the developing fur trade brought inevitable changes in the material culture of the Indians and, more important, profoundly affected their subsistence pattern, round of seasonal activities, social organization, and demography. Semipermanent villages grew up in the neighbourhood of the trading posts. With the introduction of the dog team and its growing use in fur trapping, the demand for dried fish, an easily transportable dog food, increased as did the market for furs. The natives' economic life centered more and more around the individualistic activities of the nuclear family and superseded the earlier collective activities of the local band and its network of kinship responsibilities and prequisites (McKennan 1969:95).

Of particular interest in this context is McKennan's (1969) conclusion that the disruption of societies dependent on caribou hunting as opposed to fishing was greater, because the introduction of firearms brought about individualistic production. According to McKennan, individual activities replaced the cooperative, group corralling strategies of the precontact economy. In other words, an introduced item of technology was interpreted by

McKennan (1969) as disrupting the social underpinnings of the aboriginal economy by altering the mode of production.

The final theoretical example relating fur trapping and trading to sociocultural change comes from Townsend's (1965) research among the Iliamna Dena'ina. Townsend (1975b) arrived at comparative assessments of cultural change using diachronic data on several communities in the Lake Iliamna area. Townsend (1965, 1975b) characterized Dena'ina society as being highly stratified on the basis of wealth, in contrast to the fundamentally egalitarian Yup'ik societies. Therefore, she concluded that the Dena'ina enthusiastically adopted Euroamerican trade goods in great quantities, many of which were "luxury goods." According to Townsend (1965, 1975b), the Dena'ina perceived such commodities to be the means by which personal and family wealth and, consequently status, were enhanced. The Yup'ik, on the other hand, were much less influenced by what she termed "mercantilism." She attributed this outcome to their basically egalitarian nature.

In Townsend's (1965, 1975b) view, access to trade goods intensified the nature of ranking in Dena'ina society, including more ostentatious displays and conspicuous consumption of wealth in the context of the potlatch. She argued that trade goods displaced or replaced traditional symbols of wealth. Mercantilism, according to this perspective, resulted in increased social stratification. Townsend (1965, 1975b) concluded that the subsequent destruction of aboriginal Dena'ina social organization was, in large part, the product of a loss of access to western trade goods and resultant social disintegration. Access to trade goods diminished because of the decline of the fur industry in the early American period and the withdrawal of Russian traders. The availability of western commodities, therefore, was seen by Townsend (1965, 1975b) to be both the stimulus for a period of cultural florescence and the cause of cultural decline.

The question in this context is what insights into economic change can the involvement of the inland Dena'ina in commodity or market economics provide? This example is particularly germane in light of Murphy and Steward's (1968 [1956]) conclusions which began this chapter, because the inland Dena'ina were introduced to western market economics through furbearer trapping and trading. For this reason, their case somewhat paralleled that of the economic history of the Canadian Montagnais.

TRAPPING AND TRADING: THE INLAND DENA'INA WORLD AND WORLD ECONOMICS

The inland Dena'ina were active traders prior to contact. It was well documented that the coastal Dena'ina, with whom the inland society traded, possessed beads and iron by 1778, six years before the founding of a permanent Russian settlement on Kodiak Island. Pre-Russian trade between the inland Dena'ina and those of Lake Iliamna, and with the *Dutna* living on the southwestern shores of Lake Iliamna and the Kuskokwim and Mulchatna rivers, was documented in detail in oral historic accounts. The Russians recognized the existence of the extant trade networks and made use of them during the early years of their activities in Alaska.

Primary evidence and secondary accounts concerning the economic impacts of the early Russian fur trading period on the inland Dena'ina were minimal. It is highly unlikely that the inland Dena'ina were trading for staple foods in that period of time. The most desirable and commonly exchanged commodities included metal technology, tobacco, tea, salt, lead, powder, dentalia, beads, and firearms, when available. Even flour and sugar were not items of trade in the early days. Since foods did not comprise the bulk of trade goods, it can be assumed that the inland Dena'ina were continuing their annual seasonal harvest cycle.

The later Russian period, lasting from the 1799 to the sale of Alaska to the United States in 1867, was characterized by an expansion of trade activities and facilities north of the Alaska Peninsula and into the interior. The staffing of these more distant outposts principally involved Creoles. Creole trading post managers or *baidarshchik*, like bilingual Kolmakov and his son Petr, were generally more effective in their economic and social dealings with Native peoples than were emigrant Russian administrators.

There is considerably more data regarding the economic impacts of Russian traders and trade goods on the inland Dena'ina for the later period. Because Russian-American Company records for this period of time were organized by redoubt or *odinochka* and district, it was difficult to distinguish between the activities of various ethnic groups who had economic dealings with the same trading facility (Sarafian and VanStone 1972). For example, in the case of Aleksandrovskiy Redoubt at the mouth of the Nushagak River, Aglurmiut (also spelled "Aglegmiut"), Kiatagmiut, and Kusquqvagmiut Yup'ik as well as inland Dena'ina traded at this facility. Additionally, because of the role of Natives as middlemen, the sources of furs recorded at a redoubt or *odinochka* or by district, and the ultimate dispensation of trade goods acquired at a particular facility, cannot be ascertained with any degree of certainty. Additional problems in assessing the participation of inland Dena'ina specifically in Russian trading facility exchange include major omissions in company records (Sarafian and VanStone 1972) and difficulties intrinsic in using information for purposes other than those for which they were collected.

During this period, the establishment of additional trading facilities in areas accessible to the inland Dena'ina resulted in a greater degree of contact with brokers of Euroamerican culture and economy and, assumedly, with representatives of other Native groups. For example, the reestablished *odinochka* at Iliamna was staffed with a few Aglurmiut and a Creole *baidarshchik* and his family of 10 males and 5 females (Townsend 1975b). Additionally, the *baidarshchik* was a reader in the Russian Orthodox Church and an avid proponent of Christian social and economic values. Aleksandrovskiy Redoubt was settled by a number of Aleuts and 10 Russians (Sarafian and VanStone 1972:59). Kolmakov, who was both a *baidarshchik* and Creole, was known for his ability to relate well with Native people. Kolmakov and the Creole, Lukin, were the principal players in the establishment of a redoubt on the Kuskokwim River. Townsend (1975b) argued that the role of the Creole in disseminating Russian ideology, filtered through the perspectives of their Native mothers, was underestimated in the reconstruction of the economic history of the Native peoples of southwestern Alaska. By 1821, The Russian-American Company charter theoretically required employees to get local permission before establishing an outpost, to eliminate attempts to extract tribute or taxes, and forbid the taking of hostages by force (Oswalt 1980:12).

By these later years of Russian contact, the trading posts had both a greater quantity and diversity of western commodities available to entice trade for precious furs. The contribution of the inland Dena'ina specifically to the stock of furs acquired annually at the Iliamna *odinochka* is unknown, and the value of trade goods was recorded in rubles and kopeks rather than dollars. Therefore, in this context, only the nature of the commodities exchanged for specific types of furbearer pelts and the comparative value of trade goods for 1832 and 1833 were described.

A sample of records for the Russian–American Company post at Iliamna for 1837, 1841, and 1843 indicated that furbearing species taken in exchange for trade goods included land otter, red fox, beaver, mink, lynx, muskrat, black and brown bear, marten, wolf, wolverine, and caribou ("deer skins"). To this list, Davydov (1977 [1810-1812]:145) added porcupine, squirrel, and hare. At Kolmakovskiy Redoubt, pelts traded in the period 1845 to 1860 included beaver, red fox, land otter, lynx, bear, arctic fox, marten, and wolf. Arctic fox and marten were not taken in exchange for trade goods until after the mid-1850s, and bear were only accepted during the earliest years of trade. A wolf pelt was traded in only a single documented case. The value of pelts in terms of goods for which they could be bartered increased at Kolmakovskiy between 1832 and 1836. For example, a large, prime beaver blanket, valued at 1.5 rubles in 1832, was worth 4 rubles in 1836 (Oswalt 1980:86–87).

Trade goods reported by Wrangell (1980 [1839]:12) for the Russian "colonies" in general in 1833 included wheat or rye flour, salt meat, clarified butter, rum, tea, brown sugar, refined sugar, soldier's cloth, toweling, coarse and fine linen, calico, chintz, cotton, nankeen (i.e., a Chinese cotton cloth), and leaf tobacco. Additionally, Wrangell noted that only iron had made much impact on Native technology.

The purchasing power of particular pelts for specific commodities varied temporally. Prices of trade goods were admittedly high, according to Wrangell (1980 [1839]), because of the costs of transporting them across the breadth of Siberia to coastal and interior Alaska. A pud of tea (36.1 pounds), an important trade good for the inland Dena'ina, was worth approximately 112 prime beaver pelts in 1832. Similarly, a pud of leaf tobacco was worth 25 to 30 red fox pelts during the same year (Oswalt 1980:86; Wrangell 1980 [1839]:12). The Russian-American Company reduced the price of cloth in the 1830s to discourage Native people from using furs for clothing (Oswalt 1980:87). Although it was against the Russian-American Company charter to trade firearms for furs, some *baidarshchik* were instructed to lend firearms to a few "trusted individuals" in order to improve hunting efficiency (Sarafian and VanStone 1972). Firearms also may have reached the inland Dena'ina through Native trade routes

from northeastern Alaska's Hudson Bay Company sources.

Oral historic accounts for the inland Dena'ina revealed their extensive participation in trade during the first half of the 1800s, especially for tea and tobacco. The inland Dena'ina of the Stony River were portrayed by Zagoskin (1967[1847]) as being "exclusively traders," who, by that time, were visiting Nikolayevskiy Redoubt on Cook Inlet, the *odinochka* on Iliamna Lake, and Kolmakovskiy Redoubt on the Kuskokwim. Some inland Dena'ina walked approximately 125 miles to the trading post at the old site of Tyonek to trade for gunpowder, lead, tobacco, tea, salt, and, in the American period, shells in exchange for the pelts of furbearers obtained by trapping or trade with other groups. They cared nothing for coffee and "white people's food," according to these accounts. Tyonek people often brought these same goods from the coast to the interior to trade with inland Dena'ina. People from the Stony River also went to the Kuskokwim to trade at the two stations which had been established there between 1832 and 1841 (Oswalt 1980). Traders from Kolmakovskiy Redoubt also made annual trips upriver on the Stony to trade with the inland Dena'ina (Zagoskin 1967:254).

Elders claimed that groceries generally were not available during the 1800s. Their grandparents traded for tea and tobacco when ships came into Iliamna Bay and the goods were portaged to Lake Iliamna. They maintained that trade for groceries at Iliamna followed the purchase of Alaska by the United States.

Throughout the first 60 years of the 1800s, economic change among the inland Dena'ina involved an increased reliance on a very limited number of primarily luxury or prestigious goods. There is no evidence to support the view that the Dena'ina had become reliant on trade goods as a substitute for staple foods. In fact, some have argued that the decline of both caribou and beaver in much of the area occupied by the inland Dena'ina was related to the fact that local people were supplying employees of the trading facilities of the Russian-American Company with food as well as furbearer pelts (Sarafian and VanStone 1972).

For the most part, technological change was limited to the replacement of lithic materials with metals. The Russian-American Company policy prohibited the sale of firearms to Native people. Zagoskin (1967 [1847]) claimed that the Stony River Dena'ina had access to firearms in the early

1840s. Oral histories documented that ancestral inland Dena'ina were trading for gunpowder and lead and making shot out of modified small cobbles while the Russians were still in Alaska. The degree to which firearms were held and used by the inland Dena'ina prior to the American period is a question which eludes definitive answers at the present time. Correspondingly, a precise date for the use of dog traction by the inland Dena'ina also has not been determined. Since elders in the 1980s reported that when they were young, dogs still were used principally as pack animals, it is unlikely that dog traction was used extensively during the Russian period.

Another important question is to what degree involvement in the fur trade disrupted the precontact inland Dena'ina seasonal round and settlement patterns. Because the inland Dena'ina tended not to settle around trading posts, they controlled, to a large extent, the nature and frequency of contact with Euroamericans. Since they were not dependent on food derived from furbearer trade, they continued their annual cycle of wild resource harvest necessary to sustain life as well as to obtain desired commodities for exchange.

Ranking based upon wealth and associated social status, prestige, political power connected to being a *qeshqa* and the concept of indebtedness were part of inland Dena'ina culture and society during the early historic period. Since the role of the *queshqa* already involved the accumulation of traditional wealth for conspicuous consumption and distribution, access to a greater diversity of riches from trading exacerbated this association of material well-being and social and political importance (Fall 1987; Townsend 1975b). In fact, it was the *qeshqa* most commonly controlled the middlemen trade (Fall 1987). Since the inland Dena'ina had become dependent on western commodities to both express wealth and accumulate additional goods via trade, they developed an interdependency with traders. Russian-American Company administrators specifically encouraged the indebtedness of Natives to company trading facilities (Sarafian and VanStone 1972). In the case of the inland Dena'ina, indebtedness involved the staples of social status rather than the staples of life. Therefore, the nature of relationships between the inland Dena'ina and traders was somewhat different from that described by Murphy and Steward (1968 [1956]) for the Mundurucu and Montagnais.

The *toion*, a Yakut term meaning tribal elder, was a position introduced by Russian-American Company administrators and employees to refer to individuals in Native communities who acted as intermediaries between traders and local people. They were perceived by the Russians to be responsible for maintaining satisfactory economic relationships between these two groups (Sarafian and VanStone 1972). *Toions* were given silver medals, closely accounted for by company employees. The *toion* was not necessarily a *qeshqa* in inland Dena'ina communities, but leadership roles continued to be held by the latter. In regard to the fur trade, both *qeshqa* and *toion* played important roles as middlemen. The effectiveness of a *toion* unquestionably was related to the degree to which he had locally derived prestige and high social status, as well as to his effectiveness in dealing with representatives of the company.

After 1867 and the sale of Alaska to the United States, the function of fur buyer and trader gradually was assumed by American interests. Following a year of private ownership, the assets and economic roles of the Russian-American Company were assumed by the newly formed Alaska Commercial Company (Oswalt 1967a:iv). The idea that a continuous monopoly should persist in the arena of exchanging goods for furbearer pelts with Alaska Natives was promoted, although competition with independent traders soon emerged. The Alaska Commercial Company operated three trading posts on Cook Inlet, one each at Port Graham, Kenai, and Knik (Fall 1987:29-20). By 1883, the number of Alaska commercial facilities expanded to five, of which Old Tyonek, located at Beshta Bay a few miles southwest of the contemporary community of Tyonek, was the most relevant for inland Dena'ina traders (Fall 1987). The Kenai station of the Alaska Commercial Company, and a competing firm, the Western Fur and Trading Company, were the primary sources of western commodities to the Lake Iliamna area. Trade goods were transported primarily from Kenai to an Alaska Commercial Company facility on Iliamna Bay (A.C. Point) and then portaged 12 miles overland to the community of Old Iliamna. After 1890, the center of the Kuskokwim fur trade had shifted to Bethel, at a site founded by members of the Moravian Church and far removed from the frontier of the inland Dena'ina. The Nushagak post also was reorganized under the auspices of the Alaska Commercial Company (VanStone 1967:57). Although competition between the

Alaska Commercial Company and independent firms was intense and influenced fur prices and the extension of credit, the former dominated the fur trade in southwestern Alaska. It was not until the influx of American prospectors and commercial fishermen that local entrepreneurial activities resulted in the formation of trading facilities owned and operated by non-Dena'ina residents of the area, such as that of Hans Severson in Iliamna.

Abercrombie (1900:400) reported that during the early years of American fur trade, both the Alaska Commercial Company and its primary competitor, the Western Fur and Trading Company, paid inflated prices for furs and extended almost unlimited credit to gain control of the market. After the Alaska Commercial Company acquired its competitor in the early 1880s, credit to the Dena'ina ceased, and an effort was made to reduce the state of their indebtedness (VanStone 1967:57). The cessation of credit immediately curbed the buying power of the inland Dena'ina, particularly since the values of furs declined vis-a-vis their exchange rate for trade goods and repayment of previously incurred debts.

In the days when credit was extended to trappers and indigenous traders, a relationship of economic obligation existed between the American trader and his local client. The bond between them was not characterized solely by the impersonality of market transactions or limited to immediate exchange. With the demise of credit and the increased use of cash in such transactions at the end of the 1800s, fur trade more closely paralleled western market or commodity exchange. Additionally, since independent traders continued to compete with the Alaska Commercial Company, the inland Dena'ina were able to sell furs to the highest bidder, regardless of debts which had been incurred earlier with other companies (cf, Fall 1987 regarding the upper inlet Dena'ina).

The Alaska Commercial Company provided a greater diversity of western merchandise through Iliamna than had the Russians before them. The records of the Alaska Commercial Company for the years 1884 to 1899 yielded insights into the nature of company inventories for that period. Commodities included ready-made clothing, such as pants, caps, shirts, coats, gumboots, and suits; yard goods, such as calico, blue dill (denim), toweling, and cotton; and household utensils, such as china plates, bowls, cups, saucers, and kerosene lamps. Additionally, valued trade goods included

tools, such as shovels, hammers, drills, axes, door hasps, and locks; hunting technology, such as steel traps, shotguns, 44/40 Winchester rifles, Kentucky muzzle loaders, lead shot, revolvers, gun powder, bullets, fish nets, and *baidarkas*, spices, such as pepper and mustard; and foods, such as tea, leaf tobacco, flour, butter, rice, and sugar. Upon returning to villages after trading trips to Iliamna, the inland Dena'ina shot firearms in the air to let people left behind know that they had been successful in getting the goods they had gone after. In the 1980s, elders remembered their parents describing how they purchased muzzle loaders. The number of furs needed to acquire the firearm was established by standing the muzzle loader on end and stacking the furs up until they reached the tip of the barrel. They recalled that very little money was used in trade during the late 1800s.

A greater percentage of technology used by the inland Dena'ina during the early American period was acquired from trading posts than was the case during the Russian trade era. Such technological changes influenced the organization of production. This was particularly the case when firearms or nets replaced more communal technology, such as caribou corrals and fences or fish traps and weirs. Conversely, it is apparent that reliance on essential food staples, acquired via trade, remained negligible during these years. The more frequent use of dog traction after the turn of the century influenced the number and quality of salmon harvested and processed annually. The use of dog teams allowed the inland Dena'ina to run lengthy trap lines after 1900, thereby operationalizing the incentive for trapping larger numbers of relatively less valuable pelts.

Townsend (1965) reiterated a translation of Russian Orthodox priest Shalamov's records, which stated that "the prices of furs dropped drastically, over 50 percent between 1897 and 1899," because the trading companies ". . . entered into a secret agreement to get more control over the people" (Shalamov n.d., as quoted in Townsend 1965:163):

> . . . *Indications are that considerable wealth was brought into the Tanaina [Dena'ina] area in the Late Russian Period. At this time there was an elaboration of status. The economic worth of the Iliamna area began to decrease, however. After the 1880's [sic], the Alaska Commercial Company no longer deemed it necessary to maintain a post at Old Iliamna; the furs had been depleted. The Tanaina [Dena'ina] of Iliamna never seemed to have completely given up their old means of*

Figure 78. Floyd Dennison and Brown Carlson sitting on the porch of Brown's house at Tanalian Point, spring 1938. Brown Carlson had come to the area as a prospector and trapper and was well liked and admired by the inland Dena'ina. He married Agafia Trefon Carlson. Floyd was a trapper and commercial fisherman in Bristol Bay. He and his wife, Lena, also lived at Tanalian Point. Floyd was the son of Charlie Dennison, who came to Alaska as a prospector in approximately 1900. He later became a commercial fisherman in Bristol Bay. Charlie built a home at Tanalian Point in 1935, where he established a sawmill. *Photograph Courtesy of Floyd Dennison.*

subsistence in favor of a more European type of life. . . . For this reason the culture was able to maintain itself adequately on the aboriginal subsistence base after the Russians and then the Alaska Commercial Company left. Enough trade goods still filtered in through the other traders who remained at Old Iliamna to provide necessities in the form of flour, tea, etc., but the subsistence base remained abundant because it was salmon. During the Early American Period, the economy changed from a barter and credit system to a cash system. . . .

In my opinion, the level of Tanaina [Dena'ina] integration reached its peak in the Middle and Late Russian Period. By this time the people were becoming more thoroughly adjusted to the new subsistence base of salmon and the change to a Semi–Permanent Sedentary level of complexity. Russian wealth in trade for furs poured into the area during these two periods. This augmented the other methods of integration through the potlatch and the class system. In the Early American period, a depression affected the fur business. With this stimulus removed as a source of wealth, the whole status superstructure with its integrative mechanisms began to totter (Townsend 1965:361, 378–379).

This alleged drastic decline of fur prices in approximately 1897 was also implicated by Fall (1987:21) as a major economic impact on the upper inlet Dena'ina. However, as other scholars have pointed out (Black pers. comm. 1987) and a review of selected years of Alaska Commercial Company records between 1872 and 1900 has verified, there is no evidence to substantiate this argument. Although fur prices varied between years, there were no prices for pelts as high as Townsend (1965:164) reported based on Shalamov's data. There was also no overall decline in fur prices based on these records from 1897 to 1900. For example, the value of a prime beaver pelt in Alaska Commercial Company records was $3.00 in 1896 and $3.00 in 1899. Red fox pelts fell from $1.50 in 1896 to $1.00 in 1899. Mink increased in value from 40 cents in 1895 to 50 cents in 1899. Black bear pelts, worth $3.41 in 1876, declined to $3.00 in 1886 and to $1.44 in 1887. Subsequently, they increased to $6.00 in 1890 and $15.00 in 1895, declining again to $10.00 in 1899.

There was variability in prices, quantities, and types of specific pelts taken. Correspondingly, there were variations in the prices, quantities, and nature of wares offered for exchange. In regard to the purchasing power of these pelts, it is difficult to compare the costs of goods offered for trade by the Iliamna Station between years, because invento-

ries differed, and the ways in which some commodities were described varied. For example, in 1896, steel traps ranged in price from $1.25 to $2.50, depending upon size. In 1899, the same size traps ranged from 45 cents to $1.50. A review of a sample of inventories for the Iliamna Station between 1886 and 1899 suggested that the sale or trade of food items composed a very small percentage of the overall commerce that took place at this facility.

The records of the Alaska Commercial Company indicated that there were remnants of the Russian *toion* system, which continued to function during the first four decades of the American period. In the expense accounts of the Iliamna Station for 1873 and 1876, there is documentation of gifts which were purchased for the "chiefs" of Kijik, Mulchatna, and Iliamna. Whether these were *toions* or *qeshqas* or individuals who were one and the same is unknown. However, in 1876 payment was made to both the Kijik "chief" and Kijik "trader," suggesting that possibly the *toion* functions and that of the *qeshqa* may have remained distinct in this community. Fall (1987) noted that the *qeshqas* in the upper inlet were selected as storekeepers, a function which they assumed with a great degree of ability and success. There are similar examples of this same phenomenon in the case of the inland Dena'ina after 1900.

MINERS AND MERCHANTS: THE LOCALIZATION OF ECONOMIC BROKERS

Long ago before our time, they used to have songs for every game [animal]. Now us new generations don't even know that. I was raised in Lime Village until I grew up to know. When I was six or seven years old, we didn't have anything to eat. Nowadays we have white man food and we have stores. Those days it was a long ways to the store from where we are [the Stony River] to the Kuskokwim. There wasn't very much game around here. When I was small and young, there were no moose in the Stony River area. There were caribou, but very few. Summer time when the fish came, then we'd put up fish. That is what we ate and lived on in winter. When I was young, sometimes we had one piece of fish. . . . There was nothing to eat, there were hardly any spruce hens or ptarmigan. Sometimes it took my dad and them 15 days to make a round trip [from the upper Stony River to the store on the Kuskokwim River] (Anton Evan 1980).

Figure 79 (above). Mary Ann Trefon's garden at Tanalian Point in 1915. The girl on the left is unknown, but the one on the right is Mary Ann's daughter Agafia. The garden was fenced with spruce poles to keep animals out. Many vegetables were grown here, including potatoes and rutabagas. A log cache is visible in the background. *Photograph Courtesy of Agnes Cusma.* **Figure 80** (below). Oren Hudson, pilot and operator of a flight service, holding onto the pontoons of his aircraft on Six-Mile Lake in the proximity of Nondalton, 1952. Oren, who resided in Nondalton, provided mail service for residents of that community, Iliamna, and the surrounding areas between 1950 and 1970. *Photograph Courtesy of Agnes Cusma.*

This quotation, which was derived from a segment of Anton Evan's own analysis of inland Dena'ina history, provides an appropriate introduction to the first half of the 1900s. In the previous century, the inland Dena'ina had remained relatively isolated from direct and prolonged contact with traders and trading posts.

However, by the beginning of the 1900s, changing conditions had a more protracted and intensive effect on the inland Dena'ina. After the canneries began barricading river mouths draining into Bristol Bay in the late 1880s and 1890s, there were years in which previously reliable runs of salmon became a scarce resource. Moose were not common in this area, at least during the 1800s and early 1900s. Caribou were on the decline, in part as a result of Euroamerican contact. The causes of this caribou decline at the end of the 1800s are still not well established. Pressure on caribou populations from newly arrived, non-Dena'ina traders, trappers, explorers, and prospectors may have exacerbated an otherwise natural, cyclical decline. Nonetheless, for the inland Dena'ina, it became more difficult to harvest this species in adequate numbers. The status of salmon, caribou, and moose at the turn of the century may have been pivotal in encouraging more regular uses of commercial foods. Some types of commercial foods had been available for decades but not much in demand by the inland Dena'ina.

Other events of significance at the turn of the century involved the frenetic search for gold and other minerals, which brought *Gasht'ana* men in large numbers further north into what was perceived to be previously unpopulated and unexplored, frozen wastelands. Following the discovery of gold in California in 1848, prospectors, would-be miners, and merchants moved inexorably northward, reaching what is now southeastern Alaska by 1880. Most mineral activities in the Cook Inlet area and, later, on major rivers such as the Nushagak and Kuskokwim, occurred at the very end of the 1890s and early 1900s (Fall 1987; Oswalt 1980). Some prospectors entered the Lake Clark and Stony River areas from Bristol Bay, where they had come as young men to seek their fortunes in commercial fishing, trapping, or mining. Jack Hobson, whose brother went on to settle on the arctic coast, was one of these who came in about 1900 and ended up marrying an inland Dena'ina woman. He was the first documented non-Native to settle and remain in inland Dena'ina territory.

On the Kuskokwim River, it was a gold find on the upper Innoko River in 1906 that stimulated an influx of miners between that year and 1913 (Oswalt 1980:93-94). For the vast majority, who were unsuccessful in making their fortunes through prospecting, fur trapping became a viable alternative:

> *During the early years of the present century fur prices increased, and whites began to trap along the Kuskokwim. In the spring of 1909 the harvest of eight trappers, presumably white, was valued at $30,000. At that time some 200 white trappers and prospectors lived along the river, whereas two years earlier they numbered only about a dozen. . . . However, at the beginning of World War I, fur prices dropped as much as 75 percent [Oswalt quoting Moravian cleric, Kilbuck, 1917]. In 1914 the gain by the A.C. Co. on furs traded at the old fort was $205.08, whereas the profit on general merchandise was $7134.14 (Alaska Commercial Company Records, Stanford University)* (Oswalt 1980:94).

The inland Dena'ina relished oral historic anecdotes about contact between local people and the prospectors and miners coming into the Lake Clark area and up the Kuskokwim River. Vonga Bobby from Lime Village remembered that he was taught to build and use a fish wheel before 1920 by a miner who later became a storekeeper on the Stony River. Because the fish wheel was an item of technology which functioned well on muddy and turbulent rivers unsuitable for set and drift nets, it readily was accepted by the Stony River people. Vonga also recalled the beginning of McGrath, a non-Native settlement on the upper Kuskokwim River, established by miners after the turn of the century when gold was discovered at Tokotna. He nostalgically recollected, with humor, his first sighting of a steamboat destined to bring supplies to McGrath. The Dena'ina hid all of their metal axes, as they feared that the *Gasht'ana* on the steamboat would kill them. Much to their amazement, the boat failed to even stop. In later years, the inland Dena'ina were employed to chop wood for steamboats and sold fish and meat to their crews.

The earliest claims on Lake Clark were filed in 1911 at Portage Creek. A year later, two inland Dena'ina men, in conjunction with *Gasht'ana* prospectors, filed for four quartz claims on the Kijik River. These claims were called "Nondalton Chief," "Maxim," "Lakeview," and "Kijik Queen." Although none of these claims was particularly lucrative, the search for mineral wealth continued to attract non-Dena'ina to the Lake Clark area well into the 1930s.

Of the many miners who passed through the area of the inland Dena'ina or through peripheral territories, a few learned to live like local residents and opted to remain. Some married Dena'ina women, had children, and became relatively well-integrated into society considering the fact that they were *Gasht'ana*. Since mining was not the boom many expected, these individuals and their relatives became, alternatively, trappers, traders, sawmill operators, providers of freight and transportation services, and entrepreneurs in other ventures. Because these people were virtually the first non-Dena'ina residents with whom local people had sustained relations, they overtly or covertly played the role of cultural and economic brokers in transmitting, to their Dena'ina neighbors and families, varied interpretations of middle-American culture of the first half of the 1900s. An example of such influence was articulated by an elder, Annie Delkittie, in 1986. She attributed her very life to the fact that Jack Hobson was living in Qeghnilen at the time of her birth in 1913:

> *My mother couldn't raise no kids. She had to nurse them. When she had children, every one of them died. And then I was born. When I was born, old Jack Hobson was there at the time. They told Jack Hobson that my mother can't raise children. They told Jack Hobson that she nurse her babies by breast. Old Jack Hobson told the people that maybe by nursing her children by breast may not be the best way, as some children can not be fed by breast. In those days there was no milk — nothing. Only the kind of milk was Eagle Brand milk. Only one, old Hobson said don't try to feed them [children] with your breast. And then he took a half of teaspoon of Eagle Brand milk and some water and mixed it. They didn't have any kind of bottle or nothing. They used bear guts and he [Hobson] put that milk in there and made a hole in one end and put it in her [my] mouth and that was good. Then old Jack Hobson told my mother not to use her breast. "Try that [the milk]," he say. "If I am right, then she going to grow up." Eagle Brand milk — that is why I am still living yet. . . . There were no stores nearby. Everyone went to the mountains hunting animals except my dad and Jacko, who went down the Kuskokwim to Sleetmute just to get Eagle Brand milk* (Annie Delkittie 1986).

Resident *Gasht'ana* not only engaged in entrepreneurial activities themselves, but they became the stimulus for drawing the United States government and American market economics into previously isolated and uncharted Alaskan frontiers. For example, mining, trapping, and fishing interests played a role in stimulating the mapping and analysis of natural resources in many remote areas, including the homeland of the inland Dena'ina. In the Cook Inlet area, for example, there were military expeditions, such as that of Glenn (1900), who travelled up the Susitna River; Abercrombie (1900) on the Copper River; and others more peripheral to inland Dena'ina territory (U.S. Congress, Senate Committee on Military Affairs 1900). U.S. Geological Survey and other governmental agencies sponsored expeditions directly into inland Dena'ina territory. These expeditions included that of Capps (1930) into the Chakachamna and Stony River regions; Osgood (1904a, 1904b) to Lake Clark; Martin and Katz (1912) to Lake Iliamna; Elliott (1900) to assess the fisheries resource in Bristol Bay; and other adventurous expeditions, such as that of Cook (1908). The publications of findings from these explorations further encouraged *Gasht'ana* to come into and potentially settle within inland Dena'ina territory.

Trading posts proliferated and were developed in more immediate proximity to inland Dena'ina settlements. In addition, they were intended to provide the commodities which allowed *Gasht'ana* to live lives similar to those they had left behind. In so doing, they inadvertently provided models for inland Dena'ina technological and other cultural change. Although these businesses were operated primarily by outsiders, some Iliamna residents, whose families were a part of the mercantile history of the area, also played a role in their development and operation.

By 1910, Old Iliamna was the trading center for the region. It had three stores and was the largest community (Martin and Katz 1912). Sam Foss, whose descendants remain in the Iliamna area, owned one of these stores. It is not coincidence that the first school in the region also was established in Old Iliamna in 1908. The school was the first residential institution in this area to promote a model of assimilation through the enculturation of Dena'ina children (U.S. Dept. of the Interior, Bureau of Education 1908–1912).

Hans Severson was the first person to open a store in 1914 located within an inland Dena'ina community, in this case Old Nondalton. Given the technology of the time, Severson found the logistics of providing residents of Old Nondalton with groceries and other goods difficult.

Subsequently, he relocated his store to the present site of Iliamna. He was very astute about the country and had assessed the value of furs being harvested by the inland Dena'ina. Severson built a large supply boat, which he used to get goods from Bristol and Iliamna bays, across Lake Iliamna, to the site of his store. Some inland Dena'ina sporadically worked for him as long-shoremen. They also traded both furs and gold for western commodities. An elder, Annie Delkittie, recalled that in the 1920s when she was a child, her family caught and dried fish, packed them into bundles of 40, and transported them down the Newhalen River by boat and across the portage on foot to trade with Hans Severson for goods. Severson, in turn, sold the fish to *Gasht'ana* miners to be used for dog food. In the perception of some inland Dena'ina in the 1980s, Hans Severson played an important role in their lives. He was viewed as a principal local provider of trade goods; sporadic employment; and services, such as haul-ing men across Lake Iliamna and down the Kvichak River to Bristol Bay to commercial fish. Others believed that he became wealthy at the expense of the inland Dena'ina.

Other stores sporadically sprung up within or adjacent to inland Dena'ina territory. In the 1920s, Chekok Point resident Gust Jensen's brother had a house and store at Tommy Point, where some inland Dena'ina went to trap. *Dutna* and Dena'ina acquired groceries at this store for three or four years. In approximately 1927, another ex-miner, "Old Barnhardt," opened a store on the Stony River at the site of Lime Village. He brought freight up the Stony River by boat, as he also owned a store at the confluence of the Stony and Kuskokwim rivers. Although the central Kuskokwim had a long history of trading posts, the opening of the cinnabar (mercury) mine at the present site of Red Devil encouraged a renaissance of economic activity in and around the now Yup'ik community of Sleetmute. Mary Hobson, born on the Stony River in 1919, remembered that there were many stores on the Kuskokwim River when she was a young girl.

During the early decades of the 1900s, trapping remained an important means by which western commodities were acquired by the inland Dena'ina. Not all economic intercourse occurred in the context of the store or trading post, however. Sometimes as many as half a dozen fur traders came to Old Nondalton from Seattle and Anchorage in May or June to purchase the winter and spring harvests of furs. Fur buyers conducted these commercial transactions in Old Nondalton between approximately 1912 and the late 1930s. These traders primarily were interested in beaver pelts, and people sold to the highest bidder.

In the late 1930s and early 1940s, the prices for some pelts were relatively stable. For example, beaver blankets ranged from $65 to $70, while fox skins brought between $60 and $70 during the same period. Active trappers estimated that they frequently got as many as 40 to 60 foxes a year. By the late 1950s, however, fur prices dramatically fell. Fox pelts brought only between $3 and $5 a pelt. Additionally, territorial fish and game regulations and a perceived depletion of beaver encouraged the inland Dena'ina to go further and further to obtain these animals, including along the entire Mulchatna River. It was a commonly shared sentiment among the inland Dena'ina that fur trapping was no longer worth the costs. The expense of feeding a team in excess of 20 dogs, buying steel traps and other technology, and purchasing supplies necessary for pursuing trapping resulted in the loss of viability for this economic activity.

Additionally, other sources of income became procurable, including commercial fishing. Prior to the establishment of regular air transportation in the late 1930s and early 1940s, the distribution of mail and freight was a source of employment for both inland Dena'ina men and women. For example, in the 1930s, mail and freight were carried across Lake Iliamna by boat to Severson's store, where it was picked up by inland Dena'ina teamsters. Sophie Austin, who was one of the last Dena'ina to haul freight by dog team around Lake Clark, recalled that after her husband died, this was her only means of supporting five children. She ran a team to Iliamna and, from there, around the entire shore of Lake Clark, delivering mail and freight to both Dena'ina and *Gasht'ana* residing in cabins on the lake. Katherine Bobby, a Lime Village resident, worked on freight boats and at roadhouses on the Kuskokwim and Nushagak rivers, after spending the winter and spring trapping for furs. Prior to the 1930s, some inland Dena'ina charged for packing goods across the six mile portage on the Newhalen River at a rate of one and a half cents per pound. Additionally, several local residents portaged freight 12 miles from Iliamna Bay to Lake Iliamna. The Alsworth family, located at Hardenburg Bay on Lake Cark, and Star Airways, flying out of Anchorage, displaced the local inland Dena'ina freight operations by the mid-1940s. The days of freighting by dog team and sled became a part of the past.

In the 1890s, Sheldon Jackson embarked on the grandiose scheme of importing reindeer from Siberia and Sami (Lapp) herders from northern Europe in an effort to economically civilize Alaska Natives. This plan included the establishment of a reindeer station at Eagle Bay on Lake Iliamna. Although inland Dena'ina elders recalled visiting *Dutna* herders employed in this industry and consuming deer meat during their visits, the reindeer industry had no impact on them. They were neither employed in herding nor reliant on reindeer as a source of meat and hides. They had no desire to become herders and viewed the activity with some degree of amusement.

When an elementary school was opened at Old Nondalton in the fall of 1930, an era focused on directed cultural transformation of the inland Dena'ina commenced. From the standpoint of economic change, the influences of the school were both covert and overt. In the former sense, there were attempts to instill the inland Dena'ina with western values, including the Protestant work ethic. The strong admonishments by teachers that success and prestige were associated with wage employment and the ownership of western goods diverged from inland Dena'ina values regarding industriousness and wealth in form more than in content. Role models, of course, were provided in the form of teachers and their spouses. More overt attempts to draw the inland Dena'ina of Old Nondalton into "proper" economic activities included the employment of locals in constructing the school at a wage of $2 a day, hauling freight destined for this institution, and cutting wood for $15 a cord. Additionally, school staff were instrumental in evaluating inland Dena'ina homes as being "suitable" or "unsuitable" for children, using measures of economic wealth and moral suitability based upon western criteria. Consequently, teachers functioned as social workers in recommending to territorial officials the placement of some Dena'ina children in boarding institutions away from the community and their families. The school closed during the latter part of the 1930s, but it reopened at the new site of Nondalton in the early 1940s.

The development of centers of non-Native commerce and industry within the Bristol Bay and Cook Inlet regions provided additional opportunities for sporadic wage employment of the inland Dena'ina. More importantly, they provided economic incentives for family relocations, the majority of which generally was unsuccessful. Many relocated Dena'ina eventually returned to their home communities. The development and growth of Dillingham and Naknek in Bristol Bay were associated with the commercial fishery. The impact of the commercial fishery on the inland Dena'ina, particularly of the Lake Clark area, was so significant that it warrants more detailed discussion below. The importance of Iliamna as both a trade and transportation center, initially associated with the provision of services to villages of the region and the development of the commercial fishery, later expanded in conjunction with recreational sport hunting and fishing in the Lake Clark and Lake Iliamna areas. The birth of Anchorage in 1915 was based on its selection by the federally-funded Alaska Engineering Commission as a rail center (Carberry 1979:5). The proximity of this urban center to Nondalton played a role in encouraging economically motivated relocation of some inland Dena'ina. Most residents of Nondalton did not recall ever having gone to Anchorage until the late 1940s.

HUNTERS ON THE HIGH SEAS: THE BRISTOL BAY FISHERY

The commercial fishery in Bristol Bay was a development which had considerable economic influence on the inland Dena'ina. The magnitude of this influence related to the proximity of Bristol Bay to the area occupied by the inland Dena'ina, the industry's duration over the past century, and the diversity and number of opportunities it offered for seasonal employment. More specifically, as a resource extractive industry, commercial fishing paralleled a segment of the historic economy of local Natives including the inland Dena'ina. Additionally, it provided a means for obtaining larger quantities of cash than previously had been available. During the early years, when cash was not used as the medium of exchange with local Natives, and in recent years, the commercial fishery provided stores and associated goods which might have been otherwise unavailable or scarce. Lastly, it was the most intensive and diverse source of contact of the inland Dena'ina with representatives of many non-Alaskan societies and cultures.

The first canneries in Alaska were constructed at Sitka and Klawock in southeastern Alaska in 1878. In 1882, the Cutting and Company cannery was established at Kasilof on Cook Inlet (Fall 1987:20).

Figure 81. Bristol Bay gillnetters on the Nushagak River, 1930. Many of the older men in Nondalton in the 1980s remembered commercial fishing in similar boats during the 1930s. *Photograph Courtesy of Pete Koktelash.*

In the Kenai area, a cannery belonging to the Alaska Packing Company and another owned by the Pacific Steam Whaling Company (Glenn 1900) also commenced operation in the 1880s. By 1890, these canneries were producing from 30,000 to 50,000 cases of fish per season. Sources of labor included primarily Asians and Euroamericans (Townsend 1965:204). The development of the commercial fishery at Bristol Bay, the richest sockeye spawning grounds in the world, closely followed that of Cook Inlet.

While Petroff was travelling throughout Alaska between 1880 and 1882 conducting the census of the new territory, salteries already were operating at Bristol Bay. They processed salmon and other species of fish for shipment to San Francisco and Seattle. Petroff (1884) described Bristol Bay in the following terms:

> *This district comprises the coast of the Bering Sea, between Krenitzin Strait and Cape Newenham, with the rivers Oogashik, Igagik, Naknek, Kvichak, Nusegak, Igushek and Togiak, and their tributaries. The natives of this region, numbering about 4,000, derive a very large proportion of their subsistence from the various kinds of salmon, which frequent the rivers in the greatest abundance.*

In 1883, the schooner *Neptune* brought the first cannery to Bristol Bay. It was erected on the Nushagak River for the Arctic Packing Company. Its first export of 400 cases of salmon was shipped south in 1884. During the year between 1887 and 1888, Bristol Bay canneries employed 200 Euroamericans and 400 Asians, usually referred to as "Chinese." Canneries encouraged an influx of *Dutna* to those areas in which they operated (Townsend 1965:205). By 1893, Nushagak Bay canneries were controlled by Alaska Packers Association, the firm with which the inland Dena'ina had a long–term economic relationship. With the exception of a few odd jobs, such as wood cutting (Porter 1894:69), neither the Iliamna nor the even more remote inland Dena'ina benefited from these commercial operations, in terms of earning cash or trade goods, prior to the turn of the century.

To the contrary, the early years in which these commercial fisheries operated in Bristol Bay brought about the depletion of the salmon resources upon which the inland Dena'ina depended. By 1890, the Bristol Bay canneries were producing from 30,000 to 40,000 cases of fish per season, according to a journal entry in 1897 made by the Russian Orthodox priest, John Bortnovsky (Townsend 1974:23). The technique of taking salmon commercially involved the blocking of river mouths with fish traps. An example of this fishing strategy was documented on the Kvichak River at Koggiung in 1897, where both a saltery and cannery were located. As a result, salmon were scarce or unavailable, not only during the years the rivers were blocked but also in subsequent years when their matured offspring normally would have returned to their spawning grounds. Additionally, accounts of widespread waste of commercially taken salmon were reported (e.g., Glenn 1900:647). Elliott (1900), in a survey of the salmon fishing industry, was told that 700,000 salmon were allowed to die and dumped, because it was impossible to can or ship them before they spoiled. Illegal fishing occurred in all of the commercial fisheries, according to this survey (Elliott 1900). However, the situation was somewhat alleviated by the passage of federal legislation in 1907, which prohibited commercial fishing at river mouths.

Oral historic data suggest that the involvement of the inland Dena'ina in cannery employment occurred prior to 1913. Jack Hobson came to Alaska in 1900 and worked at the Alaska Packers cannery at Koggiung in the summer of 1901. He then travelled to Lake Clark in the fall of the same year. He commercially fished every year, travelling from Qeghnilen on the Stony River until 1915, and then went to Bristol Bay from Old Nondalton until his retirement. Hobson acted as an intermediary between the inland Dena'ina and cannery managers at Bristol Bay. He facilitated their successful employment in canneries and communication in English with company personnel, since he was a fluent Dena'ina speaker. Because Hobson had obligations to the inland Dena'ina derived from his marriage to Tatiana Constantine, it is likely that assistance to them involving Bristol Bay employment may have been one means by which he fulfilled these responsibilities.

Employment of the inland Dena'ina in the industry, during at least the first two decades of the 1900s, was as cannery workers rather than fishermen. Elders recalled that cannery jobs exposed them to people from all over the world, including Chinese, Mexicans, Italians, Filipinos, Norwegians, and Natives from elsewhere in Alaska. Temporary cannery residency introduced the inland Dena'ina employees to the regular consumption of *Gasht'ana* food and the use of English as a *lingua franca*. Young men exaggerated their ages and began their summer "careers" in commercial fishing as young as 12 or

13 years. During World War I, when cannery laborers from elsewhere in the United States or foreign countries were sparse, it became even easier for inland Dena'ina to get employed. As one elder stated, "All you had to do was walk around, and the canneries would hire you." New employees were very dependent on older Dena'ina or *Gasht'ana*, such as Jack Hobson and Hans Severson, to teach them the social skills necessary to be hired. Additionally, for most Dena'ina, their jobs as slimers in the canneries or other positions, such as carpenter's helpers, were their first experiences in regular, albeit seasonal, wage employment. Wages were not very high during these early years. One man now in his 60s remembered that he took home $87.00 for an entire fishing season employed as a carpenter's helper for a cannery.

Beginning in the 1930s, the inland Dena'ina took to the sea and became commercial fishermen on boats and with gear provided to them by particular canneries. Men perceived fishing to be a much more appropriate role, since in inland Dena'ina society, it was women who processed fish. Men employed as fishermen for canneries were expected to deliver all of their harvest to the company that provided them with boats and associated fishing technology. In return, the inland Dena'ina fishermen received compensation based on the number of salmon they harvested. This arrangement resulted in a creditor-debtor relationship between the canneries for whom they fished and the fishermen, respectively. Because the cannery stores controlled the prices of commercial goods and fish and advanced both commodities and, in later years, cash to fishermen, the actual wage a fisherman received at the end of a season was much less than that for which he theoretically was paid. The nature of this relationship was similar in type, but not in magnitude, to that between trading posts and furbearer trappers in the past. Most fishermen ended each season indebted to the cannery store. They were provided bunks at the cannery for sleeping during closed periods and meals at mess halls which were segregated on the basis of ethnicity.

The adaptability of the inland Dena'ina is attested to by the apparent ease with which they took their environmental knowledge and applied it to "hunting" fish on the high seas. They applied knowledge of navigating large lakes and rivers with steep gradients in indigenous watercraft to negotiating rough seas, with major tidal fluctuations, in 28 to 30 foot, wooden plank sailing vessels.

During World II, there was a second shortage of laborers, since many aliens were not employable. Most inland Dena'ina men were fishing by this time, so women were afforded their first cannery employment opportunities. Additionally, toward the end of the 1940s, women began to fish from the beach at set net sites. Dena'ina women never systematically fished with men from boats. Men often fished with brothers, sisters' sons, sons, or with the same individuals who were their hunting and trapping partners. Women increasingly preferred set net site fishing to cannery work. Importantly, not all women went to Bristol Bay. A certain number remained behind to harvest and process subsistence salmon at summer fish camps.

Between the early 1940s and early 1950s, there were several changes in the post-war commercial fishing industry which had a profound effect on the nature of inland Dena'ina involvement in the fishery. The price of fish remained relatively low during the war, and salmon brought about five cents per fish in 1942. In 1943 many Dena'ina joined the Alaska Fishermen's Union, affiliated with the AFL-CIO. The price of salmon jumped to 12.5 cents per fish in 1944 and then to 32.5 cents in 1948.

By the early 1950s, canneries began converting sailing gillnetters into gasoline or diesel-powered watercraft. Skiffs with outboard motors alternatively were used for drift netting as well as set netting. The price of fish went up by about three cents per salmon following these technological changes. In the summer of 1953, a labor dispute resulted in some canneries bringing in their own fishermen from outside Alaska. Native fishermen, including the inland Dena'ina, no longer were provided with skiffs and outboards. In fact, some canneries stopped buying from skiff fishermen altogether. The Alaska Packers cannery at Koggiung was closed and never reopened. This turn of events was considered to be disastrous for the inland Dena'ina, since fishing was their primary source of cash. Many men were unemployed.

Finally, a small group of inland Dena'ina fishermen initiated the era of independent fishing. Using small skiffs propelled by oars or small outboard motors and short drift nets, Native fishermen harvested salmon without affiliation with any company. At first it was very difficult to get buyers, but eventually some smaller dealers began to purchase fish from independents. Effectively, this proved to be the end of cannery domination over local Native salmon fishermen and, to a lesser degree, the institution of the creditor–debtor relationship. There was a significant degree of intergroup support between Native fishermen from different communities as a result of this difficult year. Except for fishermen who continued to lease cannery boats, those with their own vessels were able to sell their catch to the highest bidder. Therefore, fishing became more lucrative, despite the variation which occurred in run strengths between years.

The inland Dena'ina were most successful in commercial fishing by combining multiple strategies. They avoided intensive capitalization involving both their boats and associated gear. They also calculated the predicted potential of each season's fishery versus their costs. If poor run strengths were predicted for the bay, Nondalton residents chose to undertake alternative economic activities. For example, during years in which extremely poor sockeye salmon runs were forecast, such as in the early 1970s, and firefighting and construction employment were abundant and provided more lucrative wage earning opportunities, the Nondalton Dena'ina were less participant in the commercial fishery than in years in which strong returns were anticipated. Additionally, small skiffs, also used for hunting, subsistence fishing, and transport, were a better overall investment than costly special purpose commercial fishing boats. Skiffs were brought back to the village rather than left unattended for most of the year on the coast. Other strategies included Nondalton Dena'ina partnerships with coastal dwelling people, who owned larger, more powerful and sophisticated boats.

Unfortunately, this multifaceted strategy for participating in the commercial fishery at Bristol Bay was not beneficial for many inland Dena'ina fishermen. In 1973, a state managed Commercial Fisheries Entry Commission (CFEC) undertook the implementation and management of a legislated limited entry system for salmon (Alaska, CFEC 1985). In 1975, the CFEC adopted regulations establishing the maximum number of permits and the point system under which such permits were to be allocated. Permits were designated to be owned by individuals, not some other productive unit more meaningful in the Dena'ina social and economic context. The criteria for the point system included a heavy weighting for participation in the fishery in 1970 and 1971, both years of severe economic depression in Bristol Bay. Additionally, criteria included the degree of "economic dependency," as measured by the percentage of individual income

derived from the fishery, and some calculation of hardship which a person would suffer if not given a permit. Other criteria included the amount of investment in vessels and gear and total years and consistency of commercial fishing activity in the bay (Alaska, CFEC 1985:14). Although not specified in the law, if a person were a "captain" (boat owner), as opposed to being a crew member, it positively influenced the permitting process. Unquestionably, this and all other criteria mentioned above were problematic in the case of the inland Dena'ina, because of the multiple strategies they had employed to remain viable participants in the Bristol Bay fishery. By 1980, there were only 25 permits held by Nondalton residents, 13 of which were drift permits and 12 set net sites. The latter continued to be considered principally a women's fishing activity. In addition, three interim use permits were allocated, while a decision was to be made on their award. Many other long-term inland Dena'ina fishermen and fisherwomen were unsuccessful in their receipt of a permit. As soon as the fishery became a limited entry system, the permits became a commodity and drastically escalated in value in the years to follow.

DILEMMAS OF CORPORATE FORAGERS: THE NONDALTON ECONOMY OF THE 1970S and 1980S

The economy of the Nondalton Dena'ina incorporated strategies for production, exchange, and consumption, which developed throughout the historic period. These strategies enabled residents to integrate cash, derived from participation in western market economic activities, in ways which were not destructive to the principal and most highly valued economic sector, that of subsistence hunting, fishing, gathering, and trapping. However, the integration did not transpire without raising some very difficult questions, dilemmas, and internal and external controversies. The solutions have demanded compromise and, by 1990, many remained unresolved.

PRODUCTION IN THE CONTEXT OF THE MODERN WORLD

There are many criteria used to describe the "importance" of subsistence hunting, fishing, trapping, and gathering to modern foragers. These have included pounds harvested per capita (e.g., Behnke 1982; Fall, Foster, and Stanek 1984;

Figure 82. The Keyes Point subdivision development on Lake Clark, 1986. Kijik Corporation, the profit-making body for inland Dena'ina shareholders primarily resident in Nondalton, was an entity created by the passage of the Alaska Native Claims Settlement Act in 1971. Kijik Corporation was the developer of this summer, recreational, home subdivision on corporate lands. *Photograph Courtesy of Gary E. Kontul and Kijik Corporation.*

Morris 1986); replacement costs of subsistence foods in dollars (e.g., Usher 1976 presented problems with this method); nutritional analyses (e.g., Heller 1967); productivity as measured through time expended in such pursuits (e.g., Fall, Foster, and Stanek 1984; Lee and DeVore 1968); and the non–dietary or sociocultural and ideological importance of these economic endeavors (e.g., Brody 1982; Ellanna 1992; Nelson 1983; Tanner 1979). None of these measures is free of controversy, and all tend to dissect and compartmentalize human cultural systems. Additionally, such analyses often exhibit partial or total disregard for the perceptions of local people in making what outsiders evaluate as "rational economic" decisions.

Between 1985 and 1990, there was overwhelming evidence that locally produced game and fish provided the vast bulk of protein consumed in the community and was, without question, the most highly desired and satisfying food. People commonly commented that *Gasht'ana* food left them feeling hungry. Harvesting local game, fish, and plant foods was considered the most pleasurable way to spend one's time and, additionally, was the source of significant prestige for men, women, and younger people. Members of all households and domestic units were observed engaging in harvest activities and consuming the fruits of their and others' endeavors.

Sockeye salmon provided the largest and most stable component of the locally derived diet of Nondalton residents throughout the historic period. Attempts at quantifying the subsistence harvest of sockeye were problematic. Variations in run strength, changing technology (e.g., the relative uses of snowmachines and ATVs versus dogs), the composition of households and domestic units, overall community size in relationship to productivity, availability of commercially produced foods, and other factors influenced the level of harvest through time. In the 1940s, when virtually all households had an average of 10 dogs consuming fish, it was necessary to harvest and process 50 bundles or 2,000 sockeye during the summer fishing season. Behnke (1982) estimated that the edible weight of sockeye in this area was four pounds per fish. Therefore, the harvest of sockeye equated to 8,000 pounds per household during the 1940s. Since contemporary conversion tables disregarded the use of salmon heads, backbones, and roe, all of which contributed to the diets of humans and dogs throughout the 1980s,

the actual contribution of sockeye based on poundage was even greater than described above.

Using the same conversion criteria, Behnke (1982) determined that sockeye contributed 2,883 pounds (or 69 percent) per household to the overall subsistence harvest of Nondalton residents in 1981 based on a survey of 40 percent of all households. Since households were not equivalent to units of production, the harvest levels of the latter can be assumed to be even larger. The use of fish for dog food as opposed to human consumption and the sparse nature of quantified harvest data for earlier years made it impossible to estimate the range of sockeye harvests for all periods of time. Several explanations for the apparent relatively lower harvest of sockeye in 1981, compared to the 1940s, included the single year temporal perspective of the data, the use of a 40 percent household sample rather than including information for the entire community, the application of the nuclear family household rather than the functional domestic unit in calculating harvest per social group, the relatively abundant availability of caribou and moose in more recent decades as compared to the 1940s, and the diminished use of dogs for transportation. The last trend seemingly was undergoing reversal during the middle to later 1980s.

In addition to netted fish, others were taken for immediate consumption by jigging and open water set hooking, primarily in March and April. These activities added to the overall quantity of fish harvested by Nondalton residents. Based on Behnke's (1982) 1981 data, freshwater fish species made up 205 pounds (or 5 percent) of each household's harvest during a single year period. In the 1980s, freshwater fish remained highly valued as a source of dietary variety. Obtaining them by jigging or hooking was considered an enjoyable and productive activity for older and middle–aged women, particularly, but also for men and younger people of both ages. During the 1980s, most freshwater fishing took place on Six–Mile Lake in the vicinity of the village, although some families made overnight or weekend trips to the Chulitna River, as they had in the past.

Since sockeye harvest estimates for all periods of time included food for both humans and dogs, terrestrial mammal meat and fat, not normally fed to dogs, played a larger role in the human diet than any calculations previously had indicated. The Nondalton Dena'ina recognized that sockeye and freshwater fish were dependable and available in abundant quantities seasonally and, therefore, were resources on which they could depend. Nonetheless, they overtly stated and covertly implied that a diet of meat and fat from caribou, moose, bear, and smaller species was central to human existence.

Behnke (1982) indicated that of the 40 percent of the households he interviewed in 1981, each took minimally 1,084 pounds of edible meat and fat, not including hides. This represented 26 percent of the total Nondalton subsistence harvest during that year. Since in the past, large game was very scarce and people traveled longer distances to obtain it, most Nondalton residents believed that particularly caribou and moose were more significant quantitatively in their overall economy of the 1980s than in any other period of time in their collective memory.

For example, between January and March 1987, there were 3,000 to 5,000 head of caribou just south of Six-Mile Lake and Lake Clark. During the winter and early spring of that year, caribou and some moose provided the core of Nondalton residents' diet. The abundance of caribou allowed for the bountiful celebration of Russian Orthodox Christmas. Additionally, enough meat was stored to provide a source of protein for the subsequent year, not only for local residents, but also for relatives in other villages and Anchorage.

In addition to fish camps near Nondalton and along the upper portions of the Newhalen River, there were minimally 28 camps on Lake Clark on the lower reaches of the Chulitna River in the 1980s. Some camps were single purpose sites. Most, however, served multiple functions. They were camps from which people fished for both salmon and freshwater species in spring, summer, and fall months; hunted caribou, moose, black and brown bear, sheep, and waterfowl in the fall, winter, and early spring; trapped furbearers in winter and spring; and gathered berries, firewood, bark, and other vegetable foods and raw materials. In addition to these more permanent camp sites, the inland Dena'ina established ad hoc camps in the course of harvesting all resources.

Subsistence production had many characteristics not shared with market or cash-earning endeavors. It was the most reliable aspect of the inland Dena'ina economy. It offered opportunities for year-round participation. All age and sex cohorts in the population were productive in some aspects of subsistence. Lastly, it was the occupation in which the vast majority of people preferred to engage. Subsistence production was considered

proper "employment," a source of economic security, and a source of "traditional" wealth and prestige. It was both described and demonstrated to be not only economics but rather the core of inland Dena'ina lives, even in the 1980s.

Cash had become a prerequisite for life in Nondalton in the 1900s and the means by which the inland Dena'ina participated in the market economy. Research involving an analysis of contemporary economies of other Alaska Native communities (such as Wolfe and Ellanna 1983; Wolfe, et al. 1984) suggested that rural indigenous peoples preferred means of acquiring cash which incorporated activities most similar to the non-market or subsistence sector of their economies and which did not involve full-time or year-round temporal commitments. In the case of the inland Dena'ina, such economic endeavors included commercial fishing, trapping, guiding, and clothing and arts and crafts production. Of these, commercial fishing was decidedly the most important economically, socially, and culturally in the 1980s.

Based on a survey conducted by Langdon (1981) in October 1980, the limited entry permit system for commercially harvested salmon taken from Bristol Bay substantially had modified the involvement of Nondalton Dena'ina in the commercial fishery. Nearly every adult male born prior to the mid-1950s, who was not incapacitated, relocated, or adopted out of the community, had engaged in commercial fishing at Bristol Bay. However, in 1980, when Nondalton had a resident population of 170, only 12 men using Nondalton addresses held drift permits. An additional 13 men or women owned set net permits. At least two of these were owned or used by non-Dena'ina men, who had married Nondalton women. Men who would have been of the age and skill level requisite to assume captaincy in the past were, in the 1980s, vying for positions on the crews of relatives, friends, or other more distant acquaintances. These included *Dutna* and non-Natives from Bristol Bay or from outside Alaska. Since most Nondalton commercial fishermen had not invested in technologically sophisticated and expensive boats and gear, by 1980 competition in this normally lucrative fishery placed them in the position of having to seek non-Native or *Dutna* "partners," who owned the technology necessary for "highline" production but lacked the essential permits.

Unfortunately, Langdon (1981) surveyed only four Nondalton fishermen and did not present disaggregated data for any community with a sample of less than five. However, some of his findings had relevance for Nondalton. For example, in 1980, Bristol Bay Native fishermen received an average of 49.4 cents per pound for sockeyes, whereas the negotiated settlement price was 57 cents. This severely depleted the earnings of all Native fishermen for that year. Langdon's (1981) conclusions indicated that local, Native fishermen made 40 percent less gross income from the fishery in 1979 than did the non-Native, non-local permit holders. Set net earnings were substantially lower than those derived by drifting for all years. Additionally, those drift permit owners with the greatest dependency ratios, or those employing the largest number of family members as crew, made the lowest average earnings (Langdon 1981:49). Langdon (1981) noted a distinction between crews which were formulated from members of extended families and those composed of unrelated individuals. Nondalton fishing crews fell into the former category. Lastly, individuals with more capital intensive vessels had higher drift earnings, with some exceptions.

Behnke (1982) also recorded information about Nondalton's participation in the Bristol Bay fishery in the early 1980s. After eight years had passed since the implementation of the limited entry system, three interim use drift permits held by Nondalton men still had not been denied or converted into regular permits, therefore creating considerable anxiety for these individuals. Minimally, one of these permits remained in question in 1987. In Nondalton, the ratio of permits per capita was 1:6.4, whereas a ratio of 1:2 was common in most Bristol Bay communities. It can be concluded, therefore, that more people were being supported by the earnings of fewer fishermen in Nondalton. Those individuals who had permits but no boats were forced to give up from 60 to 70 percent of their earnings to boat owners lacking permits (Behnke 1982). Of the 14 households which Behnke (1982:19) surveyed in 1981, half had members who had engaged in commercial fishing in 1980, with a mean gross household income of $8,442. However, these incomes ranged from $100 to $30,000, with the latter case being a household with 3 fishing members. This mean gross household income was markedly less than the average of $52,147 per permit holder for Bristol Bay resident fishermen and $71,696 for all Bristol Bay drift fishermen reported by Langdon (1981) for 1979.

By 1986, CFEC reported that there were 13 drift net permits held by individuals with Nondalton addresses. Of these, two were owned by inmarried non-Dena'ina males. Of the 11 permits owned by Dena'ina Nondalton residents, one was sold outside of the community that year to a non-Native in order to meet considerable federal tax obligations. Another permit left the productive pool of Nondalton, as it was sold to someone from the Seattle area to provide for the family of the terminally ill owner. Two others were transferred to sons and a third to the owner's mother after the deaths of the permit holders. In 1987, another of the remaining ten permits held by Nondalton Dena'ina was sold outside of the community, because the owner was in ill health and elderly and feared that his sons could not make adequate profit from fishing the permit to guarantee his and their support. Between 1987 and 1991, minimally two more drift permits were sold outside of the community. One had been left to a widow, who had no one to fish for her and lacked the experience to negotiate an association with a non-Dena'ina boat owner. The other permit, originally transferred to a mother of the deceased owner and, subsequently, retransferred to another son, was sold to a Seattle fishermen, ostensibly to resolve tax obligations and fishing boat repayment debts. By 1991, there was a maximum of seven drift permits owned by Nondalton Dena'ina. Additionally, few or no resident Dena'ina had adequate cash to repurchase a drift permit at their market value in 1991. This trend in Nondalton was typical of the status of Native owned permits elsewhere in the state (Dinneford 1986).

By the late 1980s, a Bristol Bay drift permit had a market value of in excess of $130,000. Considerable pressure to sell drift permits was put upon residents of Nondalton through a bombardment of letters from permit dealers, lawyers, and corporations enticing owners to sell. Most inland Dena'ina of Nondalton were unfamiliar with the accounting and banking techniques used by professional commercial fishermen to calculate and set aside part of each year's earnings in order to pay tax or credit obligations. Thereby, these owners involuntarily lost their permits. In other cases, an owner with multiple sons was not permitted by legislation to leave the permit to more than one of his offspring. Since this mode of inheritance disenfranchised other sons in violation of traditional cultural principles and values, the choice to sell the permit avoided internal familial confrontations. Furthermore, in cases of severe or prolonged illness and disability, and given the minimal cash available to most Dena'ina households and domestic units, selling a permit for over $100,000 was an irresistible solution to an immediate problem.

Many owners who were forced to sell permits believed that at some time in the future, they would have adequate cash to reinvest in a drift permit. Therefore, they did not perceive the sale of their permits as permanently disenfranchising them from the fishery.

In 1986, CFEC reported that 13 set net permits were held by people with addresses in Nondalton. Of these permits, one owner was a non–Dena'ina not living in the community between 1985 and 1987. Two of the remaining 12 permits were owned and one was fished by Nondalton men and women living in the Anchorage area. Three males and one *Dutna* innmarried female had received permits from their deceased or older mothers or mothers-in-law. Assuming that some of the proceeds from the three permits held by Anchorage dwelling inland Dena'ina were being shared with people in the community, 12 set net permits functioned to provide for the people of Nondalton. In 1990, several interim set net permit applications were decided in favor of inland Dena'ina women. However, some of the recipients of these permits resided in Anchorage but involved family members from Nondalton in both fishing and in the receipt of some of the proceeds. Unfortunately, the 1991 season for both set and drift net fishers was meager, due principally to market prices and associated strikes. The 1990 season as well was not lucrative. Set net permits were worth approximately one-third the value of drift permits, but their net dollar returns were higher because of low capital investment. However, set netting and cannery employment continued to be disdainful activities to many inland Dena'ina males of all ages. Based on the set net permit history to date, it could be suggested that inland Dena'ina women were less likely than men to dispense what is perceived to be wealth owned by members of kin groups to individuals who were not members of the Dena'ina community.

In the mid-1980s, money derived from commercial fishing remained the singularly most significant source of income to the inland Dena'ina of Nondalton. It was also a market activity involving extended family or domestic units. For example, during the last week of June 1986, prior to the peak of the commercial fishery, there were 24 Nondalton male residents over the age of 18 participating in the drift net fishery, including two inmarried non–Dena'ina. Additionally, there were 10 adult men and 9 women set net fishing. Although a count of all children was not made, there were at least as many Nondalton residents

under the age of 18 at Bristol Bay as adult family members. Most of these children assisted in fishing if over the age of 10. Therefore, in the summer of 1986, nearly one-third of Nondalton's population was at Bristol Bay, mostly at or near South Naknek, during the week of the survey. Three of the Nondalton drift net fishermen had their own vessels during this year. No quantitative data were gathered for other years. However, because of the intervening sale of drift permits and the generally poor fishing years in 1990 and 1991, it was estimated that a smaller percentage of the Nondalton population went to Bristol Bay compared with the 1986 data.

There were other measures of the importance of the commercial fishery to the inland Dena'ina of Nondalton during the 1980s. Most cash for capital purchases, such as snowmachines, skiffs, outboard motors, and ATVs, was obtained from money earned in fishing. A poor fishing year was always reflected in the extent to which the inland Dena'ina made such purchases. Most men scheduled other sources of wage employment to accommodate participation in the summer commercial fishery. For example, three young men, who were able to secure summer employment with the U.S. National Park Service, resigned because their jobs interfered with commercial fishing. Two others were fortunate enough to arrange time off from their jobs with this federal agency in order to fish. Commercial fishing remained the most highly valued, enjoyable, and prestigious means of obtaining cash for men and, to a large degree, women as well.

The role of furbearer trapping in the economy of Nondalton of the 1980s stood in stark contrast to that of commercial fishing. In the mid-1980s, commercial trapping was an occasional and sporadic activity, normally conducted by younger men, associated with periods of cash shortage and hunting forays, and, for some, when other sources of employment were not available. Although the ability of a man or woman to successfully trap continued to be highly valued in Nondalton, several factors contributed to diminished participation. Because fur prices always depended on world markets, the inland Dena'ina never had control over the outcome of this economic activity. Furthermore, they were unable to depend upon deriving a particular level of income from trapping during any particular year over the last four decades. While the prices paid for furs declined, the associated costs escalated. Therefore, trapping was not the best use of one's time unless it was the only option or conducted in conjunction with other productive activities. A greater degree of centralization forced the inland Dena'ina to travel farther in order to run lucrative trap lines in the absence of their families. Therefore, expensive technology and fuel became a prerequisite for successful trapping in conjunction with family and community unity and solidarity. Lastly, state and federal regulations affecting the harvest of fur-bearers and increasingly more restrictive patterns of governmental and private land ownership reduced the flexibility of land use strategies necessary to accommodate productive commercial trapping.

The participation of the inland Dena'ina in guiding was minimal throughout the years. One Nondalton man became a very successful assistant hunting guide and was to receive his guide permit when he died as the result of an accident in 1986. A few older men had been assistant guides in the past but always worked for non-Natives when employed in this capacity. By the 1980s, the Lake Clark area and its tributaries had become the source of "big business" for lodges, guides, and outfitters, catering mostly to urban or foreign sport hunters and fishermen. In all of these cases, non-Natives owned the associated businesses and facilities, resided outside of the area during off-seasons, and generally did not employ local Dena'ina. In fact, much of this industry was booked and logistically supported from urban facilities. Increased opportunities for the involvement of local people in guiding and associated tourism were argued by non-Native entrepreneurs as a major advantage in the sale of some inland Dena'ina land to individuals for summer home sites at Keyes Point. However, the non-involvement of the inland Dena'ina in guiding and tourism was principally related to the lack of training necessary for running hunting and guiding lodges, booking clients, arranging air and water transport, obtaining liability insurance, assisting sport hunters or fishers in taking "trophy" animals, and "looking after" urban adults basically helpless in the wilderness. In addition, these kinds of activities were not highly valued, desired, or a source of prestige in Nondalton in the 1980s. In fact, the activities of sport hunting and fishing minimally were perceived to be humorous. More often, however, such endeavors represented ideological antitheses to more traditional components of inland Dena'ina culture and, more importantly, were contrary to rules of respect for animals which remained central in the world view of the inland Dena'ina.

The nature of local employment opportunities during the past decades were limited and provided little incentive for acquiring education and skill training. To many inland Dena'ina, the time spent in formal western education and skill training meant abandoning or depleting opportunities for conducting the more productive, prestigious, and satisfying activities associated with hunting, fishing, trapping, and gathering. From time to time, the construction of public buildings, roads, runways, and state or federally subsidized housing involved the use of inland Dena'ina labor, usually under the supervision of *Gasht'ana* foremen or contractors. In the early 1960s, the U.S. Public Health Service installed a water and sewer system in Nondalton. In addition to employment related to construction, this facility required the training and employment of one local person and a substitute for maintaining it. In 1990, the same local person who held that position for in excess of 20 years was replaced by a non-Dena'ina from outside Nondalton. Because the Dena'ina operator had held this employment, previously he was denied access to a limited entry drift permit. In 1991, he had no regular source of income, a large family, and a seriously ill wife.

From the early 1960s throughout the 1980s, both male and female Nondalton residents were involved in forest firefighting in the summer through the auspices of the federal, and more recently, state governments. Participation in this activity was extremely variable between years, although the inland Dena'ina prided themselves in being one of the most professional firefighting teams in rural Alaska. Whereas firefighting provided an alternative or supplemental strategy to other wage-earning summer employment, its unstable nature discouraged the ability of residents to rely on it for obtaining the capital necessary to purchase snowmachines, outboard motors, skiffs, or ATVS, all of which were used for subsistence production.

Based on Behnke's (1982) work in the late 1970s and early 1980s, there were only four positions in Nondalton which had persisted over the past decade. These included the postmaster, water and sewer maintenance technician, school janitor and building superintendent, and health aide. The construction of the high school in 1978 provided the greatest number of wage earning positions in the community by adding three full-time but seasonal (nine month) positions and five part-time jobs. Additionally, maintenance of the airstrip was contracted out locally by the state.

Between 1976 and 1980, three or four Nondalton men worked in the construction industry outside the village as laborers or heavy equipment operators. Two were employed on the Alaska pipeline during its construction in the early 1970s and continued seasonal construction jobs outside the village, leaving for periods as long as four to six months at a time (Behnke 1982:14–15).

Table 6 presents jobs available in Nondalton in 1989, some approximate wages, hours per week, and duration within any given year. Some positions were not listed, as they were held solely by non-Dena'ina during the period 1985 to 1989. These included the postmaster, a position held by an inmarried non-Dena'ina. In the school, all but one of the elementary and all secondary and special education teachers and the principal were non-Dena'ina. Also, Dena'ina were not employed as the public safety officer (a position held by a Dena'ina until 1987); the mayor; and the doll factory and store managers. The two lodge operators on Six-Mile Lake and their employees, including winter caretakers; two air taxi pilots; all but three of the workers at the Keyes Point development site in the summer of 1986; and highway and public building and utility construction and survey crew bosses and many laborers were not inland Dena'ina. As is apparent from Table 6, there was more wage employment in 1989 than in the late 1970s and early 1980s (Behnke 1982). However, for multiple reasons, the economic scenario, from a western perspective, was not as positive as it appeared in the 1989 data. Road construction and the Keyes Point development employment documented in 1986 for the most part had disappeared by 1989. Turnover rates, even within a single year, were relatively high and often involved choices of priorities. Having a full-time job frequently was not as desirable as having more freedom from long-term temporal restraints, adequate time to hunt and fish, or the ability to fish at Bristol Bay. Because the inland Dena'ina continued to cling tenaciously to culturally alternative values, they often were thought to be "irresponsible" or "unreliable" by non-Dena'ina employers, including representatives of governmental agencies.

Other sources of employment were problematic. The Kiana doll factory, established for purposes of introducing an industrial employer to Nondalton, consistently failed over the years of its operation and closed regularly when funds were not available to meet the payroll. Wages were relatively low. Additionally, managers were not local and failed to evaluate or appreciate the lack of enthusiasm of Nondalton residents for this very impersonal, confining, and repetitive work. Additionally, at the end of the research period, the factory was closed due to the improper protection of employees from toxic chemicals used in the production process. In 1991, city officials were attempting to find the means to reopen the factory, using designs for a more culturally authentic product and ensuring safe and suitable working conditions. Office or "paper work" was considered by most Nondalton Dena'ina to be most suitable for and efficiently handled by women, with the exception of positions of leadership, such as those with Kijik Corporation or the Traditional Council. Positions of leadership were held by men and women.

Lastly, in general, inland Dena'ina showed little interest in becoming local entrepreneurs. Business development and the search for profit at the expense of others within the closely related community were not major motivators of local Dena'ina economics. Attempts at community-based entrepreneurial activities were generally small in scale, such as a home-based store, a local cafe, limited fuel services, and an air taxi charter service.

With the passage of the Alaska Native Claims Settlement Act (ANCSA) in December 1971, the western corporate model was applied to the structure of Native regional and village profit organizations. Kijik Corporation was one of these community institutions. In terms of its role in production for residents of Nondalton and stockholders living elsewhere, the ANCSA mandate and initial strategy of its non-Dena'ina executive director and board of directors was to model itself after other market organizations and become involved in "big business." Despite other investments, in the case of Kijik Corporation, the major thrust of development differing from that of most Native corporations was the decision to subdivide Keyes Point, a segment of Nondalton's ANCSA land settlement. Lots in this subdivision were marketed to clients interested in building summer homes in this very scenic area adjacent to a national park and preserve. In fact, Lake Clark and its surrounding environs were, ironically, of particular interest to two major groups with dichotomized interests, each having considerable political clout. On the one hand, the more

TABLE 6. NONDALTON WAGE EMPLOYMENT, 1989 [a]

Position	#/Jobs	Hrs/wk	Mns/yr	Salary($)/hr (estimated)
teacher, elementary	1	40	9	23
cook, school	1	40	9	15
assistant cook, school	1	40	9	10
custodian, school	1	40	9	17
health aide	1	20	12	12
health aide (alternate)	1	20	12	12
co-op store clerk	varied	varied	varied	6
utility maintenance, assistant	2	20	varied	20
custodian, city	1	20	12	6
secretary, city	1	40	12	10
assistant secretary, city	1	20	12	8
clerk, city	1	20	12	8
airport maintenance, state	1	varied	12	25
Kijik Corp., officer (Anchorage)	1	40	12	25
secretary, Kijik Corp. (Anchorage)	1	20	12	12
heavy equipment operator, Kijik Corp. (Keyes Point)	2	varied	4	10
caretaker, Keyes Point	1	varied	varied	10
postmaster	1	varied	12	varied
fuel delivery	1	varied	12	varied
firefighting, state	varied	80	.75	10
mayor	1	40	12	25

[a] The wage employment data were first gathered in 1986. When the authors made the decision to update the information in 1989, the number of jobs available had declined by approximately 19 to 26 positions. These were mostly seasonal jobs associated with construction on roads or at Keyes Point, manufacturing at the doll factory (which had closed), services now handled out of an urban center (such as telephone maintenance), and the assumption of some positions by non–Natives not married into the community. Some wages were estimates for 1989.

conservationist oriented clientele were attracted by the aesthetic beauty of the area and inspired by the possibility of having summer "homes" with access to non-consumptive wilderness experiences within Lake Clark National Park and Preserve. Other potential investors in the Keyes Point subdivision were more interested in the consumptive uses of resources in the area, particularly caribou, moose, sockeye, and multiple species of freshwater fish valued by sport fishermen. Although only local residents were allowed to hunt in the park proper, fishing was permitted in both the park and preserve. The preserve was open to both hunting and fishing by non-locals within the context of initially state and now newly developing federal fish and game regulations. Kijik Corporation deemed that the value derived from this type of development theoretically would benefit local people monetarily more than the increased competition for resources and contact with outsiders would prove to be a liability. In fact, in 1987 the plan had included a business consortium with a large resort developer. It was expected that a resort at Keyes Point would provide jobs for local people as guides, managers, food service workers, maids, caretakers, and clerical support.

Although a lengthy runway and some roads were constructed at Keyes Point, providing temporary laborer employment for several Nondalton residents, Kijik Corporation experienced financial difficulties common to most ANCSA-created Native corporate entities. By 1991, there were approximately 20 summer homes constructed, although many lots remained unsold and some initial buyers defaulted. In part, Kijik was affected by Alaska's economic recession of the last half of the 1980s. This recession greatly influenced property values and discouraged the sale of "luxury" real estate such as summer homes. Additionally, there were several other problems associated with Kijik obtaining adequate capital necessary to fully develop the subdivision in compliance with the covenants guaranteed to buyers. Also, the regional corporation, Bristol Bay Native Corporation, had ANCSA-legislated rights to the subsurface lands at Keyes Point. This fact made financing of these homes problematic. Lastly, some of the corporate shareholding elders were critical of the sale of Nondalton's Native lands. For all these reasons, by 1991, the Keyes Point development had not succeeded in ways originally conceived by its non-Dena'ina director and speculator. On a positive note, the corporation had sold off some of its losses and received

easement income from the U.S. National Park Service. Dena'ina had assumed full control of managing the corporation. Old age pension payments to shareholders ceased, although death benefits continued to be purchased for all shareholders by the corporation. Its financial future remained unresolved in 1991.

Behnke (1982) determined that in 1981, transfer payments, such as social security, unemployment, and other forms of social welfare, were insignificant in the overall economy of the community. Transfer payment data for Nondalton for the period 1987 to 1988 were gathered from the Alaska State Department of Health and Social Services, Division of Public Assistance (Alaska, DHSS 1988). Most state transfer payments were allocated on the basis of households rather than domestic units. Aid to Families with Dependent Children was given to from three to five families, with three being the average number for this period. Food stamps were received by from 4 to 10 families, with 6 being the most common number of households to benefit. Six to 11 individuals, rather than households, received Adult Public Assistance intended for the aged, blind, and other disabled. In this case, 7 was the norm. Unemployment data were unavailable but few individuals qualified under state law. Monetarily, transfer payments ranged from a low of $6,903 in June of 1987 to a high of $14,867 in July of 1988. The number of clients ranged from a low of 17 in August of 1987 to a high of 26 in July of 1988. The maximal number of clients and cash received were misleading, in that some households qualified for more than one type of benefit. Given these data, it can be concluded that a few households, particularly those of the elderly, received a significant proportion of their income during certain months via transfer payments for this period of time. However, the vast majority of households received no support from state transfer payments. The community overall was not supported significantly by state transfer payments, as was the case in 1981.

Most rural Alaska residents, including those of Nondalton, received energy assistance. The same was true for the elderly who were eligible for federally subsidized medicare. All Dena'ina or other Native residents qualified for health care through the auspices of the U.S. Public Health Service. This included a village health aide, occasional visiting physicians or physician assistants, and hospital care in Anchorage. However, many Nondalton residents opted to pay for private treatment outside of Nondalton in cases of serious illness or when they felt that the liabilities of U.S. Public Service Health care outweighed the financial benefits. Many elderly Nondalton residents without formal education found the processes of obtaining most state and federal services cumbersome, if not impossible.

Household income data were not collected systematically in the course of this research. However, Morris (1986) was able to calculate average individual incomes for selected years during the period 1978 to 1982 based on federal tax returns. Although these data may shed some very general insight into the nature of cash flow into the community, unfamiliarity with filing tax returns affected the accuracy of the data. Given these qualifications, in 1978, 44 federal returns were filed, with an average income of $7,181; in 1981, 77 people filed returns, with average earnings of $8,094; and in 1982, 54 returns indicated an average income of $8,560. The large variation in the number of returns filed in Alaskan Native communities was not particularly atypical, especially when a considerable proportion of income was derived from activities like firefighting, sporadic construction, and commercial fishing. Additionally, if inflation were taken into account at the rate of 10 percent per annum, real income declined between 1978 and 1981 and between 1981 and 1982 (Morris 1986).

A comparison of Nondalton incomes with those of the primarily non-Native community of Port Alsworth on Lake Clark indicated the relatively low income status of Nondalton residents during a single year. In 1982, the average income at Port Alsworth was $20,022 compared with Nondalton's $8,560. This represented a 134 percent higher income level at Port Alsworth than at Nondalton based on these data (Morris 1986:30).

DISTRIBUTION AND EXCHANGE IN THE CONTEXT OF THE MODERN WORLD

"Gift exchange," in which there is a personal relationship between the individuals who exchange goods and services, and "commodity exchange," in which impersonality and individual maximization prevail (Gregory 1982), were both operative among the inland Dena'ina of Nondalton in the 1980s. All-purpose money (cash) was involved in both types of exchange as well. Since the precise tracking of the networks, content, and context of every exchange was not feasible, examples derived from multiple years of observation provided the primary data used for addressing questions related to the role of these two types of

exchanges and the integration of cash in the Nondalton economy of the 1980s.

Cultural rules regarding the exchange of meat and fish, raw materials, vegetable foods, and other products derived from hunting, fishing, gathering, and trapping described for the past remained operative. In fact, not only did exchanges of these types occur on a daily basis, but, more importantly, the rules defining the context of "gift exchange" were known by young and old alike in Nondalton. The primary ceremony in which such principles were overtly and publicly expressed and reaffirmed was the potlatch. In the 1980s, the potlatch with its ideological, economic, social, and political implications, remained viable and functional in the context of the economy and society of the inland Dena'ina.

There are two principal theories regarding the impact of cash or all-purpose money on "traditional" hunting and gathering economies. The first, accepted by many federal and state agencies and prominent in the premises of contemporary formal economics, is that cash eventually destroys non-market or "gift" exchange. This transformation is seen to be advantageous and essential to integrating or assimilating "primitive" people into the mainstream economy of the nation-state in which they have become encapsulated. This premise disregards the sociocultural context of economic exchange or the interests of people in retaining the basic characteristics of their non-western economies. From this perspective, the total transformation of the economic system is merely a matter of time (Ortiz 1983; Schneider 1974). There is the expectation that societies in the process of such economic change exhibit naivete about handling money and learning or applying the skills of "rational economic man." It is obvious in the case of the inland Dena'ina that approximately two centuries of contact with Euroamericans, the last of which was direct and intensive, did not result in the total westernization of their economy.

Another perspective is that Alaska Native village economies are subsistence-based and "mixed." This means that such economies incorporate both subsistence and market or cash sectors. These symbiotic sectors, while integrated into a single economy, have different operative rules. That is, cash and wage labor are considered to be different from goods and services produced by or related to subsistence activities and, therefore, exchanged and accumulated by a different set of principles more similar to those found in market economies. The data derived from the inland Dena'ina raise some serious questions about the assumption that cash and services for which people are paid actually form a separate, albeit, integrated economic sector.

Has money in inland Dena'ina society taken on the role of goods produced by means of subsistence in establishing or validating social and cultural relationships between individuals or kin groups? There are many examples from the 1980s which affirmatively answer this question. When non-Dena'ina inmarried spouses without clan affiliation were adopted into appropriate opposite clans, cash was exchanged between elders of the relevant matriclans to validate the new status of the individual. Funeral and memorial potlatching in the past required the accumulation of vast stores of cherished foods, raw materials, and technology. It was the responsibility of a matrilineal clan, under the direction of its principal male leader, to accumulate such wealth. In the 1980s, highly valued Native foods and raw materials, such as pelts, were considered essential in the context of potlatching. However, western commodities and cash comprised the vast majority of material wealth dispensed in the context of this ceremony. In fact, cash was given to every representative of those clans considered to be opposite of that of the deceased. Those who assisted in mortuary and funeral procedures were compensated systematically with both goods and money. In all cases, the use of cash or purchased goods were employed in reaffirming relationships between individuals and kin groups and in validating or improving non-western social status and prestige in contemporary inland Dena'ina society.

Exchanges between inland Dena'ina and neighboring *Dutna* transpired in the contexts of festivities and spring carnivals associated with Russian Orthodox Christmas and Easter. During these events, inland Dena'ina and *Dutna* conducted intervillage visits. Subsistence derived foods, occurring in one area but not the other, were exchanged between hosts and visitors. However, an important social and economic activity was gambling associated with card playing and dog racing. Large quantities of cash, and occasionally, some costly items of technology, changed hands during the course of this friendly competition. Such gambling was distinctly not characterized by the impersonal nature of similar gaming in western society. Rather, it was seen as reaffirming relationships between individuals and groups. Modern gambling was explained as alternative to more traditional games of skill and

chance played in the historic past. In cases of personal or family loss and misfortune involving members of one of these ethnic groups, representatives of the other conducted fund-raising activities involving both cash, commodities, and subsistence goods.

Other functions of cash as employed in market economies were not adopted by the inland Dena'ina. For example, although cash and commercial goods were accumulated for potlatching, individual, family, or clan hoarding of wealth, albeit uncommon, occurred and was perceived to be "stingy" by local standards. Stratification based upon wealth remained a part of inland Dena'ina society in the 1980s. Those who were better off economically, as defined by both subsistence and monetary criteria, were of higher social status and amassed prestige. However, as in the past, the path of the modern *qeshqa* was as fine as the razor's edge, since status and prestige required having and giving simultaneously, regardless of the source and nature of one's wealth.

CONSUMPTION IN THE CONTEXT OF THE MODERN WORLD

This final consideration of the relationship between subsistence, market economics, and cash is associated with consumption by the inland Dena'ina. Money was necessary for life in all rural Alaska Native communities in the 1980s. Governmental efforts at providing rural communities with the types of infrastructure common in western cities, such as sewer and water systems and means of generating electricity, incurred costs which Native people were forced to assume above and beyond public subsidy. Increased centralization mandated the use of modern technology and fuel to continue hunting, fishing, trapping, and gathering. Therefore, the consumption of cash was described in terms of capital expenditures and daily living costs in Nondalton during the period 1989 to 1990, with some comparative data for earlier years (Behnke 1982).

Table 7 presents the costs of initial capital expenditures, the life expectancy of items purchased, and the annual costs to Nondalton residents for the years 1980 and 1989 to 1990. The selection of particular items and their life expectancy were based on what people were buying and using and what they reported as the period of time after which such technology required replacement.

As readily can be seen from Table 7, capital expenditures overall and annually increased between 1980 and 1990. The incentive to purchase larger outboard motors, four-wheel ATVs, and skiffs instead of their smaller, lesser expensive counterparts was not simply because "bigger was better." Rather, in the case of larger boats and four-wheel ATVs, they proved to be more stable and safe. They carried larger load capacities for people, gear, and resources harvested than did their smaller counterparts. Larger outboards provided greater speed and power to skiffs, allowing people to travel over more vast distances in less time and with increased efficiency. Larger snowmachines were not preferred over smaller, less powerful versions, as the latter were more maneuverable in the wooded habitat occupied by the inland Dena'ina. There was an interest in using higher powered firearms on the part of primarily younger people, although older hunters generally retained rifles of the caliber to which they had become accustomed in their youth.

In Table 7, prices were not included for sleds. Although sleds were a common and essential item of technology, they primarily were made locally. Few hand-made plank boats were visible in Nondalton in the 1980s. Many other smaller items of technology, such as fishing lines, hooks, axes, and chain saws, were not included in this table, principally because the quantity owned and the degree of variation in costs were diverse. Additionally, the prices of materials necessary for building smokehouses, cabins, fish bins, fish racks, and other critical items necessary for local production were too variable to calculate in this table. For these reasons, the costs estimated here should be considered minimal for the period 1989 to 1990. Individuals without access to these items of technology were forced to borrow them from both relatives or unrelated partners. This practice incurred a debt relationship resulting in an expectation of repayment, such as hauling wood for the lender and sharing game taken with borrowed equipment.

Housing and utility costs are also presented for 1980 and 1989 to 1990 in Table 8. In 1980, one-third of the households were heated with oil, while the remaining majority had wood-burning stoves. Because many houses were poorly insulated, heating with oil was expensive. For example, the members of one household heated solely with fuel oil purchased 10 drums during the course of the winter at a cost of $880.00. Even those who gathered their own wood purchased fuel for snowmachines to haul the wood from where it was available to the village. Fuel delivered to Iliamna by barge was less expensive, but few Nondalton residents had either the cash available or storage facilities to buy this commodity in bulk quantities and transport it to Nondalton. Another major cost was fuel for operating individually-owned generators, as the community did not have a power system in 1980. Electricity was not available in Nondalton until 1982, when an area cooperative was formed (Iliamna-Newhalen-Nondalton Electric Cooperative or INN). For example, one household with a freezer and a few other basic appliances used 30 drums of fuel oil at the cost of $88 per drum, or a total of $3,970, in the course of one winter for the generation of electricity. Many households had no access to electricity at this time and used Blazo as fuel for Coleman lanterns. One household reported consuming 120 gallons of Blazo at $5 per gallon, or $600 in the course of a year. Households commonly used six 100-pound bottles of propane for cooking, at a cost of $75 each, or a total of $450 during the year. Overall, Behnke (1982:22) estimated that one-quarter to one-third of the annual gross income of Nondalton household members was spent on fuels in 1980.

By 1989 to 1990, more families returned to heating principally with wood, although small, electrically fired, self regulating, oil furnaces were becoming popular, especially with the elderly. Freezers and other appliances, such as refrigerators, washers, televisions, and VCRs, were common in most households by 1986. Having access to electricity was valued highly by residents of the community.

As depicted in Table 8, the cost of electricity per kilowatt hour was low, primarily because of governmental subsidies. Between these two time periods, fuel costs increased dramatically for heating oil and gasoline. For example, one moderately sized house required 10 barrels of fuel oil during the course of the winter of 1989 to 1990, costing $2,090.

Air transport costs consumed a relatively large segment of expendable income for Nondalton residents in 1980 and 1989 to 1990. In 1980, air transport expenses for a round-trip fare to Naknek for participation in the commercial fishery ranged between $162 and $216, depending on the number of passengers. Scheduled round-trip flights from Nondalton to Anchorage

TABLE 7. CAPITAL EXPENDITURES, NONDALTON, 1980 AND 1989–90

Item	Cost	Life Expectancy	Annual Cost
1980			
16-foot Lund aluminum skiff	$1500	9.0 years	$166
35-hp. Mercury outboard	1800	3.8 years	824
Skidoo snowmachine (small)	1800	3.7 years	836
rifle (30.06)	300	6.8 years	44
rifle (.22)	125	13.0 years	10
shotgun (12 gauge)	275	7.5 years	37
3 dozen snares	64	1.5 years	43
2 dozen no. 2 steel traps	120	10.0 years	12
net (salmon, 50 fathoms)	350	6.0 years	58
annual cost of technology			$2030
1989–90			
16-foot Lund aluminum skiff	$1800	5.0 years	$360[a]
18-foot Lund aluminum skiff	4000	5.0 years	800
35-hp. Mercury outboard	4100	3.5 years	1171[a]
50-hp. Mercury outboard	4620	3.5 years	1320
30-hp. Suzuki outboard	2350	3.5 years	671[a]
Skidoo snowmachine (Elan)	2500	2.0 years	1250[a]
Skidoo snowmachine (Tundra)	2700	2.0 years	1350
3-wheel Suzuki all–terrain vehicle (available until 1990)	3250	2.5 years	1300[a]
4-wheel Honda all–terrain vehicle (4 x 4)	4380	2.5 years	1752
rifle (357 magnum with scope)	700	6.5 years	108
rifle (.22)	150	10.0 years	15
shotgun (12 gauge)	275	6.5 years	42
2 dozen no. 2 steel traps	140	8.0 years	18
net (salmon, 50 fathoms)	385	5.0 years	70
annual cost of technology (most expensive option)			$5475
[a] annual cost of technology (least expensive option)			$3834–4334

All costs were calculated including delivery to Nondalton. Sources: 1980 (Behnke 1982); 1989 to 1990 (field data).

TABLE 8. HOUSING AND UTILITY COSTS, NONDALTON, 1980 AND 1989-90

Item	Cost per Unit
1980	
fuel oil, heating	$105/55 gal. drum
propane	75/bottle
blazo	5/gallon
gasoline	110/55 gal. drum
water and sewer	35/month
electricity (not available unless individually generated)	
1989-90	
fuel oil, heating	$209/55 gal. drum
propane	100/bottle
gasoline	138/55 gal. drum
phone	20/month (no long distance)
water and sewer	40/month
electricity (INN Electric Coop)	.45 cents/kilowatt hour
rent (HUD payment)	90/month

Sources: 1980 (Behnke 1982); 1989 to 1990 (field data).

via Iliamna were $200. Air taxi round-trip seat fares from Nondalton to Anchorage were $150. By 1989 to 1990, scheduled flights from Nondalton to Anchorage via Iliamna cost $284 and involved two separate and unrelated carriers. Most residents of Nondalton chose to fly with Birchwood Air Taxi, which offered daily service and charged a $160 seat fare for a round-trip between Anchorage and Nondalton. This carrier allowed passengers to carry a liberal amount of luggage and freight at no extra charge and also arranged short-term credit for some village residents. Air charter costs to Bristol Bay and Lime Village also increased over the decade. These costs remained variable, depending upon the number of people travelling and the weight of baggage and freight. Frequent travel between Lime Village and Nondalton for contact with relatives was a costly expense for residents of both communities.

People in Nondalton were anxious to get telephone service and monthly rates were nominal when service began in the early 1980s. However, the frequent use of long distance services resulted in the disconnection of approximately 80 percent of original subscribers by 1987. Some of these were reinstated by the period 1989 to 1990.

Food prices for 1980 were not listed by Behnke (1982), but he estimated that they were 40 percent higher than those of Anchorage. A comparison of commercial food costs in Nondalton between 1986 and 1989 to 1990 is presented in Table 9. Although systematic contrasts between Nondalton and Anchorage commodity costs and availability were not made for ths latter period of time, the transport of goods from Anchorage or other urban centers to the village unquestionably increased Nondalton prices. A few residents with adequate cash purchased a significant portion of their food and other supplies in Anchorage during multiple purpose trips. Almost all people bought fresh produce, and other items unobtainable in the village store, in Anchorage. In most categories, the costs of commercial foods in Nondalton's cooperative store increased between 1986 and 1989 to 1990, in large part reflecting greater costs of transport.

The history of local stores in Nondalton in recent years provided some relevant insights into village consumerism and business management during the 1980s. For the past few years, the Nondalton cooperative store was operated by a non-local, experienced rural store manager from Frontier

Expediters, Inc., after having been closed for one year as the result of financial and management problems. This manager estimated that the average expenditure for commercial foods and a few dry goods per household was approximately $460 a month at the local store in 1986. Of course, this figure did not account for any Anchorage purchases. In 1986, the K'nechek Cooperative Store took in an estimated $300,000 annually, with $23,000 of that occurring between January and February. The highest expenditures, $30,000, occurred in November, correlating with Thanksgiving and American and Russian Orthodox Christmas holidays the following months. Commonly, grocery sales averaged $24,000 monthly, although the purchase of canned or frozen meat products, never a substantial portion of overall food expenditures, declined significantly during the months of August and September. Flour and sugar were the most stable commodities in terms of demand year-round. Other items varied widely, and the manager concluded that the diversity of goods purchased was associated directly with availability of cash in the community. Only members of approximately 10 households used state public assistance in the form of food stamps in 1986. Frontier Expediters, Inc. was a firm attempting to provide food to rural communities at relatively low rates, using efficient and low cost delivery and computerized ordering systems. It was their intent that the non-local manager would be able to instruct one or two local persons in the management of the store during his tenure. However, by 1991, local people, who had worked as clerks, had a relatively short tenure. No one had demonstrated an interest in assuming management of the store. Between 1985 and 1991, the only local competition to the cooperative store was an individual, who sold candy and pop in his home; a small "bread and egg" store, operated by an inmarried non-Dena'ina man and his wife, which ceased operation after a year or two; and a newly established cafe, which commenced business in spring 1987 and remained viable in 1991.

In the 1980s, Nondalton residents more or less remained marginally reliant on commercial foods, with the exception of a limited number of staples. The use of *Gasht'ana* foods, which were characterized as being more or less "luxury" or non-essential items by the inland Dena'ina, varied in relationship to cash flow in the community and the occurrence of celebrations or ceremonies, particularly potlatching. Locally harvested foods were considered both desirable and essential to the overall well-being of the community and its occupants by all residents, particularly those who were middle-aged to older adults.

THE GREAT COMPROMISE: HUNTER–GATHERER IDEOLOGIES IN A MARKET CONTEXT

Participation in western market economics was the result of historical factors over which the inland Dena'ina had limited control. Although local people were unable to govern many facets of contact, such as outside markets and the policies of trading companies, they were able to make decisions regarding the nature, intensity, and location of their interface with representatives of western, market economies. Additionally, the inland Dena'ina had a choice as to what degree Euroamerican ideologies, social organizations, and cultures were to influence the integration of principles, technologies, and values of western economies into their own culture and society.

Western economics, with its emphasis on private ownership and the individual accumulation of wealth, stood in stark contrast to more "traditional" values and behaviors of the inland Dena'ina. External forces encouraged individual maximization and social stratification as opposed to kin group or domestic unit wealth. The limited entry permit system for commercial salmon fishing, private ownership of homes and plots of land, and the organization of group wealth in the form of a business corporation rather than the band or community were examples of western economic models imposed upon the inland Dena'ina. However, for the most part these forces were resisted. Attempts of individuals or institutions to institute private ownership on inland Dena'ina lands, for example, were criticized and a source of endless gossip. There continued to be substantial leveling pressures in regard to individual wealth through traditional mechanisms of sharing and exchange, such as potlatching. Murphy and Steward's (1968 [1956]) ominous predictions of individualization of wealth which was previously "communal" had not come to pass in inland Dena'ina society.

Because Kijik Corporation was mandated by its existence and charter to make money for shareholders, a traumatic dilemma emerged with the sale of inland Dena'ina land at Keyes Point. The corporation assured shareholders that the covenants for sale of the recreational home sites provided adequate protection to local residents.

TABLE 9. MARKET BASKET SURVEY, K'NECHEK CO-OP STORE, INC.
JULY 1986 AND 1989-90

Item	Unit Cost	
	1986	1989-90
disposable diapers (Pampers, 32)	$17.95	$17.85
Crisco (6 lb.)	10.09	10.85
liquid dish washing soap (Ivory, 22 oz.)	2.85	3.19
corned beef hash (15 oz. can)	2.25	2.59
whole chicken (3 lb. 2 oz. can)	5.99	6.09
chicken sandwich spread	2.39	2.55
turkey noodle soup (Campbell 10.75 oz. can)	.95	1.05
whole kernel corn (Del Monte, 17 oz. can)	1.19	1.29
peach halves (Del Monte, 16 oz. can)	1.59	1.79
Hamburger Helper	2.45	2.89
hot chocolate (Swiss Miss, 30 oz.)	6.35	6.75
cookies (chocolate chip, 1 bag)	2.25	3.69
instant potatoes (Potato Buds, 1 lb. 12 oz)	4.55	4.69
unsweetened orange juice (Libby's, 46 oz.)	3.55	4.45
macaroni and cheese (Kraft, 7.25 oz.)	1.19	1.35
oranges (per lb.)	.99	.99
apples (red delicious, per lb.)	1.59	1.19
eggs (extra large, 1 doz.)	1.65	2.29
tomatoes (per lb.)	1.89	1.39
green peppers (per lb.)	2.95	2.45
butter (per lb.)	3.55	3.39
canned milk (12 oz.)	1.09	1.15
sugar (C and H, 5 lbs.)	3.69	4.39
apple pie filling (Wilderness, 21 oz.)	2.25	2.65
summer sausage (Oscar Meyer, 8 oz. pack)	2.15	2.59
fried chicken (Banquet, frozen, 24 oz.)	12.79	13.65
beef short ribs (per lb.)	5.39	5.35
beef rib steak (per lb.)	8.58	8.15
beef chuck roast (per lb.)	3.99	3.99
pork chops (per lb.)	4.89	5.35
dry milk (50 qt.)	30.45	38.31
	$153.48	$168.35

However, the introduction of more outsiders to an area already pressed by urban competition for resources potentially could disrupt traditional inland Dena'ina subsistence activities and the overall quality of life. In the past, resources and land were not sold or bartered away by individuals, as they were perceived to be the wealth of a group. The leaders of the corporation were primarily younger, with more education in the affairs of the western world than possessed by their elders. Although they asked for the advice of senior members of the community, their decisions set them on a course which substantially may change the life of Nondalton residents in the future. These choices were made, not out of disregard for tradition, but as a result of mandates emerging from western policies and the highly competitive market place.

As other research among contemporary northern North American hunters and gatherers has demonstrated (e.g., Wolfe and Ellanna 1983; Wolfe et al. 1984), those households with negligible cash have a difficult time in subsistence production in the contemporary world. On the other end of the continuum, however, are those whose time is solely devoted to cash-earning opportunities. Such individuals are also limited producers in the realm of subsistence production. The key to a successful economic life in Nondalton in the 1980s was maintaining balance between these two extremes.

The promise of western institutional education at elementary, secondary, and post-secondary levels for providing economic security to the young people of Nondalton went unfulfilled, primarily because rural communities lack the western economic foundation to support such hollow claims. Consequently, in the 1980s, the youth of Nondalton faced a dilemma with implications beyond the scope of mere economics. In order to find permanent, full-time employment, they were forced to leave the community in which they had rich and mutually supportive human networks and could operate with a high degree of competence and skill. Their option, to relocate in an urban and western community, placed them in a situation in which they were socially isolated and participant in a culture that was decidedly foreign. Furthermore, they had few skills for social and economic mobility in urban areas. For some, this dilemma resulted in transience between Nondalton or Lime Village and Anchorage or even outside of Alaska. Others returned disillusioned with opportunities in the outside world and much less self confidence than when they left. Yet others remained in the village with no desire to select either of these alternatives. Without the continued viability of uninterrupted hunting, fishing, trapping and gathering, the economic future of the inland Dena'ina is uncertain at best and could be considered bleak.

Figure 83. Pete Koktelash, assisting with the building of a fish caching pit, *chiqilin q'a,* Nondalton, summer 1986. *Photograph Courtesy of IMPACT, Rasmuson Library, University of Alaska Fairbanks.*

CHAPTER 11

DENA'INA PERSPECTIVE: MEMORIES OF A BRISTOL BAY FISHERMAN

THE EARLY YEARS

I was born March 15, 1905, in the Dena'ina community of Qeghnilen on the upper Stony River, the son of Gillie Koktelash and Agafia Evan Koktelash. By this time, the priests had taught our parents to give first and last names rather than just Dena'ina names to their children, and we took our father's surnames. I was called Pete Koktelash. Before I was one year of age, my mother died. One brother and one sister were born before me, but they died when they were just babies. In the years to follow, I was raised by my father and his mother's brother. My father called his mother's brother *zhala*, and I called him *chada* or grandpa. His name was also Gillie like my dad, and I think his last name was also Koktelash. He lived with us the rest of his life and always helped take care of me when I was young. Following my mother's side, I was of the *nuhzhi* clan, but my father and his *zhala* Gillie were of the opposite clan or *qqahyi*.

Life on the upper Stony River was hard for my father and *chada*. When I was eight or nine years old, in about 1913 or 1914, my dad decided that we should move to Old Nondalton to be nearer to Hans Severson's trading post at Old Nondalton. When we still lived on the upper Stony River, sometimes my father travelled to the Kuskokwim or Nushagak rivers by boat or overland to Tyonek on the coast of Cook Inlet for supplies. My dad used to say that there were no jobs and no way to make money on the upper Stony River. He knew that some of our Dena'ina relatives, who lived near Lake Clark and Lake Iliamna, had been able to get work in the canneries at Bristol Bay. That is why we moved down to Old Nondalton. Evan Koktelash, my dad's brother, already was living there. He had moved there with everyone else when they left Kijik around 1900. When we first moved to Old Nondalton, we lived with Alexie Balluta and his family until we were able to build a house of our own. Because I had no mother, I was considered to be like a brother to Sophie Hobson. Her mother, Tatiana Constantine Hobson, often made clothes and did other things for me.

Before I was old enough to go to Bristol Bay, my father and *chada* went there with other men from Old Nondalton. Those men who went at that time were Gabriel Trefon; Wassillie Trefon, whom we

also called Was; Kerosim Balluta; Alexie Karshekoff; Alexie Balluta; Stephan Karshekoff; Evan Koktelash, my father's brother, whom I also called *dada* Maxim Cusma; Vladimir Cusma; Marka Karshekoff; Pete Delkittie; and Jack Hobson. These were just about all the men of the village. The women and the younger children stayed behind with some people who were elderly or ill. They remained at fish camp putting up sockeyes, our main source of food, for the winter to come. The men usually left in late May or, more often, in early June, depending on when the salmon began running, what the weather was like, and other things. They didn't return until August, when all the fish which were canned or salted at Bristol Bay, were loaded aboard ships and sent "outside." Then everyone returned home to put up their fish for dogs.

Usually the men bought much of their winter's supply of groceries — flour, sugar, rice, beans, salt, tea, coffee beans, some cloth for the women to sew, and a few canned vegetables — from the canneries and brought it home with them. Hans Severson picked them up at Bristol Bay with his boat, the *Tern*, and hauled the men and their freight back to Iliamna. They usually left their supplies there until winter and then hauled them back to the village by dog team after the snow was good enough for them to travel. It was not too many years after we moved to Old Nondalton that I was old enough to go with the men to the bay, along with several other boys my age.

MY LIFE AS A CANNERY WORKER

When I was about 12 or 13, in 1917 or 1918, my father and *chada* decided to let me follow them to Bristol Bay. They were working at one cannery, and I was able to get a job with another, even though I was younger than the canneries said we were suppose to be to get a job. I guess the canneries really hired boys as soon as they seemed old enough to work. If you could walk around, they would hire you. My first job was with Bristol Bay Packing Company. We called it "Hungry Peterson's." It was located at a place which had been named Peterson Point by *Gasht'ana* or white men. The *Gasht'ana* had been running the commercial fishery at Bristol Bay for several years, but my people had not gone to work there until the early 1900s. When I first went to the bay, Anton Balluta, Mike Balluta, and Gillie Jacko came with me. We were all about the same age and good friends, especially Anton and I. People from the village took us by canoes or skiffs about eight or nine miles down the Newhalen River to "The Landing," which was just above the rapids. From there, we hiked across the portage to Hans Severson's store, which he had moved to Iliamna. We went down to the bay with his boat, the *Tern*, or with Kerosim Sava's boat, the *Edwin*.

We couldn't speak much English, but Hans Severson and Jack Hobson helped us get along. They were *Gasht'ana*s who could speak both English and Dena'ina. The older men who had been going to the bay for a couple of years already had learned some English from hunters and prospectors near home and, later, from other English speakers working in the canneries. We also had the help of Old Iliamna people, since some had been going to school and learning English from the early 1900s. At this time, we had never had a school at Old Nondalton.

When we got to Bristol Bay, there were people who had come from everywhere. There were Chinese, Mexicans, Italians, Filipinos, Norwegians, *Dutna,* Eskimos from other places like the Kuskokwim River, and many others. At that time, no Natives were allowed to fish. The fishermen were the Italians and Norwegians. The Dena'ina were given jobs in canneries with the Mexicans and Chinese. Our job was to "slime" the salmon before they were cooked and canned. I can't remember exactly how much we were paid at that time, but the hours we worked and the amount of money we made depended on how good the fish runs were and how many fish the canneries were able to process. During good runs or peak times, we worked day and night. Other times, work was very slow.

Cannery workers stayed in bunk houses with other people from their own area. The Dena'ina had their own bunk houses. So did the *Dutna,* the Eskimos, the Chinese, the Filipinos, and all the other groups. We called the Chinese bunk houses "Chinatown," and they had their own mess halls. The rest of the cannery workers ate together in mess halls separate from those of the fishermen. Meals were good, and we had plenty of food served family style. Sometimes we got homesick for our Dena'ina food, however. The first year I went, I wasn't used to *Gasht'ana* food, and it tasted funny. In time we got used to what they served us and to working with people from all over the world. Life wasn't so bad, and there were times we played games like *ch'enlahi,* a stick game, with our long-time neighbors, the *Dutna,* of the Newhalen River and Lake Iliamna country.

I was a cannery worker for nearly 10 years, until the early 1930s. At this time, Native people were allowed to fish, the kind of work we did normally at home. We also had become much more comfortable with English and *Gasht'ana* life in general. As fishermen, we finally had the chance to make more money, and our life at Bristol Bay greatly improved. In 1928, I married Ruth Bobby, a young girl from the upper Stony River. Now I was expected to support a family of my own.

THE DENA'INA BECOME COMMERCIAL FISHERMEN

At the time that we were hired as fishermen, commercial fishing took place in 28-to-30 foot sailing boats normally manned by only two people. Everything was done by hand with our own power, except for the wind. If there was no wind to fill our sails, we rowed and it was hard work. We set our 150-fathom nets, and pulled them in by hand. We drifted with the tide when we set net and sailed upriver or across the rivers when the wind was blowing. Most of our fishing took place at the mouth or lower parts of the Kvichak River or out in the bay itself.

The boats were owned by the canneries. Often we picked our partners before we ever left Old Nondalton. The first year I fished, Kerosim Balluta was my partner. Kerosim was married to my wife's sister, Elizabeth Bobby Balluta. Usually, the first man to get a boat from a cannery was the captain for that season. The cannery superintendents were in charge of the fishing, and they got to know who were the best fishermen and the good workers. In these days there was sort of a competition between fishermen. You had to be above average in the number of fish which you took in one year in order for the cannery superintendent to give you a boat during the next season. In a way, we were even competing against good friends and family members who also fished. We asked the tallymen, on the scows where we delivered our salmon, how many fish others boats had gotten. We tried our best to have the largest harvests. The canneries encouraged our competition by posting notices on Sundays naming which boats were the "high-liners" for that week. No one wanted to be on the crew of the low boat. During these years, we fished six days a week, taking Sundays off to rest.

When I first started fishing, I got 2 1/2 cents per fish, and, in 1933, the limit for a 12-hour opening was 1,500 salmon. In good years, we were able to take maybe 50,000 fish or make $1,500 in a season. The money earned by a boat crew was split between the two partners. During these years, that was big money, and most people didn't come close to making that much. It was not unusual for a boat to take in only 10,000 fish in a season and make $300. When partners shared that equally, $150 wasn't much for purchasing our winter's supply of dry goods. The company furnished the boat, all nets and gear; our board and room when we weren't fishing at a charge of 50 cents a day; and food, bedding, and other things we needed when we were out on the boat. If our boats or gear broke down, we replaced them at the cannery that owned our boat and to which we had to sell our salmon.

I fished for Hungry Peterson, or Bristol Bay Packers, for three years and then went to Nakeen at Squaw Point, upriver from Peterson Point. There I began fishing for A and A Packing Company. I don't know what the full name of this company really was. I fished there for one season and then went to Koggiung the following year, where I fished for Alaska Packers for the rest of my fishing career, except for one season.

In 1942, during World War II, no foreigners were allowed to either fish or work in the canneries. There were no Chinese, no Mexicans, no Filipinos, no Blacks, no one, just us Alaskans. Paul Cusma was my partner that year. Only one cannery was open at Graveyard Point run by the Libby Company, and everyone fished for them. That year, 1942, was good fishing, and salmon sold for about five cents per fish. That was also the first year any women from Nondalton or any other Alaskan village went to work in Bristol Bay. Even my wife, Ruth, worked at a cannery that year. By 1943 and 1944, most of the canneries reopened, and some Filipinos were rehired. However, some Dena'ina women continued to work as processors during these years.

In 1943, the fishermen decided to join a union, the Alaska Fishermen's Union, which was affiliated with the AFL-CIO. Cannery workers formed a separate union. By 1944, the price of salmon had increased to about 12 and 1/2 cents per fish. Membership in the union was required of all fishermen. By 1948 or 1949, the price of salmon went up to 32 and 1/2 cents per fish. During this time, everyone began fishing and processing

together. *Gasht'ana, Dutna,* Eskimo, and Dena'ina fishermen worked alongside one another and with foreigners. It was no longer the practice to keep people separate from one another. However, the outside fishermen had their own union.

I did not always have the same partner during the 1940s but fished with several different men from Nondalton and Old Iliamna, including Paul Zackar and Kerosim Sava. I always tried to pick good fishermen to be my partners, not just good friends or relatives.

We were still fishing from sailing boats at this time. Although these kind of boats required us to work a lot harder than we did when power boats came along, I personally liked them better. The 1950s was to bring about a lot of changes in the way we fished, mainly because of the introduction of gasoline and diesel-powered boats.

MODERN FISHING IN BRISTOL BAY

Between 1950 and 1952, the canneries began to convert the sail-powered gillnetters to gasoline and diesel powerboats. At this time, fishermen began using skiffs for drift netting with nine-horse Johnson outboards. Prior to this time, skiffs had been used only for set netting. Soon after, Alaska Packers brought in 10-horse Mercury outboards and furnished them, the skiffs, and nets to fishermen. The fishermen were required to sell their season's take to the cannery which furnished them with equipment. After the conversion from sails to gasoline or diesel power, the price of salmon went up to 36 cents per fish, and fishing became more efficient. We were able to take more fish during an opening with powerboats than we had been able to take with sailboats. Skiffs were limited to 50-fathom nets and large drift power-boats to 150 fathoms.

In the summer of 1953, the canneries brought their own fishermen from outside Alaska and stopped giving skiffs and outboards to local Native fishermen, mostly the men from the Nondalton, Lake Iliamna, and Bristol Bay areas. People from the Naknek area came up and told us what was going to happen during that summer. Those of us from Nondalton and other villages didn't want to give up commercial fishing. It was our main source of cash. The cannery that we had fished for many years, the Alaska Packers cannery at Koggiung, closed down in 1953 and never reopened. However, the Alaska Packers cannery at South

Figure 84. A Bristol Bay gillnetter powered by sails, used in the commercial fishery until power boats were legalized in 1952. *Photograph Courtesy of Pete Koktelash.*

Naknek remained open. The closing down of the Koggiung cannery eliminated a lot of fishermen, particularly those who used skiffs. The South Naknek cannery took only top fishermen and tried to cut out all of those who used skiffs. I never had been able to have children of my own. That year, I still fished for Alaska Packers with my adopted son, George Koktelash, as my partner. However, most Nondalton men were without jobs. Those who weren't fishing that year took their own small skiffs, most of which were about 18 feet long and 4 to 5 feet wide, and went all the way from Nondalton to Bristol Bay using outboard motors. They took their tents and other equipment, so that they could camp along the beach above the high tide line. They didn't know where they were going to get their next groceries. They didn't know where to eat, as most of them didn't have much money.

When the Nondalton men got to Bristol Bay, they got in touch with friends who lived in Naknek, and they were given surplus food so that they could get along for awhile. Those of us who were still working for Alaska Packers helped the skiff fishermen with food which we had gotten from the cannery. The skiff fishermen began fishing on their own and found an independent buyer who bought from them and then sold to the cannery. However, when the cannery got more fish than it was able to process, the buyer was unable to buy from the independent fishermen anymore. That year, skiff fishermen had to dump an entire scow full of salmon out at sea because they didn't have a buyer. All of these men without cannery jobs went broke and had no money from fishing for the following winter. Some of the men worked as laborers for a short time with the canneries at the end of the season to make enough money for gasoline to get back home. Despite our tough time, all the Native fishermen stuck together.

In 1954, I leased a cannery boat for $500 for the season and was still required to sell my fish back to cannery, since they had leased me the boat. In about 1956 or 1957, I bought a skiff from Alaska Packers. It was about 24 feet long and had an 8-foot beam. I used that skiff for 5 or 6 years.

In 1955, the Alaska Territorial Government passed a law saying that the canneries had to buy salmon from independent fishermen. The 1950s were tough for all of us. The fur prices had dropped, so we couldn't make much money trapping. The fish runs were poor and didn't really get any better until 1962. I remember that

year, because Was Trefon drowned in the summer of 1961 when he fell and was pulled overboard from his boat by a net. His son Billy was fishing with him that year, and there was nothing that he could do to save him.

That same fall George became ill and was put in the hospital. The following summer he was not able to help me fish, and I tried to fish alone. I couldn't really fish by myself, so I stayed on the beach mending nets. All fishermen at this time had a limit on the number of salmon they could take. The size of the limit depended upon the size of the boat they were using. In 1964, some men had a limit of 1,000 fish, while others could take twice as many. When fishermen went over their limit, they asked me to repair their nets, and then they gave me the fish that they couldn't sell because they were over their limit. I wrote these fish in my book as if I had caught them. In this way, I was able to make money from fishing, although I really was only repairing nets during that season. I remember not being able to sleep much that summer. As soon as I finished one net, someone else wanted me to repair his. At that time, openings were about two to three days long.

By 1968, I had completed my 49th or 50th year as a commercial fisherman in Bristol Bay. My sons, other relatives, and the canneries felt that at the age of 63, I was getting too old to fish. The following summer I unhappily decided to remain in Nondalton, though somewhat against my will. I remember how I felt when everyone left the village to go to Bristol Bay. I was lost; I thought I was going to go crazy. I had been left behind with the women, the children, the elderly, and the sickly. I didn't feel like I was neither elderly or sickly. I went up into the mountains near the village and walked around day after day. It was a very hard summer for me. A half a century was a long time to be doing the same thing every summer. It was very hard for me to stay behind.

In 1973, when the state of Alaska began issuing commercial fishing limited entry permits, I had more than enough points to qualify. George was able to get his own permit. I got mine, but it took two years to get it transferred to Leon Balluta Koktelash, my youngest adopted son, who is still fishing it today. We would never consider selling our fishing permit, since it remains a main part of our life and livelihood. Leon has continued to share the money he makes fishing with me and with my wife. Ruth, my wife, sadly died in 1987 after a long battle with cancer.

Every summer I think of Bristol Bay. I remember the past, my friends, my fishing partners, the people from different places in the world I met and worked with, the close calls we had, and the bad and good times. I miss the years I spent there as a young Dena'ina man. It remains an important part of my life.

Figure 85. (left to right) Individuals in this photograph are Dick Micey (holding cat), Chief Zackar Evanoff, Frank Evanoff, Yvdakia Evanoff, and Anisha Evanoff, at Old Nondalton, circa 1931. Zackar Evanoff was chief of Kijik when the inland Dena'ina moved to the site of Old Nondalton at the turn of the century. He remained chief until the early 1930s, when he relinquished his position to Alexie Balluta because of his advanced age. Yvdakia was Zackar's second wife, and Frank and Anisha were their children by that marriage. *Photograph. Courtesy of Ida Crater.*

CHAPTER 12

WEALTH, GENEROSITY, AND INFLUENCE: THE BALANCE OF POWER IN INLAND DENA'INA SOCIETY

Apart from highly organized chiefdoms and simple hunters and gatherers, there are many intermediate tribal peoples among whom pivotal local leaders come to prominence without yet becoming holders of office and title, of ascribed privilege and of sway over corporate political groups. They are men who "build a name" as it is said, "big-men" they may be reckoned, or "men of importance," "bulls," who rise above the common herd, who gather followers and thus achieve authority. The Melanesian "big-man" is a case in point. So too the Plains Indian "chief." The process of gathering a personal following and that of ascent to the summits of renown is marked by calculated generosity — if not true compassion. Generalized reciprocity is more or less enlisted as a starting mechanism.

Sahlins, **Stone Age Economics**, 1981 (1972)

SOME ARE MORE EQUAL THAN OTHERS: A REFLECTION ON POLITICS IN BAND SOCIETIES

For much of anthropology's history as a discipline, leadership and the allocation of power in ostensibly "egalitarian" hunting and gathering societies were portrayed characteristically as dependent upon qualities of charisma and demonstrated abilities and knowledge. In this stereotypic model, leaders of nomadic, loosely structured bands typically were referred to as "headmen." Headmen were characterized as having authority and power of limited scope and duration. Each act of influence was dependent upon the capabilities of the headman to demonstrate extraordinary abilities within the cultural context of his society. The assumption that women were not politically powerful authority figures in hunting and gathering societies was implied in use of the term "headman." Commonly, it was said that no true matriarchy had been documented.

It was generally assumed that male leaders in hunting and gathering societies were outstanding hunters and generous providers, possessing knowledge and wisdom that transcended that of the "average" man. Because of these and other personal qualities, such individuals commanded the respect of members of their society. Respect,

in turn, provided the basis of authority invoked to recommend courses of action as opposed to coercion. Headmen were expected to function in all aspects of life appropriate for their sex and age cohorts. Leadership status and associated behaviors were limited to specific actions or circumstances. Societies with these types of leaders generally were associated with environments characterized by scarce, unpredictable, and undependable resources, as argued in the paradigm of multilineal evolution (Steward 1955).

In the pursuit of knowledge about hunting and gathering societies, the anthropological perspective has become decidedly more sophisticated. Social and cultural variation among hunters and gatherers, both temporally and spatially, have been explored and commented upon, particularly in the last two decades (e.g., Lee and DeVore 1968; Schrire 1984). Within this context, the diversity of ways in which historic and contemporary hunting and gathering societies have structured the allocation of power and roles of leadership has been reconsidered, debated, and described (e.g., Leacock and Lee 1982). From the perspectives of cultural materialism and cultural ecology, the occurrence of stratified, non-egalitarian societies, in the absence of animal and plant domestication, has been attributed to the abundance of the resource base. The presence of big-men and chiefs in hunting and gathering societies, as described by Sahlins (1981 [1972]) in the quotation above, has been accepted, not merely as an anomaly, but rather as within the expected range of normal variation. This type of political organization customarily has been associated with modern foragers residing within areas with abundant and predictable resources, such as the northwest coast of North America or northwestern coastal Alaska (e.g., Bogojavlensky 1969).

Osgood (1976 [1937]) was the first ethnographer to document systematically stratification and associated aspects of political organization among the coastal Dena'ina. Townsend (1965, 1980) also documented ranked societies among the Iliamna Dena'ina based on her research in the 1960s in the community of Pedro Bay. The Iliamna Dena'ina had direct access to coastal resources and abundant salmon and freshwater marine mammal populations on Lake Iliamna. Fall (1981, 1987) provided the most comprehensive and diachronic discussion to date of Dena'ina political organization. Although his research focused on the coastal Dena'ina of upper Cook Inlet, his findings provided a meaningful model for considering leadership and the organization of power within the larger inland Dena'ina society. Compared to their coastal relatives, the inland Dena'ina were relatively nomadic and lacked direct access to marine resources, the latter considered to be a precondition for hunter and gatherer stratification in some more ecologically-oriented explanations (e.g., Lee and DeVore 1968; Oswalt 1967b; Steward 1955).

Despite their interior location and lack of direct access to marine resources, with the exception of salmon, the inland Dena'ina achieved high levels of economic productivity and participated in elaborate and formalized intracommunity, intercommunity, societal, and interethnic redistribution and trade networks. Applying the coastal Dena'ina sociopolitical model presented by Fall (1987) to ethnohistoric and oral historic data, the nature of leadership and the allocation of power among the inland Dena'ina through time was explored.

THE *QESHQA:* THE DENA'INA LEADER AS A REFLECTION OF SOCIAL ORDER

The Dena'ina *qeshqa* held a highly ranked position of leadership ". . . based on the accumulation and redistribution of wealth . . ." (Fall 1987:3). The functioning of *qeshqa* in Dena'ina societies was documented for the late 1800s and first half of the 1900s (Osgood 1976 [1937]; Townsend 1965). Records of the Russian Orthodox church and Russian American Company from the end of the 1700s and early 1800s, oral historic accounts, and the significance of the concept and status of the *qeshqa* in contemporary Dena'ina culture suggest that this institution was part of the early historic period as well (ARCA 1847-1900; Fall 1987; Oswalt 1967a).

The *qeshqa,* as described by inland Dena'ina in the 1980s, was an achieved status, associated with power derived from and authenticated by extensive knowledge, personal skills in acquiring wealth and organizing the productive and redistributive behavior of others, and demonstrated concern and generosity for the overall well-being of those in his charge. To Dena'ina residents of Nondalton in the

1980s, the term *qeshqa* meant "rich man," "head of the people," and "the chief," and incorporated well-defined economic, social, political, and spiritual expectations. The behaviors and qualities associated with achieving recognition as a *qeshqa* were, in fact, a reflection of the predominant social and valuative structure of the overall culture of the inland Dena'ina. However, individuals who achieved this status were not merely manifestations of the norms of society. Rather, they were "bigger than life," in that their achievements were superlative and intended to provide exemplary behavior unattainable by most inland Dena'ina.

The work of Sahlins (1981 [1972]) and others demonstrated the centrality of economics in the political processes of hunters and gatherers. More specifically, the way in which individuals achieve leadership statuses, their relative rank within the group, and the degree to which they influence the conduct of others are significantly correlated with economic behavior in small scale, kinship-based hunting and gathering societies. Important in this context is the ability of leaders to bring about the production, accumulation, and redistribution of material wealth.

Production in inland Dena'ina society was conducted by kin groups. Each productive unit, depending upon the nature of the activity, was organized and directed by an individual who was considered to be the head of the household, domestic unit, or family undertaking the activity. The leader was normally a male related to others in the economic group, principally through female linkages. In some cases, males who directed cooperative economic activities built and owned the means of production. For example, in the past, the most efficient means of caribou harvest occurred through the use of caribou corrals or fences. These were examples of technology controlled and/or owned by a potential or functioning *qeshqa.* In this and other cases, individuals successful in organizing and directing economic production were able to expand their realm of influence beyond that of their household or domestic unit.

According to inland Dena'ina in the 1980s, men able to achieve the status of *qeshqa* were, necessarily, personally industrious, innovative, stimulating, and economically responsible. As a result, they were capable of influencing others to demonstrate the same personal qualities. *Qeshqa* displayed these attributes both as young boys and men, suggesting the predisposition for becoming a

Figure 86. Mary Evanoff and Chief Zackar Evanoff in Kijik, circa the late 1890s. The garment between them is made of cloth and was decorated with dentalia and trade beads. Zackar Evanoff was the chief of the Kijik Dena'ina from the late 1800s until the early 1930s. He directed the relocation of the community to the site of Old Nondalton. The author of the narrative written around the photograph is unknown but, based on the text, was probably a non-Native who visited or temporarily resided within inland Dena'ina country. *Photograph Courtesy of the Alaska Historical Library, James Carter Collection.*

qeshqa. These same values were applied to the productive behavior of women. While women were not considered to be *qeshqa,* the corresponding term for "rich woman," *qiy'u,* alluded to potential leadership and stratification between women based on wealth and behavior. Leaders of productive groups were considered to be good providers, though not necessarily outstanding hunters. Their knowledge, skills at interpersonal interaction and management, wisdom regarding the environment and its proper treatment, and charisma enabled them to provide beyond the requirements of their group. In essence, they were able to produce or stimulate others to do the same, thus accumulating surplus in the form of material wealth.

Correspondingly, inland Dena'ina economic leaders were certain that family or other members of the community at large "never went without anything." The *qeshqa* had the wisdom to assess community well-being. He directed excess resources or employed his control over others to bring about the redistribution essential to achieve this end. Redistribution between members of opposite clans was exercised on a daily basis. However, ritualistic redistribution of this nature most usually occurred in the form of funeral, memorial, and other commemorative potlatches. The potlatch was the most important arena for gaining prestige and rank among the Dena'ina (Fall 1987:63; Townsend 1980; von Wrangell 1970 [1839]). Only a *qeshqa,* who was able to accumulate and acquire adequate material wealth from kin and other supporters, sponsored potlatches. In the course of this ceremony, food, raw materials, items of technology, and other goods were redistributed, thereby bringing about an economic balance between kin groups and assuring the social and material well-being of all community residents.

Fall (1987) and residents of Nondalton and Lime Village in the 1980s reported that *qeshqas* were known to guide the redistribution of wealth produced within their economic units to related communities. In fact, commonly a *qeshqa* provided for intervillage Dena'ina trade and mutual aide through the mechanism of partnerships with *qeshqas* from communities other than his own. Related *qeshqas* often directed trade between their respective kinship groups and villages. They gave one another gifts that only *qeshqas* could afford to reciprocate in kind or value. In addition, trading partnerships between inland Dena'ina and non-Dena'ina communities existed in the past

and were reflected in reciprocal relationships between residents of Nondalton and several *Dutna* communities in the 1980s. In cases of trade with non-Dena'ina, *qeshqas* facilitated and guided economic affiliations and interactions between members of communities representing different ethnic groups.

Sahlins (1963) suggested that Melanesian big-men, in their quests for prestige and efforts to amass "funds of power," in the long term often ended up giving out more than they, their kin, and other supporters retained or consumed. The same observation was made of northwest coast Indians, who occasionally potlatched themselves into poverty with the intent of gaining higher rank. In the matter of accumulating and consuming property, to what degree did the inland Dena'ina *qeshqa* conform to these examples from other ethnographic areas? Based on historic data, since the end of the 1800s, *qeshqas* were better off materially than were other members of their communities. They were able to accumulate and consume material wealth, only to the extent that they were not perceived by their supporters to be "stingy," a despised quality in the inland Dena'ina world view. Fall (1987) made the same observations about the upper Cook Inlet Dena'ina *qeshqa.*

Qeshqa wealth included both material and human resources. They were generally the first to acquire technological innovations introduced to the Dena'ina by Euroamericans, such as plank boats, outboard motors, and kerosene lamps. However, they were expected to share some of the benefits of these possessions with kin and other followers. *Qeshqas* and their relatives enjoyed a greater quantity and quality of food. Similarly, they had more wives than other men and had the means to support them and their offspring. Multiple wives were not merely passive symbols of wealth but were considered key actors in the rise to and maintenance of *qeshqa* status by the contribution of their own labor and that of their children.

Expectations of men who had achieved the rank of an inland Dena'ina *qeshqa* included political and spiritual behavior expressing an effective social conscience. Such men were called upon to provide moral support, knowledge, and guidance during times of sickness and death. They contributed the leadership necessary to organize the relocation of communities for ecological, social, economic, or spiritual reasons. They acted as advisers in times of natural disasters or hardships. In general, *qeshqas* served as buffers between members of their society and external forces, particularly during times of inter-Dena'ina and interethnic group warrfare, trade, and postcontact colonization.

There was a second class of leaders, referred to as war leaders, champions, or heroes (*veqhunuqults'elen*). Generally, they were distinguished from *qeshqa,* although these roles were not mutually exclusive. The oral history of the inland Dena'ina abounded with stories regarding the feats of Ts'enhdghulyal, one such war leader, who was involved principally in combat with the *Dutna* in the vicinity of Newhalen and other areas proximal to Lake Iliamna.

Conflicts between the inland Dena'ina and other groups provided spoils of war used by young warriors to launch careers as *qeshqas.* Hostilities commonly were associated with revenge, hostage taking, and access to land and game in the case of the *Dutna.* Although inland Dena'ina oral historic accounts of taking *Dutna* slaves were prevalent, it was implied that there was no interest in taking captured women as merely concubines. Although Fall (1987) recorded that the upper Cook Inlet people took other Dena'ina women as spoils of war, this practice cannot be established definitely for the inland society. In any event, success as a warrior and the acquisition of slaves and other spoils of war did not guarantee *qeshqa* status, since this position mandated success at managing the domestic mode of production and associated organizational skills as a means of sustaining material wealth. Again, it was the ability to organize supporters and their production that led to *qeshqa* status, rather than short-term accumulations of material wealth by means of war or other exploitive activities.

The *qeshqa,* like the Melanesian big-man, was an enterprising individual, who combined an interest in others with a notable degree of personal cunning and economic calculation (Sahlins 1963). It was the special power of this individual, his ability to attract and retain supporters and to benefit from their collective productivity as well as his own, that gave him his status, rank, and influence. Elders in 1980 were adamant that a man did not succeed through inheritance to an existing position of leadership as a *qeshqa* but attained that status because of his abilities to act uniquely and to attract about him an entourage of loyal, albeit, lesser men (Sahlins 1963). The *qeshqa,* like the big-man, had power which was functional principally within his own lineage, clan, and political faction, all of which may have been one and the same at different times and under varying conditions. Such power did not involve physical coercion. Outside of his following, a *qeshqa* minimally had respect and the indirect influence derived thereof. Like the Melanesian big-man, the larger his faction, the greater his influence. The exchange of marriage partners between members of opposite clans provided a means for enlarging and consolidating a *qeshqa's* group of supporters, both kin and members of obligatorily reciprocal clans. Ways of enlarging households or domestic units included marriage to multiple wives and support for those requiring assistance, such as widows and orphans. Unlike some big-men, however, the inland Dena'ina *qeshqa* was able to walk successfully the tightrope between perceived, unbridled greed and impoverishing generosity, thereby enabling him and his supporters to enjoy a higher material standard of life.

In the 1980s, inland Dena'ina recognized that some individuals had the qualities necessary to become *qeshqa*s. However, western bureaucracies had assumed some of the economic, social, and political roles of this Dena'ina institution. Consequently, the holistic and functional nature of the *qeshqa* had eroded in contemporary society. The nature of structural changes in leadership during the period in which contact with Euroamericans became more routine, frequent, and intense involved the role of what was entitled the *toion (duyun)* by the Russians and "chief" by English speakers.

TOIONS, CHIEFS, AND THE POLITICS OF EUROAMERICAN CONTACT

The inland Dena'ina data agreed with Townsend's (1979) and Fall's (1987) suggestions that initial Russian trade exchanges were conducted through the mechanism of *qeshqa* trading partnerships. However, both the Russian Orthodox church and Russian American Company had policies calling for the identification of an individual in each community or local group, whom they perceived to be "leaders" and with whom they could conduct business. Russian "business" involved the conversion and baptism of local people or trading for the highly valued pelts of furbearers. When the Russians contacted a new village and ascertained whom they assumed was the leader, they appointed him *toion,* or "chief," and presented him with a silver medallion bearing the image of the tsar (VanStone 1967:54-64). *Toion*s were given gifts, and their loyalty to the Russian American Company was expected to result in increased trade between supporters and trading posts. In the case of the Russian Orthodox church, leaders were trained as lay readers and became associated with the functioning of Christianity in the absence of resident clergy (Fall 1987; Smith 1980b). On the part of both the Russian American Company and Russian Orthodox church, these were efforts to formalize or institutionalize traditional leadership in a manner which interfaced more efficiently with western economic and religious systems.

Were all *toion*s, in fact, *qeshqa*s, since the traditional and early historic leadership appears to have been vested in persons of this status (Fall 1987)? Both the inland Dena'ina and upper Cook Inlet data (Fall 1987) indicated that not all *qeshqa*s became *toion*s nor were all chiefs *qeshqa*s. In any local band or community, it is likely that there was more than one *qeshqa*. Therefore, in an attempt on the part of the Russians to identify a single leader through whom they conducted business, they were forced to select between several individuals with power and factional influence. Secondly, a *qeshqa* maintained his position by perpetually demonstrating his ability to produce and redistribute wealth. In actuality, *toion*s were externally defined and selected and held their positions until their death as long as they appeared to remain loyal to their Russian benefactors. Furthermore, *qeshqa*s were expected by their followers to participate in and encourage production and stockpiling for redistribution. Conversely, the *toion* was expected by the Russian American Company to stockpile for purposes of trade. Lastly, and, most importantly, whereas *qeshqa*s served as intermediaries in traditional trade, their loyalties were to their kin and other supporters rather than to external trading partners. Fall (1987:49) described a case of a *qeshqa* who became a *toion* and, subsequently, fell from power, because he was perceived to be taking advantage of his supporters in his zeal to befriend Russian American Company agents. Because of the very nature of the role of *toion* compared to that of *qeshqa,* it was an even more difficult task to walk the tightrope of divided loyalties. Not only were the agents of the Russian American Company outsiders and non-Dena'ina, but they were not members of the *qeshqa*'s kin group or political faction. Since it was the intent of the traders to maximize their profits in their relationships, it is unlikely that a *toion* could continue to act in his own interest (i.e., that of his supporters), while assisting in their exploitation by outsiders.

The history of chieftainships within inland Dena'ina society was common knowledge in the oral tradition of Nondalton in the 1980s.

Interestingly, the inland Dena'ina word for "chief" was *duyun,* obviously a Russian loan word, as was the word for "second chief" and "church leader," *zagasik.* The inland Dena'ina system of chieftainships overtly functioned up until it was replaced in Nondalton by the city council and mayor under the auspices of incorporation as a second class city in 1971. Nonetheless, the chiefs and second chiefs, who are part of the memory culture of the inland Dena'ina, conformed more closely to the model of the *qeshqa* than to that of the Russian *toion.*

The criteria for being an inland Dena'ina chief in the 1900s included the ability to produce and to be enterprising; to be knowledgeable and wise; to look after the well-being of his people; to direct community efforts to care for widows, orphans, invalids, and the aged; to generally encourage the redistribution of wealth; to act as an intermediary between residents of the village and representatives of the outside world; and to provide spiritual guidance in times of individual, family, or societal hardship. Chiefs during this period of time had internally achieved, rather than externally ascribed, status, much in the manner of the *qeshqa.* As in the case of the *qeshqa,* chiefs were also models of Dena'ina social order and values. Second chiefs acted as apprentices to first chiefs and, if successful in the performance of their duties, were able to muster community consensus and support necessary to ascend to the status and role of first chiefs.

From this analysis, it is apparent that the Russian legacy did not destroy the core of inland Dena'ina traditional leadership. In fact, the inclusion of caring for the church and ensuring attendance as duties of the chief and second chief conformed to traditional spiritual expectations of the *qeshqa* within a different institutional framework.

The decline of the role and status of post-Russian chiefs coincided with the implementation of western political institutions as governing bodies for the inland Dena'ina. This trend was exacerbated by the unchecked growth of federal and state bureaucracies, ostensibly designed to manage all economic, social, and political aspects of inland Dena'ina life in the 1980s. Additionally, the formation of profit and nonprofit Native corporations under the auspices of ANCSA, also modeled on western institutions and values, contributed to the perception of a loss of leadership, a sentiment commonly expressed by the inland Dena'ina.

TOO MANY CHIEFS, NOT ENOUGH INDIANS: EXTERNAL POLITICAL MODELS AND THE DILUTION OF POWER

The most significant changes in inland Dena'ina polity since contact with Euroamericans involved the loss of political autonomy and the fragmentation and specialization of leadership and authority. Historically, economic, social, and political prerequisites for the continuity of inland Dena'ina society were holistically integrated with the overall culture. The *qeshqa,* as leader, functioned in all sectors of life and represented the interconnected nature of inland Dena'ina society and world view. The influence and power accompanying the role of *qeshqa* emerged from members of society and represented their values. That is, they were internally derived rather than externally imposed and consistent with the entire fabric of the social order.

Governance in modern nation-states is highly specialized and compartmentalized and may not represent the world view of many of those governed. As the inland Dena'ina were increasingly less buffered and isolated from the larger economic and political bodies into which they involuntarily became incorporated, the functions of *qeshqa* or, in later years, chiefs were formally delegated by *Gasht'ana* to external bureaucracies. For example, much of the formal enculturation of the young was forcibly institutionalized within the forum of the western school. The school and its staff served as brokers for cultural change and assimilation. Similarly, care for the aged or disabled became a designated function of state or federal agencies rather than kin groups and local leaders, despite intense efforts on the part of many to retain some degree of local responsibility for these matters. Conflict resolution was delegated to Dena'ina or, more recently, non-Native village public safety officers (VPSOs). Ultimately, jural matters were settled by non-local authorities or institutions. By the 1980s, access to and strategies for using land and resources, property ownership and distribution, social practices such as marriage and adoption, the selection of and qualifications for local "leaders," economic alternatives, and many other aspects of life theoretically fell under the influence or direct control of external political and economic institutions and their representatives.

The loss of political autonomy and leadership in the case of the inland Dena'ina, in part, was dis-guised by token local representation via memberships on boards, commissions, committees, and councils. For example, in the 1980s, local people were selected to serve on regional school and health boards, the fish and game advisory committee, and NPS subsistence commissions. Community residents "elected" mayors and city council members. Hearings or public meetings were held within the villages, ostensibly to get "local input" to decisions regarding economic development, changes in land status and educational policies, and for purposes of determining the future goals of the community. In all of these cases, the forums were structured around western models. Input was limited to a set of options that were derived, implicitly and explicitly, from western sociocultural systems and world views. For example, while the fish and game advisory committees provided input into the management of resources to the Alaska State Boards of Game and Fisheries in the form of proposals, such recommendations were forced to conform to western conceptual frameworks and associated laws regarding fish and game management. In meetings or hearings, the language, non-verbal communication, and other norms of behavior were non-Dena'ina in nature, thereby hindering effective or comfortable participation for many local representatives. In the 1980s, many of those possessing the skills to participate, such as a secondary education, were not appropriate representatives of a single community voice or view, principally because of their sex, age, interests, experience, standing in the village, opinions, or any combination of these factors.

Although created by western legislative process, the profit regional and village corporations formed under ANCSA in 1971 were intended to be Native-owned and operated market economic organizations. Most inland Dena'ina were enrolled in the Nondalton Native Corporation, now referred to as Kijik Corporation. Inappropriately, Nondalton was placed into Bristol Bay Native Corporation, with most of its membership comprising Natives of Yup'ik/Aleut (*Dutna*) ethnicity. Equally as anomalous, Lime Village was assigned to yet another Yup'ik regional entity, Calista Corporation. Most other Dena'ina, including some from Nondalton and Lime Village, were enrolled in Cook Inlet Region, Inc. based in Anchorage. As of 1974, Nondalton Native Corporation had 253 enrollees and was entitled to select 123,558 acres of land. Only 26 Dena'ina were enrolled in Lime Village's community corporation.

Figure 87. Photographs of three officers of Kijik Corporation and the Nondalton Traditional Council in 1988. (left to right) Dennis Trefon, Chairman of the Board of Directors and President of Kijik Corporation; Eleanor Johnson, First Vice President of Kijik Corporation; and Melvin Trefon, Nondalton Traditional Council President. *Photographs Courtesy of the Walsh Agency.*

As in the case of many village corporations, Kijik experienced periodic economic difficulties resulting from misfortune and unprofitable speculations. The most visible and costly of their entrepreneurial ventures, which included a fuel company and an airline, was the Keyes Point recreational housing development, representing approximately 4,000 acres, or 3 percent of Kijik's total acreage (Homelander 1986:1).

Unlike other imposed western institutions, Kijik Corporation developed some characteristics of the traditional inland Dena'ina leader. Although the corporation's mandate, like all others under ANCSA, was to earn a profit in the context of market economics, Kijik assumed social, economic, and political functions outside of the realm of normal corporate behavior. For example, like the traditional *qeshqa,* it funded potlatches, provided coffins for the deceased, until recently paid premiums for life insurance for shareholders, gave a stipend to the elderly, funded litigation protect the old village site of Kijik, acted as an intermediary between the community and the U.S. National Park Service, sought employment and education for shareholders, served as a symbol of inland Dena'ina cohesiveness for people coming in and out of Anchorage, and spearheaded the earliest conceptualization of an inland Dena'ina cultural revival. By 1991, the cultural revitalization movement and associated mental health programs, in concept or practice, were assumed by members of the traditional council, staff of the city of Nondalton, and individual, concerned residents.

Like the Russian *toion,* Kijik Corporation officers were placed in the position of meeting divided loyalties. For example, the plan to sell some inland Dena'ina lands for recreational homesites was intended to provide both cash and jobs for shareholders. In order to market the home sites, corporate directors were compelled to accommodate non-Dena'ina ideologies about land and resource use. The venture was not supported unanimously by shareholders, particularly in the case of some elders, who saw the future of the inland Dena'ina peoples and culture intricately linked with access to and control over traditional lands. Elders and some younger Dena'ina also feared the increased presence of and competition from outsiders. This is only one of many examples of the quandary in which corporation leaders found themselves throughout the 1980s.

By 1990, the relatively young leaders of Kijik Corporation and the City of Nondalton were faced with the dilemma of attempting to balance their western mandates for earning money in the market context or providing western infrastructure to the community, respectively, against the provision of social, political, and traditional economic leadership in the manner of the *qeshqa.* The traditional council continued to assume a more culturally relevant role throughout the 1980s, but it lacked the economic clout of the corporation and city. For the corporation and the city, balancing western and Dena'ina values and goals may prove to be a more formidable task than any inland Dena'ina leader has had to endure in the past. Given the chaos of multifaceted bureaucratic presence in the lives of the inland Dena'ina of the 1980s, the degree of external control over day-to-day affairs, and the schizophrenic nature of the corporate mandate, it is not surprising that residents of the community of Nondalton frequently bemoan the loss of leaders of the past and see no clear guidance for their future. In 1991, a more optimistic outlook was emerging in the form of a fledgling cultural revitalization movement, with participants from most sex and age cohorts. This effort, in conjunction with the relocation of several young families back to the community since the mid-1980s, provided the seeds for a new Nondalton society, a merger between what was considered valuable from the past and culturally relevant solutions to more contemporary, non-Dena'ina problems.

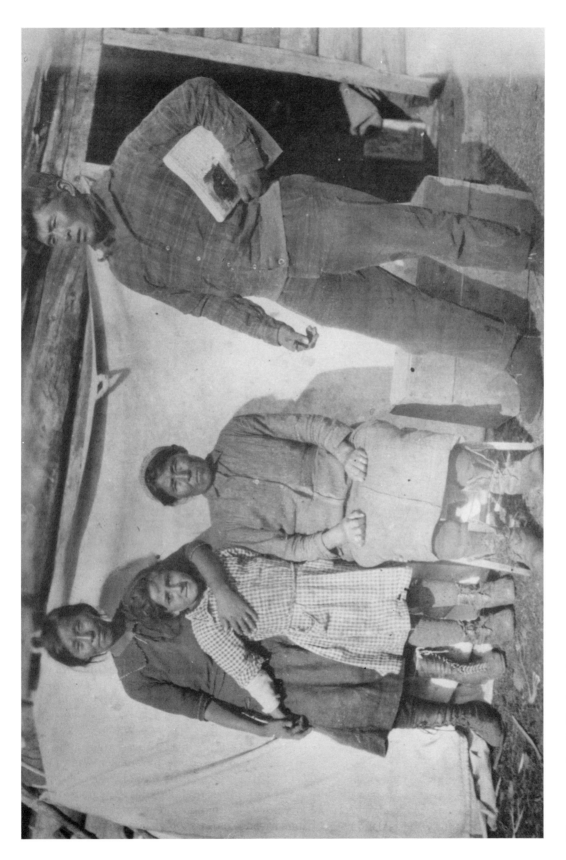

Figure 88. Agafia Trefon, Katie Trefon, Mary Ann Trefon, and Gabriel Trefon standing beside Mary Ann's house at Tanalian Point in 1926. Agafia, Katie, and Gabriel are Mary Ann's children. Her husband, Trefon Balluta, died when some of the children were relatively young. Mary Ann continued living at Tanalian with her youngest children and, at times, some of her grandchildren. Gabriel became chief of Nondalton in 1947, when the previous chief, Alexie Balluta, turned the position over to him because of advanced age and blindness. *Photograph Courtesy of Agnes Cusma.*

CHAPTER 13

DENA'INA PERSPECTIVE: THE MAKING OF A CHIEF

He was, I don't know, how would I say it. He was thinking about future. He know that things would change. He said it, the chief before him too, they use to preach like this, "It's not going to be like it is today. You guys got to change; you guys got to change with the world. You're going to have things like flying machines." Even before they even saw an airplane, they said they used to talk about peoples be flying.

Agnes Cusma, interview, 1987

RECALLING THE PAST

In Nondalton today, the elders frequently talk among themselves, remembering the past when the village had first chiefs and second chiefs. In those days, they say, people were always looking out for one another. It was the job of the chief and second chief to make sure that everyone had enough and that people would help one another. It was the chiefs, they say, who solved problems in the community. Today, with councils and mayors, the village has more problems, according to the elders. People no longer care as much for one another. The councils meet and meet, but things do not change for the better. The elders long for the ways things were in the past, when life, in their view, was better for the Dena'ina of Nondalton and the Lake Clark area.

Gabriel Trefon, son of Trefon and Mary Ann Balluta, was one of the last chiefs. He was a man who could see into the future. Yet, he urged the people of Nondalton to maintain their ties with the past and to teach their children, as they had been taught before.

When they advise each other and if a person wants to listen, then they will advise him and he will understand. He who wants to listen well to what they tell him will then be a good person. They will not be poor. They will be successful. As people, we are all different, though we don't always notice that. We are different from one another in our lives, and therefore some people who seem to support themselves, well, are in fact helpless. They don't do well. If those people are actually lazy, then that is how they act. Those who work for themselves do well. They are not helpless and they are successful people. This is why they should advise

the children (Gabriel Trefon, interviewed by Clark Davis, 1961).

Older people in Nondalton remembered Gabriel Trefon, one of the last chiefs, and the qualities that made him a leader. His personal skills, knowledge, and unique ability to know the past, while looking forward to the future, resulted in his being a highly respected member of the community. Since there were no chiefs in Nondalton in the 1980s, in the sense that Dena'ina had chiefs in the past, it was not possible to portray the life of such a man through his own recollections. Instead, we were forced to turn to the memories of others, particularly those of his children and other close relatives. In the 1980s, they were the ones in the village who knew Gabriel the best and grieved his loss the most. This chapter depicts the life of Gabriel Trefon through the eyes of Agnes Trefon Cusma, his daughter; Benny Trefon, his son; and Andrew Balluta, the brother of Phillip, Gabriel's adopted son.

SOME INSIGHTS INTO INLAND DENA'INA BOYHOOD IN THE EARLY 1900S

Gabriel Trefon was born in the village of Telaquana in 1897, the eldest of Trefon and Mary Ann Balluta's seven children. Trefon Balluta had been born at Telaquana as well in the mid-1860s. Mary Ann was from a village on the Mulchatna River. She was about 15 years younger than Trefon when they married, and she survived him by 36 years.

Gabriel was the first child born. After his birth, they gave him to Trefon's sister, whose name no one can remember today but who also lived at Telaquana. Because this sister was childless, her brother was expected to give her his first son to raise as her own. However, Trefon's sister died when Gabriel was only three years old. She had raised him "until he could put his own boots on." Gabriel thought that his aunt was his mom. After his sister died, Trefon took Gabriel back into the family.

Over the years, Trefon and Mary Ann had six other children who survived to adulthood. Gabriel's three sisters were Agafia, Alexan, and the baby of the family, Katie. His brothers were

Wassillie, Alex, and Pete. Only Katie and Alex are still living today.

Trefon Balluta was a good hunter, trapper, and fisherman. He preferred to live and run his trap line at Telaquana until Gabriel turned about five years old. In 1902, Trefon and other families at Telaquana decided to move their families closer to the larger settlement of Kijik. At that time, the Kijik people were moving to a new village location on Nuvendaltin. There was sickness at Kijik, and the priest had encouraged people to move. Besides, they say that the cemetery was too full, the land was too worn out, and there were things at Kijik that caused the illness and frightened people. Old Nondalton, the new village, was closer to the trading post at Iliamna and Bristol Bay.

Trefon moved his family first to Kijik for a short period of time and then to Tanalian Point. Tanalian was closer to the mouth of the Kijik River, where fall fishing was very good. It was also near Telaquana, where Trefon always had trapped. At the time that they moved, Trefon and Mary Ann had had two boys and one girl and already had lost a child. From that time on, Telaquana was abandoned as a village, although Gabriel continued to use Trefon's hunting and trapping areas when he became an adult. It was at Telaquana that Trefon and other relatives taught Gabriel to hunt and trap, so this place remained very important to him throughout his childhood and into his adult life. Mary Ann remained at Tanalian throughout most of her life.

One of the reasons Trefon Balluta moved down from Telaquana was that he knew there was a school in Old Iliamna. If Gabriel went to school there, he would be closer to his family if they were living at Tanalian rather than at Telaquana. Trefon wanted Gabriel to get both a *Gasht'ana* and Dena'ina education. He also wanted his family to be near a church, and Telaquana did not have one. If they wanted to attend church, they had to go to Kijik or, later, Old Nondalton. These were the only places that the priests visited.

Trefon, Mary Ann, and all of the children made a trip to Old Iliamna a year before they decided to send Gabriel to school. Gabriel was six or seven when he actually went to Old Iliamna to attend school. He lived with his mother's mother, Agafia. Agafia was originally from Mulchatna but had moved to Telaquana and then to Old Iliamna. Gabriel stayed there for 11 months and went to school during about 9 months of that time. After that year, Trefon and Mary Ann didn't want him

to stay in Old Iliamna any longer. They felt that there were too many problems and, with a population of 300, too many people there. Before he died, Gabriel frequently said how he couldn't stand life in Old Iliamna, in part because he had to "stay in one place and do nothing." Also, he was too far away from the family. So, Trefon asked Doc Dutton and Joe Kackley, two *Gasht'ana* prospectors living at Tanalian, to teach Gabriel, Pete, and Alex, to read, write, and do arithmetic.

Everyone who remembered Gabriel remembered that he was very smart. Even with only 11 months of school, he could read, write, and add well enough to later become the manager of the Alaska Packers store in Nondalton. Agnes recalled that you could ask him anything. "He was smarter than any of us; if he had gone to school at least three years, he would have been like Albert [Albert Wassillie, perceived to be an educated man]." "Each time he tally his money, sometimes he was short only a penny. He always was able to figure in his head."

Trefon Balluta was not a chief when he was at Telaquana Village. When Gabriel was a little boy, there were chiefs and second chiefs. The second chief ran around and visited different families. If he found that anyone was having a hard time, he figured out what was causing the problem. He came back to the chief and let him know what was going on. The chiefs especially were concerned about people who didn't have enough to eat. If there were people without enough food, the chief and second chief collected food from others or went out and helped the family get their own fish and meat. The chiefs were also keepers of the church. It was during his childhood that Gabriel learned what it meant to be a Dena'ina chief, by watching those who were chiefs during that time.

Zackar Evanoff was the chief who led the move of the main village at Kijik to Old Nondalton, beginning in 1901 and 1902. It was he who got people to move and remained behind until everyone had been relocated. Although he was nearly blind, old man Zackar encouraged people to attend church and told them what they were supposed to do. He remained chief until 1930 and served as an example for Gabriel throughout his childhood. Gabriel also learned that everyone in the community had to agree at a meeting that the person selected by a chief to follow him was the best choice. Chiefs also met regularly with the elders of the village to make important decisions. Gabriel saw that successful leaders had a "straight mind" and the ability to lead others. A chief had to know not only what he was doing at the present time, but he had to be able to prepare for the long-run. A Dena'ina leader couldn't just go along with white people but had to continue to teach the Dena'ina way of life as well.

Gabriel learned to hunt, fish, and trap. It was these skills that enabled him to support a family after he married and to help his mother before and after his father died in the early 1920s. Gabriel had come of age and had to prove his abilities to support a family to his fiance's *Gasht'ana* father, Jack Hobson. Before he was allowed to take his wife, Katherine, away from her family, he had to prove that he was a good provider. His years of learning from observation, instruction, and participation in hunting, trapping, fishing, and other activities successfully had prepared Gabriel for adulthood and, eventually, for the role of leader.

GABRIEL BECOMES A MAN

Gabriel was about 24 years old when he took Katherine Hobson as his wife in 1920. She was 8 years younger than him. They made Old Nondalton their home. Katherine was born in Qeghnilen, the site of the village before the Dena'ina of that area moved to present day Lime Village. She was the eldest of eight children born to Jack Hobson and Tatiana Constantine Hobson.

In approximately 1914, when Katherine was about 10 years old, her father moved the family to Old Nondalton. That is where she met Gabriel. Gabriel and Katherine travelled all the way from Old Nondalton to Lime Village to get married in the Russian Orthodox church. There was a priest from the Kuskokwim River who visited Lime Village more frequently than did the priest from Bristol Bay, who came to the church at Old Nondalton once a year.

After Gabriel and Katherine were married in Lime Village, they spent the summer there, and half of the following winter, taking care of Katherine's grandparents, Gustingen and Katherine Constantine. During other years, like in 1930, Gabriel and Katherine returned to Lime Village for shorter periods of time to visit her grandparents and to cut wood, haul water, and provide them with food. By this time, they were in their late 70s and early 80s.

In 1921, Gabriel and Katherine had Agnes, their first child, in Old Nondalton. In 1923, Benny was born. Benny was to be the last of Katherine's children, although she and Gabriel later raised three other boys. These boys were Charlie Trefon, born in 1924; Luther Hobson, born in 1931; and Phillip Balluta, born in 1936. Charlie, whose full name was Evan Charlie Trefon, was Gabriel's sister's son. Luther was Katherine's brother's son and Phillip her sister's son.

Agnes recalled that when Charlie was first adopted, Benny and she were unfamiliar with how to get along with other kids. They picked on him, although he was only three or four years old. Gabriel was afraid that Charlie would become a drifter if he remained with his stepfather. That is why Gabriel decided to adopt him. Among the Dena'ina, a woman's brother usually looked out for his sisters' children. Agnes and Benny wouldn't let Charlie sit on their mom and dad's bed, so Gabriel eventually spanked them. That was the only spanking Agnes could remember ever getting from her father.

After Gabriel got married, he continued to go up to Telaquana with his father, until Trefon was too old to make the trip any longer. Finally, in the mid-1920s, Trefon Balluta died, leaving Mary Ann with the two youngest children. Trefon was brought from Tanalian to Old Nondalton and buried there. After he was buried, Mary Ann remained at Tanalian with the children, and Gabriel helped care for them. Gabriel and his brothers took their father's first name as their surname at the suggestion of the Russian Orthodox priests.

Agnes' strongest memory of her dad was that he travelled around the country with the family all the time while he was hunting, trapping, and fishing. He used to tell them that he had been travelling around by dog team as a young man as long as he could remember. Her dad recollected that he was only about seven years old when he began to drive dogs himself. This was the way of life he wanted for his family after he was married. He didn't stop going from hunting to fishing to trapping camps with his wife and children until 1929, when the school was built in Old Nondalton. Gabriel never stayed in the village for any length of time, because he made his living from the land. Most of the money he earned came from commercial fishing in Bristol Bay back in the sailboat days or from trapping.

Agnes recalled with great detail the areas that her father took her and the rest of the family. In the spring time, the family stayed at the Chulitna River. Early in the spring, usually in April, they went to Nikabuna Lakes. They often stayed in their *chada* Hobson's cabin. As spring came to a close, the family came down the Chulitna in large, moose skin boats, where they stopped to camp on the grassy flats at Indian Point until early June. It was at Indian Point that everyone gathered. Agnes remembered that being at Indian Point was like a "vacation," where they had beaver meat parties and played games with each other and with the *Dutna* from Newhalen.

After they returned to Old Nondalton, Gabriel took his family to the fish camp he had made at Nundaltinshla. While Katherine and the kids fished at camp, Gabriel went to Bristol Bay to make money and to bring back groceries and other things bought at Iliamna. Then he returned to summer fish camp to help put up sockeye for the dogs. He took the family back to the village in the latter part of August before the Russian Orthodox holiday occurring on August 28.

No one stayed in Old Nondalton for long. Gabriel packed up his family and took them up Lake Clark to Miller Creek. Then they all walked into the mountains, looking for moose, caribou, and bear. Agnes remembered that they usually went up the Middle Fork and sometimes to Telaquana. On one trip during this time of year, her *dada* was chased up a leaning tree by a moose. The moose butted his antlers against the tree and shook it with Gabriel hanging on. Finally, Gabriel was able to kill the moose, but they had to hang it and leave it at camp. The moose was in rut, so the taste and smell were so strong that it was not edible.

In about November, Gabriel, and others camping with him, went up the Telaquana Trail for trapping. Agnes walked the Telaquana Trail three times during her life. The trapping area in Telaquana, which Gabriel had been using since the age of 17, remained a part of life until he stopped making these trips as an old man.

Everyone remembered 1926, because that was the year that there were no fish at Lake Clark or in Bristol Bay. Gabriel knew that when there were no fish at Lake Clark, he always could go to Telaquana and get salmon. He heard that salmon were coming up the Kuskokwim River. In 1926 in the middle part of August month, Gabriel, his family, and Gillie Koktelash from Old Nondalton went to Telaquana. He landed his boat with his family at Miller Creek and from there took everyone on foot to Telaquana Lake. Agnes recalled that the trip took them a week or more and that she walked every bit of the way, even though she was only about five years old.

Gabriel built a new cabin there, because the old house that had belonged to his father was too old to live in. Then he and his family went down to the outlet of the lake, where there was a fish camp and a smokehouse. The smokehouse is still standing. They stayed there for awhile, trying to get salmon with nets, but there were no fish. Gabriel had a wooden, double-ended boat at the fish camp, so he and old man Gillie fixed it up and went to the head of the lake where there was a fish pond. There were lots of fish there. Gabriel and his family put up *nudelvegh*. Then they had enough food for the whole winter.

That year, Gabriel decided to remain there with his family for the entire winter. Agnes remembered that they all thought that their grandma must have been worried about them when they didn't return to Old Nondalton after fall fishing. Trapping was really good, and Gabriel knew that he would be able to get many lynx, marten, and other furbearers at the head of the Stony River.

In 1930, the family went by dog team to Lime Village in the fall. Gabriel trapped all the way in and on the way out. The family spent the fall, spring, and summer there. There were no animals there that year, nothing. That summer Gabriel and his family went to the Lime Village fish camp, but there were no fish. One old man in the village opened up his fish cache in the ground. The fish looked like they had been buried yesterday, still real red. Katherine took some of the fish, which she shared with everyone at the settlement. The adults cooked the fish with berries for seven dogs. Using the cached fish and the dried fish Gabriel bought on the Kuskokwim river, the family did not loose a single dog. Then Gabriel and other Lime Village men went to the rivers, where there were spawning char and Dolly Varden. The freshwater fish helped both people and dogs survive throughout that difficult time.

When Gabriel and his family travelled on the Telaquana Trail, they knew of a big rock that had a cave in it. One particular trip, Agnes remembered that her dad wanted to stay there for about three nights. It was foggy right down to the ground. There were alders nearby, and Gabriel packed them into the cave for firewood. There were a lot of empty cartridges nailed into a crack in that rock. Gabriel explained that anytime hunters found a rock with a cave and spent one or more nights there, they knew it was important to leave the remains of anything that they used, such as empty cartridges, matches, and food. By doing this, they believed their luck in hunting was protected. They also left extra wood for the next traveller who needed shelter.

Agnes recollected that one fall, Gabriel and his family were hunting at Ch'gułch'ishtnu, right where a creek comes out of a canyon. This was a good place to hunt moose. It was "just like food on the table," according to Agnes. Gabriel and his family were staying at this place by themselves. Gabriel left the kids at home in the cabin, so that Katherine could chase a moose toward him. Before they left, they told the kids not to go outdoors, because they wouldn't be gone long. Gabriel was successful in getting a moose, but it started to get dark and there was moonlight. They had to quarter the moose, and then Gabriel and Katherine started back to the cabin. When it got dark inside the cabin, the kids took blankets and sleeping bags and went way down inside of them, covering themselves up. They stayed there and were very afraid in the cabin alone in the dark. The fire went out, but they were too afraid to even put more wood in the stove. Then the kids heard their parents' voices and the dog team returning to the cabin. Katherine came inside and didn't know where the kids were. She lit a lantern and looked on the floor, where she found a big pile of blankets. That is the only time Agnes could remember that her dad and mom ever left them alone in the dark.

Although the family resided in Old Nondalton during the winter after 1930, Agnes remembered that Gabriel took her to Telaquana for the last time in 1934. He was going after beaver. They travelled with two sleds, one belonging to Alex, Gabriel's brother. The family remained there the entire spring. After the snow and ice melted, Alex and Gabriel built a canoe and trapped beaver from the open water. From Telaquana, they trapped near the upper Stony River. There were some people from Lime Village trapping there as well. Gabriel took the entire family and made a trip back to Lime Village, where they remained for four days.

Then the family returned to Telaquana, where the men continued to trap and hunt moose and caribou. Game was very scarce those years. Katherine was picking *k'tl'ila,* a root that grows in riverbeds. She prepared it by either boiling it in water or frying it in oil. It tasted very sweet, much like sweet potatoes, and was eaten with trout.

During this trip, the family lived in a tent. There were two cabins there, but they always preferred living in the tent during springtime. Gabriel and the family shared a tent, and Alex had his own.

When they were ready to return to Lake Clark, they left one sleigh behind and hooked all of the dogs to the remaining one. That was a hard trip back, since the dogs were pulling the sleigh packed with beaver over earth rather than snow. All the adults and bigger kids were packing gear.

During these years, Gabriel was already known for trying to help people in need. In 1937, he went up to Lime Village to visit. It was during that trip that he brought an old, paralyzed man, Zackar Constantine, and his Koyukon wife Anisha, down to Old Nondalton. Gabriel always had a good supply of fish and game, so his family, other relatives, or people really in need of food never went hungry.

During the years that Gabriel was a productive hunter and fisherman, his trapping and commercial fishing at Bristol Bay provided enough cash for the family to get goods not available locally. Gabriel began to fish commercially when he was a very young boy. He fished for many years until about 1959, when Wassillie, his brother, drowned after falling off a boat at Bristol Bay. In the mid-1950s, Gabriel became the manager of the Alaska Packers store in Nondalton. He remained in that position for about 10 years. Many people commented on how well he managed the store, despite the fact that he had only been to school for nine months.

Agnes recalled that because her father was such a good provider, the family never went without anything that they needed, such as locally gathered foods, purchased groceries, cloth, or skins. Everyone agreed that Gabriel was one of the best providers. He was always the richest man in the village, but he was also very generous, always willing to lend things to those people who needed them.

Agnes recollected that Gabriel always wanted to be the first one to get new things from the trading post, "to be ahead of all people." He was the first Dena'ina on Lake Clark to have an outboard motor. In either 1926 or 1927, Gabriel purchased a two-and-one-half horse Johnson outboard. If the weather was good in the summer, he towed other peoples' boats to the village using the outboard so that they could attend church. Then the Coleman lamp came out next in about the mid-1920s. Although he had the first lamp, within a year almost everyone in the village also had one. After that, people stopped using the "beach light," a Dena'ina lamp made out of any kind of shallow container which held bear, moose, caribou, or fish oil and burned with a wick made out of cloth. Before the

Coleman, Gabriel used a coal oil lamp. These looked something like what people call "Aladdin lamps" today, but they didn't have a chimney. Then gasoline-operated washing machines came out. Katherine was the first woman in Old Nondalton to get one. In about 1960, Gabriel was also the first one in Nondalton to get a "snowgo." He was the first one in the village to get a "light plant," or gasoline-operated generator. He provided electricity to his household and that of Agnes and Paul Cusma. He also provided electricity to his second chief, Nick Karshekoff. The only thing he never had was running water.

Gabriel understood that things in the world were rapidly changing and that the Dena'ina of Nondalton had to take the best of both worlds. He looked forward to change and was not afraid of what was new. He always thought that if he got new things or told about new ideas or new ways of doing things, that other people in the village would follow. That is one way that he provided leadership. But he never forgot to be generous to others with the things that he had.

Gabriel's father and mother were very poor when they were young. Mary Ann, his mother, remembered never having anything when she was a girl. She always told Gabriel about what it was like to have nothing. She was determined that her life would be very different. Mary Ann used to tell Agnes to go into her cache. There were many things there, kettles and anything that you would use in a kitchen, all on shelves. She was not using the things that she had stored there. Agnes remembered her saying, "I don't care if they rot in here without anybody using them, because we never had anything when we were young." When things Gabriel bought from the trading post broke, he told Katherine to throw them away and get new ones. However, Katherine worked hard and learned to save. She never really destroyed things without a reason. Gabriel had been taught as a child never to let his family go without, and he made sure that they never did during his lifetime.

Gabriel's willingness to accept new ideas and tools, making life easier for the people of Nondalton, applied to other aspects of life as well. The site of Old Nondalton was blocked by a sand bar, which developed in front of the village. The people who lived there were unable to get their boats close to the shore and had to haul their gear out to where boats were floatable. There were other problems. The land upon which the village was built had become "worn out" and the cemetery "too crowded." In 1940, Gabriel went to the site of new

Nondalton and cut logs for a home. In 1941, he built the first house at the new village. This provided an example for others to follow, and the entire community began to move. By 1946, everyone had moved to the new site of the village. By that time, Gabriel was second chief.

Gabriel was always very concerned about the well-being of his children. He made an effort to balance their knowledge between that of the *Gasht'ana* and that of the Dena'ina. At the same time, he was not anxious to let his children go when they were ready to marry. In part, he believed strongly in traditional rules of marriage. For example, he believed that husbands and wives were chosen by families, not by individuals, and that they needed to be from the right clan. They also had to have the qualities which made them good husbands and wives in the traditional Dena'ina way. Benny was 30 years old when he finally got married, and Agnes was 23. Gabriel was "very stingy of both of us," Agnes remembered.

GABRIEL BECOMES THE NONDALTON CHIEF

Zackar Evanoff became very old and blind. He was lead around by the second chief and others who held his hand, although what he had to say was still very important in deciding how people were to behave. The priest was concerned who was chief. It was the chief who primarily communicated with the Russian Orthodox priests when they visited Old Nondalton. When the priest came in 1930, Zackar Evanoff turned his position over to Alexie Balluta, who was referred to by many people as *dada ka'a*. Alexie Balluta got this position only after everyone in the community agreed with the choice. *Dada ka'a* already had been second chief and learned from old man Evanoff. The second chief became the first chief, only if he had the qualifications for the job. Alexie Balluta made Gabriel Trefon second chief, in agreement with Zackar Evanoff's and most residents' wishes. By that time, Gabriel had proven himself to be a good provider, a generous man, and a man whom others wanted to follow. He was already on his way to the chieftainship, which was to follow some years later.

Very important in Gabriel's role as a second chief was the leadership he provided in moving the community from Old Nondalton to its present location nearer the outlet of Six-Mile Lake. Like chiefs before him, Alexie Balluta remained behind in the old village until 1946, when everyone had completed relocation. Gabriel, as second chief, was present in the new community. Alexie remained at the old site in order to assure the successful relocation of each and every family and to have an understanding of problems in both settlements. When the move was completed in 1946, Alexie Balluta had become very old and blind. In 1947, he turned the chieftainship over to Gabriel, although Alexie did not die until 1951. Nick Karshekoff was Gabriel's second chief. When Nick died in 1953, Paul Cusma, Gabriel's son-in-law, was selected to be second chief. Gabriel taught Paul about being a chief. After Gabriel's death, Harry Balluta briefly became chief. Harry was the last of the "traditional" chiefs, since decision-making was turned over to a seven member council and mayor. A traditional council remained, as it does today. Paul Cusma headed the council and became its chief, although this position was different from what it had been in the past. Gabriel was remembered as the last chief in the old Dena'ina way.

The chiefs in past days didn't have any pencil and papers to write things down. They didn't read papers or books. Instead, once a week or at least twice a month, the second chief or the chief went from one house to another to visit and talk with people. They asked peoples' opinions and went by what people said and what they had seen. If people had run out of groceries, the chiefs called a meeting. They would say, "This family hasn't got very much, and we've got to do something for them." So any family that could afford to donate groceries, did so. Boys went out, and each hauled one load of wood for the family. A family sometimes received as many as 20 loads of wood for the winter. Then the chief went up to the head of the house. If this person was young and capable, the chief would say, "Now that you've got enough to eat and you've got wood, from here on, try to help yourself." It was like a village welfare system.

During the last few years of his life, Gabriel had become a chief and a leader who shared his knowledge with younger generations through storytelling. His stories always reflected his awareness of the changes that were going on about him and his philosophies. In 1961, three years before his death, Gabriel told the following story:

Before our time, long ago, the people had things that they used as medicine. They used medicine. In the middle of "river that flows down" [Newhalen River] a rock is embedded that stands up really high. There the current wraps around it as it is embedded in midstream. The current wraps around it and the fish swim past it. Fish swim around it and the sun shines against it and "the sun passes all the way around me. Whatever flying things are here land on me and use me for recreation," that's how they would say. "The current wraps around me and then the water shapes me," it [the rock] said. "I have been shaped by the water and then fish swim past me. They [animals] have used me. My children [little rocks] drift ashore downstream from me. I am inaccessible. The sun passes all around me. They depend on me. They use me for playing." That is what they used to say. That was medicine long ago before our time. Now the ones who talk differently from us do want to know about this. Now I have told them about it. They will put it on paper. That's all (Gabriel Trefon as recorded by Clark Davis, 1961; Ellanna 1986)!

Figure 89. Individuals in this photograph are (left to right) Vladimir Cusma, Nick Karshekoff, Yvdakia Karshekoff, and Jean Karshekoff at the Old Nondalton cemetery in approximately 1936. They are standing at the site of the grave of Yvadakia's husband, Marka. Vladimir is Yvdakia's brother and Nick and Jean are children of Marka and Yvdakia. A Russian Orthodox cross and icon have been placed over his grave. *Photograph courtesy of Agnes Cusma.*

CHAPTER 14

SPIRITS, SOULS, AND ICONS: CONTINUITY AND CHANGE
IN THE INLAND DENA'INA COSMOS

Humans not only weave intricate webs of custom that regulate and order their social lives. They also spin out wider designs of the universe, the forces that govern it, and their place in it. Religious beliefs and rituals are basic in these designs. So, too, are fundamental premises about the way things and events are interrelated, the nature of time and space, the way the world is and should be.

Keesing, *Cultural Anthropology: A Contemporary Perspective*, 1976

THE UNDIVIDED WORLD

People worldwide and through time have devised cosmologies, which explain the structure and functioning of the universe. In much the same way that social norms govern interactions between individual members of a society, culturally defined views of the universe or cosmos, expressed in a system of beliefs, pattern the way humans interpret their relative places in this universe and relationships with all entities and dimensions contained therein.

Anthropologists have recognized that relationships between the social and cosmological orders exist within any given culture. It is the cosmology, or "world view," of the inland Dena'ina, and factors which have brought about shifts in this intellectual system, which are of interest in this context. The influence of formal, institutional western religion, particularly Russian Orthodoxy, and American fundamentalist Christianity and philosophy, as expressed in the forum of public educational policy and practice, provides insights into continuity and change of inland Dena'ina world views or cosmologies through time.

Western logic predominantly has delineated events and phenomena as being either "natural" or "supernatural," as defined by the "laws of nature." These two categories are perceived to be dichotomous in nature and mutually exclusive. The phenomena included in each have generally been teased apart by specialists, scientists on the one hand and clerics on the other, respectively. Unfortunately, this perception has dominated the ways in which representatives of the western world have viewed and variously interpreted the cosmologies of non-western peoples.

Although tremendous variation in substance exists, some generalizations about the intellectual order of hunters and gatherers can be made. Ties between humans and flora, fauna, and other aspects of nature are generally intense and structure traditional "religious" systems and individual and group rituals and ceremonialism (e.g., Brody 1982; Burch 1971; Nelson 1983; Tanner 1979). While there are individuals with greater than average abilities to comprehend and manipulate nonempirical phenomena on the behalf of others or society at large among hunters and gatherers, the positions of spiritual specialists commonly are not full-time, institutionalized, solely hereditary, or the exclusive occupation of the person in question.

The cosmologies of hunting and gathering peoples are embodied in ever-changing oral traditions, which include stories, knowledge, songs, "spells," and other essential information. These traditions include the past and present, personal and collective experiences of non-western peoples. They are brought to bear in explaining the nature of the world and in guiding human actions and interactions. Ideologies derived from oral traditions stand in stark contrast to the written codes or doctrines of agroindustrial societies. Such formal, codified, institutionalized rules commonly dictate behavioral norms and views about the nature of the universe in western societies. By way of contrast, hunter and gatherer ideologies, as represented in oral traditions, provide the criteria by which day-to-day decisions are made. For these non-western peoples, the cosmos, as portrayed in oral traditions, provides moral and ethical guidance and serves as a repository of knowledge and a cornerstone for ethnoscientific interpretations and analytical decision-making.

Hunter and gatherer cosmologies are holistic in nature. At one level, they mirror the ways that societies, within which they are operative, are ordered. For example, principles of reciprocity and egalitarianism, common in hunting and gathering societies, are usually reflected in the structure of their nonempirical worlds. The dichotomy between the "natural" world and what western science refers to as "supernatural" phenomena generally does not exist in hunter and gatherer world views. In the same way that social norms guide human interaction and provide the criteria by which transgressions and transgressors are evaluated, there are principles in hunting and gathering societies dictating the ways in which humans are expected to interact with animals, plants, other aspects of nature, spirits, and souls. The well-being of people is seen to be connected intimately to harmony between human and non-human inhabitants of the cosmos.

Souls, spirits, and impersonal powers of humans, non-human animals, and other phenomena are customarily cyclical in nature, influencing the living and reappearing on earth in some patterned fashion. In the case of hunters and gatherers, as economics should not be seen as isolated from kinship or kinship as distinct from politics, neither can the realm of the "natural" world be seen as separate and unique from the balance of the cosmos, nor can humans be seen as removed or above other universal phenomena. For the most part, hunters and gatherers perceive themselves as existing in a universe which is undivided.

The cosmologies or religious ideologies of northern North American hunters and gatherers, such as the northern Algonquians and Athabaskans, were described by early ethnographers and analyzed more systematically in the work of Hallowell (1955). Hallowell (1955) provided a model for more recent research focused specifically on depicting and interpreting the nature of northern Athabaskan world views (e.g., Brody 1982; Nelson 1983; Ridington 1988; Tanner 1979). Rushforth (1986:252) suggested that traditional Athabaskan religion is not as well known by anthropologists as are other aspects of culture, principally because of the absence of formal religious institutions, the personal nature of religious beliefs, and the difficulty anthropologists have in translating the meaning of religious experience. Rushforth's (1986) implication that earlier ethnographers failed to understand the nature of Athabaskan "religion" can be modified. Many ethnographers, such as Osgood (1976 [1937]) in the case of the Dena'ina, comprehended the world view of the Athabaskans about whom they conducted research. However, the ethnographic style of these earlier works, and the "outsider," or etic, perspective most commonly employed in such ethnographies, inhibited more culturally relevant expressions or discussions of the meaning of Athabaskan cosmologies, spirituality, and related behaviors.

Despite the spatial, cultural, and ecological diversity of subarctic Indians, common ideologies and practices have been noted. Young boys learn the habits of animals and skills of coping with the environments in which they live in order to become productive hunters. They are expected, simultaneously, to acquire, through observation, mythology, oral histories, and personal experiences, appropriate symbols and behaviors for ensuring proper treatment of the forces and beings of the natural world. That is, the realm of empirical knowledge, which Tanner (1979) refers to as "common sense," is not in opposition to other fields of knowledge, classified as religious ideology and practice. Both contribute to the successful production of hunters and gatherers within these societies.

Nelson (1978:229) states a similar case for the Koyukon Athabaskans of Alaska:

> *For the Koyukon, most interactions with natural entities are governed in some way by a behavioral code which maintains a proper spiritual balance between the human and non-human worlds. Let me emphasize at the outset that this is not considered an esoteric abstraction, but a matter of direct, daily concern to the Koyukon hunter-gatherer. Failure to behave according to the dictates of this code has an immediate impact on the health or success of the violator. And so, when Koyukon people are harvesting or processing natural resources, many of their decisions are based on supernatural rather than "pragmatic" or "empirical" concerns.*

In the case of subarctic Indians of North America, while religious ideologies are culturally shared by members of a group, processes of learning the ways in which animals, spirits, souls, and other aspects of the environment should be treated and the actual practice of this realm of knowledge are very individualistic in nature (e.g., McClellan 1987; Nelson 1973, 1983; Ridington 1988; Tanner 1979). Such knowledge is neither shrouded in secrecy nor commonly expressed in public ceremonies with some exceptions, such as the well documented institution of the potlatch. In effect, the most common expression of northern Algonquian or Athabaskan religious ideologies is the respectful and appropriate harvesting, processing, distribution, and consumption of wild resources. Hunting, trapping, fishing, and gathering can be viewed, from this perspective, as representing simultaneously both economic and "holy" quests on the part of the individual. The success of a producer is indicative of both one's empirical or practical skills and knowledge and the ability to act in harmony with other human and non-human entities and forces of the universe. Both Tanner (1979) and Ridington (1988) argue that the religious ideology and associated practices of subarctic hunters and gatherers are inextricably linked to ecological adaptation through the abilities of individual producers, employing the full range of knowledge, skills, symbolism, and practices necessary to repeatedly and successfully acquire wild resources.

Lastly, there is no evidence to suggest that Christianity has been successful in bringing about the total demise of traditional northern Algonquian or Athabaskan religious ideologies and practices. Tanner (1979:210-211) argues that there has been little syncretic development for the Mistassini, although he admits that " . . . their religion is a mixture of beliefs and rites derived from both the Cree and Christian traditions." Alternatively, he argues that traditional Cree views and Christianity have been applied to different social contexts. Specifically, Christianity has prevailed in Euroamerican modeled settlements, while Cree shamanistic religion functions in the "bush sector" associated with bringing home animals (Tanner 1979:211).

The detailed research of Nelson (1983) on the world view of the Koyukon is of particular relevance in this context. Nelson supports the view that traditional and Christian ideologies and related practices coexisted in Koyukon society in the late 1970s. Because of the pervasive individualistic and heterogeneous nature of Athabaskan religions, he found it difficult to characterize a single complex of Koyukon belief and practice. Nonetheless, Nelson (1983:235) concluded that the Koyukon openly had opted to select and employ elements of both their traditional religion and Christianity in their daily lives:

> *Traditional ideology is a prominent and active element in Koyukon life today. This open adherence to customary belief and practice is sharply different from the situation among other native Alaskan peoples, who are extremely reluctant to discuss or reveal such things. Elsewhere, acceptance of Christianity has caused abandonment of the old religion or has driven it underground; but not so for the Koyukon, at least in the adult generation. [Nelson quoting a Koyukon informant] "Christianity works for all people everywhere on earth, including us. But the Indian way works for us, too, so I've got to have both."*
>
> *Many Koyukon people are faithful Christians, but they are equally committed to their traditional religion. There is one expression of*
> *a general characteristic among Koyukon adults — they have attained a fairly high level of fluency in white culture without losing the vitality of their own Athapaskan lifeways. There is a native way and a white man's way, and the two can coexist comfortably. It is important to bear in mind, then, that the traditional beliefs and behavior toward nature described here are not merely the recollections of elders; they are a living part of the present-day Koyukon culture.*

The coexistence of "traditional," or early postcontact, and Christian ideologies and practices among subarctic Athabaskans, as described by Nelson above for the Koyukon, is a significant contribution to the yet fledgling understanding of subarctic North American Indian religions (Ridington 1988). However, the case of the inland Dena'ina demonstrated that not all Alaskan Natives, in fact, have abandoned or gone underground with what can be reconstructed as early contact ideologies and practices. Continuity of non-Christian ideologies and related behaviors in the face of repression from Euroamerican religious practioners and public educational policies that they influenced may be more prevalent than Nelson's (1983) conclusion suggests.

IN THE BEGINNING

The reconstruction of "traditional" inland Dena'ina cosmology, world view, or religious ideology and associated practices is unfeasible. Like other facets of culture, and based on what is known about the individualistic nature of historic Athabaskan religion, it is likely that there were variations of cosmological and associated behavioral norms among the inland Dena'ina spatially and, more importantly, temporally. Secondly, some documentation of the early contact period exists, such as the accounts of early explorers and Russian Orthodox priests. However, these accounts must be used prudently, particularly since phenomena representing world views and ideologies were the most difficult for outsiders to perceive or comprehend. These early accounts must be used with extreme caution and placed in the contexts of the culture and history of both those who were recording "history" and those who were being scrutinized (Black 1981). Such documentation, if based on the personal experiences of the writer, was usually the product of sporadic or short-term observation. In other cases, early "histories" were based on second—or third-hand accounts not subject to validation. Lastly, and possibly most importantly, the ethnocentric biases of early Euroamerican observers commonly resulted in valuative rather than descriptive views of the "savage" or "uncivilized" groups about which information was being recorded.

Other anthropological means of reconstructing the ethnohistoric period include interpretations derived from oral histories. Oral histories provide the most sound basis for delineating prominent themes, values, and associated practices emerging from the precontact period (Freeman 1976). Nonetheless, no inland Dena'ina in the 1980s, or their parents and grandparents, were born prior to contact. Given the flexibility and dynamic nature of cultural systems in general and, in specific, those of Athabaskans, one would expect inland Dena'ina oral histories in the 1980s to reflect some concepts, values, and perspectives introduced by Euroamericans.

Cornelius Osgood (1976 [1937]) conducted fieldwork among the coastal Dena'ina during the period 1931 to 1932. His well-known and important ethnography was based principally on data derived from a limited number of informants residing in the communities of Seldovia, Kachemak Bay, Kenai, Eklutna, Susitna, Tyonek, and Old Iliamna. Osgood (1976 [1937]:24) admitted to classifying the Dena'ina into a single cultural group, or "nation," largely because he lacked adequate data to distinguish between what he called "subdivisions" or "tribes" and what has been termed "societies" in this context. Additionally, he assumed that differences between Dena'ina were principally the product of ecological factors.

Osgood's summary of coastal Dena'ina religion during the period of his fieldwork is represented in the following quotation:

The religion of the Tanaina [Dena'ina] is a respectful consciousness of the activity of an animate semivisible world which exists as a shadow of their own physical environment. As far as individuals are concerned, this consciousness is a periodical thing which depends upon their temperament and is conditioned by their surroundings . . . . dreams are accepted as certain premonitions of consequent realities. Besides these casual and dream contacts with the supernatural, self-induced trances are a third means of transcending realities. This last is the way of the shamans.

The Tanaina [Dena'ina] believe that all natural objects . . . have a power relatively great or lesser than that of human beings. Toward the influence of these powers in governing individ-

ual lives, the native viewpoint is definitely fatalistic (1976 [1937]:169).

This passage stresses some themes common to subarctic Athabaskans, including the individualistic nature of Dena'ina spirituality, the holistic or undivided nature of the universe, the existence of supernatural specialists or *el'egen*, the potential power of non-human entities and forces, and the view that events are not the product of chance but ultimately the outcome of proper or improper human belief and action. With the exception of the work of Osgood (1976 [1937]), there was no comparable early systematic ethnography of the inland Dena'ina.

Osgood noted in the early 1930s that:

Ideas concerning the origin and development of the world, its gods and men, do not form a readily recognizable aspect of culture among the Northern Athapaskans. Nothing is apparently common knowledge; there is no well-known mythological pattern and only a few people seem to have any ideas or interest in the subject (Osgood 1976 [1937]:173).

Osgood's (1976 [1937]) contention, as revealed in this quotation, that there was nothing precisely equivalent to Christian tales of the genesis of the world and all life forms, to a large degree, was substantiated by inland Dena'ina oral history of the 1980s. However, there was a core of common knowledge relating to the way in which the world came to be and the nature of the relationships between humans and other phenomena of the cosmos.

In the case of the Koyukon, Nelson (1983:227) found that "explanations for the origin, design, and functioning of nature, and for proper human relationships to it, were found in stories of the Distant Time." He also noted that to the Koyukon, "Distant Time" stories were considered to be analogous to the importance of the Bible to Christians. Nelson (1983:34) noted that he was not given a great deal of information about the origins of landforms, although there were "Distant Time" stories about the genesis of features of the earth's surface.

More contemporary inland Dena'ina oral history, including descriptions of the significance of particular named places, incorporated explanations for the formation and existence of a myriad of features of landscapes they inhabited and relied upon. To the inland Dena'ina, accounts from early times (the "long, long ago") that explained the social order of the universe were more important than gods and creators. These stories told of the origins of relationships between animals and humans and between various sets of humans — such as clans, bands, and different ethnic groups — and appropriate behavioral norms emerging from the nature of these connections.

Respect for animals and other aspects of nature was a predominant theme among the inland Dena'ina of the mid-1980s and a part of what was described as "traditional Indian ways." A close bond was believed to exist, particularly between humans and the animals on which they relied. All aspects of nature were considered to be fundamentally spiritual. Human behavior was expected to reflect an elaborate code of morality and associated ethics applicable to all facets of nature. The inland Dena'ina did not perceive these values and norms to be remnants of the past but rather essential to their well-being at all times and to their ability to sustain life in their home territory. Often such values and concepts were expressed to children in the form of stories involving third parties who had violated cultural rules and associated behavioral norms which led to their ultimate fate:

In the spring of the year when it's like this, when the first fish comes upriver, they watch their children. The older people told them not to talk about things. They got the first salmon, and then they cooked it. They dished some fish out for the children. They took it out on the riverbank, and started eating. **Qeshqa** *means rich man or the head of the people — the chief. His daughter was saying things. She was saying, "Oh, this plant which she calls* **ch'deshtleg'a** *. . . , it's not alive like us, and I wonder if it's happy too." That girl, she was kicking it around and possibly broke it down. After they ate, they went back inside. Then, it started getting dark. Then it started to rain. It rained and rained and rained. Then the next thing they knew, it started snowing. And the rich girl's mother said, "No, you're not going to kill that girl. Let them take a different one. Take one of the slave's children. Take each child and kill them, and take them outdoors and cut them open and turn them over towards where the wind was coming from." Still the storm never quit. They kept doing that, one child after another, and then it just kept on snowing. So they said, "Well, there isn't much we can do. I don't think we'll all survive. Go ahead and take her life, kill her." So they took her out and then her mother gave her a bath and put bead-covered clothes on her. Put a bead necklace around her neck, braided her hair, and she put bead covered shoes on her feet, and then they took her out. And then they killed her. They cut her open and hung her up outdoors and then went back inside. And then it got*

calm. It got real calm and quiet. And then the night went by and in the morning, the morning was real good. The sun was shining. This happened just because a little girl was saying things she shouldn't be saying, about a white moss, called reindeer moss. That is why children should never talk about things that they don't know about. Anything, like plants, flowers, or birds ("The First Salmon Ritual," Ruth Koktelash, 1981; Ellanna 1986).

In the 1980s, inland Dena'ina reiterated the view that animals made themselves available for harvesting and naturally increased in number if people were in need of them. Other non-human animals, such as wolves, contributed directly to people. Wolves were perceived to be "brothers" of the Dena'ina and providers during hard times.

The oral traditions of the inland Dena'ina indicated that they perceived that virtually all men and some women, especially those past the age of menopause, had varying degrees of spiritual power. Younger women also had powers. However, because they were spiritually dangerous due to their potential fertility, they had to be taught to control their powers in this realm. The ability to conduct outstanding feats was seen as a sign that spiritual helpers gave particular people extraordinary power. In many cases, the use of assorted paraphernalia symbolized those who had more significant roles and powers than others in the spiritual realm (Honigmann 1981:719).

Among the inland Dena'ina, a person with particularly influential spiritual power, referred to generically as a "shaman" in anthropological literature, was known as *el'egen* or "a man who knows things ahead of time, who can predict the future." Such a person had knowledge about events that were to come but which were not known or predicted by the average man or woman. Inland Dena'ina in the 1980s recalled that some "old people" had visions of the changing world and predicted particularly that some day people would fly, long before aircraft were observed in their territory. *Qeshqa* commonly also were *el'egen* but not all *el'egen* were *qeshqa*.

Russian Orthodox priests who visited the inland Dena'ina in the mid-1800s and Osgood in the early 1930s noted that *el'egen* had special implements for carrying out their activities, such as dolls, masks, and rattles. As Osgood (1976 [1937]:177-178) noted among the coastal Dena'ina of the early 1930s, *el'egen* were considered to be mediators between humans and the spirit world. They predicted the future, cured the ill, and changed the weather and the course of human events. They were paid for services based on mutual agreement. The acquisition of shamanistic power was said to come through dreams. Some *el'egen* were instructed in obtaining spiritual power by fathers or grandfathers, although these were not necessarily hereditary positions. It was believed that *el'egen* obtained their power from animals and plants and from other phenomena of nature such as thunder.

El'egen had the abilities to conduct both benevolent and malevolent spiritual acts, within and between inland Dena'ina communities and between the Dena'ina and other ethnic groups. As people said in the 1980s, there were both good and bad "medicine men." "Some guys were pretty bum; some guys pretty good." The inland Dena'ina recalled a case in which a Tyonek *el'egen* conducted "witchcraft" against Mulchatna residents, bringing about the move of members of this community from one location to another. It was possible, according to the inland Dena'ina, for a father or grandfather to take back shamanistic power from a relative using it to bring harm to others. Benevolent *el'egen* often cured the ill, although there were times he or she was unsuccessful because opposing powers were too strong. In the postcontact period, opposing powers frequently were termed "devil power" in English. If curing powers were potent, *el'egen* were capable of bringing people back from the dead.

El'egen were called upon to bring about equilibrium in the universe of the inland Dena'ina, when improper human behavior resulted in chaos. Improper acts included not killing an animal immediately after taking it or trapping or shooting a wolf incidentally in the absence of proper ceremony and apology. The *el'egen* were known to have championed residents of their community by challenging monsters or "underwater creatures in large lakes" (*tatl'ah velqiz'uni*) (J. Kari 1977:235). In the 1980s, the inland Dena'ina still recalled their fear of bogeymen or *shtutnalyashyna* (J. Kari 1977:171), entities which were more than human and known to have abducted particularly women and children.

The position of *el'egen* remained overtly the focal point of inland Dena'ina "traditional" religion throughout the 1800s and may have contributed, along with the Russian Orthodox priests, to the relocation of Kijik people to the site of Old Nondalton after the measles and influenza epidemic at the turn of the century. If there is a component of inland Dena'ina "traditional"

religion that has been repressed or driven underground in the face of Christianity, it was the institution of the *el'egen*. However, the functions and significance of this figure in inland Dena'ina oral tradition clearly were not eradicated in the 1980s. Stories of the feats of *el'egen* were numerous and told with a sense of conviction and credibility. Some people considered the Russian Orthodox cross to be an amulet responsible for general good fortune, success, and safety in hunting, in much the same way as did the stone amulets used by *el'egen* of the past.

In considering "traditional" inland Dena'ina religious ideology and practice, the phenomenon of death remained the most meaningful realm of individual and collective belief and action. Although modified by Russian Orthodoxy, many non-Christian concepts related to death and spirituality persisted intact or as syncretisms into the 1980s.

In the early 1930s, Osgood (1976 [1937]:170) reported that the Cook Inlet Dena'ina perceived that each person possessed three spirits, that of the body, breath, and shadow. The shadow spirit was thought to leave the body sometime before death occurred, while the breath spirit went into the sky at death. By way of contrast, the shadow spirit was believed to linger for about 40 days before going underground, as it was loathe to leave friends and family and longed for a last farewell or for kin to bring about revenge in the case of a homicide or death from witchcraft. The shadow spirit was considered to be very dangerous to living humans during this 40-day period. In the 1980s, the inland Dena'ina demonstrated similar views about the spirits of the deceased. For example, many elders reiterated the fact that it was important to recover bodies of those who died by drowning in order that their spirits be laid to rest and not endanger surviving kin. In some cases, people who died together were buried together, in order to appease the spirit world.

For people such as the inland Dena'ina, who perceived life to be cyclical in nature, death was considered to be a critical point in transcending from one stage to another. As Osgood (1976 [1937]) noted on Cook Inlet in the early 1930s, the most important community expression of religious ideology was associated with death and the appropriate treatment of the human spirit by members of the clan of the deceased and those belonging to their reciprocal or "opposite" clan. The ceremonial recognition of death was the potlatch. Both the funeral and memorial potlatches persisted tenaciously in Nondalton for all deaths observed during the 1980s.

When the death of someone was imminent, it was the responsibility of members of the opposite clan to care for the person and his or her family. After death, those of the opposite clan washed and dressed the body of the deceased, dug the grave, carved the cross, built the coffin, and conducted final interment. The funeral and 40-day memorial potlatches were mechanisms by which members of the opposite clan were compensated for their assistance. They received food and were the recipients of the material goods belonging to the deceased and other members of his or her clan. In addition, the clan of the deceased amassed other foods and commodities for purposes of repayment. In the case of individuals who died sudden, accidental deaths, opposite clan members had similar responsibilities for recovering the body of the deceased and carrying out all other tasks described above.

Osgood (1976 [1937]:166) documented in the early 1930s that prior to the introduction of burial of the dead by the Russian Orthodox church, no method of disposal of the dead except cremation was practiced. Opposite clan members constructed a crematory of logs, two or three miles away from the community, on which the body and implements to be used by the spirit of the deceased were placed. After cremation, remaining bones were collected in a bag and placed on a pole. Osgood (1976 [1937]) also reported tremendous expressions of grief involving self-inflicted pain in the case of widows and others with close ties to the deceased. The elaborateness of the crematory and subsequent potlatches were related to the status of the individual, according to Osgood (1976:[1937]167-168).

During the period 1858 to 1860, Russian Orthodox Abbot Nicholas of the Kenai parish reported the following customs related to death, as practiced by the "Tnayna" or "Kenay" people:

> *Formerly, during paganism, the Kenay [sic] Indians, similarly to some of the other savages, burned their dead and collecting the bones in a box and set them in a cemetery. At certain times the nearest relatives came to the cemetery and mourned, crying loudly. Compassionate friends consoled them with presents. At the anniversary of the death of a relative a commemorative feast was given and all invited and uninvited guests were fed with dried fish, berries in grease and other foodstuffs. There was dancing and distribution of presents among the guests; the esteemed ones received*

> *more, the poor received less. Often a host gave all his meager possessions as presents to his guests. This custom is now seldom practiced: the Indians living near the mission headquarters ask the missionary to say requiem service at the anniversary of the death of their relative* (Travel Journal of Abbot Nicholas, Kenai, 1858-1860, as quoted in Townsend 1974 b:8.).

Although the inland Dena'ina practiced only burial of the dead in the 1980s, elders recalled stories about crematory practices of the past. Additionally, oral histories pointed to the fact that death was not merely dealt with by group ceremonies but rather involved individualized ritual and mourning. Such individual practices included making up songs about a loved one who had died or not mentioning the name of someone recently deceased. The death of a family member affected all residents of Nondalton during the 1980s and involved intense and lengthy periods of individualized grief and mourning. Mourning was both internalized and, on other occasions, expressed more publicly with restrained emotion.

CONFLICT, CONFORMITY, OR SYNCRETISM: RUSSIAN ORTHODOXY AND THE DENA'INA RESPONSE

Christianity was introduced to Alaska Natives by many different religions and denominations throughout the 1800s and early 1900s. The Russian Orthodox Greek Catholic Church, through the auspices of its American mission, was the first form of Christianity to influence those Native groups located within the sphere of economic activities undertaken by the Russian-American Company. The introduction of the inland Dena'ina to Christianity was relatively early, albeit sporadic. However, it did not involve resident clergy throughout the historic period.

The first organized attempts at establishing a Russian Orthodox mission in Alaska commenced in 1793 through the efforts of two priests and three monks. Their stated purpose was to act as overseers of the morality of the Russians as well as enlighteners of "the heathens" (i.e., Native peoples). However, the company wanted them confined to the second task (Smith 1980b:10). The mission was established on Kodiak Island the following year. From the beginning, the church and fur hunting and trading entrepreneurs were at odds about policies related to the treatment of Alaska Natives. The first resident Russians in proximity to the inland Dena'ina, who also were indirectly representative of the church, were the

Figure 90. A visit to Old Nondalton by Father Sergei Repellent from Egegik, circa 1930. He travelled to Old Nondalton on this freight sled pulled by 17 dogs. Informants report that he visited once a year by dog team and later came by boat during summer months. *Photograph Courtesy of Ida Carlson Crater.*

Figure 91. Gabriel Trefon standing by a flag at half mast because of Evan Koktelash's death in late summer 1937. The Old Nondalton Russian Orthodox church is in the background. *Photograph Courtesy of Agnes Cusma.*

staff of the *odinochka* on Lake Iliamna, established in the early 1790s.

Historical evidence indicated that Hieromonk Juvenal travelled in the direction of the Iliamna and Kvichak drainages in 1796 and, in fact, may have encountered some inland Dena'ina. Most scholars dispute the more commonly held view that Juvenal's journal (Iuvenalii 1952 [1796]) was authentic and have concluded that he actually met his death at the hands of Yup'ik people at the mouth of the Kuskokwim River rather than at Lake Iliamna (Black 1981; Oleksa 1987). Oleksa (1987) maintained, however, that local Indians and "Eskimos" of the Iliamna and Kvichak drainages proved to be largely unreceptive to Juvenal's message of Christianity during this fateful and long misinterpreted journey.

Between 1786 and 1791, there was no formal missionary activity on the Kenai Peninsula. In the 1790s, the Iliamna *odinochka* was destroyed by local people. Therefore, there was considerably less direct contact between representatives of Russian Orthodoxy and the inland Dena'ina than was to be the case after the Nushagak redoubt was established in 1819.

After the arrival of the priest Veniaminov at Unalaska in 1824, the church made an even greater effort to mitigate what was perceived by some to be the inhumane and devastating treatment of Alaska Native peoples by representatives of the Russian-American Company and their predecessors. Veniaminov personally visited the Nushagak River outpost during the period 1829 to 1832. The first chapel was constructed near Aleksandrovskiy Redoubt in 1832. Although Bishop Innocent directed his efforts toward the creation of the Nushagak Mission, this church did not receive parish status until 1841 (Afonsky 1977:57, 63).

A smallpox epidemic, which occurred between 1836 and 1840, intensified the degree of activity of Russian Orthodox clergy (Fall 1987). However, Townsend's (1981:636) conclusion that the ". . . more remote inland Dena'ina villages of Mulchatna and Kijik were little affected [by Russian Orthodox clergy] until after 1870" was erroneous based on data derived from Russian Orthodox confessionals and travel reports (ARCA 1847-1900]. These accounts indicated that priests began baptizing, chrismating, presenting liturgies, taking confessions, and gathering parish statistics at Mulchatna as early as 1847 and at Kijik minimally by 1854. In 1854, the "Iliamna area,"

including all the territory inhabited by the inland Dena'ina with the exception of the Stony River, was transferred from the Kenai to the Nushagak parish (Russian Orthodox American Messenger 1896-1907 1:14:287).

Some of the information on the inland Dena'ina gathered by Russian Orthodox priests sheds light on their status at the time of clerical visits as well as opinions held by the priests about the inland Dena'ina. Father Igumen Nikolai from the Kenai River area parish gathered data from the Mulchatna River area in 1847 and 1851, although his records never clearly delineated the number of villages existing at the time of his visits. Although Hieromonk Feofil Uspenskii of the Nushagak parish noted that he made no visits to Mulchatna during his tenure between 1853 to 1868 and no trips to any "Kenaitsy" (Dena'ina) village in 1861, confessional data for Mulchatna were recorded for most of these years. In 1863, Feofil met with the Iliamna Dena'ina and noted that there were still villages in which shamans lived and worked. However, "illegal" marriages, unions not sanctified by Russian Orthodox church ceremony, were less frequent in his parish (ARCA 1847-1900). Although not specifically commenting on the inland Dena'ina, Abbot Nicholas and Hieromonk Nikita remarked about the presence and activity of shamans and the church's struggles for power with them among the Kenai in general for the period 1858 to 1860 (ARCA 1847-1900).

After the sale of Alaska to the United States in 1867, the Russian Orthodox church continued to receive minimal financial support until the Bolshevik Revolution in 1917. By the following year, the ordained clergy was reduced to nine individuals (Smith 1980b:9). However, between 1867 and 1918, when the Nushagak parish was temporarily vacated, confessionals and priests' travel reports, particularly those of Vasilii Shishkin, provided considerable insight, from the perspective of the church's clergy, on the status of the inland Dena'ina.

During the year 1877 to 1878, Shishkin (ARCA 1847-1900) reported visiting Iliamna and providing the Dena'ina there with confessions and baptisms. He mentioned the presence of syphilis among the Dena'ina on Lake Iliamna, and reported that there was no doctor in this community. In the summer of 1878, he underwent a three-day journey to "Kichik" (Kijik) which, he reported, was also populated by "Kenaitsy." There he performed 3 days of sermons; and in one day he baptized 23 men, 13 women, 2 boys, and 2 girls. Additionally, he chrismated 30 males, 24 females, 5 boys, and 9 girls who already had been baptized during a previous visit. He performed seven marriages as well. In all, Shishkin reported that 94 people received sacraments during this visit. He commented:

The Kenaitsy most of the time of the year are spread out in the mountains for trapping, hunting, etc. and gather only on the first of August in the village of Kichik [sic] to gather fish and therefore I found it not necessary for them to build a prayer house (ARCA 1847-1900).

During this visit, the chief of the Mulchatna Dena'ina discouraged Shishkin's travel to that village, ostensibly because of low water.

In 1879, Shishkin travelled to Mulchatna, where he reported the existence of 20 "pagans" who had not been baptized. He expressed the need for teachers who could lead church services during the time that priests were away. He also commented on the necessity for having a translator of the moral and religious sermons provided by Russian Orthodox clergy.

In 1880, Shishkin's travel report (ARCA 1847-1900) described the prevalence of Dena'ina shamanism. He noted that if the weather were bad, members of the community forced the shaman to correct the situation or to cure the ill upon command. The persistence of shamanism encouraged him to reiterate the need for Russian Orthodox clergy to settle among the Dena'ina in order to convert them totally from their "vices." Shishkin noted that the good points of these people included hospitality and support of the poor. However, in Shishkin's view, the Dena'ina were plagued by the diseases of consumption and syphilis, the latter deriving mostly from their "love of passion."

In 1881, Shishkin (ARCA 1847-1900) described the seasonal round of the inland Dena'ina. Interestingly, the information he reported was very similar to that derived from Nondalton Dena'ina in the 1980s. Shishkin also recorded the use of firearms by the Dena'ina. He estimated that the people of his parish took between 2,000 to 2,500 furbearers that year. He reiterated that the Dena'ina were unwilling to give up shamanism and their "love of passion," which was particularly intense during yearly games in which people "joined together even with married females." It was common, Shishkin observed, for parents of 11-year-old girls to unite them with the best traders in order that their descendants might be "mighty" and good traders themselves. Another significant vice, he observed, was entering into marriage with rela-

tives of the "third level," based on their belief that the kin of the woman would watch over both men and children better. It is clear that Shishkin had not grasped or, alternatively, was unwilling to accept the structure and function of the system of clan affiliation and related marital patterns of the inland Dena'ina of the time. He noted that another vice was that of males who left their wives or "illegal" coresident women, thereby taking on other wives who were relatives and younger than their first wives.

In December 1881, Shishkin took two dog sleds, a junior deacon, Ioann Orlov, and five helpers and travelled up the Nushagak River. During this trip he visited the Mulchatna population after a one week portage to this area. Shishkin noted that on a previous visit, he had baptized all the "pagans" and during this trip had to give confession in one day to everyone, as people were going trapping. During that day, 27 people attended services, and Shishkin visited some homes. There were many fewer people than the 144 which had attended confession during his previous visit. He noted that in the fall of this year, nine Mulchatna Dena'ina had died of scarlet fever. The chief, Iakov Kokileashtukta, died while Shishkin was in village, and the priest performed the funeral. As Shishkin was leaving Mulchatna on his way to Kijik, he met a family from there who said that everyone had gone trapping. Therefore, he canceled his journey to that community (ARCA 1847-1900).

During a visit to Tyonek in 1881, Hieromonk Nikita's travel notes about the "Kenaitsy" provided insights into the attitudes of some clergy toward the "traditional" religious institution of shamanism at that time:

In the house of my interpreter, John Kirilov, I found the chief and other people, among whom was the local shaman, a clever fellow, either a Creole or one of the cunning Indians. He spoke Russian well and bore himself smartly. I utilized his presence to denounce him. I disclosed his deceit of his simple-minded and trusting fellow-men. I accused him of laziness and cowardice because of his refusal to partake of holy communion, I advised him to repent and in token of his repentance to surrender voluntarily the objects which he used during his shamanistic performances. He replied evasively, revising my request. It could be seen that he wished to hide or go away and undoubtedly would have done so if he had not been afraid of impairing his reputation among his followers. Then, not wishing to leave the scoundrel with even the shadow of a triumph and the listeners (including my churchman) in doubt, I, knowing the obedience of Aleuts and Kenai Indians to a priest's advice and to the church prohibitions, threatened the shaman with complete excommunication, i.e. expulsion not only from the church and holy communion, from which he excluded himself as being an unworthy member, but from the community as well in the full sense of the word. Consequently, I through my interpreter, forbid all the people of Tyonek and neighboring villages from receiving him in their houses, greeting him and speaking to him, taking him on hunting and fishing parties, giving him presents, visiting him, eating with him from the same kettle or drinking from the same cup, and having any kind of contact with him. I threatened those who refused to do so with church punishment.

It became very quiet in the house. All sat with downcast eyes. The shaman also remained silent with his head down, thinking for a minute or longer; then, without a word he left the house. In a few minutes he returned with a dirty, greasy sack and shook from it the objects of his profession, namely wooden rattles used in dancing, colored sticks, strips of wood, feathers, a doll with hair and queue, and other trinkets which were so dirty that one could not handle them without repulsion. Then one of two similar dolls were [sic] brought in by some women: All these things I burned in their presence on the street. It was amusing to see the indignation of one old woman when she saw my churchman spitting on a doll brought by her.

I doubt that the shaman surrendered everything. Anyway, this case impressed my audience tremendously. Immediately after this the chief was the first to remove the various objects from the grave of his father; the others have promised to follow his example. Giving the proper instructions to the shaman, I blessed him and promised to give him communion on my next visit if he proved by his deeds that he had relinquished his occupation entirely (Hieromonk Nikita as quoted in Townsend 1974b:11).

Hieromonk Nikita also commented on the fact that the further the clergy travelled from Kenai, the more ". . . savage in custom the people were, with no government, keeping concubines besides a wife, . . . [and not cutting] their hair, and adopt[ing] young girls to raise them as wives" (Hieromonk Nikita as quoted in Townsend 1974b:12). Other vices he observed among the Dena'ina included their fermentation of flour with sugar, playing cards and other gambling games, drinking strong tea, and using tobacco (Hieromonk Nikita as quoted in Townsend 1974b:13). Nikita was dismissed from the Russian Orthodox clergy after six years of service, because of his aggressive stance toward Native people and lack of understanding of their problems that had resulted from Russian contact (Townsend 1974b:10).

In February 1884, Shishkin (ARCA 1847-1900) visited Iliamna and Kijik Lake (Lake Clark). During this visit to Kijik, he baptized 4 boys and girls and gave confession to 40 adults. On March 1, he travelled on the Chulitna and "Qeghnilen" rivers in an attempt to reach Mulchatna, but heavy rains and high water resulted in a cancellation of this plan and a return to Nushagak. In July of the same year, he was requested by the Dena'ina to go to Iliamna because of an epidemic that resulted in two deaths. In a summary statement about this visit, Shishkin concluded that the Dena'ina are on the "good side of religious matters" but had not given up superstition. It was his belief that only access to Euroamerican medical care and resident clergy would result in the abandonment by members of his parish of their attachment to shamanism. He estimated that it would cost $60 a year to have a reader in each village in his parish and that this funding could not be provided by local people because of their poverty.

During the winter of 1884 to 1885, Shishkin (ARCA 1847-1900) did not visit either Iliamna or Kijik because of bad weather and his concern for Russian Orthodox competition with shamanism and the Moravians in the Togiak area. In January 1886, he visited Iliamna and commented about waiting for people from other villages, who were coming for groceries because of food shortages in their own areas. It is not known whether or not these were inland Dena'ina, but they arrived on February 1. Shishkin performed funeral services and chrismated 10 children. He performed the liturgy for 150 men and 90 women and performed 2 marriages. Including children, 270 people attended services during Shishkin's visit to Iliamna that year. In February 1887, Shishkin (ARCA 1847-1900) travelled to Iliamna, where he chrismated three children and gave confession to residents of Iliamna, Kijik, and Mulchatna. According to Shishkin, the Dena'ina had come intentionally from Mulchatna because of his visit. A total of 232 people attended his services. In February 1888, Shishkin (ARCA 1847-1900) attempted to go to Kijik from Iliamna but turned back because of bad weather. On March 8 of that year, he was successful in getting to Kijik, were people had come from Mulchatna to see him and were anxious to return home. After holding services for 172 people, he attempted to convince the people of Mulchatna to relocate to Kijik. Shishkin argued that they lacked a store on the Mulchatna River and, therefore, had inadequate nourishment. At the meeting which they held with Shishkin, the Mulchatna Dena'ina agreed to settle at Kijik or Lake Iliamna. Shishkin also tried to convince the Kijik people to build a prayer house, which they promised to construct during the summer of 1888. By 1889, Shishkin (ARCA 1847-1900) learned that the site of Newhalen had been settled by Dena'ina from Kijik and Mulchatna. By February of that year, Shishkin reported that the Dena'ina had become more willing to give up "pagan" beliefs and superstitions than had the people of Togiak. During the winter of 1890, he was convinced of the zeal of Native people to adopt Russian Orthodoxy and believed that the eradication of superstition and the practice of shamanism was coming about.

Townsend (1965:293), in discussing the Iliamna Dena'ina, evaluated the success of Russian Orthodoxy during the 1880s:

*The Tanaina in the 1880's [sic] wore a thin veneer of Christianity. They accepted baptism, confirmation, **miropomazaniya** and Christian burial practices, celebrated Russian Christmas and other holidays, gave up their aboriginal names for Christian ones, and attended religious services when a priest came through. Priests were welcomed and respected according to the implications of the various journals. But, it is obvious from the comments in the 1880's [sic] that beneath the Christian exterior, the aboriginal religious beliefs were still virile. A syncretism in religious beliefs and practices was arising (Townsend 1965:293).*

A Dena'ina oral historic view of Russian Orthodoxy of the 1880s is revealed in this account of an event that happened at a pond at old Kijik Point called Qil'ihtnu, which is translated "bad creek," or "evil creek." According to this story:

. . . when there was a village at Kijik, a priest came in the 1880s and took all the people and baptized them in that pond. He poured holy water in the lake [pond] and baptized all the people. At that time, men had long hair and the priest told them to cut it off — some did and some would not. Anyway, afterwards, something poured into that lake during the winter time. The ice was just broken away right into the lake. There had been no creek there before and something came out of there like a prehistoric animal and went into the lake. The holy water was responsible for making the prehistoric animal and for it becoming an evil lake. That is why it is called "Evil Creek" today (Albert Wassillie 1985).

Shishkin's (ARCA 1847-1900) administering to the spiritual well-being of the inland Dena'ina continued into the 1890s. By this time, he noted that Iliamna was populated by both Dena'ina and "Creoles." He held services in order to fight off the effects of epidemics occurring from the fall of 1888 to February 1889, in which there were 21 deaths from influenza. He travelled up the Newhalen River to Kijik Lake (Lake Clark) and to the village, where he baptized children and performed services at graves for the 16 who died between 1888 and 1889. He noted that this was the same epidemic that had occurred in Iliamna. He blessed new houses and performed services in the chapel in August for 56 men and women and additional children. In the fall of 1891, Shishkin faced considerable difficulties travelling to Iliamna because of rain and a swollen river. However, by January 1892, he arrived at Iliamna and performed a liturgy to which a few adults and children of both sexes came from the village of Kijik. During this journey, Shishkin did not visit Kijik on the advice of Iliamna residents, although he noted the importance of visits by priests in keeping Native people from "pagan" delusions or from the "heretical" missions such as the Moravians to the north. The year of 1892 was the last travel report recorded by Shishkin.

Father Vladimir Modestov was assigned to the Nushagak parish during the years 1893 to 1898. His annual report for the year 1894 (Russian Orthodox Messenger 1896-1907 3:8:224-227) noted that he travelled to Iliamna but not to "Kitcheck" (Kijik), although he saw a portion of residents of that community at Iliamna where they had relocated or temporarily resettled because of a lack of resources in their home area. It is likely that Modestov was referring to events described in the oral histories of the inland Dena'ina. Food shortages at this time were related to the Bristol Bay commercial fishing blockades of drainages used by salmon on which the inland Dena'ina depended. By 1896, Modestov reported that there were no "heretical Christians" in Kijik and that chapels in both Kijik and Iliamna existed.

Elder residents of Nondalton in the 1980s recalled that inland Dena'ina on the upper Stony River were visited by priests from the Kuskokwim River after 1900. However, in the 1890s, during a period of time in which no priest visited, a couple from Qeghnilen knew that they had been instructed by clergy encountered during their journeys to be married by a priest. They were aware that there was a mission at Nushagak. Therefore, they travelled by *baidarki,* from the upper Mulchatna River to Nushagak village. When they arrived, there was no priest there. They then travelled up the coast to the Kvichak River, up the Kvichak River to Lake Iliamna, over the portage along the rapids, up the Newhalen River, and across Lake Clark to Kijik. During this amazingly lengthy journey via *baidarki,* the couple never located a priest to marry them in the *Gasht'ana* way.

By the end of the second decade of the 1900s, there were few Russian Orthodox clergy remaining in Alaska (Smith 1980b), and contact with the inland Dena'ina appeared to have been minimal. Brotherhoods and other societies associated with the church had been established in the Kenai parish. However, none had been formed in the Nushagak parish (Townsend 1965), principally because of the great distances that separated communities, problems in converting Yup'ik populations in the vicinity of the Nushagak River, and competition from the Moravians on the coast. In the case of the inland Dena'ina, there were no Protestant attempts to convert members of the Russian Orthodox church until the 1950s.

To comprehend the nature of Russian Orthodox influence on the spirituality, ideology, cosmology, and overall culture of the inland Dena'ina, it is useful to review some of the principles by which clerics in Alaska administered their faith to residents of their respective parishes. The Russian Orthodox clergy viewed this life as preparation for eternal life. Their beliefs were drawn from the scriptures and church traditions (Mattson 1985). Their sacraments included baptism, confirmation, holy communion, confession, penance, holy orders, holy matrimony, and unction with oil (the last rites). Icons were not worshipped as objects but were meant to be images of reflection, retaining a vision of holiness.

The church's ideas about the immortality of the soul, the concept of other worlds, and the practice of individual or group ritual to influence events did not stand in necessary opposition to more indigenous inland Dena'ina beliefs. In general, Dena'ina values related to caring for those who were unable to care for themselves bore a similarity to Russian Orthodox principles of charity. The degree of individual and lay autonomy in the Russian Orthodox church, based on the church's view that anyone of the faith can conduct baptism in the absence of a priest (Black personal communication 1987), and the use of Native clergy and local readers for most services

encouraged inland Dena'ina participation in ritual, despite their limited access to clergy.

The policies of the Russian Orthodox Church in Alaska neither advocated the destruction of all aspects of Native cultures nor were they focused on wholesale assimilation, as were many of the principally Protestant denominations to follow during the American period. For the most part, the instructions under which the missionaries operated were notably humane and tolerant of Native customs not perceived to be in violent conflict with Christian moral precepts. Even some sacraments, such as marriage, were interpreted with a great deal of liberality during the first period of Native and Russian Orthodox clerical contact (Smith 1980b).

In 1899, Bishop Tikhon published "Instruction of the Most Reverend Metropolitan Innocent," which included special instructions involving the treatment of Alaska Natives (Smith 1980b). These directions designated that baptism should be preceded by instruction and should be given only to those who consented. The priests were admonished not to represent any particular government nor show open contempt for Native manners of living or insult them. Priests were to treat Native people with kindness, gentleness, pleasantness, and wisdom and, through these means, win their confidence. They were to discourage the Native practice of polygamy but not with force. Priests were not to expect Native people to observe fasting in the same way as demanded of clergy. Finally, they were to make attendance at services an absolute duty (Smith 1980b:14). Additionally, because of the small numbers of the local populations, the clergy were advised not to overextend forbidden degrees of relationship between those who wanted to marry. They were not to discourage ancient customs, so long as they were not contrary to Russian Orthodox Christianity. Even those which were could be tolerated, while not accepted. The clergy were to allow Natives who were not baptized to go to services. No matrimonial unions or contracts entered into before baptism were to be considered hindrances to the participation of Native people in the church, and no marriages outside of the church were to be annulled. The church rejected the view that the cultural heritages of all believers should be molded into a common pattern, a protest to assimilative policies practiced by other religious missions in Alaska (Smith 1980b:15).

Despite the principles of the Russian Orthodox church, from its commencement of activity in Alaska in the 1790s, to shifts in policy occurring during the Americanization of Alaska, Smith argued that the church advocated entirely new views of the cosmos and of the place of humanity in it. From Smith's (1980b) perspective, these views profoundly affected Native cultures, principally because such conceptual frameworks emerged out of "civilized" rather than hunting and gathering societies (Smith 1980b:16). VanStone (1980:177) and Oswalt (1963:40) arrived at similar conclusions regarding the relationships between "civilizing" and religious conversion. That is, they concluded that civilizing Native peoples in the context of missionization was synonymous with conversion for most denominations that proselytized in Alaska in the late 19th century.

Ethnohistoric data suggested that Russian Orthodox priests did not make the same demands with reference to changing ways of life as did the Protestant and, to a lesser degree, Roman Catholic missionaries who followed, and, in some areas, replaced them. As a result, Russian Orthodoxy came to be identified with inland Dena'ina culture in some respects. In the 1980s, most Nondalton Dena'ina viewed Russian Orthodoxy as part of their cultural heritage and "tradition." In fact, Russian Orthodoxy served as a rallying point for more conservative, tradition-oriented local residents. Mattson (1985) and Rathburn (1981) arrived at similar conclusions regarding Russian Orthodoxy as a Native institution among the Aleuts and, specifically, Koniags:

> *Regardless of how Orthodoxy was introduced to the Koniag, it has persisted. Regardless of the views of those who would see Russian missionaries forcing natives to convert, the fact is that the missionaries in Alaska were never numerous enough to exert such control over the Koniag. The 22 clergy in Alaska today is a record number. In the first 50 years of missionary work in Alaska, the church could maintain only a handful of priests, and on several occasions only one priest served all of Russian America* (Rathburn 1981:12).

Was the nature of the relationship between the Russian Orthodox Church and the inland Dena'ina that of conflict, conformity, or syncretism? In some respects and during particular stages of contact between the church and indigenous people, the relationship was characterized by all three features.

The points of greatest conflict between "traditional" or early postcontact inland Dena'ina ideology and behavior and Russian Orthodoxy, as revealed by priests' travel reports and oral histories, involved indigenous faith in and the

practice of the complex of behaviors associated with shamanism. Adherence to matrilineally based patterns of spouse selection, including the marriage of cross-cousins and arranged and polygamous unions, was opposed overtly by the church. If the coastal example described by Osgood (1976 [1937]) was relevant to the inland Dena'ina, the practice of cremation rather than burial was adamantly opposed by Russian Orthodox clergy.

The individualistic nature of inland Dena'ina religious ideology and practice, including non-Christian rituals such as the use of amulets, was less subject to critique by Russian Orthodox clergy. The delegation of liturgical responsibilities to lay readers and the role of individual responsibility in Russian Orthodoxy allowed for local and personal interpretation in a way that was culturally relevant to the inland Dena'ina. As Fall (1987:86) astutely observed, the church clergy saw themselves in a paternalistic relationship with the indigenous people of Alaska. As such, they served as protectors against the misdeeds and assimilationist policies of Russian and American traders, missionaries, teachers, and governmental officials. The Russian Orthodox church supported the continued use of indigenous languages, with attendant benefits to Dena'ina cultural continuity. In general, the church was more tolerant of cultural differences within the framework of a relatively liberal interpretation of Christian morality.

The implementation of policies of the Russian Orthodox church and practices of the inland Dena'ina over the last two centuries revealed conformity on the part of both interests. Church clergy were given directions to mitigate the impact of missionization on Native peoples in general and to liberally interpret adherence to dogma, principles of morality, and ritual to the degree that indigenous beliefs and behaviors were not in direct or overt opposition to those of Russian Orthodox Christianity. Moreover, acceptance of the faith, rather than cultural change and wholesale assimilation, was the principal aspiration of the Russian Orthodox church. On the part of the inland Dena'ina, the acceptance of burial rather than cremation, undergoing church sacraments, and constructing chapels and churches were acts of conformity to the church. Based on priests' accounts, the "eradication of" beliefs or practices associated with shamanism and marriage generally was accomplished by the early 1900s, although such behavioral and ideological modifications were slow in coming. Alternatively, rather than eradication, such beliefs and behaviors regarding shamanism and culturally-defined marriage patterns may have shifted from being overt to covert. It could be argued substantively that some aspects of shamanistic belief and "traditional" marriage patterns remained intact in the culture of the inland Dena'ina of the 1980s, despite the fact that people were well aware of aspects of their culture critiqued by church policy and clergy.

For the Iliamna Dena'ina, Townsend (1965) argued that their religion in the early 1960s was principally syncretistic, incorporating the form and function of elements of "traditional" religion with Russian Orthodoxy. Some evidence for this process of cultural interaction was observed in the case of the inland Dena'ina as well. For example, oral histories indicated that some of the most powerful *elegen* or *qeshqa* became the most active and devout lay readers in the Russian Orthodox church. Grave goods, possibly associated with earlier crematorial rites, accompanied burials in the 1980s. Both Russian Orthodox crosses and objects derived from nature were used to ensure hunting success. Prayers of thanks were offered at times of hunting achievement or in situations of danger to satisfy both "God" and the spirit world. Potlatches, overtly practiced and of the greatest ceremonial significance in the 1980s, were frequently officiated by lay readers and incorporated the use of prayers and hymns and the 40-day temporal period between death and memorial ceremonies.

Lastly, and possibly most significantly, Russian Orthodoxy did not alter the most notable features of "traditional" or early postcontact inland Dena'ina religion, that is the intricate relationships between humans and the natural world of which these indigenous peoples perceived themselves to be merely a part. Stories of long, long, ago were called upon in the 1980s as valid explanations for numerous phenomena, such as the weather conditions, animal behavior, wild resource shortages or abundances, features of local topography, illnesses, accidents, and deaths. These explanations were called upon as instructional tools in maintaining inland Dena'ina ideological and behavioral norms. The happiness and well-being of the inland Dena'ina were seen to be intimately related to their living in harmony with the universe. In a sense, Russian Orthodoxy in the 1980s was perceived to be an adjunct means for achieving this end. That is, the Nondalton Dena'ina indicated that they must have both their "Indian ways" and those of the church. In this respect, it may be accurate to conclude that Russian Orthodoxy, indeed, had become an inland Dena'ina tradition by the 1980s and was no longer seen to be exclusively a part of the world of the *Gasht'ana*.

THE AMERICANIZATION OF THE INLAND DENA'INA: THE PROTESTANT ETHIC AND EDUCATIONAL POLICY

Although the Russians were faced with both economic and ideological competition from Americans, British, Canadians, French, Spanish, and others prior to the sale of Alaska in 1867, such contact was insignificant in regard to changing the spirituality of the inland Dena'ina. The Moravians, viewed with bitter opposition by the Russian Orthodox clergy, remained centered in and around the Kuskokwim River and delta and did not penetrate inland Dena'ina territory. In the two decades following the purchase of Alaska, Protestant missionaries had not taken over the role of formal, western education, the principal institution of assimilation to be used in subsequent years. Again, because of the geographic isolation of the inland Dena'ina, they were among the last to be directly impacted by the missionary/teacher of this era.

The First Organic Act of 1884 was the initial legislation to launch what is perceived by some scholars to have been an unholy alliance between American Protestantism and the delivery of western education to Alaskan Natives (e.g., Krauss 1980). Sheldon Jackson was appointed to be the first Commissioner of Education in the Bureau of Education for Alaska under this act and served for the period 1885 to 1908. He used his position as Commissioner of Education to promote vigorously his own version of Presbyterianism in educational policy (Krauss 1980). Sheldon Jackson overtly and critically opposed the Russian Orthodox church. He boldly stated that within 25 years, Russian Orthodoxy would become history in the Territory of Alaska (Oleksa 1987:254). To accomplish his aspirations and to minimize conflicts between various Protestant groups, Jackson travelled widely throughout the United States. In the forum of an ecumenical conference in the late 1880s, he and his supporters divided Alaska Native groups and territories among various Protestant denominations. Additionally, at the turn of the century, Jackson was instrumental in bringing about the importation of reindeer and initially Chukchi and, later, Sami herders to instruct Native peoples in the "civilized" art of food production.

Figure 92. The first school in Old Nondalton in 1931. Students and a few younger adults are waving small American flags and holding up a full-sized one. *Photograph Courtesy of Ida Carlson Crater.*

The social and educational philosophy of Jackson and his followers is best illustrated in the following quotation:

Sheldon Jackson epitomized the Victorian-era American educational and social philosophy of the "melting pot" wherein all the diverse nationalities in American society were to assimilate to the Anglo-Saxon Protestant American ideal. . . . To complete the "winning of the West" and the white man's "manifest destiny," the American Indian was to be converted to the white man's religion, assimilated to his culture, and forced to abandon his Native language. The older educational policy of the Russians, Moravians, and Catholics was during this period to give way to the anti-Native policy of Jackson and the Protestant sects under his influence (Krauss 1980:22).

Although there were minimally 350 loan words from Russian in Dena'ina, the Russians had not written texts in that language or established a standard orthography (Krauss 1980). The Jacksonian policy of prohibiting the use of any Native languages in missionary schools receiving federal support and punishing any violators of this rule had a long-standing and devastating impact on the survival of Dena'ina and other Native languages. The suppression of Native languages was closely correlated with overall cultural repression, as human groups commonly employ language as a major criteria of cultural identification. Additionally, Jackson's and his supporters' interests in eliminating the use of Native languages were perceived to be key in curtailing the practice of "satanic" beliefs and practices associated with shamanism (Young 1927).

In summary, the governmentally-funded church schools were employed as instruments of social and cultural assimilation and reform, the tools of civilizing Native "heathens" and "savages." They thereby functioned as a system for the promotion of American and Protestant ideologies. In addition to bringing about the demise of Native languages, teachers and educational policies promoted the model of western science and assumed that it would replace Native world views. Teachers and their educational policies implied or expressly stated that Native cultures were inferior to those of the western world. They promoted the view that hunting, fishing, trapping, and gathering were lesser pursuits than those of animal and plant domestication and industrialization, common in western economic and social contexts. These are only a few of the messages transmitted to Native people through the auspices of western formal education.

Although Protestants indirectly challenged Russian Orthodoxy at Lake Iliamna shortly after the turn of the century (U.S. Dept. of the Interior, Bureau of Education 1908-1912) through the founding of a school and the establishment of a reindeer herd, they never penetrated inland Dena'ina territory until 1929. There were very few inland Dena'ina children that attended school at Old Iliamna. In 1929, the successor to the Bureau of Education, the Bureau of Indian Affairs (BIA), constructed a school at Old Nondalton. This school closed for a year in 1939 and was reopened at the new site of present day Nondalton. Some parents were encouraged to send their children to boarding schools outside of the region for both elementary and, in later years, secondary education.

In the 1950s, a fundamentalist, multidenominational mission was established at Pedro Bay on Lake Iliamna. This group, which referred to itself as Arctic Mission, had substantial success in converting Dena'ina residents of Pedro Bay, who had relocated there from the site of Old Iliamna (Townsend 1965). Although missionaries associated with Arctic Mission resided in Nondalton for more than a decade, by 1988 the mission functionally was abandoned and the inland Dena'ina remained firmly committed to Russian Orthodox Christianity. One of the critiques of Russian Orthodoxy by Arctic Mission representatives was that the former church ostensibly had failed to deal adequately with alcohol abuse by not establishing temperance societies or organizations and counseling programs. In the 1980s, Russian Orthodox Church clergy and active members of the congregation were concerned about the social effects of alcohol and drug abuse. The church instituted youth camps to compete with those of Arctic Mission. In 1991, some residents of Nondalton perceived the jurisdiction of the Russian Orthodox church to be appropriately more restricted to the realm of spirituality than to that of social action. Those promoting this view pursued solutions to social problems through the auspices of other institutions. Others sought the solution to "social problems" by initiating a movement of cultural revitalization, associated, in part, with increased participation in and acceptance of Russian Orthodox doctrines and the practice of faith.

Figure 93 (above). St. Nicholas Russian Orthodox Church in Nondalton in 1987. The Old Nondalton church was dismantled, hauled to the new site, and reconstructed in this location. In 1991, community members, with the help of Father David and Father Michael, completed the construction and dedication of a new church, located adjacent to the old one. For the first time in the history of the inland Dena'ina of the Lake Clark area, there was a resident priest, Father Michael, who was related to other residents of Nondalton. **Figure 94** (below). The Saint Constantine and Helen Russian Orthodox church in Lime Village in 1985.

Figure 95 (above). The alter of the old St. Nicholas Russian Orthodox church in Nondalton, 1987.
Figure 96 (below). Residents of Nondalton participating in "starring" or "slavi" during Russian Orthodox Christmas in 1987. During the week of Russian Orthodox Christmas in January, each home is visited
by lay readers, other residents of the community, and visitors. The home and inhabitants are blessed, and
gifts and food exchanged between the hosts and those who have come to provide the blessings and prayers.
This party is entering the home of lay reader Nicholai Harry Balluta.

The persistence and tenacity of inland Dena'ina ideology, behavior, and overall world view in the 1980s, given the intensity and duration of contact with *Gasht'ana* brokers of cultural change, were indicators of the centrality of ideological and valuative systems to the sociocultural matrix of this society. Most adult inland Dena'ina during the first half of the 1900s recognized the potential for the demise of their culture and society and warned their children and grandchildren that life was changing too quickly and that things were getting "too modern." They encouraged those younger than themselves to remember that they were Dena'ina and "to not turn too much to White people."

To what does one attribute the degree of continuity of inland Dena'ina cosmology, ideology, and world view throughout nearly two centuries of contact with people who have viewed the world through "glasses" colored by different cultural logics and realities? Living and talking with the inland Dena'ina of the 1980s provided some surprisingly consistent insights into this question. Informal conversations between one another and with outsiders and the elicitation of oral histories from elders inevitably lead to many variations on the theme of how the inland Dena'ina related to, felt about, used, perceived, identified with, described, and feared for the land and resources that made up the core of their world. These topics and concerns were without temporal bounds and included both "empirical" and "non-empirical" phenomena. To travel across the country, to harvest resources with proper respect, to be able to live off the land with some degree of autonomy from the larger Dena'ina society, to be able to explain the changing faces of nature with the stories of long, long ago, and to identify oneself and kin with a particular territory or camp were spiritual experiences that extended far beyond the economic, social, or political interpretations normally provided by those from outside inland Dena'ina society. Above all else, the relationship between the inland Dena'ina and nature not only formed the core of their religious ideology and practice, but also provided for cultural, social, and individual survival in the face of a rapidly changing world.

Figure 97. Ruth Koktelash in Nondaiton, summer 1987, stripping the leaves off a fireweed stem. Ruth was one of the elders assisting in the production of a videotape on a fish caching technique used by the inland Dena'ina over half a century ago. She was an important repository of inland Dena'ina history in the 1980s. This book is dedicated to her and to another elder, Albert Wassillie, both of whom regrettably did not live to see this ethnography, to which they had dedicated so much time, completed. *Photograph Courtesy of IMPACT, Rasmuson Libarary, University of Alaska Fairbanks.*

CHAPTER 15

THE POWER OF THE LAND AND THE NATURE OF THE INLAND DENA'INA

*And we might also give thought to the legacy
that they [the Koyukon] have created, by which
the people continue to live today. What is this
legacy? We often remember ancient or
traditional cultures for the monuments they
have left behind — the megaliths of
Stonehenge, the temples of Bangkok, the
pyramids of Teotihuaca'n, the great ruins of
Machu Picchu. People like the Koyukon have
created no such monuments, but they have left
something that may be unique — greater and
more significant as a human achievement.
This legacy is the land itself, enduring and
essentially unchanged despite having supported human life for countless centuries.
Koyukon people and their ancestors, bound to a
strict code of morality governing their behavior
toward nature, have been the land's stewards
and caretakers. Only because they have
nurtured it so well does this great legacy of land
exist here today. . . .*

Richard K. Nelson,
Make Prayers to the Raven, 1983

A QUESTION OF SYMBIOSIS

As in the case of the Koyukon Athabaskans,
described in the quotation above, the inland
Dena'ina, resided within and extracted a living
from the Lake Clark and the adjacent upper Stony
River areas for minimally hundreds of years
preceding Euroamerican contact. Much of the
country they occupied and depended upon was
perceived to be a vast, pristine, and relatively
unoccupied wilderness by many non-Dena'ina
throughout the historic period and, most
relevantly in this context, over the past two
decades. It was during this more recent period
that the apparently unaltered, natural beauty of
the Lake Clark area contributed to the decision to
incorporate it into "public lands" in the form of
two federal conservation units, Lake Clark
National Park and Preserve, under the auspices of
ANCSA and ANILCA legislation in 1971 and 1980,
respectively. The inland Dena'ina, like the
Koyukon Athabaskans, left this legacy of
seemingly unmodified land and resources, principally because they viewed themselves as part of
the overall ecosystem and behaved accordingly.
They lived by a code of ethics and morality in their
relationship to nature that demanded respectful
treatment of all facets of the world they occupied,
including the fauna, flora, climate, and
topographical features. The inland Dena'ina
applied the same code of ethics and system of
values to the non-empirical entities of the cosmos.
Unlike the civilizations that constructed the
monuments described by Nelson (1983) above,
subarctic hunters and gatherers like the inland
Dena'ina strove not to modify the environments in
which they lived, but rather to maintain a state of
balance or harmony with the overall universe of
which they were a part. This was, they believed,
essential to the continuance of human existence.
The inland Dena'ina maintained this symbiotic
relationship with their environment with apparent success, while sustaining the physical,
spiritual, and social well-being of individuals and
their societies through time and space.

The integrity of inland Dena'ina culture and
society in the 1980s, despite the disruptions of the
historic period, seemed to be related integrally to
their continued presence on and use of the land.
While the apparently pristine "wilderness" of the
Lake Clark area may be perceived as the legacy of
the inland Dena'ina, conversely the existence of
the inland Dena'ina in the 1980s may be viewed as
a legacy of the land. The economic, kinship,
political, and spiritual dimensions of inland
Dena'ina society and culture, during what has
been referred to as the "traditional" or early
postcontact and contemporary periods, were
intimately connected to the relationships between
these indigenous people and the totality of their
environment. If inland Dena'ina society and
culture have persisted through time, as was
argued here, they did so within the context of an
enduring relationship with a specific geographic
area and all the living and non-living aspects of
this environment.

Northern Athabaskans gained recognition among
anthropologists for the diversity and flexibility of
their social and cultural adaptations spatially and
temporally (e.g., Helm 1965; McClellan 1987;
McKennan 1969; Nelson 1973, 1983; Osgood 1976
[1937] VanStone 1974). These populations inhabited a variety of ecosystems, including, but not
limited to, high latitude boreal forests, major
riverine valleys, and the maritime coasts of the
Pacific. Through time, they adapted successfully
to ecological changes, such as vacillations in
faunal populations and significant seasonal and

long-term climatic changes. They also demonstrated an equivalent proficiency for incorporating functional aspects of neighboring cultures and for accommodating or responding to both peaceful and disputed changes in the geographical distribution of neighboring societies of both Athabaskan and non-Athabaskan origin prior to the coming of Euroamericans. A question of major importance herein is to what degree was this characteristic Athabaskan flexibility functional in the context of Euroamerican contact with the inland Dena'ina specifically?

A continued relationship between the inland Dena'ina and the land was postulated as being essential to the continuity of their society and culture. The inland Dena'ina employed diverse and innovative strategies in accommodating Euroamerican contact and westernization from the last decade of the 1700s throughout the first half of the 1900s. During this temporal span, they maintained more or less "traditional" relationships with their environment. A review of these adaptive strategies provides a useful analytical tool for assessing more contemporary issues associated with changing land and resource ownership and access.

CONTINUITY AND ADAPTATION: INLAND DENA'INA LAND USE STRATEGIES

The inland Dena'ina were never isolated culturally or socially from other Dena'ina or adjacent *Dutna* or Yupik populations. They participated in indigenous trade networks, extending from Cook Inlet, down the Stony River to its confluence with the Kuskokwim, down the Mulchatna River to areas occupied by Nushagak drainage Yup'ik, and to the areas of Lake Iliamna occupied by neighboring *Dutna*. Trade goods preceded direct Euroamerican contact. The intensity of inland Dena'ina participation in and dependence upon metal technology, trade beads, tobacco, and tea were exacerbated by the location of Russian fur trading facilities at several proximal sites on Cook Inlet and, later, at Lake Iliamna. The inland Dena'ina were more isolated from the activities of the Russian era fur traders than were their coastal relatives. It was not until the first decades of the 1800s that Russians penetrated north and into the interior of Alaska and more directly threatened the existence of indigenous and highly functional trade networks. However, these economic activities did not alter the fundamental nature of the

relationship of the inland Dena'ina with their surrounding environment.

The Russian Orthodox church directly penetrated the territory of the inland Dena'ina by the 1840s. However, the church was more interested in overlaying the dogma, rituals, and trappings of this version of Christianity than in wholesale ideological and economic assimilation. There is no ethnohistoric evidence that the Russian Orthodox clergy fully comprehended the spiritual dimensions of the relationship between the inland Dena'ina and their natural environment. The absence of resident clergy and the church's reliance on local readers did not promote year-round inland Dena'ina settlement in or about chapel or church sites or other significant social and cultural change, although clergy may have influenced the relocation of Mulchatna and Kijik populations. Additionally, the church did not encourage sedentism at the expense of reduced participation in trapping, as such policies would have been met with disfavor on the part of the Russian-American Company. By the American period, the inland Dena'ina considered Russian Orthodoxy, as it had been integrated, to be more of a "traditional" than introduced institution. Continuity of inland Dena'ina spirituality and syncretism were more enduring than conflict in the association of the Dena'ina with the Russian Orthodox church.

The inland Dena'ina were impacted by epidemics in the 1800s, resulting in a population decline throughout at least the first half of the 1900s. The relative magnitude of population decimations among the inland group was not as well documented as that of coastal Dena'ina populations. The factor of isolation may have played a role in mitigating the spread of disease among the inland Dena'ina.

For example, Wolfe (1982) argued that the major impact of the epidemic of 1900 on Alaska Natives was the synergistic effects of disease and the corresponding collapse of economic and social support systems among groups in which large numbers of people were ill either simultaneously or successively. Manifestations of this phenomenon included the abandonment of villages and territories; consolidation of populations, usually in the vicinity of western trading facilities; increased sedentism; and a corresponding disruption of traditional economic activities. In the case of the inland Dena'ina, centralization preceded sedentism, but it does not appear that territories were abandoned or economic activities ceased during this period of time. Additionally, there is no evidence that areas used by the inland Dena'ina for resource harvesting diminished in size or that their reliance on locally harvested staples decreased until well into the middle of the 1900s. These later changes were more directly related to the commencement of mandatory western education in federal schools and a decline in the fur market than to the effects of disease.

By the early 1880s, the commercial salmon fishery in Bristol Bay had influenced the inland Dena'ina by providing sources of commercially-produced goods and, a decade later, employment. The participation of men in commercial fishing during mid-summer months encouraged relocation of some Stony River Dena'ina to Kijik and then to Old Nondalton. Women, children, and elderly or infirm adults were left to conduct the majority of the local subsistence fishery in the absence of the men. The Bristol Bay commercial fishery was a significant factor in depleting salmon runs on the Kvichak and Nushagak rivers in the early years of its operation. The Dena'ina responded to this economic crisis by fishing the Stony and Mulchatna river drainages and by increasing their reliance on freshwater fish and small game.

Throughout the early decades of the 1900s, both commercial trapping and fishing provided an impetus for the development of federal and territorial fish and game regulations. That was the first time during which the inland Dena'ina were affected by a resource management regime derived from without their own system of land tenure and use and reflective of western concepts and values. Increasing attention on the part of governmental representatives to the harvesting activities of both indigenous and non-indigenous peoples paralleled the expansion of federal and territorial interest in and control over the land used and occupied by the inland Dena'ina. The influx of miners to this area at the turn of the century increased resource competition and introduced the concept of private property. The inland Dena'ina of the 1980s reflected upon their apprehension about the potential repercussions of ignoring these poorly understood, western precepts regarding the taking of game and fish. In some cases and during particular years, trapping territories were changed to accommodate such regulations. For the most part, however, internally functional systems of communication enabled residents to continue harvesting and using long-standing methods, means, and periods without suffering externally generated sanctions.

Generally, what were some of the other responses of the inland Dena'ina to 150 years of Euroamerican contact? The four local bands were consolidated into two by the 1930s. Increased sedentism was not a corollary of centralization until after the late 1950s and early 1960s. In fact, villages continued to function as they had in the past. They remained centers for inland Dena'ina ceremonialism, such as potlatches, and the focus for the continuity of social and political interaction among and between community residents. People continued to move between hunting, fishing, and trapping camps, with periodic visits to the community for the distribution of harvested resources through mechanisms of reciprocity. Additionally, rituals associated with the sporadic visits of Russian Orthodox priests or the celebration of church holidays by lay readers took place in the community context. Provisioning of the nomadic inland Dena'ina with trade goods, although still very limited at this time, also occurred in the context of the village or at nearby commercial trade centers. The seasonal round of the early 1900s basically remained intact until the 1950s and 1960s.

Changes in the seasonal cycle and land use patterns resulting from early Euroamerican contact involved an intensification and lengthening of extant trapping seasons and the possible development of the concept of individually "owned" trap lines, which were the "property" of males based on principles of usufruct rights and inheritance. Village residential units or households reflected a trend toward nuclear family occupation and away from the large, semisubterranean, multiple family dwellings of the prehistoric and early historic periods (VanStone and Townsend 1970). However, the social organization of hunting, trapping, and fishing remained grounded in the domestic unit organized around more traditional principles of matriclan affiliation.

The introduction of western, institutional education ushered the inland Dena'ina into a contact period with decidedly greater implications for indigenous settlement patterns and local resource uses. Although the first school marginally available to the inland Dena'ina had been established at the site of Old Iliamna by the end of the first decade of the 1900s, few people chose to send their children there. By 1929, the tentacles of western educational bureaucracy penetrated directly into inland Dena'ina country, resulting in the establishment of a school at Old Nondalton.

Parents were coerced by officials representing federal policy into affording their children the "opportunity" to receive an elementary education. Some families adapted to this situation by employing the strategy of leaving school-aged children with elderly parents or older children in the village. These adults continued the seasonal round of resource harvest activities with children younger or older than the age of mandatory school attendance. In some cases, men continued their seasonal round with greater mobility from a central-based village, since the use of dog traction was an alternative mode of transport after the turn of the century. In other instances, men left adult women and children in the village for parts of the seasonal round, particularly during winter trapping and hunting activities. During spring and fall, however, many adult women accompanied their husbands, fathers, and other male relatives with children who theoretically were mandated to attend school, much to the dismay of resident teachers.

According to elders in Nondalton in the 1980s, giving up their mobility was perceived to be the greatest personal, social, and cultural sacrifice made in the context of western contact. During a visit to the old village site of Telaquana, Agnes Cusma responded to a question about the impact of schools on the inland Dena'ina.

> *Well, they [Dena'ina people in the past] let peo-*
> *ple move around. That's why we know how to*
> *make our living out in the sticks. You take*
> *those kids down there [in Nondalton] now —*
> *nobody would [know how to make a living] —*
> *drop them off like this, they're going to starve.*
> *They wouldn't know which way to survive even*
> *though they may know how to read and write*
> (Agnes Cusma, interview, 1986).

By the end of the 1920s, a much greater array of western goods was being used by the inland Dena'ina, although wild game, fish, and plant resources remained the principal components of their diet. Access to western commodities required sporadic employment, such as commercial fishing, hauling freight and mail by dog team, longshoring, providing meat and logs to miners, and trapping until the fur market became depressed after World War II. Although cash was always in very short supply, the integration of subsistence and cash economies was well underway. However, the subsistence component of this economy remained central to the economic, social, and cultural well-being of the inland Dena'ina.

Western technology facilitated the sustained mobility of large segments of this society in the face of increased pressures toward sedentism. Dog traction replaced travel by foot and the use of dogs for pack. Large, plank watercraft, with which the inland Dena'ina had become familiar while participating in the commercial fishery, displaced birch bark canoes and skin-covered *baidarki* and *niggiday*. A few families had access to small outboard motors and commonly towed the boats of relatives or partners. By the 1950s, aircraft transport provided more diverse and efficient provisioning of local stores and increased opportunities for the inland Dena'ina to travel outside of their area.

Well into the middle of the 1900s, many inland Dena'ina families employed multiple strategies for perpetuating a way of life that focused upon their longstanding relationships with the land and all it provided. This bond was expressed not only in those endeavors normally described as "economic" in nature but also in the configuration of the social and ideological systems of the inland Dena'ina. None of these changes fundamentally inhibited or restricted the ability of the inland Dena'ina to move across, use, and participate in more "traditionally" spiritual relationships with the territory associated with their society. By that time, there were a few resident non-Dena'ina; the concept of private ownership was introduced in the forms of mining claims, allotments, and homesteads; externally generated fish and game regulations proliferated; and competition for resources by large game hunters and sport fishers increased. Nonetheless, the area of the inland Dena'ina remained relatively remote. Ways in which local people used "their country" were mostly a matter of personal and family choice, as dictated by available economic and social alternatives and pressures. Western technology provided the vehicle for maintaining extensive land use from larger and more permanently established communities, especially after the settlement of the new site of Nondalton in the early 1940s.

It was, ironically, the passage of the Alaska Native Claims Settlement Act (ANCSA, 1971) and the associated allocation and designation of federal and state lands under both ANCSA and the Alaska National Interest Lands Conservation Act (ANILCA, 1980) that emerged as the greatest potential threats to inland Dena'ina economic, social, political, and overall cultural continuity in the 1980s. These forms of legislation directly or indirectly provided conditions for the formation of profit-oriented Dena'ina organizations mirrored after western corporations and the associated sale of inland Dena'ina lands. They also designated most lands used by the inland Dena'ina as "public lands." These conditions intensified competition and conflicts between what was termed "sport," "commercial," "non-consumptive," "recreational," and "subsistence" uses of fish and game resources, thereby leading to high profile, external management and regulation of those resources important to local people.

OWNERSHIP AND ACCESS: CULTURAL SYSTEMS IN CONFLICT

The legislative change in the status of Alaska from territory to state in 1958, implemented in 1959, was to be followed by increasing efforts on the part of state and federal governments, special interest groups, and Alaska Natives to settle issues related to land claims and rights, natural resource extraction, economic development, and concerns about the growing population of Alaska in the context of finite resources. To some, Alaska was conceptualization as the "last frontier." Depending upon the perspectives of interested parties, it was a country abounding in resources and lands available for exploitation or, alternatively, for incomparable aesthetic pleasures. It was the source of wealth and opportunity for the rugged individualist, a place on the fringes of governmental control and interference. Others perceived that the "frontier" era had come to a close, and that Alaska had "come of age" with statehood. From this perspective, Alaska was seen as essential to the well-being of the populace of the United States at large.

Alaska was promoted by conservationists as the last vestige of wilderness and natural beauty, once typifying the United States. Therefore, as was common in the conservationist ideologies of the United States (Callicott 1982), it required preservation in its allegedly virgin, unaltered state. Developmental interests argued that Alaska was a critical, if not the last, "cache" of extractive resources needed to turn the wheels of the growing industrialized society dependent upon petrochemicals. Alaska Natives, who, at best, had been treated as second-class citizens throughout most of the Euroamerican history, recognized the implications of the interests of these outside groups and wanted their own stake in and rights to land and resources preserved and protected under law. It was clear to Alaska Natives that in the spectrum of debates about how "best" Alaska and

its resources could be used, they had to seek some way to protect their culturally different and vastly diverse ways of life and those of subsequent generations.

For the inland Dena'ina, as for most other Alaska Natives, this protection came with the passages of ANCSA in 1971 and ANILCA in 1980, although, in hindsight, such was not to be the case. Both of these legislative acts ultimately resulted in the formal privatization and publicization of lands, which once constituted the territory of the inland Dena'ina through unwritten laws, norms, and principles of land tenure and resource use.

Although the criteria for village affiliation with any one of 12 regional corporations formed under ANCSA was claimed to be cultural, linguistic, and ecological homogeneity, that was not the case for the inland Dena'ina. Lime Village on the Stony River was placed within the boundaries of the predominantly Yup'ik Calista Corporation, Inc. Nondalton and the southwestern portions of Lake Clark and Six-Mile Lake became part of a largely Yup'ik organization, Bristol Bay Native Corporation (BBNC). The northeastern portion of Lake Clark, including the sites of Kijik and Telaquana, was incorporated into the principally coastal Dena'ina and otherwise ethnically and culturally diverse urban entity, Cook Inlet Region, Inc. (CIRI). While Nondalton and Lime Village were allocated land as community corporations, when eventually conveyed, such acreage represented only a fraction of the territory used by members of this society into the 1980s. The three regional, profit corporations (Calista, BBNC, and CIRI) relevant in this context had subsurface rights and consequent control over many aspects of the territory conveyed to the village corporations and those areas designated as "historic and cemetery sites" under 14(h)1 of ANCSA.

With the exception of the estimated 74 Native allotment applications, each potentially entitling the holder to 160 acres, either conveyed or pending in 1989 (Gerhard pers. comm. 1989) as a result of the Alaska Native Allotment Act of 1906, and some private parcels, including "homesites," the vast majority of the territory occupied and used by the inland Dena'ina was designated as federally-controlled "public lands" and included within the boundaries of Lake Clark National Park and Preserve (LCNPP). The management of this park and preserve was intended to focus on the protection of the Bristol Bay watershed, scenic wilderness beauty, habitat, and the well-being of particular game species (LCNPP 1986:10), as well as to carry out other general goals of the National

Park Service (NPS) Organic Act of 1916 (LCNPP 1986:10). Section 1302 of ANILCA provided NPS in general, and LCNPP in specific, with the authority to acquire additional lands within the park and preserve by means of purchase, donation, exchange, or other methods (USNPS, LCNPP 1986:11-12).

To date, land issues, as opposed to resource access, involving Kijik Corporation and LCNPP generally have been resolved in the spirit of compromise, conciliation, and cooperation. Though many residents of Nondalton resented the formation of the park and preserve, others perceived "their country" to be better protected by federal than state governmental authority. For example, LCNPP management was concerned about the protection of the Tazimina River drainage, which enters Six-Mile Lake almost directly across from the village of Nondalton. In 1989, Kijik Corporation and BBNC received approximately one million dollars from NPS for easements along approximately one-third of the Tazimina River (Hutchison pers. comm. 1989; Kijik Corporation pers. comm. 1989). In exchange, Kijik agreed not to develop or subdivide the areas contained within this easement. In 1989, LCNPP management was interested in arriving at a similar agreement for the remaining two-thirds of the Tazimina drainage.

Some inland Dena'ina concurred with LCNPP's attempts to thwart an effort on the part of a Port Alsworth group known as Tanalian Corporation to receive title to 2,240 acres of land under the auspices of ANCSA. Since the inland Dena'ina once occupied Tanalian Point, that site was perceived to be part of their territory rather than that of the members of Tanalian Corporation or NPS. This feeling, on the part of most Nondalton residents, was extended to other sites on Lake Clark and adjacent areas now owned by private individuals or businesses.

Additionally, Kijik Corporation, Nondalton City and Traditional councils, CIRI, and NPS jointly and successfully fought the efforts of a non-Native individual to obtain the historic site of Kijik as a homesite. The inland Dena'ina were greatly concerned about the granting of a homesite to a private party at the location of Kijik, which was the home of elderly inland Dena'ina now living in Nondalton and the ancestors of the majority of this group. Furthermore, this site contained 200 to 300 Dena'ina graves, from which the claimant allegedly destroyed Russian Orthodox crosses, and substantial and irreplaceable material remains of

inland Dena'ina cultural history. The site remained an important location for both fishing and hunting activities of the inland Dena'ina throughout the 1980s.

In the late 1980s, the issue of greatest actual and potential conflict between Kijik Corporation and LCNPP was the recreational homesite development at Keyes Point. Although this issue was discussed diplomatically on both sides, it was the intent of Kijik Corporation that the development of these summer homesites would benefit stockholders and residents of Nondalton economically. It was the concern of LCNPP and NPS staff that the Keyes Point development could result in environmental degradation and increased consumptive uses of the park and preserve, antithetical to dominant NPS philsophies regarding the conservation of "public lands" (Callicott 1982). Negotiations between Kijik Corporation and LCNPP management resulted in stipulations in the homesite contracts which met some of the federal agency's concerns.

Lastly, control over inland Dena'ina land outside of LCNPP potentially may be affected by the formation of the Lake and Peninsula Borough in 1989. This political unit included a culturally, economically, and linguistically diverse area, extending from Ivanof Bay and Perryville on the Alaska Peninsula to the southwest, to Port Alsworth in the northeast, including Nondalton to the west and the majority of the western shoreline of Cook Inlet. The formation of the borough passed by a slim margin in 1989. Glen Alsworth, Sr., of Port Alsworth ran unopposed as first mayor of the new borough.

In general terms, by the 1980s, the indigenous inland Dena'ina systems of land use, occupancy, and tenure had been undermined, in large part, by changing land statuses emergent directly and indirectly from external sources of authority. Because of the privatization and publicization of what was once inland Dena'ina territory, people no longer were free to move across, establish camps, harvest resources, or assert their identity within the area occupied by them and their ancestors. In effect, they had lost much of the flexibility of more traditional land use associated with usufruct rights and social and spiritual connections to their area. The long-term implications of these changes in land status for the cultural and social survival of the inland Dena'ina were unknown and remained a critical question for community leaders in 1991.

In the 1980s, the other major category of issues — setting inland Dena'ina cultural values, concepts, ideologies, and behavior into conflict with those of the larger western society — related to access to fish, game, and plant resources. Behnke (1978:104), in a study intended to anticipate the effects of the formation of LCNPP on inland Dena'ina economy and related features of society, noted the potential for conflict in the case of regulations controlling the harvest of fish, game, and plant resources. In the case of access to local resources in the 1980s, management authorities involved the Alaska Department of Fish and Game (ADFG) and NPS. There were multiple issues since the passage of the state subsistence law in 1978 that implied or involved cultural conflict throughout this period.

From statehood until 1978, all resource harvests, with the exception of those specifically under international or federal jurisdiction, were regulated by the Alaska Department of Fish and Game (ADFG) on state and private lands; navigable waters; and, under U.S. Department of the Interior guidelines, federal lands. The passage of the state's "subsistence law" in 1978 was intended to continue state management of resources on federal lands by compliance with the priority for rural subsistence uses on national lands mandated by ANILCA. Both state and federal policies of resource management created more restrictive conditions for the harvest of local resources for "subsistence" and, in the case of salmon and furbearers, commercial purposes. Restrictions came in the form of often arbitrarily determined seasons, bag limits, gender of animals harvested, means of access, hunting and fishing technology, and other management tools. Many regulations were culturally irrelevant or insensitive to the conditions under which Alaska Natives in general, and the inland Dena'ina specifically, lived. A series of legal challenges to the state's attempts to manage fish and game within the subsistence priority for rural uses mandated by federal law resulted in the assumption of management of resources on federal lands by federal agencies in the early 1990s. As of this writing, consistent federal management policies had not been finalized.

Prior to the assumption of federal management on national lands, state management problems were exacerbated by additional regulations associated with the harvest of resources in national parks, preserves, or other categories of "public lands." For example, subsistence hunting was permitted by law in newly created national land units, such as LCNPP, and regulations were to be developed in conjunction with a subsistence commission composed of local representatives. While access to hunting within the park proper was restricted to those "domiciled" within a "resident zone" and who qualified as "rural," the identification of individuals considered eligible remained complex and unclarified in 1991 and was of major concern to Nondalton residents. In the case of LCNPP, an emotional and potentially explosive issue regarded the harvest of trees for fuel or building materials, a resource issue of significant concern to NPS managers throughout the 1980s.

Fundamental to cultural conflicts regarding management regimes and associated fish and game regulations in the early 1990s, as in earlier decades, was a fundamental belief on the part of rural Alaska Natives and state and federal agencies that each knew and applied sound principles of wildlife management and distrusted those abilities of the others.

Native concepts of management were based on indigenous values and rules for behaviors regarding the entirety of environments in which hunters and gatherers lived and made a living, including all fauna and flora. Such systems also incorporated both empirical and non-empirical rules and sanctions emergent from "traditional" management systems. It has been argued that hunters and gatherers worldwide had systems which operated to maintain maximum sustained yields and monitored ecological dynamics and processes affecting the occurrence and abundance of resources (e.g., Williams and Hunn 1982). Nelson (1982) argued this point for the Koyukon Athabaskans in the 1970s, stating that their system included both ecological and empirical dimensions and incorporated ". . . an interpretation of natural history which we [westerners] would call 'supernatural'" (Nelson 1982:211). He went on to say that the ideological knowledge of the Koyukon included a well-developed conservation ethic and strict prohibitions against excessive use and waste. Such transgressions were punished by supernatural forces. Thus, empirical and "supernatural" knowledge were combined, in the case of the Koyukon, to create an effective management system for locally available resources.

Two examples of the distrust of the inland Dena'ina of state fish and game management were illustrative of intrinsic cultural conflict between indigenous and western management systems. Albert Wassillie, who was a member of the local

Fish and Game Advisory Committee in the 1980s, reiterated on several occasions the lack of understanding on the part of ADFG biologists of the interactions between beavers, salmon spawning, and bears in the vicinity of the old village site of Kijik:

> *All those places the beaver damage, all those spawning grounds. And trying to get the fish and wildlife [making reference to ADFG], you know, [to understand]. But everywhere in Kijik, the spawning grounds is spoiled cause of the beaver, nobody traps the beaver and it is getting worse and worse. The fish and wildlife wouldn't believe that. They try to tell us where the beaver is, that's where the salmon likes to go. That isn't true. So, there's no more spawning grounds there. The bears have a hard time to get these salmon too 'cause it's flooded out* (Albert Wassillie, interview, 1985).

In another example, Mike Delkittie, also a member of the local Fish and Game Advisory Committee, was lamenting the lack of understanding on the part of ADFG biologists and managers and international migratory waterfowl governing bodies regarding inland Dena'ina access to and use of these species during spring and fall seasons, the former being considered illegal for many decades:

> *There's a lot of bird migration through here in spring time which we've been kind of arguing with the fish and game guys about. But we don't get too much chance of that [migratory waterfowl hunting] in the fall time 'cause they don't migrate back through this area. They come through pretty heavy in the spring time, but when it's time to hunt them [the legal fall season], they [ducks and geese] go back along the coastline. We get nothing through here. They just kind of come through, then they make a U–turn or something like that, so those guys [regional members of the Fish and Game Advisory Committee] are still battling that* (Mike Delkittie, interview, 1986).

In the case of views commonly held by state and federal resource managers, it was often assumed that an understanding of wildlife ecology and the application of measures to ensure sustained yield required a relatively extensive and specialized formal western education. Since the philosophy of western wildlife management emerged from societies with economies based on the domestication of animals and plants for sustenance, it customarily is assumed that hunters and gatherers "exploit" resources at every opportunity without regard for the overall well-being of animal and plant stocks and general ecological conditions. In addition, it is conjectured by resource managers and much of the lay populace

that hunters and gatherers traditionally maintained relatively small populations and used "primitive technologies," thereby providing less threat specifically to animal populations than do modern foragers. This assumption leads to several conclusions. Since modern hunting and gathering societies have grown in size and acquired and employed western technology in subsistence endeavors, it follows, given the western scientific paradigm, that modern foragers have become a deadly threat to the well-being of faunal and floral populations and overall environments. They lack western education and, therefore, the knowledge to conserve or protect resources. Consequently, it is necessary to impose external management regimes in order to ensure the survival of endangered species, the sustained yield of all fauna and flora, and an overall healthy environment. If non-empirical indigenous ideologies for resource management were even identified by biologists, they generally were thought to be antithetical to the concepts of western science underlying governmental fish and game management regimes.

Fledgling efforts to bring about a greater degree of mutual understanding and trust between Alaskan Natives and state and federal resource management and regulatory agencies and staff commenced statewide during the 1980s but not without considerable resistance on all sides. Included in these efforts were attempts at statewide, national, and international communication aimed at achieving mutual recognition of different, but equally credible, bases of knowledge. All would agree, however, that by 1991, there was a significant gap between indigenous and western resource management concepts, values, and systems. Concurrently, the development of mutual respect for the relevant knowledge of these very different regimes had not been realized, nor had issues of conflict regarding resource access and harvest diminished. For example, Nondalton residents, who customarily relied on brown bear as a source of fat, meat, and, in past years raw materials, found the state regulation permitting them to take only one bear every four years incomprehensible. The inland Dena'ina felt that this seemingly irrational regulation caused them severe nutritional, cultural, and spiritual hardship; was intended to favor sport users of this resource and their professional guides; and had no sound non-empirical or empirical foundation.

The nature of the processes of privatization and publicization of land ownership and largely external, non–Dena'ina control of resource access suggest that the inland Dena'ina now face their greatest threat and challenge to the maintenance of their social and cultural identity. Land and resource managers, planners, and those in positions of power to make public policy should be informed and carry forth their mandates responsibly in the face of these concerns. In the 1980s, despite problems associated with functioning economically and politically within a culturally different and large nation-state, the inland Dena'ina were aware of the challenges and opportunities facing them as a society and culture. They were cognizant of the fact that maintenance of their relationships to the land was central to their continued viability as a society, the integrity of their culture, and their well-being as individuals.

LASTING IMPRESSIONS

Five years of living with the inland Dena'ina, sharing in their rich oral history, participating in their celebrations, empathizing with them in times of grief, learning about the things they value most and those which they disdain, accompanying them on hunting and fishing forays by boat in summer and fall and on snowmachines during winter months, and hearing them recount the changes they have experienced in their collective and individual lifetimes have left what can only be termed "lasting impressions" of a society and peoples, a life way abstracted in this ethnography. Those aspects of inland Dena'ina beliefs, values, and behaviors, which serve as the threads of the fabric of their culture, made up the content of these indelible impressions and were highlighted herein.

Anthropologists have characterized Athabaskan cultures as being adaptively flexible. The inland Dena'ina of the 1980s highlighted the ultimate reality of this often stereotypic, impersonal, sterile, and hollow-sounding generalization. Several examples illustrate this point.

When this study commenced, the non–Dena'ina co-author operated under the assumption that those who comprised inland Dena'ina society were merely the residents of Nondalton and Lime Village. In a matter of weeks, it was clear that a significant sector of the functional society flowed freely between Anchorage and the villages, as medical, educational, employment, recreational, and other needs dictated. These were not migrant "urban Natives" but rather families and individu-

als who continued to participate fully in the social, economic, political, and cultural life of their Dena'ina society. They left "home" temporarily to attain certain goals which they identified as important in the contemporary context. As in the past, they valued mobility in and of itself. Yet, there was never any question about their identity as inland Dena'ina, any loss of recognition of kin and associated reciprocal obligations, or doubt about where "home" really was.

As we gathered kinship terms and the names of matriclans and teased out the nature of interclan association and reciprocity in the context of this study, older inland Dena'ina, initially delighted with the opportunity to discuss their favorite topic of kinship, became concerned that younger members of the community were not adequately fluent in this realm of knowledge. As a result, they informally suggested to the only Dena'ina teacher that children be taught their clan affiliation in school. In fact, the topic of teaching matriclan affiliation and genealogical connections to young people in the home was on the agenda of more than one traditional council and Kijik Corporation shareholder meeting. At an informal meeting held during spring 1991 regarding cultural revitalization and the mental, physical, and social health of the residents of Nondalton, the importance of the transmission of this knowledge between generations was reiterated. Inland Dena'ina elders, concerned about the fact that the children of inmarried females were left clanless, conducted several spontaneous adoptions, thereby providing a place in the kinship system for inmarried women and their offspring.

In the realm of land use, during a trip up the Chulitna River in search of moose or caribou during a wet and cold early September day, our boat party landed on what appeared, to the untrained eye, to be an inhospitable river bank. We were all very wet and cold and had not eaten for some time. Within a matter of minutes, this location was transformed into a comfortable and warm camp, as had undoubtedly occurred many times in the past. Spruce poles were located and modified to provide the structure for the tent. Relatively dry wood, kindling, and moss were gathered adeptly and placed inside what first appeared to be merely a rusted fuel container. This object was quickly transformed into an efficient stove for warming us and heating water and food. Spruce boughs became our floor and were more thickly distributed in that part of the tent which was to be our sleeping area. Water was collected from the river and fish lines set for obtaining fresh food for dinner. Within an hour, we had finished eating and, over tea, older members of the party were telling of the many times in the past that this place had provided shelter for individuals or groups of hunters, trappers, and fishermen. Each and every physical detail of the site was familiar, and many points in the surrounding area had place names in Dena'ina. Additionally, on this day, the site had been surveyed for any evidence of proximal moose and caribou. Thus, this camp provided not only shelter from the elements but, more importantly, was one of many places in which inland Dena'ina traditions were perpetuated on an annual basis.

Another feature of inland Dena'ina culture that stood in stark contrast to the contemporary, western emphasis on modernization and disdain for the obsolescence of the past is the importance of traditional knowledge in Dena'ina society, as transmitted through verbal forms of communication. It commonly is thought that this realm of knowledge among hunters and gatherers is principally historical in orientation and content, as implied in categorizing such phenomena "oral history." It is often assumed by western scholars and lay readers that oral histories have negligible applicability to the present or future. Such is not the case among the inland Dena'ina. Regardless of the topic of interviews conducted during the course of this research, adults of all ages called upon a knowledge base encompassed in such "histories." This repository of inland Dena'ina wisdom explained every aspect of the world of the past and present and some expectations for the future. Traditional stories included information concerning how all life came to be, the relationships between the living world and other features of nature and between entities of the empirical and non-empirical cosmos, the reasons for particular rules of behavior among Dena'ina and between them and other peoples and beings, the sanctions which result from breaking social and cultural norms, and values and their significance to the well-being of society and individuals. This knowledge was not perceived to be a relic of past times but rather essential to the continuity of life at whatever point in time. Contemporary misfortunes, successes, prosperity, unusual occurrences, expectations and their potential for fulfillment, community and individual problems requiring resolution, and many other phenomena were explained in the context of this base of knowledge that was firmly grounded in the past or in "tradition" but flexible enough in nature to accommodate a changing world.

For the most part, the inland Dena'ina of the 1980s saw their tradition as viable and applicable to the solution of contemporary problems and challenges. They perceived it to be as valuable, though not a sole alternative, to knowledge transmitted in the context of western educational institutions. They saw inland Dena'ina and *Gasht'ana* knowledge as being complementary in the face of modern world issues, but felt that the former was more significant in providing for the continuity of their society as distinctively Dena'ina in nature. This was a value held by most people of all ages. The inland Dena'ina of the 1980s were optimistic, albeit not to the point of complacency, that traditional values and norms had applicability in contemporary times and that they, as a society and culture, would endure into the future.

At the end of the study period, a well-meaning *Gasht'ana* planner from Bristol Bay Native Association was requested by the non-Dena'ina mayor of Nondalton to assist the community in developing a five-year plan. In the course of the meetings to accomplish this task, which were attended by a small number but broad cross-section of residents of the community, participants were asked to identify "problems" which needed solving and goals which the people of Nondalton wished to achieve and by what means. This was to be the first step in the planning process.

It was apparent to the residents of Nondalton and anyone who knew them well that there were problems intrinsic to this endeavor, the greatest being that neither the meeting agenda nor the planner had any grounding in inland Dena'ina culture or tradition. The content, process, and forum were inconsistent with inland Dena'ina sociopolitical processes still operative in the 1980s, both covertly and overtly. Although appreciative of the efforts of the planner, outside the context of the meeting, many middle-aged inland Dena'ina adults humorously and satirically referred to the fact that their future was assured through this planning process. In an equally humorous vein, however, they expressed interest in the perception on the part of the planner that they lacked the ability to determine the course of their own future without a written plan of limited duration; guided, at least initially, by an outsider; employing a process foreign to their culture; and, most importantly, in the absence of the application of their traditional knowledge base. This meeting stood in stark contrast to another with similar broad intent conducted by Nondalton residents in the spring of 1991. Although the forum was a meeting, its attendance was informally generated, its conduct was undertaken by many adults in attendance, people of all ages were urged to speak, and problems and solutions were identified by the inland Dena'ina within their own cultural context.

In Nondalton in the 1980s, there was a concern on the part of adults that young people were spending too much time in school and watching television and videos, thereby not paying adequate attention to incorporating the traditional knowledge base in their overall socialization. By way of contrast, young people expressed overtly and covertly a sense of growing inland Dena'ina cultural revitalization. For example, they valued selecting Dena'ina spouses and raising their children in the community. They valued the opinions and knowledge of elders and, although mostly not bilingual, commonly employed Dena'ina kinship terms and expressions. They often professed their ability to understand, if not speak, their Native language, and many criticized the policy of the school district in discontinuing bilingual education in recent years. Most vehemently, they expressed their identification with the land and its resources and highly valued their abilities to hunt, fish, trap, and gather. They put a premium on having the temporal, spatial, and technological opportunities to conduct these activities.

To inland Dena'ina of all ages, a person like Albert Wassillie was highly valued for his knowledge. He was perceived to be a living repository of traditional wisdom, a fluent Dena'ina speaker, and the only person in the village who had become fully literate in his Native language. Residents lauded his efforts to use this aptitude to put inland Dena'ina tradition into written form. In some ways, Albert epitomized the importance of the land and its resources to the inland Dena'ina of the 1980s by recalling his effort to live autonomously but with the land in the 1970s:

One year, it was 1971, I went to chatchitnu to trap. I spent three months up there by myself. I just took an airplane up there and stayed all winter. I had an axe, couple of axes, and Swede saw and snowshoes, and tent. I didn't even have a radio. I never see people for three months — like a hermit. There was so much animal up there, I couldn't starve. Caribou, they'd go in my yard, so many caribou, lots of moose. When I was young, I used to travel alone. I used to like to go alone. But now, I couldn't do it. I've had a couple of [health] difficulties. That time I stayed three months, and then the plane came up. I was almost out of food like coffee, sugar, and tea. . . . But I caught 16 beaver in one week. I will never forget this time (Albert Wassillie, interview, 1985).

Unfortunately, Albert, who gave so much to this ethnography, did not live to see its completion. If one is to talk about lasting impressions of inland Dena'ina culture, they can be seen as embodied in Albert Wassillie, Pete and Ruth Koktelash, Sophie Austin, Agnes Cusma, and others like them. These are people who behaved as and perceived themselves to be traditional inland Dena'ina but were able to excel in the world which had vastly changed during their lifetimes. They had the respect of inland Dena'ina and *Gasht'ana* alike. Their commitment to and association with their environment were preeminent in their lives, even when they became physically unable to undertake the activities they commonly had undertaken in their youth. They looked to the past for wisdom, but never with bitterness, and to the future with optimism and confidence in themselves and in the ability of their culture and society to survive intact. These values and qualities, aspirations and optimism, were more apparent in many of the young people in 1991 than appeared to be the case in 1985. To the authors, this was the essence of the lasting impressions and legacy of the inland Dena'ina.

Figure 98. Pete Koktelash, thinking of his years as an inland Dena'ina and Bristol Bay fisherman and sharing stories about those days with younger people in Nondalton. This photograph was taken in 1986. In the early summer of 1991, at the age of 87, Pete remained one of the most knowledgeable and vigorous elders in the community. During June 1991, Pete hosted a high school teacher from Wisconsin, who was taking a field course to learn about the inland Dena'ina. With a twinkling eye, Pete told him stories about his life, showed him photographs, and taught him to fish in the local style, thereby, in only a short time, meaningfully sharing with another, albeit a *Gasht'ana,* what it meant to be an inland Dena'ina man.

APPENDIX A

FISH AND GAME RESOURCES USED BY THE INLAND DENA'INA OF NONDALTON

This appendix lists animal species used during the lifetimes of inland Dena'ina from the Lake Clark and upper Stony River areas residing in Nondalton between 1985 and 1990. For each species, names of each animal are provided in inland Dena'ina; English, employing the most commonly used term in the study area; and Latin, respectively. Species are presented in categories of fish, game, and fowl. Attempts to organize these species within these larger categories or for the list overall by the criterion of relative "importance" was not possible, as no methodology was employed for eliciting these data on the basis of such a measure. That is, "importance" was not quantified in terms of numbers of animals harvested, relative contribution to the overall diet, food versus raw material sources, or any other criteria. Relative importance of particular species varied by seasons, years, the place of origin and sex of the person discussing the animal in question, and other sociocultural factors. For example, periodic demographic fluctuations of some species contributed to a situation in which others were relatively more important, at that time, because of their stability or abundance. Stability and abundance of any particular resource were distinct from the criterion of dietary preference. Preference also varied from season to season, year to year, place of birth and lifetime residences of persons selecting particular species. Other criteria employed by local people to calculate, at any given time, the relative "importance" of a particular species included the overall configuration of resource availability, ease of harvest, sex and age roles, and other sociocultural variables. Future research usefully might focus, methodologically and theoretically, on gathering data on the basis of these variables and others.

Animal species that were traded to the inland Dena'ina, but harvested in other areas, were not included in this context. Plants were omitted, as they are the subject of a separate publication that was a product of the larger study (P. Kari 1987). Therefore, the inclusion of plants in this context would have been redundant.

Particular acknowledgement should be given to Dr. James Kari, Alaska Native Language Center, University of Alaska Fairbanks. His Dena'ina dictionary (J. Kari 1977) provided the basis for most faunal terms presented in Dena'ina in this appendix. Additionally, Albert Wassillie, who was literate in Dena'ina, assisted with faunal terms not listed in the dictionary (J. Kari 1977) or in cases in which there was undocumented dialectical variation. Lastly, our sincere appreciation to Dr. Dale Taylor, U.S. National Park Service, Alaska Region, for correcting the "scientific" names portrayed in this appendix.

Inland Dena'ina Name	Common English Name	Scientific Name
k'q'uya	sockeye (red) salmon	*Oncorhynchus nerka*
liq'aka'a	king (chinook) salmon	*O. tschawytscha*
nulay	dog (chum) salmon	*O. keta*
nusdlaghi	silver (coho) salmon	*O. kisutch*
qughuna	pink (humpy) salmon	*O. gorbushca*
hulehga	whitefish, Alaska	*Coregonus nelsoni*
qhelghuli	whitefish, pygmy	*Prosopium coulteri*
q'untuq'	whitefish, humpback	*Coregonus pidschian*
hesten	whitefish, round	*Prosopium cyliwdruceum*
telay	whitefish, broad	*Coregonus nasus*
ch'dat'an	arctic grayling	*Thymallus arcticus*
ghelguts'i	pike, northern	*Esox lucius*
duch'ehdi	long nose sucker	*Catostomus*
tuni	rainbow trout	*Salmo gairdneri*
qak'elay	Dolly Varden	*Salvelinus malma*
ghelguts'i k'una	least cisco	*Coregonus sardinella*
zhuk'udghuzha	lake trout	*Salmo namaycush*
vat	arctic char	*Salvelinus alpinus*
dghili juna	dwarf common char	(see note below)
ch'unya	freshwater ling cod, burbot	*Lota lota*
huzheghi	blackfish, Alaska	*Dallia pectoralis*
vek'eha qilani	stickleback	*Gasterosteous sp.*
vejex	caribou	*Rangifer tarandus*
k'uhda'i	moose	*Alces alces*
yeghedishla	black bear	*Ursus americanus*
ggagga	brown (grizzly bear)	*U. arctos*
nudyi	Dall sheep	*Ovis dalli*

Note: Local Dena'ina and non-Dena'ina refer to any small trout with spots as "eastern brook trout." These fish are actually dwarf common char instead (McNard pers. comm. 1988).

Inland Dena'ina Name	Common English Name	Scientific Name
chu	beaver	*Castor canadensis*
qunsha	arctic ground squirrel	*Spermophilus parryii*
neghvaya	rabbit, snowshoe hare	*Lepus americanus*
ggehkegh	Alaska hare	*L. othus*
nini	porcupine	*Erethizon dorsatum*
k'qushiya	marmot, "whistler"	*Marmota caligata*
tułchuda	muskrat	*Ondatra zibethicus*
tiqin	wolf	*Canis lupus*
q'anlcha	red fox	*Vulpes vulpes*
chavadushga (Russian)	cross fox (color phase of red fox)	*V. vulpes*
ts'elga	red squirrel	*Tamiasciurus hudsonicus*
k'cheqhuxa	marten	*Martes americana*
kughuljena	short-tailed weasel, ermine	*Mustela erminea*
kina	least weasel	*M. rixosa*
tak'ich'a	mink	*M. vison*
idashla	wolverine	*Gulo gulo*
aggeya (Yup'ik)	river otter	*Lutra canadensis*
kazhna	lynx	*Lynx lynx*
tava	tundra swan	*Olor columbianus*
dult'iya	trumpeter swan	*O. buccinator*
ndalvay	Canada goose	*Branta canadensis*
chulyin viy'a	black brant	*B. nigricans*
k'dut'aq'a	white-fronted goose	*Anser albifrons*
ch'iluzhena	snow goose	*Chen caerulescens*
chadatl'ech'i	mallard	*Anas platyrhynchos*
tsendghinlggesh	pintail	*A. acuta*
sheshinya	American wigeon	*A. americana*
veduzhizha dghiłtali, vedushqula	northern shoveler	*A. clypeata*
qulchixa	green-winged teal	*A. crecca*

Inland Dena'ina Name	Common English Name	Scientific Name
veq'es dasdeli	canvasback	*Aythya valisineria*
vech'enlna q'enk'elggeyi	greater scaup (bluebill)	*A. marila*
tsiq'unya	goldeneye	*Bucephala clangula*
sukna tsighał	bufflehead	*B. albeola*
ahhanya	oldsquaw	*Clangula hyemalis*
tus qet'ay	harlequin duck	*Histrionicus histrionicus*
venchix va'idetsiggi	black scoter	*Melanitta nigra*
venaq'a qa'ilch'eli	white-winged scoter	*M. deglandi*
venchix va'ilch'eli	surf scoter	*M. perspicillata*
cheghesh	common merganzer	*Mergus merganzer*
yucheghesh	red-breasted merganzer	*M. serrator*
ełdyin	spruce grouse	*Canachites canadensis*
k'delneni	ruffed grouse (willow grouse)	*Bonasa umbellus*
q'ach'ema	willow ptarmigan	*Lagopus lagopus*
jel q'ach'ema	rock ptarmigan	*L. mutus*
qatsinłggat	white-tailed ptarmigan	*L. leucurus*
k'ełteli	sharp-tailed grouse	*Pedioecetes phasianellus*
ndał	sandhill crane	*Grus canadensis*
dujeni	common loon	*Gavia immer*
shdutvuyi	red-throated loon	*G. stellata*
taqa'a	red-necked grebe	*Podiceps grisegena*

APPENDIX B

DENA'INA PLACE NAMES USED IN THE TEXT

Dena'ina Place Name	English Equivalent [a]
Chałchitnu	Chilchitna River
Chaq'ah Tugget	bay on Lake Clark [b]
Chałchi Kaq'	site at the mouth of the Chilchitna River [b]
Chatnashtl'ech'i	mountain southeast of Cairn Mountain [b]
Chayi Ch'dedlish Kiyiq'	Chayi ("tea") Point (Russian)
Chikalushen Tustes	Chickalusion Pass (personal coastal Dena'ina name)
Ch'ak'daltnu	Kijik River
Ch'alitnu	Chulitna River
Ch'alitnu Hdakaq'	mouth of the Chulitna River [b]
Ch'dat'antnu	Black Creek
Ch'ghitalishla	creek one mile south of the new site of Nondalton [b]
Ch'kentałqeyitnu	creek north of Currant Creek [b]
Ch'qi'un Vena	Alexey Lake
Ch'gułch'ishtnu	"where a creek comes out of a canyon" [b]
Ch'qułch'ishtnu	"willow sprout creek" or Trail Creek
Ch'ul'egitnu	Dennis Creek
Chun Tałen	south fork of the Chulitna River Delta [b]
Chuqutenghehtnu	Chokotonk River, Little Lake Clark
Dazlit Dazdlu	located at the head of the Swift River [b]
Denyihtnu'	canyon on the Mulchatna River [b]
Dghilishla	mountain south of Kijik Lake [b]
Dilah Vena	Telaquana Lake
Dilah Vena Q'estsiq'	Telaquana Lake outlet

[a] Dena'ina place names taken from J. Kari (1977), P. Kari (1983), J. Kari and P. Kari (1982), Ellanna 1986, and from field data gathered by Albert Wassillie and Andrew Balluta. Literal translations of the Dena'ina terms can be found in the published sources named above.

[b] No English name documented.

Dena'ina Place Name	English Equivalent[a]
Dilah Vena Tustes	Telaquana Pass
Dilah Vetnu	Telaquana River
Hek'dichen	Hungry Creek
Hek'dichen Hdakaq'	mouth of Hungry Creek [b]
Hggezh	a pass to the Lower Tazimina Lake [b]
Hłsaynenq'	"first land," area of the upper Stony River, piedmont plateau west of the Alaska Range [b]
Hłsit	site on Tishimna Lake [b]
Hłsit Vena	Tishimna Lake
Hqak'elaxtnu	Moose Creek
Huch'altnu or Huch'alitnu	Swift River
Huk'esdlik'itnu	creek that runs into the Koksetna River [b]
Hukughitenitnu	creek at the head of K'q'uya Vena [b]
Hulehga Tahviłq'	slough on the north fork of the Chulitna delta [b]
Husuyghiqan Hni'a	Flat Island
Igiugig	the channel connecting Six-Mile Lake to Lake Clark (Yup'ik)
K'a Ka'a	valley on the upper Chilikadrotna River [b]
Kijeghi Tsayeh	Owl Bluff
K'adela Vena	Snipe Lake
K'chanlentnu	Lynx Creek
K'ezghaxtnu	Gagaryah Creek
K'ilghech'	valley south of College Creek [b]
K'qizaghetnu	Stony River
K'q'uya Vena	Kijik Lake
Łih Vena	Whitefish Lake
Łiq'a Qilanhtnu	Tlilakila River or Big River
Łiq'a T'el'iht	Tommy Point

Dena'ina Place Name	English Equivalent[a]
Nan Qelah	site at the mouth of Miller Creek [b]
Nan Qelah Vetnu	Miller Creek
Nduk'eyux Dghil'u	Telaquana Mountain
Nikugh Vena	Nikabuna Lake
Nikugh Vetnu	Neacola River
Nilan Q'estsiq'	Lake Iliamna outlet [b]
Nilavena, Nilan Vena	Lake Iliamna
Niłqidlen Vena	Twin Lakes
Nli Z'un Vetnu	second creek below Fish Village [b]
Nizdlu Dghil'u	Lime Hill north of Stony River [b]
Nuch'nastninhtnu	portion of the Mulchatna River above Mosquito Creek [b]
Nuch'natninhtnu	Mosquito Creek
Nuch'tnashtnunhtnu	Currant Creek
Nughilqutnu	Tazimina River
Nughil Vetnu	Newhalen River
Nunch'qelchixi Vena	Fishtrap Lake
Nundaltin	Six-Mile Lake
Nundaltin Q'estsig'	outlet of Six-Mile Lake [b]
Nundaltinshla	about six miles toward Lake Iliamna on the Newhalen River [b]
Nunk'dushjexa	the hills above the mouth of Bonanza Creek [b]
Nusdnigi Q'aghdeq	valley on the Koksetna River [b]
Nuvendaltin	Nondalton
Qalnigi Tunilen	creek that runs into Chulitna Bay [b]
Qankuhtnu	south fork of the Hoholitna River [b]
Qedeq Vena	lake east of Kutokbuna Lake [b]
Qeghnilen	Qeghnilen village or "canyon village"
Qenlghishi Vena	Kontrashibuna Lake
Qinghuy Dghil'u	a mountain north of Long Lake [b]

Dena'ina Place Name	English Equivalent[a]
Qinghuch'una	mountain at the head of the first creek from the north which runs into the Chulitna River [b]
Qinghuyi Vena	Long Lake
Qiyhi Qelahi or Dghil'u	Groundhog Mountain
Qizhjeh	Kijik village
Qizhjeh Vena	Lake Clark
Qizhjeh Vena Tustes	Lake Clark Pass
Qukdeli	Koktuli Creek (name of Yup'ik origin)
Q'aghdeg Vat'esluh Vena	Middle Pickerel Lake
Q'eteni	a ridge at the base of Telaquana Mountain [b]
Q'uk'tsatnu	Caribou Creek or Koksetna River
Shagela Vena	"trout lake" [b]
Sheh Kaq'	site at the mouth of Springway Creek [b]
Shehtnu	Springway Creek
Skihdulchin	a creek running from the mountain called Unhnidi [b]
Tałchatnaq'	Hook Creek
Tanilen Vetnu	lower Tanalian River
Tanilen Vetnu Tustes	pass from Tazimina Lake to Lake Clark at the mouth of the Tanalian River [b]
Taz'in Vena	Lower Tazimina Lake
Tich'eqan	a hill on Bonanza Creek [b]
Tich'eqantnu Gguya	Little Bonanza Creek
Tinch'ghilkaq'	the mouth of Can Creek [b]
Tinch'ghiltnu	Can Creek
Tleghtitnu	Hoholitna River
Ts'atanaltsegh	creek below Fish Village [b]
Tsayeh Ka'ahtnu	Sheep Canyon
Tsilak'idghutnu	Chilikadrotna River or Middle Fork
Tsilak'idghutnu Hdakaq or Niłaghedlen	mouth of the Chilikadrotna River [b]
Tuk'eleh	south creek of the Kijik River delta [b]

Dena'ina Place Name	English Equivalent [a]
Tutnutl'ech'a	Two Lakes
Tutnutl'ech'a Tustes	Merrill Pass
Unhnidi	Hoknede
Unqeghnich'en Tazin Vena	Upper Tazimina Lake
Unqeghnich'en	North Pickerel Lake
Vałts'atnaq'	Mulchatna River
Vandaztuntnu	outlet of Turqoise Lake [b]
Vandaztun Vena	"caribou hair lake" or Turquoise Lake
Vata'esluh Vena	South Pickerel Lake
Vatsilyaxi	hill north of the Stony River [b]
Vendash Vena	Tundra Lake
Vendashtnu	Stink River
Venkdah Vena	lake north of Half Cabin Lake [b]
Venq'deltihi	mountain range north of the Chulitna River [b]
Yusdi Ghuyiq'	Indian Point
Yuzheghnitnu	Ptarmigan Creek

APPENDIX C

GLOSSARY

affines: Affines are relatives by marriage; that is, spouses and in-laws. Affines are distinguished from consanguines or relatives by birth.

age of death by year of birth: Age of death by year of birth can be portrayed in a diagram used to represent visually the age of death on one axis and the year of birth on the other. Such an analytical tool correlates these two variables and can represent longevity within a population at any given point of time in relationship to the birth cohorts of members of the population.

age of death by year of death: Age of death by year of death is a graphical representation of the age of death on one axis and the year of death on the other. Age of death by year of death graphically represents population decimations and the cohorts of the population affected. It visually highlights patterned deaths associated with factors such as diseases, famines, health practices, and accessibility of health care.

agnate: An agnate is a member of the same patrilineal descent group as ego. See patrilineal descent.

ala: A Dena'ina term of address referring to one's older brother.

alliance: An alliance is an affinal relationship between descent groups and is maintained across generations through recurrent or prescribed marriage between members of one group with members of another.

ATV: ATV is the acronym for an all-terrain-vehicle, such as three or four-wheel Honda motor "bikes."

avunculate: Avunculate is the term for the institution most commonly found in matrilineal societies, in which male offspring are raised or trained by a mother's brother. Female offspring also are provided with considerable guidance and inheritance from this maternal uncle.

avunculocality: Avunculocality is the term for postmarital residence of a couple with the husband's maternal uncle.

babiche: A term referring to strips of caribou or moose rawhide used as rope for snowshoe webbing and other purposes by Athabaskans.

baidarshchik: A Russian term for creole (people of mixed Native and non-Native parentage) trading post managers.

band: A band is an association of families related by kinship or marriage, occupying a common territory. Localized bands are the most common organizational social unit among many hunting and gathering societies consisting of up to approximately 100 people. Size and composition of bands vary according to seasonal variation, subsistence and ritual activities, and environmental characteristics. Anthropologists have distinguished between regional bands, composed of multiple local bands; local bands, as described above; and special purpose task groups, which unify for conducting a short-term cooperative economic activity. In this ethnography, the term society has been used in a manner synonymously with that of regional band.

baidarki: A Russian term for a kayak-like, one person or two person skin boat.

bilateral: Bilateral descent is kinship affiliation traced through both parents.

bride service: The services rendered by a man to those from whom he has received a wife. This practice usually involves residence of this man with the family of his bride or bride-to-be.

chada: A Dena'ina term of address and reference for one's grandfather or old man of the same generation.

ch'deshtleg'a: The Dena'ina term for fireweed, *Epilobium angustifolium*. See P. Kari 1987 for more detailed information about Dena'ina floral knowledge and uses.

ch'enlahi: A "traditional" Dena'ina stick gambling game.

ch'qidetnik'en: The Dena'ina term for "lazy person," or an individual who could not support himself.

cheyatda: A Dena'ina term of address for grandfather.

chida: A Dena'ina term of address and reference for grandmother or old woman of the same generation.

child-woman ratio: The child-woman ratio is the ratio of children under 5 years old to women of childbearing age. It is computed by dividing the number of children under 5 years old in the population by the number of women 15 to 49 years old natality and multiplying by 1,000. This ratio is also sometimes called the fertility ratio or natality. The computation formula for the child-woman ratio is:

$$\frac{\text{number of children under 5 years old}}{\text{number of women 15 to 49 years old}} \ \textbf{x} \ \ 1000$$

chiqilin q'a: A Dena'ina term for an underground, pit-like cache for the storage and fermentation of fish.

chishlaht'an: one of the eight Dena'ina matrilineal clans (matriclans), the "independent" or "paint" clan.

chulyin: A Dena'ina term for raven, considered to be a trickster in Dena'ina and other northern Athabaskan mythologies but also having considerable spiritual power.

clan: A clan is a unilineal (one-line) corporate descent group, either determined matrilineally (a matriclan) or patrilineally (a patriclan), based upon stipulated descent from an often mythological ancestor, such as a mineral, plant, animal, or celestial body. A clan may consist of several lineages which are not coresidential. A clan is also known as a sib in some anthropological literature.

cognate: A cognate is a consanguineal relative or relative by birth, either male or female.

cohort: A cohort consists of a group of individuals who experience the same significant demographic event during a specific period of time, often a year. Members of a cohort are subsequently identified on the basis of this common demographic experience. For example, a birth cohort is all of the individuals born during the same year or years. For purposes of U.S. Census data gathering and demographic analysis, a population is often broken down into five year cohorts — ages 0 to 4, 5 to 9, 10 to 14, 15 to 19, and so on.

consanguines: Consanguines are relatives by birth or "blood" relatives. This category usually includes parents, siblings, and offspring. Consanguines are distinguished from affines.

cross-cousins: Cross-cousins are children of siblings of the opposite sex or more distant cousins classified by the same terminology. For example, a person's cross-cousins would include minimally his mother's brother's children and father's sister's children.

Crow terminology: The Crow terminology kinship system, often associated with matrilineality, is a system for naming relatives. Different categories distinguish between maternal and paternal lineal relatives. Cross-cousins are not of ego's generation but equate with individuals of either older or younger generations depending upon whether the linking relative is of the opposite sex on mother's as opposed to father's side. Parallel-cousins are equated with brothers and sisters. The preferred marriage partners are cross-cousins (see Figure 41 and Table 4 of the text).

dada: A Dena'ina term of reference and address for father or father's brother and other relatives of younger or older generations with the same kinship status to ego.

Dashtl'ech'na: A Dena'ina term for "Black people" or Afroamericans.

Deg Hit'an (Kenaniq' Hit'an): A Dena'ina term for Ingalik Athabaskans from the Kuskokwim and Yukon rivers.

dependency ratio: The dependency ratio is the ratio of children under the age of 15 and adults 60 and over (the assumed dependent segment of a population) to individuals between ages 15 and 59 (the assumed productive segment of a population) multiplied by 100. A dependency ratio of 100 indicates 1 dependent for each worker. When the ratio is low, the population may be well-off, since the producers may not have to work as hard to support the dependents. The computation formula for the dependency ratio is:

$$\frac{\text{number of persons under 15 and over 60}}{\text{number of persons aged 15 to 59}} \ \textbf{x} \ \ 100$$

descent group: A descent group is a kin-based group with membership based on a particular rule of descent; see matrilineal and patrilineal descent.

dineh: A harpoon-like fish spear with detachable head.

Duntsiht'an (Dunch'ench'dna): A Lime Village Dena'ina term for "southern people" or lower Lake Iliamna or lower Lake Clark Dena'ina. Nondalton people use this term for residents of lower Lake Iliamna.

Dutna: "Aleuts," term applied to Yup'ik speakers of the Naknek River, Bristol Bay, and the southwestern end of Lake Iliamna. These people refer to themselves as "Aleuts," although they differ culturally and linguistically from the people indigenous to the Aleutian Islands.

duyun: A Dena'ina version of the Russian term "toion," meaning "chief." This term should be distinguished from the role of "traditional" inland Dena'ina leader of *qeshqa*.

el'egen: A Dena'ina term for shaman or spiritual leader, a person who can predict the future and modify events influencing the Dena'ina (misleadingly referred to as "medicine man" in lay literature).

endogamy: Endogamy is the rule or set of rules that requires individuals to marry within their social group. The criteria for membership in the marriage universe or social group is determined by its members.

exogamy: Exogamy is the rule or set of rules that requires individuals to marry outside their social group, membership in which is determined by the society or culture represented by the group.

fecundity: Fecundity is the physiological capacity to reproduce rather than actual reproduction. One's fertility is limited by one's fecundity and is usually far below it.

fertility: Fertility has two meanings: (1) the quality of being fertile (capable of reproducing); and (2) the birthrate of a population. Broadly, fertility refers to the birth factor in a population undergoing change. In a more restricted and common meaning, fertility statistics come from either the birth registration system or from censuses and surveys.

Gasht'ana: A Dena'ina term for "White" people or Euroamericans.

ggahyi: One of eight Dena'ina matriclans, referred to in English as the "raven" clan.

hdenlyahi: A Dena'ina noun meaning "that which grows," or, in a more general sense, plant life.

highliner: A boat or fisherman who takes the biggest catch in a commercial fishing period or season.

huch'ghinu: A Dena'ina term for "winter camp."

ida: A Dena'ina term for partnerships between males. Also used for female "good friends" or the female version of "partners"; male or female cross cousins.

Ilavnaht'an: The Lime Village Dena'ina term for the Lake Iliamna Dena'ina. Terms used by one group for another are frequently distinct, depending on perceived "closeness" or "distance" from the group that is being described.

infant mortality: Infant mortality refers to deaths of children under 1 year of age. The infant mortality rate is the number of deaths of children under 1 year of age during the year divided by the number of births during the year, multiplied by 1000. Infant mortality rates are lower in developed nations and may be affected rather quickly by health programs aimed at the problems of infants. The infant mortality rate may be altered more rapidly than the general death rate. The computation formula for the infant mortality rate is:

$$\frac{\text{number of deaths of children} < 1 \text{ year during the year}}{\text{number of births during the year}} \times 1000$$

k'eniquzdun: A Dena'ina name for a potential son-in-law, or "man performing bride service."

k'ighali: A Dena'ina game of skill, the goal of which is to spear grass balls.

k'kali: One of eight inland Dena'ina clans, known in English as the "fishtail" clan.

k'tl'ila: A Dena'ina term for a sweet tasting vine fried in oil or boiled in water.

kukuht'an: An inland Dena'ina term for one of eight matriclans, known in English as the "downriver" clan.

kuya: A Dena'ina term for a woman's grandchild of either sex.

levirate: The levirate is a marriage pattern in which a female, after her husband's death, marries one of her husband's brothers, or another male member of his lineage who stands in relationship of brother to the deceased. This institution functions to maintain affinal ties between kinship groups, such as families, lineages, or clans.

lineage: A lineage is a unilineal descent group, based upon genealogically demonstrated descent either through males (patrilineage) or females (matrilineage). Members of a lineage trace their descent to a known common ancestor. A lineage may or may not be localized.

lingua franca: Lingua franca is a term for a trade language used in an interethnic contact and economic exchange. In the case of the Dena'ina, first Russian and later English were the lingua franca of trade with Euroamericans. Native language lingua franca undoubtedly operated before contact with Euroamericans.

liq'a k'eyenazggeni: A Dena'ina term for a wooden rack used to dry fish.

litl'en nuch'etdeh: A Dena'ina term for spring camp.

longevity: Longevity refers to the length of life of individuals in a population.

marriage universe: A marriage universe is a category of persons from which an individual should choose a spouse.

matriarchy: A matriarchy is a theoretical social system in which females both overtly and covertly dominate males and wield the greatest degree of power. Although women in some matrilineal societies hold considerable political and/or religious power, no examples of a real matriarchy have been documented among human societies.

matrilineal descent (matrilineality): Matrilineal descent is tracing an individual's descent through his or her mother's side. This form of descent tracing is much less common than patrilineal descent worldwide. Matrilineal descent is also referred to as matrilineality. The inland Dena'ina determined descent matrilineally.

matrilocity: This term refers to post-marital residence of a couple with the wife's mother's family. See also uxoralocality.

mean age: Mean age is calculated by adding all ages of individuals in the population, then dividing by the number of individuals in the population. Mean age is distinguished from median age and modal age in the following ways. Median age refers to the middle age in a given population. There are just as many individuals older than the median age as there are younger. Modal age is the most frequently occurring age, regardless of where it lies in the age of distribution of the population.

$$\frac{\text{mean}}{\text{age}} = \frac{\text{sum of all ages of individuals in population}}{\text{total number of individuals in population}}$$

miropomazaniya: A Russian Orthodix ceremony involving the anointing of an individual with oil.

moiety: Moiety is a term used by anthropologists to describe a dual division of society into two kinship groups. Each side is composed of multiple clans and is usually, but not exclusively, exogamous. Each half is commonly identified with a common ancestor, usually of a mythical nature.

morbidity: Morbidity refers to the relative incidence of disease in a population. A population with high morbidity often also has high mortality, as even the survivors of disease may be weakened and more susceptible to death.

mortality: Mortality refers to rates and percentages of death in a population. It also refers to deaths, specifically with respect to certain characteristics. Mortality can denote the actual number of deaths in a given population at a given time or it can refer to the proportion of deaths to the whole population. Mortality is generally high at birth and throughout the first years of life, then declines steadily in an extraordinarily predictable manner.

mothers' age at birth: Mothers' age at birth simply refers to the age of the mothers when they gave birth to their children. This is a useful measure for comparing birth practices between women of different generations, temporal periods, and cultures.

nanutset nakenaghech' sutdu'a: This Dena'ina phrase refers to "stories and history before our time" or from long, long ago.

naqeli nuch'etdeh: A Dena'ina term referring to fall fish camp.

naqeliteh ch'k'ezdlu: A Dena'ina term referring to fall trapping.

natality: Natality is often used as a general term representing the role of births in population change and human reproduction. It also is used synonymously with the concept of child-woman ratio.

nch'equyi: A Dena'ina term for dip net used for fishing.

neolocality: Neolocality is the postmarital residence of a couple with neither the husband's nor the wife's kin group. That is, residence after marriage is at a locale spatially not linked with either spouse's kin.

nichil: A Dena'ina term for the traditional semisubterranean, multi-family dwelling with attached bath house.

niggiday: A Dena'ina term for a semi-permanent open boat, covered with the hides of moose or caribou skin. Such boats were commonly used for hauling meat, fish, and freight from spring camps.

nivagi: A Dena'ina term for "Indian ice cream," made of pounded whitefish, bear grease, and berries.

nudelvay: A Dena'ina term for dried, spawned-out, and filleted sockeye salmon.

nuhzi: One of eight inland Dena'ina clans, referred to in English as the "neat" or "clean" clan.

nusdlaghi: A Dena'ina term for silver salmon.

odinochka: A Russian term for small trading posts. Such facilities were important in furbearer trading during the early Russian-American period in Alaska.

outside: "Outside" is an Alaskan term for the contiguous United States (also referred to as the "lower 48").

parallel-cousins: Parallel-cousins are children of siblings of the same sex or more distant cousins classified by the same terminology. Specifically, parallel-cousins would include minimally one's father's brother's children and mother's sister's children.

patrilineal descent (patrilineality): Patrilineal descent is a means of determining kinship by tracing descent through one's father's side. This form of descent is much more common worldwide than matrilineal descent. This type of descent is often termed patrilineality.

patrilocality: This term literally refers to postmarital residence of a newly married couple with husband's father. See also virilocality.

polyandry: Polyandry is a form of polygamy in which one female is married to more than one male simultaneously. This form of marriage is very rare and often only a temporary arrangement.

polygamy: Marriage to more than one spouse simultaneously. One form, polygyny has been very common worldwide, while another, polyandry, is relatively uncommon.

polygyny: Polygyny is a form of polygamy in which one male is married to more than one female simultaneously. This marriage form is often reserved for older, prestigious, more wealthy, or more highly productive male members of a social group.

population growth: This is a measure of population increase. Such growth is reflected in greater fertility and/or increased longevity. A population that is growing slowly has a higher proportion of old people than one that is increasingly rapidly. Conversely, a population that is experiencing rapid growth has a higher proportion of infants and children. A population pyramid can provide a rough view of the general growth of a given population.

population pyramid: A population pyramid is a visual representation of the age and sex composition of a population graphed on vertical and horizontal axes. It gives a detailed picture of the age and sex structure of a population and is usually based upon five-year age groups or cohorts. The pyramid consists of bars depicting age groups in ascending order from lowest in age to highest. The bars for males are usually placed on the left of a central vertical axis; those for females are on the right of the axis. The length of the bars from the central axis delineates the number of individuals in each age group. The age scale is shown vertically, often to the left of the pyramid, but sometimes straddling the central axis. In some cases the age scale is shown on both sides of the pyramid, perhaps combining both age and year of birth. A healthy population generally has a pyramid with a large base, a gradual narrowing to the top, and a balance of males and females. A growing population normally approximates the form of a pyramid from which the name of this diagram is derived. Populations with small bases (few children), a significant imbalance between sexes of any age, but particularly those who are reproductively active, or few individuals of old age may indicate population imbalance, decline, or other conditions.

postmarital residence: Postmarital residence refers to the locale where a couple establishes itself after marriage. The most common form described for non-western populations is virilocal, whereas the most usual form in industrialized societies is neolocal.

promyshlinniki: A Russian term for fur hunters or trappers and traders. These were the first Russians who had contact with the indigenous peoples of Alaska.

q'atl'anht'an: One of eight inland Dena'ina matriclans, referred to in English as "head of the lake" clan.

q'ich'idya: A Dena'ina term for a "rock rabbit" or pika. An important character in inland Dena'ina oral tradition.

qeshqa: A Dena'ina term which translates "rich man." These persons were usually male and acted as "traditional" Dena'ina leaders or headmen.

qiy'u: A Dena'ina term for "rich woman." Though not the same as the male *qeshqa*, it may be assumed to be a female parallel of that position.

qunsha: A Dena'ina term for ground squirrel.

sex ratio: The sex ratio of a population is usually defined as the number of males per 100 females. A sex ratio above 100 indicates an excess of males; a sex ratio below 100 indicates an excess of females. The sex ratio at birth is the number of males per 100 female live births. This sex ratio is above 100 for most countries with relatively complete demographic data, usually ranging between 104 and 105.2. The computation formula for sex ratio is:

$$\frac{\text{number of males}}{\text{number of females}} \times 100$$

shaman: A shaman, as employed in anthropological literature, is a part-time spiritual or "religious" specialist, serving as an intermediary between the spiritual and the empirical worlds. To this purpose, shamans frequently undertake journeys to the spirit worlds below or above the physical one in a state of trance. With the aid of spirit helpers, shamans are possessors of divinatory and curing powers. In some societies, shamans are perceived to be both "good" and "bad." Men with unusual personal qualities, post-menopausal women, hermaphrodites, or transsexual individuals often underwent shamanistic training or apprenticeship. Shamanism is most characteristically found among hunting and gathering societies.

shan nuch'etdeh: A Dena'ina term for summer fish camp.

nakani, nant'ina, shtutnalyashna: Athabaskan and Dena'ina terms for "bogeyman," "wild man," or "drifter," often assumed to be from a neighboring ethnic group. These potentially malevolent creatures sneak up, scare, or harm humans.

sib: See clan.

slavi (**starring**): A Russian Orthodox Christmas ceremony during which the houses and their inhabitants are blessed.

slimer, to slime: A term commonly applied to the processing of fish either domestically or within the context of a commercial cannery operation. This refers to the removal of the slime from fish before they are cooked.

sororate: The sororate is a marriage pattern in which a man, whose wife is deceased, marries one of his wife's sisters or another female member of her kinship group designated as that woman's "sister." This is a means by which marriage, perceived as an alliance between families or groups, can continue the group affiliation.

sutdu'a: Dena'ina "stories" or oral history and tradition. These are the primary means by which information is transmitted between generations in non-literate societies. These stories are told also for entertainment. They provide the principal source of socialization and enculturation of children in such societies.

syncretism: A term usually applied to spiritual or religious phenomena or movements. Syncretism is the combination of elements from different religious or cultural traditions.

Tahtna: A Dena'ina term for Russians.

tatl'ah veł qiz'uni: A Dena'ina word for "underwater creatures in large lakes" or sea "monsters."

taz'in: A Dena'ina term for a fish trap.

Tnayna: An inland Dena'ina term for "Kenai people" or the Kenaitsy.

toion: Siberian Yakut term meaning "tribal elder." Used by the Russians to designate "chiefs" or the persons they perceived to be leaders and with whom they conducted business. See Dena'ina *duyun*.

tsiya: A Dena'ina term for a man's grandchild of either sex.

tulchina: One of eight Dena'ina matriclans, referred to in English as the "water" clan.

tunch'edał: A Dena'ina term which refers to fall hunting.

tuqesi: A Dena'ina term which refers to barbed fish spears.

Ułchena: A Dena'ina term for Alutiiq speakers of Prince William Sound, Kodiak Island, and the eastern half of the Kenai Peninsula. These indigenous people refer to themselves as "Aleut" but are culturally distinct from the Native people who traditionally occupied the Aleutian Islands.

unilineal descent (unilineality): Unilineal descent is descent traced through one genealogical line only, either the male (patrilineality) or the female (matrilineality).

uxorilocality: Uxorilocality is the postmarital residence of a couple with the wife's kinship group.

vach'ala: The Dena'ina term for father's sister, her female children, and the female descendants of these children. *Vach'ala* were "traditionally" preferred marriage partners.

valgas: A Russian term for skiff or small, wooden boat.

vaqilin: A Dena'ina term for the skin-covered baidarki, as termed by the Russians, or kayak-like boat. Such watercraft are similar to those used by Yupik (Eskimo) neighbors. In later years, they were covered with canvas instead of hides.

vashla: A Dena'ina term for the woman's knife, which has a blade of semilunar shape.

veghunuqults'ełen: Dena'ina legendary heroes.

vejex: A Dena'ina term for caribou.

virilocality: Virilocality is postmarital residence of a couple with the husband's kinship group. Also see patrilocality.

yeghedishla: A Dena'ina term for black bear.

Yun'eht'an: A Dena'ina term for Athabaskans from the upper Kuskokwim River.

Yup'ik or Yupik: The most southerly of the "Eskimo" people of North America. The first term refers to the language and people described as "central" or "mainland" Yup'ik, distributed today from the middle of Norton Sound to Bristol Bay. The second term is used to designate the language and culture for all representatives of this southerly "Eskimo" group, of which the Alutiiq are members.

yusdi gulchina: An inland Dena'ina term for one of eight matriclans, referred to in English as "end of the point" clan.

zagasik: A Russian loan word for "church leader" or "second chief."

zhala: A Dena'ina term of reference for mother's brother or father's sister's husband.

Note: Most of the orthography for Dena'ina terms was derived from that of J. Kari (1977). Many kinship terms not presented in this context can be found in Figure 41 and Table 4. It is assumed that terms not included in this glossary, but unfamiliar to the reader, are either identified in the text or could be found in a standard college dictionary. Only those terms, likely to be unfamiliar to non-anthropologists or to someone unfamiliar with the Dena'ina language and used most frequently in the text, are included here.

BIBLIOGRAPHY [a]

Abercrombie, W.R.
1900 A Supplementary Expedition to the
Copper River Valley, 1884. *In*
Compilation of Narratives of Explorations
in Alaska. Pp. 383-408. Washington, D.C.:
U.S. Government Printing Office.

Aberle, David F.
1974 [1961] Matrilineal Descent in
Cross-Cultural Perspective. *In* Matrilineal
Kinship, D.M. Schneider and K. Gough,
eds. Pp. 655-727. Berkeley: University of
California Press.

Ackerman, Robert E.
1975 The Kenaitze People. Phoenix: Indian
Tribal Series.

Afonsky, Bishop Gregory
1977 A History of the Orthodox Church in
Alaska (1794-1917). Kodiak: St.
Herman's Theological Seminary.

Alaska Commercial Company (ACC) Records
1872-1899 Iliamna Trading Post.
Manuscript. Fairbanks: University of
Alaska Fairbanks, Elmer Rasmuson
Library, Archives.

1875-1903 Tyonek Trading Post.
Manuscript. Fairbanks: University of
Alaska Fairbanks, Elmer Rasmuson
Library, Archives.

Alaska Commercial Fisheries Entry
Commission (CFEC)
1985 Unpublished data.

Alaska Department of Health and Social
Services, Division of Public Assistance
1985 Regulations, September 1985.

1988 Unpublished data.

Alaska Department of Community and Regional
Affairs (DCRA), Division of Community
Planning
1974a Selected 1970 Census Data for Alaska
Communities, Part IV — Southwestern
Alaska. Juneau: DCRA.

1974b Selected 1970 Census Data for Alaska
Communities, Part V — Southcentral
Alaska. Juneau: DCRA.

1979 Middle Kuskokwim Region
Community Profiles, A Background for
Planning: Lime Village. Anchorage:
Darbyshire and Associates.

1982 Alaska Peninsula/Iliamna Lake
Regional Profiles. Juneau: DCRA,
Division of Community Planning.

Alaska Department of Labor
1983 Alaska Population Overview, 1982.
Juneau: Department of Labor, Research
and Analysis Section.

Alaskan Russian Church Archives (ARCA)
1847-1900 Kenai Parish Confessional Lists;
Nushagak Parish Confessional Lists; Index
to Baptisms, Marriages, and Deaths,
1816-1866; and Fr. Vasilii Shishkin, Travel
Journals, 1877, 1882, 1883, and 1887, and
Yearly Reports, 1877 and 1883 (Tape 1,
Sides 1 and 2; Tape 2, Sides 1 and 2).
Reels 145-147 and 339-342. Microfilm 139.
Washington, D.C.: Library of Congress.
Fairbanks: University of Alaska
Fairbanks, Elmer Rasmuson Library,
Alaska Polar Regions.

Altman, Jon C.
1987 Hunter-Gatherers Today: An
Aboriginal Economy in North Australia.
Canberra: Australian Institute of
Aboriginal Studies.

Andreyev, A.I.
1952 Russian Discoveries in the Pacific and
in North America in the Eighteenth and
Nineteenth Centuries. C. Ginsburg, trans.
Ann Arbor: J.W. Edwards.

Applebaum, Herbert, ed.
1987 Perspectives in Cultural Anthropology.
Albany: State University of New York.

Asch, Michael I.
1977 The Dene Economy. *In* Dene Nation:
The Colony Within, M. Watkins, ed. Pp.
47-61. Toronto: The University of
Toronto Press.

1980 Steps toward the Analysis of
Athabaskan Social Organization. Arctic
Anthropology XVII(2):46-51.

[a] This bibliography is intended to provide a comprehensive list of literature related to the inland Dena'ina and theoretical issues in cultural and social anthropology considered in the context of this work. Since it is intended to be a comprehensive bibliography of the inland Dena'ina of the Lake Clark and upper Stony River areas, it is not limited to references cited in the ethnography.

Bacon, Glenn, J. Kari, T. Cole, C. W. Mobley,
    and R. J. Carlson
    1982 Cultural Resource Assessment: Beluga
    Study Area, Southcentral Alaska.
    Anchorage: U.S. Forest Service, Soil
    Conservation Service.

Bancroft, Hubert H.
    1970 [1886] History of Alaska, 1730-1885.
    Darien: Hafner Publishing Co.

Barry, Mary J.
    1973 History of Mining on the Kenai
    Peninsula. Anchorage: Northwest
    Publishing Co.

Bates, Robert H.
    1983 Some Core Assumptions in
    Development Economics. *In* Economic
    Anthropology: Topics and Theories, S.
    Ortiz, ed. Pp. 361-398. Lanham:
    University Press of America.

Bearne, Colin, trans. and Richard A. Pierce, ed.
    1976 A Selection from G.I. Davydov: An
    Account of TwoVoyages to America.
    Arctic Anthropology XIII(2):1-30.

    1978 The Russian Orthodox Religious
    Mission in America, 1794-1837: with
    Materials Concerning the Life and Works
    of the Monk German, and Ethnographic
    Notes by the Hieromonk Gideon.
    Kingston: Limestone Press.

Behnke, Steven R.
    1978 Resource Use and Subsistence in the
    Vicinity of the Proposed Lake Clark
    National Park, Alaska, and Additions to
    Katmai National Monument. Occasional
    Paper No. 15. Fairbanks: University of
    Alaska, Fairbanks, Anthropology and
    Historic Preservation, Cooperative Park
    Studies Unit.

    1979 Personal communication.

    1981 Subsistence Use of Brown Bear in the
    Bristol Bay Area: A Review of Available
    Information. Technical Paper No. 46.
    Dillingham: Alaska Department of Fish
    and Game, Division of Subsistence.

    1982 Wildlife Utilization and the Economy
    of Nondalton. Technical Paper No. 47.
    Dillingham: Alaska Department of Fish
    and Game, Division of Subsistence.

Bensin, Basil
    1967 Russian Orthodox Church in Alaska,
    1794-1967. Sitka: Russian Orthodox
    Greek Catholic Church of North America,
    Diocese of Alaska.

Beresford, William
    1789 A Voyage Round the World: But More
    Particularly to the Northwest Coast of
    America, Performed in 1785, 1786, 1787
    and 1788, in the King George and Queen
    Charlotte. George Dixon, ed. London:
    George Goulding.

Binford, Lewis and W. N. Chasko
    1976 Nunamiut Demographic History. A
    Provocative Case. *In* Demographic
    Anthropology. Ezra W. B. Zubrow, ed.
    Pp. 63-144. Albuquerque: University of
    New Mexico Press.

Birkedal, Ted
    1991 Personal communication.

Bishop, Charles A.
    1981 Northeastern Indian Concepts of
    Conservation and the Fur Trade: A
    Critique of Calvin Martin's Thesis. *In*
    Indians, Animals and the Fur Trade, S.
    Krech III, ed. Pp. 39-58. Athens:
    University of Georgia Press.

Bishop, Charles A. and Shepard Krech III
    1980 Matriorganization: The Basis of
    Aboriginal Subarctic Social Organization.
    Arctic Anthropology XVII(2):34-45.

Black, Lydia T.
    1981 "The Daily Journal of Reverend
    Father Juvenal": A Cautionary Tale.
    Ethnohistory 28(1):33-57.

    1987 Personal communication.

Bobby, P., et al.
    1978 *K'qizaghetnu Ht'ana* (Stories from
    Lime Village). Anchorage: National
    Bilingual Materials Development Center.

Bogojavlensky, Sergei
    1969 Imaangmiut Eskimo Careers:
    Skinboats in Bering Strait. Ph.D.
    dissertation, Harvard University,
    Cambridge, MA.

Brelsford, Gregg
    1975 Cook Inlet Region Inventory of Native
    Historic Sites and Cemeteries. Anchorage:
    Cook Inlet Native Association.

Brody, Hugh
    1982 Maps and Dreams. New York:
    Pantheon Books.

Burch, Ernest S., Jr.
1971 The Nonempirical Environment of the Arctic Alaskan Eskimo. Southwest Journal of Anthropology 27:148-165.

1975 Eskimo Kinsmen. New York: West Publishing Co.

1981 The Traditional Eskimo Hunters of Point Hope, Alaska: 1800-1875. Barrow: North Slope Borough.

Callicott, J. Baird
1982 Traditional American Indian and Western European Attitudes toward Nature: An Overview. Environmental Ethics 4(4):293-318.

Capps, Stephen R.
1930 The Chakachamna Stony Region. *In* Mineral Resources in Alaska. U.S. Geological Survey Bulletin 813-B. Pp. 97-123. Washington, D.C.: U.S. Government Printing Office.

1935 The Southern Alaska Range. U.S. Geological Survey Bulletin 862. Washington, D.C.: U.S. Government Printing Office.

Carberry, Michael J.
1979 Patterns of the Past: An Inventory of Anchorage's Heritage Resources. Anchorage: Municipality of Anchorage, Historic Landmarks Preservation Commission.

Chance, Norman
1990 The Inupiat and Arctic Alaska: An Ethnography of Development. Fort Worth: Holt, Rinehart and Winston.

Clark, Donald W.
1981 Prehistory of the Western Subarctic. *In* Handbook of North American Indians, Subarctic, Vol. 6, June Helm, ed. Pp. 107-129. Washington, D.C.: Smithsonian Institution.

Cook, Frederick A.
1908 To the Top of the Continent: Discovery, Exploration, and Adventure in Sub-Arctic Alaska. New York: Doubleday, Page, and Co.

Cusma, Agnes
1986 Interview.

Dall, William H.
1870 On the Distribution of the Native Tribes in Alaska and Adjacent Territory. *In* Proceedings of the American Association for the Advancement of Science for 1869. Pp. 263-273. Salem: American Association for the Advancement of Science.

1886 The Native Tribes of Alaska: Addresses to Proceedings of the American Association for the Advancement of Science for 1885. Pp. 363-379. Salem: Salem Press.

1896 Geographical Notes on Alaska. Journal (Bulletin) of the American Geological Society 28(1):1-20.

1970 [1870] Alaska and Its Resources. New York: Arno Press.

Damas, David, ed.
1969 Contributions to Anthropology: Band Societies. Montreal: Crown Copyrights.

Davis, Nancy Yaw
1987 History of Research in Subarctic Alaska. *In* Handbook of North American Indians, Subarctic, Vol. 6, J. Helm, ed. Pp. 43-48. Washington, D.C.: Smithsonian Institution.

Davydov, Gavriil I.
1977 [1810-1812] Two Voyages to Russian America, 1802-1807. Colin Bearne, trans., Richard A. Pierce, ed. Kingston: Limestone Press.

Delkittie, Annie
1986 Interview.

Delkittie, Michael
1986 Interview.

de Laguna, Frederica
1957 Some Problems of Objectivity in Ethnology. Man 227, 228:179-182.

1971 Matrilineal Kin Groups in Northwestern North America. *In* Proceedings: Northern Athabaskan Conference, 1971. Mercury Series, Canadian Ethnology Service, Paper No. 27, Vol. 1. Pp. 17-145. Ottawa: National Museum of Man.

1975 [1934] The Archaeology of Cook Inlet, Alaska. Anchorage: The Alaska Historical Society.

Dinneford, E. and B. Hart
1986 Changes in the Distribution of Permit Ownership in Alaska's Limited Fisheries: 1975-1985. CFEC Report Number 86-6. Juneau: Alaska Commercial Fisheries Entry Commission.

Dixon, E. James
    1979 Lower Cook Inlet Cultural Resource
        Study: Final Report. Fairbanks:
        University of Alaska Museum.

Dumond, Don E.
    1973 Review of Kijik: An Historic Tanaina
        Settlement by James W. VanStone and
        Joan B. Townsend. American Antiquity
        38(2):247-248.

    1978 A Chronology of Native Alaskan
        Subsistence Systems. In Alaska Native
        Culture and History, Y. Kotani and W.B.
        Workman, eds. Senri Ethnological Studies
        No. 4. Pp. 23-49. Osaka: National
        Museum of Ethnology.

Ellanna, Linda J.
    1990 Demographic Change, Sedentism, and
        Western Contact: An Inland Dena'ina
        Athabaskan Case Study. In Oceania
        Monograph, No. 39. Hunter-Gatherer
        Demography: Past and Present,
        B. Meehan and N. White, eds. Pp.
        101-116. Sydney: University of Sydney.

    1992 Land, Resources, and Cultural
        Identity: Public Policy and Contemporary
        Hunter-Gatherers in Alaska. Human
        Organization (in press).

Ellanna, Linda J., ed.
    1986 Lake Clark Sociocultural Study, Phase
        I. Anchorage: U.S. National Park Service,
        Alaska Region.

Ellanna, Linda J., George K. Sherrod, and
    Steven Langdon
    1992 Subsistence Mapping: The Spatial
        Component of Hunter-Gatherer Ecology.
        Lanham: Academic Press of America (in
        press).

Elliott, Charles P.
    1900 Salmon Fishing Grounds and
        Canneries. In Compilation of Narratives
        of Explorations in Alaska. Pp. 738-741.
        Washington, D.C.: U.S. Government
        Printing Office.

Evan, Anton
    1976 Interview.

    1980 Interview.

    1985 Interview.

Fall, James A.
    1981 Patterns of Upper Inlet Tanaina
        Leadership, 1741-1918. Ph.D. dissertation,
        University of Wisconsin, Madison, WI.

    1987 The Upper Inlet Tanaina.
        Anthropological Papers of the University
        of Alaska 21(1-2):1-80.

    1990 Personal communication.

Fall, James A., Dan J. Foster and Ronald T.
    Stanek
    1984 The Use of Fish and Wildlife Resources
        in Tyonek, Alaska. Technical Paper No.
        105. Anchorage: Alaska Department of
        Fish and Game, Division of Subsistence.

Fall, J. A., J. M. Morris, J. Schichnes, and M.
    Chythlook
    1986 Freshwater Fish Harvests by the
        Communities of the Bristol Bay Region,
        Southwest Alaska: A Research Design.
        Anchorage: Alaska Department of Fish
        and Game, Division of Subsistence.

Federova, Svetlana G.
    1973 [1971] The Russian Population in
        Alaska and California, Late 18th Century
        to 1867. Richard A. Pierce, ed., and Alton
        S. Donnelly, trans. Kingston: Limestone
        Press.

    1975 Ethnic Processes in Russian America.
        Antoinette Shalkop, trans. Occasional
        Paper No. 1. Anchorage: Anchorage
        Historical and Fine Arts Museum.

Fienup-Riordan, Ann
    1984 Regional Groups on the
        Yukon-Kuskokwim Delta. Etudes Inuit
        Studies 8:63-95.

Freeman, Milton M.R.
    1970 Not by Bread Alone: Anthropological
        Perspectives on Optimum Population. In
        Optimum Population for Britain, L.R.
        Taylor, ed. Pp. 139-149. London:
        Academic Press.

    1971 The Significance of Demographic
        Change Occurring in the Canadian East
        Arctic. Anthropologica 13(1-2):215-236.

Freeman, Milton M.R., ed.
    1976 Inuit Land Use and Occupancy
        Project. 3 Vols. Ottawa: Minister of
        Supply and Services, Canada.

Gerhard, Robert
    1989 Personal communication.

Glenn, Edward F.
    1900 Explorations in and about Cook Inlet,
        1899. In Compilations of Narratives of
        Explorations in Alaska. Pp. 713-724.
        Washington, D.C.: U.S. Government
        Printing Office.

Gough, Kathleen
    1974 [1961] Variation in Residence. *In*
        Matrilineal Kinship, D.M. Schneider and
        K. Gough, eds. Pp. 545-613. Berkeley:
        University of California Press.

Greenberg, J., Christy Turner, II, and Stephen
    Zegura
    1986 The Settlement of the Americas: A
        Comparison of the Linguistic, Dental, and
        Genetic Evidence. Current Anthropology
        27(5):477-497.

Gregory, C.A.
    1982 Gifts and Commodities. New York:
        Academic Press, Inc.

Gsovski, Vladimir
    1950 Russian Administration of Alaska and
        the Status of the Alaskan Natives,
        Prepared by the Chief of the Foreign Law
        Section. Library of Congress, Law
        Library, Senate Document 152, 81st
        Congress, 2nd session. Washington, D.C.:
        U.S. Government Printing Office.

Guédon, Marie-Francoise
    1974 People of Tetlin, Why Are You
        Singing? National Museum of Man
        Mercury Series No. 9. Ottawa: National
        Museum of Man.

Hallowell, A.I.
    1955 Culture and Experience. Philadelphia:
        University of Pennsylvania Press.

Hammerich, Louis L.
    1968 Some Linguistic Problems in the
        Arctic. Acta Artica 1960:83-89.

Harmon, David
    1987 Cultural Diversity, Human
        Subsistence, and the National Park Ideal.
        Environmental Ethics 9(2):147-158.

Helm, June
    1965 Bilaterality in the Socio-Organization
        of the Arctic Drainage Dene. Ethnology
        4(4): 361-385.

    1968 The Nature of Dogrib Socioterritorial
        Groups. *In* Man the Hunter, I. DeVore
        and R. Lee, eds. Pp. 118-125. Chicago:
        Aldine Press.

    1969 Relationships between Settlement
        Pattern and Community Pattern. *In*
        Contributions to Anthropology: Ecological
        Essays, D. Damas, ed. Pp. 151-152.
        National Museums of Canada, Bulletin
        No. 230. Ottawa: National Museums of
        Canada.

    1976 The Indians of the Subarctic: A
        Critical Bibliography. Bloomington:
        Indiana University Press.

    1985 Horde, Band, and Tribe: Northern
        Approaches. Third Annual Presidential
        Lecture, February 1985, The University of
        Iowa, Iowa City, Iowa.

Helm, J., T. Alliband, T. Birk, V. Lewison, S.
    Reisner, C. Sturtevant, and S. Witowski
    1975 The Contact History of the Subarctic
        Athapascans: An Overview. *In*
        Proceedings: Northern Athapascan
        Conference, 1971. Vol. I, A. McFayden,
        ed. Pp. 302-349. Ottawa: National
        Museums of Canada, Canadian Ethnology
        Service.

Helm, June and Eleanor Leacock
    1971 Hunting Tribes of Subarctic Canada.
        In The North American Indians in
        Historical Perspective, E.B. Leacock and
        N.O. Laurie, eds. New York: Random
        House.

Helm, June and Royce Kurtz
    1984 Subarctic Athapaskan Bibliography:
        1984. Iowa City: Department of
        Anthropology, University of Iowa.

Hippler, Arthur E. and John R. Wood
    1974 The Subarctic Athabascans: A
        Selected Annotated Bibliography.
        Fairbanks: University of Alaska,
        Fairbanks, Institute of Social, Economic
        and Government Research.

Hirschmann, Fred, ed.
    1986 Lake Clark, Lake Iliamna Country.
        Alaska Geographic 13(4):1-152.

Hoagland, Alison K.
    1982 A Survey of the Historical
        Architectural Resources in Lake Clark
        National Park and Preserve. Unpublished
        report. Anchorage: U.S. National Park
        Service, Lake Clark National Park and
        Preserve.

Hobson, Steve
    1981 Interview.

Hoijer, Harry
    1956 Athabascan Kinship Systems.
        American Anthropologist 58:309-333.

    1963 The Athapaskan Languages. *In*
        University of California Publications in
        Linguistics, 29, Studies in Athapaskan
        Languages, H. Hoijer, ed. Pp. 1-29.
        Berkeley: University of California Press.

Homelander
    1986a   1(1).

    1986b   1(2).

    1987   2(4).

Honigmann, John J.
    1981 Expressive Aspects of Subarctic Indian
    Culture. *In* Handbook of North American
    Indians, Subarctic, Vol. 6, June Helm, ed.
    Pp. 718-738. Washington, D.C.:
    Smithsonian Institution.

Hornberger, Sara
    1985-1986 Unpublished field notes.

Hosley, Edward M.
    1977 A Reexamination of the Salmon
    Dependence of the Pacific Drainage
    Culture Athapaskans. *In* Problems in the
    Prehistory of the North American
    Subarctic: The Athapaskan Question,
    J.W. Helm, et al. Pp. 124-129. Calgary:
    University of Calgary, Archaeological
    Association.

    1980 The Aboriginal Social Organization of
    the Pacific Drainage Dene: The
    Matrilineal Basis. Arctic Anthropology
    XVII(2): 12-16.

House of Representatives. Standing Committee
    on Aboriginal Affairs
    1987 Return to Country: The Aboriginal
    Homelands Movement in Australia.
    Canberra: Australian Government
    Publishing Service.

Hrdlička, Ales
    1944 Alaska Diary, 1926-1931. Lancaster:
    Jacques Cattel Press.

Hutchison, Andrew
    1989 Personal communication.

Iuvenalii, Khovorukh (Juvenhal,
    Ieromonakh)
    1952 A Daily Journal Kept by the Rev.
    Father Juvenal, One of the Earliest
    Missionaries to Alaska, 1796. B.G.
    Hoffman, comp. *In* Kroeber Society
    Anthropological Papers 6:26-59.

Jacobsen, Johan Adrian
    1977 Alaska Voyage, 1881-1883: An
    Expedition to the Northwest Coast of
    North America. Trans. by Erna Gunther
    from the German text of Adrian Woldt.
    Chicago: University of Chicago Press.

Jones, Randall M.
    1983 Alaskan Athabaskan Bibliography.
    Fairbanks: University of Alaska,
    Fairbanks, Central Alaska Curriculum
    Consortium.

Kalifornsky, Peter
    1974 *Ch'enlahi Sukdu.* The Gambling
    Story. Fairbanks: University of Alaska,
    Fairbanks, Alaska Native Language
    Center.

Kari, James
    n.d. Iliamna Lake — Western Cook Inlet
    South of Tuxedni Bay Place Names List.
    Unpublished. Fairbanks: University of
    Alaska, Fairbanks, Alaska Native
    Language Center.

    1975a A Classification of Tanaina Dialects.
    Anthropological Papers of the University
    of Alaska 17(2):49-53.

    1975b *Dena'ina T'qit'ach:* The Way the
    Tanaina Are. Collected by James Kari.
    Fairbanks: University of Alaska,
    Fairbanks, Alaska Native Language
    Center.

    1977 Linguistic Diffusion between Tanaina
    and Ahtna. International Journal of
    American Linguistics 43(4):274-288.

    1985 Some Linguistic Insights into Dena'ina
    Prehistory. Paper presented to the
    American Society for Ethnohistory, Nov.
    7-10, 1985, Chicago.

Kari, James, comp.
    1977 Dena'ina Noun Dictionary. Fairbanks:
    University of Alaska, Fairbanks, Alaska
    Native Language Center.

Kari, James, ed. and comp.
    1980 *Q'udi Heyi Nilch'diluyi Sukdu'a.* This
    Year's Collected Stories (Dena'ina Stories
    From Tyonek and Iliamna Lake). James
    Kari, trans. and ed. Anchorage: National
    Bilingual Materials Development Center
    and University of Alaska.

Kari, James and Priscilla Kari
    1982 *Dena'ina Elnena:* Tanaina Country.
    Fairbanks: University of Alaska,
    Fairbanks: Alaska Native Language
    Center.

Kari, Priscilla Russell
    1983 Land Use and Economy of Lime
    Village. Technical Paper No. 80. Juneau:
    Alaska Department of Fish and Game,
    Division of Subsistence.

    1985 Wild Resource Use and the Economy
    of Stony River Village. Technical Paper
    No. 108. Juneau: Alaska Department of
    Fish and Game, Division of Subsistence.

1987 Tanaina Plantlore: *Dena'ina K'et'una.* Anchorage: U.S. National Park Service, Alaska Region.

Keesing, Roger M.
1975 Kin Groups and Social Structure. New York: Holt, Rinehart and Winston.

1976 Cultural Anthropology: A Contemporary Perspective. New York: Holt, Rinehart and Winston.

Kijik Corporation
1983 Unpublished "Amendment of Bylaws."

1986 Board of Directors Packet, 1986. Anchorage: Kijik Corporation.

1987 Interim Report to Shareholders for the Year Ended June 30, 1987. Anchorage: Kijik Corporation.

1989 Personal communication.

Koktelash, Ruth
1981 Interview.

Krauss, Michael E.
1964 Proto-Athapaskan-Eyak and the Problem of Na-Dene (Part I). International Journal of American Linguistics 30(2):118-131.

1965 Proto-Athapaskan-Eyak and the Problem of Na-Dene (Part II). International Journal of American Linguistics 31(1):18-28.

1973 Na-Dene. *In* Linguistics in North America, Current Trends in Linguistics, Vol. 10, Thomas A. Sebeok, ed. Pp. 903-978. The Hague: Mouton.

1978 Na-Dene and Eskimo-Aleut. *In* The Languages of Native America, L. Campbell and M. Methuen, eds. Austin: University of Texas Press.

1980 Alaska Native Languages: Past, Present and Future. Alaska Native Language Center Research Paper, No. 4. Fairbanks: University of Alaska, Fairbanks, Alaska Native Language Center.

1982 [1974] Native Peoples and Languages of Alaska (Map). Fairbanks: University of Alaska, Fairbanks, Alaska Native Language Center.

1990 Personal communication.

Krauss, Michael E. and Victor K. Golla
1981 Northern Athapaskan Languages. *In* Handbook of North American Indians, Vol. 6, June Helm, ed. Pp. 67-85. Washington, D.C.: Smithsonian Institution.

Krauss, Michael E. and Mary Jane McGary
1980 Alaska Native Languages: A Bibliographical Catalogue. Part One: Indian Languages. Alaska Native Language Center Research Paper, No. 3. Fairbanks: University of Alaska, Fairbanks, Alaska Native Language Center.

Krech, III, Shepard
1976 The Eastern Kutchin and the Fur Trade, 1800-1869. Ethnohistory 23(3):213-253.

1978 On the Aboriginal Population of the Kutchin. Arctic Anthropology XV(1):89-104.

1979 Disease, Starvation, and Northern Athapascan Social Organization. American Ethnologist 5(4):710-732.

1981 "Throwing Bad Medicine": Sorcery, Disease, and the Fur Trade among the Kutchin and other Northern Athapaskans. *In* Indians, Animals and the Fur Trade, S. Krech, III, ed. Pp. 73-108. Athens: The University of Georgia Press.

Krech, III, Shepard, ed.
1981 Indians, Animals, and the Fur Trade: A Critique of *Keepers of the Game.* Athens: The University of Georgia Press.

Langdon, Steve
1981 The 1980 Salmon Season and Bristol Bay Native Fishermen: Performance and Prospects. Anchorage: University of Alaska Anchorage.

1991 The Integration of Cash and Subsistence in Southwest Alaska Yup'ik Eskimo Communities. *In* Cash, Commoditisation and Changing Foragers, N. Peterson and T. Matsuyama, eds. Pp. 223-268. Senri Ethological Studies, No. 31. Osaka: National Museum of Ethnology.

Langness, L. L. and Gelya Frank
1985 Lives: An Anthropological Approach to Biography. Novato: Chandler and Sharp Publishers, Inc.

Laughlin, William S.
1972 Ecology and Population Structure in the Arctic. *In* The Structure of Human Populations, G.A. Harrison and A.J. Boyce, eds. Pp. 379-392. London: Oxford University Press.

Leacock, Eleanor and Richard Lee, eds.
1982 Politics and History in Band Societies. Cambridge: Cambridge University Press.

Lee, Richard B. and Irven DeVore, eds.
1968 Man the Hunter. Chicago: Aldine Publishing Company.

Lisiansky, Urey
1814 A Voyage Round the World in the Years 1803, 1804, 1805 and 1806; Performed by Order of His Imperial Majesty Alexander the First, Emperor of Russia, in the Ship Neva. London: John Booth.

Livingston, John A.
1981 The Fallacy of Wildlife Conservation. Toronto: McClelland and Stewart.

Lynch, Alice J.
1982 Qizhjeh: The Historic Tanaina Village of Kijik and the Kijik Archaeological District. Occasional Paper No. 32. Fairbanks: University of Alaska, Fairbanks, Anthropology and Historic Preservation, Cooperative Park Studies Unit.

Malinowski, Bronislaw
1961 [1922] Argonauts of the Western Pacific. New York: E.P. Dutton and Company, Inc.

Malthus, T.R.
1803 [1798] An Essay on the Principle of Population. London: J. Johnson.

Marcus, George E. and M. J. Fischer
1986 Anthropology as Cultural Critique. Chicago: The University of Chicago Press.

Martin, Calvin
1978 Keepers of the Game: Indian-Animal Relationships and the Fur Trade. Berkeley: University of California Press.

1981 The War Between Indians and Animals. *In* Indians, Animals, and the Fur Trade, S. Krech, III, ed. Pp. 11-18. Athens: University of Georgia Press.

Martin, George Curtis and F.J. Katz
1912 A Geologic Reconnaissance of the Iliamna Region, Alaska. Department of the Interior, U.S. Geological Survey Bulletin 485. Washington, D.C.: U.S. Government Printing Office.

Mattson, Elizabeth M.B.
1985 Orthodoxy and the Aleuts: The Historical Significance of the Russian Orthodox Mission to Alaska. Ph.D. dissertation, Department of History, University of Idaho, Moscow, ID.

Mauss, Marcel
1967 [1925] The Gift. New York: W.W. Norton & Company, Inc.

McClellan, Catharine
1964 Culture Contacts in the Early Historic Period in Northwestern North America. Arctic Anthropology II:3-15.

1975 My Old People Say: An Ethnographic Survey of the Southern Yukon Territory. Publication in Ethnology No. 6. Ottawa: National Museums of Canada.

1987 Part of the Land, Part of the Water: A History of the Yukon Indians. Vancouver: Douglas and McIntyre.

1990 Personal communication.

McKennan, Robert A.
1969 Athapaskan Groupings and Social Organization in Central Alaska. Anthropological Series 84. National Museum of Canada Bulletin 228:93-115.

McNard, Mack
1988 Personal communication.

Mishakoff, Dick
1961 Interview.

Morris, Judith M.
1986 Subsistence Production and Exchange in the Iliamna Lake Region, Southwest Alaska, 1982-1983. Technical Paper No. 136. Juneau: Alaska Department of Fish and Game, Division of Subsistence.

Murie, Olaus J.
1935 Alaska-Yukon Caribou. U.S. Bureau of Biological Survey, North American Fauna 54. Washington, D.C.: U.S. Government Printing Office. (Reprinted in 1967 by Shorey Book Store, Seattle.)

Murphy, Robert F. and Julian H. Steward
1968 [1956] Tappers and Trappers: Parallel Process in Acculturation. *In* Man in Adaptation: The Cultural Present, Y. A. Cohen, ed. Pp. 214-234. Chicago: Aldine.

Needham, Rodney, ed.,
    1971 Rethinking Kinship and Marriage.
    London: Tavistock.

Nelson, Richard K.
    1973 Hunters of the Northern Forest.
    Chicago: University of Chicago Press.

    1978 Athapaskan Subsistence Adaptations
    in Alaska. *In* Alaska Native History and
    Culture, Y. Kotani and W. B. Workman,
    eds. Second International Symposium,
    Senri Ethnological Studies, No. 4. Pp.
    205-232. Osaka: National Museum of
    Ethnology.

    1983 Make Prayers to the Raven. Chicago:
    University of Chicago Press.

    1986 Raven's People. *In* Interior Alaska: A
    Journey through Time. R.M. Thorson,
    J.S. Aigner, R.D. and M.L. Guthrie, W.S.
    Schneider, and R.K. Nelson, ed. Pp.
    195-250. Anchorage: Alaska Geographic
    Society.

Nelson, R. K., K. Mautner, G. R. Bane
    1982 Tracks in the Wildland: A Portrayal of
    Koyukon and Nunamiut Subsistence.
    Fairbanks: University of Alaska,
    Fairbanks, Cooperative Park Studies
    Unit.'

Nietschmann, Bernard
    1973 Between Land and Water. New York:
    Seminar Press.

Nondalton Natives
    1979 Unpublished Articles of Incorporation
    of Nondalton Natives.

Norton, Susan
    1980 The Vital Question: Are Reconstituted
    Families Representative of the General
    Population? *In* Genealogical
    Demography, B. Dyke and W.T. Merrill,
    eds. Pp. 11-21. New York: Academic
    Press.

Oleksa, Michael, ed.
    1987 Alaska Missionary Spirituality. New
    York: Paulist Press.

Orth, Donald J.
    1971 Dictionary of Alaska Place Names.
    Geological Survey Professional Paper 567.
    Washington, D.C.: U.S. Government
    Printing Office.

Ortiz, Sutti, ed.
    1983 Economic Anthropology: Topics and
    Theories. Monographs in Economic
    Anthropology, No. 1. Lanham: University
    Press of America.

Osgood, Cornelius
    1933 Tanaina Culture. American
    Anthropologist 35(4):695-717.

    1936 The Distribution of Northern
    Athapaskan Indians. Yale University
    Publications in Anthropology, No. 7. New
    Haven: Yale University Press.

    1970 [1940] Ingalik Material Culture. Yale
    University Publications in Anthropology,
    No. 22. New Haven: Human Relations
    Area Files Press.

    1976 [1937] The Ethnography of the
    Tanaina. Yale University Publications in
    Anthropology, No. 16. New Haven:
    Human Relations Area Files Press.

Osgood, Wilfred H.
    1904a A Biological Reconnaissance of the
    Base of the Alaska Peninsula. North
    American Fauna #24. Washington, D.C.:
    U.S. Government Printing Office.

    1904b Lake Clark: A Little Known Alaskan
    Lake. National Geographic 15(8):326-331.

Oswalt, Wendell H.
    1962 Historical Populations in Western
    Alaska and Migration Theory.
    Anthropological Papers of the University
    of Alaska 11(1):1-14.

    1963 Mission of Change. San Marino:
    Huntington Library.

    1967a Alaska Commercial Company
    Records: 1868-1911 Register. College:
    University of Alaska Library.

    1967b Alaskan Eskimo. San Francisco:
    Chandler Publishing Co.

    1980 Kolmakovskiy Redoubt: The
    Ethnoarcheology of a Russian Fort in
    Alaska. Los Angeles: University of
    California, The Institute of Archaeology.

Overturf, Jan H.
    1984 Regional Subsistence Bibliography,
    Vol. IV, Southcentral Alaska, No. I.
    Technical Paper No. 97. Juneau: Alaska
    Department of Fish and Game, Division of
    Subsistence.

Park, William
    n.d. The Land Beyond. Unpublished
    manuscript.

Peterson, Nicolas
1991 Cash, Commoditisation and Changing Foragers. *In* Cash, Commoditisation and Changing Foragers, N. Peterson and T. Matsuyama, eds. Pp. 1-16. Senri Ethnological Studies No. 30. Osaka: National Museum of Ethnology.

Petroff, Ivan
1884 Report on the Population, Industries, and Resources of Alaska, 1880. Tenth Census of the U.S., 1880, Vol. 8. Washington D.C.: U.S. Government Printing Office.

Pierce, Richard A., ed.
1976 A Selection from G.I. Davydov: An Account of Two Voyages to America. Translated from the Russian by C. Bearne. Arctic Anthropology XIII(2):1-30.

Powers, W. Roger
1990 Personal communication.

Rathburn, Robert R.
1981 The Russian Orthodox Church as a Native Institution among the Koniag Eskimo of Kodiak, Alaska. Arctic Anthropology XVIII(1):12-22.

Regan, Tom, ed.
1982 All That Dwell Therein: Animal Rights and Environmental Ethics. Berkeley: University of California Press.

Richardson, J.
1851 Arctic Search Adventure: A Journal of a Boat-Voyage through Rupert's Land and the Arctic Sea. 2 vols. London.

Ridington, Robin
1988 Knowledge, Power, and the Individual in Subarctic Hunting Societies. American Anthropologist 90(1):98-110.

Rollins, Alden M., comp.
1978 Census Alaska: Number of Inhabitants, 1792-1970. Anchorage: University of Alaska, Anchorage, Library.

Roth, Eric
1981 Historic Population Structure of a Northern Athabaskan Bush Community: Old Crow Village,Yukon Territory. Arctic Anthropology XVIII(1):33-43.

Russian Orthodox American Messenger, 1896-1907

Sahlins, Marshall
1963 Poor Man, Rich Man, Big Man, Chief: Political Types in Melanesia and Polynesia. Comparative Studies in Society and History 5(31):285-303.

1981 [1972] Stone Age Economics. New York: Aldine Publishing Co.

Sarafian, W. L. and J. W. VanStone
1972 The Records of the Russian American Company as a Source for the Ethnohistory of the Nushagak River Region, Alaska. Anthropological Papers of the University of Alaska 15(2): 53-78.

Scherer, Joanna Cohan
1981 Repository Sources of Subarctic Photographs. Arctic Anthropology XVIII(2):59-65.

Schneider, David M.
1974 [1961] The Distinctive Features of Matrilineal Descent Groups. *In* Matrilineal Kinship, D.M. Schneider and K. Gough, eds. Pp. 1-35. Berkeley: University of California Press.

1980 American Kinship. Chicago: University of Chicago Press.

Schneider, David M. and Kathleen Gough, ed.
1974 [1961] Matrilineal Kinship. Berkeley: University of California Press.

Schneider, Harold K.
1974 Economic Man: The Anthropology of Economics. Salem: Sheffield Publishing Company.

Schrire, Carmel
1984 Wild Surmises on Savage Thoughts. *In* Past and Present in Hunter Gatherer Studies, C. Schrire, ed. Pp. 1-25. New York: Academic Press, Inc.

Selkregg, Lidia L.
1976 Alaska Regional Profiles: Southwest Region. Anchorage: University of Alaska, Arctic Environmental Information and Data Center.

Service, Elman R.
1971 Primitive Social Organization. New York: Random House.

Shinkwin, Anne and Mary Pete
1984 Yup'ik Eskimo Societies: A Case Study. Etudes Inuit Studies 8:95-112.

Siebert, Erna V.
1980 Northern Athapaskan Collections of the First Half of the Nineteenth Century. David Kraus, trans., J.W. VanStone, ed. Arctic Anthropology XVII(1):49-76.

Skoog, Ronald
1968 Ecology of the Caribou (*Tangifer
torandus granti*) in Alaska. Ph.D.
dissertation, University of California,
Berkeley.

Smith, Barbara S.
1980a Russian Orthodoxy in Alaska: A
History, Inventory and Analysis of the
Church Archives in Alaska with an
Annotated Bibliography. Anchorage:
Alaska Historical Commission.

1980b Orthodoxy and Native Americans:
The Alaskan Mission. Orthodox Church
in America. Department of History and
Archives Historical Society Occasional
Papers No. 1. Crestwood: St. Vladimir's
Seminary Press.

Smith, George S. and Harvey M. Shields
1977 Archaeological Survey of Selected
Portions of the Proposed Lake Clark
National Park: Lake Clark, Lake
Telaquana, Turquoise Lake, Twin Lakes,
Fishtrap Lake, Lachabuna Lake and Snipe
Lake. Occasional Paper No. 7. Fairbanks:
University of Alaska, Fairbanks,
Anthropology and Historic Preservation
Cooperative Park Studies Unit.

Smith, Philip Sidney
1917 The Lake Clark-Central Kuskokwim
Region, Alaska. U.S. Geological Survey
Bulletin 655. Washington, D.C.: U.S.
Government Printing Office.

Snow, Dean R.
1981 *Keepers of the Game* and the Nature of
Explanation. *In* Indians, Animals, and
the Fur Trade, S. Krech, III, ed. Pp.
59-72. Athens: University of Georgia
Press.

Sprott, Julie E.
1987 Cancer Causation Beliefs in an
Alaskan Village. Paper submitted for
presentation to the Arctic Science
Conference, September 1987. University
of Alaska Anchorage.

St. Nicholas Baptismal Records
1951-1986 Unpublished baptismal records of
the Russian Orthodox Church of
Nondalton, Alaska.

Steward, Julian
1955 Theory of Culture Change. Urbana:
University of Illinois Press.

Sudkamp, Anne C.
1985 Russian Orthodox Brotherhoods and
Temperance Societies in the Kenai Parish.
Unpublished paper.

1986 Population Boom in Mulchatna,
1876-1877: Fact or Fiction? Unpublished
paper.

Tanner, Adrian
1979 Bringing Home Animals. New York:
St. Martin's Press.

Tenenbaum, Joan, comp.
1976a *Dghiliq' Sukdu'a* (Mountain
Stories). Fairbanks: University of Alaska,
Fairbanks, Alaska Native Language
Center.

1976b *Nanutset K'ughun Nit T'qul'an Qegh
Nuhqulnik* (Stories of the Wars They Had
Before Our Time). Fairbanks: University
of Alaska, Fairbanks, Alaska Native
Language Center.

1984 *Dena'ina Sukdu'a*: Traditional Stories
of the Tanaina Athabascans. Fairbanks:
University of Alaska, Fairbanks: Alaska
Native Language Center.

Tikhmenev, P. A.
1978 [1861-1863] A History of the
Russian-American Company. Seattle:
University of Washington Press.

1979 [1861-1863] A History of the
Russian-American Company. Volume Two:
Documents. Kingston: The Limestone
Press.

Townsend, Joan B.
1963 Ethnographic Notes on the Pedro Bay
Tanaina. Anthropologica, New Series 5(2).

1965 Ethnohistory and Cultural Change of
the Iliamna Tanaina. Ph.D. dissertation,
Dept. of Anthropology, University of
California, Los Angeles. Ann Arbor:
University Microfilms.

1970a Tanaina Archaeology in the Iliamna
Lake Region, Alaska. Bulletin of the
Canadian Archeological Association
2:36-43.

1970b Tanaina Ethnohistory: An Example
of a Method for the Study of Cultural
Change. *In* Ethnohistory in Southwestern
Alaska and the Southern Yukon, M.
Lantis, ed. Pp. 71-102. Lexington:
University of Kentucky Press.

1970c The Tanaina of Southwestern Alaska:
An Historical Synopsis. *In* Western
Canadian Journal of Anthropology
2(1):2-16. (Special Issue: Athabascan
Studies, Regna Darrell, ed.)

1974a Ethnoarchaeology in Nineteenth Century Southern and Western Alaska: An Interpretive Model. Ethnohistory 20(4):393-412.

1974b Journals of Nineteenth Century Russian Priests to the Tanaina: Cook Inlet, Alaska. Arctic Anthropology XI(1):1-30.

1975a Alaskan Natives and the Russian American Company: Variations in Relationships. *In* Proceedings of the 2nd Congress, Canadian Ethnology Society, J. Freedman and J.H. Barkow, eds., Vol. 2. Pp. 555-570. National Museum of Man Mercury Series, Ethnology Service Paper 28.

1975b Mercantilism and Societal Change: An Ethnohistoric Examination of Some Essential Variables. Ethnohistory 22(1):21-32.

1979 Indian or Eskimo? Interaction and Identity in Southern Alaska. Arctic Anthropology XVI(2):160-182.

1980 Ranked Societies of the Alaskan Pacific Rim. *In* Alaska Native History and Culture, Y. Kotani and W. B. Workman, eds. Second International Symposium, Senri Ethnological Studies, No. 4. Pp. 123-156. Osaka: National Museum of Ethnology.

1981 Tanaina. *In* Handbook of North American Indians, Subarctic, Vol. 6, J. Helm, ed. Pp. 623-640. Washington, D.C.: Smithsonian Institution.

Townsend, Joan B. and Sam-Joe Townsend
1961 Archaeological Investigations at Pedro Bay, Alaska. Anthropological Papers of the University of Alaska 10(1):25-58.

1964 Additional Artifacts from Iliamna Lake, Alaska. Anthropological Papers of the University of Alaska 12(1):14-16.

Trefon, Gabriel
1961 Interview.

Trefon, Martha
1986 Interview.

U.S. Congress, P.L. 92-203
1971 Alaska Native Claims Settlement Act.

U.S. Congress, P.L. 95-341
1978 American Indian Religious Freedom Act.

U.S. Congress, P.L. 96-487
1980 Alaska National Interest Lands Conservation Act.

U.S. Congress, P.L. 101-610
1990 National American Graves Protection and Repatriation Act.

U.S. Congress, Senate Committee on Military Affairs
1900 Compilation of Narratives of Explorations in Alaska. Washington, D.C.: U.S. Government Printing Office.

U.S. Department of the Interior, Bureau of the Census
1913 Thirteenth Census of the United States, Taken in the Year 1910: Abstract of the Census, Supplement for Alaska. Washington, D.C.: U.S. Government Printing Office.

1921 Fourteenth Census of the United States, Taken in the Year 1920: Volume I, Population 1920. Washington, D.C.: U.S. Government Printing Office.

1932 Fifteenth Census of the United States: 1930. Outlying Territories and Possessions. Washington, D.C.: U.S. Government Printing Office.

1947 Sixteenth Census of the United States: 1940. Population, Vol. I, Number of Inhabitants. Washington, D.C.: U.S. Government Printing Office.

1952 United States Census of the Population: 1950, Number of Inhabitants: Alaska. Washington, D.C.: U.S. Government Printing Office.

1961 The Eighteenth Decennial Census of the United States. Census of Population: 1960, Vol. 1, Part A. Washington, D.C.: U.S. Government Printing Office.

1972 1970 Census of Population. Vol. I, Part A, Section I, Alaska. Washington, D.C.: U.S. Government Printing Office.

U.S. Department of the Interior, Bureau of Education
1908-1912 An Inventory of the Records of the BIA, Alaska Division, General Correspondence 1903-1935. Juneau: Division of State Libraries and Museums, Alaska Historical Library.

U.S. Department of the Interior, Bureau of Indian Affairs, ANCSA Office
1987a Report of Investigation for Telaquana Fish Camp, Cook Inlet Region, Inc. Anchorage: BIA, ANCSA Office.

1987b Report of Investigation for Telaquana Fish Village Cemetery, Cook Inlet Region, Inc. Anchorage: BIA, ANCSA Office.

1987c Report of Investigation for Chałchishtna Village, Cook Inlet Region, Incorporated (CINA). Anchorage: CINA.

U.S. Department of the Interior, National Park Service
1970 National Register of Historic Places, Kijik (Qizhjeh). Anchorage: U.S. National Park Service, Alaska Region.

1984 General Management Plan and Environmental Assessment, Lake Clark National Park and Preserve, Alaska. Anchorage: U.S. National Park Service, Alaska Region.

1985a Cultural Resources Management Guideline, FPS-28. Washington, D.C.: U.S. National Park Service.

1985b Work Plan/Task Directive, Lake Clark National Park and Preserve Sociocultural Study. Unpublished memorandum of agreement.

1986 Draft Land Protection Plan. Anchorage: Lake Clark National Park and Preserve.

1987a Courier 32(2).

1987b Native American Relationships Policy. Federal Register 52(14):2452.

U.S. Public Health Service
1980 Unpublished data.

University of Alaska, Fairbanks, Alaska Native Language Center
n.d. Alaska Native Language Center. Tanaina Tape Index.

Usher, Peter
1976 Evaluating Country Food in the Northern Native Economy. Arctic 29(2):105-120.

Van Gennep, Arnold
1960 [1909] The Rites of Passage. Chicago: University of Chicago Press.

Van Horne, Bea
1975 The Lake Clark Area, Vol. I: Planning for People, Wildlife and the Land. Santa Cruz: Environmental Studies Program, University of California.

VanStone, James W.
1962 Notes on Nineteenth Century Trade in the Kotzebue Sound Area, Alaska. Arctic Anthropology 1(1):126-128.

1967 Eskimos of the Nushagak River: An Ethnographic History. Seattle: University of Washington Press.

1970 Introduction to Baron F.P. von Wrangell's Observations on the Eskimos and Indians of Alaska. Arctic Anthropology 6(2):1-4.

1974 Athapaskan Adaptations: Hunters and Fishermen of the Subarctic Forests. Arlington Heights: Harlan Davidson, Inc.

1980 Alaska Natives and the White Man's Religion: A Culture Interface in Historical Perspective. *In* Exploration in Alaska, Captain Cook Commemorative Lectures, A. Shalkop, ed. Pp. 175-179. Anchorage: Cook Inlet Historical Society.

1981 Eskimo and Indian Settlements in Southwestern Alaska, 1902: A Photographic Record. Field Museum of Natural History Bulletin 52(6):4-9.

1984 Exploration and Contact History of Western Alaska. *In* Handbook of North American Indians, Arctic, Vol. 5, D. Damas, ed. Pp. 149-160. Washington, D.C.: Smithsonian Institution.

1985 Personal communication.

VanStone, James W., ed. and David H. Kraus, trans.
1973 V.S. Khromchenko's Coastal Explorations in Southwestern Alaska, 1822. Fieldiana: Anthropology, Volume 64. Chicago: Field Museum of Natural History.

VanStone, James W. and Joan B. Townsend
1970 Kijik: An Historical Tanaina Indian Settlement. Fieldiana: Anthropology, Vol. 59. Chicago: Field Museum of National History.

Vaudrin, Bill
1969 Tanaina Tales From Alaska. Civilizations of the American Indian Series 96. Norman: University of Oklahoma Press.

von Wrangell, Ferdinand Petrovich
1970 [1839] The Inhabitants of the Northwest Coast of North America. James VanStone, trans. and ed. Arctic Anthropology VI(2):5-20.

1980 [1839] Russian America, Statistical and Ethnographic Information. Translated from the German edition of 1839 by Mary Sadovski, Richard Pierce, ed. Kingston: The Limestone Press.

Ware, Timothy
1985 The Russian Orthodox Church. New York: Viking Penguin Inc.

Wassillie, Albert
1985 Interview.

Wassillie, Albert, comp., and James Kari, ed.
    1980a *K'ich'ighi*: Dena'ina Riddles.
        Anchorage: National Bilingual Materials
        Development Center, University of
        Alaska.

    1980b *Nuvendaltin Hi'ana Sukdu'a*
        (Nondalton People's Stories). Anchorage:
        National Bilingual Materials Development
        Center, University of Alaska.

Williams, Nancy M. and Eugene S. Hunn, eds.
    1982 Resource Managers: North American
        and Australian Hunter-Gatherers.
        Canberra: Australian Institute of
        Aboriginal Studies.

Wolf, Eric R.
    1982 Europe and the People without
        History. Berkeley: University of
        California Press.

Wolfe, Robert J.
    1982 The Great Sickness, 1900: An
        Epidemic of Measles and Influenza in a
        Virgin Soil Population. Proceedings of the
        American Philosophical Society
        126(2):90-121.

Wolfe, Robert J. and Linda J. Ellanna, comp.
    1983 Resource Use and Socioeconomic
        Systems: Case Studies of Fishing and
        Hunting in Alaskan Communities.
        Technical Paper No. 61. Juneau: Alaska
        Department of Fish and Game, Division of
        Subsistence.

Wolfe, R.J., S. Langdon, J. Gross, J. Wright, G.
    Sherrod, L. Ellanna, and V. Sumida
    1984 Subsistence-Based Economies in
        Coastal Communities of Southwest
        Alaska. Technical Paper No. 89. Juneau:
        Alaska Department of Fish and Game,
        Division of Subsistence.

Workman, Karen
    1991 Personal communication.

Workman, William B.
    1978 Continuity and Change in the
        Prehistoric Record from Southern Alaska.
        In Alaska Native Culture and History, Y.
        Kotani and W.B. Workman, eds. Senri
        Ethnological Series, No. 4. Pp. 49-103.
        Osaka: National Museum of Ethnology.

    1974 Prehistory of the Southern Kenai
        Peninsula. The Native, Russian and
        American Experience of the Kenai Area of
        Alaska. Orthodox Alaska 5(3-4):11-25.

Wright, John M., Judith Morris, and Robert
    Schroeder
    1985 Bristol Bay Regional Subsistence
        Profile. Technical Paper No. 114.
        Juneau: Alaska Department of Fish and
        Game, Division of Subsistence.

Young, S. Hall
    1927 Hall Young of Alaska: An
        Autobiography. New York: Fleming H.
        Revell Co.

Zagoskin, Lavrentiy Alekseyevich
    1967 [1847] Lieutenant Zagoskin's Travels in
        Russian America, 1842-1844. H. Michael,
        trans. Toronto: University of Toronto
        Press.

Zubrow, Ezra B.W.
    1973 Prehistoric Carrying Capacity: A
        Model. Menlo Park: Cummings
        Publishing Co.

INDEX